States of Violence

THE COMPARATIVE STUDIES IN SOCIETY AND HISTORY BOOK SERIES

Raymond Grew, Series Editor

Comparing Muslim Societies:
Knowledge and the State in a World Civilization
Juan R. I. Cole, editor

Colonialism and Culture
Nicholas B. Dirks, editor

Constructing Culture and Power in Latin America
Daniel H. Levine, editor

Time: Histories and Ethnologies
Diane Owen Hughes and Thomas R. Trautmann, editors

Cultures of Scholarship
S. C. Humphreys, editor

Comparing Jewish Societies
Todd M. Endelman, editor

The Construction of Minorities: Cases for Comparison
Across Time and Around the World
André Burguière and Raymond Grew, editors

States of Violence
Fernando Coronil and Julie Skurski, editors

States of Violence

Fernando Coronil
and
Julie Skurski,
Editors

THE UNIVERSITY OF MICHIGAN PRESS
Ann Arbor

2009   2008   2007   2006   4   3   2   1

A CIP catalog record for this book is available from the British Library.

Library of Congress Cataloging-in-Publication Data

States of violence / Fernando Coronil and Julie Skurski, editors.
        p. cm. — (Comparative studies in society and history book
series)
      Includes bibliographical references.
      ISBN-13: 978-0-472-09893-4 (cloth : alk. paper)
      ISBN-10: 0-472-09893-4 (cloth : alk. paper)
      ISBN-13: 978-0-472-06893-7 (pbk. : alk. paper)
      ISBN-10: 0-472-06893-8 (pbk. : alk. paper)   1. Violence.
2. Political violence.   3. State, The.   4. Power (Social sciences)
I. Coronil, Fernando, 1944–   II. Skurski, Julie, 1945–   III. Series.
HM886.S83   2005
303.6—dc22   2005017996

This book is dedicated to
RAYMOND GREW,
whose vision and commitment
made it possible.

Acknowledgments

The editors wish to thank E. Valentine Daniel for his help in guiding this work from the outset. We would like to acknowledge in particular the contributions of the graduate student participants in the seminar and the conference out of which this volume grew, for their insightful commentaries on all the papers. We thank Laurent Dubois for his work on the conference, James Schaeffer of *CSSH* for his dedicated support of this project, and above all Ray Grew for his sense of vision and unflagging encouragement. To David Akin, whose superb work was essential in the final completion of this book, our gratitude. The order of our names on the volume and the introduction do not reflect relative contributions of work or ideas; this was a wholly collaborative effort.

Grateful acknowledgment is given to *Comparative Studies in Society and History (CSSH)* for permission to reproduce the following articles in revised form:

"Civilization and Barbarism: Cattle Frontiers in Latin America" by Silvio R. Duncan Baretta and John Markoff first appeared in *CSSH* 20: 587–620.

"Dismembering and Remembering the Nation: The Semantics of Political Violence in Venezuela" by Fernando Coronil and Julie Skurski originally appeared in *CSSH* 33: 288–337.

"Mad Mullahs and Englishmen: Discourse in the Colonial Encounter" by David Edwards originally appeared in *CSSH* 31: 649–70.

"Tea Talk: Violent Measures in the Discursive Practices of Sri Lanka's Estate Tamils" by E. Valentine Daniel originally appeared in *CSSH* 35: 568–600.

"Banditry, Myth, and Terror in Cyprus and other Mediterranean Societies" by Paul Sant Cassia originally appeared in *CSSH* 35: 773–95.

"Of Crowds and Empires: Afro-Asian Riots and European Expansion, 1857 to 1882" by Juan R. I. Cole originally appeared in *CSSH* 31: 106–33.

Contents

Illustrations

Fig. 1. A poster commemorating the Amparo contained the elements of the Amparo iconography: the faces of the two survivors, the Arauca River, the boat, and a bamboo cross draped with peasant clothes. Produced by two church-related human rights groups (comision Justicia y Paz and SECORVE), the poster was designed by Cerezo Barredo and is captioned, "for the protection and dignity of man, we will forge justice."

Fig. 2. José Augusto Arias and Wollmer Gregorio Pinilla, survivors of the Amparo massacre, in the Caracas church in which they received sanctuary: Sagrado Corazon, Petare.

Fig. 3. Relatives of those who died in the Amparo massacre next to the collective grave of the victims.

Fig. 4. Singing the national anthem and waving the flag, workers and barrio residents head toward a commercial district on 27 February 1989, and a policeman joins the march.

Fig. 5. People controlled the streets in downtown Caracas by blocking them off.

Fig. 6. Once they controlled the streets, people began looting. Here they enter a small store, carrying off whatever they can.

Fig. 7. During the initial stage of *saqueo popular* (popular looting), the police watched without interfering.

Fig. 8. On the second day of looting (28 February 1989), constitutional guarantees were suspended. The military and the police began a heavy armed attack on the looters and barrios.

Fig. 9. A body lies in the street as people wait in line for food.

Fig. 10. A policeman shoots at looters while others carry away the dead and wounded.

Introduction: States of Violence and the Violence of States

Julie Skurski and Fernando Coronil

Political violence has become searingly visible in the contemporary world, as civil war, ethnic cleansing, and mass social dislocation have marked the post-Cold War social landscape with ineffaceable wounds. In this era of uncertainties associated with the collapse of modernist illusions and the celebration of postmodern disillusions, the harm wrought by political conflicts and state repression have become a deadly certainty for many people the world over. With the spread of destructio n unconstrained by the norms of conventional warfare or strategies of the Cold War (which Subcomandante Marcos called "the Third World War," resulting in over twenty million deaths in the Third World [1997]), violence has emerged in public consciousness as an independent cause of destruction; a U.S. news-paper headline states simply, "Violence leaves four dead in the Middle East." Yet the depiction of violence as an agent responsible for destruction cannot quell the disquieting awareness that its understanding continues to escape us.

Despite its tangible material effects, political violence is an elusive phe-nomenon. In the dramatic and public forms with which it is identified, such as riots, civil insurgencies, massacres, and terrorism, political vio-lence appears as a brute physical force that ruptures the flow of everyday life. Its factuality is reinforced by the possibility of measuring its effects, of counting the dead and maimed bodies and quantifying the material destruction. When seen in terms of its techniques, strategies, and objec-tives, violence appears as a tool wielded in the pursuit of power. Yet through its devastating effects and the surplus of emotion that accompa-nies its deployment, violence reverses its appearance; its quality of excess, and its capacity to overwhelm meaning, give it the character of a force that controls humans rather than an instrument used by them. It seemingly establishes its own logic and language and becomes its own justification, driving people beyond the recognized limits of their humanity. In this metamorphosis of effect into cause, violence is transfigured into an entity, an autonomous agent that disrupts order and stands against society, an asocial force beyond the normal and the normative.

This volume forms part of a growing scholarly effort to counter the reification of violence by analyzing it as a complex set of practices, representations, and experiences, and by investigating rather than reproducing its appearance as a tool of power and an asocial force. Focusing on the relations between the state and the domestic order, it directs analytical attention to contests over the establishment and representation of meanings and addresses the impact of state-centered categories and narratives on the organization and collective remembering of violence. Recognizing that the reification of violence itself has political implications, these essays locate violence in relation to the organization, legitimation, and contestation of power. These processes implicate the state and political actors but extend far beyond them, encompassing the constitution and denial of collective identities in the public and private spheres. They involve multiple forms and different intensities of violence whose analysis blurs conceptual boundaries between the violent and the non-violent, the conjunctural and the structural, the legal and the illegal, the physical and the psychological, the quotidian and the exceptional, the public and the private, the state and civil society.

We take as the historical frame for this work the creation of the West since the colonization of the Americas, the development and global expansion of capitalism, and the formation of colonial empires and nation-states. In contrast to accounts of history that present the rise of modern nations as entailing the gradual elimination or containment of violence through the state's monopolization of the regulation and organization of civil society, these essays explore the role of violence in the formation and transformation of modern nations. By examining contests over meaning and power entailed in the mutual constitution of metropolitan centers and colonial or postcolonial peripheries, they unsettle a historiography that has denied the violence of these contests or sanitized it within narratives of civilizing progress.

Reflecting the impact of theoretical currents developed in recent years, including colonial studies, cultural studies, feminist theory, and the linguistic turn, these essays approach violence as a constitutive dimension of modern states and societies. In contrast to familiar teleological approaches in which the modern state strives to expel violence from the civil order, violence they see as being produced within it. By illuminating the links between violent ruptures and the routine maintenance of order, they expand as much as they redefine the conceptual field within which political violence is viewed. Seen from this perspective, practices and discourses of violence, like currents that shape the ocean floor, sculpt social landscapes, imperceptibly chiseling their configuration and casting life chances.

The Extraordinary in the Ordinary

The mystification of political violence has resulted in part from its identification with its most extreme manifestations, such as wars, state-sponsored terror, and genocidal campaigns. This familiar equation creates the appearance that violence exists as a separate category, an identification that exerts its own kind of coercion. The view that violence is distinct from the civil order tends to legitimate everyday forms of violence and to reify its extraordinary occurrences, placing them outside the social rather than recognizing their continuities with quotidian practices.

These essays point to the ordinariness of seemingly extraordinary violence and recognize the exceptional in everyday practices of force and coercion: the constitution of cattle frontiers in Latin America as shifting peripheries of violence tied to centers of power (Baretta and Markoff); the processes linking rural banditry, state repression, and codes of justice and terror in the Mediterranean (Cassia); the politics and social foundations of urban crowd actions in colonial Egypt (Cole); the semantics of anti-free market urban protests and state massacres in Venezuela (Coronil and Skurski); the cultural paradigms underlying narratives of colonial rule in northern India (Edwards); the ethnicization of violence among groups of miners in apartheid South Africa (Moodie); the semeiotics of plantation labor and resistance to colonial authority in Sri Lanka (Daniel); the aestheticized optics of state surveillance in Northern Ireland (Feldman); the legal regulation of male sexual violence and classification of female bodies in India (Das); and the ideologies of prison discipline and reform in the United States (Bright).

This volume is part of an emerging body of work that explores the intersections among violence, power, the state, and memory (e.g., Chatterjee and Jeganathan 2000; Corradi, Fagen, and Garretón 1992; Das 1995b; Kleinman, Das, and Lock 1997; Nordstrom and Robben 1995; Warren

1993; Sluka 2000). The analytical broadening of the concept of political violence, the concept of social suffering, and the attention to structural violence and to the violence of everyday life, as Arthur Kleinman argues, have problematized how violence is conceptualized, categorized, represented, and given voice. "Current taxonomies of violence—public versus domestic, ordinary as against extreme political violence—are inadequate to understand either the uses of violence in the social world or the multiplicity of its effects in experiences of suffering, collective and individual" (2000: 227). The inadequacy of existing approaches suggests not only the need to rethink the categories with which we work (Farmer 1997). It raises the need to make the conditions in which violence becomes constituted as a subject an integral part of our analysis. As many of the articles here demonstrate, violence does not present itself unmediated to observers or participants, but is named, recognized, and experienced in terms of authorizing concepts and relations of power.

While their antecedents are not always acknowledged, current discussions of violence build on earlier debates that confronted prevailing theories of order with the realities of profound social disruption. The notion that social conditions can be agents of violence is rooted in nineteenth-century critiques of capitalism offered primarily by Marxists and Socialists. The most influential contemporary formulations of this idea have been put forth by critics of imperial and neocolonial relations writing from the perspective of the periphery. Latin American liberation theologians, for example, have asserted since the 1960s that structural violence is an active force affecting the majority of people throughout the world (Boff 1987; Torres 1968). "Violence does not first appear on the scene when somebody fires a gun or blows up a building," reflects a U.S. scholar of liberation theology, for "the situation is already violent" (MacAfee Brown, quoted by Reinders 1988: 5). So too, Frantz Fanon argues in his searing critique of colonialism, there is "a kind of complicit agreement, a sort of homogeneity" linking "the violence of the colonies and that peaceful violence that the world is steeped in" (1963: 81). Fanon counterposes these intertwined forms of normal violence in the metropolis and the colonies to the liberating violence of the "damned of the earth," which "frees the native from his inferiority complex and from his despair and inaction; it makes him fearless and restores his self-respect" (1963: 94). From these and other antecedents formed by engagement with relations of inequality, there has developed the recognition that violence resides in different realms of social life and individual experience, shaping contexts, moving among subjects, and altering meanings.

Defining Violence

Our title, "States of Violence," recognizes this complexity and suggests the unacknowledged ambiguities associated with violence. Although widely treated as a known and objective entity, violence eludes definition. Neither the *Encyclopedia of the Social Sciences* or the *Dictionary of Concepts in Cultural Anthropology* has an entry for it. In its standard meaning, violence refers to the unwanted use of physical force that results in harm, degradation, or death (Keane 1996: 66–67). As this usage indicates, violence is commonly associated with the destruction of life, the material world, and meaning. Raymond Williams, attending to the varying forms that violence takes, and not wanting to privilege its physical dimension, recognizes meanings that extend from the use of force to the threat to property or dignity, and that encompass the symbolic representation of these actions (1976). These definitions suggest the difficulty of delimiting violence and lead us to ask about its role in the production as well as in the destruction of social relations. If we attend to its broad range of meanings, the concept of violence points to a multiplicity of social connections that link physical and psychological force, individual and structural harm, pain and pleasure, degradation and liberation, the violent and the non-violent (Asad 1997).

The authors here offer a broad understanding of violence that raises fundamental questions about the practices and categories through which we order and know society. Bright calls into question the category of inmate "prison violence," analyzing its evolution in the United States in relation to successive penitentiary ideologies whose coercive discipline is based on claims of scientific knowledge. Das's discussion of rape laws and their adjudication in India shows that the apparent opposition between law and violence can be seen as a constitutive relationship, for the legal system encodes and regulates violence against women with respect to categories of both male and national honor. The isolation of a violent act, as Daniel shows in his analysis of Sri Lankan plantation agricultural practices, severs the act from the dense semeiotics of gesture, language, and discipline in the context of coercive conditions within which the act makes a statement. Violence may also be present in its seeming absence, as Feldman argues, for it is implicated in the formation of the senses, shaping practices of visual objectification that are integral to overtly violent acts yet that appear as external to them. Violence is present as well in the essentialism that posits violence as the natural characteristic of certain groups, whether bandits, racial others, tribal peoples, or simply the poor, a point discussed in several articles. The one author here who offers a definition of violence, Moodie, specifies that it pertains to a certain type of conflict and does not treat violence as an abstraction. He considers violence to be "action which causes or threatens to cause physical hurt to the person or property of another," a definition that fits his analysis of "ethnic" conflict in South African gold mines and media representations of it. Taken together, these essays analyze violence as it is officially defined and as it is contested, and they explore the assumptions and invisible histories that permit certain practices to escape definition as violent.

Violent Definitions

The invisibility of these histories makes evident that violence itself participates in the definition of violence. As Teresa de Lauretis has argued concerning the gendering of violence, the notion of a "rhetoric of violence" assumes that "some kind of discursive representation is at work not only in the concept of 'violence' but in the social practices of violence as well. The (semiotic) relation of the social to the discursive is thus posed from the start" (1989: 240). The terms in which de Lauretis conceptualizes the relation between violence and rhetoric, as well as between the social and the discursive, underline key problems in defining violence, including the difficulty of developing an analytical vocabulary that can distinguish different orders of experience without creating unwarranted divisions among them. Regarding these orders as part of a shared semiotic field, she argues that "once a connection is assumed between violence and rhetoric, the two terms begin to slide and, soon enough, the connection will appear to be reversible" (ibid.).

Linking Foucault's discussion of the power of discursive formations with Derrida's analysis of the "violence of the letter," de Lauretis argues: "From the Foucauldian notion of a rhetoric of violence, an order of language which speaks violence—names certain behaviors and events as violent, but not others, and constructs objects and subjects of violence, and hence violence as a social fact—it is easy to slide into the reverse notion of a language which, itself, produces violence" (ibid.). If the rhetoric of violence is thus inseparable from the violence of rhetoric, the complex exchange between violence and its representations may be seen as an ongoing interchange between different semiotic domains in the course of which certain narratives become hegemonic while others are marginalized. While hegemonic rhetorical violence has the effect of rendering visible some forms of violence and obscuring others, political violence has the potential to upset the stability of dominant narratives and to bring to the surface their underlying assumptions. The devastating impact of World War I on Europe undermined assumptions about the inevitability of Western progress and the universality of Western reason. In his essay "Critique of Violence," written in the aftermath of the war, Walter Benjamin sought to make visible the links between violence and order through a discussion of the place of violence in natural and positive law. While natural law sees violence as an inherent datum of nature and judges all existing law only by criticizing its ends, positive law views violence as the product of history and judges all evolving law only by criticizing its means (1978: 278). This distinction between natural and positive law has contemporary relevance, given the ongoing tension between sociobiological and constructivist understanding of violence. Concerned that Darwinism had rekindled natural law explanations of violence in the post-war military climate, Benjamin criticized Darwinian biology for its "thoroughly dogmatic manner" of regarding violence "as the only original means, besides natural selection, appropriate to all the vital ends of nature" (ibid.). Yet his goal was not to contrast natural and positive law, but to discuss their common foundations and shared assumptions concerning the relation of means and ends.

By examining violence in relation to the legality of war, capital punishment, and labor strikes, Benjamin distinguishes between the violence that posits the law and the violence that preserves it. According to him, both natural and positive law "meet in their common basic dogma: just ends can be attained by justified means, justified means used for just ends." "While for natural law ends are primordial, for positive law means are fundamental. Natural law attempts, by the justness of the ends, to 'justify' the means, positive law to 'guarantee' the justness of the ends through the justification of the means." Both schools of law thus treat violence as involving the relations of means and ends within the legal system and neither fully recognizes the circularity of their position and the need to develop independent criteria for establishing both just ends and justified means. Moreover, neither view considers justified forms of violence outside the law, one of Benjamin's central concerns. From the perspective of his messianic conception of history, he argues for the necessity of a kind of non-legal violence that works not as a means of legality, but as a manifestation of redemptive power. He called this "divine violence," a form of violence that neither constitutes nor preserves the law, but rather de-poses it. For Benjamin, if there was to be salvation, it was necessary to posit a form of violence different from all those envisaged by the law, a conception that confirmed his understanding of the indispensability of violence in human affairs. "Every conceivable solution to human problems, not to speak of deliverance from the confines of all the world-historical conditions of existence obtaining hitherto, remains impossible if violence is totally excluded in principle" (293).

Writing at the close of the twentieth century, Italian philosopher Giorgio Agamben draws on Foucault's discussion of biopolitics and on Schmitt's analysis of the sovereign to develop Benjamin's argument into a discussion of sovereignty as the "power over life." He argues that Schmitt's discussion of "sovereign violence" also "opens a zone of indistinction between law and nature, outside and inside, violence and law." But for Agamben, far from undoing the dialectic between law-constituting and law-preserving violence, "the sovereign is precisely the one who maintains the possibility of deciding on the two to the very degree that he renders them indistinguishable from each other" (1998: 64). "As long as the state of exception is distinguished from the normal case, the dialectic between the violence that posits the law and the violence that preserves it is not truly broken, and the sovereign decision even appears simply as the medium in which the passage from the one to the other takes place." In this sense, sovereign violence both posits the law, "since it affirms that an otherwise forbidden act is permitted," and conserves it, "since the content of the new law is only the conservation of the old one" (ibid.). Central to this dialectic is the notion of sovereignty as power over life which, according to Agamben, has developed in a disenchanted world together with the sacralization of what Benjamin called "bare, natural life." Modernity, paradoxically, entails a social order in which the secular state has power over the sacred, "naked life" of individuals (1998: 65).

It is significant that Agamben's analysis of sovereign violence links political and legal ethics to the issue of human potentiality and of cultural difference. Yet, as in Benjamin's essay on violence, his discussion of exceptional and normal states as well as of possible social orders assumes Europe as the standard and thus does not consider the pervasive significance of colonialism in the making of the modern world. Instead, an analytical perspective informed by the legacy of colonialism questions sharp distinctions between states of normality and of exception, and makes it necessary to consider the possibilities opened by violence in light of an already existing global order of differences; an approach attentive to colonial relations pluralizes and further politicizes the connections among violence, potentiality, and ethics.

Despite this shortcoming, the discussions of these authors make evident the enormous difficulty of defining violence, distinguishing its various forms, and evaluating it ethically and politically. Any definition of violence already assumes a partial standpoint sustained by violent relations. This book responds to the indispensability as well as to the inadequacy of definitions by relating violence to that which appears to be non-violent. Using different strategies and modes of analysis, the essays in this volume seek to construct and examine the contexts within which violence is recognized or concealed, while deconstructing violence as a naturalized subject. They show that while political violence is associated with acts of transgression and aggression against central values, it is also present in the mechanisms that preserve order and legality and in the practices that seek to institute new visions of society.

Considering the State

The ambiguity of the title *States of Violence* suggests the differing and often unacknowledged domains within which power and violence are organized. State refers in part to the central node of institutions and ideologies from which territorial rule is exercised and the right to control the administration of violence is claimed. However, state also refers to the condition of being—experiential, corporal, and affective—of individuals or collectivities. If the state as political center is normally aligned with permanence and with the domain of law and reason, state as a condition is related to the transitory and to the realm of the psyche and emotion. Through its uncomfortable juxtaposition of meanings, this title reveals suppressed associations, bringing together the stable and the transient, the institutional and the experiential, and inviting recognition of the multiple intersections of practices of governance and processes of feeling.

State, meaning condition, may seem to collide with the claim of the modern state, particularly in its liberal form, to stand above the fray of conflicts and passions as a neutral agent of order. Yet if we see beyond its self-proclaimed role, it is clear that the state is profoundly involved in the structuring and representation of the moral order and in the shaping of affective ties and allegiances. It helps define the moral categories and standards of civilized life on which practices of inclusion and exclusion are based and identities constructed, and it buttresses the norms of civility against which respectability and belonging are measured and by which marginality and transgression are established (Stoler 1991). Concerned with its ability to command allegiance and obedience, the state presents itself in moral terms that range from the benevolent to the punitive, while it cultivates state-centered affective orientations that range from love to fear (Berlant 1991; Sommer 1991; Stoler 2001). It categorizes and engages with its opponents in the language of its ethical universe, presenting its use of force as a moral necessity. Our title calls attention to these mutually reinforcing domains of state reasons, actions, and affects.

By suggesting complicity between states and violence, it also invites us to question statist narratives and to explore teleological assumptions at the core of Western theories of state rule. For while violence lies at the heart of the modern world, influential social theories and historical narratives present it as residing on the margins of modernity. The modern state has been identified as the agent of reason and progress, legitimating its authority to define and defend order through its regulation of legalized violence. For traditional Western theory the state acts as the neutral adjudicator of conflict, eliminating illegitimate violence from daily life and controlling its legal application (Keane 1996; Poole 1994). The historical and social sciences, intimately connected with processes of state formation and with the division of the world between metropolitan centers and subaltern peripheries (de Certeau 1984; Wallerstein 1999; Pletch 1981), have reproduced this distinction, seeing the state as exercising and regulating the legitimate use of force (Das 1992). These disciplines have generally counterposed the state to violence and have placed law, regulatory practices, and the state's use of force on the side of historical development and civilization.

The identification of the modern state with freedom, in contrast to premodern and non-Western forms of rule, has been furthered, Chakrabarty argues, by "histories that either implicitly or explicitly celebrate the advent of the modern state and the idea of citizenship," playing down "the repression and violence that are as instrumental in the victory of the modern as is the persuasive power of its rhetorical strategies." In the "self-fashioning of the West," violence is connected to idealism, as coercive measures are presented as tied to projects of progress, reform, and development (2000:

44–45). State violence in the multiple forms that accompany nationalism and colonialism, both internal and external, becomes normalized as the necessary hand of modernity.

Poles of Power

State discourse obscures the range of relationships on which the state is based as well as the state's capacity to affect historical events and their representation. Given the intimate association between processes of state formation and of knowledge production, the analyst's task of representing violence involves a self-critical effort to listen to subaltern as well as official voices and to remain sensitive to the limits of what can be said and to the eloquence of silences.

Several of the cases discussed here illuminate the historical connections between poles of power and the complex web of social relations existing within subordinated sectors. Rather than accept the naturalized depiction of certain categories of people as inherently violent, these authors examine the structural constraints, social conditions, and sets of meanings within which people act. Moodie demonstrates that conflicts among miners in South Africa's gold mines under apartheid have been unjustifiably depicted as an expression of tribal animosities, ignoring the impact of divisive company policies on workers' lives within the confines of the mines. Miners' forms of solidarity and targeted violence evolved in response to these conditions, cutting across ethnic boundaries to reflect collective goals. In Egypt and in Venezuela, violent urban protests classified as "riots" were officially presented as irrational expressions of collective emotion and incapacity for self-rule. Yet if we read the actions and listen to the language of their participants, asking how they address social inequalities and collective memories, we may delineate the logic and form of expression these protests take (Cole, Coronil and Skurski). In other instances, where social sectors lie at the margins of state control and maintain a degree of autonomy—among peasant bandits, frontier communities, and tribal peoples in the Mediterranean, Latin America, and India—forms of violence may be analyzed not only as a response to power, but as constituents of alternative forms of sociality (Cassia, Baretta and Markoff, Edwards).

Through attention to the mediation and interiorization of violence, we may analyze situations in which the possibilities for expression and interpretation are severely limited. Regimes of regimented labor regulation on

Sri Lankan colonial tea plantations, Daniel shows, confined workers to the arena of agronomic discourse as the terrain of struggle on which to define personhood and contest authority. The carceral order of the U.S. penitentiary that Bright examines denied prisoners interaction and arenas of self-making in response to changing ideologies of prisoner reform and discipline. Thus, as Bright asserts, the subject of "prison violence" is steeped in ambiguity, for "prisons are both producers and containers of violence," structuring, creating, and suppressing violence in highly differentiated and modulated forms. Within this totalizing institution inmate forms of violence can be delineated, but prisoners' "violence cannot be interpreted," remaining an opaque response to regimes of control that themselves reflect the social conditions and ideologies that define criminality as a problem to be treated.

The invisibility of relations of domination is an effect of power in the panoptic regime of routinized state violence in Northern Ireland that Feldman examines. Power is embedded within technologies and disciplines of ocularity, such as marksmanship and photography, based on "the circuit of visibility" and "the power relation ignited within this circuit between detached technical instruments of visualization and those bodies surveilled and objectified by vision and/or violence." These disciplines of ocularity fix the image of those surveilled, creating them as objects of an unseen power, akin to the objectifying operations of discourses that fix, detach, and frame their objects of observation. The landscape of violence in Northern Ireland takes form as much through its representation as through the invisibility of its operations or the occlusion of its agents and instruments. In this context, the concealment of violence is a condition of its performance. Ethnographic analysis participates in this concealment when it reproduces the realist monopoly on the construction of facticity and ignores "alternate perceptual postures."

The routinized operations of legal systems center on the evaluation of acts defined as criminal and violent, concealing the links between law and violence, Das argues. The categories embedded in India's rape laws and wielded by its judges classify types of females and zones of their bodies in such a way that women's and girls' experiences and intentions become both legally irrelevant and unknowable. The law recognizes the existence of rape on the basis of evidence provided by female bodies in accord with their categorization as appropriate or inappropriate objects of male desire. This production of legal knowledge dismembers a female, placing her and her severed parts at the disposal of state and masculine authority.

Although women and girls may speak to the court, their intentions are discounted and male voices receive recognition.

Representation

The issue of representation is inseparable from the forms and intensities of violence and from the temporal circumstances within which people live through and beyond it. Torture "hyperindividuates" the victim by means of pain that is incommunicable and unshareable, Daniel concludes from his extensive work on Sri Lankan civil violence. Placed beyond the limits of language, the victims' attempts at narrating their suffering either fail or are emotionally empty. Although the expression of terror may find a voice through other people, as in artistic forms emerging from a collectivity subjected to terror, the "excess" of violence often renders it unspeakable for its immediate victims (Daniel 1996: 142–45).

The limits of language as a means to express overwhelming horror present scholars and interpreters with a challenge that is at once human and intellectual. Overpowering violence, Daniel asserts, calls into question the notion of "culture" and the hope of meaning that we place in it (1996: 210). The academic concept of "culture" has been identified with the capacity to totalize and harmonize social life, to make it comprehensible at ever higher levels of abstraction. But violence confronts scholars with realities that can be neither incorporated into nor explained by "culture," realities that press against the human limits of expression and question assumptions about the social order.

The concept of culture as harmonizing and inclusionary has been closely wedded to Western theories of the state and history, informing the widely held teleological assumption that culture evolves from the primitive to the advanced and finds its highest form in the rational nation-state (Daniel 1996: 202). Yet the realities of devastating national conflicts and internal repression wielded by and in the name of the state now appear for many analysts to be incompatible with this view, reflecting instead exclusions that are constitutive of the nation-state and of nationalist discourse (see e.g., Feldman 1991; Das 1995b; Eley and Suny 1996; Cooper and Stoler 1997; Warren 1998; Gould 1998; Chakrabarty 2000; Grandin 2000; Sluka 2000).

The enormously violent Partition of India that created two "artificial states" was propelled by a nationalist logic of statehood; it sought to expel those deemed alien to the nation and to forcibly incorporate within it those claimed by the nation as members (Das 1995a). In her wide-ranging body of work on the consequences of the Partition and on the links among violence, gender, and nationalist ideology, Das investigates the relationships among language, silence, gesture, and suffering. She examines questions that have important implications for those who investigate violence. Can suffering be expressed, known, or shared? What is the relationship of the observer to those who suffer from violence? She notes that under extreme conditions, "as human understanding gives way, language is struck dumb." When violence annihilates language it creates its own fear; "a relapse into a dumb condition is not only a sign of this period but is also a part of the terror itself." Yet silence does not bring an end to communication or to understanding; thus for the analyst, "it is the silences that need to be addressed" (1995b: 184, 191).

Certain forms of silence emerge in response to loss, shaping processes of collective reconstitution and healing. "Veils of silence" covered breaches of norms resulting from the Partition, allowing violated women to be reabsorbed into the community (1995a: 218). Silence also helped shape memories of violence that remained at the surface but were kept enclosed through a shared language of allusion and limits (2000: 209). A "zone of silence" surrounded events too painful for women to narrate, memories that enclosed a "poisonous knowledge" that was maintained within the self rather than seeking direct expression (1997: 84).

Does the violent destruction of meaning negate the possibility of knowing another's pain? While pain may destroy the capacity to communicate, Das asserts, the expression of pain nevertheless establishes a relationship of communication. It asks for recognition, and thus initiates a social connection; in return it may elicit a response and become transformed into shared suffering. As it is brought out of the zone of the unknowable and the individual, pain passes into another's body, shaping the moral community (1995b, 1997). This helps bridge the gap between victim and observer and suggests a way in which "relating to the pain of others can become witness to a moral life" (1995b: 194–95). Witnessing does not necessarily imply that investigators should seek to unearth and give voice to hidden narratives; rather it suggests the importance of following the cultural forms that connect pain and language among a people, forms that indicate the particular social paths that recognition and healing can take.

As these discussions show, analysts of violence must also face the tension in their own use of language between the destruction of sense by suffering and the need to make sense of suffering. Recurrent questions about the poetics and ethics of representing the lives of others take on special significance when the subject is violence and the pain it inflicts. Given its polyvalent structure and capacity to engage our senses and emotions, there is the risk of turning violence into a sensational object of interest, pleasure, or profit (Feldman 1991; Daniel 1996; Kleinman and Kleinman 1997; Rabasa 2000). The call to act as a witness of a moral life shows how much the epistemological field is actually a part of the domain of politics. While this domain offers no stable ground for answers, it makes the public effect of our work a critical standard, focusing attention on the victims of violence rather than on the theorists of its representation. Yet perhaps it needs to be remembered that the risk attending the representation of violence is not exclusive to it, for no representation is immaculate or free from aesthetic framing. The social suffering inflicted by violence only makes trivializing or exoticizing modes of objectification more offensive. Social suffering intensifies the urgent need to produce forms of understanding that make the conditions from which it arises intolerable.

The Location of Violence

The modern state's discourse of historical progress is organized around dichotomies of progress and backwardness, law and criminality, reason and irrationality. These taxonomies define violence in terms of spatial and temporal locations, weaving violence into practices of social classification and economic differentiation. Through their attention to the spatial, the essays here show that just as violence is located in spaces saturated with particular histories, these histories are shaped by the spaces in which they develop; they allow us to analyze, in Doreen Massey's terms, the relationship between the social construction of space and the spatial construction of the social (1994: 254). Spaces of violence may be distant from centers of state control or reside on their internal frontiers; they may be closely regulated public sites or human bodies defined in spatial terms. Whether cast as an opposition between centers of state reason and peripheries of disorderly backwardness (Baretta and Markoff, Edwards), as the threat of subversion and anarchy within zones of conflict (Cassia, Coronil and Skurski, Feldman), or as the need to confine and classify transgressive figures (Bright, Das, Moodie), the conceptualization and organization of the spatial is integral to the formation of violence.

Spatial classifications typically draw boundaries around political and administrative units, concealing the constitutive relations that link local conflicts to global processes. In contrast, these studies highlight such links, exposing the inadequacies of analyses that assume violence to be explained by cultural and political differences and individual proclivities. In the case of the U.S. prison system discussed by Bright, transformations in the economy and in political discourse affected not only the formal ordering of the prison and its ideologies of rehabilitation and discipline, but also forms of violence and complicity between prison bosses and inmates, as they developed sophisticated mechanisms of collusion and control. Similarly, ethnic conflict in South African gold mines, Moodie shows, was related to shifts in the national economy rather than to the dynamics of the mining camps seen as isolated units. Changes in management's organization of production affected both work patterns and relations among the miners, modifying their modes of ritualized combat and leading to open confrontations. These clashes did not reflect workers' primordial ethnic ties, but rather their response to increasingly divisive conditions.

In the world of Tamil estate workers, Daniel shows, words that expressed a system of exact measures and rules for tea cultivation served to establish hegemonic notions of capitalist rationality and progress. The two modalities of "tea talk," agricultural and agronomic, articulated two distinct moral and historical universes related to each other by practices of domination and a narrative of progress that were supported by state power. These forms of "tea talk" not only brought different historical universes in contact with each other, but helped redefine the social landscape. A Tamil worker's preference for apparently inexact methods of pruning, such as "knee height," instead of the exact fifteen inches above the ground demanded by colonial manuals, did not impede him from leaving his mark on the agricultural field, or in response to humiliation, cutting his supervisor's arm exactly fifteen inches below the elbow. At this micro-scale, spatial discourses and forms of measurement have long been a site of social struggle.

Under changing international conditions involving movements of people and capital and shifts in state policy and international relations, spaces controlled by the state may be transformed into areas where state power is challenged, while peripheral zones may move to the center of national attention. Urban violence in nineteenth-century Alexandria, Cole argues, formed part of a broader revolt that provoked a crisis of the local state and of imperialism in the region. War, immigration, and debt crisis heightened nationalist tensions and anti-European sentiments in Egypt, drawing working people into protests located along urban boundaries defined by national and ethnic identifications. A century later in Venezuela, the advent of a debt crisis and the dismantling of state protectionism brought state repression at the frontier, while in the capital city the poor who lived on the urban margins assaulted businesses in the center (Coronil and Skurski). Military forces retaliated by drawing boundaries around working-class zones, making residential areas the target of massive firepower, and invading homes and neighborhoods to seek out those deemed criminal and subversive. Zones of conflict extended to the public cemetery, where concealed mass graves of the massacred became the site of demands by relatives that the dead be recognized as citizens possessing rights. These events redrew the national political landscape, establishing a temporal rupture that marked a newly visible set of spatialized social fissures.

In times of conflict the organization of spatial divisions and of distinctions between public and private arenas are disrupted, introducing fear into ordinary movements and domestic spaces, as Feldman shows in his discussion of Northern Ireland. As surveillance renders the private visible, and being seen can be akin to being made a target, the boundaries of bodies and residences are routinely transgressed and political opponents are constituted through their visual objectification. This diffuse system of control is embedded within the colonial history of Belfast and the creation of bounded "ethnic landscapes," reflecting the constitutive relationship between the British state's strategies of depiction and Northern Ireland's history of domination. Visual realism, Feldman argues, makes and transforms its objects rather than simply reflecting them. In the context of nationalist projects, it is directed at the domination of space and rests on the creation of fields of ethnic, racial, and topographic homogeneity. Ethnic landscapes thus carry the marks of violence recorded in social memory and repeated in ongoing acts through which political space becomes circumscribed.

Civilizing Violence

The discourse of civilization and barbarism has had a constitutive role in the definition and global expansion of the West, delineating a landscape marked by zones of danger that represent a challenge as well as a threat to the state. This discourse casts violence as the marker of the primitive irrationality that civilized states are divinely and historically mandated to overcome, a sign of the disorder and savagery that lie at their borders. Although it has shaped the modern colonial "civilizing mission" directed at native salvation and reform, its historical origins in the Spanish and Portuguese empires have been obscured. For while northern European powers defined themselves through opposition to the Spanish Crown's reputedly barbarous colonial practices, the distinctions and teleology on which Spanish colonialism was based became incorporated into and transformed by the projects of its rivals, and have continued to inform imperial and state relations at the global level (Mignolo 2000).

The classification of groups and cultures within hierarchical and evolutionary frameworks has been at once an organizing political principle and an object of contention within the civilizing project. The effort to civilize the Indians in the Americas during the Conquest was premised on distinctions between "peaceful" and "wild" (or "barbarous") peoples, distinctions around which projects of conversion and coerced labor were built (Castro-Klarén 2001, Hulme 1986). The political ramifications of such distinctions and their implication in the state-sanctioned use of violence has been a subject of dispute since the "Great Debate" (1557) in which Fray Bartolomé de las Casas argued before the Spanish Crown that Indians were pacific rather than barbarous and should be gently converted and taught to labor rather than forcibly converted and enslaved (Brading 1991). His influential critique of arbitrary violence and his call for justice simultaneously undermined the wars of conquest and legitimated the colonial enterprise by reinforcing the universalizing claims of Catholicism (Rabasa 2000: 26). The debate thus wove violence into a moral and political complex of meanings associated with the colonial state and its historical teleology.

The moral and religious principles on which Spain's colonizing project rested were bound up with state economic practices through which regional centers and peripheries were constituted as interrelated poles. While the relationships between them transformed over time, they continued to be defined by the discourse of civilization and barbarism. As Baretta and Markoff show, the expulsion and flight of Indians, blacks, and *mestizos* to cattle frontiers created ambiguous zones of freedom and exclusion that were seen as external to civilized society even as they were economically and ideologically constitutive of urban centers. Over time, the expansion of capitalist relations meant that plains activities once viewed as customary and legitimate, such as hunting wild cattle, became defined as banditry and their practitioners classified as criminals. This categorization justified state repressive actions against autonomous plainsmen and the eradication of their social basis.

The repression of banditry has frequently been tied to post-Enlightenment state building and to discourses of law and reason. In periods when the colonial state has sought to establish its legitimacy or the national state has promoted capitalist relations, the role of the state as the ultimate producer of the contrast between reason and violence has become more visible. The state in Cyprus and Greece, acting as the representative of abstract law and the agent of reason, construed the bandit as a practitioner of savage, personalized violence and as standing for a place and time that represented the backwardness the state sought to eradicate, Cassia argues. Yet the state's persecution and public execution of bandits did not insure the acceptance of state reason nor eliminate such forms of resistance, for though it strengthened state power it also threatened state legitimacy among the communities that produced and were victimized by bandits.

In this cautionary analysis Cassia reminds us that the tendency to romanticize or to demonize bandits, as well as to assign them to a precapitalist past, has lain primarily with the state, political commentators, and intellectuals. At the local level, however, moral categories shift and boundaries between the state and the outlaw are blurred. The often moralizing and simplifying accounts constructed by national and foreign elites shape the histories that are taken as authoritative, codifying the opposition between the state and banditry, delegitimizing non state violence, and obscuring the views of those whom the state dominates. People such as the illiterate plainsmen of Latin America, as Markoff comments, leave little record through which we can discern their skeptical response to the moral claims made by the discourse of civilization and barbarism. In the official histories of Latin American and European nations, bandits and other frontier populations appear as an obstacle to the nation's progress, while the structural conditions that shaped them and the moral codes they lived by are ignored.

Yet on occasion it is possible to discern counter narratives to official discourse, with its colonizing assumptions. In an illuminating counterpoint, Edwards sets the rhetorical strategies and narrative conventions of British colonial representatives against those of the Mad Mullah and other *fakirs* who led tribal opposition to British rule in northern India in the late nineteenth century. The analysis of these conventions suggests why the official British account of a tribal uprising and its defeat by colonial forces has failed to gain acceptance in local memory, while the account of the Mullah's miraculous triumph over these forces is maintained in local narrative. Colonial officials' discourse of civilization and barbarism presented the advance of British civilization as both an irresistible natural force and a providential social force that promised to domesticate uncivilized peoples. Military power was seen as a legitimate instrument in the cause of reason against tribal peoples' "fanaticism" and their opposition to colonial "good government." The counter-discourse of miracles wielded by the Mullahs provided an alternative cultural paradigm, imparting divine purpose to events and linking believers to their ordained fulfillment. Set within conventions of opposition to despotic authority, this paradigm helped Muslim tribes place limits on the British ability to control understandings of history through their use of force. By making a contextualized analysis, Edwards shows, we may be able to dislodge from its position of privilege the discourse of civilization and barbarism and grasp how counter identities are mobilized. To do so requires that scholars include within their analysis a critique of the colonizing categories and teleologies that are embedded in official historiography (Guha 1988).

Religious unreason, associated with backwardness and danger, has also been seen by colonial powers as responsible for urban violence. The clashes in Alexandria, Egypt, linked to the 'Urabi revolt were regarded as the action of "enraged, fanatical Muslim mobs" and explained in terms of ancient religious antagonisms and despotic traditions that demonstrated the need for the civilizing establishment of European rule, Cole argues. These ideas, in turn, played a role in England's bombardment and invasion of Egypt, fundamentally altering the politics of the region. The European construction of regional conflicts in terms of religious animosities and elite political manipulation concealed the destabilizing effects on Egypt of increasing colonial intervention and of the growing local presence of a diverse European working population. In European accounts of the revolt, Cole contends, important factors were concealed, perpetuating an elite-centered view of local political life. The notion of the "riot" applied to these events reflected the perspective of colonial authorities and was laden with moral and legal evaluations that criminalized collective actions. The reductionist hierarchies implicit in the discourse of riots also erased the complex politics of non-elite social actors, attributing to them homogenizing religious motives while ignoring the impact on them of international social and economic changes.

The term "riot" reflects a legal and moral evaluation of collective acts in terms of a state-centered teleology. From the modernizing state's perspective, riots signal the breakdown of reason and the failure of civilizing controls; those who riot both cause destruction and unleash backwardness.

From an opposition perspective, however, such actions may be seen as a popular protest against the state's violation of the terms on which its own claims to hegemony rest. Such conflicting discourses concerning the state and violence came into contention in response to mass protests in Venezuela against the government's IMF austerity program, according to Coronil and Skurski. The material destruction the protests caused and the state massacre of hundreds of people signified a rupture in the Cold War era populist pact that had promised national progress and prosperity through state-promoted modernization. Prior to this rupture, the discourse of civilizing progress had effectively been wielded by the state against critics of the development project, depicting them as a subversive threat to the social order. Yet contradictory strands in nationalist discourse, which combined anti-elitist tenets with developmentalist goals, provided the principles on which a broad opposition discourse was built. As the pact became undone, its basis in exclusionary and colonizing principles became apparent. Thus, when the state used force against the protests and defined them as an outbreak of anarchy, it encountered an opposition discourse of popular justice that cast the state as the savage and asserted continuities between the regime's quotidian exclusionary practices and its exceptional repression of the "disturbances."

The popular challenge to the Venezuelan state discourse of modernization reflected conflicts occurring throughout Latin America since the 1960s, as dictatorships having U.S. support brought massive repression against "forces of subversion." In constructing the opposition between state/civilization and subversion/barbarism, regimes created an unseen enemy that penetrated the social body and demanded specialized techniques of violence. Ranging from the bureaucratized violence of the Argentine "Dirty War," fought in defense of "Western Christian civilization," to the genocidal scorched-earth campaigns of the Guatemalan military regime, the colonial discourse of conquest against forces of backwardness was mobilized and refashioned to create the promise of national historical redemption through a modernizing crusade (Carmack 1988; Graziano 1992; Warren 1998). The demise of these regimes and of this form of civilizing discourse has subsequently shifted attention from the violence directly wielded by the state to the underlying continuities between military and democratic regimes and to the conditions of structural violence and legal impunity yet to be transformed by democratization (Caldeira and Holston 1999; NACLA 2000). With the state's claimed mission of pacifying disorder unfinished, its policing agencies define the threat of violence as residing among the primitives, subversives, and criminals who have a continuing presence within the nation.

Engendering Violence

The production and representation of gender hierarchies is integral to the relationship between the state and the social order. Yet the naturalization of gender identities has not only concealed the historical origins of these ties, but grounded the ideological division between the state, seen as a public sphere of male activity, and the family, seen as a subordinate, private sphere identified with female activity. This volume problematizes the dichotomy between the public and private spheres and the gender identities associated with them. It shows how the state itself is constituted through gendered practices, such as discourses of national honor, rational civility, the colonial mission, and the realist gaze. It also shows how the state participates in the production of gendered subjects by such means as legal codes, penal institutions, and labor regimes, and how it marginalizes gendered Others, such as primitive bandits, defiled women, or unruly prisoners. This construction of gender identities as well as the gendering of collective projects involves the constant and often coercive fixing of meanings. If states are sustained by violence, the silencing of gender through its naturalization constitutes an often perversely violent manner of buttressing gender inequalities.

Gender-blind approaches to imperial and nationalist projects and to anti-colonial movements have reproduced these projects' universalizing claims and have ignored a fundamental basis of inequities. Exploring new terrain, recent studies informed by feminist and postcolonial perspectives have analyzed the hidden continuities between gender hierarchies and the state, examining the social imaginary and the material relations on which these projects draw and that they help fashion (e.g., Bederman 1995; Berlant 1997; Das 1995b; Dore and Molyneux 2000; Enloe 1993; Eley and Suny 1996; Franco 1999; Gutman and Pease 1993; Hall 2000; Mayer 2000; Mosse 1996; Pateman 1988; Stoler 1997; Taylor 1997; Yuval-Davis 1997). They show that both imperial states and anti-colonial nationalisms have linked constructs of masculinity to the state in their efforts to mobilize support and to configure an ideal collective identity. While the vision of progress and liberation such projects promise may emphasize the defense of women, the concept of their defense has been formed within imperial hierarchies that differentiate among women on a civilizatory and racial scale (Newman 1999) and it has been subordinated to the unifying demands and homogenizing claims of the nation within which women become subsumed (Chatterjee 1993).

Among the naturalized renderings of gender that inform state projects, the association between masculinity and violence has had a vitally important role, shaping the racialized concepts of progress and power that propel Western projects of expansion and unification. Integral to state formation, this association has helped define concepts of political leadership and of moral worth embedded within colonial and nationalist projects. Male violence has often been made the marker of primitive forms of society that survive at the margins of state control and modernizing progress. Yet among the rural sectors identified with violent forms of masculinity discussed here—frontier plainsmen in Latin America and bandits in Greece and Cyprus—local modes of violence did not develop independently of the state, but in relation to it, reflecting complex ties of incorporation as well as of opposition. State power was exercised through local male networks and forms of authority at the same time that state repression was directed against local leaders and aspects of rural life. Codes of masculinity associated with banditry were both seen as reflections of backwardness and made a component of the state.

Within these regions, violent practices were constitutive of collective identity and political relations, intertwining concepts of power, gender, and honor. At the local level, men's skills with weapons and codes of personal bravery valorized violence as a symbolic and practical medium of masculinity—a sign of local authority, opposition to the state, and male superiority. In the Mediterranean regions Cassia discusses, women stood for collective reproduction and honor among the communities producing banditry. As figures vital for the construction of masculine identity, women were both protected and attacked, respected and defiled. Made the object of male actions and the sign of masculinity, the subordination of women was necessary for male leaders: women's physical safety was threatened in contests between rival men, their protection was claimed by the state, and their identity questioned if they transgressed the normative gender order.

However, most scholarship has overlooked the difficult-to-discern system of gender relations sustaining banditry and cattle frontiers, and has thus helped reproduce the male-centered perspective of state and subaltern discourses (Markoff, this volume; Socolow 1998). Analytical attention to male activity, as well as the identification of political power with the public sphere, has obscured the role of women and has limited the analysis of gender in the formation of the state and of the social order. This is but one of many instances in which analysis converges with and reflects the universalizing discourse of the nation, concealing the continuities between colonial and nationalist projects and the reproduction and fixing of gender—and racial—hierarchies this has entailed (Chatterjee 1993; Dore and Molyneux 2000).

These gendered relations have been assumed by nationalist discourse and state projects to constitute the natural foundations of society, as well as to be an object of their modernizing reform. In Latin America, the glorification of the postcolonial state has been cast in masculine terms of military strength and rational enlightenment, granting the state the mission to uplift and control a backward people, ambiguously gendered as both docile and dangerous (Skurski 1996). Nationalist discourse has claimed that the masculine state protects the people against internal and external threats, while state repression and torture have sought to feminize political opponents (Coronil and Skurski, this volume; Franco 1999; Taylor 1997).

Although the issue of women is concealed by the universalizing language of citizens' rights, it is central for understanding the links between violence and the postcolonial state, Veena Das argues. The massive violence against women carried out during India's Partition was constitutive of the states of India and Pakistan, as women's bodies, through rape, mutilation, and abduction, were made "political signs, territories on which the political programmes of the rioting communities of men were inscribed." In response, official efforts to recover abducted women were made evidence of the new states' civilization and modernity. Legitimated as the defense of national honor, these forced returns and classifications in fact established new articulations between the domain of kinship and the domain of politics, treating women as reproducers of the nation and investing existing norms of familial control with yet greater authority and rigidity (Das 1995a: 212–14).

Since independence, India's legal regulation of sexual violence against women has classified sexuality in accord with a standard of male normality and has sorted women on the basis of their sexual availability. Legal discourse, Das shows, has defined women in terms of their reproductive capacities and their assumed sexual tendencies, denying them agency and rights while normalizing male sexual assault as an expression of natural male tendencies. The quotidian relationship between legal discourse and violence in the production of gender identities can be seen in the judicial system's interpretation of assaults on female bodies as signs communicated among men, or in the denial, as with marital rape, that certain assaults constitute violence. These established assumptions about gender and sexuality have shaped and been shaped by collective violence occurring when the normative system has collapsed, as during the Partition; the violation of gender categories of honor has been a crucial arena in which to effect the destruction and the assertion of collective forms of belonging.

The processes of gendered abstraction by which subjects, citizens, and non-citizens are constructed intersect with institutional practices for which violence is constitutive of categories of people. The gendered division of labor and agronomic discourses on Sri Lankan tea plantations shaped identities within the colonial order, creating the practices and language through which control and resistance were exercised. Within the labor regime of apartheid South Africa, where coerced gender segregation severed black men from their communities, the gold mines became a quasi-carceral system in which violence was attributed to groups of men as an expression of their ethnicity. High-security prisons for men in the United States sought to punish and reform prisoners according to differing theories of criminality and personhood integrally linked to shifting gender regimes of labor and capital. The British state's militarized system of control in Northern Ireland presented itself in gender-neutral terms while building into its abstract language and technology gendered relations of hierarchy, domination, and disembodiment. Through interlocking institutions and practices that have masculinity as their norm, the production of homogenizing concepts of men and women regarded as typifying the nation has been given specific content.

The Ordinary as Extraordinary

A focus on the contexts, practices, and discourses within which political violence takes form and is understood runs throughout these essays. Through their attention to the interactions between human action and historical context they circumvent the structure/agency dichotomy that characterizes much social analysis, showing that processes of structuration and subject-formation are inseparable and that the lines dividing contexts and texts, and structures and actors are fluid. In these studies we see that structures act, actors structure, and contexts not only form, but are formed, transformed, and deformed by violence. Their close examination of specific fields of power challenges easy distinctions between the violent and the peaceful, the state and the civil, the lawful and the criminal, as well as between extraordinary and quotidian forms of violence.

The attention to these fields of power reveals that violence varies widely in both its forms and effects; it may free the present from certain constraints of the past, can renew the hold of the dead upon the living, or it can turn the present into an engulfing reality that weighs upon the past. As Daniel writes of displaced Tamils subjected to the "burgeoning of the present in their lives":

> The quality of their life seems nothing but an assemblage of instances, disruption their source of possibility, interruption their only reverie, shock their only trance, surprise the basis for their openness to the world, the recalcitrant other the only route to their inner selves, chaos their only community, brute force the main impress of power, action the only manifestation of their feelings, doubt the mark of their innocence, contiguity the ground of their freedom, the timbre of tokens the tone of their lives, suspicion their principal trope, and the moment the determinant of their mood (2000: 339).

While violence can create a sense of potentiality, it can obliterate expectations, certainties, and context itself. Inextricably linked to the exercise of power, violent practices are a medium through which values and visions of life are established, contested, and destroyed.

In her essay on violence, Hannah Arendt asserts that warfare is related neither to the human species' "secret death wish" nor to its "irrepressible instinct of aggression," but to "the simple fact that no substitute for this final arbiter in international affairs has yet appeared on the political scene" (1970: 5). Yet as we have seen in this collection, violence is deeply implicated in state practices as well as in states of being that are not confined to the conventions of war; it participates in the formation of institutions and subjectivities as well as in their transformation and destruction. In its multiple expressions, ranging from warfare to peace, violence is a constant if often invisible arbiter of interactions. During the current era of neoliberal globalization, the diverse "violences" of everyday life under conditions of poverty and coercion (Kleinman 2000) constitute an invisible war (Marcos 1997), a final arbiter that works through multiple mediations. As states and markets change, form and power become more diffuse and global, violence as an arbiter of interactions takes on more varied and diffuse forms as well, even as it continues to be wielded as concentrated direct force.

A critical effort to examine statist assumptions that define, normalize, and conceal violence propels the studies here, leading them to follow uncommon paths and to seek the traces of violence within ordinary practices of power and signification. However, this effort finds itself in tension with the effort to construct a position from which to assert the presence of violence and to evaluate its effects. The conceptual, moral, and empirical difficulties of finding such a stance have become evident with the current critique of universalizing Eurocentric assumptions, master narratives, and imperial projects. If violence cannot be seen as a given empirical object, as we have argued, this opens up complex questions as to how it can be appropriately viewed and evaluated without reproducing the inequities of power within which it is embedded.

Paradoxically, instances of massive and undeniable violence mark the limits of efforts to describe and account for violence, rather than offering a foundation for them. Responding to the devastation of European soldiers who returned home after World War I, Walter Benjamin asserted that the most striking lack they encountered in their barren world was an impoverished language unable to express the suffering people had undergone; words were inadequate to experience. As he observed, a history in which "every document of civilization is at the same time a document of barbarism" offers no vantage point free from its violence (1969: 256). The implication of language and morality, law and culture in the organization of this history binds them to the very terms of its formation.

The awareness that there is no neutral analytical position independent of the object studied does not imply the futility of analysis, however. It opens up the possibilities for studies that are attentive to the political and ethical implications of the subjects they choose and of the terms in which they present them. Differing conceptions of life—of personal and collective freedom, of autonomy and sovereignty, of justice and goodness—are at stake in the practice of violence as much as in its study. If there is a certain risk in seeing violence as an inherent component of modern state orders, there is a larger danger in accepting statist narratives that deny its presence. Instead we may see the violence of states as well as states of violence as signs of the limits of these orders, and of the presence within them of alternative social visions.

REFERENCES

Agamben, Giorgio. 1998. *Homo Sacer: Sovereign Power and Bare Life.* Stanford: Stanford University Press.

Arendt, Hannah. 1970. *On Violence.* New York: Harcourt, Brace and World.

Asad, Talal. 1997. "On Torture, or Cruel, Inhuman, and Degrading Treatment." In, Arthur Kleinman, Veena Das, and Margaret Lock, eds., *Social Suffering.* Berkeley: University of California Press, 285–308.

Bederman, Gail. 1995. *Manliness and Civilization: A Cultural History of Gender and Race in the United States, 1880–1917.* Berkeley: University of California Press.

Benjamin, Walter. 1969. "Theses on the Philosophy of History." In *Illuminations.* New York: Schocken Books.

———. 1978. "Critique of Violence." In *Reflections.* New York: Harcourt Brace Jovanovich.

Berlant, Lauren. 1991. *The Anatomy of National Fantasy. Hawthorne, Utopia, and Everyday Life.* Chicago: University of Chicago Press.

———. 1997. *The Queen of America Goes to Washington City. Essays on Sex and Citizenship.* Durham, N.C.: Duke University Press.

Boff, Leonardo. 1987. *Introducing Liberation Theology.* Maryknoll, N.Y.: Orbis Books.

Brading, D. A. 1991. *The First America: The Spanish Monarchy, Creole Patriots, and the Liberal State, 1492–1867.* New York: Cambridge University Press.

Caldeira, Teresa P. R. and James Holston. 1999. "Democracy and Violence in Brazil." *Comparative Studies in Society and History* 41, 4: 691–729.

Carmack, Robert M. 1988. *Harvest of Violence. Guatemala's Indians in the Counterinsurgency War.* Norman: University of Oklahoma Press.

Castro-Klarén, Sara. 2001. "Historiography on the Ground: The Toledo Circle and Guamán Poma." In, Ileana Rodríguez, ed., *The Latin American Subaltern Studies Reader.* Durham, N.C.: Duke University Press.

Certeau, Michel de. 1984. *The Practice of Everyday Life.* Berkeley: University of California Press.

Chakrabarty, Dipesh. 2000. *Provincializing Europe: Postcolonial Thought and Historical Difference.* Princeton: Princeton University Press.

Chatterjee, Partha. 1993. *The Nation and Its Fragments.* Princeton: Princeton University Press.

Chatterjee, Partha and Pradeep Jeganathan. 2000. *Community, Gender and Violence.* New York: Columbia University Press.

Cooper, Fredrick and Ann Laura Stoler, eds. 1997. *Tensions of Empire. Colonial Culture in a Bourgeois World.* Berkeley: University of California Press.

Corradi, Juan F., Patricia Weiss Fagen, and Manuel Antonio Garretón, eds. 1992.

Fear at the Edge. State Terror and Resistance in Latin America. Berkeley: University of California Press.

Daniel, E. Valentine. 1996. *Charred Lullabies: Chapters in an Anthropography of Violence.* Princeton: Princeton University Press.

———. 2000. "Mood, Moment, and Mind." In, Veena Das, Arthur Kleinman, Mamphela Ramphele, and Pamela Reynolds, eds., *Violence and Subjectivity.* Berkeley: University of California Press.

Das, Veena, ed. 1992. *Communities, Riots and Survivors in South.* New Delhi: Oxford University Press.

———. 1995a. "National Honor and Practical Kinship: Unwanted Women and Children." In, Faye D. Ginsburg and Rayna Rapp, eds., *Conceiving the New World Order.* Berkeley: University of California Press.

———. 1995b. *Critical Events: An Anthropological Perspective on Contemporary India.* Delhi: Oxford University Press.

———. 1997. "Language and Body: Transactions in the Construction of Pain." In, Arthur Kleinman, Veena Das, and Margaret Lock, eds., *Social Suffering.* Berkeley: University of California Press.

———. 2000. "The Act of Witnessing: Violence, Poisonous Knowledge, and Subjectivity." In, Veena Das, Arthur Kleinman, Mamphela Ramphele, and Pamela Reynolds, eds., *Violence and Subjectivity.* Berkeley: University of California Press.

de Laurctis, Teresa. 1989. "The Violence of Rhetoric: Considerations on Representation and Gender." In *The Violence of Representation: Literature and the History of Violence.* New York: Routledge.

Dore, Elizabeth and Maxine Molyneux, eds. 2000. *Hidden Histories of Gender and the State in Latin America.* Durham, N.C.: Duke University Press.

Eley, Geoff and Ronald Grigor Suny. 1996. *Becoming National.* New York: Oxford University Press.

Enloe, Cynthia. 1993. *The Morning After. Sexual Politics at the End of the Cold War.* Berkeley: University of California Press.

Fanon, Franz. 1963. *The Wretched of the Earth.* New York: Grove Press.

Farmer, Paul. 1997. "On Suffering and Structural Violence: A View from Below." In, Arthur Kleinman, Veena Das, and Margaret Lock, eds., *Social Suffering.* Berkeley: University of California Press.

Feldman, Allen. 1991. *Formations of Violence: The Narrative of the Body and Political Terror in Northern Ireland.* Chicago: University of Chicago Press.

Franco, Jean. 1999. *Critical Passions. Selected Essays.* Durham, N.C.: Duke University Press.

Gould, Jeffrey L. 1998. *To Die in This Way: Nicaraguan Indians and the Myth of Mestizaje, 1880–1965.* Durham, N.C.: Duke University Press.

Grandin, Greg. 2000. *The Blood of Guatemala: A History of Race and Nation.* Durham, N.C.: Duke University Press.

Graziano, Frank. 1992. *Divine Violence. Spectacle, Psychosexuality, and Radical Christianity in the Argentine "Dirty War."* Denver: Westview Press.

Guha, Ranajit. 1988. "The Prose of Counter-Insurgency." In, Ranajit Guha and Gayatri Spivak, eds., *Selected Subaltern Studies.* New York: Oxford University Press.

Guttman, Amy and Donald Pease, eds. 1993. *Cultures of United States Imperialism.* Durham, N.C.: Duke University Press.

Hall, Catherine. 2000. *Gendered Nations: Nationalism and the Gender Order in the Long Nineteenth Century.* Oxford: Berg Press.

Hulme, Peter. 1986. *Colonial Encounters: Europe and the Native Caribbean, 1492–1797.* New York: Methuen.

Keane, John. 1996. *Reflections on Violence.* New York: Verso.

Kleinman, Arthur. 2000. "The Violences of Everyday Life: The Multiple Forms and Dynamics of Social Violence." In, Veena Das, Arthur Kleinman, Mamphela Ramphele, and Pamela Reynolds, eds., *Violence and Subjectivity.* Berkeley: University of California Press.

Kleinman, Arthur and Joan Kleinman. 1997. "The Appeal of Experience; The Dismay of Images: Cultural Appropriations of Suffering in Our Times." In *Social Suffering.* Berkeley: University of California Press.

Kleinman, Arthur, Veena Das, and Margaret Lock, eds. 1997. *Social Suffering.* Berkeley: University of California Press.

Marcos, Subcomandante. 1997. "La 4e Guerre Mondiale a commencé." *Le Monde diplomatique,* 1 August: 4–5.

Massey, Doreen. 1994. *Space, Place and Gender.* Minneapolis: University of Minnesota Press.

Mayer, Tamar, ed. 2000. *Gender Ironies of Nationalism: Sexing the Nation.* London: Routledge.

Mignolo, Walter D. 2000. *Local Histories/Global Designs: Coloniality, Subaltern Knowledges, and Border Thinking.* Princeton: Princeton University Press.

Mosse, George L. 1996. *The Image of Man: The Creation of Modern Masculinity.* New York: Oxford University Press.

NACLA. 2000. *Rethinking Human Rights.* Vol. 34: 1.

Newman, Louise Michele. 1999. *White Women's Rights: The Racial Origins of Feminism in the United States.* New York: Oxford University Press.

Nordstrom, Carolyn and Antonius C.G.M. Robben. 1995. *Fieldwork Under Fire. Contemporary Studies of Violence and Survival.* Berkeley: University of California Press.

Pateman, Carol. 1988. *The Sexual Contract.* Cambridge: Polity.

Pletch, Carl. 1981. "The Three Worlds, or the Division of Social Scientific Labor, circa 1950–1975." *Comparative Studies in Society and History* 23, 4: 565–90.

Poole, Deborah, ed. 1994. *Unruly Order. Violence, Power, and Cultural Identity in the High Provinces of Southern Perú.* Denver: Westview Press.

Rabasa, José. 2000. *Writing Violence on the Northern Frontier: The Historiography of Sixteenth-Century New Mexico and Florida and the Legacy of Conquest.* Durham, N.C.: Duke University Press.

Reinders, J.S. 1988. *Violence, Victims and Rights. A Reappraisal of the Argument from Institutionalized Violence with Special Reference to Latin American Liberation Theology.* Amsterdam: Free University Press.

Skurski, Julie. 1996. "The Ambiguities of Authenticity in Latin America: *Doña Bárbara* and the Construction of National Identity." In, Geoff Eley and Ronald Grigor Suny, eds., *Becoming National.* New York: Oxford University Press.

Sluka, Jeffrey, ed. 2000. *Death Squad. The Anthropology of State Terror.* Philadelphia: University of Pennsylvania Press.

Socolow, Susan Migden. 1998. "Women of the Buenos Aires Frontier, 1740–1810 (or the Gaucho Turned Upside Down)." In, Donna Guy and Thomas Sheridan, eds., *Contested Ground.* Tucson: University of Arizona Press.

Sommer, Doris. 1991. *Foundational Fictions: National Romances of Latin America.* Berkeley: University of California Press.

Stoler, Ann. 1991. "Carnal Knowledge and Imperial Power: Gender, Race, and Morality in Colonial Asia." In, Micaela di Leonardo, ed., *Gender at the Crossroads of Knowledge.* Berkeley: University of California Press.

———. 1997. *Race and the Education of Desire: Foucault's History of Sexuality and the Colonial Order of Things.* Durham, N.C.: Duke University Press.

——— 2001. "Tense and Tender Ties: The Politics of Comparison in North American History and (Post) Colonial Studies." *Journal of American History* 88: 829–65.

Taylor, Diana. 1997. *Disappearing Acts: Spectacles of Gender and Nationalism in Argentina's "Dirty War."* Durham, N.C.: Duke University Press.

Torres, Camilo. 1968. *Camilo Torres: His Life and His Message.* Springfield, Ill.: Templegate Publishers.

Wallerstein, Immanuel. 1999. *The End of the World as We Know It: Social Science for the Twenty-first Century.* Minneapolis: University of Minnesota Press.

Warren, Kay. 1993. "Interpreting La Violencia in Guatemala: Shapes of Maya Silence and Resistance." In, Kay Warren, ed., *The Violence Within: Cultural and Political Opposition in Divided Nations.* Boulder: Westview Press.

———. 1998. *Indigenous Movements and Their Critics: Pan-Maya Activism in Guatemala.* Princeton: Princeton University Press.

Williams, Raymond. 1976. *Keywords: A Vocabulary of Culture and Society.* New York: Oxford University Press.

Yuval-Davis, Nira. 1997. *Gender and Nation.* London: Sage Publications.

Civilization and Barbarism:
Cattle Frontiers in Latin America

Silvio R. Duncan Baretta and John Markoff

In looking at yesterday's frontiers (or at today's industrialized world), social analysts tend to see violence as a straightforward and uncomplicated phenomenon: when openly used, it is a direct way of settling disputes; when it is not used but available, it is a necessary—and, at least in the short run, sufficient—condition of domination.[1] As a background condition violence is readily forgotten. Such is the case even in the study of the various affronts to authority that are lumped under the rubric of "collective behavior." One speaks of violent "episodes" arising from the "breakdown" of various routine social mechanisms. By the same token, all the interesting problems in political theory seem to lie in the area of how to control people in every other conceivable manner: through the establishment of a normative consensus, through ideologies, through the creation of common interests, or through bargains and deals. Sufficient consideration is not usually given to the varied and subtle effects of these ways in which the capacity for violence is structured in social life. But consequences follow for any society from the presence or absence of full-time military specialists, from the forms of their organization, from the regional distribution of control of organized violence, from the advantages and disadvantages associated with the use of force, and from the norms associated with such use.

Cattle frontiers in Latin America provide a good context for developing these general considerations. The tradition of violence in New World frontiers is usually simply taken for granted. In this essay we will show that violence was complex in structure and closely linked to the ways in which, in large areas of Latin America, centers and peripheries formed each other. We shall take up the economic, political, and cultural environments

33

within which the cattle frontiers of Latin America developed their remarkable forms of social life. The physical characteristics of the regions were important, but so were the moral categories used to describe the people of the frontiers, the degree of control of peripheral landholders by central administrators (and vice versa) and the changing nature of the European market. We can then examine the frontiers themselves and the ways in which these regions attracted, produced, and supported specialists in violence. This regional specialization at first suited Iberian administrators, whose resources for the direct control of large areas were severely limited; but well before the twentieth century the way of life of the people of the frontiers became an obstacle to would-be state-makers.

We shall begin with a sketch of the development of the cattle industry, which exhibited broadly similar political, economic, and social patterns across the diverse geography of areas ranging from northern Mexico to portions of Argentina. Underlying the similarities in regions so far apart was their character as pastoral frontiers. The early colonizers introduced the cattle that rapidly proliferated into vast herds of wild animals during the sixteenth and seventeenth centuries. In northern Mexico, on the plains around the Orinoco and on the vast grasslands that cover the southernmost part of Brazil, Uruguay, and a large part of Argentina, horsemen—variously called *gauchos, llaneros, vaqueros*—created a society based on the hunting of cattle. Raising cattle was at first far less important than hunting them; careful breeding was impossible in the unpoliced, unfenced, and thinly populated territories. In at least some regions, an *estancia* scarcely referred to a ranch at first, but only to a vaguely defined area encompassing grazing rights. Property rights over grazing lands began in different ways and at different times on the various frontiers; strict enforcement of these rights, however, was always accompanied by attempts to rationalize production and was related to the development of internal or external markets. The most dramatic example of this process appears to be the *rioplatense* region of southern South America. There the passage from the hunting to the raising of cattle was stimulated in the first half of the eighteenth century by administrative measures to protect the depleted herds.[2] Nonetheless, the major impulse for the emergence of large-scale ranches had to wait for the eighteenth-century liberalization of mercantilist trade restrictions and the final collapse of these restrictions with independence. Rationalization of production resulted from the rising prices of hides in the international market and from the prominence of jerked beef as an export industry in the first years of the nineteenth century.

As part of the rationalization drive landlords and states sought to tame the independent frontier populations, and the settled ranchhand increasingly predominated as the cattle-hunting nomad disappeared. The late nineteenth and early twentieth centuries saw the completion of this process as the barbed wire fence began to define unambiguous ranch boundaries and permitted the systematic breeding of tamer (and tastier) cattle that eclipsed the wilder longhorns. The development of refrigerated ships and railroads expanded the possibilities of edible exports beyond the jerked beef made from the original tough animals—close kin to the fighting bulls—and, as often, the structure of production accommodated itself to the opportunities of the market. The introduction of barbed wire effectively closed the heroic era of cattle frontiers by destroying the freedom of movement essential to the forms of social organization that had grown up in these areas.[3]

This rough sequence varied; Rio Grande do Sul, for example, adopted wire fencing somewhat later than neighboring Uruguay. This implies that there was a considerable overlap of the different periods: cattle hunting coexisted with well-defined ranches for a long period as did fenced and unfenced properties.

Creating Frontiers

Frontiers and the Cost of Protection

Frederic Lane observes that one cost of an economic activity is the cost of its protection from violent disruption.[4] One of the major activities of a government is to supply this protection through control of violence, a service paid for by taxation. Historically, it may frequently be unclear to what degree a particular government was engaged in a protection racket, in which enterprises had to ward off *governmental* violence by payments of some sort. The protection industry is a natural monopoly, at least on land. Competition impairs the quality of the service, since no single protector can completely guarantee the security of a client against a powerful rival. Competition also makes protection much more expensive.

From Lane's analysis a fruitful conceptualization of frontiers can be derived. As he points out, they are places, where no one has an enduring monopoly on violence. At a given level of technological development, an optimum size exists for an area being protected. Below this size resources are inefficiently used and above it governmental control tends to vanish.

There may or may not be another political unit "on the other side." If so, the two political centers may raise each other's protection costs drastically. Uruguay is an area which Spain and Portugal (and later Argentina and Brazil) found too costly to protect against the other party (and the Uruguayans). Frontiers are, then, boundaries beyond the sphere of the routine action of centrally located violence-producing enterprises, although they may well be within the range of isolated attacks.

For the governments of Spain and Portugal protection, or more precisely their capacity to produce and sell it, was a scarce resource which had to be wisely allocated. Naturally, it was allocated to those regions that could yield maximum returns for the cost of governing. The process of selection favored areas with dense native populations whose labor was allocated to Spaniards (under *encomienda*), such as central Mexico or the South American *altiplano;* it also favored regions with mines, like northern Mexico. Cattle raising in Mexico started in the empty spaces between mines; it was promoted by the Spanish government with the specific purpose of securing the roads against nomad raids through some form of settlement. It is not surprising that diminishing returns from mining in the seventeenth century, together with financial need, led the Crown practically to relinquish control over the northern territory to powerful private citizens.[5] It simply did not pay to govern the semi-arid region once the silver had been extracted. This process was not unique. Buenos Aires was a backwater in the early colonial era because it had neither settled natives nor mines of silver or gold;[6] consequently, the Spanish Crown had little immediate interest in controlling that region.

Cattle frontiers were largely the result of economic choices made by governments. Factors taken into consideration were the quality of the physical environment, particularly land; the presence of a relatively dense native population; and the existence of mines. Regions with marginal land, no mines, and low population density tended to be those in which governments delegated their authority to private citizens more often than in other regions. These men paid the costs of colonization and defense, but they were compensated through the acquisition—by legal and not so legal means—of huge tracts of land.

Cattle tended to concentrate precisely in these areas for a variety of reasons. Herds were driven out of more densely settled land by intervention of political authorities, who were concerned about the welfare of the Indians, or at least about the Indians' value as an exploitable resource. Such was the case in sixteenth-century Mexico.[7] The eventual destination of the herds was usually land that could not have supported large agrarian populations in any event (at least prior to the development of modern agricultural technology). In addition, ranching required only a small labor force. Moreover, the mobility of cattle made these animals an obvious resource to bring along on military expeditions in advance of other forms of European penetration, putting cattle herds on what Morissey has called "the cutting edge" of the conquest.[8] Finally, given a territory where no monopoly of violence existed, the ideal investments were those—like cattle ranching—that required small amounts of fixed capital.

Once the formation of a cattle frontier was far advanced, it tended to become a self-locking process. For one thing, the animals themselves modified their physical environment; heavy and hungry beasts made potential cropland marginal and reduced prairie to scrub. More important, in our view, than these physical transformations were the effects on the social environment. The expansion of cattle raising had the effect of uprooting the few settled Indians living in those areas. These Indians, as well as those who had been nomads before the Europeans arrived, quickly learned the use of horses.[9] The result was a native population capable of surviving and waging continuous warfare in areas such as Argentina, southern Chile, or northern Mexico. The Indians' ability to handle cattle, moreover, was soon comparable to that of Spanish or mestizo cowboys. Finally, the low population density, the abundance of wild cattle in the early colonial period, and the absence of an organization that had a monopoly on violence attracted criminals and vagrants to frontier areas, as Góngora[10] observes. Adept in the rough skills of cattle raising, which as we shall see, were very similar to those of premodern warfare, these men could easily make a living by plundering and by smuggling cattle; they were another source of the continuous turmoil of these regions.

This brief overview illustrates, in Owen Lattimore's fine phrase, the degree to which civilization was the "mother of barbarism."[11] The imperial expansion of strong centers, he has argued (most forcefully for the case of China), may itself create the dangerous and supposedly primitive mobile raiders who menace outlying areas. Contact with the Indian populations of the Empire's frontiers was made through cattle, through vagrants, through military incursions, and through Catholic missions, the latter being the only "civilizing" influence on the native populations. The result was a kind of continuous warfare, as mentioned above, which was also *systematic.* The Crown could not, in the short run, occupy immense marginal areas filled only with herds. The Indians had, therefore, time to probe the Spanish organization and attack the least protected cattle raisers and the weakest military outposts. We would suggest that an important part of this process was the inevitable formation of ties between natives and white or mestizo vagrants.[12] The latter were men who knew the Spanish much better than the Indians did and had no bonds of loyalty to the political center. They could make a profitable living by assuming the role of mediators—today conducting the natives in war raids and tomorrow negotiating peace with Spanish officials.[13]

Violence and political negotiation were then at the center of the social and economic life of Latin American cattle frontiers. In the economic sphere, it is apparent that a frontier cattleman also had to be a diplomat and a captain of war. Business success certainly depended on skill with weapons and on military leadership. But it very likely also depended on having informal contacts with regular bands of nomads, on choosing the right occasions to fight or to buy protection from such bands, and on having the right connections with smugglers. Gaining wealth depended on finding adequate solutions to the problem of the control of violence in a society in which many had access to military skills and military tools. Such solutions could consist, as pointed out above, only in the establishment of one's own armed group or in bargaining with others who also had a degree of control over the use of force. In the political sphere, a major problem for Crown officials was to maintain peace in the absence of a clear military superiority over nomadic bands, Indian or otherwise.[14] This implied negotiations, and probably tacit agreements that guaranteed these bands a fair economic gain. Without ever mentioning it, officials were probably good buyers in what one might call the protection market.[15]

Mestizo, Vagrant, Barbarian: The Moral and Legal Status of Frontier Populations

We have considered above how the locations of Latin American cattle frontiers were constrained by the physical environment, the level of technology, and the overall goals of the Spanish conquerors. But, as Lattimore observes, an unchanging physical environment can acquire changing meanings for a changing society. A new discovery can make a mountain range irrelevant as a "natural" limit for expansion. Modifications in policy can turn marginal areas into civilized ones if the policy is sustained for long enough. That social change produces frontier change leads to the axiomatic statement that frontiers are of social, not geographic origin.

Only after the concept of a frontier exists can it be attached by the community that has conceived it to a geographical configuration. The consciousness of belonging to a group, a group that includes certain people and excludes others, must precede the conscious claim for that group of the right to live or move about within a particular territory. . . .[16]

The "consciousness of belonging to a group" recalls of course other, nonterritorial forms of social exclusion. Kai Erikson has proposed that communities need to produce negative models systematically, so as to demarcate for their members acceptable behavior.[17] The dislocation produced by the clash between Spanish and Indian civilizations challenged the norms which defined membership in the Spanish (and Indian) communities. Church and Crown authorities were therefore concerned with enforcing and reinforcing these norms. At the same time, the clash produced a number of individuals of mixed cultural and racial status who were ideal targets for hostile accusations of deviance. It is not surprising that some of these individuals moved away from the territory controlled by the political center and became an important element in the formation of frontier societies. A full understanding of the moral and legal status of frontier populations demands therefore a brief general examination of the history of social exclusion in Latin America. Racial and cultural mixtures, as major concerns of the ideologies that the conquerors constructed to justify colonial domination, are central to such a history.

The Spanish Crown professed the conversion of Indians to be the main reason for its presence in America. The new society was seen as composed of two distinct groups, Christians and Indians. Conversion of the latter seemed to demand their concentration in settlements on the assumption that this would facilitate their adoption of civilized customs. There was an elaborate program of transformation of Indians and their society: they should dress like Europeans, acquire disciplined habits, and learn the Catholic faith. Spaniards were seen as instrumental to this program. They would be "teachers of morality," especially through good examples which should serve as inspiration to the natives. The image of the good citizen of the New World was that of a settled peasant, married and working the land. There was even a faith in the healing power of settled agricultural labor: Bartolomé de las Casas believed that it would regenerate the morals of former vagrants.[18]

It is clear, therefore, that the Spanish policy was also a pedagogic doctrine, a set of precepts to transform and educate natives (and, more generally, all those without Christian faith). This doctrine soon clashed with some New World realities. Instead of furnishing living models of the Christian virtues, the Spanish all too often stood revealed as models of the usual human vices. Interracial contacts often took place within the institutions of highly coercive forms of labor control; petty conquistadors wandered over the land and routinely violated the moral norms of Spanish society. Thus multiple impacts of the whites upon the social life of the Indians were frequently contrary to the values of those engaged in the construction of ideological justifications for Iberian colonization. This climate promoted the emergence of a theory quite the reverse of the earlier one. As Spaniards[19] came to be considered bad examples, their contacts with Indians were to be minimized and strictly regulated. This was the origin of the policy of residential segregation, whose development and decay is carefully traced by Mörner. The same conditions further reinforced the doctrine of population concentration in small peasant settlements (*pueblos*). In addition to being morally commendable such a policy had obvious economic and military advantages.[20]

Whatever the shifting policies and rationales, the actual ability of administrators or churchmen to prevent miscegenation was nonexistent. Whether children were the result of concubinage or more casual relations, conventions were routinely flouted. "Mestizo" and "illegitimate" became almost synonymous words, an identification reinforced by the tendency to regard legitimate children of whatever parentage as *criollos* or "American Spaniards." The developing racial typifications that helped legitimate the authority of European masters could draw, in the instance of the mestizo, upon an already established moral and legal condemnation of violation of sexual norms.[21] This condemnation helped to remove from the mestizo the support of those sectors of state and church which had been well disposed, in the early phases of colonization, toward a policy of racial assimilation.

Regardless of official attitudes, mestizos also had to deal with the social prejudices of Spaniards toward Indians. Differences in habits, culture, education, and social esteem produced strong resistance to mixed marriages among white males, who believed that honor demanded union with European women. This reinforced the idea of the superiority of pure Spanish blood, an idea useful in warding off political and social competition by growing numbers of those of mixed blood.[22] Some mestizos responded to discrimination by turning to vagrancy. Lacking stable work, stealing in many cases, and having irregular contacts with the natives, they soon were regarded (along with mulattoes) as the class of people who might set Indians the worst possible example.[23] Vagrancy therefore added strength to racial prejudice, particularly as vagrants were the exact opposite of the Crown's definition of respectability.

Similar processes led to discrimination against other groups. Blacks had to cope with the stigma of slavery. They were prohibited from marrying whites or Indians, lest their children gain their freedom. Mixed bloods had to endure a heightened form of the disdain that whites displayed in milder ways toward the mestizo group.

Color of skin was turned therefore into an unambiguous statement of a person's condition as a violator of norms, one likely to have a dubious origin, to be a vagrant or, more generally, a pernicious element. Dark-skinned individuals were the negative models of colonial Latin America. From the official point of view, their exclusion reasserted the fundamental ideals of the colonial enterprise: the creation of a society of settlers who had families and worked the land.[24] There was of course a great distance between the goals that might have guided the state and church officials in the first years of colonization and the goals of powerful whites and later officials. For the latter the ultimate aim was not the conversion of the heathen. Social exclusion was for them a means of maintaining the distance between the conqueror and the conquered—a distance needed to keep intact the social and political order, the white monopoly of offices, and especially the control of labor. It is not surprising then that mestizos, escaped slaves, or freedmen made their way to the savannas. The racial ideologies of the European rulers helped to define the frontier as the location of freedom.

Composed mostly of nonwhites or whites of irregular life, frontier populations were subject to these general forms of exclusion.[25] Fears of a race war in the first years of independence gave eloquent testimony of the tensions created by discrimination all over Spanish America. Frontier populations were largely responsible for such fears because of their military prowess and their resentment against the white elite, as the example of the Venezuelan *llaneros* clearly shows.[26]

The mixture of terror and contempt that frontier inhabitants inspired in urbanites could not be attributed solely to their racial status; it was also a consequence of their culture and life style. Territorial boundaries were linked to social exclusion. The images of the mestizo or of the vagrant were only components of a broader image of the cowboy as essentially foreign to the values of Europe and of the city; a society had developed that seemed radically opposed, in its norms and daily activities to that of the urban centers of the colonial world. Frontier populations came to be considered as "barbarians" by the spokesmen of the same civilization that had created them out of its clash with Indian societies.

The image of the barbarian was found in the early reports of colonial administrators[27] but it became widespread only in the post-independence period. One reason was, of course, the general mobilization of frontier populations during the independence wars, a mobilization that persisted as many military leaders found in armed conflict a quick path to riches and power. If it was the gauchos and *llaneros* who had annihilated the Spanish forces, the would-be state-makers of the new republics found these warriors a major problem. Border populations reciprocated the feelings of urban dwellers[28] and were easily roused for attacks upon cities and political centers. For frustrated political liberals who were attempting to explain to themselves their failures at state-building along the lines that seemed to be succeeding in the United States, the horsemen of the interior became a suitable target for blame. At the same time, cities had grown more cosmopolitan with independence, due to greater commercial and cultural exchanges with Europe, particularly England.[29] As distance increased between European (or Europeanized) urbanites and a hinterland population mobilized for war, the image of the barbarian became even more firmly attached to the latter.

No one has depicted more vividly than Sarmiento the reciprocal exclusion between the cultures of townsmen and horsemen in his *Civilization and Barbarism,* a polemic against the era of Rosas. But there are many other examples. The declining years of the Monagas regime in mid-nineteenth-century Venezuela were characterized by one observer as a "struggle between Civilization and Barbarism." During the 1893–1895 civil war in Rio Grande do Sul, the advancing gauchos of Saravia were, again, described as "barbarians." As a final witness, we cite a former participant in frontier culture, José Antonio Páez. Writing of the rigors of his early life, years later, "in a room with furniture by an agreeable fire," he tells us that the ranches of today "differ as much from those I knew in my youth as civilization differs from barbarism."[30]

The ideology that equated frontiersman and barbarian provided a justification for the solutions which the newly independent Latin American states sought for their problems. The difficulties were old ones— scarcity of labor for public and private purposes, vagrancy, and the heightened threat of political instability caused in part by frontier populations endowed with military skills. These problems all required that the nomadic horsemen of border areas be dealt with in one way or another.

Given their status as outcasts who did not belong to civilization,[31] the methods adopted were also old—similar, indeed, to those of the colonial era. Legislation against vagrancy, forced recruitment into armies and public works, and maintenance or elaboration of the debt peonage system were considered necessary, given the lack of discipline and the antisocial habits of frontier cowboys. In a word, as the value of cattle rose and former colonies were threatened with political disintegration, the need to settle and discipline populations became more pressing than ever before. The ideology that saw gauchos and *llaneros* as uncontrollable barbarians became an adequate framework for justifying the cruel methods employed by the political elites as a response.[32]

The rejection of the hinterland by urbanites with European identifications, who were drawn to the British economy or the U.S. polity, testifies to the fact that cattle frontiers were shaped by interactions with the larger structures of which they formed a part. National societies and the international environment created constraints and changes which had profound effects upon the frontiers. Economic opportunities were of one sort when Iberian mercantilism reigned and of quite another sort when the European market was opened. As the demands of the industrializing West, most importantly England, replaced the views of Iberian administrators, the cultural setting of the frontiers also changed.

The Nature of Frontier Regions

The Political Economy of Cattle Raising

Chevalier[33] argues that in northern Mexico size was a central feature of the production unit. Late sixteenth-century cattle raising was profitable only on a large scale, due to the low prices of meat in Mexico City and elsewhere. This in turn, he adds, implied considerable investment in cowboys, slaves, and *estancias,* and hence extreme concentration of land. This argument must be modified since ranching is about as far removed from a labor-intensive activity as can be imagined. Rodríguez Molas[34] even suggests (perhaps with exaggeration) that in the late eighteenth century it was possible to manage an area of 250,000 hectares with only four or five slaves in the Banda Oriental. *Estancias* were flexible, and their needs for capital could be brought down to almost nothing if necessary,[35] to a few slaves for a vast extension of land. However, *estancias* so thinly staffed were probably rare, given the need for protection from bandits, Indians, and other ranchers. No one could hold 250,000 hectares with only a handful of men. A protective staff was essential if herds were to expand without reinvestment, both to keep predatory cattle hunters away and to make raids upon the animals of others. An important consequence follows: if very large extensions of land could be managed with a tiny labor force, a landowner with even a small work force could easily expand his holdings. This was certainly true at least in the phase of the formation of great properties, when both land and wild cattle could be had at no cost. Chevalier's argument holds in general, therefore. There was a tendency both to concentration and expansion inherent to the cattle industry. It would be difficult for the small stockman to compete with the cattle baron.

In the early stages entrance into business was not always determined by possession of land, but in some regions by pasturage rights. Only rights to specific grazing sites were conferred on individuals in Mexico during the sixteenth century, although signs of rudimentary property rights were already present.[36] In the region of Buenos Aires, by contrast, property rights were already established by the beginning of the seventeenth century, access to land being a necessary condition of access to cattle.[37] In all cases, however, the tendency to expand was driving powerful men to concentrate animals and territory in their hands. Such increases were especially easy to accomplish in frontiers such as northern Mexico,[38] where the control of the Spanish administration was particularly weak. In Buenos Aires province at the end of the eighteenth century, laws defined the minimum extension of property required to be considered a cattle raiser. Those who fell short of that considerable minimum had to sell out.[39]

Cattle raising undoubtedly contributed to the widespread vagrancy produced by the clash of Iberian civilization with the natives of the New World. The rural lower classes were blocked from achieving the landholding status that defined an individual as a member of the political community. Denied ownership and social honor, the lower classes—many of them mestizos, but also Indians, mulattos, free or runaway blacks, and even a few whites—were left with two alternatives: life as a settled peon on one of the great ranches, or vagrancy. Many chose the latter. Once a vagrant, an individual was a threat to landowners. He might easily become an independent rustler or bandit. He was likely to be integrated into commercial networks which landowners might not control,[40] particularly those linked to smuggling of hides and animals, as was the case in the extensive and illegal commerce across the border of Brazil and the Banda Oriental until the late nineteenth century.

No less important, a successful life as a vagrant cowboy could only perpetuate an image of a life of freedom which was a threat to landowner and bureaucrat alike. It is hard to tell how widely diffused was the belief in "cheap meat and freedom," but the continuing flow of escaped slaves and army deserters (and cramped *criollo* sons of the urban elites) to the frontier suggests that the myth of "the barbarian" was accompanied by a potent counter-myth.[41] The *estancieros,* themselves in large part responsible for the problem, became champions of harsh measures to repress vagrancy as access to the world market raised the value of hides (and later, meat). On the one hand they needed labor; on the other, each vagrant was a very real menace to orderly business. Government repression (in the form of forced recruitment into army or public works), however, was as much a problem as a solution. Even though many peons might be intimidated into accepting a settled life within the confines of an *estancia* or hacienda, repression also caused much turmoil. Very likely it actually increased nomadism in nineteenth-century Argentina, as gauchos fled to avoid forced recruitment. Similarly, the brutality of army life created a class of deserters.[42]

The point to stress is that vagrancy was inseparable from cattle raising, or rather from the specific form of the organization of cattle raising that was obtained on Latin American frontiers. The most notable feature of this organization was undoubtedly the control by *estancieros* of military and judicial means in their own bailiwicks and often at the national level. Such control took varying forms according to time and place, from direct monopoly of offices by great ranchers to alliances with "justices of the peace" who held considerable power in their own right.[43] In one way or another, it ensured that *estancieros* obtained the command over land and labor that characterized frontier cattle raising in Latin America.[44]

Even though one talks about sales of land and wages of peons, land and labor were not sold in a free, competitive market until late in the nineteenth century. This is illustrated, for instance, by the higher wages that temporary labor, as compared to permanent, commanded in nineteenth-century Buenos Aires province. (The latter received nonmonetary compensation in the form of protection from the abuses of forced recruitment into the army.) It is also illustrated by the startling discovery of Tulio Halperin-Donghi, that the expansion of cattle raising in the *campaña* of Buenos Aires province did not respond to oscillations in world prices,[45] which he finds possible because of the high level of profits and the modest initial investment required by cattle raising. Such was no doubt the case;

but it was also the case that *estancieros* were able to restrict access to land and manipulate a scarce labor supply through their control of military and judicial functions. Control over labor was important not because it permitted a compression of wages, since ranches did not require many hands in any case; far more important was the capacity that judicial and military resources gave *estancieros* to obtain permanent workers, whom they protected from forced recruitment. The same capacity enabled them to repress vagrants, whose effects upon a rationalized cattle business were particularly harmful.

The same system prevailed in one form or another in other cattle frontiers. In Venezuela the devices used were very similar to those of Argentina: anti-vagrancy laws, requirement of identity cards for those traveling within the country, and forced recruitment.[46] In northern Mexico, workers were attached to property mainly through debt peonage, and deserters were fiercely pursued.[47] Cattle frontiers in Latin America therefore confirm Evsey Domar's thesis that the joint presence of scarce labor and abundant land is likely to produce highly coercive forms of labor control, provided that governments make appropriate political decisions.[48] "Appropriate decisions" are necessary to block the access that would give rise to a class of free farmers. We think it within the spirit of Domar's model, of which the "second serfdom" in eastern Europe is probably the best known example, to note that in the Latin American case military success opened up more territory, while forced conscription was itself a cause of labor scarcity. The actions of governments, then, helped to create the conditions against which those actions were directed.

The Respectable and the Illegal

The preceding sections may have produced the impression that on the frontiers vagrants and nonvagrants stood in profound opposition. Nothing was farther from the truth. Wanderers were in permanent conflict with *estancieros* and authorities but had close connections with stable peons and with the occasional small proprietor. This continuity was more noticeable in areas like southern Chile, where small properties and a significant settled agriculture (vineyards) coexisted with cattle raising, and where there was still unoccupied land as late as the eighteenth century.[49] But it certainly was also present in other areas, such as Argentina, in which forced conscription would often strike vagrants and stable workers indiscriminately.[50] There were therefore two sources for such continuity: on the one hand, settled *estancia* hands were probably aware that for administrators and landowners they were potential vagrants, almost as pernicious as the actual ones. Our earlier observations have shown that an extended definition of vagrancy existed in a frontier, encompassing anyone who had no access to land; the inclusiveness of the actual definition varied according to economic and military needs. On the other hand, there certainly were many ties between nomads and settled peons, cowboys and *campesinos.*

The most direct evidence of the continuity between nomadic[51] and stable populations is provided by Góngora[52] for southern Chile. Using judicial records, he established the fact that vagrants were frequently said to be either *peones gañanes* (or the equivalent) or small proprietors. This finding clearly shows a frequent transition from settled to nomadic life, and almost certainly the opposite transition as well. The conclusion is inevitable that many wanderers had extensive ties of kinship and friendship with settled people. It also seems likely that permanent nomadism and permanent geographical stability were two extremes, and that most of the population in cattle frontiers belonged to neither. This movement between nomadism and permanent geographical stability also took place in nineteenth-century Argentina, as *estancia* hands were thrown into vagrant existence by forced recruitment. And Chevalier[53] remarks that vagabonds in northern Mexico frequently changed their employers and location and that friends and accomplices of theirs could be found in every isolated *estancia.*[54] In short, wars, forced recruitment, the continuous expansion of great estates, and the judicial repression of vagabonds continuously created new wanderers and kept the old ones in movement. It is then not unlikely that many people in these areas would have been vagrants at least once in their lives,[55] and that they would have shared social ties and cultural norms with the nomadic sector of the population.

An equally remarkable bond was that of the common skills shared by frontier inhabitants, skills which, as could be expected, were developed in their dealing with cattle. Observers agree on the excellence of their horsemanship and on the care they gave their horses. Working with cattle required the use of tools that were virtually weapons—such as the lasso, the *garrocha* (a long pike), and the *desjarretadera,* a crescent-shaped blade mounted on a long pole, which enabled riders to cut a bull's hamstrings without dismounting. It could obviously be wielded against people with very effective results. Traveling with cattle in a world of poor roads and no long-distance communication led to the cultivation of tracking almost as an art form.[56] All such skills had immediate application in the realm of premodern warfare: gauchos and *vaqueros* formed a natural cavalry, equipped with lances and other required weapons and talents. Furthermore, the hard life combined with a protein diet extraordinarily high by premodern standards gave these men a high degree of physical endurance,[57] another useful trait for the long exertions required by war. We may add that the significance of the horse as a symbol of the conqueror made frontier horsemen natural war leaders for the settled *campesinos*.[58] Finally, work routines organized around the horse and the hunt or the cattle drive, a continual infusion of wanderers, and a culture that assigned a low value to proprietary rights in land—a point to which we shall return—all contributed to a life style which made sustained combat over long distances easily acceptable. (That this is a problematic characteristic is shown by the difficulties that leaders the world over have had in moving peasant armies away from their base of operations.)

These skills could be, and were, used both in illegal endeavors like banditry or smuggling and in legal ones such as serving in the frontier police. There was a striking similarity between these two uses. The difference in way of life was so minute that the administration of Rio de la Plata recruited its anti-smuggling *Cuerpo de Blandengues* from among the outlaws themselves.[59] Landowners might have their own armed guards for protection not merely against "official" bandits but against the depredations of the militia as well.[60]

Finally, the cultural continuity that resulted from the constant interaction between Europeans and Indians has to be mentioned. Exchanges of personnel and of technology occurred all over frontier areas as the Spanish sometimes fought the Indians, sometimes employed them as auxiliaries, sometimes attempted to buy them off (perhaps with cattle), and sometimes tried to put them into settlements and teach them the art of ranching. Indians became adept in the use of horses and hunted the new cattle (or in North America, the buffalo). More generally, they acquired the skills of the cattle industry (including rustling), while Europeans acquired new foods and even new weapons, such as the *boleadora*.[61] Although the administrative capacity of central governments to sustain warfare was far greater than that of the Indians, the technology of weaponry was not entirely unequal.[62] The peaceful exchanges included the possibility of living with natives who provided an important source of refuge for vagrants or hunted criminals. Góngora remarks that they not only lived among Indians occasionally, but also conducted them on expeditions of pillage.[63] The society of the frontier was mixed both racially and culturally, with people competing as well as cooperating; exchanging ideas and genes as well as blows; but participating in a culture mysterious to the administrators of Caracas or Mexico City.[64]

It seems clear then that a great number of kinship and friendship ties existed between the sedentary and the nomadic, the legal and the illegal sectors of frontier populations, that a sizable circulation of personnel took place between them, and that the skills shared by individuals in frontier areas were equally useful in peace and in war, in settled and in mobile forms of existence. These continuities formed a basis for their moral outlook on issues such as property rights or the legitimacy of authority. Many among them certainly had economic interests in the continuation of banditry, smuggling, or illegal trade with Indians, as well as in the existence of a police force that provided legal coverage for participation in illegal activities. Many more must have had relatives engaged in such activities, and all shared common skills and a common culture. In addition, a negative basis for this moral outlook was provided by the various forms of social exclusion suffered on the frontier, whose inhabitants were labeled as pernicious elements and barbarians, and whose settled peons and small proprietors were easily thrown into nomadic life.

In a situation in which violence was persistently used for the purpose of controlling the poor and denying them access to land, it is no surprise that the cowboys developed their own version of the values of the powerful. They seem to have considered fields as common property, in which they were backed by Iberian tradition;[65] they probably considered cattle rustling an act of justice, a reparation which was their due; and rebellion against political authority was rebellion against oppression.

We would propose that there is a parallel here to the sense of justice that E. P. Thompson has suggested for European crowds. Emilio Coni observes that, in the colonial period, in principle all wild cattle belonged to the king. Municipal authorities, however, took the position that licenses for *vaquerías* could be granted to private citizens and justified their actions by arguing that all wild cattle were descended from runaway animals that had once been the property of *estancieros*. It is understandable that nomadic gauchos did not accept these claims. They probably believed that stealing from private citizens was legitimate, since the latter were violating the king's property rights. In any case, townsmen certainly had no more rights to hunt or take possession of wild animals than did nomadic gauchos. In Venezuela, shrewd cowboys would sabotage branding to take advantage later of traditional claims on unmarked animals.[66]

The violence of the lower classes, then, was acceptable within the moral terms of the frontier. The underclass was participating in a set of values shared at least in part by elites. If seizure of a neighbor's livestock was a widely practiced form of expansion, then we should not be surprised that successful rustlers were highly prized as foremen or overseers. That these moral norms were shared by all sectors of the population is shown by the pervasiveness of smuggling, cattle theft, and constant conflict with state officers.[67] Góngora[68] observes that settled families lacking title to their land used to protect bandits in southern Chile. The frontier tradition of opposing authority is also well known,[69] a tradition often politically exploited by sectors of the Latin American elites. The continual desertions of gauchos from frontier posts in nineteenth-century Argentina exemplifies yet another strand of this defiance. In a word, the lower classes apparently shared a mentality of resistance to oppression that gave banditry a character of social rebellion[70] and legitimated open political revolt. It is this common mentality that cemented the numerous material ties that unified nomadic and sedentary populations.

It is important to acknowledge, however, the ambiguous character of the resistance of frontier inhabitants to central authorities. Their rebelliousness was a moving force behind their illegal activities, but these activities served their material interests equally well. Frontier *caudillos* and their followers, for instance, almost regularly switched sides in political struggles.[71] The transition in the independence wars in Venezuela from the terrifying royalist *llaneros* of Boves to the equally terrifying republican *llaneros* of Páez is merely the most famous instance. Without denying that convenience and calculation played a part in these sudden shifts, it is also necessary to consider the effects of the social organization of frontiers upon the forms given to rebellion by frontiersmen. In the case of political frontiers, such as the one between the colonial empires of Portugal and Spain, and later between Brazil and Uruguay, it is easily understandable that individuals developed economic, kinship, and friendship connections with people "on the other side"; it is also understandable that their interests and loyalties became split, to the point at which they could (conveniently) identify with either nationality.[72]

The "other side" did not have to be a competing political center, however. It could be one among the multiple bands of smugglers, bandits, or Indians with whom frontier inhabitants had several kinds of links. In brief, the ties that unified legal and illegal, vagrant and settled forms of existence gave individuals in those areas an open choice between joining "barbarism" or living in relative conformity with the prescriptions for respectability. We claimed above that a frequent transition between these forms of existence characterized the lives of many frontier inhabitants; similarly, it characterized their politics. Most frontier chieftains—and their followers as well—felt that banditry and smuggling were acceptable ways of earning a livelihood, but so was obtaining a pardon and joining the border police.

One can say that the economic and social organization of frontiers created a class that specialized in expediency, whose only commitment was to preserve the order that made possible the profitable utilization of such expediency. This may be part of the explanation for the puzzling lack of interest in land reform by movements that counted cowboys among their participants.[73] Frontier horsemen were interested solely in the defense of a life style that they considered legitimate, one that assumed an abundance of cattle and land made accessible to all and considered violence a proper means of subsistence. They fought for those who granted them these rights which they took as natural; and this could even include political authorities, who themselves utilized vagrant populations for armed conflict.[74]

Brokers between Urban Elites and Frontier Outcasts

Of the vagabonds engaged in rustling, smuggling, and illegal trade, there were those who lived by themselves, killing animals for food or for the sale of their hides. But many of these wandering horsemen were in regular contact with an entrepreneur, who bought their products in order to resell them. This figure was very often the *pulpero,* a small merchant who owned a food and liquor store. In some cases the *pulpero* was associated with powerful *estancieros,*[75] who did not hesitate to sponsor illegal enterprises that they could control. The *pulpero* hired vagrants and then hired himself and his men to the great landowner. It was through this process of "contracting and sub-contracting" that *estancieros* controlled the vast contraband network of animals between the Banda Oriental and southern Brazil in the eighteenth century.[76] The same relationship might prevail between the great rancher and the chief of a band of smugglers and cattle hunters.[77]

If *pulperos* and smuggling chiefs controlled the access of vagrants to jobs, their command over labor was a source of strength in negotiation with *estancieros.*[78] On cattle frontiers, where hands were scarce and undisciplined, the establishment of control over people was almost a guarantee of power and upward mobility. While *estancieros* had command over stable peons, the existence of a significant number of mobile people opened opportunities for entrepreneurs who specialized in recruiting and establishing links with wanderers. The *pulpero* was one such entrepreneur because he dealt in food and drink. Another was the captain of war.[79]

There certainly were captains of war who were primarily in the business of the economic exploitation of violence. In its more primitive forms such exploitation took the form of pillage—a common procedure in frontier areas, frequently intertwined with regular trade. Góngora observes that plunder was endemic to the area of contact with Indians in southern Chile during the eighteenth century.[80] It is clear that a population that did not acknowledge property rights and accepted violence as a legitimate means of earning a livelihood would follow successful war chiefs who ensured loyalty by distributing the fruits of raids. This process is well documented for the *llaneros* of Venezuela during the independence war by Carrera Damas, who relates the continuous pillage to their extreme poverty, exacerbated during the war period. We can add that such poverty, typical of all cattle frontiers, was certainly conducive to the formation of a mentality in which violence became a legitimate way to acquire wealth. This was so clearly understood that Boves, a royalist chief in the Venezuelan conflict, issued his men documents granting rights to future pillage.[81]

Besides routinized plunder, there were probably more subtle forms of economic exploitation of violence. Nepomuceno Saravia[82] testified that his uncle, Aparicio Saravia, exacted a war tax in order to support his army in the Uruguayan conflicts of the early twentieth century. He took special care, however, to prevent devastation or unnecessary pillage. This controlled use of violence shows that the general understood the necessity of not ruining his source of maintenance, and perhaps even bargaining with the owners of wealth. Saravia's objectives were primarily political rather than economic, but his methods were probably not unusual among chiefs interested in building a patrimony through the exploitation of violence. These men would have been in the business of selling protection,[83] their major asset their capacity to control and organize the natural warriors of cattle frontiers. It is probable that many powerful landowners started their upward movement as successful military chiefs.[84]

Whatever their strategy in the pursuit of wealth, captains of war, *pulperos,* and smuggling chiefs were all intermediaries—willing or unwilling—between cities and frontier populations. Their control over frontier populations provided urban elites with the soldiers who fought many of their battles. Similarly, they were the individuals who organized and directed cowboys in the tasks required by the primitive cattle industry. Through the agency of these men, barbarians promoted the progress of cities and created the fortunes of merchants engaged in the import-export business. Civilization therefore was not only the "mother of barbarism"; it was also its child.

The Decline of the Barbarian

The post-independence period saw the gradual fading of the frontier horsemen and their way of life. With the end of the almost continuous wars that characterized the era of *caudillo* politics, armed activity, which was well adapted to the abilities of frontier inhabitants, and which allowed them to express their permanent opposition to authority and discipline, disappeared. Furthermore, with improved communications, governments asserted their control over the remaining frontier areas. With no wars to fight and no further land to occupy, armies were no longer dependent on the recruitment, forced or otherwise, of vagrants for frontier outposts. The development of military technology had made obsolete the ways of fighting of the gauchos and *llaneros*. The city and state had broken free from dependence on the barbarians.

Moreover, the internal organization of frontier areas was changing. Revolts had often accompanied attempts to consolidate private property and to settle the population in these regions.[85] Among the most dramatic were the final rebellions, directed against the introduction of wire fencing. In the 1880s bands of gauchos fought persistently in Argentina, defending their old system of life.[86] Enclosure of fields was one reason for the great civil war that swept southern Brazil between 1893 and 1895;[87] another was the improved capacity of the central administration to control smuggling on the Uruguayan border.

The effects of wire fences were multiple. For one thing, they decreased the need of ranches for settled laborers,[88] a need already very low. They also made possible for the first time the effective policing of cattle and property; vagrants were therefore cut off from their sources of food and profits and illegal trade was far more difficult. Additionally, wire fences established a clear-cut separation between stable and nomadic populations, since nomadism ceased to be a feasible alternative to misery and repression. Without the continuous exchanges they had once had with sedentary people, the remaining wanderers lost their access to the social network that made vagrancy possible. They no longer had friends or relatives to shelter them against police action. Thus fences destroyed the relations of reciprocity between vagrants and nonvagrants; in so doing, they eliminated the former and radically changed the lives of the latter.

The Culture of Violence

Chevalier observes that material ambition was not the only drive that propelled Spanish conquerors: there was also a search for glory, an awareness that they were doing "great things." He adds that they had a strong sense of military honor and a deep religiosity that enabled them to face danger without hesitation. In 1519, the founders of Vera Cruz sought a papal bull that would absolve of sin those dying during the enterprise of conquest. Such a bull, they claimed, would free them from any restraint in the course of combat.

It is not surprising that many of these traits survived in modified form in Latin American cattle frontiers. The constant state of armed conflict attracted people endowed with a "keen sense of [military] honor" and also produced individuals with these characteristics. A man's rank within frontier communities depended at least partly on his courage and on skills related to military endeavors, such as riding and fighting. Chevalier observes that pastimes like bullfighting, obviously functional for those who needed fighting men, were encouraged by the emerging Mexican aristocracy. The reason was that they kept men in fighting trim and provided an outlet for their turbulence.[89]

There are numerous testimonials to the value attributed to courage and dueling skills by frontier populations. Rodríguez Molas[90] says that they enjoyed exhibiting their dexterity with knives and their fearlessness in facing death. Their goal was to be renowned as men of courage. And Chevalier's observation on the cultivation of riding and bullfighting, quoted above, attests to the same thing, that is, to the prestige associated with exposure to risk. These testimonies seem to indicate that there was more to frontier violence than its utilitarian aspect, linked to needs for defense and to economic gain. Violence was also an expressive activity. By this we mean that violence took on the character of play,[91] a voluntary activity in which people engaged for enjoyment. Above all, it was an activity that involved competition and gave men an opportunity to demonstrate their prowess.

Violence, in the form of play, was an occasion for mutual recognition for the members of frontier communities. One of its main attractions consisted precisely in the fact that such recognition could not be denied to anybody who played in accordance with the rules, and won (or to anybody who was skillful, if the play did not take the forms of a contest). In this sense, violent games, such as dueling and bullfighting, became an occasion for people to test their individual worth and to make their bid for a superior status in the community.

The reasons for the centrality of the expressive component of violence in the social life of frontiers are apparent. We have observed above that wealth and power during the colonial and the early post-independence periods, which in Latin America depended largely on access to land, were denied to most individuals in cattle areas. Similarly, we pointed out that these outcasts had developed their own forms of social organization. The centrality of violence to this social organization can be explained by recognizing that military honor was the only component in the Iberian cultural heritage that could be achieved by all people, without distinction of birth or possessions.[92] In other words, achievement of honor through exposure to risk was a democratic affair. For a society of vagrants and outcasts there could be no better focus for the construction of an identity and for the gaining of self-respect. The powerful could deny a man everything except the badges he had earned through his courage and his fighting abilities. The cult of military values, a basic element in the life of the Spanish aristocracy, became for the lower classes a sort of ideology of the oppressed—their only route to the achievement of recognition. As observed above, the upper classes could use these outcast warriors for their own purposes, even though they were often unable to control them.

We should note here the significance of the private possession of a horse for riding, generally associated in Western Europe with a restricted military class of nobles. In Latin America, where horses were more abundant, access to the quality of mounted warrior was democratized. It was relatively easy for many to become *caballeros* in the most literal sense. One anthropologist has described a group of German immigrants to Rio Grande do Sul, farmers who nevertheless came to ape the nearby gauchos. In short order these German ex-peasants and their children were refusing to walk when they could mount a horse; and the tavern brawl was no longer a matter of fists, but of knives.[93]

Honor had to be achieved, but even more important, it had to be recognized by one's peers. Consequently, gauchos, *charros,* and *llaneros* expected their valor to be accepted by all, and in particular by their enemies—the harshest test to which they could submit themselves. An excellent example occurs in Érico Verissimo's *O Tempo e o Vento*.[94] Licurgo Cambará, Republican chief of the town of Santa Fé, was surrounded by Federalists in his own house. Though his wife was in difficult labor he did not ask for a truce in order to call a doctor, since, in his view, enemies would have interpreted such an action as weakness.

The need for recognition meant that the opponent in a war or duel was not simply an opponent but also an audience.[95] An enemy gave the certification needed to validate properly those claims to honor on which membership in the community depended. Indeed exploits were largely aimed at arousing admiration among enemies. A good example of a feat of this kind was to steal an artillery piece by lassoing it and then pull it from the enemy's lines to one's own.[96] The significant thing is that a mission of obvious tactical importance did not become the object of a concerted action but was accomplished in such a way as to allow spectacular demonstration of prowess. When both sides in a war had the support of segments of a frontier's population a "mirror effect" took place, each party striving to prove more daring than the opponent. This effect helps to account for the astonishing military accomplishments of both Republicans and Federalists in the civil war of 1893 in Rio Grande do Sul, accomplishments that surprise even utterly objective analysts today.[97] It can explain the extreme brutality that often characterized the military actions of gauchos and *llaneros*. Terror, once it began, became, as much as prowess, an object of competition between the warring sides. The result was an uncontrolled exchange of atrocities.[98]

The culture of violence then refers to the achievement of membership within frontier communities through the pursuit of military honor. This achievement was elusive, however. Honor could be lost, and was tested anew in every interaction with others. Individuals needed enemies, since they were recognized as full members of the community only by proving their personal valor. Without enemies, one was not a man. The culture of violence tended therefore to generate personal rivalries, and individuals were extremely prone to interpret other people's actions as insults. This process of including people in the community through generating opposition among them was the essence of the culture of violence in Latin American cattle frontiers.

Our analysis of honor may be deepened by looking at other cultural strands. Érico Verissimo's fiction testifies to a widespread fatalism, as does the famous *Martin Fierro*. More striking still was the extent of gambling,[99] which was pervasive among men, as several authors indicate. Apparently they did not hesitate to lose all their money in games of chance and in buying drinks, as witnessed by their permanent debt to the *pulperos.*[100] The stakes were often high: sometimes they even involved land, when a proprietor happened to be playing.[101] People constantly exposed themselves to risks; risks were considered inevitable, part of a flow of events over which one's actions had very little control. The underlying philosophy would seem to have been that in a frontier environment life and property could be lost at any moment in violent action; in that sense, existence took on the nature of a permanent gamble. The pervasiveness of games of chance among individuals was therefore an abbreviated statement of their views on life. This fatalistic approach was the other side of the constant pursuit of military honor, the only way one could sustain the psychological burden of permanent exposure to death.

These considerations bring us back to a theme touched upon before: the democratic character of the pursuit of honor. It is now clear what this means: that then, as now, all men are equal before chance and death. It was around this tenet of the Iberian cultural tradition that frontier people built their society and their self-conceptions. Violence for them was not simply anarchy and destruction; properly delimited, it was the realm in which individuals could prove themselves worthy members of their community.

Conclusion

We have attempted to describe the kinds of violence that developed in Latin American borderlands, and their social and economic uses. Frontiers were seen as areas where governments did not monopolize the production of protection services and whose populations were excluded from and opposed to the culture of the cities. We have seen that economic constraints determined which areas would be frontiers: usually those with no mines and sparse settlements. Because of the absence of firm governmental control and their "barbarian" way of life, frontiers became a harbor for people labeled as deviants or criminals; because of their sparse population, they became ideal sites, given adequate physical conditions, for the huge herds of cattle that could not expand in the more intensively agricultural regions. We have shown how particular forms of social organization and economic enterprise grew around these basic elements; how violence was exploited for purposes of economic gain; how cattle-raising skills were transferred to the realms of banditry and primitive warfare;

and how violence became, paradoxically, a means of integration in frontier communities.

We have also attempted to show that there was no sharp cleavage to be drawn on the frontiers between peon and gaucho, bandit and ranchhand, smuggler and policeman. While admiring the careful work of Emilio Coni, we must totally reject his view of the gaucho as a "marginal," in the sense of one having no links with regular social life.[102] Frontiers were shaped by the politics, economics, and culture of the Latin American societies of which they were a part and which they shaped in turn. Moreover, the life of cattle frontiers was constrained by still larger processes. The British smuggling of the eighteenth century and the open British market of the nineteenth century were vital for raising the value of hides and later of meat; British and Americans provided models of civilization; British and American financiers built the railroads that opened up the interiors; Americans sometimes even introduced barbed wire, which made possible a strict enforcement of property rights over cattle and land.[103]

These and other changes in national and international contexts accounted for the declining trajectory of frontier societies in the nineteenth century. As bureaucratic capacities developed, as the telegraph and the railroad penetrated the outlying areas, as the repeating rifle and modern artillery brought about the current capital-intensive form of warfare, professional armies acquired increasing advantages while the charge of mounted lancers lost its decisive character.[104] The *guerra gaucha* of Páez or Güemes had overwhelmed the Spanish forces; the losing tactics of Aparicio and Gumercindo Saravia in Uruguay and Brazil several generations later were more spectacular than anything else.[105] The barbarians who had been necessary, if problematic, allies for landed elites, urban meatpackers, and central administrators had become merely a source of turmoil.

If the military skills of gauchos and *llaneros* were rendered less consequential, the cultural differentiation of frontier cowboy and urbanite has been longer lasting. In the early nineteenth century, the French traveler Arsène Isabelle described a victorious gaucho force entering Buenos Aires as a frightening and wholly foreign horde.[106] As late as 1930, following the accession to power of Getúlio Vargas, General Flores da Cunha of Rio Grande do Sul made good on his promise to tether the horses of his troops to the obelisk in Rio de Janeiro before going home.[107] Twentieth-century regionalism in southern Brazil and the classical opposition between Buenos Aires and continental Argentina are memories of the ancient hostility between centers and frontiers—memories, however, which had until recently kept their political efficacy.[108]

The transformation of the life style of the American cowboy is a part of the broader process of the modern creation of a disciplined labor force. The establishment of external controls in the form of police and custodial institutions and internal controls, through the diffusion of appropriate cultural models and the formulation of therapies, are currently under much study in Europe and North America. We are now developing the social histories of the factory, army, school, prison, mental hospital, police.[109] To these we need to add, for Latin America, the social history of the great estate and especially of its most neglected variant, the ranch. Cowboys have played a role in the history of major countries in Latin America out of all proportion to their small numbers. May one hope that the current explosion of first-rate research on agrarian societies will come to include work on large-scale stock raising as well as on settled agriculture?

Appendix: On Freedom and Well-Being on the Frontiers

The literature on the Latin American cowboy raises an important and perplexing issue: this is the quite remarkable disagreement about the degree of freedom and well-being enjoyed by ranchhands. On the one hand we have a seemingly endless narration of brutality by Rodríguez Molas, well in accord with the Domar thesis on the coercive consequences apt to accompany the simultaneous presence of scarce labor and abundant land. Indeed a reader of Rodríguez Molas finds it hard to imagine a ranch without stocks and whips. On the other hand we have the claims of a "gaucho democracy," a form of social and racial egalitarianism fostered by the easy access of individuals to horses and weapons, and by the constant border wars. This image is no doubt romanticized but it is hard to dismiss, especially in the face of the more sophisticated argument of Carlos Rama that the mobility and responsibility of ranch life were incompatible with slavery. A sensitive and careful scholar like Halperin-Donghi admits to some puzzlement because in the era that saw a dramatic intensification of repressive measures by state, judge, and landlord, witnesses favorably compared the lot of the Argentine peon with that of the contemporary European peasant.[110] We can hardly settle such an issue here for the appropriate research has not yet been done, but we may make several points.

In the first place, the level of repressive discipline in frontier areas varied in time and space. Friedrich Katz has argued that during the Porfiriato debt peonage was much less prevalent than it had been earlier in northern Mexico,[111] due to the opening of alternative work opportunities in mines and in U.S. ranches. These new opportunities undermined the ability of *hacendados* to block the access of a scarce labor force to land: some tenants succeeded in exchanging their labor-power for large plots and formed an agricultural middle class. Cowboys, less interested in land, obtained higher wages. Variations also occurred in Argentina. Roughly speaking, an upward movement in the value of cattle products seems to have been accompanied by an increase in complaints against vagrancy, as well as by an increase in disciplinary measures and in military attempts to open new territories. This is documented in an unsystematic fashion by Rodríguez Molas.[112] In Argentina coercion expanded when rising demand produced a simultaneous increase in the value of labor and in the opening of new land; in northern Mexico harshness decreased as *hacendados* lost their monopoly of employment opportunities and found no alternative political means to keep labor under tight control.

In the second place we have the issue of variations in the methods, as well as in the severity, of repression. A comparison between Argentina and northern Mexico once again is helpful. Argentine proprietors made use of debt peonage as a device to attach people to land,[113] but they also relied extensively (as did Venezuelan proprietors) on government-backed repression. By contrast, in northern Mexico debt serfdom was the major means of labor control until the era of Díaz, when, as Katz argues, cowboys came to enjoy high levels of wages and of personal freedom. It is apparent that the strength of the coercive alliance of state and landlord varied greatly across historical and geographical situations, and these variations affected the methods (in addition to the levels) of repression. An explanation for these differences can be suggested. In Argentina cattle barons and meat-packers, long central to national politics,[114] could force the passage and implementation of laws designed to solve their specific labor problems. Bluntly put, they could rely on the government because they were the government. Mexico, however, was economically far more differentiated than Argentina; only in the great revolution of the early twentieth century did the ranch country fight its way into the Mexican political centers. Northern "lords" therefore had to make use of debt serfdom rather than government coercion; once the former method failed them, they were compelled to make significant concessions to their workers. It is interesting to add that Rio Grande do Sul, another cattle region long deprived of political power within a large and economically differentiated nation, also did not exhibit the variety of governmental measures to control ranchhands that were used in Argentina.

We may propose yet another reason for the improvement in the wages and way of life of Mexican cowboys. Despite concessions, northern *hacendados* whose large holdings might have a diversified production, still relied to some extent on coercion, particularly in areas far from mines and from the U.S. border. The coercion itself, we suggest, required them to pay their armed, mobile ranchhands well so that they might maintain their private armies. In contrast, the settled peons of Argentina received important nonmonetary compensation by being sheltered from state repression, a factor that was absent in the northern zones of Porfirian Mexico.[115]

Finally, we should indicate that there probably were significant differences in the brutality of disciplinary measures from ranch to ranch within a single historical and geographical situation. The simultaneous need of the cowboys for protection and of the landlord for armed retainers, mutual needs forged by a hostile environment, must have led to a social system easily tipped in two rather different directions. The *estanciero* as absolute master and the *estanciero* forced to grant major concessions to his armed mobile, and volatile workers must have existed side by side.[116]

Even though we agree with Cardoso's devastating criticism of the myth of "gaucho democracy,"[117] we would suggest that in Latin America the cowboy could easily represent a life of freedom, and that not merely because of the romantic image associated with the horseman. Here were terribly poor people, often part of a racially defined underclass who, in spite of the harshness of their lives, were free from many of the indignities of laborers on agricultural haciendas or plantations. This was true for at least *some* cowboys. The contrast with other types of agricultural workers must have been striking, particularly since horsemen were often associated with the landlord as his private enforcers of the law. To become a cowboy must have been a cherished dream of many of the rural underclass.

NOTES

1. We thank John Marx, Santiago Real de Azúa, Daniel Regan, Harold Sims, and João Carlos Brum Torres for valuable suggestions.

2. Emilio Coni, *Historia de las vaquerías de Rio de la Plata 1555–1750* (Buenos Aires: Editorial Devenir, 1956). Jesuit missionaries also promoted rationalization prior to the integration of Latin American cattle ranching into the world market. See Magnus Mörner, *The Political and Economic Activities of the Jesuits in the La Plata Region: The Hapsburg Era* (Stockholm: Library and Institute of Ibero-American Studies, 1953).

3. Joseph L. Love, *Rio Grande do Sul and Brazilian Regionalism, 1882–1930* (Stanford: Stanford University Press, 1971), esp. chs. 1 and 2; S. da Costa Franco, "O sentido histórico da revolução de 1893," in *Fundamentos da cultura rio-grandense,* Quinta Série (Porto Alegre: Gráfica da Universidade [Do Rio Grande do Sul], 1962), 193–216; Fernando O. Assunçao, *El gaucho, su espacio y su tiempo* (Montevideo: Bolsilibros Arca 1969); Ricardo Rodríguez Molas, *Historia social del gaucho* (Buenos Aires: Ediciones Marú, 1968); Tulio Halperin-Donghi, "La expansión ganadera en la campaña de Buenos Aires (1810–1852)," *Desarrollo Económico* 3 (1963): 57–110; Coni, *Historia de la Vaquerías* and *El gaucho, Argentina-Brasil-Uruguay* (Buenos Aires: Ediciones Solar, 1969); François Cheva-lier, *La formation des grandes domaines au Mexique. Terre et société aux XVIe–XVIIe siécles* (Paris: Institut d'Ethnologie, 1952); Donald D. Brand, "The Early History of the Range Cattle Industry in Northern Mexico," *Agricultural His-tory* 35 (1961): 132–39; W. H. Dusenberry, *The Mexican Mesta: The Administra-tion of Ranching in Colonial Mexico* (Urbana: University of Illinois Press, 1963); Odie B. Faulk, "Ranching in Spanish Texas," *Hispanic American Historical Review* 45 (1965): 257–66; Julio de Armas, "Nacimiento de la ganadería vene-zolana," *Revista Shell* 3 (1954): 26–35; Preston E. James, "The Possibilities of Cat-tle Production in Venezuela," *Bulletin of the Geographical Society of Philadelphia* 22 (1924): 45–56.

4. Four of Frederic Lane's essays collected in *Venice and History* (Baltimore: The Johns Hopkins University Press, 1966) deal with this subject: "National Wealth and Protection Costs," "The Economic Meaning of War and Protection," "Force and Enterprise in the Creation of Oceanic Commerce," and "Economic Consequences of Organized Violence."

5. Chevalier, *Formation des grandes domaines,* 44, 46, 51ff.

6. See Rodríguez Molas, *Historia social del gaucho,* 61; Assunçao, *El gaucho,* 32–34, 42; and Mörner, *Political and Economic Activities of the Jesuits,* 47.

7. Chevalier, *Formation des grandes domaines,* 116–17; Charles Gibson, *The Aztecs Under Spanish Rule. A History of the Indians of the Valley of Mexico, 1519–1810* (Stanford: Stanford University Press, 1964), 90, 280–81.

8. Richard J. Morissey, "The Northward Expansion of Cattle Ranching in New Spain, 1500–1600," *Agricultural History* 25 (1951): 115–21.

9. Roger M. Denhardt, "The Horse in the New Spain and the Border-lands," *Agricultural History* 25 (1951): 145–50. This happened despite Spanish attempts to restrict the access of Indians to horses (Mörner, *Political and Economic Activities of the Jesuits,* 37; Coni, *El gaucho,* 91).

10. Mario Góngora, *Vagabundaje y sociedad fronteriza en Chile (siglos XVII a XIX)* (Santiago: Centro de Estudios Socio-Económicos de la Facultad de Cien-cias Económicas de la Universidad de Chile, 1966), 5–6, 11ff.; "Vagabondage et société pastorale en Amérique Latine," *Annales: Economies, Sociétés, Civiizations* 21 (1966): 159–77; see esp. 160ff.

11. Owen Lattimore, "La civilisation, mère de Barbarie?" *Annales: Economies, Sociétés, Civilisations* 17 (1962): 95–108; "The Frontier in History," *Relazioni del X Congresso Internazionale di Scienze Storiche,* Vol. I (Firenze: Sansoni, 1955), 103–38.

12. These ties were the object of serious concern for the Spanish Crown, which made strenuous efforts to limit and regulate them. The best work on the subject is Magnus Mörner, *La Corona española y los foraneos en los pueblos de indios de América* (Stockholm: Almqvist & Wiksell, 1970). On different kinds of interactions between Indians and non-Indians in frontier areas see for instance Assunçao, *El gaucho,* 42–48; Chevalier, *Formation des grandes domaines,* 10–12, 43–47; Góngora, *Vagabundaje,* 22–27; Coni, *El gaucho,* 182. Finally, Louis de Armond describes the systematic character of frontier warfare in colonial Chile. He notes that many mestizos deserted the army and joined the Indian tribes and that the latter soon learned Spanish war tactics. It seems likely that deserters played a role in the improvement of Indian war methods. See his, "Frontier Warfare in Colonial Chile," *Pacific Historical Review* 23 (1954): 125–32.

13. On the role of the mestizo as mediator see Eric Wolf, "Aspects of Group Relations in a Complex Society: Mexico," *American Anthropologist* 58 (1956): 1065–78. For an extended example see Vito Alessio Robles, *Coahuila y Texas en la época colonial* (México: Editorial Cultura, 1938), 118ff.

14. On the difficulties faced by frontier administrators see Lattimore, "The Frontier," 126.

15. Alessio Robles (*Coahuila y Texas,* 165) documents Spanish deliveries of food and clothes to Indians in northern Mexico in order to maintain peace.

16. Lattimore, "The Frontier," 108.

17. Kai T. Erikson, *Wayward Puritans* (New York: John Wiley & Sons, Inc., 1966). The examination of the complex relationships between territorial and non-territorial forms of social exclusion is a difficult—and fascinating—area for theoretical and empirical explorations. Some of the relationships are more or less obvious, such as the tendency of frontiers to attract deviants of several kinds. Besides this recruitment effect, one can suggest that the type of territorial frontier a nation has bears on the kind of political deviant its authorities are likely to "discover" and label. The presence of a powerful enemy "on the other side" for instance, will have authorities concerned with an internal "fifth column." Examples of this process are commonplace in today's world. A systematic examination of the subject is lacking, even though suggestions can be found in Erikson, 157–59.

18. Mörner, *La Corona,* 21–23, 29.

19. These "Spaniards" almost certainly include mestizos who had been assimilated to the white group, as was common in the early period of colonization. For a discussion of the inclusiveness of the term Spaniard at this time see Mörner, *La Corona,* 113.

20. Mörner, *La Corona,* 27–35, 155–60.

21. During the brief period in which mestizos were not yet sufficiently numerous to constitute a major problem for the obsessed categorizers of the developing "society of castes," recognition of illegitimate children and assimilation into Spanish society happened often. Magnus Mörner, *Race Mixture in the History of Latin America* (Boston: Little, Brown and Company, 1967), 25–33, 40ff., 55.

22. Richard Konetzke, "Los mestizos en la legislación colonial," *Revista de Estudios Politicos* 112 (1960): 113–29, esp. 124ff. Magnus Mörner suggests that the increase in the numbers of mestizos helped to set them apart as a special group ("El mestizaje en la historia de Ibero-América. Informe sobre el estado actual de la investigación," in *El mestizaje en la historia de Ibero-América* [Mexico: Instituto Panamericano de Geografia e Historia, 1961], 33.)

23. Mörner, *La Corona*, 30, 105.

24. Portuguese racial policy, according to Mörner, responded to the same "basic conditions and motivations" as the Spanish one; see *Race Mixture,* 49–52.

25. René Echaiz offers the interesting suggestion that frontier mestizos were even more stigmatized than their counterparts in central areas, since they resulted from unions with very primitive, nomadic Indians, themselves far more stigmatized than the pacified Indians of the center. They also were often children of kidnapped white women. For these reasons, he argues, frontier mixed bloods were assimilated in the Indian group much more frequently than mestizos in the urban areas. See René León Echaiz, *Interpretación histórica del huaso chileno* (Santiago: Editorial Universitaria, 1955), 19–20.

26. Mörner, *Race Mixture,* 89; Germán Carrera Damas, *Boves—Aspectos socioeconómicos de la Guerra de Independencia* (Caracas: Ediciones de la Biblioteca de la Universidad Central de Venezuela, 1972), 29ff.

27. For example, in a report of Don Alfonso Carrió de la Bandera. "Visitador de Postas y Correos de Su Majestad," quoted at length in Assunçao, *El gaucho,* 173–74. The term "barbarian" was current as a designation for intractable Indians who had to be defeated or settled. The *indio bárbaro* (as opposed to the *indio de razón*) was a moral category that could be drawn on to describe the cowboy, just as the English stereotype of the Irish laborer—or of laborers generally—provided a model for the assignment of negative traits to blacks in the forging of U.S. racism (Eugene D. Genovese, *Roll, Jordan, Roll. The World the Slaves Made* [New York: Random House, 1976], 298–99).

28. As Joseph Love describes it, the Brazilian gaucho clearly distinguished himself from the three other races of humanity: the *baianos* (other Brazilians), the *castelhanos* (Spanish-speakers), and the *gringos* (other foreigners). See Love, *Rio Grande do Sul,* 12. Frontier cowboys all over Latin America felt that those who did not ride were beneath contempt—the "equestrian conception of the world" as Góngora puts it. Poor as these people were, their disdain for the work of settled agriculturalists was so intense that attempts to develop the Argentine pampas for anything but stock-raising in the mid-nineteenth century required paying enor-

mous wages to Irish immigrant laborers; three weeks of such earnings permitted them to quit for sheep raising. James R. Scobie, *Revolution on the Pampas: A Social History of Argentine Wheat, 1860–1910* (Austin: University of Texas Press, 1964), 14.

29. See Tulio Halperin-Donghi, *The Aftermath of Revolution in Latin America* (New York: Harper & Row, 1973), ch. 3, esp. 85ff.

30. The English translation of *Civilización y Barbarie* is available as D. F. Sarmiento, *Life in the Argentine Republic in the Days of the Tyrants* (New York: Collier, 1961); Robert L. Gilmore, *Caudillism and Militarism in Venezuela, 1810–1910* (Athens: Ohio University Press, 1964), 82; June E. Hahner, *Civilian-Military Relations in Brazil, 1889–1898* (Columbia, S.C.: University of South Carolina Press, 1969), 141–42; José Antonio Páez, *Autobiografía* (New York: H. R. Elliot, 1946), I, 5, 7.

31. Rodríguez Molas, *Historia social del gaucho*, 317–22.

32. Thus even the liberal enemies of Rosas participated in elaborating, ironically, a partial legitimation of his repressive rule. The liberal Argentine Sarmiento argued with disgust (whose force derives from the admiration with which it is mingled) that the strange savages of the interior had overwhelmed the European cosmopolites and produce monsters like Facundo and Rosas. The conservative Venezuelan Vallenilla Lanz differed only in approving the tyranny he regards, with Sarmiento, as founded on the barbarians. Both men, incidentally, saw only the ways in which the physical environment shaped the cowboy; both missed the significance of the forms of exclusion practiced by the urban centers and are utterly unconscious of their own contributions to the image of the barbarian.

33. Chevalier, *Formation des grandes domaines*, 115.

34. Rodríguez Molas, *Historia social del gaucho*, 80.

35. Halperin-Donghi indeed makes the opposite claim from that of Chevalier, namely that extensive cattle raising needed little capital investment. See *Aftermath of Revolution*, 60, 67–69. He argues that in the political chaos of the Independence period cattle could expand in Venezuela and Buenos Aires province precisely for this reason, while mining languished in other parts of the New World. We would add that protection costs were very likely lower for the cattle business, since cowboys could substitute for police as suppliers of needed violence.

36. Chevalier, *Formation des grandes domaines*, 108–9, 120ff.

37. Rodríguez Molas, *Historia social del gaucho*, 22, 61.

38. For examples of expedients used to build large herds and properties see, for instance, Chevalier, *Formation des grandes domaines*, 270ff.; Rodríguez Molas, *Historia social del gaucho*, 75; Juan Carlos Caravaglia, "Las actividades agropecuarias en el marco de la vida económica del Pueblo de Indios de Nuestra Señora de los Santos Reyes Magos de Yapeyú: 1768–1806," in Enrique Flores-cano, ed., *Haciendas, latifundios y plantaciones en América Latina* (Mexico: Siglo XXI, 1975), 464–85.

39. Rodríguez Molas, *Historia social del gaucho*, 173–74.

40. Some of the largest landowners did control illegal commerce; see Caravaglia, "Actividades agropecuarias," 481. This was hardly true of all of them.

41. Caravaglia shows that Indians frequently deserted the strictly organized missionary settlements, attracted by the high wages paid in the *vaquerías* and, presumably, by the life-style of the gauchos ("Actividades agropecuarias, 474).

42. Rodríguez Molas, *Historia social del gaucho*, 273, 362. For the role of military recruitment in post-independence Venezuela see Gilmore, *Caudillism and Militarism*, 36–37.

43. Rodríguez Molas, *Historia social del gaucho*, 456–57.

44. This was, of course, a general characteristic of rural agricultural enterprises in Latin America. See Magnus Mörner, "La hacienda hispanoamericana: Examen de las investigaciones y debates recientes," in Enrique Florescano, ed., *Haciendas, latifundios, y plantaciones en América Latina*. Mexico: Siglo Veintiuno, 1975), 15–48, esp. 23.

45. Halperin-Donghi, "Expansión ganadera," 62, 100.

46. See Gilmore, *Caudillism and Militarism*, ch. 7, esp. 137; Carrera Damas, *Boves*, 201ff; Laureano Vallenilla Lanz, *Cesarismo Democrático-estudio sobre las bases sociológicas de la constitución efectiva de Venezuela* (Caracas: Tipografia Garrido, 1952), 112–13.

47. Chevalier, *Formation des grandes domaines*, 363ff; Mörner, "La hacienda," 32–33.

48. Evsey D. Domar, "The Causes of Slavery or Serfdom: A Hypothesis," *Journal of Economic History*, 30 (1970): 18–32.

49. Góngora, *Vagabundaje*, 18–21.

50. Rodríguez Molas, *Historia social del gaucho*, 273, 400–401. The relatively inefficient protection afforded by landowners to settled workers, paradoxically, fitted well into the coercive system that attached labor to land. Total efficiency would have been counter productive, since cowboys would have grown confident enough to press wage and other demands upon the cattle raisers. Even though the landowners sometimes resented the conscription raids of the regular forces, such raids helped them to keep the climate of terror that ensured total control over labor; only a worker's submission would move a landowner to attempt to rescue him in the case of forced conscription. Cattle raisers profited from their protection failures.

51. Lacking a better word, we have been employing the term "nomad" in a loose fashion and not in a technical sense. To what extent frontier populations in Latin America really resembled nomadic societies is an important issue, especially in view of various comparisons found in the literature from Sarmiento onwards. Unfortunately, we cannot settle the question. Gauchos and *llaneros* did not constitute tribes, nor did their migrations follow any consistent geographical cycle. These, among others, are characteristics of nomadic societies as described by

anthropologists; see for instance Elizabeth E. Bacon, "Types of Pastoral Nomadism in Central and Southwest Asia," *Southwestern Journal of Anthropology* 10 (1954): 44–68. Manoelito de Ornellas argues the essential similarity of gauchos and nomads in *Gaúchos e beduinos (A origem étnica e a formação social do Rio Grande do Sul)* (Rio de Janeiro: Livraria José Olympio Editora, 1956). See also Coni, *El gaucho,* 177–78.

52. Góngora, *Vagabundaje,* 27–28.

53. Chevalier, *Formation des grandes domaines,* 142–43.

54. Assunçao, *El gaucho,* also observes the existence of a continuity between vagrant and settled populations in the area which today is Uruguay; see 14, 161.

55. Assunçao, *El gaucho* proposes that gauchos followed patterned careers. Vagrants and adventurers during their youth, they would settle down in later phases of their lives. See 189–90.

56. See Sarmiento's descriptions of the *rastreador* and the *baqueano,* in *Life in the Argentine Republic,* 44–49.

57. General Páez, in his charmingly narcissistic account of his youth, credits the harsh privations of *estancia* life for his later successful career as *caudillo.* "This was the school where I acquired the athletic robustness that often was so extremely useful to me later on. My body, from blows received, turned into iron" (*Autobiografía,* 8). On the robustness of *llaneros* and the misfortunes of the Spanish army in the Venezuelan savanna, see Vallenilla Lanz, *Cesarismo,* 13ff.

58. We follow here a suggestion of Eric Wolf, *Peasant Wars of the Twentieth Century* (New York: Harper Torchbooks, 1969), 29. Note that the leader of the greatest peasant uprising in twentieth-century Latin America, Emiliano Zapata, did not dress like a *Zapatista*—like a peasant of the Mexican south—but like a *charro* (he had broken horses in the Mexican army).

59. Assunçao, *El gaucho,* 212–14. Tulio Halperin-Donghi, *Politics, Economy and Society in Argentina in the Revolutionary Period* (Cambridge: Cambridge University Press, 1975), 278. Notice that "recruitment" could have multiple meanings. Governments were eager to enter into agreement with captains of war that they could not control; men like José Artigas could therefore move from the leadership of a band of smugglers to a captaincy in the *Blandengues.* Recruitment could also mean forced conscription.

60. Góngora, *Vagabundaje,* 25–27; Dante de Laytano, *Fazenda de Criação de Gado* (Porto Alegre: Oficinas Gráficas da Imprensa Oficial, 1950), 23.

61. Jack D. Forbes, *Apache, Navaho and Spaniard* (Norman: University of Oklahoma Press, 1960); Philip Wayne Powell, *Soldiers, Indians and Silver* (Berkeley: University of California Press, 1952) and "Spanish Warfare against the Chichimecas in the 1570s" *Hispanic American Historical Review* 24 (1944): 580–604; Oakah L. Jones, "Pueblo Indian Auxiliaries in New Mexico, 1763–1821" *New Mexico Historical Review* 37 (1962): 81–109; Góngora, *Vagabundaje,*

Assunçao, *El gaucho;* Rodríguez Molas, *Historia social del gaucho;* de Armond, "Frontier Warfare."

62. One Spanish official favored giving the Indians guns on the grounds that a mounted archer was as good a warrior as existed; the guns might at least make them dependent on the Spanish. See Max L. Moorehead, *The Apache Frontier, Jacobo Ugarte and Spanish-Indian Relations in Northern New Spain, 1769–1791* (Norman: University of Oklahoma Press, 1968), 127–28. As for equestrian skills, it has been claimed that Indians improved on the techniques received from the Europeans. See Tomás Lago, *El Huaso* (Santiago: Editorial Universitaria, S.A., 1953), 56–62.

63. Góngora, *Vagabundaje,* 23.

64. While the frontier culture was neither aboriginal to America nor dominant in Iberia, it is hard to assess the extent to which the Latin American frontier culture may have been a transplant of an Iberian cattle-raising culture similarly developed on the Christian-Moslem frontier. See Charles Julian Bishko, "The Peninsular Background of Latin American Cattle Ranching," *Hispanic American Historical Review* 32 (1952): 491–515, and "The Castillian as Plainsman: The Medieval Ranching Frontier in La Mancha and Extremadura," in Archibald R. Lewis and Thomas F. McGann, eds., *The New World Looks at Its History* (Austin: University of Texas Press, 1967), 47–69. At least one pioneer in bringing cattle to sixteenth-century Venezuela had been a rancher in Spain (de Armas, "Nacimiento de la ganadería venozolana," 33). No doubt there are other continuities of personnel, but the scale of New World ranching is without Iberian parallel.

65. Chevalier, *Formation des grandes domaines,* 105ff.

66. E. P. Thompson, "The Moral Economy of the English Crowd in the Eighteenth Century," *Past and Present* 50 (1971): 71–136; Assunçao, *El gaucho,* 144–246; de Ornellas, *Gaúchos e beduinos,* 141, Coni, *Historia de la Vaquerías,* 11, 17; Eleazar Cordova-Bello, "Aspectos históricos de la ganadería en el Oriente Venezolano y Guayana," *Revista de Historia* 3 (1962): 71.

67. The conflicting attempts of a local governor and of the far more distant royal authorities to regulate the ranching industry in eighteenth-century Texas was undermined by the resistance not only of Indians, rustlers, and frontier soldiers but mission fathers and ranchers as well (Faulk, "Ranching").

68. Góngora, *Vagabundaje,* 19. Coni observes that warnings of friends frequently allowed gaucho outlaws to elude capture. *El gaucho,* 177.

69. Góngora, *Vagabundaje,* 35–37; Rodríguez Molas, *Historia social del gaucho,* 465–66.

70. Eric Hobsbawm deserves credit for vividly demonstrating the interest of bandits although his work is weakened by a lack of interest in distinguishing the origins, nature, and consequences of banditry from those of the *myth* of banditry. See his *Bandits* (New York: Dell, 1969), and *Primitive Rebels* (New York: Norton, 1959).

71. An example of the ease with which one could switch sides is given in

Sarmiento's stunning portrait of Uruguay's Rivera: "General Rivera began his study of the grounds in 1804, when making war upon the government as an outlaw; afterwards, he waged war upon the outlaws as a government officer; next upon the king as a patriot; and later, upon the patriots as a peasant; upon the Argentines as a Brazilian chieftain; and upon Lavalleja as President; upon President Oribe as a proscribed chieftain; and, finally, upon Rosas, the ally of Oribe, as a general of Uruguay; in all of which positions he has had an abundance of time to learn something of the art of the Baqueano [pathfinder]." Sarmiento, *Life in the Argentine Republic*, 49.

72. It was a custom of families on the Brazilian-Uruguayan border to make their sons citizens of both countries to protect them from the consequences of defeat in revolutionary warfare. Double nationality could evidently be used to escape the consequences of common crimes. See Nepomuceno Saravia García, *Memorias de Aparicio Saravia* (Montevideo: Editorial Medina, 1956), 18.

73. Martin Güemes, a major Argentine chief, tried to use a land-reform program to build support among gauchos linked to other power brokers in Salta province, but it appears no one was interested. This left him dependent on the local elites (Roger M. Haigh, *Martin Güemes: Tyrant or Tool? A Study of the Sources of Power of an Argentine Caudillo* [Fort Worth: Texas Christian University Press, 1968], 43–49). For Venezuela see Carrera Damas, *Boves*, 198–200, and for a probable instance from colonial Argentina see Rodríguez Molas, *Historia social del gaucho*, 78. The Villista movement in the Mexican revolution, in spite of the moral influence of the Zapatistas, was not concerned with land reform in the usual sense. Rather, as Friedrich Katz has shown, the Villista land program was organized almost completely to pay off Villa's soldiers—not to mention his generals. Friedrich Katz, "Agrarian Changes in Northern Mexico in the Period of Villista Rule, 1913–1915." Paper presented at the Fourth International Congress of Mexican Studies, 1973. On the drastic differences of Zapatista and Villista delegates at the Aguascalientes Convention see Robert E. Quirk, *The Mexican Revolution, 1914–1915* (New York: Norton, 1970), 213.

74. This analysis of the mobilization of cowboys seems not to apply to the contemporary world. The spread of class and party politics has probably affected cowboys as much as other sectors of the rural population, as demonstrated by the integration of Colombian *llaneros* in a movement of a socialist bent during the 1950s. See Germán Guzmán Campos, Orlando Fals Borda, and Eduardo Umaña Luna, *La Violencia en Colombia* (Bogotá: Ediciones Tercer Mundo, 1962–1964), esp. vol. II, 55–151. The contemporary *llaneros*, like the rest of us, find lawyers to help draft political position papers.

75. The *pulpero* was in some cases the overseer (*capataz*) of a ranch and in others the rancher himself. See Assunçao, *El gaucho*, 203. On entrepreneurs who sponsored large-scale *vaquerías* with legal authorization see Coni, *El gaucho*, 63; and *Vaquerías*, 50–52.

76. Caravaglia, "Actividades agropecuarias," 481–83. For further evidence on the process of "contracting and sub-contracting" in frontier regions see Coni, *El gaucho* 178.

77. Assunçao, *El gaucho,* 146–51.

78. We are talking about those *estancieros* who lived in cities and were powerful officers or merchants. The small proprietor could well be a *pulpero* or smuggling chief himself.

79. Assunçao remarks that the smuggling chief and the military leader were often the same person. The wars of independence and the era of *caudillismo* propelled bands of smugglers into adopting violence as their way of life and means of subsistence—especially since the turmoil seriously disrupted the cattle business. Another reason was the growing rationalization of whatever *estancias* were still operating, which tended to make cattle hunting obsolete (*El gaucho,* 207, 212). Military leaders were also contrabandists (as in the case of Boves); in many cases they had been overseers of cattle ranches, or *pulperos.* See Coni, *El gaucho,* 175; Vallenilla Lanz, *Cesarismo,* 76–79.

80. Góngora, *Vagabundaje,* 22.

81. Carrera Damas, *Boves,* 182, 184–85, 193–202. Vallenilla Lanz observes that Boves and Páez, the two greatest *caudillos* of the independence period, had been in trouble with the colonial justice due to their illegal activities. See his *Disgregación e integración. Ensayo sobre la formación de la nacionalidad venezolana* (Caracas: Tip Universal, 1930), Vol. 1, 188, fn. 2.

82. Saravia García, *Memorias,* 472, 483–84.

83. In their fine article on *caudillismo,* Eric Wolf and Edward Hansen emphasize the pervasiveness of pillage as a means of acquiring wealth but fail to emphasize that the selling of protection was as important an activity as direct pillage for Latin American *caudillos.* The successful *caudillo* had the business acumen to realize the possibilities of this form of exploitation of violence, as becomes clear in the impressive list of their entrepreneurial qualities compiled by Wolf and Hansen. See their "Caudillo Politics: A Structural Analysis," *Comparative Studies in Society and History* 9 (1967): 168–79.

84. One might add that the armies of many chieftains started as small frontier bands that generally evolved into forces controlling nationwide extensions (Góngora, *Vagabundaje,* 36). Mörner proposes investigating the question of whether military power precedes ownership of great estates or vice-versa for all types of rural enterprise in Latin America ("La hacienda," 25).

85. Carrera Damas, *Boves,* 201ff., singles out the anti-vagrancy laws and the attempts of *hacendados* to appropriate the vast Venezuelan fields as the major reason why *llaneros* initially sided with royalists in the Independence War. Similarly, Góngora points out how a mentality of resistance to state authority—particularly to military service—fed continuous guerrilla warfare in Chile in the early 1800s. *Vagabundaje,* 34–36.

86. Rodríguez Molas, *Historia social del gaucho,* 465ff.

87. Franco, "Revolução de 1893," 203.

88. Fewer cowboys were necessary because a major task was no longer needed: keeping the animals within the boundaries of unfenced properties.

89. Chevalier, *Formation des grandes domaines,* 25, 27, 401.

90. Rodríguez Molas, *Historia social del gaucho,* 107–68. On the Spanish fondness for dangerous displays of riding skills see Lago, *Huaso,* 72, 124.

91. The following conception of play and of violence as a playful activity is based on J. Huizinga, *Homo Ludens: A Study of the Play Element in Culture* (Boston: Beacon Press, 1955), esp. ch. 1.

92. Religion was also a universal component—all could, or rather *should,* be Catholic. But being Catholic did not bring social honor to anybody, while excelling in the arts of war did.

93. Emilio Willems, "Acculturation and the Horse Complex Among German-Brazilians," *American Anthropologist* 46 (1944): 153–61.

94. Érico Verissimo, *O Tempo e o vento* (Porto Alegre: Editora Globo, n.d.), I, ch. VII.

95. Impressive evidence of this fact is given by the gaucho version of the duel with knives. The goal in such a duel was not to kill the opponent, but to mark him. In looking at his own face the loser would have to acknowledge for the rest of his life the courage and skill of the winner. He would literally be a captive audience. See Sarmiento, *Life in the Argentine Republic,* 64. Death in these duels was described as "a misfortune."

96. For documentation of such occurrences see Alfredo Aragón, *El desarme del ejército federal por la revolución de 1913* (Paris: Imprimeries Wallhoff et Roche, 1915), 68; Assunçao, *El gaucho,* 197; de Ornellas, *Gaúchos e beduinos,* 124.

97. For instance, Franco, "Revolução de 1893," 207.

98. Even in the absence of this "mirror effect," frontier chieftains had a keen perception of the dramatic (in addition to the physical) uses of terror to assert their domination over a frightened audience. Sarmiento's classic description of Facundo is an excellent example (*Life in the Argentine Republic,* 70–81).

99. Rodríguez Molas, *Historia social del gaucho,* 30; Góngora, *Vagabundaje,* 9; Saravia García, *Memorias,* 46.

100. Obviously, the *pulperos* had also other methods to force debts upon *peons.* See Rodríguez Molas, *Historia social del gaucho,* 236.

101. Saravia García, *Memorias,* 20. Ornellas observes that bets on horse races were very high (*Gaúchos e beduinos,* 350). Tomás Lago notes that excesses in gambling were frequent and that authorities sometimes intervened to restrict them. He cites a set of 1785 regulations which, among other things, established limits for horse-racing bets in the Santiago area (*Huaso,* 83). One can only guess at the extremes that gambling reached in the uncontrolled frontiers.

102. For Coni's views on this matter see *Vaquerías,* 87ff; *El gaucho,* 12, 58, 67,

128–29. He even adds that "gauchification" was a process of European cultural decay, originated in the close contact and daily exchanges with Indians (*El gaucho,* 61). The careful researcher in Coni, however, has to admit the existence of continuities between gauchos and the settled sectors of the population (*El gaucho,* 148). Elsewhere, he asserts that there were constant additions to the numbers of gaucho bands (*El gaucho,* 151). If the latter were totally cut off from regular life, where would these constant additions come from?

103. Stanley J. Stein and Barbara H. Stein, *The Colonial Heritage of Latin America. Essays on Economic Dependence in Perspective* (New York: Oxford University Press, 1970); Mark Wasserman, "Oligarquía e intereses extranjeros en Chihuahua durante el porfiriato," *Historia Mexicana* 22 (1973): 279–319. On the introduction of the barbed wire by Americans see Brand, "Early History of the Range Cattle Industry," 136.

104. On the modernization of armies see Gilmore, *Caudillism and Militarism;* Jorge A. Lozoya, *El ejército mexicano (1911–1965)* (Mexico: El Colegio de México, 1970); Magnus Mörner, "Caudillos y militares en la evolución hispano-americana," *Journal of Inter-American Studies* 2 (1960): 295–310.

105. A detailed description of their adventures can be found in Saravia García, *Memorias.* Although this work is a nephew's tribute to the heroism of General Saravia, the desperate situation of those relying on the tools and tactics of the *guerra gaucha* is evident.

106. Arsène Isabelle, *Viagem ao Rio da Prata e ao Rio Grande do Sul* (Rio de Janeiro: Zelio Valverde, 1949).

107. See Carlos E. Cortés, *Gaucho Politics in Brazil* (Albuquerque: University of New Mexico Press, 1974), 23.

108. A good study of the impact of Rio Grande do Sul's regionalism on Brazilian politics up to 1930 is Love, *Rio Grande do Sul;* on Argentina see James R. Scobie, *La lucha por la consolidación de la nacionalidad Argentina, 1852–1862* (Buenos Aires: Librería Hachette, 1964). A full explication of regionalism would be far beyond the possibilities of this essay, but we must at least suggest that cattle frontiers seem to promote significant and enduring geographical cleavages in national politics. Nineteenth-century Venezuelan politics was dominated by the *llanos,* until the Andean chieftains seized power in 1899. Although not the classical *llano* country, the Andean provinces also had complex links to the cattle industry. See Charles C. Griffin, "Regionalism's Role in Venezuelan Politics," *Interamerican Quarterly* 3 (1941): 21–35; Winfield J. Burggraaff, "Venezuelan Regionalism and the Rise of Táchira," *Américas* 25 (1968): 160–67; Vallenilla Lanz, *Disgregación,* 121. The great Mexican revolution was, among other things, a claim to power by northerners against the famous Mexico City—Vera Cruz axis that had dominated political life. See Paul W. Drake, "Mexican Regionalism Reconsidered," *Journal of Inter-American Studies and World Affairs* 12 (1970): 401–15; Barry Carr, "Las peculiaridades del norte mexicano: 1880–1927. Ensayo de interpretación," *Histo-*

ria Mexicana 22 (1973): 320–46; Peter H. Smith, "La politica dentro de la revolución: el congreso constituyente de 1916–1917," *Historia Mexicana* 22 (1973): 363–95.

109. See Michel Foucault, *Folie et déraison: Histoire de la folie á l'âge classique* (Paris: Gallimard, 1972); and *Surveiller et punir. Naissance de la Raison* (Paris: Gallimard, 1975); Herbert G. Gutman, *Work, Culture and Society in Industrializing America: Essays in American Working-Class and Social History* (New York: Knopf, 1976); E. P. Thompson, "Time, Work Discipline and Industrial Capitalism," *Past and Present,* 1967, 57–97; André Zysberg, "La société des galériens au milieu du XVIIIe siècle"; Michelle Perrot, "Délinquance et Système pénitentiaire en France au XIXe siècle" and Gérard Bleandou and Guy LeGaufey, "Naissance des asiles d'aliénés (Auxerre-Paris)": all three are in *Annales: Economies, Sociétés, Civilisations* 30 (1975): 43–65, 67–94, 93–121; Pierre Deyon, *Le Temps des prisons. Essai sur l'histoire de la délinquance et les origines du système pénitentiaire* (Paris: Editions Universitaires, 1975); Samuel Bowles and Herbert Gintis, *Schooling in Capitalist America: Education and the Contradictions of Economic Life* (New York: Basic Books, 1976); David H. Bailey, "The Police and Political Development in Europe," in Charles Tilly, ed., *The Formation of National States in Western Europe* (Princeton: Princeton University Press, 1975).

110. Carlos M. Rama, "The Passing of the Afro-Uruguayans from Caste Society into Class Society," in Magnus Mörner, ed., *Race and Class in Latin America* (New York: Columbia University Press, 1970), 28–50, esp. 32. Halperin-Donghi, "Expansión ganadera," 101.

111. Friedrich Katz, "Labor Conditions on Haciendas in Porfirian Mexico: Some Trends and Tendencies," *Hispanic American Historical Review* 54 (1974): 31ff.

112. Rodríguez Molas, *Historia social del gaucho,* 24–26, 134–35, 255, 316–17.

113. Halperin-Donghi, "Expansión ganadera," 99ff.

114. Peter Smith, *Politics and Beef in Argentine: Patterns of Conflict and Change* (New York: Columbia University Press, 1969).

115. Katz, "Labor Conditions," 33; Halperin-Donghi, "Expansión ganadera," 100ff.

116. Katz, "Labor Conditions," 31.

117. Fernando Henrique Cardoso, *Capitalismo e Escravidão no Brasil Meridional* (São Paulo: Difusão Europeia do Livro, 1962), esp. 119–32.

Afterword, 2002

John Markoff

"What's past is prologue": I take this opportunity to look back on a paper first published twenty-three years ago in light of the themes of the University of Michigan's conference on States of Violence; to identify shortcomings in that paper is to suggest some promising avenues for further investigation.[1]

First of all, since Silvio Baretta and I wrote that paper, there have been some valuable additions to the historical literature on the cattle frontiers of Iberoamerica. Richard W. Slatta has penetratingly treated the impact of rationalized ranching and increasingly effective state authority in nineteenth-century Argentina, Thomas Hall has set northern New Spain within its global context, Jane Rausch has surveyed the entire history of the Colombian *llanos* and John Chasteen is clarifying the sanguinary politics of the Uruguayan-Brazilian frontier in the late nineteenth century.[2] At the time we were working on "Civilization and Barbarism" the Venezuelan and Chilean were the least well researched among the major cattle frontiers; they remain so.[3] Finally, valuable comparative treatments have appeared.[4]

We devoted some attention to banditry in relation to domination: where does banditry fit in the dealings of large landowners and those with little or no land, of state officials with peripheral regions? This theme has been much more extensively explored since we wrote, in and out of Latin America, as in Paul Sant Cassia's essay in this volume.[5]

In a different vein, economic historians have been addressing Domar's stimulating thesis on the economic sources of coercive forms of labor deployment such as those that played such a role in Latin American frontiers. It may be that some of this work would permit a theoretical statement that is more responsive to the variations across space and time in coercive patterns than Domar's model of labor scarcity.[6]

Our essay was concerned with oppositions and the construction of oppositions: how did administrators and outlaws, wanderers and settled people, Europeans and Indians, city dwellers and frontier dwellers, ranch hands and ranchers, not to mention those on horseback and those on foot, define themselves in relation to the other. One French historian has suggested that civilizations define themselves "by their barbarians."[7] One opposition that we failed to consider, however, was the construction of male and female identities. A number of conference participants pointed out that we said nothing of frontier women. I have little doubt that this is a significant missing dimension. We missed an opportunity to enrich our discussion of the cowboys' culture as specifically masculine. The norms surrounding violence were clearly part of a sense of what a "man" was. Consider weaponry. Richard Slatta's comparative survey greatly clarifies a point left implicit in our essay: from the pampas to northern Mexico, cowboys felt the use of firearms unmanly, a disdain not shared by the Anglos further north.[8]

Such notions of what is proper for men and women are shaped in the interactions of men and women and omitting the latter risks deforming the portrayal of the former. Unfortunately, little has been written that would, in my view, permit us to speak with much confidence on this subject. The literature suggests a few tentative generalizations. We think that cattle frontiers had far fewer women than men; that nineteenth-century ranch owners were likelier to have a family life than were ranch hands; and that ranch hands spent long periods without women in barracks, on trail drives, or in shacks tending isolated parts of the great ranches. If we go back before the nineteenth century, we know even less. But there are too many sentimental depictions of gauchos being torn from woman and child by the police or the military recruiters to dismiss such attachments as a nullity.

If, as is to be wished, new research subjects Latin American frontiers to the same sort of scrutiny that the western frontier of the United States has undergone, even the few big generalizations may begin to appear shaky. Susan Socolow, for example, finds that in the mid-eighteenth century about 45 percent of the inhabitants of rural Buenos Aires province were women. Yes, men significantly outnumbered women, but much less so than conventionally assumed. These women assumed a variety of economic roles, although the raising of large animals was—and here the conventional picture is confirmed—exclusively male. Nor was it common for women to reside on the ranches.[9] But once one recognizes something as fundamental as their existence, the sorts of relationships between the earlier cattle hunters or the later settled ranchhands and the women of the frontier becomes a matter it would be good to know a great deal more about. And, more broadly, it seems to me that we know next to nothing about sexuality in this very male world. (Perhaps someone on the current research frontier zone of the history of sexuality will tackle this.)

One conference participant asked specifically whether omitting women made it impossible to understand the replacement of the labor force or the socialization of future workers. On this very specific issue of recruitment, it seems likely that relatively few cowboys managed to acquire enough land to bring up future cowboys (of course ranch owners could pass on their position). Many cowboys came from elsewhere; young cowboys were often breaking family traditions, not following them. (*A propos,* Socolow shows immigration into frontier Buenos Aires province to have been over-whelmingly male.)[10]

What made such external recruitment possible was the very scant labor requirements. In nineteenth-century Argentina it took about five riders for each thousand head of cattle on a drive.[11] Labor requirements were radically reduced, cyclically, in winter. The long-term trend was toward further reduction, as technological innovations like wire fencing and social innovations like more secure and better-defined land titles simplified the task of policing the roads and controlling the movement of cattle and men. The strengthened bureaucratic and military authority reduced the value of private cavalry forces.

One might expand the general theme of the shifting boundaries of cultural categories by considering the deployment of frontier imagery in the elaboration of national identities from the late nineteenth century to the present in fiction, history-writing, and film. Silvio Baretta and I argued that a variety of processes tended to conflate dark skin, criminality, barbarism, and frontier from the colonial period on. When the frontiers, now safely in the past, were re-appropriated into national mythology in the *gauchesco* literature of Argentina and Uruguay, for example, or the history writing of Frederick Jackson Turner in the United States, the cowboys, now national types, were no longer to be marginalized, and became retrospectively whitened so that the typical *gaucho* of Argentine consciousness or the North American cowpuncher of Hollywood westerns is generally, unambiguously, white. (Let me speculate that in countries where cowboys did not enter into national self-identity, the retrospective whitening in film or print was less pronounced. Mexican film cowboys could be mestizos.) Since every U.S. school kid knows there were cowboys and Indians, joined in opposition, we considered beginning the paper: "In Chile, the first cowboys were Indians."[12]

Although we contended that core and periphery shaped and shape one another, our paper was a great deal clearer about the impact of imperial centers on their frontiers than the reverse. In part this is a deficiency of perspective: we would have to shift from the pampas and *llanos* to the New World's urban centers as well as to the towns and countryside of Iberia to trace the impact of periphery on core. New foods and medicines, new wealth, were acquired along with the bolstering of a sense of purpose in the peoples of the western end of Eurasia, whose mission it was to bring civilization to the barbarians and tame the savages. In identifying those they subdued as wild, cruel, ignorant, and immoral, Europeans could see themselves, in contrast, as just and enlightened and their own violence as pacificatory. (Europeans could compete with each other for the mantle of enlightened world dominion by extending such condemnations to each other as in the English deployment of Spanish cruelty and ignorance in the Americas to minimize their own activities in the way of ethnic cleansing, but that is another story.) The strength of identifications forged at the peripheries of empire continues in the conflicts in the imperial cities themselves, now that migrants from the peripheries are settling in those cities.[13]

What is a frontier as an object of inquiry? We took up cattle frontiers in Latin America, but what is specific to these regions and what resembles other frontiers that differ in topography, in productive labor, in the relationship to imperial centers? Is the capacity of our pastoralists to resist, and their consequent ambivalent relationship to central authority, like or unlike that of equally difficult to govern hill peoples or desert dwellers? In what ways are our propositions applicable to the nineteenth-century cowboys of the United States and Canada? And what of regional differences within Latin America?

If we, rather broadly, see frontiers as regions at the limits of central power,[14] then it seems likely that a great deal is happening there. New World frontiers were variously described by Europeans as deserts and as gardens.[15] People flee to them from settled routines, or the demands of elites, or the exactions of states, and thus frontiers are associated with notions of freedom. And on the other hand, because conditions are harsh, uncertain, and dangerous, people are brought there by force, held there by coercion, and disciplined by violence under the control of those seeking profit or geopolitical advantage. The Americas appear early in Europe's imaginary as a place of opportunity for the adventurous, but of those who crossed the Atlantic in the early modern period more were Africans in chains than European fortune-seekers. Even among ocean-crossing Europeans, there were many in various forms of unfreedom.

But how did these frontiers appear to the indigenous peoples of the Americas? Were there analogous polarities of freedom and unfreedom in their early experience of European penetration: some finding release from established routines in new forms of livelihood; some, especially among local elites, finding a freedom from traditional constraints in obtaining from Europeans previously unavailable resources (in return for supplying those Europeans with food, or local knowledge, or coerced laborers);[16] and many others finding new forms of subjugation? Baretta and I suggested that for plebeians transplanted from an Iberia whose very language of hierarchy divided those on horse from those on foot, *caballeros* and *peones,* an equestrian life had an aura of freedom about it. Could the availability of horses also have meant new freedoms for some Indians, while others, sedentary agriculturalists, were now prey to formidable mounted warriors?

In "Civilization and Barbarism," we grappled with contrasting images of the frontier as a place of freedom and a place of servitude. But perhaps we did not stress sufficiently the creative potential of such a mix. Administrators, elites and townsfolk may elaborate conceptions of civilization and barbarism, but out on the range many official claims must have rung hollow. In a frontier very distant from the one we explored, David Edwards' essay in this volume shows the incapacity of British punitive expeditions to control the lesson drawn from violent events at the limits of effective imperial control in India. Winston Churchill's journalism presents as a salutary lesson to Muslim fanatics what is remembered in Afghanistan as a triumph for the faith. Our Latin American cowboys, largely illiterate, have not left us much in the way of personal testimony, but it is difficult to imagine them regarding with anything but skepticism the moral claims of authorities who, for example, recruited anti-smuggling police from among outlaws.

Marcus Rediker and Peter Linebaugh have been suggesting that the working people of a very different frontier, the Atlantic, where the authority of merchant masters and admiralties was challenged incessantly by mutiny and piracy, was particularly explosive, precisely because of the intermingling of freedom and servitude that I have suggested to be widely characteristic of frontiers. The sailor who can defy authority by jumping ship worked side-by-side with slaves unloading cargo all over the Western

Hemisphere, exchanging information on how slaves could escape by ship and how sailors could dispose of pilfered merchandise on shore.[17] The multilingual, multiethnic mix of port cities was social dynamite. (There seem to be similar features in the Egyptian ports of Juan Cole's paper, but group boundaries—the Muslim-Christian divide particularly—seem firmer in his account than divisions in the early modern Atlantic world.) And in piracy a model of an alternative form of employment existed, free of state authority (until capture) and with a far more egalitarian mode of decision-making than that which characterized merchant or military ships.[18]

Frontiers, including cattle frontiers, are places where authority—neither secure nor nonexistent—is open to challenge, and where polarities of order and chaos assume many guises. As nineteenth-century European cities filled with those who could no longer make a go of it in the countryside, some European elites now discovered that it was their own urban lower classes who were the barbarians (and at least in the case of early nineteenth-century France, they used that very word).[19]

So these images survive.[20] The essay by Fernando Coronil and Julie Skurski shows them to be very much alive in contemporary Venezuela in the current discourse of the political elite and in the resonance of the novel *Doña Bárbara*. (And when we think how widely read in Latin America generally that novel was, we get a hint of the continuing power of similar polarities in other countries.)

Although the specific, geographically constituted cattle frontiers were not permanent, perhaps it may be said that authority always has its limits, and that shorn of their spatial image, frontiers are pervasive. We find them on Sri Lankan tea plantations, in South African gold mines, and in U.S. prisons. And on those frontiers we find oppositional definitions of groups, we find claims of order and claims of freedom, and we find definitions of violence that explain violence as they create it.

NOTES

1. I thank all the organizers and participants in this event and especially Stacy Cherry, Fernando Coronil, Valentine Daniel, David Edwards, Anjan Ghosh, David Pedersen, and Julie Skurski for their comments. This postscript also benefited from discussions with Thomas Hall and Erik Zissu.

2. Richard W. Slatta, *Gauchos and the Vanishing Frontier* (Lincoln: University

of Nebraska Press, 1983); Thomas Hall, *Social Change in the Southwest, 1350–1880* (Lawrence: University of Kansas Press, 1989); Jane M. Rausch, *A Tropical Plains Frontier: The Llanos of Colombia, 1531–1831* (Albuquerque: University of New Mexico Press, 1984), and *The Llanos Frontier in Colombian History, 1830–1930* (Albuquerque: University of New Mexico Press, 1993); John C. Chasteen, "Fighting Words: The Discourse of Insurgency in Latin American History," *Latin American Research Review* 28 (1993): 83–111; "Background to Civil War: The Process of Land Tenure in Brazil's Southern Borderland, 1801–1893," *Hispanic American Historical Review* 71 (1991): 737–60; and *Heroes on Horseback. A Life and Times of the Last Gaucho Caudillos* (Albuquerque: University of New Mexico Press, 1995).

3. Noteworthy in filling in the Venezuelan gap has been Miquel Izard: "Sin domicilio fijo, senda segura, ni destino conocido: Los llaneros de Apure a finales del período colonial," *Boletín Americanista* 33 (1983): 13–83; "Ni cuatreros ni montoneros, llaneros," *Boletín Americanista* 31 (1981): 83–142; "Oligarcas temblad, viva la libertad. Los llaneros y la Guerra Federal," *Boletín Americanista* 32 (1982): 227–77; "Ya era hora de emprender la lucha para que en el ancho feudo de la violencia reinase algún día la justicia," *Boletín Americanista* 34 (1984): 75–124; "Sin el menor arraigo ni responsabilidad. Llaneros y ganadería a principios del siglo XIX," *Boletín Americanista* 37 (1987): 109–42.

4. Richard W. Slatta, *Cowboys of the Americas* (New Haven and London: Yale University Press, 1990), and *Comparing Cowboys and Frontiers* (Norman: University of Oklahoma Press, 1997); Donna J. Guy and Thomas E. Sheridan, *Contested Ground. Comparative Frontiers on the Northern and Southern Edges of the Spanish Empire* (Tucson: University of Arizona Press, 1998).

5. Richard W. Slatta, ed., *Bandidos: The Varieties of Latin American Banditry* (New York: Greenwood Press, 1987).

6. For example, Mario Pastore, "Trabajo forzado indígena y campesinado mestizo libre en el Paraguay: Una visión de sus causas basada en la teoría de la búsqueda de rentas económicas," *Revista Paraguaya de Sociología* 32 (1995): 39–75.

7. Bronislaw Baczko quoted in Pierre Michel, *Les Barbares, 1789–1848. Un myth romantique* (Lyon: Presses Universitaires de Lyon, 1981), 11.

8. See Slatta, *Cowboys of the Americas,* 43, 150. Perhaps a code of self-reliance cast a precision machine like a firearm as an alien and expensive artifact when the cultural traits of Latin American frontiers developed in the colonial period; in the nineteenth-century U.S. West, the purchase of factory-made tools may have seemed a routine, unremarkable, and natural activity.

9. Susan Migden Socolow, "Women of the Buenos Aires Frontier, 1740–1810 (or the Gaucho Turned Upside Down)," in Donna J. Guy and Thomas E. Sheridan, eds., *Contested Ground. Comparative Frontiers on the Northern and Southern Edges of the Spanish Empire* (Tucson: University of Arizona Press, 1998).

10. Socolow, "Women of the Buenos Aires Frontier," 72–73.

11. Slatta, *Cowboys of the Americas,* 80.

12. We abandoned that sentence out of doubts that the Chilean history was known with certainty.

13. Even more generally, attempts to control peripheries have been dynamic sources of change for cores. See, for example, William McNeill's discussion of the role of the steppe frontier across several millennia of Eurasian history in *The Rise of the West: A History of the Human Community* (Chicago: University of Chicago Press, 1991).

14. John Markoff, "Frontier Societies," in Peter N. Stearns, ed., *Encyclopedia of Social History* (New York and London: Garland Publishing Company, 1994), 289–91.

15. There is a fine, concise discussion in Slatta, *Cowboys of the Americas.*

16. See Eric Wolf's observations on the opportunities that the European presence presented elites in the Americas and Africa, in *Europe and the People Without History* (Berkeley: University of California Press, 1982).

17. Peter Linebaugh and Marcus Rediker, *The Many-Headed Hydra: Sailors, Slaves, Commoners and the Hidden History of the Revolutionary Atlantic* (Boston: Beacon Press, 2000).

18. Marcus Rediker, *Between the Devil and the Deep Blue Sea* (Cambridge: Cambridge University Press, 1987).

19. Louis Chavalier, *Classes laborieuses et classes dangereuses à Paris pendant la première moitié du XIXe siècle* (Paris: Plon, 1958), 453–68; Pierre Michel, *Les Barbares, 1789–1848. Un Myth Romantique* (Lyon: Presses Universitaires de Lyon, 1981).

20. For some very rich discussions of the idea of the frontier in the United States, which may suggest Iberoamerican parallels and contrasts, see Richard Maxwell Brown, "Violence," in *The Oxford History of the American West,* Clyde A. Milner II, Carol A. O'Connor, and Martha A. Sandweiss, eds. (New York, Oxford University Press, 1994), 393–426; Richard White, *"It's Your Misfortune and None of My Own": A History of the American West* (Norman, Okla.: University of Oklahoma Press, 1991); Richard C. Poulsen, *The Landscape of the Mind. Cultural Transformations of the American West* (New York: Peter Lang, 1992); and Richard Slotkin's three books, *Regeneration through Violence: The Mythology of the American Frontier, 1600–1860* (Middletown, Conn.: Wesleyan University Press, 1973); *The Fatal Environment. The Myth of the Frontier in the Age of Industrialization, 1800–1890* (New York: Atheneum, 1985); *Gunfighter Nation: The Myth of the Frontier in Twentieth Century America* (New York: Atheneum, 1992).

Dismembering and Remembering the Nation: The Semantics of Political Violence in Venezuela

Fernando Coronil and Julie Skurski

Y la muerte del pueblo fué como siempre ha sido:
como si no muriera nadie, nada,
como si fueran piedras las que caen
sobre la tierra, o agua sobre el agua.
> —Pablo Neruda[1]

Violence and History

Although political violence has played a central part in the formation of nations, its historical constitution and its role in representing nations have received scant attention. All too frequently the explanation of violence is equated with the identification of its causes, its form is accounted for by its function, and its function is seen in instrumental terms; violence is reduced to a practical tool used by opposing social actors in pursuit of conflicting ends. Whether treated as a cause, function, or instrument, violence is generally assumed rather than examined in its concreteness. Little attention is paid to its specific manifestations, to the way its effects are inseparably related to the means through which it is exerted, and to the meanings that inform its deployment and interpretation. In contrast, typological approaches that postulate a correspondence between types of societies and forms of violence often recognize the opacity of violence yet lose sight of the historical depth and specificity of its manifestations.[2]

Moments of political violence may appear shatteringly similar in their grim outcome and in the sheer physicality of the destruction they inflict. Yet these moments, even those regarded as spontaneous outbursts, are shaped by each society's particular history and myths of collective identity and are energized by sedimented menuxies of threats to the collectivity. In a critique of what he called the "spasmodic view of popular history," E. P. Thompson warned against viewing popular protest as a simple reaction to increasing prices, as if riots were the automatic response to economic stimuli, the result of compulsive rather than intentional historical agents (1971). Just as riots are not a direct response to hunger, state repression is not simply a means to control popular unrest. Seemingly spontaneous popular action develops through the enactment of shared understandings and the enunciation of novel statements in a familiar idiom, while the state's use of force as a means to control unrest draws a vision of the natural ordering of society that is based on quotidian relations of domination. The immediacy and apparent naturalness of moments of collective violence may conceal their intentionality and socially constructed significance.

Violence is wielded and resisted in the idiom of a society's distinctive history. When it becomes a force in contending efforts to affirm or restructure a given vision of order, it simultaneously dis-orders and re-orders, established understandings and arrangements. Aggression becomes inseparable from transgression, the rupture of conceptual and physical boundaries indivisible from the construction of new orders of significance. Violence pushes the limits of the permissible, opening up spaces where customary and unexpected meanings and practices are brought together in unprecedented ways, illuminating hidden historical landscapes in a flash, and leaving behind the opaque memory of ungraspable territories. In the crisis of meaning that violence conceives, the territoriality of nations and the corporeality of people become privileged mediums for reorganizing the body politic and for forcibly controlling the movement of persons and ideas within the nation's material and cultural space. Statements to the collectivity are indelibly inscribed upon and made through the body, as it becomes a medium for searing assertions of power. The body is defiantly risked in the attempt to subvert ordinary restrictions and to avenge daily affronts. Individual biography and collective history seem momentarily united, as history and the body become each other's terrains.

Contending collective memories and differing accounts of an uncertain present shape these terrains. In this paper we examine two conflicts between the state and popular sectors in Venezuela and explore the making and representation of events regarded at the time as landmarks in that nation's history. We locate these conflicts in the context of their making, as they were conditioned at once by a colonial legacy and by a reordering of worldwide capitalist relations. As the hidden hand of finance capital

and the visible hand of intellectual fashion etch the indeterminate boundaries of the postmodern map of the world, the contours of this landscape
reveal the hold of transformed colonial relations in the age of postcolonial
empires.[3]

History and the Massacres

The outbreaks of collective violence and civil unrest analyzed here were
responses to social-economic transformations that in the last two decades
have disrupted the bases of the populist political system based upon petro-
leum-rent distribution and have challenged the assumptions that had long
sustained it. These conflicts became nodal points in the redefinition of the
discourse of democracy, as dominant and opposition forces clashed over
the interpretation of the events and their implications. The first conflict, a
massacre that expressed the deepening crisis of the protectionist model of
development and the hardening of the political system, occurred at the end
of the 1988 presidential electoral campaign. It appeared far removed from
the fanfare and display of politics, yet its message was directed to a
national political audience. Fourteen villagers from the border town of
Amparo were killed on 29 October 1988, on a remote cattle savanna on the
Arauca River dividing southwest Venezuela from Colombia. A government counterinsurgency brigade claimed the villagers were guerrillas killed
by its troops in an armed encounter. Opponents contended that the government brigade had ambushed and disguised the innocent victims as a
way of creating the appearance of a subversive threat to the nation. Electoral competition permitted these counterclaims to be amplified and vali-
dated within centers of power. As a result of sustained protest, the military
encounter was publicly redefined as the Amparo massacre: an attack on
innocent citizens who had no protection (*amparo*) against state violence
and the manipulation of appearances.[4]

The second conflict, lasting from 27 February to 3 March 1989, was an
urban social uprising in response to which the government used massive
force: by official count, 277 people died; by unofficial estimate, over 1,000
people were killed. This event reflected accumulated frustration with the
nation's rapid economic decline and its political and economic corruption.
It was detonated by the clash between the expectations of political and
economic renewal raised by the electoral campaign; and anger at newly
elected President Pérez's abrupt adoption of a stringent International
Monetary Fund (IMF) austerity program. In multiple unplanned protests

over sharp price increases and food shortages, an estimated one million people spontaneously looted thousands of stores and factories in the capital and most major cities, in effect erasing state control of the street.[5] During five days the state responded to mass looting, redistribution, and destruction with containment, repression, and retaliation. It constituted by far the most massive and severely repressed such riot in the history of Latin America.[6]

The violent conflicts we discuss here shook assumptions concerning the relationship between civilization and barbarism, leader and *pueblo,* and state and citizen that have ordered populist discourse. In order to understand these unusual incidents of repression, protest, and revolt, we first look at the context in which they occurred. We then briefly examine dominant representations of the nation's history and promised future that articulate these relationships and became paradigms within populist discourse: the Bolívarian ideal of unity between leader and masses codified in official discourse and in the novel *Doña Bárbara.*[7]

The concept of democracy, which is the central term in Venezuela's dominant political discourse, draws on historical memories of autocratic rule and economic stagnation to validate the political party-led system of capitalist promotion. Dominant discourse holds democracy to be the nation's greatest achievement as well as the necessary condition for its progress. It closely links democracy to development, attributing Venezuela's rapid growth and prestige concerning political freedom and human rights to its multiparty system of government and construes the democratic regime to be the nation's guardian, entrusted with directing the flow of oil income to benefit the interests of the *pueblo* and the nation.[8] This conception of democracy builds implicitly on the memory of the nation's strife-filled history of *caudillo* rule and military strongmen, which lasted with brief interruptions until 1958; it rests as well on the memory of armed leftist opposition to the young democracy that occurred in the early 1960s. Populist discourse has linked internal threats to democracy from the right and the left to the presence of foreign threats to national sovereignty. In an effort to buttress its legitimacy and to strengthen its control of dissent, the democratic regime has kept alive the image of threats that reside concealed within the polity and at its borders, seeking the chance to return.[9]

The Venezuelan economy began a decline at the close of the 1970s into what became a crisis by the mid-1980s. It had experienced a short-lived euphoric oil boom, brought on by skyrocketing world oil prices, during

President Carlos Andrés Pérez's first term of office (1974–1979). His government launched an extraordinarily ambitious program to industrialize the economy, with the stated goal of freeing the nation from its dependence on oil exports.[10] The promise of rapid development, coupled with a protected economy in which state oil-rent distribution generously supported patronage-based political parties, raised expectations and defused opposition. But the program heightened tendencies within the rent-based system: a level of consumption that far outran production, concentration of power within the state and its allied economic groups, and corruption at the highest levels of the political and economic ruling elite. Moreover, the oil boom added a factor that had been virtually absent from the Venezuelan economy since 1930, a large foreign debt.[11]

The unanticipated drop in world oil prices in the 1980s, the likelihood of which the country's leaders had ignored when they contracted the debt, propelled a downward slide of the economy.[12] In 1986, under President Jaime Lusinchi (1984–1989), Venezuela signed a costly debt-renegotiation agreement with the international banks.[13] It meant that repayment of the debt, rather than the state's promotion of development and social programs, received political priority. The financial sector and large economic groups with assets abroad and diversified investments at home profited; capital flight accelerated as the wealthy deposited in foreign banks an estimated 60 billion dollars, or twice the national debt, while domestic real income fell by 50 percent over this period. The debt service paid during Lusinchi's administration came to 30 billion dollars and consumed 50 percent of the nation's foreign exchange, while the debt principal was only reduced from 35 to 32 billion dollars. Although these changes undermined the basis of the protectionist model and powerful business organizations made gains in their promotion of free-market policies, the political elite maintained the rhetoric of populist nationalism. As the expectations fueled by this rhetoric clashed with deteriorating conditions, political protest and disaffection with the nation's political leadership increased.

The rentier state's economic independence from a taxpayer base has permitted the Venezuelan political system, like those of other nations primarily dependent on exporting oil or other primary products, to become highly state-centered and unresponsive to demands from the public, thus discouraging the development of independent interests and organizations within civil society. Mechanisms of political reciprocity and accountability have remained restricted, elected officials obtain their position through their place in their party's hierarchy, and the expression of local demands is channeled through highly politicized structures.[14] Presidential campaigns, then, are the occasion for the promise of a dialogue between politicians and electorate to be momentarily constructed and consumed as an image.[15] Costly and lengthy, these campaigns orchestrate a national theater of democracy in which candidates seek to display mass support and their followers seek to position themselves favorably within the changing configuration of clientelistic ties.

The presidential election of 1988 prompted conflicting responses. The campaign brought to the fore a deep current of skepticism as regards electoral promises, yet it opened a space for opposition voices and raised hopes for economic improvement. It was a struggle not only between parties, but within the ruling party, Acción Democrática (AD), as the Pérez and Lusinchi factions fought for control of its apparatus.[16] In the context of the campaign, fissures within AD facilitated public criticism of widespread administrative corruption and repression.

The election on 4 December brought two unprecedented results: for the first time in Venezuelan history a former president was reelected, and voter abstention, previously below 10 percent, now reached 20 percent. In addition, the left increased its representation in Congress, and Pérez's leading opponent made inroads in areas of AD allegiance. In comparison to Pérez's first victory (1973), which brought forth triumphant celebrations in the streets, this one was edged with skepticism and critique. Many wary voters had decided that Pérez might dare to bring about dramatic change, but they had weak allegiance to his party.[17]

It was widely believed that Pérez would bring an improvement in economic conditions. A leader of major initiatives during the oil boom of 1974–1978, he had maintained his image as a decisive man of action who could defy domestic and international powers in defense of the nation and the *pueblo* (people).[18] His spectacular inaugural celebration on 2 February 1989 confirmed his image, for it convoked a wide spectrum of political leaders from 108 countries and issued a call to debtor nations to lobby against the oppressive policies of international banks and the IMF.[19] Yet, unknown to the general public, Pérez was sending a quiet message to the banks at the negotiating table, where he offered to fulfill stringent conditions.

Within days of his inauguration, Pérez gravely announced the content of his inaugural promise to *sincerar* (to make sincere or truthful) the economy. The free market would cleanse it of monopolies and artificial practices, allowing it to become productive. The means consisted of a strict austerity program, administered rapidly and in a large dose, like a strong medicine.[20] He informed the public, which was largely unfamiliar with the consequences of such policies, that subsidies for basic goods would be eliminated, price controls ended, exchange rates unified and the currency allowed to fluctuate, tariffs lowered, interest rates freed, and the price of government services increased. Rejecting labor demands, he did not institute a wage raise, job freeze, or welfare measures. Instead, he offered the hope that international banks would quickly provide Venezuela with fresh money to tide it over its pressing situation, and would forgive a significant percentage of its outstanding debt, making strict austerity a brief treatment on the path to economic recovery. His promise was to establish solid economic foundations for Venezuela's democracy. Just as protectionist import-substituting industrialization had been established thirty years earlier in the name of strengthening democracy, it was now to be dismantled for the same reason.

The Bolívarian Ideal

Venezuelan nationalist discourse conceives of history as the uncertain advance of civilization over barbarism. In the struggle between these contending forces, the never fully achieved goal of locating the nation within the flow of world progress is felt to be constantly undermined by outside enemies and by the no-less-threatening savagery of the land and people within. Nationalist discourse has constructed history as the ongoing effort to conquer the natural and social geography, freeing the nation from the external and internal forces that undermine sovereignty and obstruct its progress. Accounts of foreign threats, rebellions, dictatorships, and industrialization campaigns chart a course of incomplete progress in which significant discontinuities and recurrent new beginnings mark the nation's spasmodic advance.

This view of history as conquest, represented spatially as the colonizing movement from the center toward the peripheral frontier, is embedded in numerous narratives recounting the nation's foundation. Official history has constructed certain events and figures as templates of the nation's civilizing project, embodiments of foundational relationships in terms of which the present is intended to be read and the future constructed. The epic tale of Simón Bolívar's battle to achieve South America's independence from Spain is the master narrative for nationalist discourse. It recounts Bolívar's victory against external forces, followed by incomplete success at home; this fusing of victory and defeat renders it particularly compelling as a model for projects which call for national unity to pursue an ever-receding goal of modernity.

Official history presents Simón Bolívar, a member of one of the largest landholding families of the Creole oligarchy, as a providential leader empowered to represent the elite and speak for the unformed masses.[21] Depicted as a political and military genius with a unique capacity to communicate with and lead the common man, he brought over to the revolutionary cause the unruly *llaneros,* mestizo plainsmen who initially supported the Spanish crown during the Independence War (1811–1821). At the outset, the *llaneros* and rebel slaves made devastating attacks on the families and estates of the landed oligarchy, turning the conflict into a civil war with racial dimensions.[22] Only after Bolívar allied with the *llanero* leader José Antonio Páez, promising the distribution of estate property to his troops and the manumission of slaves, could the patriots' side command broad support and defeat the royalists. The narrative of Bolívar's triumph depicts the patrician hero as having redirected the rebel masses' anarchic energies toward the construction of a liberal national order. This image has been encoded as a model of the union between civilizing force and barbarous energy that must be reproduced in the struggle to achieve historical progress.[23]

Nationalist discourse has suppressed from official history the oligarchy's prolonged resistance to slave abolition and its failure after the war to command broad allegiance from the population. Its attempts to govern throughout the turbulent nineteenth century were rent by *caudillo*-led revolts and defined by fear of the masses.[24] Throughout this period contending regional *caudillos* offered their rural followers the opportunity to loot (*saquear*) the haciendas of the landed elite as recompense during their repeated assaults on power, and slave and peasant uprisings resulted as well in looting of the propertied. "Looting" (*saqueo*) also described in popular terminology the relationship of the *caudillo* victor to the state; his object of conquest was the state apparatus, which he could then loot by wielding his political power for personal enrichment.[25]

Only when foreign capital developed the petroleum industry in the 1920s did the economic elite—as it changed from an agrarian to a commercial base and allied politically with the middle class—offer a model of the national community that had broad social appeal. Popular and elite nationalism then found common ground in the project to democratize oil wealth and to modernize Venezuela through state protectionism (Coronil

1987). As the foundations of the state changed, the image of Bolívar as a tutelary leader of an unformed *pueblo* became a template for the construction of the nationalist development project. The Bolívarian ideal of the national community became elaborated and institutionalized within populist discourse and the democratic regime, linking the past to the hoped-for future and legitimizing the role of reformist parties. The massacres and the popular unrest we discuss here were intimately related forms of contestation and transformation of this ideal.

Populist Nationalism: *Doña Bárbara*

"A canoe travels up the Arauca River." This line opens the novel *Doña Bárbara,* written by Rómulo Gallegos during the regime of the *caudillo* autocrat Juan Vicente Gómez (1908–1935),[26] quickly acclaimed by the dictator's supporters as well as his opponents as the greatest literary expression of national identity. The novel's first line locates the reader on a journey inward in space and backward in time, at the social edges of the nation, where the Conquest is incomplete. The Arauca River crosses the Llanos in the state of Apure, marking Venezuela's southern frontier with Colombia. It traverses a sparsely populated region once inhabited by cattle hunters and contrabandists who were the troops for warring *caudillos* in the nineteenth century. To follow the river upstream, it is understood, is to enter a primitive social world, one that the novel constructs as an emblem of the backward nation.[27] The novel maps this space as the symbolic site for the construction of a new national identity. The establishment of the rule of law, private property, and legal marital union, it promises, will eliminate despotism and backwardness and domesticate savage man and untamed nature.

The boat carries Santos Luzardo (Holy Light), a lawyer from the capital who returns to his origins and faces challenges that make him complete as a man and as an historical agent. He confronts and tames the two sides of barbarism: the destructive (savage) dimension embodied by the powerful yet seductive *metiza* (mixed race) horsewoman Doña Bárbara (a symbol of the dictator Gómez) and the innocent (wild) dimension embodied by her beautiful but primitive and untutored daughter Marisela (an emblem of the *pueblo*). Doña Bárbara (Lady Barbarian) rules despotically through her knowledge of primitive people and nature, using Indian sorcery and murderous henchmen to monopolize land and to corrupt authority. Santos Luzardo resolves to defeat her and to replace the rule of force by the rule of law. If he fails and succumbs to her temptations to act outside the law, he risks repeating the fate of her discarded alcoholic lover, Lorenzo Barquero—a once-brilliant lawyer and Luzardo's cousin whom she had seduced and made her a pawn. In order to transform the Llanos, Santos Luzardo cannot simply eliminate Doña Bárbara. He must domesticate and instruct the helpless Marisela, who is as innocent as untamed nature, in proper feminine speech and behavior. Once she becomes aware of her own backwardness and attempts to overcome it, Marisela is eligible for his love. Luzardo then courts her, and their promised union signals the end of Doña Bárbara's despotic rule. Their union marks as well the end of open-range cattle ranching and the beginning of modem production, as ranches are fenced to delimit their boundaries and cattle are raised in bounded spaces.

A foundational fiction that depicts the path to nation-building through an allegorical romance,[28] the narrative charts the domestication of unconquered nature and uncivilized humans. The rule of law replaces the rule of violence, and the dominion of matrimonial love supplants the reign of sexual conquest. The relationship between energy and law, passion and love, the *pueblo* and the state, is transformed from one of coercion and opposition into one of attraction and union. Marriage between the elite and the *pueblo* will create, it promises, national historical progress. The modern state, capitalism, and the bourgeois family will be harmoniously wed.[29]

An unacknowledged tension underlying this apparently linear tale of the triumph of progress organizes this myth's capacity to act as a template within the populist project. The novel closes with Doña Bárbara's disappearance but not her elimination. Overcome by her impossible love for Luzardo and by her newfound sentiment for her daughter, she renounces her power and returns downriver to her origins. A submerged presence, her reappearance is an unknown potential. She resides in the land and in the collective psyche. Luzardo and Marisela must struggle against the pull of savage barbarism, for ultimately it lies within themselves and the *pueblo*, requiring careful taming and containment.

This ambiguity, the sense of attraction and repulsion toward the repressed side of the popular, has structured the construction of the nation's populist discourse.[30] In his early writing, Gallegos called for enlightened leaders to achieve the "containment of barbarism" whose "dark instinctual tendencies" were the energy that "rushes like a river overflowing its bed" (1954: 101). In the allegorical romance of *Doña Bárbara,* the river of instinctual energy represents the attraction and repulsion toward the repressed side of the people that is central to populist discourse.

As an allegorical tale of national, class, and family foundation, *Doña Bárbara* brings Bolívar back to earth, creating a powerful image of the modernizing leader who courts the untutored *pueblo,* ruling by consent rather than coercion. This hopeful view of national transformation became imaginable only with the growth of the oil industry in the 1920s and with the progress it promised. The emerging middle-class leaders of the 1930s and 1940s, many of whom were involved in clandestine political activities against the dictatorship and in the organization of nascent parties in the hinterland, saw themselves heroically reflected in this novel. For a certain social sector, it became a template for action, an image of the conquest of modernity.[31] As AD gained power in the 1940s, a formative period for the nation's present political leadership, the novel was canonized by populist discourse and educational curriculum. *Doña Bárbara* attained the status of nationalist myth, charting the nation's development as an ever-present process of conquest.

The Amparo Massacre

The Theater of Violence

A canoe travels up the Arauca River. Thus began a drama on 29 October 1988—the beginning of a history that would be retold in opposing versions from competing sites of power and incorporated into alternative images of the nation. The boat with sixteen men entered a densely wooded branch of the river, the Caño Colorado, on a Saturday morning. Peasants far from the site heard massive outbursts of gunfire, followed by shooting from military helicopters. Within hours reporters were flown to the scene by the military. General Camejo Arias, regional commander of the border counterinsurgency brigade CEJAP,[32] announced a successful encounter with fifty heavily armed members of Colombia's ELN (National Liberation Army) guerrilla organization who had planned to sabotage oil pipes and kidnap ranchers within Venezuela. He stated that sixteen guerrillas had been killed, although the twenty-member security brigade reported no injuries.[33] Photos of bodies with ELN insignia and lying next to guns on the river shore quickly appeared in the press. President Lusinchi congratulated the General for controlling threats to Venezuela's borders and to its democracy.[34]

Two days later voices challenging this version emerged in the press and were taken up by diverse sectors. The claims came from the outraged townspeople of Amparo located across the river from Colombia: The dead men were not Colombians but Venezuelans; they were not guerrillas but unarmed fishermen and workers, family men on a fishing expedition; they were preparing not the sabotage of oil pipes but the most popular weekend pastime of fishing and sharing a pot of soup (*sancocho*) and rum by the banks of the river. Above all, there were not sixteen dead men but fourteen. Two men had escaped by swimming through the swampy stream as helicopters searched for them overhead. With the aid of a neighboring rancher and the local police chief, they had returned to town in terror the next day to tell the story of the ambush. Fearing reprisals, they took refuge in the police station. When the National Guard and the DISIP asserted they were going to remove them from Amparo for questioning, a mass of angry townspeople impeded them from doing so, and the police chief, risking his life, threatened to shoot the DISIP officials if they insisted. Alarmed by the prospect of a civil disturbance, government authorities contacted Congressman Walter Márquez of the socialist party Movimiento al Socialismo (MAS), a well-known political activist in the border region, to mediate the situation.[35] The survivors were released into his custody, and he began what was to become a long campaign in their defense.

The government's effort to impose its version of reality began with the concealment of the victims' bodies and the discrediting of the townspeople's claims. The bodies, after being viewed by the press, were brought back to Amparo by the military and hastily buried, without the legally required autopsy, so that they could not reveal what had been done to them. Townspeople, Congressman Márquez, and journalists at the scene soon offered evidence that contradicted the government's claims. In response to growing denunciations, General Camejo Arias gave a televised declaration on 4 November in which he dismissed the veracity of the survivors' statements and claimed that intelligence reports confirmed that the men were linked to the ELN, had criminal and subversive records, and were on a sabotage mission.[36] They had offered armed resistance to the CEJAP brigade and were killed in action. President Lusinchi supported the General, insisting that these criminal guerrillas were part of a campaign to subvert democracy. He dismissed the denials of guerrilla ties by the people of Amparo, for the "golden rule of the clandestine struggle" is that you cannot tell "even those most closely related to you what you are doing."[37]

Investigation of the case began on two fronts: President Lusinchi assigned it to a military court, and a multiparty congressional commission began its own investigation shortly thereafter. By placing the case under military jurisdiction, the government shrouded it in the military's rules of secrecy and shielded it from the pressures of politicians and the press. Military judges, moreover, were likely to be personally and institutionally disposed in favor of the CEJAP. In effect, Judge Ricardo Pérez Gutiérrez, a close ally of General Camejo Arias, obstructed the investigation and maintained a hostile stance toward the survivors, José Augusto Arias and Wollmer Gregorio Pinilla.[38] Congress named a five-man, multiparty commission on 9 November, headed by a congressional ally of Carlos Andrés Pérez, to take testimony from officials and draw up an independent report.[39] Four days after the massacre, in direct disagreement with President Lusinchi, Pérez denied in a press conference that the villagers were subversives. He noted that many were members of AD who had supported his campaign, and he promised that justice would be applied.[40] His campaign rival, Eduardo Fernández of the Social Christian Party (Comité Organizador Partido Electoral Independiente, or COPEI), visited Amparo, an AD stronghold, and promised retribution for the victims' families.

In all likelihood, the massacre would have gained little national notice and the commission would not have been formed had it not occurred at the end of the electoral campaign. But the President's attempt to cast the deaths at Amparo in terms of the defense of democracy from external threat associated the concept of democracy with the narrow manipulation of power and appearances contrasted with the electoral campaign's effort to represent democracy in its most inclusive and popular terms. Lusinchi's stance brought to the fore the image of arbitrary rule established through coercion: it evoked the return of Doña Bárbara, devising and manipulating her own law.

The centrist presidential candidates, finding the regime's credibility threatened, hastened to defend democracy by demonstrating that the democratic system rested on the rule of law, not force, and that it defended national rather than particularistic interests. As opposition grew from outside the confines of the political elite, in the press and in leftist circles, the Congress and the center parties sought to preempt the opposition, claiming for themselves the ability to uphold democracy's principles of legality and justice. Beyond their attempt to obtain electoral gain lay the effort to reproduce the moral-political bases on which the regime rested. In this process, dominant discourse created its own centrist opposition to the official line of argument, establishing a counterpoint between differing dimensions of democracy. Political leaders shifted the focus of appeal from the external threat to democracy, which Lusinchi evoked, to the submerged internal threat to democracy, which the collective lack of faith in democratic institutions would allegedly allow to reappear. Playing on the memory of civil strife and dictatorship, they cast the investigation as proof that the state, directed by the existing political elite, had the capacity to correct what they depicted as personal abuses of power, not structural problems.

Official, centrist, and opposition interpretations of the events emerged through many channels. The congressional commission called the directors of security agencies and the CEJAP brigade members to testify. These men reiterated the official claim that the fishermen were subversives and denounced Arias and Pinilla as guerrillas who were posing as innocent survivors. Although they cited unspecified intelligence reports, they primarily based their argument on the assumption that the dead men were the type of person—poor, uneducated border villagers of no means or reputation—who could be presumed to be allied with subversives.[41] General Camejo Arias asserted to the commission, "They are implicated in crime, because of that symbiosis that exists, that union that exists between crime and non-crime, in that mixture that exists between men from Colombia and men from Venezuela . . . In those river areas there is practically nobody who is not involved in some kind of crime however small it might be, out there everyone is involved" (Republica de Venezuela 1989: 459). Barbarism still resides on the Llanos.

Cracks immediately appeared in this story, revealing a carelessly devised simulacrum. Government officials could not produce police records for the victims, and neither Venezuelan nor Colombian military intelligence agencies corroborated the claims of their records as subversives.[42] Reporters and congressmen visiting the site of the attack with the survivors filmed them on repeated occasions reenacting their escape (they swam skillfully through the waters, disproving their accusers' contentions) and found at the scene discarded cans of acid and clothes that were taken off the fishermen; the shell casings they found were only from M-19 rifles, the DISIP's weapon.[43] They noted that the weapons displayed with the dead men were few and insignificant and that relatives of the victims had observed that the bodies were disfigured and had been shot in the head and back. The autopsy that the Colombian officials performed on a Venezuelan victim soon after his death stated that he had been shot in the back, his skull crushed by heavy blows, and his face burned with acid.

One month after the attack, due to delays imposed by Judge Pérez Gutiérrez, the congressional commission obtained an order for the bodies to be exhumed and an autopsy performed. In an open field, with congressmen, journalists, and family members looking on, forensic doctors found evidence that the men had been shot point-blank from behind, some tortured and mutilated, their bones crushed, and their tattoos and faces burned.[44] The judge prevented the release of the autopsy report, but news of what witnesses had observed was published, shocking the public. Evidence accumulated that the CEJAP's leaders had organized the ambush with General Camejo Arias' knowledge, were aware of the planned Saturday fishing outing, and were possibly instrumental in organizing it. They dressed several of the dead men in ELN uniforms (which lacked bullet holes) and had placed a few guns next to them.[45] This simulacrum of subversion was constructed for national, not local consumption, for it was clear that the townspeople of Amparo would recognize the victims. The assumption was that they were too powerless—and terrified—to counter the government's claims. Made more potent by the extremity and starkness of its elements, Amparo became a symbol because of the ways in which power and identity were constructed within the realm of everyday life. Explanations for the massacre's occurrence were incomplete, yet the issue of the massacre awoke broad public interest and the growing sentiment, outside of the conservative upper class, that the men had been victimized.

The fate of the survivors was emblematic of the inversion of order that the state could effect. After hearing testimony from the survivors and the CEJAP members, on 14 November Judge Pérez Gutiérrez ordered the arrest of Arias and Pinilla on charges of military rebellion, provoking protests at this conversion of the victims into the accused. Congressman Márquez had kept them in hiding, but they feared for their lives if they turned themselves in as was expected. Márquez took the public by surprise by clandestinely obtaining refuge for them in the Mexican ambassador's house on 21 November. On 9 December Arias and Pinilla were flown to Mexico after its government granted them political refuge. This international acknowledgment that their safety could not be assured undermined the official version of events and the government's image regarding human rights.

Once Pérez was elected president, the case appeared to reverse its direction. Pérez had promised to change its terms, and he sought to have Amparo removed as a point of political pressure by the time of his inauguration in February. An arrest order was issued for the CEJAP members on 30 December on charges of falsifying a crime, illicit use of arms, and homicide. After President-elect Pérez assured them of safe treatment, Arias and Pinilla returned to Venezuela on 2 January and turned themselves in.[46] When a higher military court ruled there was no evidence against them, the charges were dropped and they were freed on 17 January. With their assailants now detained, they returned to Amparo amidst celebrations, accompanied by representatives of a newly formed network of human rights activists, clergy, and political leaders. Critics noted, however, that the massacre's planners, in particular Camejo Arias and Lopéz Sisco, remained in power, and the pressures to obstruct the case were enormous.

In this period of electoral transition, the congressional commission forged the emerging dominant version of events. Its report to Congress on 18 January 1989, concluded that an armed confrontation had not occurred and recommended that this "different event" be investigated judicially. It questioned that the victims were guerrillas and detailed the false and contradictory testimony given by the attack's planners and participants. While it criticized individual military officers, including General Camejo Arias and Judge Pérez Gutiérrez, it recommended that the DISIP be removed from the CEJAP and that military forces alone should direct a coordinated policy of development and defense of Venezuela's border.[47] Approved by the major parties, this report was portrayed as a validation of Venezuela's democratic processes. Acclaiming this achievement, Pérez promised to reorganize these security agencies and achieve justice for the victims as soon as he took office.

Alternative Representations

How did the opposition depict the massacre? In this seemingly open political system, issues of presidential and military credibility are hedged by unwritten rules bound by the mandate not to question the integrity of government institutions. Only after President Pérez was in office did opposition leaders offer fuller outlines of an alternative explanation, for they felt the threat of retaliation had lessened. The opposition version of events suggested that the Amparo massacre was carried out to further the interests of a highly placed set of intelligence, military, and business figures having strong economic interests in the border region. Backed by his documentation of this and previous cases of CEJAP violence obtained through confidential contacts, Walter Márquez argued that powerful regional interests backed the counterinsurgency brigade's ascent as a "subversive manufacturing machine."[48] He stressed that the DISIP, whose commanders controlled the CEJAP, had become a politically privileged paramilitary organization involved in illicit activities in the western border area through which it expanded its power and buttressed that of its landowner and business allies. Ideologically fueled by extreme anticommunism, the foreign-trained commandos reputedly charged ranchers for protection from subversives; at the same time, in alliance with ranchers, the DIST terrorized peasants and Indians, so they would not defend their lands from encroachment by powerful landowners, many of whom were retired military men.

The Amparo attack, the opposition version claimed, had a history that included several prior DIST and CEJAP massacres of alleged subversives.[49] The border brigade had manufactured subversives—generally undocumented Colombian workers who were lured into ambushes and brutally killed, their bodies then displayed as guerrillas. These supposed subversives were used to justify continuing government and rancher support for the DIST and its autonomy in the region.[50] The previous massacres had not created a public outcry, in part because they involved Colombians or (in earlier years) Venezuelan leftists and because they did not take place during an electoral period. Each confrontation further justified the DISIP's power and augmented the president's image as the defender of a threatened democracy, while spreading fear among different sectors of the population.

The subtext of the opposition account of men and their abuses was that a woman who epitomized the calculated manipulation of power connected this murky network of strongmen directly to President Lusinchi—his longtime mistress, Blanca Ibáñez. Her relationship to him and her extensive political influence could not be mentioned in the press (the Secretary of the Press exerted direct pressures on the media) but were widely recognized. Although she formally held the minor post of Secretary to the President, she had become a central figure in his administration.[51] For those with power, she held the key to influencing decisions about government appointments and investments; for those without power, she was a distributor of presidential favors to the poor in charitable events and in the barrios, not unlike Eva Perón. Her distribution of patronage was tied closely to the securing of political control and to the repression of dissent.

She made the DISIP her special province, influencing the appointment of its directors and maintaining close links to its commander of operations, López Sisco, and his ally, General Camejo Arias. Critics maintained that through a combination of patronage and surveillance she had constructed a fiefdom of power that extended ties into the upper levels of economic and political activity, playing a role in Lusinchi's ability to silence dissent and to sustain the appearance of consent to his policies.

The opposition's accusations about responsibility for the Amparo massacre made unspoken reference to this reality. The sustained criticism of the Amparo massacre, seemingly focused on the abuses of an uncontrolled intelligence unit, implicated the specific forms through which power was exerted during this administration. Within the opposition, opinions differed as to whether these forms were limited to this administration or whether the relations of power that outlasted the tenure of the Lusinchi presidency were at stake.[52]

The Credibility of Power

Occurring at a time of political transition, the Amparo massacre jolted interpretive schemes, provoking a sense of indignation among sectors of the urban populace ordinarily uninterested in the fate of rural people and inclined to believe accusations of their criminality.[53] In protest against the government's cover-up, student-led demonstrations occurred during November in Caracas and other major cities, many of which ended in property destruction and police violence. A large demonstration in Caracas, The March for Life (10 November), brought together a wide spectrum of groups, using puppets and street theater to depict the massacre, in a march downtown to Congress. In the emerging contestatory interpretation, the government was the oppressor and the *pueblo* the innocent victim. A crescendo of protests, in which Christian-based groups and activist clergy were vocal, created images of the Amparo fishermen as symbols of a martyred *pueblo.* They articulated a widely circulating opposition view: the Amparo victims stand for all of us. They are *desamparados*—forsaken, without legal protection, rights, or even identity. They are ordinary people, pawns in a system of inverted values. They are victims of government manipulation—deceived, used, and discarded.

The Amparo massacre resonated in the public imagination with the foundational tale of civilization and barbarism on the Llanos: the Arauca River in the state of Apure, the lawless frontier ruled by force, outbursts of savagery, and the helplessness of the *pueblo* in the face of personalized power. Many people were quick to relate the event to Gallegos' novel.[54] The drama of *Doña Bárbara* appeared to have been reenacted in Amparo, but who played what role in the tale? Was the CEJAP a representative of the law or a repressive tool like Doña Bárbara's henchmen? Were the men in the canoe barbarous subversives or innocent people of the *pueblo*, personifications of Marisela? Was Blanca Ibáñez the ruthless Doña Bárbara, and President Lusinchi her submissive lover, Lorenzo Barquero? Or were they the representatives of civilizing order, Santos Luzardo, in this drama? Or was Walter Márquez or Carlos Andrés Pérez the incarnation of Santos Luzardo? Or was he absent entirely?

Counter interpretations of the massacre challenged not just the official version of events but the government's capacity to construct its own image. Throughout its tenure, the Lusinchi administration had relied on obscuring reality to maintain its public support. While it confronted the debt crisis by denying that a crisis existed, it financed state expenditures with Venezuela's international reserves, consuming them entirely by the end of his administration. Through polished propaganda focused on the president's affable personality, the administration reassured the public that the state's paternalistic role would remain unaltered. But a report by Amnesty International delivered to the government in July 1988 prior to the Amparo massacre documented the administration's escalating suppression of political protest and its constant police and military violence against the poor.[55] The state reproduced ever more overtly its official image as the protector of an anarchic *pueblo*, while silencing its critics as "subversives."

By the end of Lusinchi's administration, dwindling resources made the illusion of abundance and progress increasingly tenuous. The Amparo massacre occurred not at the hopeful dawn of petrodollar-fueled growth when *Doña Bárbara* was written, but fifty years later when credit and credibility were running out for the protectionist model of national development. Without projects to feed the promise of national development or the pacifying illusion of individual upward mobility, the political space of the nation shrank to a parochial arena. The threat of finding the path of historical progress blocked had become real for the citizens and for the nation.

Our interpretation of the Amparo massacre suggests that the Venezuelan state asserted its authority in a theatrical mode, constructing a drama whose plot reenacted the civilizing myth of the state as the scriptwriter.

This simulacrum—the representation of the illusion of representing the real—rests on the controlled tension between fact and appearance, between attention to evidence and disregard for conflicting information, and thus on the willingness to allow cracks in the performance to reveal the arbitrariness of authority. Fear grows out of these cracks.[56] As in detective stories in which certain clues are left behind in order to induce a misreading, the visible marks of artifice in the misrepresentations of politics are not necessarily to be treated as faults, but as signs to be deciphered.

El Masacrón

The Great Turn

When Carlos Andrés Pérez was elected on 4 December 1988, many, including opposition leaders, believed he would restore the tutelary bond between leader and *pueblo* and halt the nation's shrinkage and backward slide.[57] His first term of office saw providential wealth raise living standards and establish Venezuela as a leader of Latin American economic integration. Thus despite Pérez's links to corruption and to the debt, he represented for one current of collective memory the Bolívarian promise that the state would battle for social justice and economic independence. The electoral campaign had raised the hope that his presidency would signal an end to retrogression, a reopening of the nation to progress.

"The river overflowed its bed" (*El rio se salió de la madre*) was the headline of an opinion article in the newspaper *El Nacional,* 4 March 1989, describing the outpouring of people into the streets of fourteen cities during five days of popular unrest and looting that shook Venezuela between 27 February and 3 March.[58] These events constituted the most massive as well as the most violently suppressed urban protest in Venezuelan history. On 27 February, masses of people took over the streets of most of the nation's major cities, particularly in the capital region, protesting increasing prices and looting stores.[59] Once the government recovered from its initial paralyzing shock, it responded with the suspension of constitutional guarantees and a storm of bullets. Thousands were wounded and arrested, and the official death toll reached 277. Unofficial estimates which observers from many fields circulated confidentially, however, estimated there were well over one thousand fatalities.[60]

No comparable social upheaval, in terms of the extent of the looting or the ferocity of the repression, had taken place in contemporary Latin America in response to an economic austerity plan. The total number of people reported killed in fifty different protest events occurring between 1976 and 1986 in thirteen countries was under two hundred; the most violent single incident had been the 1984 riots in the Dominican Republic which claimed sixty lives (Walton 1989: 188). While the so-called IMF riots were frequent during this span, according to Walton they generally grew out of organized protest, such as strikes and demonstrations, and they tended to select certain targets, both political and business. The Venezuelan riots, however, did not emerge from organized efforts, although they were preceded by years of sporadic conflicts in certain cities, and the looting was aimed at a broad range of businesses, encompassing street vendors and modem supermarkets, workshops, and factories.

The events that shook state authority and fragmented the social territory also disrupted established interpretive schemes, resisting the efforts of official and opposition forces to fix them with a name. Official discourse neutrally labeled the conflict "27-F" and "the events" (*los sucesos*). The terms "the disturbances" or the "big jolt" (*el sacudón*), which suggest a passing disruption of the normal order, became widely accepted in the media. Opposition discourse introduced the terms "social explosion," "popular uprising" (*pobluda*) and "the big massacre" (*el masacrón*). The stark label "the war" was common among professionals, expressing the social fracture that the middle class had experienced. It recalled as well the feared return of the civil wars that marked the nineteenth century, whose memory has been kept present by government leaders. These differing classifications reflect the uncertain attempts to control the historical construction of events that overflowed traditional channels of contestation and categories of collective agency.

What had happened between 2 February, when Pérez's spectacular inauguration took place, and 27 February? On assuming the presidency, pressured by an acute shortage of funds, President Pérez took up the internationalist strand of Venezuela's Bolívarian nationalist ideology in an effort to refocus the state's civilizing mission.[61] He defined Venezuela as a leader of the debtor nations' battle against domination by international banks, a promoter of Latin America's unity against threats to its independence. This image built on the anticolonial component of nationalist discourse that equates national independence with equality and depicts the quest to free nations from foreign domination as a moral struggle. By evoking these shared assumptions, with their resonance of social justice, Pérez sought a legitimating link with official history for the government's policies.

On assuming the presidency, Pérez initiated his administration with an attack on the IMF and international lenders in the name of an imagined community of Latin American borrowers. Yet at the same time his administration—committed to an IMF-inspired austerity economic program yet urgently needing new loans—sought to persuade the international banking community of its commitment to rationalizing the economy. Thus, Pérez criticized both the IMF and the domestic protectionist policies that had created a sick economy in need of emergency treatment. The prescription was the cleansing medicine of an austerity program. Through rhetorical jujitsu, the obligatory was made to appear as desirable, the imposed as self-chosen.

The crucial task in the new economic strategy, and a condition the banks made for obtaining new loans, was to open the protective shell that had insulated the nation against international competition throughout most of the twentieth century. Ideologically constructed as a momentous historical change, this decision redefined Venezuela's place in history and in the world. From this perspective, the protected and subsidized market had fostered parasitical capitalists, inefficient industries, and corrupt politicians. But lacking the oxygen of abundant petrodollars, protectionism was asphyxiating the nation. Insulation from international competition had meant isolation from economic competence. Opening the nation to the world market meant building bridges to capitalism, allowing its rationality to flow into the nation. This new policy, which meant the decline of many small businesses, was suddenly presented as common sense. It received the strongest endorsement from wealthy businessmen and politicians able to retain power through the transition. This manner of pursuing modernity also made the nation vulnerable to world-market relations. The state had created an exceptionally sheltered domestic space—a fertile ground for cultivating hierarchical alliances and weaving illusions of social harmony. Opening this shell also meant tearing down this web of relations and shared understandings.

With the acceptance of the curative rationality of the free market, an important change occurred in the discourse of nationalist modernization. The achievement of a healthy economy became valorized as the nation's primary goal—above that of forming a developed *pueblo*. Although these goals had coexisted in parallel fashion in the discourse of protectionist modernization, arguments now openly privileged the economy's demands, subordinating those of the *pueblo*. The civilizing relationship that weds state and *pueblo* and engenders national progress no longer appeared as a protective bond. The dismembering of this bond was dramatically prefigured by the Amparo massacre. The border *llaneros* again became the emblems of the *pueblo*, but they were now transformed into a subversive threat to be silenced and written upon, evoking collective memories of the conquest.

With the ascent of a populist variant of free-market discourse under Pérez, the *pueblo* was presented as the undisciplined and lazy product of an unproductive economy, a symptom of the sickness caused by easy money obtained during years of abundant oil rents. The official effort to explain the crisis without seriously implicating the nation's ruling elite presented Venezuelans as wanton consumers. The assumption was that if the state's protectionist structures were dismantled, people would turn to productive work, for they needed the discipline and the instruction that the market could provide. The new administration introduced its adjustment program using a moral language of reform. Although it spoke of the need to reform individual behavior, it did not address social reform, which had long been central to protectionist discourse. The latter had promised to correct social inequities by intervening in the organization of the market. Instead, free-market discourse promised to correct economic distortions by reorienting individual behavior and perceptions.

In an oft-repeated lament, Pérez claimed that Venezuelans had been living in a world of illusion and false expectations. They must now face reality. On 16 February, Pérez announced *El gran viraje* (The Great Turn): the move from artificial to real capitalism. The government would soon cut tariffs, remove price controls and subsidies, and unify the exchange rate at market levels, thus eliminating the preferential rates that had continued to subsidize imports subsequent to official devaluations. While these measures would take time to design and implement, the expectation of their advent, together with a shortage of foreign exchange, prompted a series of escalating processes.

The reality that consumers faced diverged wildly from one of market rationality. Confronted with the imminent dismantling of protectionism and the rising costs of imports, manufacturers cut back production and businesses hoarded products. Several weeks before Pérez's inauguration, in an effort to drive prices up, businesses withheld government-regulated food and consumer items from the stores. Angry confrontations in markets and grocery stores between sellers and consumers escalated as consumers found that supplies of basic goods were rationed in stores, and they accused sellers of hoarding and of favoring their preferred customers. These confrontations occurred far from the large businesses that oligopolistically controlled commerce; they took place above all where the middle class and the poor shopped, in stores often run by Portuguese, Chinese, and Lebanese immigrants who many thought to be avaricious and unscrupulous.

Commercial hoarding was met by consumer hoarding. Shortages and anticipated price hikes provoked consumer runs on products, a snowballing desire to stock up on necessities in preparation for the disruption of production or for some unknown eventuality. In uncertain times, hoarding provided a vague sense of protection, but only those with means could afford to hoard to any degree. Soon for the urban poor—for those who shopped daily and had no refrigerator and certainly no savings—the inability to purchase corn meal, bread, milk, oil, flour, beans, sugar, coffee, salt, soap, and toilet paper with their money at the store; to be told at their neighborhood grocery *no hay* (there is none); and to search anxiously across the city for stores rumored to have the needed products fed a mounting anger. Their sense of affront at a deceptive political system reflected in the tyranny of profiteering businesses grew as supplies diminished.

As the austerity program's outlines became known, consumer anxiety changed to panic. Consumers learned from large press headlines and blaring radio programs that the price of such staples as bread, pasta, powdered milk, beans, and cooking oil would soon triple and quadruple. Wage earners felt threatened by rising prices and the prospect of unemployment in a shrinking economy, and the marginally employed felt unprotected. Confidence in progress turned into fear of sliding backwards. The working classes no longer felt they shared a common space under the umbrella of the state, and the middle class saw its chance for ascent removed. Although some people hoped to hold their ground, and a few even to improve their lot, most realized they were left out and slipping down, a change of fate in a country where, during half a century, a significant segment of the urban population (which is 80 percent of the nation) had grown accustomed to rising living standards.

In this context, the government announced a doubling of gasoline prices, to take effect on 26 February, as a first step towards reaching world prices. The government had decided to increase the state oil company's income by no longer subsidizing gasoline. In this oil-exporting nation, a hike in gas prices was not a simple mercantile decision. It implicated the bond that united the national community: an imagined shared ownership of the nation's petroleum resources based on its founding legal code. The state's legitimacy was intimately tied to its ability to control the nation's formerly foreign-owned oil industry in the name of the entire *pueblo*.[62] To equate oil with other commodities on the international market and to demand that people pay dearly for what was considered to be their national birthright was to rupture a moral bond established between the state and the *pueblo*.

This rupture was symbolized when the collective transport association, arguing that transportation fares had to reflect the increased costs of vehicles and parts, decided to raise bus and van fares by over 100 percent on Monday, 27 February, in defiance of the government's 30 percent ceiling.[63] Already resented by working-class commuters and students for their poor service, the privately owned transport companies' aggressive stance now provoked outrage. Passengers had no alternative transportation to the city and were down to their last change before receiving their pay at work at the end of the month. The abrupt doubling of bus fares crystallized the sense that people were being deceived and abused by the government and business, and it brought them together in the street, a place where both protest and the inversion of authority could occur. Before the battle in the streets began on Monday, 27 February, the domestic space had already become a battleground between different moral and economic orders.

The Events/The War: Popular Expansion

Popular protest began at dawn on 27 February in the working-class town of Guarenas outside Caracas, as well as in the Caracas bus terminal, where workers and students congregated at an early hour.[64] Protesters, some led by students chanting antigovernment slogans, initially blocked collective transport vehicles. Soon people turned against grocery stores and food markets. Leaders, generally young men who broke store locks with crowbars and smashed windows, emerged, urging people to take what was theirs. The people surging into the stores found to their outrage that stored deposits of subsidized basic food stuffs that had disappeared from the market were waiting to be sold at marked-up prices. Cases of powdered milk, cornmeal, pasta, and coffee were passed to the street and distributed, as the outnumbered police looked on. Some policemen, themselves poorly paid, helped looting take place in an orderly fashion or took part.[65] A collective decision to occupy the streets and invade the stores, suspending the rules regulating public movement and commerce, took shape. The street became the site for the contestation of market and political controls widely regarded as immoral and oppressive.

Diffuse and decentered, the protest multiplied in commercial areas near working-class neighborhoods, following the city's principal streets. These avenues and freeways, the channels along which the news was quickly communicated to the major commercial centers by the city's numerous motorcycle messengers, were also vulnerable arteries that protesters blocked off with barriers, bringing traffic to a halt. Most public transportation ceased. Trapped delivery trucks were besieged, their goods carried off and distributed. By the end of the workday in Caracas, astonished downtown employees left their jobs to find the streets filled with people doing free shopping, calmly carting off food and even large appliances. A photograph of a man carrying a side of beef on his back in a burned-out street became one of the most reproduced images of the disturbances. The upheaval was soon disseminated throughout the vast barrio periphery, the lower-class residential areas of unplanned construction in which shanties, cinderblock houses, and housing projects crowd precariously on the hills surrounding the valley of Caracas and in the interstices of the city, in deep ravines that wind half-hidden near middle-class and wealthy neighborhoods.

In this *saqueo popular* (popular looting), people came down from the hills and up from the ravines, streaming toward local stores in the streets ringing the city The term *saqueo popular* had a double meaning. The Venezuelan political and economic elite was widely accused of looting the national treasury, for it had engaged in notorious corruption and had taken twice the amount of the national debt out of the country in a massive flight of capital. Now it was the turn for the rest of the population to obtain things without working. Middle-class families in neighborhoods traversed by deep ravines, where looting had been initiated by slum dwellers, participated in the *saqueo,* driving their cars to the stores, in a few cases having their servants help with the heavier goods. At this early stage, when popular action had not encountered government repression and was limited in scope, observers of diverse social origins related with empathy to the call for *saqueo popular.*

In many barrios a loose organization within and among families emerged. Young men, risking serious injury from glass and metal, broke into new stores and processing plants and expanded the area of popular action. Women and children followed them into food and clothing stores, at times forming lines for the removal of groceries and shoes. Those who could not or dared not participate, such as the old and women with young children, received goods brought to their homes by others. People exchanged among themselves what they had obtained in quantity and carved up the sides of beef and pork they had carried away. As a woman later approvingly observed, "Money was no longer important. In a matter of hours we went back to the age of barter." In the industrial Antímano sector of Caracas, hillside residents attacked the Ronco pasta factory, loaded the large stores of pasta they found there onto the company's trucks, and distributed them throughout the area. "We made sure," a driver and father of several children said proudly, "that everybody got their package of pasta."[66] Enderson, an impoverished fourteen-year-old, said he broke into stores and threw food at the people outside, shouting "*¡come, pueblo!*" (eat, people!). For him looting was not theft, for he said, "it is not the people's fault that prices are going up, it is the government's fault. People have to eat.[67] That morning there was nothing to eat at my mother's house."

Looting dissolved momentarily money's ability to regulate collective life. The invasion of business establishments rendered meaningless the barriers that money normally imposes between commodities and consumers, between public and private space. In the midst of an uncertain and dangerous situation there were overtones of a village fiesta—a sudden abundance of liquor and grilled meat shared at impromptu gatherings in the poor neighborhoods on the hills circling Caracas. Bottles of champagne and brandy made a surprise appearance at parties now enlivened by dance music broadcast throughout the hills from newly acquired audio equipment. The smoke of barbecues mixed with that of burning stores. Against the "etiquette of equality"[68] that ruled street behavior in this self-defined egalitarian society, the poor sought to assert, even if only momentarily, their image of real relations of equality.

During this initial period, when rules were transgressed and categories confused, exhilaration and fear competed for control of the situation. Exhilaration followed from the collective assertion of popular understandings over official explanation. Through countless acts of defiance, which included burning some police stations and local AD offices, people spoke about their rejection of not only their immiseration, but the deceptive reasons routinely put forth to explain it and of the institutions supporting it.[69] On 27 February several hundred motorcycle delivery men, *motorizados,* surrounded the FEDECAMARAS building, the headquarters of the nation's largest business associations and a symbol of the business class that has benefited from government policies. Business leaders briefly caught inside spread rumors of alarm concerning attacks on the propertied. Some took their families out of the country, and many privately called on the president to act.

Looting, however, was the major means of protest. It was largely indiscriminate, as people generally looted areas close to where they resided. Many were drawn into looting out of concern to protect themselves against an uncertain future. At a moment perceived to be the onset of a crisis, they sought to obtain both expensive goods that had ceased to be attainable and food for their families. Raul, a young university-educated father from the barrio La Vega, watched in shock from his house as people rushed down the hill to loot the stores. When he looked at his little daughter he said, "I saw her turn into a can of milk. All I could think of was, how was I going to feed her." That night he accepted cans of powdered milk taken from a neighboring store that a friend brought him.

"*El pueblo tiene hambre*" (The people are hungry), the slogan widely painted on walls, was the explanation most frequently offered by participants for the uprising. It imaged shared experiences uniting strangers who were anonymously joined in the simultaneous looting briefly televised to the country and the world. Hunger was regarded as a natural cause for revolt, but it was a shorthand expression referring, through the image of food, to what was regarded as unnecessary deprivation and insult in a country that had both wealth and democracy. With their revolt, people bluntly shattered the officially constructed illusion that the economy could be adjusted with popular acquiescence. Reflecting with surprise on their collective action, many observed, "We are no longer a passive *pueblo.*" They expressed a sense of moral affront at the manipulation and silencing of popular demands that was the cumulative experience of this oil- and rent-based democracy. If, as Pérez demanded, it was time to face reality, this was what it looked like from the popular perspective.

The link between hunger and revolt connected notions about political action and rights, leaders and people, which were given blurred expression during the disturbances. In a striking gesture to appropriate the most hallowed official signs of nationhood, protesters in many instances sang, as they broke open stores, the opening line of the national anthem, "*Gloria al bravo pueblo que el yugo lanzó*" (Glory to the brave and angry people who threw off their yoke). They sang it both when they waved the national flag and when they faced the attack of the military in lines drawn in the streets between an unarmed people and occupying troops. This hymn to popular revolt linked anger to courage, political freedom to social justice. Invoked in official contexts, such as the state ceremonial occasion and the school salute to the flag, the hymn embalmed the *bravo pueblo* in the distant past, to sing it simultaneously in a popular assault on the street was to resuscitate it as a living critique, not a ratification of authority.

"*El pueblo está bravo*" (the people are angry), painted on walls and repeated by protesters, rebutted the official glorification of a silent *pueblo*. Popular anger was inseparable from indignation at being deceived. "*Se han burlado de nosotros*" (they have mocked us), "*basta del engaño*" (an end to deception) declared looters and sympathetic observers (many from the middle class) at the outbreak of the disturbances. When in the polyphony of this mass upheaval, people asserted that "*el pueblo habló*" (the people have spoken), their actions indicated their refusal to remain passive.

Hunger initially rendered the looting understandable, even legitimate. A consensus in many sectors condoned the popular appropriation of food as being just. Given the anxiety over food shortages intensifying over weeks, a shared sensibility had begun to exist concerning market threats to survival. Women were particularly adamant that people's right to food meant that the taking of food fell into a different moral category than other goods. For many women their participation in looting was their first public transgression of authority and was seen as an act of family defense. Looters also took clothes, appliances, furniture, hardware, and even unusable computers. Before the government intervened, on the afternoon of the second day, the television news showed live scenes of people (in the middle-class San Bernadino sector of Caracas), unhindered by authorities, calmly carrying audio equipment and videocassette recorders, and loading cars with furniture. Hunger for consumer commodities other than food violated elite and middle-class notions of what should rightfully be accessible to poor people. The idea took hold that not necessity but lust for material goods was fueling the looting. The terms robbery and vandalism spread, supplanting popular looting, as tales circulated of the destruction of stores, cars, and shopkeepers' houses. Attacks on property escalated, as looters ripped out equipment and plumbing, hitting not only commerce and factories but medical and educational facilities. Many businesses were set on fire, spreading the sense that limits were no longer being respected.

Intense popular anger was directed at immigrant shopkeepers—the

Portuguese, Chinese, and Lebanese merchants in daily contact with barrio residents who were long suspected of hoarding and overpricing clothing and food. Their threatening practices were symbolized by the fact that they did not extend credit, which was a tradition among Venezuelan small shopkeepers. For the urban poor, these businessmen were the visible face of cold capitalism and became the target of their rage. *"No se fía"* (We don't give credit) was the sign often displayed in their stores. Even the residences of many immigrant storekeepers who had long lived in the barrios were looted. Although they regarded themselves as being part of the *pueblo,* the crowd attacked them as being *burgueses* (bourgeois or the rich).[70] Venezuelan shopkeepers in some cases painted "I am Venezuelan" on the metal sheets covering their store windows in an effort to dissuade looters from attacking.

Fear set in, driving people to affix blame for the worsening course of events. The multi-layered fear that emerged had two main sources: fear of uncontrolled popular criminality and fear of official repression. Both state action and state absence were cause for terror, compounded by the uncertainty as to whether the present government would be able to survive at all. In this seemingly solid democracy, no local system of political groupings was found to help reestablish order in the barrios; and no words of explanation were offered by the political leadership. As a resident of the devastated barrio La Vega stated, "All of a sudden there were no more *adecos* (members of the ruling party AD) to be found anywhere. They took their pictures of Carlos Andrés out of their windows and joined in the looting." Among the elite and the middle class, the fear that the disturbances were a threat to all private property and social order took hold. Some of the very wealthy left the country in their private jets. The middle class sought to band together to protect their property, often organizing armed defense groups among neighbors.

Gaps in the state's leadership and the coordination of its agencies became visible. Although the government's civilian leadership was hesitant, the military was suddenly decisive in the streets. On the morning of the 28th the military began to occupy the cities, ordering all businesses to close. By the end of the day, as assaults on businesses grew bolder and extended to small factories, troops cleared the streets by opening fire on the crowds of looters. People turned to the television for word from the government and found images of looting.

The President eventually spoke. He defined the disturbances as a protest of the poor that reflected longstanding social injustices (*El*

Nacional, 1 March 1989). With this statement he placed responsibility on past policies and differentiated himself from those who blamed the upheaval on subversives, criminals, or illegal immigrants (though some members of Pérez's cabinet did so). With grim private sector leaders at his side, he declared a general wage raise and a four-month freeze on firings—both measures that business had until then opposed. However, Pérez offered no purpose around which to unite as a nation, no promise for the future; rather, he underlined, as on many occasions, the exceptional ties he had built in the international arena. The audience to which he was primarily speaking, in effect well outside the borders of the country, sat in the government and bank offices of Venezuela's creditors; he sought to communicate that Venezuela required concessions on its debt in order to avoid future upheavals, but that he was well in control of the present situation.[71] To his domestic audience he issued a demand for acquiescence. Pérez tersely announced that constitutional guarantees, including freedom of the press, were suspended and that a curfew, to begin within hours, would be in effect from 6 P.M. until 6 A.M. until further notice. His role as an international leader remained, but now it was one without a *pueblo.*

The suspension of guarantees led to a sharp escalation of state violence against the poor. When the Minister of the Interior Alejandro Izaguirre, a seasoned AD leader (regarded as a man of the people and nicknamed "The Policeman") appeared on television on 1 March to announce government measures, he was overcome by nervous exhaustion and rendered speechless on camera. Disney cartoons replaced him without explanation. The leadership of the party had been meeting since the previous day to discuss how to control the situation and was divided concerning the use of force. Although initially delayed, it had been used massively by the time of his television appearance. The traditional language of populism did not prepare Izaguirre to represent the state in this conjuncture.

The eruption of the *pueblo* into public view deeply troubled the Venezuelan political leadership. On 1 March, at the height of government violence, AD's president and founder Gonzalo Barrios lamented that the international media had televised abroad "the horror, the primitive, the uncontrollable, from a civilized point of view, of the looting that took place in Caracas" (Sanín 1989: 143). He regretted that the events had shown "the entire world the other face of Venezuela, the face of slums, of the hungry masses, of marginal people" (*El Nacional,* 4 March 1989). This was the face that the government violently sought to conceal. Gonzalo Barrios cast the government's decision to use massive violence in terms that evoked the state's civilizing mission. In the congressional debate of 1 March, the eighty-eight-year-old apostle of Venezuelan democracy, widely regarded for his wit and political acumen, concluded his speech by recounting a story that had "captivated" him because of its "implicit irony." The story concerned a British general who wanted to subdue one of the "less primitive tribes" of Africa. The general sent as his emissary a missionary who had lived among the indigenous people in order to convince them that British occupation would be to their benefit. The missionary told them of the hospitals, schools, means of communication, and laws they would receive from the British. The African chief recognized the value of this offer but rejected it, arguing that its acceptance would cause his people to lose their soul. The missionary, on reporting the chief's refusal to the General, suggested that the chief was right. "The General," Barrios said, "naturally paid no attention to the missionary and gave orders to blast the natives with gunfire (*plomo cerrado*), as often occurs in disputes among civilized nations." Barrios concluded, in a tone of ironic understatement, that if the congressmen decided to reject President Pérez's austerity program and the repressive measures taken to defend it, the nation would begin a backward slide. "I think that Venezuela would not necessarily return to loincloths and arrows, because we have well-grounded structures and progress, but we could go back to a situation in which luxuries like Rolls Royces and fancy televisions would disappear" (Sanín 1989: 155). This unabashed inscription of state policies within a colonial framework—the acceptance of massive state violence to oblige acquiescence and forestall greater decline, and the identification of popular protesters as a "primitive tribe" and of congressmen as "civilizing generals"—went unnoticed, for the opposition shared its underlying premises.

The War/The Events: State Repression

The state's actions slowly took form, as it attempted to control, define and conceal the events that were underway. Ten thousand troops were airlifted into Caracas which, because of its valley location, had been cut off by road from the rest of the country, interrupting its food supply. With a naturalness that stunned the barrio population, the military and police forces undertook to drive people out of the streets and to mark territorial boundaries delimiting the frontiers that the poor must not cross. Scenes of soldiers and police firing on looters in barrios were not televised nationally but were broadcast on United States and European news, bringing an unwelcome shock of recognition to Venezuelans with satellite dishes who discovered a disturbing new image of the nation through the eyes of the international media.

The militarization of the conflict under the suspension of most constitutional guarantees meant that "order" was reestablished in the barrios by means of massive violence, both indiscriminate and directed, despite the fact, as critics later argued, that the constitutional guarantee of the right to life had not been suspended. The military displayed its presence, stationing tanks to protect government and corporate offices, major shopping centers, and the borders of wealthy neighborhoods. But outside of a few shopping centers, these had not been targets of the looters. Rather these outposts signaled the boundaries to be defended from the assault of the "marginals" (residents of the barrios).

Government repression brought to an end the expansive phase of the disturbances marked by the popular occupation of the street. Pockets of gunfire directed at government forces by so-called anti-socials in certain barrios and housing projects became the focus of government attention. They were presented as revealing the true face of the disturbances: the anarchic and criminal effort to subvert democracy through violence. In the context of deep collective fear, the idea hardened that despite broad social participation in the looting the disturbances emanated from the feared *cerros* (hillside barrios) ringing Caracas.

According to dominant notions, the very poor and the criminal, living in sub-human conditions in shanties and housing projects, lead a basically lawless existence in these zones. The *cerros* are regarded as the haven for various categories of *antisociales: malandros* (thugs), drug dealers, dark-skinned foreigners, and remnants of urban guerrilla groups. They allow the reproduction of those who occupy the margins of civilized life: the criminal, the subversive, and the alien. The dominant discourse soon constructed these disturbances as the unleashing of this primitive mass upon the city's center. At this moment of crisis, otherness was projected onto the city's barrios, as if the residents of these socially diverse areas in their entirety constituted a threat to the civilized order. As General Camejo Arias had said of the border region where the Amparo massacre occurred, "everyone there is a criminal."

Collective fears fragmented the urban population along the lines they traced. Many barrio residents feared that marauding savagery might emerge within their midst. They believed that neighboring barrios, often situated higher up the hill and populated by recent immigrants, would attack their homes and property. The army and police, attempting to divide the poor through the spread of panic,[72] planted rumors that mobs of impoverished foreigners and criminals were leading night assaults on houses. Although the rumored assaults never materialized, barrio residents stood guard on their rooftops and in the streets, drawing gunfire from the troops. Although people in the barrios sought to defend themselves from their neighbors, people in wealthy districts armed themselves against the barrios. Residents of luxury apartments bordering on the barrios formed armed brigades with police approval, and Rambo-style groups of wealthy youths brandished sophisticated automatic weapons that the upper middle class had been bringing into the country for some time.

The government's armed agencies deployed violence in multiple forms, communicating in practice to the poor the distinct forms of otherness by which they could be encompassed. The military faced the barrio population as a military enemy, the police confronted it as a criminal gang, and the DISIP and other intelligence police treated it as a subversive agent. Their crosscutting attacks created confusion and panic, fragmenting the poor yet more. After the initial exhilaration of defiance, most of the population hoped for the reestablishment of order and for an end to uncertainty and destruction; and they often welcomed the young soldiers of rural origin who were posted in their neighborhood. But military officers responded to the subversion of order by defining the barrios as the source of that subversion. Their population became the enemy to be controlled, driven back, and broken. The death of an Army officer leading a search for snipers was made the symbol of democracy under siege, one which political and entertainment figures elaborated upon in televised statements and during the broadcast of his military funeral.

The battle lines were drawn in border areas at the edges of large barrios, particularly those with a reputation for criminality and subversion, from which encroachment by mobs of the poor was thought to be a threat to major commercial and government establishments. But government forces, ill-prepared for civil conflict, did not carry out a strategically planned operation. The sound of supposed sniper fire provoked massive gunfire from nervous, inexperienced Army troops who were rural recruits taught to fear urban subversives. The erratic and disproportionate character of their assault was their response to the menacing image of the popular threat. Claiming that heavily armed snipers were providing intense resistance, military officers ordered high-powered automatic artillery fire to be directed at the exposed faces of the *cerros* and high-rise housing projects for hours at a time, perforating their thin walls.[73] A soldier warned Josefina, a working woman from Petare whose house overlooked a shopping center, "This hill has been taken. Stay inside. Anybody who moves will be shot." Stunned by this announcement, she and her family stayed on the floor for two days.

Police and security forces used the period of suspended legality to round up criminals, settle personal accounts, raid houses, and terrorize certain barrios. Policemen who knew the criminals and illegal aliens in a neighborhood sought them out in their houses and the streets, in some cases shooting them down or taking them away to unknown sites. For these operations some agents did not use their official weapon but an unregistered personal gun called the *cochina* (the dirty one, literally, the female pig).[74] Security forces also used a tactic developed in demonstrations and on the university campus to provoke incidents and turn public opinion: masked gunmen known as *encapuchados* (hooded ones) in civilian clothes shot at people, often from motorcycles, creating panic. It was impossible to determine whether they were police, criminals, or subversives. Terror became faceless.

Intelligence forces put into effect counterinsurgency measures. They detained and in some cases tortured activists from barrio cultural organizations and from student and political groups. The only cases to cause a public outcry were those of university student leaders and prominent Jesuit priests residing in the barrio La Vega, one of whom was the vicerector of the prestigious Andrés Bello Catholic University and an editor of the magazine *SIC*, Luis Ugalde.[75] The intention was to identify publicly members of the left intelligentsia with subversion and to define them for the future as an alien threat.

The identities of casualties from the barrios were rapidly erased. Their massive number and the places and circumstances in which they occurred rendered them subversive. Understaffed hospitals and morgues were overrun with corpses, and norms and procedures were suspended in chaotic streets where unidentified armed authorities ruled.[76] Records that could substantiate the widely circulating estimates of a high death toll were not maintained, and bodies disappeared from the streets. The Minister of Defense calmly insisted, even as gunfire continued through the nights, that order had been restored and the death toll was low. The media soon ceased reporting news of casualties. Death was the occasion to imprint upon the poor their marginality to civilized society.

The morgue was the site for the encounter between the poor and their own invisibility, as people sought in vain to recover the bodies of their relatives and friends. Some knew that a person's body had been sent there after witnessing their death. Others arrived after fruitless quests at overflowing jails and hospitals. Unclaimed decomposing bodies were stacked in the morgue hallways where, defying rules and the stench, relatives searched among them. The city's supply of coffins ran out. Eventually many family members were told by indifferent morgue workers to end their vigil. Loads of cadavers, they said, had been taken en masse to an unmarked mass grave in the Caracas public cemetery—in garbage bags.

The geography of the sprawling old Cementerio del Sur replicates that of Caracas. Past the crypts and statues in the center area that belong to families with names and means, there rises a crowded periphery of untended hillsides with rough-hewn paths and barely visible crosses. Cemetery workers confirmed that a mass grave had been opened in an elevated area named La Nueva Peste (The New Plague), the successor to a mass grave for victims of an epidemic in the past. Visited at night by trucks, an unknown number of bodies in bags unregistered in the records had been covered there.

Images of bodies picked up and tossed into trucks, dumped in garbage bags and buried in unknown sites by tractors, took hold of the collective imagination. Repeated and magnified in the barrios, they objectified for the poor their own erasure, the futility of attempting to establish their individual claims. A month after the massacre, Yvonne Pirela, a textile worker, vainly sought an order to exhume the body of her son from La Nueva Peste. The court official impatiently told her, "But Señora, the bags they were in are broken. Everything has become one mass by now. Forget it."[77]

Just as many bodies were erased, so were the figures of the casualties. After initial estimates of several hundred dead in Caracas, the media quickly stopped giving information on the number of fatalities. The government, denying unofficial estimates of over 1,000 dead and hundreds wounded and maimed, has maintained that 277 people died.[78] Because conditions were chaotic and people alarmed, the tendency at the moment for many people was to hold exaggerated notions of the deaths involved, which rumors placed in the thousands. However, the government has not released the names of the dead and has refused repeated legal efforts by newly formed groups of the victims' families, such as the Committee against Forgetting and the Committee of Relatives of the Innocent Victims of February–March (COFAVIC), to obtain the exhumation of the mass graves.

The Revelation: The Nation's Primitivity

The startling suddenness of the popular protest brought often candid commentary, yet its complexity and newness defied description. Uncertain on a changing ground, commentators sought the stable footing of established foundations. One such premise, concealed in normal times, concerned the intrinsic backwardness of the country. It was as if by overflowing the river bed, the masses had uncovered the hidden but familiar bedrock of the nation's identity: its primitivity. The evaluation of the nature, source, and significance of the nation's backwardness had been the obscure object of literary and political attention, distinguishing oligarchic and populist views of the nation. For the elite, the upheaval brought repressed understandings of this troublesome issue to the surface. At the height of the crisis, when people gained control of the streets, submerged populist assumptions converged with the oligarchic conception of the *pueblo* as backward masses. While under ordinary conditions populist rhetoric depicts the *pueblo* in positive terms, as virtuous, albeit ignorant, and therefore in need of guidance, during this crisis the element of ignorance was brought to the foreground in order to present the *pueblo* as savage: prone to lose control if not adequately harnessed and ready to plunge the nation into chaos if not swiftly repressed. It is not surprising, therefore, that on 4 March an outspoken journalist such as Alfredo Peña would employ without qualms the image of the *pueblo* as an uncontrolled river.

Ambivalence toward the *pueblo* did not disappear but was displaced. According to Peña, popular protest had been justified. The problem arose because the masses, without adequate political or trade union organizations, had no means of expressing themselves. Although the economic crisis in Venezuela was less serious than in Argentina and Uruguay, the masses in those countries remained controlled because they had representative parties and trade unions. "Without leadership they [the masses] become anarchic or overcome their leadership, overflow the river bed—and the unruly come to lead the movement" (*El Nacional,* 4 March 1989). The masses were right in being upset, he reasoned, but wrong in their form of protest.

In the congressional debate of 6 March, the leader of the moderate left party (MAS), Teodoro Petkoff, suggested that the protesters were not organized workers but people pushed to the edges of society—to prostitution, drugs, and alcoholism. Petkoff argued that the Venezuela that "erupted like a volcano" on 27 February was not "the Venezuela of workers organized in trade unions or associations. No, it was another Venezuela, it was the non-organized Venezuela, the Venezuela that has been piling up in a huge bag of wretched poverty." According to him, the Venezuela that "came down from the hills or up from the ravines" was "a Venezuela of hungry people, of people who are not part of the conventional organization of society." This Venezuela had produced "the roar of a wounded animal." He blamed the politicians of the ruling parties for having created this other Venezuela, labeling them Doctor Frankensteins: "They created a monster, And this monster came out to complain, came out to demand its share of the immense petroleum booty of all these years."[79] (República de Venezuela 1989).

As hidden assumptions surfaced during the riots, they took on novel meanings and were recast by changing conditions. The opposition between civilization and barbarism now equated rationality with the free market—the domain of the modernizing elite, and backwardness with state protection—the province of the needy masses, corrupt politicians, and inefficient businessmen. This division became graphically imaged in the layout of the cities, as the borders between rich and poor neighborhoods became military and moral battlegrounds, frontiers separating different kinds of people. In ever more binding ways, the ruling elite established its fraternity across international lines, for its overriding concern was with international financial flows rather than with the organization of the domestic market. It interpreted popular protest as a reaction against capitalist rationality, denying the multi-layered critique of injustice it contained—a protest at once against new free-market measures and against a politically constructed economy characterized by corruption, inflation, scarcity, and the hoarding of basic goods.[80]

Bodily Inscriptions and the Body Politic

Having represented the *pueblo* as a barbarous mass blind to the force of reason, the governing elite found justification for using blinding force against it. The ferocious deployment of state violence at the center stage of national politics blocked from view the significance of popular protest as a critique of the social order. Through the display of force, the government represented the protesting *pueblo* as a multi-headed monstrous threat that assumed the form of subversives, foreigners, drug dealers, Cuban agents, guerrillas, and common criminals—all dangerously invisible.[81] In this light, the mass killings were a way of constructing the *pueblo* as an irrational mass and the government as the sole defender of reason. Through the massacre, the logic of the Spanish Conquest was reinscribed on new bodies. For this conquest, government leadership endorsed the civilizing mission of heavy gunfire (*Plomo cerrado*), modeled itself after representatives of the imperialist English state and imaged the popular sectors as African natives. The nation was split in two.

The uprising of the *pueblo* changed the anatomy of the nation. From the perspective of the elite, the masses now embodied the menace of barbarism surfacing anywhere in the body politic, not just at its frontiers. Borders were no longer solely located at the nation's outer edges but had become internalized, turning into the arteries that irrigate the country with poor people. Wherever there were people at the margins—the *marginales*—a threat was seen. Caracas, once the showcase of modernity, appeared fragmented by the slums that surround it, as well as by those that grow like wild grass in the multiple ravines that crosscut the city.

The elite confronted the fractured body politic by enunciating its own contradictory relationship to the *pueblo,* deepening national divisions while calling for the restoration of unity. The Defense Minister directed the removal of alien elements at the same time that politicians called for renewed communication with the *pueblo.* Employing the paternalistic terms of elite discourse, the leader of the Christian Democratic party, ex-president Rafael Caldera, reprimanded the national political leadership for having distanced itself "from the *pueblo* who feel, who live, who sometimes express themselves in an improper fashion, and sometimes look for forms of expression that border on barbarism, but that must be understood. We have to reestablish communication with them" (Sanín 1989: 138).

As violence provoked a crescendo of fear, the Minister of Defense General Italo Alliegro became the public hero in the reestablishment of order. His capacity to express a combination of authority and sympathetic concern and to invoke democratic principles as the reason for military action made him the personification of the ideal leader for the moment of crisis. By the time troops were withdrawn and the media had defined the riots as vandalism and resistance as subversion, suppressing initial reports of military and police abuses, Alliegro's smiling face appeared on magazine covers and his name topped public opinion polls in popularity.[82] As in Barrios' colonial allegory, conquest was a time for generals, not politicians—but generals of a populist mold.[83]

At the moment officially construed as a historical crossroad in the nation's ascent towards modernity, threatening images of the people as savages—overflowing rivers that undermine order, primitive force that blocks national progress, barbarous masses that assault property and reason—made violence against them seem acceptable, necessary. The death of the *pueblo* was made to appear inconsequential, inscribed in the collective imagination through images of the poor as an anonymous mass of savages, as refuse to be discarded in garbage bags, as if the poor, in death as in life, were one mass.

The Barbarism of Civilization

Discovered by our men. . . . the natives' obstinacy was such that, unwilling to surrender, although assured of their lives, they resorted to arrows, shooting the entire supply in their quivers from above. When all had been used, in desperation they pulled out from their own bodies those the Spaniards' Indian allies had fired from below. They placed them in their bows with pieces of flesh still clinging to the tips and fired them again on their original owners. The Spaniards, appalled at such barbarity, at length brought them down with bullets, impaled them and left their corpses on the hill as a lesson in terror for others.

—José Oviedo y Baños[84]

Twelve Indians, two of whom were children, were massacred . . . in the Rómulo Gallegos District of the state of Apure, a few kilometers from the Colombian border. The bodies of the Indians were found in a lake. All of them had been stabbed to death and their bodies had been quartered. . . . Murders of indigenous people are constantly denounced in this area, but on this occasion it could be proven because the cadavers were found. The crime was committed during Easter, but a survivor only now made public this information.

—*El Diario de Caracas*, 27 April 1989[85]

The corporeality of people has served as a privileged medium for the political imagination in Latin America, as states that have but partial control over populations and territories have inscribed on the bodies of their subjects assertions of power directed to collective audiences. These inscriptions encode not only the reasons of state but the unquestioned foundations of these reasons, the bedrock of common sense that makes a social landscape seem natural. In this respect, physical violence, not unlike printing, is a vehicle for making and encoding history whose specific form and significance cannot be understood outside that history. Times of crisis show more clearly that these assumptions are reinterpreted and transformed from the standpoint of the present rather than being reproduced unchanged. In making history, people remake their history, recasting the past through a contemporary optic. The waking terrors of the living are the nightmare through which the past is imagined.

A colonial history that engraved upon bodies the denunciation of the victim's crimes informed the Amparo massacre. Similarly, a tradition of conquest weighed upon the state's treatment of the *masacrón* victims as an anonymous mass. But if both instances reconfigured the present in terms of the past, they also reconstructed the past in terms of the present, making salient suppressed conceptions of the poor as disposable savages. In accord with shifts in domestic and international conditions, the terms of nationalist discourse acquired new accents. "I would have killed all those savages, as I am sure they would have killed us if they had a chance. They hate us," Sofia, a wealthy young lawyer and Harvard-trained business woman, told us as she shaped her arm into a machine gun and pointed her finger toward the slums that surround her office in a skyscraper overlooking the hills from which looters had descended.

For the last half-century, state affluence held social conflict in check. During this time, petroleum abundance and torrential money flows brought rapid social and geographical mobility and helped redraw social identities. But as petroleum money dried up, the social world built upon the fluid foundations of this easy money began to crack. With the crisis of credit came a crisis of credibility. Not surprisingly, the poor were to be the victims and the demons of the ensuing social reordering. In the turmoil of meaning provoked by the mass uprising, dominant discourse transformed the *pueblo* from the virtuous foundation of democracy into a savage threat to its existence—a barbaric presence.

As the debt crisis has set the stage for the civilizing advance of the free market, the *pueblo* is being redefined as an aggregate of citizens at the same time that the meaning of citizenship is being recast through practice. With the ascent of free-market ideology and the displacement of the moral economy of protectionism by the morality of capital, a rupture of customary bonds uniting leaders and masses, state and people, has pushed the poor to the border of the body politic. In this new configuration of social relations, boundaries are transformed into frontiers that separate the civilized from the barbarous. Without state protection, people are being left free to choose progress. Hand in hand, the logics of conquest and of the free market converge to impress upon people the changing meaning of their social anonymity.

State power was exercised, in characteristic fashion in a dramaturgical mode by means of performances designed to establish an account of reality through the persuasiveness of power; they intended less to convince than to produce acquiescence. When the reproduction of state authority is so deeply intertwined with the construction of its representation, politics centers on the artifice of its making. The makeshift or contrived character of certain political representations, visible in the theatrical display of state violence during both massacres, may actually express a form of constructing power rather than a deficiency in its organization.[86]

In each massacre the state attempted not simply to represent reality, but to show that it had the power to write the plot, to decide who belongs at center stage, who is at the margins, who is in the audience, and who is shut outside. When people dared to act, transgressing spatial and conceptual boundaries, the state counteracted by turning them into actors of different dramas. By transforming peasants into guerrillas and protesters into savages, the state sought simultaneously to control their actions and to reconstitute the *pueblo* as the usual chorus in the wings of the theater of populism. At the margins of this official drama, however, people spoke lines of their own making, challenging the plot of a modernizing project that was based on their silence. Less than four weeks after Pérez's inauguration as President, in response to the state's attempt to make commodities reflect the unmediated rationality of the free market, people responded with fury by "spontaneously" freeing commodities from the market. This spontaneity at once revealed the hidden activity of sedimented memories and experiences, and made explicit a popular critique of relations of rule that was embedded in quotidian life. Through their actions, people pried open a space through which to glimpse a different social imaginary by ignoring the state's drama (which they called the *farse*) and attacking for a moment the theatre itself.

While popular violence was circumscribed, centering on material barriers between things and people, state violence was unbounded, as if its aim were to trap popular will; with heavy gunfire it cast a net around streets and slums, targeting the poor and their homes. The planning and execution of the Amparo massacre assumed an implicit definition of the *pueblo* as passive and disposable, and the February–March massacre was presented as a natural government reaction to an explosion of popular savagery. As with apparently spontaneous popular action, the very naturalness of state activity revealed the invisible work of historical memory through which not only the governing elite but large sectors of the population interpreted the sources of danger and the meaning of rights.

It will be as difficult to remember as it is hard to forget just how order was reimposed. While people inscribed with their bodies their presence upon the state, the state inscribed its power upon their bodies.[87] To achieve the reestablishment of stability, the state can no longer assume that there are compliant actors or a passive audience; it must modulate its actions in accord with its memory and with its altered perception of what the *pueblo* might do. As the state continues to present the drama of modernization on stage, people murmur in the aisles, walk out, and talk outside. We may be able to hear these voices questioning the assumption that the death of the *pueblo* may take place "as if no one, nothing had died, as if they were stones failing on the ground, or water on the water."

Violence and Modernity

Are the events we discuss here, then, just further exotic tales about the violent character of distant others, a confirmation of the premodern character of contemporary Latin American states? A myth central to modernity, whose paternity can be traced to Hegel and Foucault (1979), contends that, as heirs to the Enlightenment, modem states establish their authority by embodying not divine will or force but reason. The modem state, it asserts, having domesticated the bloody theater of violence of the ancien regime, replaces publicly inflicted physical punishment with a myriad of disciplinary procedures that permeate the body politic and engender the modern soul. From this perspective, state violence as a reason of state marks the premodern domain, in which the state writes its texts on the bodies of its citizens, presumably because premodern souls grasp its reasons concretely.

Our analysis questions a viewpoint that divides history into neat ascending stages and is blind to the violence through which modem states secure their hegemony. The forms of state violence may indeed vary in different societies, in part reflecting how their mechanisms of social control—what Gramsci called their "trench systems"[88]—protect states from political and economic threats. State violence is thus inseparable from other forms of social violence, the exceptional deployment of state force from the quotidian practice of social domination. But whenever states violently reproduce the conditions of their existence by imposing the standards of their rule through force, we may glimpse how myths of authority are grounded on the terrain of history and how, as Benjamin suggests, documents of civilization are at the same time documents of barbarism (1969: 256).

In this discussion we have sought to advance an argument for understanding political violence as an opaque historical artifact, that is, as a set of practices and cultural forms whose meanings can only be deciphered by understanding the historical memory and the social relations of the society within which it arises, takes form, and achieves effects. As violence becomes embodied in practices and objectified in institutions, technologies, and icons, it becomes modular; commoditized and taught in multiple forms, it circulates in markets that cross boundaries.[89] "I only wish I could have been trained in Israel like López Sisco, for there they teach you to be a killer-machine," a DISIP member assigned to guard the Amparo survivors told us as he caressed his favorite weapon, a Magnum, and praised its superiority over his revolver and submachine gun. The irony that his idol had led the massacre of the Amparo fishermen whom he was guarding highlights another historical irony, that the barbarity attributed to the periphery has been historically forged in conjunction with the barbarity of the centers of civilization, where it parades in the guise of reason, morality, and technique.[90] Because history is the offspring of such ironies, we must seek the specific historical character of violence behind the outward similarity of its mechanisms and consequences. By situating these massacres within the history of their making, we have tried to observe how they were represented, to decode the semantics of violence, and to listen to what was said.

Listening to violence entails exploring a terrain in which the construction of meaning is contested through the deployment of competing modes of meaning-making. If, building on de Certeau's work, we view society as being constituted by "heterogeneous places" in which a "forest of narrativities" (1986: 201, 183) engenders multiple conceptions of reality, we may hear a multitude of submerged voices speaking through a variety of semantic fields. Narrativities of violence form a dense forest with deceptively homogeneous contours. While Foucault posits the existence of a clear correlation between types of society and forms of state violence, our analysis suggests that these typological correspondences may be partial and shifting, for the surface similarity of the elements composing the forest of violence obscures how the power of these forms derives from their complex articulation with each other on heterogeneous social terrains.

In the Amparo and February massacres state violence took place at once as a spectacular theatrical performance and as a hidden technical operation. Neocolonial societies, by making particularly visible the ongoing imbrications of heterogeneous historical forms, also illuminate the emerging landscape of the postcolonial world. At a moment in history when the globalization of space is being achieved through simultaneous integration and fracture, inclusion and exclusion, transmuted colonial relations remain dynamic forces within processes of global change. The events we analyze in this paper are moments in this worldwide reordering of body politics. Through them we may glimpse the movement from a world organized by what Tom Nairn calls the uniformed imperialism of direct political control and territorially fixed markets (1977: 356) to one shaped by what we call the multiform imperial controls of fluid-finance capital, a world of increasingly de-territorialized markets and shifting political, economic, and cultural boundaries. The Venezuelan riots and massacres, as people who lived through them know, are inseparable from the hidden violence of postmodern empires.

Epilogue

As this article has sought to show, the two instances of political violence analyzed here entailed heated contests over their interpretation. At the time of their occurrence, the state sought to impose its vision of reality and to disqualify alternative views. Afterwards, it sought to bury the memory of these events and to reinstate politics as usual, removing challenges to its authority from center stage. This is not the place to examine the complex aftermath of these events and the struggles over their memory. But one outcome, because of its ongoing significance, deserves brief mention.

Even before he was elected president in 1998 with a mandate to renovate the state, Lieutenant Coronel Hugo Chávez defined the Caracazo as emblematic of the anti-popular character of the established party regime and as a turning point in Venezuelan history. Middle-level military officers affiliated with Chávez's "Bolivarian Revolutionary Movement" (founded in 1982) claim that the 1989 popular protests and their violent repression, in which they were obliged to participate, reinforced their commitment to overthrow the regime that had massacred hundreds of innocent people and turned the military into a brutal agent of state violence. At first they sought to do so by launching an unsuccessful coup d'état in 1992, led by Chávez, and afterwards by using electoral and constitutional means. Since he began his rule in 1999, Chávez's "peaceful revolution" has redefined not just the political system, but also official Venezuelan history. If the old regime sought to restrict the memory of 27 February by presenting it as a shameful upsurge of barbarism that must be contained, Chávez's government memorializes it in annual marches and state discourse as the foundation of a revolution that claims to have united the military and the people in struggle against those responsible for dismembering the nation.

NOTES

Acknowledgments: Research for this paper was supported by the Michigan Society of Fellows and the Spencer Foundation. In Venezuela we were affiliated with the Centro de Estudios Latinaméricanos Rómulo Gallegos; we would like to thank all these institutions for their interest and support. Our research at the time of the Amparo Massacre and the February riots involved extensive observation and interviews with a wide range of people. These included the presidential candidates and their campaign organizers, members of the business community, the Amparo survivors and relatives of victims, members of the human rights community, people participating in and affected by the February riots, clergy, opposition activists, and security agents. Our statements about collective states or agencies reflect a necessarily simplified assessment of extremely complex and contradictory realities, the further discussion of which we are developing in a longer work. Versions of this article have been presented at the Annual Meeting of the American Anthropology Association, Washington D.C., November 1989, and the Annual Meeting of the American Ethnological Association, Atlanta, April 1990. At the University of Michigan versions were presented to the Michigan Society of Fellows, the Program for the Study of Social Transformations, the Graduate Student Association for Latin American Studies, and the Program in History and Anthropology; and at The University of Chicago to the Workshop on Comparative Nationalism. We would like to express our gratitude for the constructive comments we received. In addition we wish to thank Roger Rouse for many helpful discussions, and John Comaroff, Raymond Grew, Richard Thrits, Tom Wolfe, and an anonymous reviewer for their valuable insights. Finally, we would like to acknowledge the cooperation of many people in Venezuela who shared with us their understanding of these conflicts.

    1. From Pablo Neruda's *Canto General.* These verses refer to a massacre of Chilean workers in 1946. The English translation reads:

And the death of the people was as it has always been:
as if no one, nothing had died,
as if they were stones failing on the ground,
or water on the water

2. In contrast to predominant approaches to this subject, the works by Baretta and Markoff (1978), Taussig (1987), and Thompson (1971) illustrate attempts to examine the historical construction and cultural forms of violence.

3. This issue is addressed by Coronil in a critique of postmodern discourses on colonialism (1989).

4. Ironically, the word *amparo* means protection or shelter and is also a judicial measure affording defendants legal protection. In a society in which personal fortune is closely tied to one's patronage relations, to be *desamparado*, or unprotected, is to be socially alone and vulnerable.

5. This figure is necessarily tentative. Journalist Jack Sweeny calculates that in Caracas alone between 500,000 and 750,000 people participated in the riots (*Veneconomía*, March 1989).

6. See Walton (1989) for a careful comparative analysis of protests in Latin America against debt-related austerity programs.

7. First published in 1929, *Doña Bárbara* (1959) was written by Rómulo Gallegos, a pedagogue and author of several noted novels, and a founder of Acción Democrática Party (AD). He became Venezuela's first freely elected president in 1948.

8. The nation's petroleum-export industry began under the autocratic rule of General Juan Vicente Gómez (1908–1935) and buttressed his monopolistic hold over wealth and power. During the transition toward pluralism after 1936, Acción Democrática governed briefly (1945–1948), but was overthrown by the military. Pérez Jimenez headed a repressive military regime (1948–1958) during which oil wealth benefited a growing commercial bourgeoisie.

9. Leftist guerrillas were active in the early 1960s in opposition to the alliances that President Rómulo Betancourt (founder of AD and mentor of Carlos Andrés Pérez) made with domestic and foreign capital. The government launched a successful (but costly in terms of rights and lives) counterinsurgency campaign directed by Minister of the Interior Carlos Andrés Pérez. The guerrillas failed to win support among the peasants who were loyal to AD but found some backing in the capital's large working-class periphery (*barrios*). The defeated guerrilla groups were formally pacified in 1970, but the barrios have remained the base for occasional small radical groups and continue to be seen as the primary site of subversive threats to democratic order. See Ellner (1980).

10. World oil prices quadrupled in late 1973 and remained high until the close of the decade, when they again doubled. Government income from oil (which ranges from 60–75 percent of its total income and accounts for over 90 percent of export earnings) quadrupled just before newly elected Carlos Andrés Pérez took office. Pérez's program, which claimed it would bring about Venezuela's Second Independence, emphasized capital—intensive heavy industry (petrochemicals, steel, aluminum, hydroelectric power). Although it ignored the social impact of these projects, it directed large sums of money into subsidizing popular consump-

tion and services. Together with the increase in construction and luxury consumption, this created an illusion of prosperity. See Walton (1989) for the "appearance of development" created through borrowing in Latin America.

11. With a foreign debt of 33 billion dollars and a population of approximately 20 million, Venezuela's per capita foreign debt is the highest in Latin America. A number of sources discuss the oil boom and its consequences. For an analysis of the petroleum boom and the effects it had on cultural forms and institutional practices, see Coronil (1987). For the impact of the oil boom on industrial policy, see Coronil and Skurski (1982). Mommer's innovative work analyzes the historical development and the logic of the rent-based economy (1983, 1988). For examples of critical evaluations of the administrations of Pérez and his successors, see Hellinger (1985), Malavé Mata (1987), and Proceso Político (1978).

12. The president who followed Pérez, Luis Herrera Campins of the Social Christian Party (COPEI), also contracted large debts, encouraged once again by a brief rebound of oil prices in 1979. But the nation's finances worsened rapidly, and the currency, the Bolívar (basically stable since the 1920s), was abruptly devalued in 1983.

13. Pérez and Lusinchi are leaders of the centrist-reformist party, Acción Democrática (founded in 1941). Longtime party leaders and former allies, they are both powerful national figures and now head rival factions within the party. AD, the nation's leading party, is historically associated with populist reform and a nationalist oil policy. It relies heavily on making pacts with political and economic elites, rests on patronage distribution rather than mobilization and exerts political control over the major labor and peasant federations. There are few good analyses of AD. See Blank (1973), Ellner (1982), Martz (1966), and Moleiro (1978). For the rhetoric and imagery utilized by the party, see Britto García (1988). For theoretical discussions of Latin American populism, see Hennessy (1976) and Laclau (1977).

14. An electoral-reform program began to take effect in 1990, but structural constraints, both financial and administrative, limit the autonomy of local officials. See the magazine *SIC* for analysis of changes in the electoral system. On the political party system see Arroyo Talavera (1988), Hein and Stenzel (1973), Hellinger (1985), Levine (1973), Magallanes (1986, 1987), and Romero (1986).

15. Venezuela's electoral democracy was established in 1958, and power has changed hands peacefully every five years since 1959. The Social Christian Party has governed twice in this period, 1969–1974 under Caldera, and 1979–1984 under Herrera Campíns, but AD has governed during the remaining terms. Given the political stability of Venezuela's multiparty system in an era marked by violent military takeovers in much of the continent, its elections have been much studied. See Lubrano and Sánchez (1987), Marta Sosa (1984), Martz and Baloyra (1976), Martz and Meyer (1977), Rangel (1973, 1982), Rangel and Duno (1979), and Silva Michelena and Sontag (1979),

16. Lusinchi had backed his ally, Senator Lepage, for the party's nomination during its primary. Pérez mobilized support from the labor sector to win the nomination.

17. Pérez ("the man with energy") defeated his leading opponent, Eduardo Fernández ("the Tiger") of COPEI, by a 13 percent margin, receiving an unusually high 53 percent of the 7,321,281 votes cast. Teodoro Petkoff, the candidate of the allied socialist parties MAS and MIR, received 2.7 percent of the vote; these parties received 10 percent of the congressional vote, depriving AD of its majority. Lusinchi's administration had been marked by parochialism, paternalistic clientelism, and increasing repression, directed on occasion against highly placed critics of his policies. In contrast to Lusinchi, Pérez had a cosmopolitan image, international experience, and a record of incorporating rather then excluding critics. His electoral victory aided the chances that his supporter would gain positions of control in the party apparatus.

18. The term *pueblo* has a dual set of meanings. On the one hand, it encompasses the entire citizenry of Venezuela and is invoked in relation to the nation's defense and the memory of its independence. On the other hand, the term refers to people who have lower-class (popular) origins and is widely used as a substitute for social class categories when referring to the poor, who are the majority of the population. Its connotations, charged with ambiguity, vary with context, speaker, and audience.

19. Twenty-two heads of state attended the inauguration, which had an international and elite style. Various proponents of revising the terms of third-world debt attended, among them Germany's Willy Brandt, Spain's Felipe González, and the United States' Jimmy Carter. Vice President Dan Quayle of the United States was present on his first official international trip. Nicaragua's Daniel Ortega and Cuba's Fidel Castro (on his first trip to Venezuela since 1959) drew great attention; their presence augmented Pérez's image as a leader willing to challenge foreign and conservative pressures.

20. The program was the standard package of measures that the International Monetary Fund (IMF) requires of debtor nations in order for them to qualify for new loans. Variants of it have been applied in many countries and have often provoked violent protests. While Pérez continued to criticize the IMF, his team of negotiators, with international reserves alarmingly low and interest payments on the debt suspended, agreed to meet IMF conditions so as to obtain new loans.

21. See Carrera Damas (1972) for a study of the cult of Bolívar as a civic religion.

22. On the extreme polarization of colonial society and the social content of the war, see Carrera Damas (1968), Lynch (1973), and Izard (1981). On the piecemeal abolition of slavery and the racial dimension to social conflict in the post-independence period, see Lombardi (1971), Matthews (1977), and Fundación John Boulton (1976).

23. See Stallybrass and White (1986) on the construction of categories of high and low as an element in class formation.

24. The wars of the nineteenth century were fought largely with plainsmen from the cattle frontier, the Llanos, and the threat of anarchy became closely identified with this population formed at the social margins. See Baretta and Markoff's (1978) comparative analysis of violence and cattle frontiers.

25. The right to loot was established practice during the Independence War on the part of Bolívar as well as his *llanero* opponent, Boves. It was a necessity, given the lack of supplies and money to support the troops. The looting of the national treasury, now a common image in contemporary politics, was seen in the nineteenth century as part of the spoils a political leader offered his followers. This was acknowledged in a saying of the time: "I don't ask to be given anything, I just ask to be placed where there is something." Baretta and Markoff suggest the foundations of looting in the practice of cattle rustling on the Llanos, governed by notions of social justice and common property (1978). For the practice of *saqueo,* see Brito Figueroa (1966), Britto García (1988), Carrera Damas (1972), Gilmore (1964), and Matthews (1977).

26. Under Gómez, who rose to power under Cipriano Castro (1899–1908), Andeans monopolized control of the state and of choice property. Gómez put an end to *caudillismo,* as a system of regional strongmen vying to control the state, and centralized state power. He ruled as a *hacendado* patriarch, with personal mystique and the ability to use repression without hesitation, and used state power to achieve the greatest accumulation of wealth in land and industry in Latin America. He continues to be a controversial and historically opaque figure. See Pino Iturrieta (1985), Segnini (1982), Sosa (1985), and Velásquez (1986).

27. Critics canonized it as a "novel of the land" and only recently have located it. In relation to nationalist discourse. See Howard (1976), Dessau (1980), Scharer-Nussberger (1979), Skurski (1991), and Sommer (1991).

28. See Doris Sommer for an innovative study of foundational fictions, Latin American novels (1991) that allegorically relate national integration and family romance.

29. On the construction of the colonized subject and on the National Symbolic, see Lauren Berlant (1988, 1991). Her comments concerning the nation and utopia have benefited this analysis.

30. For an analysis of *Doña Bárbara* as a nationalist myth that incorporates the Bolívarian model within the populist project, see Skurski (1994).

31. Our interviews with political figures of this era confirm the impact of *Doña Bárbara* on the emerging political leadership's self-conception and vision of progress. Also see Dessau (1980) and Howard (1976).

32. The CEJAP (Comando Específico "General en Jefe José Antonio Páez") was named after the llanero caudillo hero of the Independence War. It brought together members of the Army, the Policía Técnica Judicial (PTJ), and the Dirección de los Servicios de Inteligencia y Prevención (DISIP), a paramilitary intelli-

gence police specialized in counterinsurgency. Created on 28 October 1987 under the Border Law, the CEJAP had broad powers to act against suspected subversives and contrabandists. General Camejo Arias was its regional commander, but the chief of operations of the DISIP, Henry López Sisco, was its leader. López Sisco, trained abroad in counterinsurgency, had previously gained notoriety as the leader of DISIP's armed attacks on so-called subversives.

33. López Sisco, the brigade's commander, was not present, as he had been injured days earlier during preparations for the attack. Nine DISIP members, seven PTJ members, and four soldiers participated in the attack.

34. This event helped depict Lusinchi as a defender of the national territory at a time when Carlos Andrés Pérez was accused by opposition candidates as having reached a secret agreement with Colombia concerning a longstanding border dispute on the oil-rich coast.

35. Márquez is locally known for his battles against landowner and military abuses in the border region. Trained as a historian, he has backed peasant land claims with research into obscure land titles. From a modest family in a small Andean town and disabled since infancy by a crippling disease, Márquez has acquired a hero's status in the region as a defender of the powerless.

36. One of the victims was a Colombian from the town of Arauca, across the river from Amparo. The residents of the border area move freely between Venezuela and Colombia, and intermarriage and dual citizenship are common. Commerce between the two towns is heavy, and goods are often carried across the river in both directions by fishing boat owners, depending on fluctuations in currency values and the prices of goods. Residents regard most of this movement as trade rather than contraband.

37. *El Nacional,* 5 November 1988.

38. Arias and Pinilla, thirty-five and twenty-six years of age, are both natives of Amparo, single, and irregularly employed. Arias, who served in the army, works for a land surveying company. Pinilla, who has close family in Colombia, works on fishing boats during the Arauca River's flood season. Neither had known political or religious affiliations. Prior to the attack they were acquaintances but became close over the following months of obligatory companionship.

39. Three members were added to the commission. They included Walter Márquez and Congressman Raul Esté, elected on the Communist Party slate. Esté had investigated earlier DISIP massacres, led by López Sisco, against claimed subversives. See Esté (1987).

40. Pérez remained closely tied to the military leadership, and his assertions were seen as more than campaign rhetoric.

41. Guerrilla forces are linked to contraband, robbery, and kidnapping activities, and thus a criminal record was used as presumption of possible guerrilla ties. In the border regions especially, guerrilla identification carried no necessary assumption of ideological affiliation.

42. A few had been jailed for drunkenness and fights. Officials of Venezuela's

and Colombia's military intelligence agencies (the director of the Dirección de Administración Social [DAS] in Arauca, Colombia, Francisco Alberto González, and the national director of the Dirección General Sectorial de Inteligencia Militar [DIM] in Venezuela, German Rodríguez Citraro) denied Camejo Arias' claim that the men had a record for criminal or subversive acts. The DIM director's testimony undermined the official account and indicated opposition by military intelligence to the autonomy granted the DIST (a civilian police agency) under Lusinchi. A sign of this tension is the DIM's offer to bring Walter Márquez and the survivors to Caracas in its airplane.

43. *El Diario de Caracas,* 15 Nov. 1988, 8.

44. The official autopsy has not been released on the grounds that the legal case has not been concluded. However journalist Fabricio Ojeda reported details of its findings, including evidence of the torture of seven men, and the castration of one. (*El Nacional,* "En una 'orgía de sangre' mataron a los pescadores" [Fishermen killed in "orgy of blood"], 24 and 25 Mar. 1989, pp. D 10, D 11). A Colombian informer also participated in the attack but remained hidden until December. Fragments of his confession to the military intelligence agency (DIM) leaked to the press describe the assault's organization and how a DISIP member, Hipólito, forced him to shoot a wounded survivor as a "test of courage" (*El Nacional,* "La confesión de Yaruro" [Yaruro's confession], 10 April 1989, p. D 17).

45. A locally feared DIST member of the CEJAP (César Rincones, or Hipólito) who resided in Amparo was seen before the ambush with the owner of the fishing boat. Some speculate he promoted the outing by offering the boat owner money to carry contraband. After the attack, he attempted to force the release of the survivors from the local jail, but the police chief resisted.

46. Nevertheless, conflicts continued between different factions of power. On their return the survivors were again under the control of Judge Pérez Gutiérrez (backed by Camejo Arias and Lusinchi) who jailed them for two weeks and who treated the jailed CEJAP members with open friendliness. He was instrumental in the reversal of the case that occurred after the presidential inauguration, resulting in the freedom of the attackers and the accusation of the survivors.

47. It called for an investigation of Judge Pérez Gutiérrez's obstructionist behavior. For the text of the report, widely reported in the press, see República de Venezuela (1989).

48. The leftist members of the commission were guarded in revealing their information to the press about the powerful landed, military, and political interests that supported the CEJAP. They also took care not to be seen as maligning the military as an institution. Márquez quietly received support from military intelligence officials, who were critical of DISIP incursions into their field and of DISIP-led attacks tarnishing the army's reputation (personal interviews with Walter Márquez, Jan. 1989). The backers of the DISIP issued death threats to Márquez and to discredit him organized a costly right-wing advertising campaign that was

paid for by a branch of Lyndon Larouch's party based in the United States. It portrayed the Gnostic church to which Márquez belongs as a satanic sect and a guerrilla front (*El Nacional,* 28 Jan.–3 Feb. 1989).

49. Congressman Márquez compiled information placing the Amparo massacre within the context of previous massacres, all of which involved General Camejo Arias, the DISIP's López Sisco, and Judge Pérez Gutiérrez, carried out in 1988 by the CEJAP: Cotufí (ten dead) in January, Las Gaviotas (two dead) in April, Los Totumitos (five dead) in July, El Vallado (three dead) in October (*El Nacional* 1 Feb. 1989; El Diario *de Caracas,* 18 Mar. 1989; personal interviews with Márquez, 1989). This information matches that of Congressman Raul Esté concerning earlier DISIP massacres at Cantaura and Yumare. Esté stresses the ideological intentions of the attacks to quell dissent (personal interviews with Esté, Nov. 1988, Jan. and July 1989).

50. These death factories have been documented in detail by United States journalist Ralph Schusler in investigative reports in *El Diario de Caracas* (13 and 22 Dec. 1988) and *El Nacional* (1, 2, and 3 May 1989). Schusler was fired from his job at the English-language newspaper *The Daily Journal* after he questioned Carlos Andrés Pérez concerning the Amparo massacre at a press conference. His articles, based on interviews with survivors, describe how Colombians were brought across the border by DISIP agents on the promise of ranch work only to be killed, often after torture.

51. Lusinchi was the first president to bring his mistress into a position of power. He broke another unofficial political rule by bringing divorce proceedings against his wife of many years, the pediatrician Gladys Lusinchi, while he was in office, moving into quarters at his executive office with Ibáñez. Most critics focused on Ibáñez, defining her as exerting sinister control over the easygoing Lusinchi. Criticism of her power, which was backed by use of the DISIP, entered the national press in August 1988 when the elder AD leader Luis Piñerúa opposed the party's effort to slate her for a congressional seat (see *The New York Times,* 23 Jan. 1988). Beroes (1990) and Piñerúa (1988) refer to her intromission in political, police, and military affairs.

52. Two months after Pérez took office, military and political pressure began to reverse the Amparo case. On 6 April a military court headed by a *compadre* of Camejo Arias ordered the CEJAP members released on a legal technicality. The survivors, fearing for their lives with their assailants free, sought sanctuary from the church; they spent one month in Caracas in a church in a working-class area of Petare. Clergy active in human rights, particularly Fathers Matías Camuñas and Antonio García, and Sister Lali Lacarra, placed them in contact with barrio Christian-based groups. In a cruel irony, the government kept them guarded by members of the DISIP under the guise of protecting them. Underlining the deep relations of complicity involved in the Amparo massacre, the Supreme Court refused to hear the case, and the Martial Court declared on 25 April 1990 that the incident

at Amparo had in fact been an armed encounter and that Arias and Pinilla were guerrillas posing as survivors; simultaneously President Pérez ordered the investigation of Judge Pérez Gutiérrez to be dropped (*El Nacional,* 26 April 1990). In a shift reflecting internal disagreement, the Supreme Court then rejected the military court's ruling in August 1990 and agreed that it would hear the case. See the magazine *SIC* and the human rights newsletter *PROVEA* for accounts of developments.

53. For an excellent discussion of the negative associations historically attached to the Venezuelan peasantry, see Roseberry (1986).

54. The Spanish news magazine *Cambio 16* opened its 11 November 1988 article on the Amparo massacre by making reference to the novel's setting.

55. See Amnesty International (1987, 1988). Prominent media and political figures had been attacked through loss of their jobs, by physical assault, or censorship for having criticized government corruption, particularly in relation to Blanca Ibáñez. The report on human rights connects DISIP and police attacks on prominent figures to the abuse and deaths of numerous ordinary citizens, many of whom were labeled as criminals.

56. This mode of exercising state power relies on techniques for forming political subjects and gaining their conformity to political rule analogous to those which supported the culture of the baroque in seventeenth-century Spain. The baroque, Maravall (1986) argues, was a culture of state-building in a time of crisis that arose as part of the state's effort to move and to control a mass of anonymous, potentially disruptive subjects. Its theatrical character grew from the orchestration of appearances by the combination of terror and propaganda, the excessive use of force, and the overproduction of rational formulas. We thank Rafael Sánchez for his comments on these issues. See Comaroff (1989) for the quotidian theater of the civilizing process.

57. "The big massacre" is the phrase used in the African context by human rights groups and protest singers.

58. The author, Alfredo Peña, is an influential political commentator.

59. See *Veneconomía,* March 1989, and *SIC,* April 1989, for excellent reporting and analysis of the events of the week.

60. The estimate of 1,000 to 1,200 deaths is based on our interviews with highly placed figures in the media, the military, the political arena, and the health field. The United States Department of State Report (1990) acknowledges this estimate and details the military's deliberate armed attack on the population.

61. President Pérez suddenly learned that the total amount of Venezuela's international reserves was only 200 million dollars, which necessitated an abrupt change of policy.

62. Venezuelan legislation continued the Spanish colonial legal definition of the subsoil, and thus of petroleum, as the property of the state. In 1976 President Pérez nationalized the oil industry with generous compensation.

63. The private owners of the varied buses, vans, and cars providing most urban transportation argued that escalating costs for the repair and replacement of vehicles made even a provisional ceiling intolerable. Drivers also refused to honor the student half-fare payments. The leaders of the bus association were affiliated with AD but refused to abide by a fare agreement, a symptom of AD's diminishing capacity to control its members.

64. For vivid descriptions and photos of the outbreak and spread of the riots in the Caracas area by journalists on the scene, see the photo essays by *El Nacional* (1989, 1990) and Catalá (1989). For analysis of the riots, see *Cuadernos del CENDES* 10; Sanín (1989).

65. The Metropolitan Police, like the looters, have low wages, are of lower-class origins, and generally live in the barrios. Outnumbered by looters, at the outset they interfered little or actively cooperated, although in some cases they shot at looters. Observers have stated that the government issued orders initially to respond with minimal violence to the protests.

66. This section draws on personal interviews conducted with residents of barrios in Antímano, La Vega, El Valle, El Cementerio, and Petare in the days immediately following the riots. See *El Nacional* (1989) for an account of the situation in Antímano and the role of the police in negotiating women's orderly looting of groceries, which was termed shopping, while men were kept at a distance.

67. Personal interview, 29 Aug. 1990.

68. We are indebted to Roger Rouse for this expression and for his observations concerning behavior in the street.

69. The information concerning attacks on small factories and on police and party centers was kept out of the media, while news of sniper fire on troops and police was amplified.

70. There was much variation in these situations. In many cases neighbors banded together to defend a neighborhood store owned by immigrants from attack by looters from outside the barrio.

71. On 28 Feb. the commission negotiating the restructuring of the debt proceeded to sign a letter of intent with the IMF in New York, committing the government to the austerity program despite the outbreak of the riots. See *SIC,* April 1989 for its contents.

72. Interview with a reporter who investigated the sources of such rumors, and *El Nacional* (1989). This tactic was also used in Chile in 1973 by the forces opposed to President Allende. See *PROVEA* (1989).

73. In Caracas, certain sectors were the object of particularly heavy gunfire: the *23 de Enero* housing projects located near the capitol building and a perennial site of political and criminal resistance; barrios in El Valle near the wholesale food market and a military deposit; and barrios in Petare near market and military sites and bordering on upper-middle-class residential zones.

74. Personal interview with a member of a security force, 27 July 1989. Many

relatives of such victims were later afraid to denounce deaths that occurred in this way because of their own illegal status or activities and their daily fear of police retaliation (personal interviews with members of The Committee for the Disappeared).

75. See "Carta al Director de la DIM," *SIC*, Lll: 516 (July 1989), 274–75, for an account of the detention of six Jesuit priests who live in the barrio La Vega. For an account of the torture of a student activist see Roland Denis, "El encuentro," *Punto*, 15 Feb. 1990, 10.

76. Personal interview with a forensic doctor who worked in the Bello Monte Morgue of Caracas continuously for three days during the riots (April 1989).

77. Personal interviews with cemetery employees, journalists, and relatives of victims.

78. The actual number of those killed nationwide is unknown and is very difficult to ascertain. Many more were injured, some disabled for life. Two policemen and two members of the Army were reported killed, Undoubtedly considerable time will pass before reliable confirmation of these estimates can be obtained.

79. Petkoff is a leader of the left known for his role as a guerrilla leader in the sixties and for having led the division of the Communist Party of Venezuela after the Soviet invasion of Czechoslovakia. A proponent of social democracy, he received 2.6 percent of the presidential vote in 1988.

80. Even coins were scarce as speculators melted them for their nickel content, making the Venezuelan currency's loss of value poignantly visible.

81. Among the conservative elite the rumor circulated and was published in the press that Fidel Castro, after attending the inauguration, had left behind 300 trained agents who had organized the riots.

82. Indicative of his political star quality, Alliegro exerted the erotic attraction characteristic of the successful male populist leader. Newspapers noted that he was besieged by lovely young women reporters, and women often commented he would make an attractive president.

83. Alliegro's appointment as the Minister of Defense expired in June 1989 (he began under Lusinchi) but was not renewed. It was rumored that the AD leadership feared the effects of Alliegro's popularity if he were to remain. Only after his obligatory retirement from the military could Alliegro speak to the press about his opinions. In a televised interview on the anniversary of the riots Alliegro criticized the Pérez government for having applied its program too rapidly and without measures to aid the poor. He expressed interest in becoming the representative of a new "Independent" political coalition (*El Diario de Caracas*, 28 Feb. 1990).

84. *Oviedo y Baños* (1987), 196. This is an eighteenth-century account of the Conquest, based on original records, written from the perspective of the colonial elite.

85. This brief article, titled "Twelve Indians Were Massacred," was buried in the middle of the newspaper. Unlike the Amparo massacre, the victims were not

identified, and the incident went unnoticed. See Coppens (1975) for a prior Indian massacre in this region.

86. See Coronil and Skurski (1991) for a discussion of the double discourse of nationalism as it negotiates the ambiguous bases of authority in postcolonial societies.

87. We are indebted to Kathleen Canning, William Sewell, and Jane Burbank for their comments concerning the impact of popular action on the body politic. Although we do not see the emergence of a counter-hegemonic discourse, the events we discuss here indicate that the demobilizing promise of the modernization project has lost some of its hold. In the municipal elections of December 1989, held for the first time under a new electoral law, 80 percent of the electorate abstained; the media label it was given, the electoral jolt (*el sacudón electoral*), drew a parallel to the riots.

88. Gramsci's conception of the fluid and shifting relationship between the state and civil society whereby "state functions" are sometimes taken up by civil society suggests a non-essentialist view of state power. See Forgacs (1988).

89. This formulation draws on Anderson's discussion of nationalism as a "cultural artifact" that has become "modular" (1983). In highlighting the opaque and historical character of violence, however, we want to underline both its multivocal semantic structure and its historically specific significance. While the modular character of violence leads to a process of standardization, even of commodification, its significance always remains specific and must be ascertained by locating it within a particular field of social forces; no cultural analysis of violence detached from specific historical contexts can account for its meaning.

90. Taussig examines mutual constitution of colonizer and colonized through histories and stories of terror and wildness (1987).

REFERENCES

Amnesty International. 1987. *Political Prisoners in Venezuela.* London: Amnesty International Publications.
———. 1988. *Memorandum al gobierno de Venezuela.* London: Amnesty International Publications.
Anderson, Benedict. 1983. *Imagined Communities.* London: Verso.
Arroyo Talavera, Eduardo. 1988. *Elecciones y negociaciones: Los límites de la democracia en Venezuela.* Caracas: Fondo Editorial CONICIT.
Baretta, Silvio, R. Duncan, and John Markoff. 1978. "Civilization and Barbarism: Cattle Frontiers in Latin America." *Comparative Studies in Society and History* 20, 4: 587–605.
Benjamin, Walter. 1969. *Illuminations.* Schocken Books: New York.
Berlant, Lauren. 1988. "Race, Gender, and Nation in *The Color Purple.*" *Critical Inquiry* 14 (Summer): 831–59.

———. 1991. *The Anatomy of National Fantasy: Hawthorne, Utopia, and Everyday Life.* Chicago: University of Chicago Press.

Beroes, Agustin. 1990. *RECADI: La gran estafa.* Caracas: Planeta.

Blank, David Eugene. 1973. *Politics in Venezuela.* Boston: Little, Brown and Co.

Brito Figueroa, Federico. 1966. *Historia económica y social de Venezuela.* Caracas: Universidad Central de Venezuela.

Britto García, Luis. 1988. *La máscara del poder: Del gendarme necesario al demócrata necesario.* Caracas: Alfadil.

Carrera Damas, Germán. 1968. *Boves: Aspectos socioeconómicos de la Guerra de Independencia.* Caracas: Ediciones de la Bibioteca de la Universidad Central.

———. 1972. *El culto a Bolívar.* Caracas: Universidad Central de Venezuela.

Catalá, José Agustín. 1989. *El estallido de febrero.* Caracas: Ediciones Centauro.

Certeau, Michel de. 1986. *Heterologies: Discourse on the Other.* Translated by Brian Massumi. Minneapolis: University of Minnesota Press.

Comaroff, John L. 1989. "Images of Empire, Contests of Conscience: Models of Colonial Domination in South Africa." *American Ethnologist* 16, 4.

Coppens, Walter. 1975. *Los Cuiva de San Estéban de Capanaparo.* Caracas: Fundación La Salle de Ciencias Naturales.

Coronil, Fernando. 1987. The Black El Dorado: Money Fetishism, Democracy and Capitalism in Venezuela. Ph.D. dissertation, The University of Chicago.

———. 1989. "Discovering America Again: The Politics of Selfhood in the Age of Post-Colonial Empires." In *Discourses on Colonialism,* Rolena Adorno and Walter Mignolo, eds. *Dispositio* XIV: 36–39.

Coronil, Fernando and Julie Skurski. 1982. "Reproducing Dependency. Auto Industry Policy and Petrodollar Circulation in Venezuela." *International Organization* 36, 1 (Winter): 61–94.

———. 1991. "Country and City in a Colonial Landscape: Double Discourse and the Geopolitics of Truth in Latin America." In *View from the Border: Essays in Honor of Raymond William,* Dennis Dworkin and Leslie Roman, eds. New York: Routledge.

Dessau, A. 1980. "Realidad social, dimensión histórica y método artístico en Doña Bárbara, de Rómulo Gallegos." In *Relectura de Rómulo Gallegos,* Instituto Internacional de Literatura Iberoamericana. Caracas: Ediciones del Centro de Estudios Latinoaméricanos Rómulo Gallegos.

Ellner, Steven. 1980. "Political Party Dynamics in Venezuela and the Outbreak of Guerrilla Warfare." *Inter-American Economic Affairs* 34, 2 (Autumn): 3–24.

———. 1982. "Populism in Venezuela, 1935–48: Betancourt and 'Acción Democrática.' In Michael L. Conniff, ed., *Latin American Populism in Comparative Perspective.* Albuquerque: University of New Mexico Press.

El Nacional. 1989. *El día que bajaron los cerros.* Caracas: Editorial Ateneo de Caracas.

———. 1990. *27 de Febrero: Cuando la muerte tomó las calles.* Caracas: Editorial Ateneo de Caracas.

Esté, Raúl. 1987. *La masacre de Yumare.* Caracas: Fondo Editorial "Carlos Aponte."

Forgacs, David, ed. 1988. A Gramsci Reader: Selected Writings, 1916–1935. London: Lawrence and Wishart.

Foucault, Michel. 1979. *Discipline and Punish: Birth of the Prison.* New York: Vintage Books.

Fundación John Boulton. 1976. *Política y economía en Venezuela, 1810–1976.* Caracas: Fundación John Boulton.

Gallegos, Rómulo. 1954. *Una posición en la vida.* Mexico: Ediciones Humanismo.

———. 1959. *Doña Bárbara,* in *Obras Completas,* Torno 1. Madrid: Aguilar.

Gilmore, Robert L. 1964. *Caudillism and Militarism in Venezuela, 1810–1910.* Athens: Ohio University Press.

Hein, Wolfgang and Conrad Stenzel. 1973. "The Capitalist State and Underdevelopment in Latin America: The Case of Venezuela." *Kapitalistate* 2.

Hellinger, Daniel. 1985. "Democracy in Venezuela." *Latin American Perspectives* 12: 75–82.

Hennessey, Atis Tair. 1976. "Fascism and Populism in latin America." *Fascism, a Reader's Guide,* Walter Loquer, ed. Berkeley: University of California Press.

Howard, Harrison Sabin. 1976. *Rómulo Gallegos y la revolución burguesa de Venezuela.* Caracas: Monte Avila Editores.

Izard, Miguel. 1981. El *miedo a la revolución.* Madrid: Editorial Universal.

Laclau, Ernest. 1977. *Nationalism, Populism, and Ideology.* London: Verso Books.

Levine, Daniel H. 1973. *Conflict and Political Change in Venezuela.* Princeton: Princeton University Press.

Lombardi, John V. Venezuela. 1971. *The Decline and Abolition of Negro Slavery in Venezuela, 1820–1854.* Westport, Conn.: Greenwood Press.

Lubrano, Aldo and Rosa Haydee Sánchez. 1987. *Del hombre complete a Jaime es como tú. Recuento de un proceso electoral venezolano.* Caracas: Vadell Hermanos.

Lynch, John. 1973. *The Spanish-American Revolutions, 1808–1826.* New York: W. W. Norton.

Magallanes, Manuel Vicente, ed. 1986. *Reformas electorales y partidos políticos.* Caracas: Publicaciones del Consejo Supremo Electoral.

———. 1987. *Sistemas electorales, acceso al sistema politico, y sistema de partidos.* Caracas: Publicaciones del Consejo Supremo Electoral.

Malavé Mata, Héctor. 1987. *Los extravios del poder.* Caracas: Universidad Central de Venezuela.

Maravall, José Antonio. 1986. *Culture of the Baroque: Analysis of a Historical Structure,* Terry Cochran, trans. Minneapolis: University of Minnesota Press.

Marta Sosa, Joaquin. 1984. *Venezuela: Elecciones y transformación social.* Caracas: Ediciones Centauro.

Martz, John. 1966. *Acción Democrática: Evolution of a Modern Political Party in Venezuela.* Princeton: Princeton University Press.

Martz, John and David J. Myers, eds. 1977. *Venezuela: The Democratic Experience.* New York: Praeger Publishers.

Martz, John and Enrique Baloyra. 1976. *Electoral Mobilization and Public Opinion: The Venezuelan Campaign of 1973.* Chapel Hill: University of North Carolina Press.

Matthews, Robert D., Jr. 1977. *Violencia rural en Venezuela, 1840–1858.* Caracas: Editorial Ateneo de Caracas.

Moleiro, Moisés. 1978. *El partido del pueblo.* Valencia: Vadell Hermanos.

Mommer, Bernard. 1983. *Petroleo, renta del suelo e historia.* Mérida: Universidad de los Andes.

———. 1988. *La cuestión petrolera.* Caracas: Fondo Editorial Trópikos.

Nairn, Tom. 1981. *The Break-up of Britain.* London: Verso Edition.

Neruda, Pablo. 1978. *Canto General.* Caracas: Biblioteca Ayacucho.

Oviedo y Baños, José. 1987. *The Conquest and Settlement of Venezuela.* Berkeley: University of California Press.

Piñerúa, Luis. 1988. *Luis Piñerúa: Enfrentamiento con el poder.* Caracas: Ediciones Centauro.

Pino Iturrieta, Elías, ed. 1985. *Juan Vicente Gómez y su época.* Caracas: Monte Avila.

Proceso Político. 1978. *CAP: 5 años.* Caracas: Equipo Proceso Político.

PROVEA. 1989. Informe Annual. Caracas: Ediciones PROVEA.

Rangel, Domingo Alberto. 1973. *Los Mercaderes del voto.* Valencia: Vadell Hermanos.

———. 1982. *Fin de Fiesta.* Valencia: Vadell Hermanos.

Rangel, Domingo Alberto and Pedro Duno. 1979. *La pipa rota: Las elecciones de 1978.* Caracas: Vadell Hermanos.

República de Venezuela. 1989. *Gaceta del Congreso,* XVIII, I (March 1988–January 1989).

Romero, Ambal. 1986. *La miseria del populismo.* Caracas: Ediciones Centauro.

Roseberry, William. 1986. "Images of the Peasant in the Consciousness of the Venezuelan Proletariat." In *Proletarians and Protest,* Michael Hanagan and Charles Stephenson, eds. Westport, Conn.: Greenwood Press.

Sanín. 1989. *Los muertos de la deuda.* Caracas: Ediciones Centauro.

Scharer-Nussberger, Maya. 1979. *Rómulo Gallegos: El mundo inconcluso.* Caracas: Monte Avila Editores.

Segnini, Yolanda. 1982. *La consolidación del régimen de Juan Vicente Gómez.* Caracas: Biblioteca de la Academia Nacional de la Historia.

Silva Michelena, José Agustín, and Heinz Rudolf Sontag. 1979. *El proceso electoral de 1978.* Caracas: Editorial Ateneo de Caracas.

Skurski, Julie. 1994. "The Ambiguities of Authenticity in Latin America: Doña Bárbara and the Construction of National Identity," *Poetics Today* 15.4 (Winter 1994): 605–42.

Sommer, Doris. 1991. *Foundational Fictions: When History was Romance.* Berkeley: University of California Press.

Sosa, Arturo A., ed. 1985. *Ensayos sobre el pensamiento politico positivista venezolano.* Caracas: Ediciones Centauro.

Stallybrass, Peter; Allon White. 1986. *The Politics & Poetics of Transgression.* Ithaca: Cornell University Press.

Taussig, Michael. 1987. *Shamanism, Colonialism, and the Wild Man.* Chicago: The University of Chicago Press.

Thompson, E. P. 1971. "The Moral Economy of the English Crowd in the Eighteenth Century." *Past and Present* 50: 76–136.

United States, Department of State. 1990. "Report to Congress on Principal Human Rights Concerns in Venezuela" (February).

Velásquez, Ramón J., et al. 1986. *Juan Vicente Gómez ante la historia.* San Cristóbal: Biblioteca de autories y temas Tachirenses.

Walton, John. 1989. "Debt, Protest, and the State in Latin America." In Susan Eckstein, ed., *Power and Popular Protest.* Berkeley: University of California Press.

PERIODICALS

The Daily Journal
El Diario de Caracas
El Nacional
El Universal
NOTIcrítica
PROVEA
Punto
Referencias
SIC
Ultimas Noticias
Veneconomía

Fig. 1. A poster commemorating the Amparo contained the elements of the Amparo iconography: the faces of the two survivors, the Arauca River, the boat, and a bamboo cross draped with peasant clothes. Produced by two church-related human rights groups (comision Justicia y Paz and SECORVE), the poster was designed by Cerezo Barredo and is captioned, "for the protection and dignity of man, we will forge justice."

Fig. 2. José Augusto Arias and Wollmer Gregorio Pinilla, survivors of the Amparo massacre, in the Caracas church in which they received sanctuary: Sagrado Corazon, Petare. (Courtesy of Julie Skurski.)

Fig. 3. Relatives of those who died in the Amparo massacre next to the collective grave of the victims. (Courtesy of Francisco Oliveros.)

Fig. 4. Singing the national anthem and waving the flag, workers and barrio residents head toward a commercial district on 27 February 1989, and a policeman joins the march. (Courtesy of José Cohén.)

Fig. 5. People controlled the streets in downtown Caracas by blocking them off. (Courtesy of José Cohén.)

Fig. 6. Once they controlled the streets, people began looting. Here they enter a small store, carrying off whatever they can. (Courtesy of Frasso.)

Fig. 7. During the initial stage of *saqueo popular* (popular looting), the police watched without interfering. (Courtesy of José Cohén.)

Fig. 8. On the second day of looting (28 February 1989), constitutional guarantees were suspended. The military and the police began a heavy armed attack on the looters and barrios. (Courtesy of José Cohén.)

Fig. 9. A body lies in the street as people wait in line for food. (Courtesy of José Cohén.)

Fig. 10. A policeman shoots at looters while others carry away the dead and wounded. (Courtesy of José Cohén.)

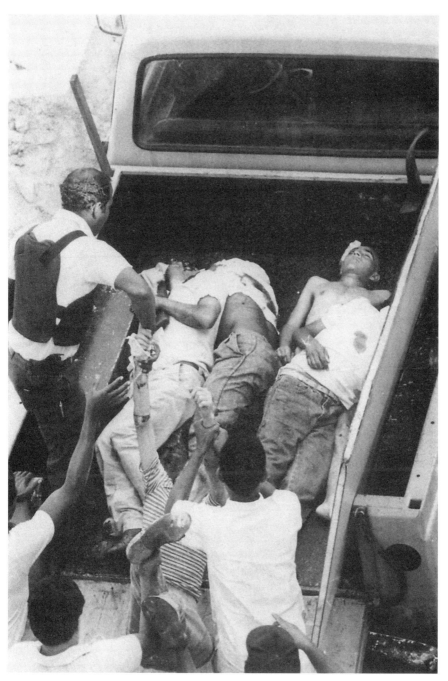

Fig. 11. The police and military heaped the dead bodies in cars and trucks. (Courtesy of José Cohén.)

Mad Mullahs and Englishmen: Discourse in the Colonial Encounter

David B. Edwards

A Passage to India: Winston Churchill on the Afghan Frontier

Winston Churchill was winning money at the Goodwood Races when he heard the news that a tribal uprising had broken out on the northwest frontier of India. Within a matter of hours, the young cavalry officer, who was then on home leave from his regiment in Bangalore, booked return passage on the Indian Mail. He also sent off a telegram to an old family friend, General Sir Bindon Blood, who had been appointed to head the column that was being dispatched to relieve the two garrisons at Malakand and Chakdara then under siege. General Blood had once made a casual promise to Churchill that he would include him in a future campaign, and with this promise in mind Churchill set off for the frontier.[1]

To understand Churchill's excitement, one must consider the circumstances. The year was 1897. That summer all of England was celebrating the Diamond Jubilee of Queen Victoria, who had been on the British throne for twenty-five years.[2] The day before the news of the frontier uprising reached London, Churchill delivered his first public address before a picnic meeting of the Primrose League of Bath, in which his principal theme was maintaining the grand expansion of the empire that had been accomplished during the quarter-century of Victoria's reign. Despite the lamentations of "croakers" who proclaimed that the British empire must someday go the way of Babylon, Carthage, and Rome, Churchill argued that the British government must continue to "pursue that course marked out for us by an all-wise hand and carry out our mission of bearing peace, civilisation and good government to the uttermost ends of the earth."[3]

The uprisings were an opportunity for Churchill to authenticate with action what he had proclaimed in words. Though only a minor conflict in absolute terms, the frontier uprisings had larger implications. "Northern savages, impelled by fanaticism or allured by plunder," had invaded the plains, and it was now time for the imperial power to demonstrate its mettle: "It is impossible for the British government to be content with repelling an injury—it must be avenged. So we in our turn are to invade Afridis & Orakzais and others who have dared violate the Pax Britannica."[4]

On arriving in India, Churchill learned that General Blood had been unable to secure the formal appointment for him that he had sought, but that the general had managed to get him posted to his staff as a war correspondent. With the additional assistance of his mother back in London, Churchill succeeded in getting a newspaper—*The Daily Telegraph*—to publish his dispatches which would chronicle the movements of General Blood's detachment as it went about the business of punishing those tribes that had shown the temerity to rise up against Her Majesty's government. Churchill's correspondence from this period shows his initial disappointment at not being given a formal staff position. In retrospect, however, we can see the advantage that this failure gained him; for despite his noncombatant status, Churchill was still permitted to act in the military capacity of leading men in the field and was awarded official commendations for his exertions. Even more important for a man who saw his future in the political rather than the military arena, his newspaper reports received a wide readership and won him many admirers, including such influential figures as the Prince of Wales and the Prime Minister, Lord Salisbury.[5]

That Churchill's fame as a public figure really began with this frontier disturbance is sufficient to make the episode of interest, but this essay is not concerned with the way in which Churchill's experience on the northwest frontier affected his political career. Neither am I interested in developing a chronology of events nor producing an analysis of the objective causes for the outbreak of hostility against the British government. Rather, I want to focus on the process of historical representation in the colonial context by isolating those elements in imperial accounts that are the most obviously figurative in nature and rhetorical in function.

The procedure of this paper is thus contrary to most historical treatments of colonial encounters. Instead of using documents and narrative accounts to develop a chronological ordering of factual events, I use those same documents and accounts to glean rhetorical elements that are usually excluded from consideration because it is thought that their polemical cast obscures our understanding of what actually happened at a particular time and place. While recognizing the need for the historical facts which allow us to determine the social, economic, and political factors that impel individuals and groups to violent action, I will nevertheless try to show the utility of looking at some of the more artificial or fictive features found in historical sources as a means of grasping the cultural and discursive bases of political action. In keeping with this, Churchill's prose is used not for the determination of "what really happened" but as a mine for metaphors. The analytical strategy that I pursue here is to focus on the controlling metaphors of imperial discourse in order to ascertain what they stood for and signified and how they achieved their desired end.

At the same time, I examine the rhetorical discourse of the imperial protagonist, specifically, the so-called mad mullahs who incited the border tribes to rise up against the colonial invaders and who became the primary focus of British rage and ridicule through their impudence. Here again, the focus of my interest is neither on what happened as that can be reconstructed from native accounts; nor am I concerned with trying to reconstitute the protagonists' point of view. Instead, my concern is with the discourse itself and the organizing figures that give it meaningful coherence and affective force. In particular, I will focus on the logic and significance of the miracle stories that were a vital element in the local understanding of the events of 1897 and that more generally have shown themselves to be a persistent feature in the political rhetoric of those who resist colonization.

Based on this analysis, I present two accounts of a single battle, each of which depicts history in a manner that reflects the cultural preconceptions of their societies as well as the organizing logic deriving from their particular rhetorical styles. Though apparently dissimilar and inassimilable, these separate histories share similar rhetorical features and work toward the common end of representing history in culturally meaningful ways.

The Uprisings of 1897

From the perspective of the local political authorities, the frontier disturbances that Churchill took such pains to witness began in an unexpected way and were initiated from an unexpected source. For some months, British officials had been reporting improved relations with the local people of the Swat valley after several years of hostility. A postal service had been established in the region; a medical dispensary located beside the Chakdara fort was treating patients from the neighboring communities;

and British officers found that they could ride "about freely among the fierce hill men" and were even being "invited to settle many disputes, which would formerly have been left to armed force."[6]

In early July, however, the first hints of disaffection began to appear. The native markets were reported to be in turmoil over rumors that "great events were impending."[7] At the center of these reports was a religious mendicant known as the "Mad Fakir" or "Mad Mullah," who was openly proclaiming the commencement of a holy war and the imminent occurrence of miraculous events:

> About the 20th and 21st the Fakir began giving out that he had heavenly hosts with him, that his mission was to turn the British off the Malakand and out of Peshawar, as our rule of 60 years there was up. He claimed to have been visited by all deceased Fakirs, who told him the mouths of our guns and rifles would be closed, and that our bullets would be turned to water; that he had only to throw stones into the Swat river, and each stone he threw would have on us the effect of a gun. He gave out that he had no need of human assistance, as the heavenly hosts with him were sufficient.[8]

On the afternoon of 26 July, the Mad Fakir set off to attack the British garrisons at Chakdara and Malakand. Followed at first by a few of his fellow religious mendicants (*faqir*) and a handful of teenage boys, the Mad Fakir attracted new supporters with each village he passed—some five thousand in all by the time he reached the fort at Chakdara. Although their weaponry consisted mostly of primitive flintlocks, swords, and staves, the followers of the Fakir mounted an assault that lasted seven days and might have led to the capture of the Chakdara garrison had it not been for the arrival of General Blood's relief column on the second of August.

The timely appearance of the cavalry succeeded in breaking the Chakdara siege, but no sooner had this uprising subsided than others began. In the Mohmand territory, west of Swat, "a priest of great age and of peculiar holiness, known to fame as the Hadda Mullah," led his followers in an attack against the Hindu-controlled market at Shankargar and the neighboring fort at Shabqader.[9] Further south, the Akka Khel Mullah led Afridi tribesmen from the Tirah against British installations protecting the Khyber Pass while other religious leaders mounted similar operations against posts in the Kurram Valley and along the Samana Ridge.

Although none of these attacks succeeded, they were worrisome to the British administration because of their apparent coordination. Since the infamous Mutiny of 1857, India had been free of widespread insurrection but the passing of time and the ensuing peace had failed to assuage the residual fear inspired by that episode. During the travails of 1857 one of the saving graces for the British had been the failure of the northern tribes to join the general upheaval; it had been mainly concluded from this experience that, however tough an opponent the tribes were on their home ground, their potential danger to the Raj was mitigated by their inability to make common cause with their fellow tribes outside their immediate environs. Such was the received wisdom, but here were these notoriously fractious tribes mounting coordinated assaults on well-fortified garrisons and demonstrating a degree of organization unprecedented in the history of British rule.

In his various reports from the frontier, Churchill played on the deep-seated fears of his audience by presenting a picture of savage tribesmen possessed by an extraordinary fervor. This portrayal certainly made for good reading and a devoted readership; it also gave Churchill—an otherwise insignificant junior officer—an uncommon platform for espousing his views on the way in which the government should be running its operation in India. He expressed these views in the context of explaining why it was that the tribes had chosen to rise up against British rule when it had appeared that political relations were on the mend and the material conditions of life for the tribes were so clearly superior since the advent of a British presence in the region. In Churchill's view, a number of outside factors had first to be taken into account to understand the timing of the uprisings, such as the recent Turkish victory over the Greek army (which was said to be encouraging hopes of a Muslim revival) and the seizure of Aden and the Suez Canal (which was said to be hampering British efforts to bring troop reinforcements from Europe).

These external events "united to produce a 'boom' in Mohammedanism" that local religious leaders quickly exploited. Their motivation was not difficult to discern: They had the "quick intelligence" to recognize that "contact with civilisation assails the superstition, and credulity, on which the wealth and influence of the Mullah depend."[10] So long as British arms produced security in the region and an increase in trade and communication with the outside world, the authority of the mullahs was bound to suffer. Therefore, it was critical for them to find a pretext to fight back and reassert their former authority among their tribal followers.

The success of this endeavor was not solely the product of outside forces. Local conditions had also to be favorable. In particular, the exertions by local religious leaders required an additional catalyst, specifically the appearance of an extraordinary figure—a Mad Mullah—who could transform the propaganda of the local mullahs into popular action: "What Peter the Hermit was to the regular bishops and cardinals of the Church, the Mad Mullah was to the ordinary priesthood of the Afghan border. A wild enthusiast, convinced alike of his Divine mission and miraculous powers, he preached a crusade, or Jehad, against the infidel."[11]

Given the numerous rational disincentives to rebellion, the only logical reason why the tribes would choose to act against their own best interests was "fanaticism," a social condition set in motion by the combined actions of a visionary who "fired the mine" and the backstage machinations of "crafty politicians" like the Mullah of Hadda who "seized the opportunity and fanned the flame."[12] Thus, at the instigation of the religious leadership, "a vast, but silent agitation was begun." "Messengers passed to and fro among the tribes. Whispers of war, a holy war, were breathed to a race intensely passionate and fanatical. Vast and mysterious agencies, the force of which are incomprehensible to rational minds, were employed. The tribes were taught to expect prodigious events."[13]

Central to the appeal of the visionary leader was the people's belief that he could perform miracles. "Had the 'Mad Mullah' called on them to follow him to attack Malakand and Chakdara they would have refused. Instead he worked miracles."[14] Some of these "miracles" have readily discernible explanations. For instance, the claim that the impoverished Fakir could feed thousands was due to the steady stream of guests who visited him each day and brought with them small offerings of food or money that allowed him to continually replenish his stores. Other miracles, such as the Fakir's claim that he could make himself invisible, were effective simply because of the "extraordinary credulity" of the people and the Fakir's own remarkable skill at manipulating this credulity and making it appear that his power derived entirely from otherworldly sources: "Finally he declared that he would destroy the infidel. He wanted no help. No one should share the honours. The heavens would open and an army would descend. The more he protested he did not want them the more exceedingly they came."[15]

Miracles occupy an important place in the development of Churchill's polemic. For him, the existence of religious leaders claiming miraculous powers and the readiness of the local people to believe such claims provides irrefutable evidence of the barbaric nature of the adversary and their constitutional predisposition to fanaticism in the conduct of political relations. "Were [the tribes] amenable to logical reasoning, the improvement in their condition and the strength of their adversaries would have convinced them of the folly of an outbreak. But in a land of fanatics common sense does not exist." Given this absence of rational calculation, it is "useless, and often dangerous, to argue with an Afghan," and since "his actions interfere with the safety of our Empire he must be crushed.[16]

Miracles and Metaphors

Central to Churchill's polemic—developed from his explanation of the causes of the uprisings of 1897 and his own conclusions as to the appropriate response of the British government—is the use of miracles as evidence of the fanatical nature of the local people. Establishing the enemy as fanatical denies him moral status and affords those whose moral superiority is thus affirmed a free hand in defending their interests. The analytical challenge presented by Churchill's discourse is whether it is possible to reclaim the moral status that has been thus revoked. One way to accomplish this reclamation is to decipher the meaning of miracles or at least begin to gauge the significance of miracles in the culture of the frontier tribes.

According to Islamic theological doctrines (to which all local cultural beliefs refer at least in part), there are two kinds of miracles: those associated with the prophets, and those associated with the saints, which are called *karamat. Karamat* are "the miraculous gifts and graces with which Allah surrounds, protects and aids his saints."[17] The existence of miracles presupposes the willingness of God to intervene in human affairs and also the limits of human knowledge of the world in which they live. Thus, it is believed that in addition to the world of appearance (*zahir*) there is a second, hidden realm known as the *batin.* Outside of God and his prophets, only God's "friends" (the *aulia*) have been vouchsafed personal knowledge of the *batin;* they alone among living men have been endowed with the capacity to mediate between the realms of *zabir* and *batin* through the performance of miracles.

Despite the fact that belief in miracles is a common feature of Muslim cultures, few scholars have paid much attention to the subject; most references tend to be anecdotal rather than analytical. One reason for this lacuna is without doubt the difficulty of making sense of miracles and negotiating between the subjective experience of those who believe in miracles as actual events in the world and the observer's skepticism that such things could take place. A way out of this impasse is offered by Michael Gilsenan, who has focused on the way in which saintly miracles operate in and through popular discourse. A central point in his analysis is that miracles are experienced first as stories, whatever they may be in reality. These stories, generally "endless versions and varieties of the 'the same' miracle," comprise what is known of the *batin* and reveal to the believer recurring instances of God's presence in human affairs.[18] The ubiquity of miracles in everyday discourse creates a predisposition to interpret events as reflections of a non-empirical causality, so that everyday congruencies of circumstance that might normally be dismissed as coincidences, luck, or happenstance are continually subjected to scrutiny for evidence of the involvement of some external agency. Simply stated, saints and the miracles they perform provide "a scheme of interpretation by means of which [people] explain and apprehend the multiple hazards and changes that play so great a part in their lives."[19]

Gilsenan's approach may not tell us what miracles are, but it does suggest a comparison by which we can bridge the difference between cultural perspectives. That comparison is between miracles and metaphors. Like miracles, metaphors mediate between discontinuous domains of experience, make the inchoate subject to the determination of the familiar, and generally provide a moral ground to the experience of events.[20] The suggestion that miracles are like metaphors should not of course be taken as a statement as to the empirical status of miracles; rather, the seeking out of likeness is at least in part an analytical response to the impulse to make miracles conform to our parameters of rationality by saying what they are. Being unable to say what miracles are, we are on safer ground when we offer suggestions as to what they might be *like* in our cultural domain. The objective here is to find a way of translating between separate cultural discourses without sacrificing the integrity of either.

One difficulty in making a connection between miracles and metaphors has to do with our own limited notion of what metaphors are and how they operate, which tends to reduce metaphoric relationships to statements of mere likeness. The effectiveness of metaphor stems less from the similarity between two objects than in the mutability of perception itself. Metaphors have the power to transform the real and make it seem to be something other than what it had always seemed before. They achieve their effect by violating the separation of objects and physical processes.

They disrupt the categories by which we organize the world and, in doing so, fuel the suspicion that the world may not be as it appears and that our knowledge of it is less than what it should be. Thus, the potency of metaphor derives from the possibility that a resemblance recognized on the surface of language will cause a fundamental transformation in the way we perceive, organize, and express our experience of the world.

Miracles have much the same effect but begin from the place metaphors arrive at—that appearances are not what they seem. Metaphors seek relationship on the level of appearance and go through appearance to the more fundamental connections linking discrete phenomena in the world. Miracles, however, assume the falsity of appearance and demonstrate to those who believe in their possibility that the world exceeds our understanding. Thus, while metaphors suggest that appearances are illusionary and, consequently, that our control over the world is less than we believe it to be, miracles assume the deception of appearance and the forfeiture of control as a condition of being in the world.

Another basis of comparison between metaphors and miracles has to do with their placement as figures of speech in social discourse. Following the lead of Kenneth Burke, a number of scholars have examined the role of metaphor in political rhetoric over the last fifteen years; their work has led to a profound sense of the ways in which figurative language does not "just express the pertinence of certain cultural axioms to given social conditions, it provides the semantic conditions through which actors deal with that reality."[21] Instead of using this body of work as a point of departure, however, I want to refer to another source which, while less familiar, allows us to keep our focus on the nineteenth-century context of events. This source is an unpublished and unfinished paper entitled, "The Scaffolding of Rhetoric," that Winston Churchill was writing during the summer of 1897 on the nature of effective political oratory.[22]

In Churchill's view, the "direct, though not the admitted, object" of political rhetoric is "to allay the commonplace influences and critical faculties" of an audience. One primary attribute which an orator needs for accomplishing this objective is a "striking presence" caused, for example, by a slight speech impediment or even a physical deformity. It matters also that the orator himself believes—if only momentarily—in what he is saying: "The orator is the embodiment of the passions of the multitude. Before he can inspire them with any emotion he must be swayed by it himself."[23]

Besides the personal qualities of the speaker, the quality of the speech itself is significant, and in this regard Churchill points to a number of elements in a speech which may collectively cause an audience to be affected. These elements include the correctness of diction, rhythm of phrasing, and the overall accumulation of argument that creates a coherent picture and allows the audience to "anticipate the conclusion." More important than these factors, however, is the use of an "apt analogy" through which the orator can "translate an established truth into simple language" or "adventurously aspire to reveal the unknown." While admitting that "argument by analogy leads to conviction rather than to proof, and has often led to glaring error," Churchill discerns that the reason why analogies are so effective in oratory is that they "favor the belief that the unknown is only an extension of the known: that the abstract and the concrete are ruled by similar principles: that the finite and the infinite are homogeneous. An apt analogy connects or appears to connect these distant spheres."[24]

Using Churchill's analysis as a point of departure, we can identify certain similarities between the rhetorical principles governing traditional political discourse and those governing the charismatic discourse of the Mad Fakir. The first matter to consider in this regard is the person of the Mad Fakir himself.[25] While we don't have any evidence as to the appearance of the Fakir, we can tell something about his identity from the names by which he was known. The first of these names was *sartor faqir* ("bareheaded *faqir*"), apparently referring to the fact that he did not wear a turban or other head-covering and probably indicating that he was unconcerned with the usual markers of social propriety. The second name was *lewanai faqir* ("crazy *faqir*"), which does not convey the same sense as that intended by the British when they referred to Muslim leaders as "mad." Thus, rather than being thought of as "irrational" or "fanatical," the Fakir was believed to be subject to a species of "madness" or "intoxication" brought on when a holy man comes in proximity to God and is overwhelmed by the experience.

As to the identifying features of the Mad Fakir, British intelligence records don't contain a great deal of information on the personality of the Fakir or his life prior to the summer of 1897, but they do show a man who lived outside the boundaries of normal social interaction. Thus, for example, we know that before he drew the fire of the British the Fakir had managed to antagonize local mullahs by his declarations that certain of their religious teachings were wrong; he was also apparently ostracized at one point for failing to follow local custom by avenging his son when he was murdered in a dispute. The Fakir was also thought to have traveled extensively, perhaps to Central Asia or Arabia, and was rumored to have met with the Afghan Amir in Kabul. Whether or not these stories are true, they contribute to a picture of a man who was different from others in his society, who went places that other people did not go, and who acted in ways other people did not act. The significance of this is not merely that we are dealing with someone who, in Churchill's terms, had a "striking presence," but who also occupied a traditional sort of role that made him fully capable of performing the miraculous acts claimed by him.

In Swat, as elsewhere in the Indian subcontinent, the religious mendicant is a familiar figure on market streets and in the vicinity of shrines. Most are ignored, except when they pester passers-by for donations; many people feel resentment toward them, doubting the sincerity of their religious conviction and secretly suspecting that most of those who become *faqir*s do so to avoid work and smoke hashish. At the same time, however, not all of those who distrust the motives of *faqir*s would be openly willing to declare their opinions of the matter; and the reason for this hesitancy is at least in part that there are too many stories that attest to the unhappy fate of those who abuse devotees of God.

Thus, as portrayed in popular legend, the *faqir* (also referred to as a *dervish* or *malang*) is presented as precisely the sort of person we presume the Mad Fakir to have been: an outsider of indeterminate background and unpredictable demeanor who flouts local pieties and fails to show proper respect for those in power. Traditional narratives centered around *faqir*s typically begin with the appearance of a stranger who performs some action that incurs the anger of a local despot who tries to punish the miscreant. Before he can accomplish this end, however, roles are reversed; and the ruler becomes the one who is punished, usually through some miraculous event that brings about his demise.[26]

The obvious moral of such stories is, first, that however abject and despised a *faqir* might appear, this very same person might be one of God's chosen. Consequently, whatever one's feelings of disdain, it is better to emulate the wise men of the legends who give alms and food to beggars and thereby keep clear of God's wrath. The other implication of these popular tales is that it is more often the powerful who are at fault in God's eyes than those who eschew wealth and comfort. God is forever aware of the actions of men, and his punishment of those who abuse their positions is certain and may be inflicted through the most unlikely of agents. Whether or not he intended to draw on this legacy, the Fakir was able to attract a large number of adherents to his cause in part because of the existence of these paradigmatic stories of *faqirs* combating despotic authority. By claiming "to have been visited by all deceased Fakirs," the Fakir called attention to a cultural category and his presumptive status as representative of all those who have devoted themselves to the mendicant life in the past and the present.[27]

Similarly, in predicting that heavenly hosts would descend, that bullets would be turned to water, and that a pot of rice would feed a multitude, he was not "making up" stories but rather drawing on and adapting narrative traditions with which most people were familiar. Thus, the miracles the Fakir claimed for the future represented events that had happened in the past; this gave them a historical and familiar character that made them believable in the first instance. At the same time, miracles function like "apt analogies" in political rhetoric in that they "allay commonplace influences and critical faculties" by making the unknown "an extension of the known." The essential talent of all great political orators is their ability to "appeal to the everyday knowledge of the hearer" in such a way that the hearer will be tempted "to decide the problems that have baffled his powers of reason by the standard of the nursery and the heart."[28] The particular genius of the charismatic religious leader is his ability to make a preexisting belief in miracles the basis for how people apprehend the reality around them.

Like metaphors, miracle stories make concrete but inchoate experience subordinate to the abstract design of the eternal, while also making the eternal immediate and perceptible in the concrete. When reality is seen through the lens of miracles, transient events are experienced as coherent and directed towards the fulfillment of a larger design unfolding in time. Miracles thus convey a sense of unity to events that are normally experienced as discontinuous and enable those sensible to the continuity of events to see themselves as part of an ongoing story moving toward its necessary and predetermined conclusion. It matters not that those who believe in the miracles do not understand the nature of the eternal, which in any case is beyond their comprehension. What matters is that the situation before them—a situation which has no apparent solution—is seen not only to have an outcome but a self-evident one.

Extending our comparison of miracles and metaphors, we can say that the efficacy of both figures derives not only from their capacity for making people "see" the world in a certain way but also from the fact that they implicate their audiences in their own resolution. This is to say that both types of figures carry with them an implicit sense of moral culpability, so that those who "see" the world anew also "feel" themselves as responsible for achieving the outcome predicated by the figure. An example of the moral determinance of metaphor can be seen in the following dispatch written by Churchill and published in *The Daily Telegraph:* "Starting with the assumption that our Empire in India is worth holding, and admitting the possibility that others besides ourselves might wish to possess it, it obviously becomes our duty to adopt measures for its safety. . . . The most natural way of preventing an enemy from entering a house is to hold the door and windows; and the general consensus of opinion is that to secure India it is necessary to hold the passes of the mountains."[29]

The Londoner reading his newspaper over breakfast may know nothing of India, but he recognizes the imperative of defending what is his and taking reasonable precautions to prevent others from getting the idea that his property could be theirs. What he does not know about India is excluded by the figure. The weight of this familiar knowledge from the realm of his own experience leads him to ignore what he does not understand—India—and to accept the logic of similarity over the mystery of difference. In this way, the metaphor serves literally to domesticate what is strange while also pointing to the moral necessity of pursuing a particular line of political action that derives from the sense of inevitability imparted by the figure.

The sense of inevitability is contained in two additional metaphors Churchill quoted in his paper, "The Scaffolding of Rhetoric," and which again have to do with the discourse of imperial control:

They (Frontier wars) are but the surf that marks the edge and advance of the wave of civilization.
Our rule in India is, as it were, a sheet of oil spread over and keeping free from storms a vast and profound ocean of humanity.[30]

The first of these, penned by Lord Salisbury, then prime minister, uses nature to inculcate a sense of the futility of opposing an inexorable process—the advance of civilization. Never mind that the metaphor also implies that civilization is static rather than progressive; the dominant image is of the wave advancing against ineffective resistance. The second example, attributed to Lord Randolph Churchill, implicates the same natural phenomenon but to a different end. Civilization is not nature here, but the element that tames and subdues nature (i.e., the uncivilized peoples of India).

While we might be tempted to dismiss these analogies as mere "figures of speech," it is clear that such figures empower those who use them, and do so in a way that is not much different from miracles. Thus, both the miracles of the Mad Fakir and the analogies of the young Tory present to the imagination of those responsive to them "a series of vivid impressions which are replaced before they can be too closely examined and vanish before they can be assailed."[31] Along with the impressions they create, the figures also engender a sense of providence operating in ineluctable and inexorable ways in human affairs; this in turn inculcates an attitude both of anticipation for what will happen in the future and of personal culpability for the proper resolution of the situation framed by the figure.

Tales of Jarobi Glen

In the preceding analysis we have sought to define a ground of intelligibility between two very different modes of political discourse. One central feature of this analysis has been a consideration of the relationship between miracles and metaphors as the organizing figures for these two modes of discourse. The desired effect of this exercise has been to make that which is strange familiar (miracles after all are not so different from metaphors) while also estranging what has become too familiar (metaphors may actually partake of the miraculous). In the final section, I want to put intelligibility to the test by considering how two accounts of the same battle told from opposite points of view reflect the discursive properties of their cultures and, more particularly, how miracles and metaphors function in each.

The histories to be examined involve the final encounter between British troops and the principal ally of the Mad Fakir: the Mullah of Hadda. The first account, which tells of the British traverse of the Mohmand tribal territory toward the end of the summer of 1897, is taken from a chapter entitled, "A Mohmand Paradise: Home of the Hadda Mullah." This chapter was part of a history of the uprisings written by H. Woosnam Mills, one of Churchill's fellow correspondents, for the *Civil & Military Gazette* of Lahore.[32] The second account tells the story of how the Mullah of Hadda dealt with the British troops that had been sent to capture him. This story is a local interpretation of the concluding events of 1897 and was told to me by Maulavi Ahmad Gul Ruhani, the son of one of the Mullah's principal deputies and now an Afghan refugee in Pakistan.

The events described took place towards the end of September. The

Swat uprising had collapsed over a month earlier, and the Swat Fakir was in the upper reaches of the Swat valley to which he had fled to avoid capture by British troops. After relieving the Chakdara and Malakand garrisons, General Blood's column—designated as the Malakand Field Force—assumed the role of a punitive expedition. In this capacity, General Blood's troops first secured the submission of the villages of lower Swat directly involved in the siege on the Malakand and Chakdara forts. They then turned west to force the surrender of the Mohmand and Mahmund tribes, which had joined in supporting the Hadda Mullah in his attack on the Shabqader fort. Blood's Malakand Field Force was joined in the field by a second column—the Mohmand Field Force under General Elles—that had marched towards the Mohmand country from the south. The explicit objective of the combined operation was to disperse and punish the tribes that had undertaken the assault on the market at Shankargar. Beyond this, the British contingent also hoped to apprehend the author of their discontents—the Mullah of Hadda—in his home village of Jarobi, which was located in the most inaccessible part of the Mohmand territory virtually astride the border between India and Afghanistan.

As they marched toward the Mullah's stronghold, the British had encountered stiff resistance while crossing the Bedmanai Pass, some miles from Jarobi. In the final approach, their only difficulty was the fatigue induced by stifling heat and "tier upon tier of dusty waste-stretches." The aridity and barrenness of the landscape was sufficiently oppressive to cause the author to wonder if, in fact, the much fabled "Jarobi, the valley of the Mohmands, which overflows with milk and honey" was "but a myth."[33] Such doubts were assuaged, however, upon crossing the pass leading into the undefended valley.

Surrounded by forests of walnut and pine and graced with green fields of Indian corn, the village of Jarobi stood on a knoll with a deep grove at its foot and beneath "wooded spurs which rose away from behind it melting away into the bleak barrenness of the separating range." Before the troops could proceed into the valley, however, the drama of a moment long anticipated was suddenly and strangely interrupted: "As the first white men shaded their eyes to the scene, the elements joined, and as if in disapprobation of the sacrilegious advance, dense storm clouds rolled over the peaks and vivid lightning played above the sacred spot, while the artillery of heaven reverberated across the peaceful valley; an ominous forecast of the rude awakening which was about to come."[34]

The odd congruence of natural and human events did not deter the col-

umn from continuing with its mission. At the moment that the monsoon
was gathering above them, miners from the Bengal Sappers began their
work of destruction, first blowing up the tower that commanded the
entrance to the valley and then proceeding on to the village itself, which
they also intended to burn. As they began to climb the knoll on which the
village stood, the threatening storm finally broke: "The heavy clouds
brought up rain and hail, and a bitter wind chilled all to the bone."[35]

To the accompaniment of thunder and lightning, the miners entered a
village that was virtually but not entirely deserted. Five swordsmen
secreted in the Mullah's mosque charged out at the advance party but were
dispatched in a fusillade of answering fire. While a detachment of the Sappers "applied the fatal torch," other troops continued on past the village
towards a defile through which the Mullah was believed to have made his
retreat. Here, at the narrowest point in the gorge, they came under serious
attack for the first time. Artillery support was called up, which briefly
"made beautiful practice on the hills," but since darkness was approaching
and "the main object of the expedition had been attained," the retire was
sounded. Harassing fire did not prevent an orderly retreat, and "by 5-30
the whole of the troops engaged were in camp."[36]

All that remained before "the curtain was finally rung down" was for
General Blood's troops to conduct a "Political walk-round." For the most
part, this consisted of a demonstration of force and intimidation, one
aspect of which was the prying loose of money, arms, grain, and forage
from tribes that "owed" them for having acted in a hostile fashion towards
the government of India.[37] Hostages were also taken from those tribes failing to turn over the stipulated penalties, new passes and routes were recon-
noitered; and all the while an orderly and unhurried retreat was negotiated. On 7 October, the Mohmand Field Force returned to Peshawar.
While the expedition was judged a complete success, the one mitigating
failure was their inability to capture the Mullah of Hadda himself. Even
here, however, there was consolation in the form of "a good story" that
was told of the Mullah's fall from grace: "[D]uring the attack on the Bad-
manai Pass, the Hadda Mullah was seen personally riding among the
flying foe, but his pony fell in an awkward place, and they put him into a
litter and carried him off. There were women close by, refugees from the
villages, who cursed him in their choicest tongue for the troubles he had
brought upon them."[38]

Before commenting on the preceding history, let us turn to the second
account that has been preserved, this one among the Mullah's followers.

The narrative was recounted to me by an Afghan refugee living in Pakistan, who is the son of one of the Mullah of Hadda's chief disciples and is himself a religious scholar of some renown. The story was told during the course of an interview in Peshawar in 1984 and was introduced with the statement that it was a story "we have heard from our elders." "One day the late respected Najm-ud-Din Akhundzada [the Mullah of Hadda], may peace be upon him, gathered [his forces] in Jarobi, and from there they attacked the English and assaulted them and did jihad against them. The English were faced with great trouble because of him. Finally, they concentrated their forces near [Jarobi].

In this rendition of events, the British commander is said to have met with the elders of the village and threatened to destroy Jarobi and kill their women and children if they did not surrender the Mullah. This caused them "great worry, grief, and sorrow," which led the elders to seek counsel from the Mullah himself. On being told the situation, the Mullah responded that he would go and sit on a nearby mountain. They should inform the British commander that he had been sent away and that it was now "between you and him." The Hadda Mullah then went to the mountain and began to recite his *nawafil* [voluntary] prayers as the village elders relayed his message to the British commander.

The commander ordered his soldiers—foot and cavalry—to go and surround *Sahib-i Mobarak* [blessed master] and take him alive and bring him. From there, the English forces moved and were running and finally had almost reached him. The God of the universe, in answer to his blessed prayers—he was busy humbly and secretly praying to God, he was praying to his only Creator, he was busy and prayed to him and took refuge in God—by the blessing of God, bees swarmed down on the English, and the bees attacked, and on every one of their soldiers, [there were] hundreds of bees and they stung them. Some fell from their horses, and some fell while running, and some died, and some fled. Thus, they faced defeat, and they came and told their commander that, "We were faced with this kind of plague and disaster that all of our bodies, from poison, how painful, and we couldn't reach there. God sent bees against us."

Faced with this severe defeat, there was nothing for the British commander to do but order his troops to carry away the dead bodies of those killed by the bees. The story ends with the commander's admission of defeat: "Against this *faqir*, who has spent his life in the clothes of poverty and piety, our power cannot affect him even if there is no one with him and he is unarmed. This is truly a *faqir* with *karamat*."

The above narrative and a few similar versions that I have also recorded appear to represent the only generally preserved accounts of the uprising of 1897. There are no dates attached to the story; the only reason we know that the narrative concerns the same events as those in the first account is the setting in Jarobi and the involvement of the Mullah of Hadda. Older informants who have been asked to recount additional stories from this time that they might have heard from their elders do not recall any others. This is the story they remember; while there are significant variations in how the story is told and what elements are emphasized, the miracle of the bees is the central event in all of the versions.

In considering the relationship between these two narratives, it is appropriate to begin by mentioning the elements that they share in common. This would include the following "facts." The British came to Jarobi to capture the Mullah, but he was absent from the village. After a confrontation in the mountains outside the village, the British retired from the valley without capturing the Mullah. Finally, both accounts come to closure through an act of submission on the part of the other. The most intriguing element common to both narratives is certainly the "natural" event that occurs, for it is in this phenomenon that we recognize that indeed this is the same moment differently cast in two forms of remembrance. It is also in the representation of this "storm" that we see the most telling difference in the cultural perspectives of the protagonists.

Thus, for Mills, the onset of a violent hailstorm at the moment of their arrival at "the promised land . . . overflowing with milk and honey" is given an ironic significance. The odd synchronicity of these natural and human events leads the author to introduce the notion of a supernatural intelligence conspiring to resist "the sacrilegious advance." The "artillery of heaven" however is no match for the "destroying cartridge" of the Sappers, and the (super)natural intervention proves to be no more than "an ominous forecast" of the more potent "awakening" about to come through the agency of the Mohmand Field Force. The effect of this passage is to appropriate and, through irony, dissolve the Islamic sacred world view within the framework of the rational. In the second narrative irony is also implied, but in relation to those who believe themselves to be all-powerful while being in fact powerless before God. This is demonstrated in the miraculous defeat of the enemy forces and then elaborated in the final epitaph, which has the British commander—the traditional Islamic despot recast in colonial uniform—admit his helplessness before a poor and humble *faqir.*

Lifting the Veil: The Lives of a Metaphor

The different metaphysical principles embodied in the two narratives can both be exemplified by reference to the same organizing figure—one that conveys very different meanings to each side of the confrontation. That figure is contained in the phrase, "lifting the veil" or "lifting the *purdah.*" On one level, this figure expresses the moral duty of civilized society (reprising Churchill's Primrose League speech) to bear "peace, civilization and good government to the uttermost ends of the earth." Since the tribes lived in what Churchill termed "the unpenetrated gloom of barbarism," it was incumbent upon those blessed by enlightenment to push back the curtain of irrationality and superstition and dispel the gloom. This figure also symbolizes the more immediate and expedient act of asserting political dominion. This sense of the figure is illustrated by H. Woosnam Mills' use of the phrase at the end of his account of the Mohmand expedition: "As far as the Baizais [Mohmands] are concerned, they never can boast that their *purdah* has not been lifted, that a Sirkar's force has not swept through their country, and in accordance with the nature of things, it may be fairly presumed that they will keep clear of raids in our territory for many a long day."[39]

Similar instances of the metaphor could be cited. In each, the overt meaning of the phrase has to do with the political division of space between tribal and British realms and the inviolability that had previously characterized the tribal territories. The figure conveys the sense of overcoming an impediment to imperial rule but does so in terms that are culturally significant to those over whom the colonial power seeks to assert its authority. Specifically, it appropriates the emotionally charged symbol of *purdah,* the cloth screen or veil used to conceal women and the private space of the home from the public gaze of outsiders. As employed by Mills, the nature of the appropriation is clearly spelled out: invading tribal space is an act of penetrating private space and, as such, an affront to tribal honor that is equivalent to having one's domestic quarters inspected by strangers. The British troops are the ones in a position to boast. Their force is the greater one; the tribe's must endure the shame of trespass.

By construing the invasion in these terms, colonial writers like Mills were, of course, putting the best slant on the political reality of limited rule. Despite their superiority in weapons and organization, the British found permanent occupation of the tribal territories to be impractical, if not impossible. Consequently, the effectiveness of campaigns such as the Mohmand expedition depended as much on the exercise of symbolic domination as on actual control. In this instance, symbolic domination was achieved through the act of trespass itself, which was also an act of observation. As Foucault demonstrated, observation is both a condition and an expression of power; but here the particular salience of observation is in relation to the tribal context—a context in which public and private space are strictly defined. Trespass is an offense requiring armed retaliation, and the sight of a restricted other can by itself constitute a capital offense.[40] Although few British officers were familiar with the cultural dynamics of honor among the frontier tribes, they were well aware that tribesmen, like their own subject populations in India, placed considerable importance on the sanctity of *purdah;* they also realized that the act—figurative or literal—of "lifting the veil" was a way of empowering themselves (in their own terms) by unmanning their adversaries (in theirs).

That is one way to interpret the metaphor of "lifting the veil." But there is another, and it is this other interpretation which allows us to understand how the Mullah and his followers achieved their own symbolic victory during the encounter in Jarobi glen. This alternative interpretation derives from the mystical significance of the phrase "lifting the veil" as it has been developed in such works of Sufi philosophy as the eleventh-century treatise *Kashflal-Mahjub* by 'Ali bin Uthman al-Hujwiri (better known in the subcontinent as Data Ganj Baksh). The title of this treatise, which can be translated as "The Unveiling of the Veiled," refers to the process by which mankind can be made aware of "the subtlety of spiritual truth."[41]

As expounded in this text, humans exist in a state of ignorance, or "veiledness," in which they are unable to comprehend God's presence in the world. Only the prophets and "God's saints and His chosen friends" have personal knowledge of God. For them, the veil has been lifted and the truth revealed. However, God's saints must live among men, and because men have a tendency to misconstrue God and worship that which is other than God, the saints must veil their own nature from those around them. Only in extreme circumstances—such as when a saint is ridiculed or endangered or when God's own preeminence is profaned—does God perform what are perceived as miracles through the agency of His saint. "A miracle cannot be manifested except in the state of unveiledness (*kashf*), which is the rank of proximity (*qurb*)."[42] Therefore, saints must leave the state of humanity and approach God. When they do so, the veil obscuring their relationship to the divine is pulled back and, for a brief instant, God acts through them to demonstrate His own dominance over human affairs.

Although caution must be exercised in making connections between the universe of learned writings and the domain of political relations, it can be argued that the figure of the lifted veil has a paradigmatic significance informing the particular story we are considering and reflects in a more general way the relationship between the divine and worldly realms and the role of the saints in mediating this relationship. In the story of the bees, divine intervention is brought about when the Mullah moves outside the bounds of human society to devote himself completely to God. The narrator of the story notes several times that the Mullah was absorbed in worshipping God, and he specifically mentions that the Mullah was engaged in *"nawafil"* prayers—a significant detail. Given the narrator's background as a religious scholar, it is reasonable to suppose that he is familiar with the well-known tradition from the life of Prophet Mohammad, according to which God told Mohammad: "When My servant seeks to approach Me through super[er]ogatory works, I entirely love him. And when I love him I become the hearing through which he heareth, the sight through which he seeth, the hand with which he graspeth, the foot with which he walketh."[43]

This tradition is a principal part of the evidence for the belief that men can enter into a state of "nearness" to God through acts of supererogatory worship (*qurb an-nawafil*) and that God will show His love to those who enter this state through the performance of miracles. Thus, by engaging in *nawafil* prayers, the Hadda Mullah entered the state of "unveiledness" within which a miracle could be manifested and the Mullah's power as God's "friend" revealed to others.[44]

This act of mystical unveiling is the central focus of the second historical narrative, as the political act of lifting the veil is of the first. Thus juxtaposed, the unveiling in the first becomes an ironic counterpoint of the second, for the British attempt to lift the veil concealing the Mullah provides the condition for the revelation of God's miraculous control over human affairs. This is, of course, quite contrary to what British officials intended to accomplish through their punitive campaign, and it leads to the conclusion that if it is power that allows the British to create their image of the mad mullah, then it is the capacity of these same mullahs to use the condition of powerlessness to recreate themselves or at least to be retrospectively recreated through the transformative vehicle of miracle stories.

The British effort to make the Mullah visible and subject to the constraints of their metaphors, their plots, and their terms of narrative closure may effect this end for themselves. It failed in relation to the tribes, however, for the simple reason that they have succeeded in remembering the encounter in a way reflecting their own sense of the moral determinacy of history as expressed in narrative form. Reports of the Mullah's defeat gather dust in British archives. No one particularly recalls that in 1897 British troops managed to penetrate to the very heart of tribal territory. What is remembered is that a long dead saint was saved by the miraculous appearance of bees. Through this story, a divine act of intervention that reaffirmed the Mullah's status as one of God's elect has eclipsed evidence of his human vulnerability and his defeat at the hands of the British. Defeat thereby provided the condition for the Mullah's perpetuation in local myth, and it is within this domain that the possibility of future miracles is perpetuated.

Conclusion

In developing my analysis of the tribal uprisings of 1897, I have focused on two individuals in particular: an obscure, and possibly unbalanced, religious mendicant who set out to claim the Mughal throne of India, and a young military officer and journalist who would go on to become the most famous political leader in the world and the greatest orator of his age. The extremes could not be greater in certain respects; but commonalities nonetheless exist that unite these two disparate figures, not the least being their ability to inspire a crowd with their words. While the Fakir's talents in this regard proved to be evanescent and only Churchill's would be of enduring importance, there was nevertheless a similarity in the way they went about their business that was founded on the common features of metaphors and miracles as figures of political discourse.

By way of illustrating the convergent and divergent features of metaphor and miracle, I have concluded this paper with an examination of two parallel historical accounts having to do with the last encounter between the Mohmand Field Force and the forces of the Mullah of Hadda. The primary concern here has not been the battle itself but its transformation into distinct modes and traditions of historical representation. Central to this analysis has been the exegesis of a figure of speech—

"lifting the veil"—which has provided the focus for a consideration not only of the common ground but also of the differences between the metaphor and miracle. We have seen that, for the British, the phrase expressed the dominance of reason over superstition and civilization over barbarism, but did so in a way that demonstrated it to be an act of hegemonic appropriation in which their superiority as the dominant group could be cast in the cultural terms of the subordinate group. For the followers of the Mullah, the phrase "lifting the veil" symbolized something entirely different: the hidden nature of divine power in the world and the inevitable failure of all political dominion, save that of God. Thus, a single figure of speech led in opposite directions that were culturally unintelligible and logically antagonistic. Both examples, however, expressed not only a common reliance on symbols for the creation of meaning and the legitimation of action but also a shared desire to make action fit within the bounds of an encompassing moral system. This above all else is a function of discourse and specifically figurative language, and it is this which we see emerging in the gathering storm over Jarobi glen.

NOTES

Acknowledgments: Some of the research on which this paper is based was conducted in Peshawar, Pakistan between November 1982 and June 1984, supported by predoctoral grants from the Fulbright-Hays Commission and the National Science Foundation. I would also like to acknowledge the comments and suggestions received as this paper has gone through various incarnations. In particular, I must thank Lois Beck, John Bowen, Steven Caton, Holly Edwards, Raymond Grew, Susan Harding, and Aram Yengoyan.

1. For background on Churchill's activities in the summer of 1897, see Winston Churchill, *My Early Life—A Roving Commission* (London: MacMillan, 1943); Ted Morgan, *Churchill: Young Man in a Hurry, 1874–1915* (New York: Simon & Schuster, 1982), 89–93; and William Manchester, *The Last Lion, Winston Spencer Churchill, Visions of Glory 1874–1932* (Boston: Little Brown, 1983), 249–58.

2. On the state of empire in the year of the Diamond Jubilee, see Jan Morris, *Pax Britannica: The Climax of Empire* (New York: Harcourt Brace Jovanovich, 1968); and Byron Farwell, *Queen Victoria's Little Wars* (New York: W. W. Norton, 1972), 311–17. On the uprisings of 1897, see also H. L. Nevill, *Campaigns on the North-West Frontier* (Lahore: Sang-e-Meel Publications, 1977); Lionel James,

The Indian Frontier War: Being an Account of the Mohmand and Tirah Expeditions,
1897 (London: William Heinemann, 1898); A. H. McMahon and A.D.G. Ramsay,
Report on the Tribes of Dir, Swat and Bajour (Peshawar: Saeed Book Bank, 1981);
and Akbar S. Ahmed, *Millennium and Charisma among Swat Pathans* (London:
Routledge & Kegan Paul, 1976).

3. Quoted in Randolph S. Churchill, ed., *Winston S. Churchill Companion*
1896–1900 (Boston: Houghton Mifflin, 1967), vol. 1, pt. 2, 774.

4. Ibid., 789, 783–84.

5. Cf., ibid., 881, for the Prince of Wales' letter to Churchill in which he
praises his writings.

6. Winston Churchill, "The Story of the Malakand Field Force—An Episode
of Frontier War," in his *Frontiers and Wars* (London: Eyre & Spottiswoode 1962),
28.

7. Ibid., 29.

8. Letter from Harold Deane, Malakand Political Agent to the Secretary,
Foreign Department, Government of India, 8 Aug. 1897 [Punjab Civil Secre-
tariat/Foreign Department/Frontier File (PCS/FD/FF) Sept. 1897]. Government
of India documents cited in this article were examined in the archives section of the
Peshawar Library. The filing system employed in this archive does not necessarily
correspond to those found in other Government of India archives.

9. W. Churchill, op. cit. (1962), 66.

10. Ibid., 28–29; for the original dispatches from which the book-length
account was drafted, see Fredrick Woods, ed., *Young Winston's War: The Original*
Dispatches of Winston S. Churchill, War Correspondent, 1897–1900 (London: Leo
Cooper Ltd., 1972), 9–10.

11. W. Churchill, op. cit. (1962), 29.

12. Woods (1972), 29.

13. Churchill (1962), 28.

14. Woods, op. cit. (1972), 29–30.

15. Ibid., 30.

16. Ibid., 10.

17. "Kararna," in, H.A.R. Gibb and J. H. Krarners, eds., *Shorter Encyclopedia*
of Islam (Leiden: E. J. Brill, 1974), 216.

18. Michael Gilsenan, *Recognizing Islam: Religion and Society in the Modern*
Arab World (New York: Pantheon Books, 1982), 75. See also *Gilsenan, Saint and*
Sufi in Modern Egypt: An Essay in the Sociology of Religion (Oxford: Clarendon
Press, 1973), esp. 20–35.

19. Gilesnan (1982), 83–84.

20. J. Christopher Crocker, "The Social Functions of Rhetorical Forms," in,
J. David Sapir and J. Christopher Crocker, eds., *The Social Use of Metaphor:*
Essays on the Anthropology of Rhetoric (Philadelphia: University of Pennsylvania
Press, 1977), 33–66; James W. Fernandez, *Persuasions and Performances: The Play*

of Tropes in Culture (Bloomington: Indiana University Press, 1986), 8–11; and Robert Paine, "When Saying is Doing," in, Robert Paine, ed., *Politically Speaking: Cross-Cultural Studies of Rhetoric* (Philadelphia: Institute for the Study of Human Issues, 1981), 9–24.

21. J. Crocker, op. cit., 46.

22. R. S. Churchill, op. cit., 816–21.

23. Ibid., 818.

24. Ibid., 818–19.

25. Biographical information on the Mad Fakir comes from a telegraph dated 8 August 1897, from the Deputy Commissioner (Peshawar) to the Secretary, Government of the Punjab; and from the "Political Diary of the Political Agent, Khyber Agency." (Both documents were examined in the archival section of the Peshawar Library.)

26. A typical example of this kind of story is found in Niamatullah's *History of the Afghans* (London: Susil Gupta, 1965). In one of the chronicles that make up this history, a ruler named Islam Shah decides to punish a dervish accused of opening a shop to waste "his whole time in conversation with the women of the town" (169). The dervish is brought before the king who denounces him and has him bastinadoed. The dervish is silent throughout the ordeal until the end when the king threatens to have him burned for any future violation of the law. To this, the *faqir* replies, "Burn me, if thou dost not burn thyself." The next morning, a boil appears on the king which shortly becomes a burning inflammation that spreads throughout his body. When the king attempts to find the dervish to beg forgiveness, the man is nowhere to be found, and the king soon dies of his affliction (169–70).

27. The similarity between miracle stories told of different saints was described as early as 1882 by a scholar named R. C. Temple, who noticed the close resemblance between stories pertaining to the Akhund of Swat and those having to do with otherwise unrelated saints from the Punjab and Sindh. See R. C. Temple, "Twice-Told Tales Regarding the Akhund of Swat," *The Indian Antiquary* 9 (Nov. 1882), 325–26.

28. R. S. Churchill, op. cit., 819.

29. Woods, op. cit., 9–10.

30. R. S. Churchill, op. cit., 820.

31. Ibid., 818.

32. H. Woosnam Mills, *The Pathan Revolts in North-West India* (Lahore: Sang-e-Meel Publications, 1979; orig. pub. in Lahore by The Civil and Military Gazette Press, 1897).

33. Ibid., 161.

34. Ibid., 163.

35. Ibid., 161.

36. Ibid., 163–64.

37. Ibid., 165.

38. Ibid.

39. Ibid.

40. Michel Foucault, *Discipline and Punish: The Birth of the Prison* (New York: Vintage Books, 1979). In the prison context studied by Foucault, the rationalization of power demanded that all marks of the individual's personal identity be transformed into signs of institutional dominance. In a similar way, dominance on the frontier is exercised by having that which is most intimately linked to the identity of tribal culture appropriated and made part of the political language of the foreign power.

41. 'Ali Bin Uthman al-Hujwiri, *The Kashf al-Mahjub,* R. A. Nicholson, trans. (Lahore: Islamic Book Foundation, 1980), 4.

42. Ibid., 226.

43. Al-Bukhari, Rikak, quoted in Gibb and Kramers, eds., op. cit., 432 ("Nafila").

44. See Annemarie Schimmel, *Mystical Dimensions of Islam* (Chapel Hill: University of North Carolina Press, 1975), 133; and Al-Hujwiri, op. cit., 226–27.

Tea Talk: Violent Measures in the Discursive Practices of Sri Lanka's Estate Tamils

E. Valentine Daniel

If interpretation is the violent or surreptitious appropriation of a system of rules . . . in order to impose direction, to bend it to a new will, to force its participation in a different game, and to subject it to secondary rules, then the development of humanity is a series of interpretations. The role of genealogy is to record its [effective] history; [the history of the event]. [By "event" is meant] the reversal of a relationship of forces, the usurpation of power, [and the appropriation of a vocabulary turned against those who had once used it].
> —Michel Foucault, Nietzsche, Genealogy, History

Discourse lives . . . beyond itself in a living impulse toward the object; if we detach ourselves completely from this impulse all we have left is the naked corpse of the word, from which we learn nothing at all about the social situation or the fate of a given word in life. To study the word as such, ignoring the impulse that reaches out beyond it, is just as senseless as to study psychological experience outside the context of the real life toward which it was directed and by which it is determined.
> —Mikhail Bakhtin, *The Dialogical Imagination*

At the most manifest level, this paper is about agricultural and agronomic terminology as found in the discourse of Tamil-speaking workers on Sri Lanka's tea plantations, or tea estates, as they are called there. My use of the terms agricultural and agronomic in this context is admittedly idiosyncratic. In the tea estates of Sri Lanka, two kinds of agricultural (in the unmarked sense) terminology are in use, one belonging to managerial agriculture, and the other to folk agriculture. But by and large, the tea estate is the regime of managerial agriculture, whereas in village India, folk agri-culture prevails. I call the class of terms belonging to managerial agri-culture "agronomic terminology," and reserve the term "agricultural ter-minology" for the domain of folk agriculture. By analyzing four commu-nicative events that I observed and recorded on tea estates in Sri Lanka, I attempt to show how these two terminological worlds interact.[1] The nature of that interaction is such that the dominant terminology of agron-omy may be seen to be deconstructed by the subdominant terminology of village agriculture.[2]

This essay is also about several other issues, even if they are expressed only obliquely or implicitly, apart from agricultural and agronomic termi-nology. First, and in a sense only briefly attended to, this article is about the accident of colonialism in a certain place and time. Much of the aca-demic writing on colonialism has opted to attend to the history of the col-onizer and his doings, rather than focus on the effects that colonialism has had and continues to have, in its own peculiarly transformative fashion, on the people it had once overtly subjugated. This essay runs counter to this trend.

Second, a theoretical point. This article is informed by a semeiotic[3] and is, therefore, concerned about the activity of signs, the signs of an aspect of a people's life in which a distorted and subalterned past is being recovered. Perforce, it is a semeiotic which, in contradistinction to much of tradi-tional semiology and semiotics, attempts to come to terms with the neglected dimension of power. But how should the activity of signs be con-ceptualized? Genealogically, as Foucault would have it, or determinedly, as Bakhtin might have preferred?[4] Given the form and content of the ethnographic material, taking sides on this question would be to settle on a meta-narrative that would undermine these contradictory impulses that I found to constitute the very communicative events I wish to analyze. To recover is not the same as to uncover or to discover. Recovery, in the sense used here, is more akin to regaining one's balance, albeit in a new place and time; it is a coming to terms with contemporary forces that buffet without allowing these forces to overwhelm. Recoveries often do entail radical rearrangement of meanings and forms, but they do not necessarily presume radical ruptures nor deny all continuity, all memory—whether real or imagined—and all familiarity. In this essay I have attempted to pre-serve the apparent contradictions of the Bakhtinian and Foucauldian positions as a pervasive backdrop against which the task of recovering the past in such prosaic linguistic fabrications as agricultural terminology is enacted. Words, and even words used as terms, like all symbols, grow. They traverse space and time. They are transformed and transform. In the topic under examination in this essay, that which has risen to the surface, that which has transferred itself onto tape and has been transcribed onto ethnographic parchment, bears but a strange resemblance to the agricultural world of village India. These transformations are not passive records of history but active embodiments of the genealogy of the relations of power. Third, and returning to the manifest content of this article, this essay is not only about certain terms and their link to standards and measures peculiar to the world of tea but also the manner in which they give expression to contained violence. I use "contain" in both senses: to have and to limit.

Let us then make our entry into the discursive practices of Sri Lanka's estate Tamils through a more detailed examination of these terms and expressions. I shall begin by providing a brief historical sketch of Sri Lanka's estate Tamils and then move on to explicate two broadly conceived terminological types, the approximate and the precise, used by these Tamils. Following this, I shall sketch a semeiotic by which the distinction between agriculture and agronomy may be theorized. Next, I shall present and analyze several communicative events in which agricultural and agronomic terminology constitute and are constituted by a people's lived experience, a people's world. In conclusion, I shall attempt to pull together the theoretical threads that weave through this essay to give its design a measure of tautness and greater visibility.

An Abbreviated History of Sri Lanka's Estate Tamils

The first group of Tamil laborers were brought from the villages of South India to the island of Ceylon in 1834. Offices for the sole purpose of recruitment sprang up in Tiruchirapalli, Madurai, Madras, and other cities of the Madras Presidency in South India. Within a short time, the greater part of the recruiting was done in the villages themselves, by men of some influence. South Indian villagers recall that these recruiters tended to be the younger brothers of a village headman or caste-*panchayat* headman. As such, they were driven to claim, by other means and in other places, the power they were deprived of in their natal villages.[5] Most of these men accompanied their labor gangs in their migration to Ceylon, and there they became labor supervisors known as *kankanis*.[6]

What these pioneer workers first confronted on the island was not cultivated land ready to be appropriated from the local peasants, but thick, virgin tropical forests. Through the labor of this immigrant group and that of subsequent waves of immigrants, these forests were transformed into coffee and, later, tea estates. The earliest immigrants were exclusively men. In later years, especially after tea began to replace coffee in 1867, women and children joined the men.

From the very beginning, the structure of the society of these immigrants was to be different from that of village India, re-formed to suit the interests and requirements of a capitalist estate economy. The multiple crops of village India were replaced by a single cash crop. Unlike village India, where most of what was grown in the village was consumed by its residents, on the estate almost the entire production of this single crop was to be exported. Caste distinctions that might have been kept clear by distinct residential patterns in village India were threatened and often effaced as all workers were compelled to live in identical, barracks-style line rooms,[7] regardless of caste. Caste-specific occupations became less important, and in some cases even disappeared, because all the residents of an estate had to work towards the rationalized end of manufacturing coffee or tea at a profit. Even though many other cultural changes followed, the culture of estate Tamils never lost its sense of continuity with village India.

From Agricultural Approximations to Agronomic Precision

One of the most remarkable changes in the lives of these immigrant workers was that, with a few exceptions, they were not allowed to cultivate any land for growing cereals or vegetables for their own consumption, so the land they worked on did not directly yield their subsistence. This was due less to the unavailability of land for personal gardening and more to their labor having been leased for the sole purpose of growing tea. In the agronomy displacing agriculture was found an agency that was committed to the constitution of a "totally useful time" and the elimination of "anything that might disturb or distract."[8] The workers' rice, dhal, cereals, spices, vegetables, flour, sugar, and oil were provided for them by the company shop, known as the Cooperative Store. A few *kankanis* and some staff members owned one or two milk cows. But cow's milk was beyond the purchasing power of most laborers. Their drink was the dark brew of a heavily sweetened low-grade tea dust.

Forced to give up the old agriculture for the new agronomy, these Tamils were also subjected to the hegemonic pressures of new agronomic terminology and its attendant discursive practices. This new terminology, they learned, belonged to a rationalized system which favored precision over approximation, universal standards, and units of measurement over contextualized ones. The island's Tea Research Institute, founded in 1925 on St. Coomb's estate near the town of Talawakelle, continues to be one of the most prestigious dispensers of these precise terminologies.

The British, who owned and operated the tea estates for over a century saw precision as much in terms of fairness as in terms of efficiency. Precise scales were ordered to assure accurate weighing of green leaf and fairness to all the tea pluckers. From the point of view of the British superintendent (the title given a tea estate manager), it would have been dreadfully unfair to use two unmatched scales in two different weighing sheds. Similarly, precision was imperative in the measurements used to construct living quarters for the workers. It assured uniformity, and uniformity assured equality, and equality guaranteed fairness. The concern with precision was carried so far that attempts by individual workers to expand their living space or even to reorganize it within the prescribed dimensions incurred the management's instant disapproval. In memoranda and letters that these early planters wrote to their subordinates and to their parent companies in England, the words fairness, justness, precision, and uniformity are used as if they meant the same thing. Nevertheless, the precise by no means displaced the approximate in terminology. Rather, the two have continued to coexist, constituting a contradictory consciousness in estate Tamil culture and society. In recent times, as we shall soon see, one has begun to deconstruct the other in unexpected and intriguing ways.

The Precise

Writing of another place and another time, Foucault reminds us that "precision and application are, with regularity, the fundamental virtues of disciplinary time."[9] On the side of precision, distance is rendered in feet, yards, and miles;[10] area in square feet, square yards, and acres; weight in ounces and pounds; volume in quarts and gallons; wages in rupees and cents; labor power in number of pounds of tea picked, feet of trenches dug, number of bushes pruned, and acres of field fertilized, and so forth; rain fall in inches or centimeters; and time in minutes, hours, days, weeks, months, and years. Accordingly, a trench should be 1 foot deep, 12 feet long, and 8 feet wide; a line room 100 square feet; the total number of bushes that yield 100 pounds of made tea must be fertilized with 10 percent nitrogen; 5 ounces of pernox (a chemical) are mixed in 1 gallon water; eighteen to twenty-four laborers are needed for each acre of hard pruning, fourteen laborers per acre for skiffing; and wages of 12 rupees per day are to be paid for pruning and 7 rupees per day for picking tea. Prince among the list of precise items is time. For most women, who have to prepare breakfast and a parceled lunch, the 4:30 A.M. gong at the tea factory signals their time to arise from bed; for the men it could be the 5:30 or even the 6:00 bell. *Perattu,* a word unknown to India's Tamils, dominates their attention in the morning. None of the laborers with whom I spoke was aware that this word originated from the English word, parade, so thorough has been its assimilation into estate Tamil. But what is *perattu?* Is it the march to the field site? Or is it the lining up at the site in order to receive the day's work order? It is not clear. In either event, it is a review, "an ostentatious examination,"[11] especially when the superintendent suddenly appears, as a commanding officer before his troops. The workers who rise at the gong of the factory bell gather at muster when the conch blows at 6:30 A.M., break for lunch when the conch blows at 12:00 noon, and return to work when the conch blows at 1:00 P.M., and quit work when the conch blows at 4:30 P.M. The conch is no longer a real conch shell (*canku*), but the piercing wail of the tea factory's steam siren. The laborers call it a *canku* anyway. It is only one of the many means by which "time penetrates the body and with it all meticulous controls of power."[12] The list of precise measures goes on and on, constituting the tone and texture of this new disciplinary regime, this agronomic world.[13] And time is the harbinger of this list and this world.

Guards in khaki, parades and musters, troops of workers, rows of bushes, rows of line houses, line of shirkers, lines in books, names on lines, rows of books, columns in rows, numbers in columns, check rolls,[14] roll calls, and conch (bugle?) calls, discipline, punctuality, and other discursive units of eighteenth- and nineteenth-century Europe impel an apparently willing labor force to consent, signifying the militarization and radical remaking of the relations among people as well as between people and land. If the conch announces the beginning of work (or war) for Hindus, it also announces the beginning of prayer. The discipline required in work (and war) finds its "elective affinity," to borrow a phrase from Max Weber, in the discipline intrinsic to devotion but one robbed of all dignity.[15] The traditional *namaskaram,* the Hindu greeting of god and fellow man, in which palms are held together in front of the chest, is replaced by *salam,* an Arabic word, and a European gesture. The gesture is a salute, but a docile one, in which the shoulders are drawn in and head appropriately lowered.

The Approximate and the "Little Extra"

In the extra-agronomic context, as might be expected, there is a wealth of approximate terms employed. In the kitchen, rice and dhal are measured in *cuntu*s (from the Arabic, *Sunduq* via the Sinhala *hunduva*[16]) and *kottu*s (a corruption of "quart"). A *cuntu* is ideally a cigarette tin, not unusually a condensed milk tin, and sometimes a half of a coconut shell; of the right size of course. The Sinhala, *hunduva,* as a token of indigenous agricultural terminology, had always been an approximate measure. The conversion of the precise quart into the approximate *kottu* is an example of the power of approximation over the precise. In fact, the assimilation of the quart in this manner into estate Tamil is so complete that the primary meaning of *kottu* is not a unit of measure, per se, but a container of a certain approximate size and shape.

The stores on the estates claim to own a set of the few standardized measuring instruments available. Until about fifteen years ago, the salesmen in these stores used a combination of dry measures, such as *cuntus, kottus* and bushels, and weights, such as ounces and pounds, to measure the various kinds of goods they sold. They used dry measures for rice, dhal, and other cereals, and pounds and ounces for such items as sugar, tamarind, and incense.

Since the early 1970s, the metric system of weights has replaced both the former dry measures and the measures of weights. The salesman likes this change, not only because the new system is more rational than the old, but because the use of a scale as opposed to a measuring container gives him greater flexibility, which in turn gives him greater power. In the case of the *cuntu* and *kottu* the salesman used to scoop up the grain or sugar and fill the measuring container to overflowing, and then, with the help of a stick, level off the excess. The quantity that he was free to play with in this manner was limited, depending on whether he pressed the stick tightly upon the rim of the container or only grazed it gently. With the scale, he has far greater discretionary powers. When a salesman weighs dhal, rice, flour, or sugar, he is more likely to underweigh than weigh precisely. He does this by pouring the contents of the scale's pan into the newspaper cone before the pointer of the scale has had time to come to rest. But he is free to—and, more often than not, will—throw in a little extra. The customer rarely demands that he re-weigh the item already in the cone, for he would not trust the scale anyway. He may, however, ask the salesman to throw in a little more of the extra. The salesman might oblige, especially if the customer is one who belongs to the "he may be needed by us" category (*namakku ventiyavar*).

One is classified into the needed category for reasons that may range from the immediate to the deferred. An example of the immediate would be when a customer is able to oblige the salesman with a few logs of firewood from the estate's store, which he will "lose" during transportation at a point mutually known to him and the salesman, to be picked up by the latter at a specified time after dusk. To the deferred category belongs a case known to me in which the salesman never stinted on the little extra to a certain customer whose son was doing well in school and was considered to have a good chance of becoming a clerk in the estate office and who then, it was thought, would be able to wield sufficient clout to find an appropriate bridegroom for the salesman's daughter, then only ten years old. The dynamic involved here entails, to, quote Appadurai, "a logic of cross-reference, whereby one set of objects or phenomena is measured by explicit or implicit measures of other objects or phenomena of [this] world of reckoning" (1986: 12).

The little extra[17] is an important cultural category. At weddings and other occasions where gifts are exchanged, it is important that whenever the gift is in cash the amount be in odd numbers: 51 or 101 rupees. That extra one is symbolic of generosity and prosperity on the part of the giver.[18] When an untouchable places her empty pot at the well to be filled by the woman of a clean *jati* who has access to the well, the latter will invariably pour enough water so that the vessel brims over with that little extra.

When a man's kinsfolk go to the house of a potential bride to initiate marriage negotiations, they are invariably invited to partake of a feast.[19] This feast is most important, among other reasons, for assessing whether or not the prospective bride has it in her to be a Dhanalakshmi, the goddess of wealth. The signs noted are kinesic ones, observed especially by the women, as she serves her guests. How does she hold the serving spoon? How much rice does she scoop up (it need not be full)? How many times does she scoop up rice? Does she tap the neck of the spoon on the edge of the container to release the rice that is stuck to the spoon? At which point along the length of the stem of the spoon does she tap on the edge of the serving container! (A miserly woman will fail to tap her spoon or will tap it in such a way that the stuck rice does not fall back into the vessel and, therefore, the amount of rice she scoops up afresh will not be as much as it should be. But sticky rice could be a stickier affair. Too much tapping, indicating excessive glutinousness, could raise questions about the young lady's or her mother's cooking skills.) Most important, does she place that little extra on the guest's leaf, even after the latter has said, "enough!, enough!"?[20] All these signs together, especially the last, indicate whether or not the girl is blessed with the capacity and the gift of being generous and bountiful—a Dhanalakshmi. All these signs, if they are to be considered auspicious, must be completely free of any indications of attempts at measuring, especially, measuring precisely.

Agronomic Approximation

Approximate measures have perfused the highly rationalized world of tea estates as well. The factory officer who pays a laborer for tending to his garden on company time (against company rules) will be given a container full of tea (again, against company rules) and a little extra. The gestural language is not unlike that which one finds in village India when the landlord gives his field hands a certain number of *patis* of grain each, as agreed upon by some tacit contract, in return for their services, and then a little extra. The contextually determined measures and standards true of village India are also true of the agronomic tea estates. Ask the *kankani* how many men he needs for pruning a given field. "Ten to twelve" comes the answer. "How many hours will it take?" "Seven to eight hours." Ask the pruner how many inches below the surface he should skiff a bush. "At the right level," replies the pruner readily. "The manual says, two inches below the surface."[21] "We don't carry books and measuring sticks." And any planter knows (having learned from the experienced laborer) that the manual's accuracy is more a sign of agronomic obsessiveness than scientific accuracy. "Some bushes need to be cut two inches below the surface, some three inches, some even four." "What about 'cut-across' pruning?" I ask. "At knee level," comes back the reply. The book says, fifteen inches from the ground, and knees are not high-precision measuring sticks. In practice that matters very little.[22]

When tea pluckers bring their baskets full of tea to be weighed by the field supervisor at the weighing shed, the tea is dumped into a gunny sack and hooked onto a spring (salter) scale.[23] The scale faces the supervisor and not the picker. And even if it were to face her, the scale's reading is an average observed between the extreme points of the pointer's oscillations. "Letchumi, twenty-seven pounds!" "No, it cannot be. It must be at least thirty-five," protests Letchumi. "You held your basket in the waterfall on your way here. Too much water here. I have deducted eight pounds for water." "How can you do that? There must be at least three pounds of rain water, no?" "Well, rain is water too." "Mariyayi, twenty-seven pounds." Mariyayi does not complain. She knows that she is a poorer picker than Letchumi, but her husband makes up for it by carrying firewood to the supervisor's quarters. "Kamatchi, thirty-two pounds"—even though the scale oscillates around thirty, with rain water and all. But the supervisor knows that she recently lost her kinsman in the communal riots. And so it goes. Fair and unfair, all of them are approximations.

There are two quintessential approximations irrevocably built into the manufacture of tea. The first is the standard by which the ripeness of *koruntu* (the leaf bud and the two leaves that sprout at its base) is determined. "When do you pick a *koruntu*?" "When it is just right. The bud should not be too closed, nor too open." The second is to decide when the withering of green leaf should be stopped and the rolling of the leaf (in special cones and rollers or, more recently, in retrovane-rollers) begin. The answer again is, "when it is just right." Any manual that tries to be more precise than that is wrong.[24] In the third major step in the manufacture of tea, measurement (of humidity and temperature) is nowadays increasingly employed over judgment. This is the step of interrupting the rolling (technically called, roll-breaking) every half an hour or so for about ten minutes before subjecting the leaf to a second rolling. On the average, five or six rolls can be done, and during each roll-break, the *dhool,* the rolled tea that does not pass across the roll-breaking sieves, is extracted out for fermentation. The leaves that pass across the sieves are put back into the roller and rolled again.

A Semeiotic of Agriculture and Agronomy Broadly Conceived

In general, agricultural measures tend to be phenomenological seconds, and agronomic measures phenomenological thirds. The semeiotic terminology comes from C. S. Peirce. Briefly, he argues that whatsoever is capable of presenting itself to the mind for contemplation has three aspects to it: Firstness, Secondness, and Thirdness. In this essay we are least concerned with Firstness, which is associated with potentiality. Secondness, associated with actuality, is emphasized by existents—the here and the now, the contextually delimited and determined. The universal, the conventional, and the context-free characterize Thirdness, which is associated with generality.

Of the numerous sign-types Peirce wrote about, the best known are the iconic, indexical, and the symbolic.[25] They each describe the nature of the type of bond that holds together a sign and its object. The iconic sign which falls under the broad phenomenological category of Firstness is a sign that signifies by virtue of its resemblance to (or even identity with) the object for which it stands; the indexical sign which falls under the broad phenomenological category of Secondness signifies by virtue of its contiguity to the object for which it stands; and the symbolic sign which falls under the broad phenomenological category of Thirdness signifies by virtue of a convention that determines that it stands for a certain object in a given way. In prescinding the object-sign relationship from the triadically constituted sign as a whole, the necessary third correlate of the sign, the interpretant (to whom/what such a representation stands) is provisionally left out of consideration. I shall consider interpretants in a slightly different theoretical context later in this essay.

Statues and metaphors (iconic conventions) rely on resemblance for their significant import and therefore are iconic. Smoke and fire, lightning and thunder, the rise in temperature and the rise of mercury in a thermometer are, to one degree or another, indexical. The actual effect of the object on the sign or their invariable contiguity dominates these processes of signification. Even though in nature we most readily find the manifestation of indexical signs, culture provides us with its share of indexical signs as well. In many languages, as is well known, a certain dialect or accent could be indexical of the status or gender of one or another interlocutor. On tea estates, even when a superintendent is a native Tamil speaker, he may choose to adopt an Englishman's Tamil accent. In doing so, he indexes his status as a manager to plantation workers and his distance from them, whereas in village India, such an affectation would be taken for a speech impediment. As for symbols, human existence is perfused with them. Words as signs stand for their objects only by dint of convention. That sixteen ounces make up a pound is a convention and, therefore, symbolic. So is the convention that twelve inches make a foot, much more so now than when the king's foot provided the standard.[26] To be sure, most signs that human beings traffic in are compounds of all three significative modes. But what is at issue is emphasis, dominance, and determination.

Let us consider determination, for this is important for seeing the crucial difference between agriculture and agronomy. Let us designate the measuring implements, the *cuntu* and the liter as *cuntu*^{i} and liter^i so as to differentiate them from their corresponding concepts, *cuntu*^{c} and liter^c, treating *cuntu*^{i}–*cuntu*^{c} and liter^i–liter^c, as tokens of the agricultural and agricultural domains respectively. A semeiotic object is said to determine its sign, and the sign represents the object to a third, the interpretant. Continuing to bracket out the third correlate, the interpretant, and focusing our attention on the sign and object, we may understand the property of determination as an active one and that of representation as a passive one.[27] In the case of liter^i–liter^c, the semeiotic object is the abstract standard of measure, the liter^c, and each actual measuring implement, the liter^i, its sign. Stated differently, a liter^i is iconic of (i.e., it resembles) the semeiotic object, the liter^c. This object is none other than a conventional symbol and therefore, a semeiotic Third, a general idea. Or at least, it is the conventional and the general that is placed in the foreground. In the case of *cuntu*^{i}–*cuntu*^{c}, matters are turned around. Here, it is the measuring implement, a *cuntu*^{i}—a cigarette tin, condensed milk tin or coconut half-shell—that is put forward as the semeiotic object. The abstract idea of a quantity of measure, the *cuntu*^{c}, is the sign determined by this object. The *cuntu*^{c} is an icon of a *cuntu*^{i} and not vice versa. Nevertheless, both the liter^i–liter^c, and the *cuntu*^{i}–*cuntu*^{c} are similar to the extent that they are both ultimately based on iconicity. But the semeiotic object for a liter a is a symbolic (conventional) type; while the semeiotic object for the *cuntu* is an indexical token. Types emphasize generals; tokens emphasize instances.

In determination, the vector of determination for liter moves from the general idea—the conventional liter, to the actual token—the measuring implement. The vector of determination for *cuntu* proceeds from the actual implement, to the general convention. The convention of the liter is active, and the actual is passive; but for the *cuntu*, the actual is active, and the convention is passive. This groundedness (pun intended) is seen to operate with the same agricultural insistence in the case of the *vafa* measure, so astutely explicated by Appadurai (1981).

Measures as abstract standards are located in an environment of other abstract/ideational/general objects and are held together by mutual interrelations. But being conventional, their relationships strive toward a constant and invariable structure. Conventions, by definition, move towards stability and fixity and away from caprice and surprise. They invite limitations upon possibilities and lend themselves to the generalities capable of being rendered into conversion tables. Measuring implements are also located in their own environment of objects, what we commonly call real objects. This environment is a fluid and variable environment, the variations of which allow for the variability of the instruments as well. Such measuring implements, as objects in and of actualities (or acts), are fraught with surprise and caprice. Acts *qua* acts are pre-conventional and highly variable.

The abstract domain of standards and measures is populated with objects that have been normalized and regularized, objects (as concepts) that have been tamed and disciplined. The domain of actualities, by contrast, by being populated by emergent objects—be they cigarette tins of various sizes or fields of various slopes or people of various moods—determine representations that are themselves variable and flexible. An object that determines its representation from within a regularized domain determines regular representations, such as in the case of standardized measures like the liter. An object that determines its representations from within a domain of variables determines variable representations, the case of the *cuntu.* Implicit in the communicative events that follow and their analyses, we shall see, at varying levels of activity is the interplay among the determining semeiotic vectors discussed above.

Four Communicative Events in Their Ethnographic Settings

Pruning (Kavvattu Vettal)

If left unpruned, the tea bush will not be a bush but a tree, producing flowers and seeds instead of a flush of pluckable buds. Pruning stimulates growth yet keeps it in a permanent vegetative state. Finally, pruning maintains the bush at a height that lends itself to efficient and productive picking. One prunes with a quick, precise, and powerful stroke of arm and wrist, using the knife called a *kavvattu katti.* Because this skill requires considerable muscle strength, only adult males prune. A weak stroke results in splitting the stem; too ungainly or too free a stroke could damage stems that are not meant to be cut by that stroke; an imprecise hack could result in a poorly angled cut.

There are three types of pruning: skiffing, cut-across pruning, and clean pruning. Skiffing is called *mecai vettu* in Tamil. In skiffing, according to the manual, the bushes are trimmed two inches from the top with a *kavvattu katti.* As in all types of pruning, the bush is pruned along the gradient of the hill upon which it grows, and yet each branch pruned is cut at an angle (*cacci vettu*), so that the cut edge faces the center of the bush.

Skiffing allows a bush to be picked after thirty-five to forty days. Consequently, this form of pruning is often resorted to as an alternative to the more radical types of pruning, which prevent the bushes from being picked for anywhere from 90 to 150 days. The word *mecai* means table; thus, a *mecai vettu* literally is a kind of pruning that makes the surface of a bush like that of a table. Cutting across, the second kind of pruning, is called *mel vettu* in Tamil, meaning an upper cut. The bush is pruned with a *kavvattu katti,* at a height of about fifteen inches above the ground, approximately across the middle of the bush. The Tamil laborer describes it as knee level, obviously making ingenious adjustments to varying heights of knee joints and variously dispositioned tea bushes. The tea planter's manual, on the other hand, specifies with agronomic precision that this middle cut should be made fifteen inches above the ground. Knee level is admittedly approximate, but its approximation tends to be consistently in the best interest of the healthy growth of each tea bush. As in skiffing, the angle of the cut in cut-across pruning slants inward, towards the center of the bush. Following such a pruning, the bush may not be picked for at least ninety days.

The third and the most difficult kind of pruning, hard pruning or clean pruning, is called *adi vettu* in Tamil. Here, the manual specifies that the bush is pruned either with a *kavvattu katti* or a hand saw (*val*), eight inches above the ground, which the laborer measures as a span one and one-half of the width of the hand (*onnarai jan*). The hard pruning cut is described in the manual as not angled but horizontal. In Tamil, this cut is simply called *pottu vetta* because the exposed surface of the cut stem resembles a *pottu,* the auspicious circular mark that Tamil women and sometimes men wear on their foreheads. And any Tamil knows that if a stem is cut at an angle, the *pottu* will be oblong and not circular as it ought to be. Formerly, in clean pruning the bush is reduced to leafless stumpy stems. Nowadays, two variations of clean pruning are practiced in the belief that a radical clean pruning might be too severe on the bush. In the first variation, rim-clean pruning, the outermost rim of branches are spared radical pruning. In the second, lung pruning, a single leafy branch is spared. When a bush is hardpruned, the manual says, it may not be harvested for "125 days." The *kankani* says, "120 or 130 days."

Communicative Event 1: The Story of the Perumal Cut

Most of the tea estates of Sri Lanka are located at elevations ranging from 3,000 to 7,000 feet. The higher reaches of the estate that Poocchi Kankani has worked all his life rises above 7,000 feet. In these higher elevations in particular, the mornings have dense fog and are cold. In the words of Poocchi, one of my principal informants:

Those who gather at muster, the field supervisors included, especially the field supervisors, would rather be back in their line houses, on the cow dung-plastered floor, on mats, under wart blankets. In those days, only a few supervisors used to sleep on cots. Now all of them do. Therefore, to warm up ourselves, to make our blood flow, and to keep us from thinking about our line houses, we talk a lot, and that too, very loudly. The supervisors yell, swear, curse, and find fault. "You seeker of vaginas, where did you learn to hold the knife like that? Was it from your wife?" The male worker mutters back a wise crack or breaks out laughing. To a female worker a supervisor may even say, "You daughter of a harlot, who gave you a name today? Look at her how she works! Look at her, like a newlywed bride she is." If the laborer is a young woman she will giggle. An older woman might shoot back, "Why, it was your father who gave me a name." The other women would break into laughter. No one really means what they say. It is all meant to make the blood flow, the sun to rise, and the mist to disappear.[28] This kind of banter goes back and forth, until they start working like machines, at a constant pace, without speeding up now and slowing down there. The only thought is to finish their assigned acreage covered as soon as possible so that they could go home or off to a second job. Then they might even start to pick faster so that they could exceed the minimum poundage and earn additional money for the extra pounds they pick.

Around noon, the sun gets hot and the workers get hungry. Now when the supervisor wants something done in a certain way, he may shout, but he tempers it with a joke. "Go ahead and work like a tortoise. Both of us are going to be here till seven at night or until we fall dead from hunger."

New superintendents, especially the *cinna dorais* (assistant superintendents—until recently, mostly Britons) are not sensitive to the time of the day and the tempers of the workers. They learn from whoever taught them, that the only way to get work out of our people is to shout at them, treat them like dogs, pelt them with obscenities.

Many years ago there was such a *cinna dorai*. And in those days there was a young lad named Perumal. It was past one o'clock in the afternoon, and Perumal was doing a cut-across prune. The *cinna dorai* came tearing through the bushes in his khaki shorts, stockings, hat, and boots. They can run that way because of their boots. It is not good for the bushes to run through them like that. But the *cinna dorai* don't care. It shows their power. Their authority. They think it scares us when they come rushing down like that. "Give me that knife you son of a harlot," this *cinna dorai* said. "Let me show you how to prune a tea bush." Perumal handed the *dorai* the knife without saying a word. He watched the *dorai* swing at the bush, shouting "Like this, like this. Fifteen inches above the ground. Fifteen inches above the ground." It was clear that the *cinna dorai* didn't know pruning from shaving off pubic hair. The stems were splitting down the middle, and instead of the slanted cut he was performing the (horizontal) *pottu vettu.* Perumal felt his blood boil and rise to his head. In his stomach was hunger. He held out his left hand, in a gesture of asking for his knife back, saying, "here *dorai,* please, not like that, not like that. Please, let me show you fifteen inches." The *dorai* returned the knife to him with contempt, blade-side first, noticing neither the anger in Perumal's eyes, the dangerous sarcasm in his voice, nor that he had asked for the knife with his *left* hand. Like a flash of lightning, Perumal returned the knife's handle to the grip of the other hand, his right hand, and swung at the Englishman with the word, "*ippati!*" (like this!) The next thing you saw was the Englishman's arm, severed from below his elbow, writhe in the drain, spouting blood. It was exactly fifteen inches long.

Ever since, this infamous swipe has been known as the Perumal cut.

Estate life is filled with such recallings and retellings, reminding one of Foucault's distinction between enlightenment historiographies and effective histories. The former are typified by their pretensions to examine things furthest from themselves, whereas "effective history," as in the Perumal story, "shortens its vision to those things nearest to it—especially the body."[29] "The body," Foucault remarks, "is the inscribed surface of events (traced by language and dissolved by ideas) . . . a volume in perpetual disintegration. Genealogy . . . is thus situated within the articulation of the body and history."[30] In "Perumal's Cut," the implicated body is a white man's. As metaphor, it has become the body of a condemned man. But the effect is not only that Perumal, as judge and executioner, left his mark on the Englishman's body and shortened its power, but also that this body has become public property, available for useful appropriation by the collective memory of a subordinated people against future oppression.

Draining (Kan Vettutal)

Digging drains, like pruning, is considered to be hard work and, therefore, is done by men. The skill required for cutting drains is not as exacting as that required in pruning. This difference is reflected in the difference in wages; pruners are paid twelve or even twelve and a half rupees per day, whereas drain diggers earn only nine. The *kankani* plays an important rule in determining the gradient of the drain and limiting it to a ratio of 1:120 as it follows the contours of the hill. A measuring stick and string are carried around to serve the purpose of determining this and the distances between the terraced drains. Nevertheless, the most respected *kankani* is one who is able to plan and direct the digging of perfect drains by using only his eyes, feet, legs, and experience.

Drains check erosion and channel the flow of rain water during the monsoons. They are cut with *manvettis* at thirty-foot intervals along the contours of the hills. For those familiar with nineteenth-century sensibilities, the view across the valley of a given hill's drains along its contours might take on the appearance of the flounces of a Victorian gown. These drains are two and a half feet deep, two feet wide, and twelve to fifteen feet long. At the end of each drain a three-foot-long platform or *tittu* is made, after which the next drain continues. Whenever a drain is dug, the soil is thrown onto the upper slope of the hill; to do otherwise would of course either fill up a lower drain previously dug, make the digging of such a drain extremely difficult, or even gradually cover the tea bushes in the lower slopes.

Communicative Event II: "Down-Piling"

Behavioral modes motivated by short-term goals or hedonism are often analogized to digging a drain and throwing the soil down the slope of a hill. Initially, it appears to be so easy and only natural to shovel something downhill. But eventually one brings about either destruction or creates for oneself a staggering amount of work. In recent years, "down-piling," as this action is called in technical jargon, has come to serve as a general description of the work habits of recently hired Sinhala laborers, and as a metaphor of the Sri Lankan government's policies toward Tamils of recent Indian origin.

Late one morning, I was taken to the field by a Sinhala tea estate manager. He wished to show me how a Sinhala worker was digging a drain. He had been down-piling all morning. "He is the gov'ment," clipped the manager in his quasi-British accent, with overdone diphthongs, glottal stop and all. "'Aw the gov'ment does is dompile." Obviously "dompiling" to this Sinhalese gentleman planter was not mere technological terminology, a symbol, but also an index. Or more precisely it was a "shifter," in Silverstein's terminology, symbolically contributing to the referential content of the discourse as well as indexically implicating aspects of the context of utterance, in this case, the status of the speaker.[31] The accent indicated that he belonged to that proud lineage of planters whose ancestral members were British and whose pedigree he wished to be identified with by virtue of his dialect. Subsequently, I was to learn that this idiom of down-piling, which had its origin in the agricultural terminology of tea estates, has recently gained considerable currency among Tamil workers themselves, used with an ironic twist. More on this shortly.

Down-piling, as enunciated by our mimic man,[32] our anglicized but not-quite-English gentleman planter, is a vestige and metonym of colonial discourse. To be sure, not all Sinhala managers resort to British-English, nor are the Sinhalese managers the only ones who do so. Of the proportionately fewer Tamil and Burgher managers as well, there are those who fondly assume such an affectation. Accompanying the assumed dialect is the British style of life: bungalows, men servants who are addressed as boys, scotch, a desire for "English vegetables," khaki shorts, white stockings, safari bat, and rugger. In an earlier day, mimicry had been an ambivalent fetish of the mimic man, who was at once both empowered and disempowered by the condescending validation of the white man, who thought he had the last word and could say, "almost as good as an Englishman, but not quite," or could remark on "the slippage, the excess, the difference."[33] However, I have yet to know of a white colonialist or a student of colonialism to have remarked, let alone observed, that the subalterns too see these same slippages, excesses and difference, even though they read them differently. In their view from below, the subalterns had found some comfort and frivolity in seeing mimic man as one of their kind, who regardless of what he might have intended, had also ended up reducing the white man's airs to laughable size. If they found him to be the reassuringly ambivalent repository of mimicry; they also found him to be the embodiment of mockery. Even when menacing, his bark had failed to convey the convictions of a beast. Mimicry of this kind was all too human. Now, with the white man gone, mimicry is no longer funny; it is not even human. The simulacrum remains but is abandoned by its original and by the parodic relief it had offered. The shadow has become the demon, the mask the monster. Old metaphors have created new interpretants in new discursive fields. Down-piling itself has acquired currency in a different discourse, a discourse in which mimic man is top dog; and he bites.

In 1972 and 1974, the Sri Lankan government nationalized its tea estates and introduced several sweeping reforms that had far-reaching consequences for estate Tamils and for the Sinhala villagers who lived in the peripheries of these estates. Prior to 1970, the privately owned estates, both foreign and local, maintained a ratio of two registered laborers per acre of cultivated land. In estate Tamil parlance, when a laborer is registered he is said to have a name and when he is not, he does not have a name.

The available work on all estates invariably exceeded the capacity of the number of registered workers. This state of affairs worked to management's advantage. An army of nameless young men, women, and children were available on call to pick up the slack whenever weather conditions or management decisions called for extra labor. The ratio of workers with names and those without names was 60:40. These nameless workers were either paid minimal hourly wages or subcontracted by registered workers afraid of losing their jobs by being unable to complete the amount of work for which they had contracted. Wages thus earned were called *kai kacu,* or 'hand cash.' At least 75 percent of these seasonal or stand-by workers were anything but seasonal and did anything but stand by, for most of them worked throughout the year, saving millions of rupees for the management, which would have otherwise had to pay out regular wages and benefits to workers with names. When the tea estates were nationalized, the government mandated that the ratio of workers to cultivated land must be increased from two to five workers per acre. This policy was enacted with the professed intention of reducing the severe underemployment among estate Tamil youth and providing employment for the unemployed Sinhala population of the surrounding villages. In order to assure the latter, the government mandated that two Sinhala workers had to be hired for every Tamil worker employed.

In the case of the Tamils, the purported goal of reducing under-employment was undermined by another policy mandated under the government's land-reform bill. As a consequence of this bill, parts of many estates were recolonized by Sinhala villagers, driving thousands of unemployed and homeless Tamil laborers into the cities of Kandy and Colombo. Many other Tamil estate workers became refugees and fled to the northern and eastern provinces. A number of these refugees were transformed into bonded laborers who worked for Sri Lankan Tamil land owners for wages and in conditions far more deplorable than on the tea estates. These apparently contradictory policies of the government are described as "down-piling." The effect of these reforms for estate Tamils has been to substitute unemployment and homelessness for under-employment and poor housing. Most significant, these reforms have helped transplant a docile and ideologically and experientially parochial youth to the socio-cultural environments of the cities and the rural areas of the north and east, where they have become hardened and radicalized.

The recently incorporated Sinhala peasant[34] has devised a work schedule of extreme convenience for himself and much inconvenience to the management. But since the management is none other than the government, no single manager need have his reputation on the line with respect to the mentioned inconvenience, even though some of the old hands, especially those who were trained under Englishmen and whose habits of thought continue to conform to the good old days when profit was all that mattered, are quite troubled by the economically detrimental work habits of most of the newly incorporated Sinhala workers. These work habits range from incompetence, as pointed out to me by the Sinhala gentleman planter, to the more intractable habit of well-timed absenteeism. The latter works in the following manner.

According to the revised set of rules, no worker may lose his or her name (registration) as long as he or she reports to work at least one day a month. Many Sinhala peasants now registered on tea estates choose not to come to work when the weather is bad or when the work is heavy. For the Sinhala worker, bad weather is by definition rainy weather, for work in general picks up its pace when the rains come. For instance, weeds grow far more luxuriantly in foul than fair weather. The same goes for tea. Rainy weather is also the ideal time for pruning. When the sun is out, the weeds sparse, and the picking light, Sinhala workers willingly show up. The only heavy work to which an unlucky worker could be assigned during some of these sunny days is cutting drains. There are some sunny days when there is not even an hour's worth of work per laborer per day. These days are everyone's favorite under the new regime, for regardless of the number of hours worked, anyone who shows up in the morning is guaranteed a full day's wages.

Both management and Tamil laborers think that the sole purpose of Sinhala absenteeism is work avoidance. This is only partly true at best. Some peasants have traditionally worked at other jobs in the local towns, such as domestic servants, bakers, waiters, vegetable venders, carpenters, and truck unloaders. Peasants do not live in the estates' line rooms. They live in their own huts and houses which need repairs, such as fixing the roofs during the heavy rains. But there is work outdoors as well. If weeds grow profusely in tea estates, they also grow in the peasants' own gardens of vegetables and cash crops. Some Sinhala laborers have rice fields to tend to, flood waters to channel appropriately, or fields to plough. Whatever the case may be, having a name on the tea estates is a great insurance against hard times. The Tamils who have few outside options for work, and have no choice but to do the hard work in bad weather, are resentful of the new arrangement. Since the early 1970s, many young Tamil men too have opted for absenteeism of convenience. Some of these men have found alternate part-time jobs in the local towns; some spend their time at home; others have actively launched into political activities of consciousness-raising and organizing resistance groups in case there is another outbreak of communal violence against them. This brings me to my last example of down-piling.

A forty-five-year-old Tamil man used the expression down-piling to describe the work habits of the Tamil youth of the day who were following the work habits of the Sinhalese. His hegemonic logic traced the consequences of these habits from the neglect of tea bushes, to the drop in tea prices, to the drop in revenue to the government, to the deprivation of essentials to the Sinhala people, to taking out their frustrations on the Tamils. His eighteen-year-old son, resentful because his father had ordered him to work regularly on the estates and not keep the company of the other "idle young men who waste their time talking politics," retorted indignantly, saying, "it is you [old] people who have been 'down-piling' all these years. You have even buried your children. From the Sinhalese we can learn how not to down-pile." Instead of chastising his son for insubordination, the father's response amounted to admitting the charges. "Why then," he said, "don't we go to the *ūr* (to our ancestral village in India). There are no hills there" (i.e., one cannot down-pile there).[35]

Tipping (Mattam Vettutal)

The leaves picked off a tea bush, called *koruntu,* include the tender bud at the very tip of a branch and the two leaves at its base from between which it sprouts. Before picking *koruntu* off a recently pruned tea bush, the pluckers lay light, eight-foot-long sticks known as *matta kampu* (literally 'leveling stick') atop a row of bushes. Then they pick only the twin leaves and bud that rise above the recumbent sticks. Before removing the sticks and moving further down the row of bushes, the workers nip off the small stems protruding above the level of the sticks, thereby grading the bushes in keeping with the hills' slopes. Tipping is done with a two-inch-long *koppi katti,* which has a hooked tip.

From the rim of the crown of a pruned stem, a snatch of fresh stems bud and grow (*kavvattu vatiliruntu potanci varum* means the leaves grow in profusion from the cut stem). The parent stem from which these stemlets grow is called the *potai vatu* (*potai,* 'sprout' or 'burst forth'; *vatu,* 'stem' or 'branch'). When a stem is not pruned on time, it grows long and erect except for the tip, which angles like the neck and head of a deer. A stem thus grown is called the *tai vatu* (literally, 'the mother branch'). After a tea bush has been tipped, picking continues every seven days, on the average, until the next pruning cycle. Between cycles, the same bushes are picked by the same picker. Thus, it is in each plucker's interest to tip with care and tend to their bushes.

Communicative Event III: Betrayal

Of the many *jati*s represented on estates, the Kallar and the Parayans are the most numerous, and for this reason they have traditionally competed for leadership. In the 1950s, the Kallar began to dominate the trade unions and their dominance culminated in the nomination of their leader, Thondaman, as minister of Housing and Rural Development in 1977 by Sri Lanka's President, J. R. Jayawardane. The unchallenged rise of Kallar leadership began in the 1950s when the Parayans lost one of their most charismatic leaders, P. Vellayan.

In the communal riots of 1983, when scores of estate Tamils were killed by Sinhala mobs, many workers saw S. Thondaman, by his very position as minister in a Sinhala government, as having betrayed the Tamils. Some remembered Vellayan, who was a victim of violence, much like the many Tamils who were killed in 1983. The following was a song of a *valluvan* (a Parayan priest) which I obtained from an estate in the Hatton district:

atiyōta vettinānā ācāmi—vellayan
mutiyōta cānjānā enjāmi—tontayanum
tāivātum valarattum māmi
pottum potanji valarātā collu kaccāmi?

[Even as throated pedigree grows
Unpruned with the mother stem,
Tell me,
Chanter of Buddhist prayers!
Burst forth will it not in gay profusion
A crown of buds around the *pottu* of my Lord,
Vellayan,
That uncrowned bush,
Hewn at the base
By a villain's knife?]

(author's translation)

In Tamil, the poem ends with the words, "tell me Katchami"; or rather, "tell me you Buddhists who chant *"Buddham saranangatchami"*; or even more expansively, "you who claim to follow a non-violent religion, tell me." The word *tontaiyan* in the second line literally means the throated one (from *tontai,* meaning throat). But to any estate worker, it also sounds like part of the minister's name, Thondaman, even though the *thondai* in the minister's name has nothing to do with throat but means "a great length of time." Thus Thondaman means "chieftain from time immemorial," or "Lord of a long line of chieftains," or "Lord of pedigree." The skill of the poet here is to merge the literal sense of the "throated one" with the minister's name which it evokes through homophony. But no sooner is the name of Thondaman brought into consciousness than he, the "Lord of pedigree," is brought into the foreground and the throated one recedes to lurk in the shadows. But from there it does its semeiotic work. It splits the minister's name into two unintended morphemes: *thondai,* meaning "throat," and *man,* which means "deer." Once linked to deer, *tontai* is no longer merely "throat" but becomes "neck." To secure this meaning, the poet yokes it with "the mother stem." To render the first two lines (the third line in the Tamil original) more literally: "Let the throated one and the mother stem grow together or grow alike." As you will recall, the mother stem on the tea bush is an unpruned (uncultured) stem whose posture is like that of a proud deer. But an unpruned stem is useless. One cannot pick from it the useful *koruntu.* It has been detected and will soon be cut down. Sound and sense have combined to cast a clearly outlined shadow: a deer, sometimes a pet of the rich, self-absorbed in its pedigree and beauty, with extended neck and veins pulsing, unaware of the rapid shifts in the tones of history. The poet goes on to note that the cutting down of Vellayan did not destroy him, even though the villain who wielded the knife might have expected just that. Instead, what we have is a crown of new leaves sprouting from the rim where once a well-crowned bush was supported. He who was cut down then (perhaps prematurely) is beginning to re-emerge now, and he who has continued to grow proudly long after he should have been pruned is nearing his end, like a deer that has stood still for too long a time, extending its neck, tempting the knife to do its job.

Tea Picking (Koruntu Etuttal)

Picking green tea leaves, women's work, constitutes the central and most conspicuous activity in a tea estate. The pluckers gather at muster by 6:15 A.M., and are in the fields among the bushes by 6:30. As indicated earlier, pluckers pick *koruntu,* the two tender green leaves at the very tip of a branch and the slightly curled leaf bud growing between them. This is done with a single nip of the tender stem at the base of the third leaf, held between the thumbnail and forefinger, and a simultaneous slight twist of the wrist. The other fingers tuck the nipped-off *koruntu* into the palms of the hands, where the leaves are held lightly so as not to braise them. When her hands are too full for the comfort of the leaves, she tosses the hands full of leaves into the basket (*kutai*) that hangs against her back from a rope strung over her head; and the emptied hands return in a flash to pick more *koruntu.*

A bush may be over- or under-picked. A bush may be over-picked in four ways. In the first two, the bush may not be harmed, but if caught the picker will be heavily penalized. The first entails the picking of the third leaf (*kattai ilai*), growing at the base of the *koruntu ,* along with or in addition to the *koruntu .* The second entails the picking of mature leaves (*karattai itai*). A *karattai ilai* is not merely mature but also coarse. If, during inspection, the supervisor finds either a *kattai ilai* or a *karattai ilai* in a woman's basket, he is likely to penalize her by deducting from her total poundage far more than she might have gained from having picked the mature leaves. The picking of a *karattai ilai* is seen as a far more serious violation than the picking of a *kattai ilai.* The third and fourth forms of over-picking adversely affect the healthy growth of the bush. In the third, the picker picks the *koruntu* off the side or peripheral branches (*pakka vatu*). Such picking curtails the horizontal spread of these branches, thereby depriving the soil underneath the bush of the invaluable shade needed to retard the growth of weeds which, if allowed to grow, compete with the tea bush for the nutrition of the soil. The fourth way of over-picking a bush is to pick the *arumpu,* or an unopened bud. In an *arumpu* the two tender base leaves that characterize the *koruntu* are either still barely separated from the terminal bud or are one with it. When an *arumpu* is picked, the stem that bore it, being too tender to support the sprouting of a new bud, withers, turns brown, and rolls back on itself. A new bud can sprout from this stem only after the withered stem is nipped with a knife.

The bush can also be under-picked. Under-picking directly affects the picker's poundage in two ways. First, she picks less than she might have. Second, if a *koruntu* is not picked in time, the next time around, the sprig will have grown into a mature stem or leaf, unfit for picking.

While picking tea leaves, a picker also carries with her a *koppi katti,* a six-inch-long knife with a curved beak which looks like a miniature version of a *kavvattu katti.* This knife is used to nip off bits of stem called *vanki koruntu.* A *vanki koruntu* is formed when there is a long space between the two leaves of the *koruntu* and the fourth leaf (*kattai ilai*) and when the *koruntu* is nipped so close to the twin leaves that there is left behind a long protrusion of leafless stem. As long as this length of stem remains, a new bud cannot sprout.

The tea bush, upon which so much of a woman's activity is concentrated, has also become the source of a profusion of metaphors for children, most often that of female children. The similarity between a child forced to work in the field at a very young age or subjected to excessive discipline and deprived of the privileges of childhood freedom and a bush whose peripheral branches are picked is obvious to a Tamil tea worker. Such discipline and deprivation are seen as misdirected, the actions of selfish, greedy, or short-sighted parents. To paraphrase one of my informants: the nourishing soil of healthy mystery is exposed to the scorching rays of premature knowledge, which in turn encourage the growth of the weeds of bad thoughts and habits capable of retarding, choking, and even killing the growth of a child and a family with a good name.

The experience of dislocation and displacement suffered by Tamil workers, especially the young, in the wake of the land reforms in 1974 and the series of communal violence since then, has been described as "the picking of *koruntu* from the peripheral branches." In this instance the over-picking is attributed not to the parents but to circumstances of fate. Those who never left the estates see the young raised in urban areas returning to the estates for brief visits as hardened and corrupt and characteristically displaying a thorough disregard for the old ways of deference and respect to elders and authority.

The men among these youth who return to the estates defy the custom of dressing down, wearing long trousers, shoes and Seiko watches and, above all, refusing to step to the edge of the road when the manager of the estate rides by on his motor bike or in his car. The same lack of deference is shown toward the staff of the estate, with more immediate and discomforting consequences for the kinsmen who still reside in and work on the estates.

The staff constitutes a middle category of estate employees who on the one hand ingratiate themselves to the estate manager (or superintendent) and are supremely arrogant toward Tamil laborers on the other. These are the mini-mimic men. They include office clerks, field supervisors, factory officers, the cooperative store clerks, and sometimes the truck drivers. Their intermediary position makes them acutely sensitive to the self-assuredness of the youth raised in the cities. The airs of these young people expose the vulnerability of their own position. Unable or afraid to take out their revenge on the visitor, members of the estate's staff make life extremely difficult for the parents, especially the mother of the young man. As a tea picker, the mother is the most vulnerable target of the vindictiveness of field supervisors. Her basket of tea may be underweighed; she may be falsely accused of wetting her load in the local waterfall; or she may be sent to pick tea on a hill where the bushes are old and are known for their poor yield. The list of possible reprisals could easily be extended, and is in practice.

The returnees see their parents, especially their fathers, as *matta kampus,* the eight-foot-long leveling stick set upon the bushes before tea picking. The contemptuous allusion is that their fathers are so servile that they are willing even to lie flat on their backs if called upon to substitute for a leveling stick. Throughout their lives, the women are most often compared to the *koruntu.* If the *koruntu* of the peripheral branches ought not to be picked, the *koruntu* of the central branches must be picked, when they are just right, no sooner, no later. To marry off a girl when she is too young is described as picking an *arumpu.* A virgin in her mid- to late-teens is likened to a *koruntu,* ripe for picking. A woman in her mid-twenties is compared to a *kattai ilai,* the third leaf, and an old maid is a *karattai ilai,* a mature and coarse leaf.

Communicative Event IV: Rage and Hope

A young girl who had left the estate in 1974 when she was twenty to work as a domestic servant in Colombo returned to the estate of her birth. She was welcomed back by her maternal uncle's wife with the words, "you left us as a *koruntu* and you come back as a *kattai ilai.*" Stung by this unkind remark, the girl's mother embarked upon a bitter tirade against the people and life on tea estates and proceeded to proclaim to all her plans for leaving the island for her husband's ancestral village in South India. In the following excerpt from her speech, I have attempted to provide a translation of one of the most eloquent orations of rage I have ever heard in any other language. Apart from revealing the manner in which she summons agricultural and agronomical images to make her point, I have attempted to highlight, for the reader who does not know Tamil, her use of alliteration by providing, wherever possible, italicized Tamil equivalents within brackets. The Tamil original follows the translation.

Damn the third leaf [*kattai ilaiyavatu*] and damn the stemlets [*kampavatu*]. Why don't you who are losing your luster [*mankal* also means dimming wit] suck [*umpu* (obscene)] on the *vanki* stem [sterile and useless protrusion]. This sucking [*umpal*] and this hell [*ural*] suits this land just fine. None of this can be pulled off in our [plural possessive exclusive] country [village India]. What business does a widow [*kompanat-ti*] have with a young virgin [*kumari*] and a tender sprout [*komntu*]. Cursed saturnine coarse leaf [*karattai ilai*]! Perish here. Go on, eat in silence [also in secret] kilo-loads of squeezed rice from the Sinhala man's [*cinkalavan*] hand. The foreign land [*cimai*] where we [*nanka,* first person exclusive, plural] are bound for, there are none of these tea sprouts (looks at daughter while she says this) and kilos [*koruntavatu kilovavatu*]. [There], ears of rice [*katir* also means ray of sun] and grain [*payir*] will pour [he measured out] in *palam*-loads [an Indian unit of measure]. You who weed five acres to earn five rupees in wages [*kuli*] how big you talk! In my grandfather's field of five *kottais,* for the barber who helps harvest the field for one day they pay him ten *patis.* . . . [As for you], you will climb the mountain [*malai*] and look for the level [*mattam* also implies, "lying down like the leveling stick"], I shall be on the level [*mat-*

tam] and look at the mountain [*malai*]. Once I board that ship [*kappal*] I shall not even lift my eyes [*kan*] to look back at these rowdy asses [*kavali karutaikal*] or this evil eye of a jungle [*kantishti katu*].

[*kattai ilaiyāvatu kāmpāvatu. ēn, manki pōra nī vanki koruntai ūmpēn. inta ūmpalum ūralum into ūrukku tān cari. komariyōteyum koruntōteyum kompanāttikku enna vēlai? cci cani karatta ilai! nī inka keta. cinkalavankaiyila pecanja cōtta pēcāma kilo kanak-kā tinnu. nānka pōra cimayila inta koruntum kīlōvunketaiyātu. katirum payirum palam palamā kottum. anji rūva kūlikku anji ēkkar kalai putunkira onakku enna pēccu. namma tāttāta anji kōttai vayalila nellarukkira ampattanukku oru nālukku pattu pati alappānka . . . ni malaiyila eri mattatta paru. nān mattattilayiruntu malaiya pāk-kirēn. anta kappalila ērunatum into kāvāli karutaikalayum kantishti kāttayum kannāla tirumpi kūta pākkamāttēn.*]

Apart from being impressed by this woman's remarkable ear for reverberating sounds and rhythms, phonemic metonymy, the analysis of which I must defer for another occasion, I was also struck by the number of agricultural and agronomical images she drew upon. At one level her verbal outrage is directed at her adversary. But at another level it is directed at Sri Lanka in general and the agronomic culture of tea in particular. I wish to turn my attention mainly to the latter.

This woman (I shall call her Celvi), like thousands of other Tamils of recent Indian origin, was actively planning her departure to India. When the Citizenship Act was first passed in 1948, almost none of the estate Tamils wished to return to India. India was, for most of them, as alien as Italy is to most Italian Americans. They knew India as their ancestral home, but they also knew it to be a land of great hardship, harsh climate, and chronic poverty. From the few who had been to village India they learned that even though their lot on the estates was a difficult one, it was luxury compared to life in an Indian village. By the time the Sirima-Shastri Pact[36] had been signed, the Tamils of Sri Lanka had already been the victims of three anti-Tamil riots; and the Sri Lankan government's own attempts to repatriate a section of these Tamils had taken an earnest turn. Yet, year after year, the quota of repatriations was not met. Some who had emigrated to the districts of Ramnadhapuram and Tirunelveli in the late 1960s and early 1970s re-immigrated to Sri Lanka to escape the severe drought that was consuming Southern India during those years. Many of these 'illicit immigrants,' as they are called in Sri Lankan English, were caught while attempting to land on the northern shores of the island and were blackmailed into working for indigenous Tamil land owners as indentured agricultural laborers.

After the events of July 1983, the overwhelming majority of estate Tamils, including many who had opted for Sri Lankan citizenship under the Sirima-Shastri Pact and had thereby given up all claims to Indian citizenship, were attempting to leave for India. For the first time that anyone could remember, India was on the receiving end of illicit immigrants. If we look at Celvi's harangue against this background, we see how she systematically invokes Sri Lankan tea estates' agronomic images in order to present, through them, an entirely tenebrous picture of Sri Lanka, a picture which the greater part of the estate Tamil community has come to share.

Celvi finds everything about the tea bush damnable. A bush that these Tamils had treated as a deity had now become a vehicle by means of which she could express obscenities. The piece of protruding stem is no longer a test of her care and attention for the tea bush, a blemish that beckons her to trim it away with her knife. Instead, it has become a withered penis that only her worst and contempt-worthy enemy would suck (*umpal*) on. Then again, by the metonymic juxtaposition of *ural* (hell) with *umpal,* hell becomes not merely a place of suffering—which indeed Sri Lanka had become—but also one of obscene iniquity. She opens her tirade with the disparaging metaphor of the third leaf that her sister-in-law had used on her daughter. She then follows it with a series of undesirables, such as *kampu* (picked pieces of stem) and *vanki koruntu* (unpicked, but protruding pieces of stem). All three are, agronomically speaking, of the same order of undesirables. But with the last in that series, she has yoked it with connotations of obscene morality on the part of her adversary. In a quick, cutting sentence Celvi reminds her that a widow like her could not possibly know anything about a *kumari* (young virgin, like her daughter) or its metaphor, *koruntu,* and in so doing indirectly restores her daughter to the status of a *koruntu.* Having done this, she reduces her sister-in-law to *the most* undesirable find in a tea picker's basket of tea leaves, a *karattai ilai* (a coarse, old leaf). Then she moves on to terminology of measures.

Celvi identifies her sister-in-law's state of being condemned to remain in a hell of an island as being condemned to eat kilo-loads of cooked rice, or more exactly, leavings, from the Sinhala man's hand. The word kilo comes to bear connotations of servility, bondage, even immoral concubinage. Before she contrasts this with a positively valued unit of measure found in village India, she interjects a transitional sentence in which she identifies *koruntu,* that most precious product of the tea estate, with the contemptible kilo. The fact that she looks (not very happily) at her daughter when she says *koruntu* and the fact that she follows it up with the next sentence, in which she speaks of bountiful *katir* in India, she is indicating that India, unlike Sri Lanka, will give her not daughters (even if they were *koruntu*), but sons. (Her son's name is Kadiresan).

Celvi refers to India as *cimai. Cimai* has undergone a double-inversion. It is a Tamil word originally used to mean something like homeland, or the place of birth to which one periodically returns. This usage is still prevalent in South India. Once domiciled in Sri Lanka's estate country, this word came to apply meaningfully and conspicuously only to the British superintendents who were, after all, the only ones who could afford to and did return to their homeland, to spend their furlough there. Despite inconspicuous exceptions, the tea estate laborers were [largely] confined—first economically and, subsequently, emotionally—to the estates. Thus, *cimai* came to mean England. Now, in Celvi's vocabulary, the word had taken another turn, spiraling up to a new point in its evolution. She calls India *cimai.* By identifying India with England she is identifying India with England's presumed prosperity. In that land, rice and grain will be measured not in kilos but in *palam*s. Quite clearly, a *palam,* as far as Celvi is concerned, is a unit of measure found in India and, therefore, must be a generous one. By contrasting this measure with the kilo of the preceding sentence, she clearly wishes to set this presumed contrast in clear relief. In fact, a palam as a unit of measure is a mere idea, a trace of a tradition, and one that has no practical usage among the Tamils of Sri Lanka. Furthermore, it is, ironically, quite small. More agronomical and agricultural terminology follows. The miserly wages her sister-in-law *cams* are described as *kuli,* which also refers to a person of servile status (hence, the word coolie, now naturalized into English). Furthermore, she earns these wages by doing one of the lowliest of jobs on the estate, weeding. Even the barber in India does more honorable work, the harvesting of sun-warmed sheaves of rice. Celvi's adversary weeds acres. The barber in India who works in her grandfather's fields works in *kottais,* which is not strictly a measure of area, but of yield of grain (8 *pati* equal 1 *marakkal;* 12 *marakkal* equal 1 *kalam;* 7/8 *kalam* equal 1 *kottai*). It also means fortress. And the barber is not paid humiliating *kuli* but in *patis* of grain, the traditional payment in village India that signifies a traditional bond between landlord and field hand.

Then comes the comparison of the terrain: the flat desirable plains of village India against the arduous mountains of Sri Lanka's tea estates. In India, the mountain is only something to look at and enjoy (or perhaps gloat over in that one does not have to work on it). In Sri Lanka, one labors on the mountains and looks down enviously upon the plains. The sentence also implies having to prostrate one's self flat on one's back or belly, like a leveling stick, in the most abject servility, if and when management calls upon one to do so. And the final contrast is between India, the *ūr* (home, the civilized village to which one belongs) and Sri Lanka, the *katu,* or jungle, which is inhabited by wild animals and is an immense evil eye.[37]

These transformations are not passive records of history but active embodiments of the genealogy of power relations. The evolution of these terms (even if only by chance, as Foucault would have us see matters) illustrates their embodiment in semeiotic practice in space and time as they came to be articulated as a "metonymical concatenation of deviation from the norm [while concurrently engaging in] a progressive creation of metaphors."[38]

Word has come back that India is not the utopia it was imagined to be. Some have described it as a worse hell than Sri Lanka. Repatriots, the quaint term for those who return and are returned, are swindled and cheated from the time when they first disembark from the boat until they reached their remembered villages. Many repatriots are destitute. Some have become beggars in the streets of Madurai, Madras, and other cities and towns in South India; some women have turned to prostitution. The minister and labor union leader, Thondaman, who was sung of as a villain by the poet in 1983, has survived radical changes in the governing party, played his cards deftly, won pay increases and citizenship for his people, and has thereby regained considerable support from them. The view of him as a traitor is retained only by a recalcitrant minority. But the poet thinks something has changed: "The old days are gone. They say the tea bush lives only a hundred and twenty years. 1867 to 1967. It's over. We may stay, we may leave. But we won't be tea estate workers for much longer. There is the factory (pointing at the tea factory). Here is the fire (pointing to his chest). Bring the two together. Finished!"

Conclusion

The history of South Indian Tamil workers who migrated to Ceylon (later Sri Lanka) is one of confinement and limitations upon choices. In recent years, under the force of anti-Tamil ethnic violence, estate Tamils have been moved to make choices, and in the mid-1980s, many of them were choosing to recover, in reality and in their imaginations, what they had lost in their villages of ancestral India. An agronomy that had relentlessly imposed limitations upon the variability of the natural environment had also, through its colonial agents, attempted to impose limitations on the variability of the cultural environment—sometimes by force, but more often by consent both subtle and complex—by making available a vocabulary that marked the boundaries of permissible discourse. What may have at first appeared as mere terms, convenient, universal and neutral in values, turned out to be the very signs that contained and carried forth the hegemony of agronomy and its capitalist concomitants through time as signs of history. These terms had become metaphor, metonym, and synecdoche, in Hayden White's sense, of these workers' very existence.[39]

Consent, so central to Gramsci's understanding of hegemony, is not a simple mental state. Rather, it entails a contradictory consciousness in the subaltern, "mixing approbation and apathy, resistance and resignation."[40] Counter-hegemonic forces find their impulsion in a variety of semeiotic pools. In the case of these estate workers, a recovered past of an agricultural world of approximations provides one such pool.

It is commonplace to note that a past thus recovered is inextricably linked to the present. But such a past cannot and must not be understood in purely temporal terms. Rather, what I wish to define as past and present is more akin to Walter Benjamin's pairing of the past and the now in the image: "It isn't that the past casts its light on the present or the present casts its light on the past; rather, an image is that in which the past and the now flash into a constellation. In other words, image is dialectics at a standstill. For while the relation of the present to the past is a purely temporal, continuous one, the relation of the Then to the Now is dialectical-isn't development but image [,] capable of leaping out (*sprunghaft*). Only dialectical images are genuine (i.e., not archaic images); and the place one encounters them is language."[41]

To call these recoveries signs is also to ask what manner of signs they are. They clearly signify many things, some of which we have already considered in the body of this essay and do not need to be recounted. But it is worth considering the manner of their signification, their mode and mood. For this let us briefly return to C. S. Peirce, who describes several trichotomous, hierarchically ordered types of signs, including triads of interpretants. By interpretant he meant the significant effect of signs upon a third; or more simply, the means by which interpretation is effected. In one of the trichotomies Peirce mentions the production of three hierarchically nested effects: gratification, action, and self-control. He also called these, respectively, the emotional interpretant, the energetic interpretant, and the logic interpretant. As in all genuine hierarchies, each subsequent kind of interpretant subsumes the former, but not vice versa. Thus, logical interpretants contain impulses of (physical or mental) effort and emotions; energetic interpretants, non-conceptual effort and emotions; and emotion interpretants, only a welling of feelings before action or thought take form.[42]

Had Antonio Gramsci had access to Peirce's arcane vocabulary and chosen to use it, he might well have characterized hegemony as actions constituted by logical interpretants, the kinds that contain—in both senses of the term—energetic and emotional interpretants. When Peirce wrote of logical interpretants, he had in mind a world constituted by the repose of habit. Of course, Peirce, the ever-sanguine utopian, attributed to human beings the habit of "taking and laying aside habits,"[43] the "self-analyzing habit,"[44] or the habit of self-control.[45] In the world of logical interpretants, reason is expected to exert its "gentle force" of reasonableness. There are of course lower-order habits, wherein matter is not apart from mind but is merely "mind whose habits have become fixed so as to lose the power of forming them and losing them."[46] Here we have self-control without agency, as it were. In a hegemonic regime a la Gramsci, this lower order of habits constitutes the logical interpretants of the socio-cultural domain or a significant part thereof.

In the communicative events considered here, we see a deconstruction of the hierarchic encompassment of persuasive reason. In a hegemonic universe, not only do logical interpretants form an intricately linked script that spreads its mantle over underlying layers of emotional and energetic interpretants, concealing and calming them, but, moreover, logical interpretants are also inscribed in the other interpretants in minuscule, though inconspicuously. The conch that sounds for muster, sounds for prayer too. In the communicative events we have considered, logical interpretants are dismantled to expose and make viable underlying emotional and energetic interpretants. Words and acts linked together in imperceptible minuscules are disarticulated, thrown asunder, scattered about, and transformed into conspicuously quaint—if not monstrous—majuscules.

In language, metaphors and poetry are privileged repositories of emotional interpretants. Peirce also names gratification and recognition as principle attributes of emotional interpretants. Gratification, though, must be seen not only as the fulfillment of desire but also, perhaps more important, as the acute realization of its non-fulfillment, as the realization of what deprivation really is. In recent years, thanks to the dismantling of the hegemony of logical interpretants, the Tamils of Sri Lanka's estates have awakened in the grip of such a realization. Recognition is, in Peirce's scheme, an iconic function, literally, of cognizing again. As already indicated, an icon is a sign that resembles its object. The recovery of resemblances, then, is at the heart of recognition. But re-cognizing is not only cognizing what was but what might be as well. Such recognitions invoke a past as much as they chart out a future, a future that could subvert and avoid familiar hegemonies. Whether the past in question is real or imagined is only of philosophical interest. Suffice it to note that the objects of iconic signs may be real existents or only imaginary entities. Wherein does the power of emotional interpretants lie? Wherein the power to transform?

The word emotion brings to mind a welling of feeling, an overflowing of affect. This is certainly true of the communicative events we have considered. Emotional interpretants find their sources in re-cognitions as well as re-membrances, both of which are iconic functions. But the iconic bases of these emotional interpretants provide another insight into the source of their power. As Peirce observed, iconic signs are also diagrammatic. And diagrams select features for representation, disregarding the rest. Mathematical equations are among the most powerful icons. In their very leanness they reveal connections in the object they represent that, without these icons, would have laid concealed in the amplitude of the object. Likewise, the most effective metaphors are lean and can be mean. Metaphors wrench words from their context. But if they destroy, they also reveal. "Fourth leaf!" Mimicry, another iconic function, can turn into mockery; mockery to the undermining of hegemonic conceit. "Dompiling." Metaphors and mimicry employ the iconic function only to index, to point, to throw into clear relief.

The laying bare of energetic interpretants is likewise the result of the dismantling of the hegemonic dominance of logical interpretants, the world of habit. Uncontained by logical interpretants and driven by emotional interpretants they contain, energetic interpretants lead to spontaneous action. Ungoverned by the courtesies of rule-governed behavior, energetic interpretants explode. Their meanings are precipitated, not before, nor after, but in the act, the Perumal cut.

I have not presented these communicative events merely for linguistic show and tell or to display the poetic genius of a people. I have presented them as instances of indigenous interpretations, the writing of effective history. I have attempted to capture such interpretation, such writing, in the act. Bearing this in mind, I would like to end where I began, quoting Foucault: "If interpretation is the violent or surreptitious appropriation of a system of rules . . . in order to impose direction, to bend it to a new will, to force its participation in a different game, and to subject it to secondary rules, then the development of humanity is a series of interpretations. The role of genealogy is to record its [effective] history; the history of the event]. [By "event" is meant], the reversal of a relationship of forces, the usurpation of power, [and] the appropriation of a vocabulary tamed against those who had once used it."[47]

NOTES

Acknowledgments: The original draft of this essay was written for and presented at a workshop on "Agricultural Terminology," in New Orleans in 1986, funded by the Social Science Research Council and the American Council of Learned Societies. A year at the Institute for Advanced Study, Princeton, enabled me, among other things, to rewrite the paper extensively. That wonderful year was made possible by a grant from the National Endowment for the Humanities. A subsequent draft was presented at a second SSRC/ACLS workshop in New Hampshire in 1987. Revised drafts were also read at seminars at the Institute for Advanced Study at Princeton, The University of Chicago, and at The University of Michigan. Participants at all these fora made significant contributions towards the improvement of this essay. I would like to single out for special thanks the following individuals from whose comments I benefited greatly: Arjun Appadurai, Susan Bean, Bernard Cohn, Nicholas Dirks, Carol Eastman, Richard Kurin, David Ludden, Harry Powers, Franklin Pressler, David Spain, and my wife, Margaret Hocy-Daniels.

1. Anthropological fieldwork on which material for this essay has been drawn was carried out in 1971, 1974, 1976, 1983–1984, and 1987. The most extensive research of 1983–1984, funded by a grant from the Social Science Research Council, is gratefully acknowledged.

2. Carol Eastman (personal communication) directed my attention to the cultural versus nomic distinction in agriculture and agronomy, the former indicating practice-generated behavior and the latter rule-governed behavior. By extension one may note the nominalist epistemology of agronomy and the realist epistemology of agriculture. The former imposes a name (order) on the world; the latter indicates names as real emergents from the world.

3. Peirce's (and my) rationale for this spelling are twofold: "(1) There is no

more reason for semeiotics or semiotics than for logics or dietetics, (2) Both the spelling and the pronunciation should (in this case at least) be signs of etymology; that is, should make it evident that the derivation is from Greek *sememe* (sign), not from Latin *semi-* (half)." There is nothing halfway about semeiotic—it is all about signs, and it is about all signs. And the o in semiotic should be long because it has behind it a Greek omega, not an omicron" (Max H. Fisch 1978: 32).

4. In my book, *Charred Lullabies: Chapters in an Anthropography of Violence* (Princeton University Press, 1996), I have addressed this apparent dilemma more amply.

5. Even if primogeniture is not strictly observed in South India, it is known to assert itself in times of material scarcity.

6. For the sake of simplicity, clarity, and convenience, I have chosen to indicate the plurals of Tamil words by adding an "s" in roman type (not italicized) to the end of a word.

7. In many estates, a line room consists of an open front porch, a middle room and a kitchen, the total unit measuring 10 feet by 10 feet. One can find as many as twenty-five such rooms in a single row.

8. Foucault 1979: 150.

9. Ibid. What may appear as a liberal use of Foucault in this essay is in fact a cautious one. I have been cognizant of the inappropriateness of imposing European problematics onto Asian ones. However, the appropriateness of extending Foucault's study of the birth of the disciplinary regime in Europe to facilitate the understanding of the social formations of nineteenth-century plantations in Europe's colonies cannot be minimized.

10. Since the late 1960s, the shift has been gradually made to the metric system of weights and measures. Even though the conversion was to have been officially completed by 1970, the adoption of the metric system is uneven in the manufacture of tea. In the manuals and account books (especially as they near the point of export), the metric has fully replaced the older English system of weights and measures. In the field, however, the English system persists.

11. Foucault 1979: 188.

12. Ibid., 152.

13. For an interesting glimpse into this world, see the *Annual Reports* of the Tea Research Institute (1966, 1967) and also its "One Day Course in Tea Production" (1963).

14. The name given to the huge ledgers in which are recorded the names and productivity (among other matters) of individual workers.

15. Weber 1948: 284–85.

16. Both Sinhalese and Tamils have forgotten the Arabic origin of this word. Most Sinhalese believe that *hunduva* came from the Tamil *cundu,* and the Tamils believe that it came from Sinhala; but both treat it as a thoroughly domesticated "folk-measure."

17. The idea of "a little extra" is not conveyed in a single expression but in a variety of verbal and gestural forms. One of the commoner forms such an expression takes is to be found in the utterance (with appropriate hand gesture, facial expression, and head movement), *"cumma konjam pattu potunka"* (literally: just or simply / a little / look or take note of / and give).

18. For a more detailed analysis of the symbolic import of the odd-numbered gift, see my *Fluid Signs* (1984: 131–35).

19. Material on which this paragraph is based was gathered in the field during my 1973–1974 research in Tamil Nadu.

20. For a more enhanced understanding of the intricate play of signs in the context of food and feasts in a South Indian community that is unrivalled in its celebration of "gastro-politics," see Appadurai (1981: 494–511).

21. For example, see R. J. Johnson, *Johnson's Note Book for Tea Planters* (1962).

22. The kind of pruning and the length of the pruning cycle varies according to elevation and climate. In the low country (below approximately 2,000 feet) rim-lung pruning or cut-across pruning is carried out every two years; in the mid-country (between approximately 2,000 and 4,000 feet) cut-across pruning with lungs; in the up-country (above approximately 4,000 feet), clean pruning with no lungs is the norm (see fig. 12). The branches that are spared the pruner's knife are called lungs, presumably because they help the plant to breathe, while the rest of the bush is subjected to radical surgery of sorts.

23. The scale indicates both pounds and kilograms. The announcement of the weights, which continue to be called out in pounds, may or may not be recorded at this stage in kilograms. Quite often conversions are done at the very end of the bookkeeping process in the estate offices and factories.

24. Sanderson 1964: 146–56.

25. I prefer the adjectival forms, iconic, indexical, and symbolic to the nominal forms, icon, index, and symbol because the latter misleadingly convey the sense that there can be signs that are exclusively icons, or indexes, or symbols. Not so. All signs partake of mixed signifying modes, with one mode rending to dominate in the manner in which significance is effected.

26. The origin of the foot as a unit is often said to be traceable to the length of a certain French monarch's foot.

27. Parmentier 1985.

28. If a *kankani* feels that he has "over-abused" someone, he will compensate her by giving her bonus pounds at the day's end at the weighing shed.

29. Foucault 1984: 89.

30. Ibid., 83.

31. Silverstein 1976.

32. See Homi Bhabha's essay (1984: 127–42), in which mimicry is somewhat differently inflected but which nonetheless considerably influences my own thoughts on the subject.

33. Homi Bhabha 1984: 125–33.

34. The Sinhala peasant worker who resides in his or her own neighboring village is to be distinguished from the few Sinhala resident workers. What follows applies only to the peasants.

35. Only a few years earlier, the same response could have been read as sarcasm. This was not true in 1984, when I recorded this episode.

36. This refers to the pact reached in October 1964, between the then prime ministers of Sri Lanka and India, Sirimavo Bandaranaike and Lal Bhadur Shastri, respectively. According to this pact, of the estimated 975,000 persons of recent Indian origin in Sri Lanka who were stateless, 525,000 (together with the natural increase in their number) were to be granted Indian citizenship and repatriated to India over fifteen years; 300,000 (together with the natural increase in their number) were to be granted Sri Lankan citizenship over the same period of time; the status and future of the remaining 150,000 (and the natural increase in their number) were to be decided on in a separate, future agreement between the two governments.

37. Daniel 1984: ch. 2.

38. Kristeva 1980: 40.

39. White 1973: 31–33.

40. Gramsci 1971: 326–27, 333; Lears 1985: 568.

41. Benjamin 1983–1984: 1–40.

42. Peirce, 1958: 5.474–76. In keeping with convention, the number to the left of the decimal point indicates the volume and that to the right indicates the paragraph.

43. Ibid., (6.101).

44. Ibid., (5.491).

45. Peirce n.d. (MS, 612,7). MS refers to Peirce's unpublished manuscripts, identified in terms of the numbers used by The Houghton Library at Harvard.

46. Pierce 1958: 6.101.

47. Foucault 1984: 88.

REFERENCES

Appadurai, Arjun. 1981. "Gastro-politics in Hindu South Asia." *American Ethnologist* 8, 3: 494–11.

———. 1986. "The Terminology of Measurement in the Peasant Community of Maharashtra." Paper presented at workshop on "Agricultural Terminology," in New Orleans.

Bakhtin, Mikhail M. 1981. *The Dialogical Imagination: Four Essays by Bakhtin,* Michael Holquist, ed. Austin: University of Texas Press.

Bhabha, Homi. 1984. "Of Mimicry and Man: The Ambivalence of Colonial Discourse." *October,* 125–33.

Benjamin, Walter. 1983–1984. "Theoretics of Knowledge; Theory of Progress," Leigh Hafrey and Richard Sieburth, trans. *The Philosophical Forum* 15, 1–2: 1–40.

Daniel, E. Valentine. 1984. *Fluid Signs: Being a Person the Tamil Way.* Berkeley: University of California Press.

———. 1996. *Charred Lullabies: Chapters in an Anthropography of Violence.* Princeton: Princeton University Press.

Fisch, Max H. 1978. "Peirce's General Theory of Signs." In, Thomas Sebeok, ed., *Sight, Sound and Sense.* Bloomington: Indiana University Press.

Foucault, Michel. 1979. *Discipline and Punish: The Birth of the Prison.* New York: Vintage Books.

———. 1984. "Nietzsche, Genealogy, History." In, Paul Rabinow, ed., *Foucault Reader.* New York: Pantheon Books.

Gramsci, Antonio. 1971. *Selections from the Prison Notebooks.* New York: International Publishers.

Johnson, R. J. 1962. *Johnson's Notebook for Tea Planters.* Lake House Press: Colombo.

Kristeva, Julia. 1980. *Desire in Language.* New York: Columbia University Press.

Lears, T. J. Jackson. 1985. "The Concept of Cultural Hegemony: Problems and Possibilities." *The American Historical Review* 90, 3 (June): 568.

Parmentier, Richard. 1985. "Signs' Place in Medias Res: Peirce's Concept of Semiotic Mediation." In, Richard Parmentier and Elizabeth Mertz, eds., *Semiotic Mediation.* New York: Academic Press.

Peirce, Charles S. 1958. *Collected Papers, Vols. 1–8.* Cambridge, Mass.: Harvard University Press.

———. n.d. Unpublished Manuscripts. Cambridge, Mass.: Houghton Library, Harvard University.

Sanderson, G. W. 1964. "The Theory of Withering in Tea Manufacture." *Tea Quarterly* 35, 3: 146–56.

Silverstein, Michael. 1976. "Shifters, Linguistic Categories, and Cultural Description." In, Keith H. Basso and Henry A. Selby, eds., *Meaning in Anthropology.* Albuquerque: University of New Mexico Press.

Tea Research Institute. 1963. *One Day Course in Tea Production.* St. Coombs, Ceylon.

———. 1966 and 1967. *Annual Reports.* St. Coombs, Ceylon.

Weber, Max. 1948. *From Max Weber: Essays in Sociology.* H. H. Gerth and C. Wright Mills, trans. and ed. New York: Oxford University Press.

White, Hayden, 1973. *Metahistory.* Baltimore: Johns Hopkins University Press.

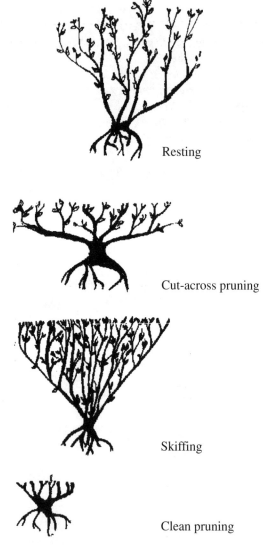

Resting

Cut-across pruning

Skiffing

Clean pruning

Fig. 12. If left unpruned, the tea bush will not be a bush but a tree (see "resting," above). Pruning stimulates growth and maintains the bush at the proper height for picking. There are three types of pruning: skiffing, cut-across pruning, and clean pruning. (Courtesy of E. Valentine Daniel.)

"Better Occasional Murders than Frequent Adulteries": Discourses on Banditry, Violence, and Sacrifice in the Mediterranean

Paul Sant Cassia

Banditry and Its Ambiguities

Fernand Braudel once observed that "banditry" was "an ill-defined word if ever there was one" (1972, 1: 102). Subsequent debate has confirmed his view. This article is not an exercise in semantics, but explores the concept of banditry from a different set of perspectives than the parameters set by the Hobsbawm-Blok debate in its various manifestations. As is well known, Hobsbawm (1969) and others (Joseph 1990) viewed banditry in populist-romantic terms (banditry expresses pre-political sentiments and a desire for a just world). Alternatively, it has been seen by hard-nosed empiricist revisionists (Blok 1972; Vanderwood 1981; Driessen 1983; Hart 1987; Koliopoulos 1987; Slatta 1987) as collectively, politically repressive and individually interested. In this paper I take the view that this debate, if pursued further along this line, risks becoming increasingly sterile and marginal to contemporary scholarship. I suggest that Hobsbawm essentialized the concept in terms that were too narrowly Marxist, and thus forced the discussion into certain directions that prevent us from addressing important issues about criminality, representation, violence, the psychology and sociology of terror, and how bandit myths may be created and used within nation-states or societies aspiring to nationhood.

Conversely, I argue that Blok and his followers do not take discourses on banditry into account. Banditry is not just a specific form of lawlessness in the countryside which can be harnessed by political forces. "Banditry" is a statist definition of certain types of violent behavior, not necessarily seen in the same way at the grassroots. It operates between the state-imposed system of law, the courts, social order, and so forth, and the local system of vengeance and grassroots conceptions of justice. It is a specific form of arbitrary personal prepotence and agency that has its own "aesthetic" and accompanying discourses, and thrives on, and constitutes itself through, the production of overdetermined signs and symbols. This personal power and symbolization may well have cumulative political (class) implications, but not necessarily in the way one would automatically assume. As a form of extreme personal power, "banditry" can survive after its formal conditions have disappeared. As an expression of agency, involving violence to persons and things, banditry is illegal in state-defined terms, but it may well extract consent or complicity at the grassroots. How authorities have responded to this form of prepotence (either through extreme savagery or cooption of strong-arm men) has itself influenced grassroots responses to agency there. The state is therefore complicit in the construction and interpretation of banditry.

Even more fundamental in the modern state's project of homogenizing and nationalizing time and space is that the state has used banditry as a means to produce discourses on order, time, legality, justice and legitimacy (of the state), and local cultures. In its shaping by functionaries, intellectuals, writers, politicians, and investigators of all sorts, banditry has had a disemic identity. Since the nineteenth century there have been two discourses on banditry, intimately tied with the nation state and the geography of its imagination. First, *bandites d'honneur,* heroes of the vendetta, personal honor, "saints," or saint-like, on the periphery of society, are always presented on the horizon of the past, as traces of a nostalgic world that has been lost forever. The closer one gets to it, the more it appears to recede. Conversely, there are "contemporary bandits" involved in such things as protection rackets, common robberies, and murder. An extreme form is contemporary political brigandage which merges with political terrorism, blending political programs, covert violence, and protection rackets. "Genuine" banditry always seems to have existed in the past, never in the present. "Banditry" can therefore be seen a metaphor of, and from, time. Through these two poles the state constructs discourses about order and legitimacy, whilst also stereotyping regions as inhabiting a "different time" than that of the modern state, and thus legitimating savage repression. But because banditry is often a myth of nation-statehood which legitimates itself by reference to popular culture, notions of freedom can be used by those resisting the state or carving out their own power domains.

As a category, banditry is thus a state historiographic discourse about order, ordering, justice, and freedom. In contrast to Hobsbawm, I do not claim that the symbolism of banditry is "true" but concealed (even from its practitioners). Neither do I claim with Blok that it is "false," and distorting (even from its victims). Rather, I suggest that banditry has a symbolizing or inherently ambiguous signifying role for the construction of power within the nation state.

Banditry can be approached as a legal category, a social category, a social representation, and as a series of stories and myths. Its meaning has changed across time. As a *legal category* it may be "part of the metalanguage of crime rather than crime itself" (Moss 1979: 478). Adopting a statist definition, one could consider banditry to be the consistent, relatively long-term flouting of the laws of the state by groups of individuals. They are so supported and protected by a local population or potentates, either spontaneously or through a complex combination of covert and overt threats and incentives, that their betrayal to the state's agents conflicts with dominant grassroots moral sentiments. Officially a bandit may be "a man who responds to a summons by taking to the maquis,"[1] although he may become something more than that. From the perspective of the "bandit" himself the situation may be viewed quite differently: as a man who "killed an enemy and took to the maquis abandoning wife and family to avoid public justice and private revenge" (Wilson 1988: 339).

As a *social category* "banditry" employs a specific form of personalized violence within a state framework, formally delegitimized by the state, but which may evoke notions of justice against the rule of law. Thus, as a *social representation* banditry may be polyvalent or even disemic and may encompass diametrically opposed sets of values: violence and generosity, secrecy and openness, and incorporation in and exclusion from the moral community (Herzfeld 1985). Banditry can be seen as an idealized "redistribution" of material and/or symbolic value through the emplotment of violence as a series of performative signs linking the parties to the "exchange." Finally, as *a series of stories* that should not be told but are told just the same, it socializes a depoliticized individualized interpretation of its consequences. Banditry thus often blinds its witnesses to its political consequences.

The Political Economy of Violence

In this essay I am interested in exploring the social and economic conditions of banditry with reference to Cyprus and other Mediterranean and

Latin American societies. I contextualize banditry in discourses by the state and intellectuals, and try to show how the significance of banditry changed across time. By analyzing the use of extreme violence that accompanied banditry at the grassroots and the violence of its suppression, I suggest that the bandit figure in the Ancien Regime was not so much a noble figure but a tragic one, a sacrificial victim of the interaction of the state and the local community. I then show how banditry assumed different nuances from the Enlightenment onwards and was enmeshed in the process of constructing a folk culture as well as problematizing regional and local identities. Finally I try to deconstruct a particular example of banditry in Cyprus.

I begin by examining banditry in various Mediterranean and Latin American societies, and Cyprus, to show why British colonial rule was initially unable to impose its monopoly of violence—a heritage of the previous Ottoman administration—on the Cypriot countryside. I then suggest that we ought to go beyond the confines of the parameters of the debate between the "essentialists" (Hobsbawm, et al.) and the "revisionists" (Blok, et al.). I argue that the sentiments inspired by the bandits should not be seen, as Hobsbawm argues, as a yearning for a pre-political just world, nor should the terror they instill merely be understood as a means to keep the peasants docile, as Blok argues. I suggest that most accounts of banditry fail to tackle two interrelated factors: the extreme signification of violence that often accompanies "banditry," and the complex sociology of terror. For the first I suggest that the signs of extreme violence that accompany banditry, both in its practice and *in its repression* (especially, but not exclusively in the "Ancien Regime") may provide clues as to why bandits appeared to have become popular symbols to the populace then. It is not because they practiced extreme violence and revenge; it is rather because, when caught and juridically processed, their bodies became the subject of publicly demonstrated state power. By his public execution and suffering the bandit is conjured up as a victim of a terrible state power, and thus as sacrifice. Rather than seeing the violent actions of bandits as a yearning for a pre-political just world (a product of romantic imaginings of the nation state which peopled its landscape with figures from the past, such as the noble bandit), we must recognize that it is in their violent executions that "bandits" witness both the transcendent notions of retribution-justice, and that a pre-political just world that can only be realized, like the sufferings of saints, as an imagined utopia outside of time.

Secondly, as an exchange between individuals, banditry often employs a specific set of finely graded messages involving violence to the body and property of the victim. Violence employed in banditry (as against other forms of social engagement) is resolutely personalized. It is targeted specifically against persons, and things as properties of persons, and displayed through stories. "Reason" dictates that such excess "personalized" violence could not but of necessity have had a personal genesis of which it is an expression. Banditry displays itself socially in the form "retribution as justice," where the ferocity of signification of an imploding vortex of "reciprocity" between two parties renders it a private affair not to be witnessed to the state.

The above suggests we must reconfigure the functionality of fear. Fear is a necessary but not a sufficient cause for the persistence of banditry, and the decline of banditry cannot be attributed merely to the state's increasing monopoly of violence, as Blok suggests. Banditry can often survive and indeed resurface, even in contexts in which the state is strong; and terror and its conscious unpredictability can be seen as constituting a special type of authority. Such authority is often accepted implicitly by the grassroots and hence legitimated as being in opposition to the state. Furthermore, wider factors must be adduced to explain the persistence of banditry and its reemergence. These include both economic and political factors. The nature of capital accumulation, transformation through reinvestment, or disaccumulation all contribute in different ways to the particular evolution of banditry in specific contexts. Finally, myths of banditry are significant in that in certain contexts they have been incorporated in nationalist or regionalist rhetoric and can be used to legitimate subsequent examples of lawlessness in the countryside.

A significant feature of banditry in the Mediterranean and Latin America is its political dimension. This includes the way it has been subsequently presented at the local and national levels. Throughout the Mediterranean and Latin America, banditry has often been incorporated in nationalist and regional rhetoric in various complex ways, at least as far back as the eighteenth century. *Brigantaggio Politico* had already emerged as a central feature of Corsican independence strategies against Genoa under Paoli and Gaffori in the mid-eighteenth century (Carrington 1971). Political banditry often required outside support to be successful. This was the case in Corsica and in southern Italy (Calabria), and Sicily, in the early nineteenth century where "our chivalrous brigand-allies" were supported by the British against the French (Douglas 1994: 322). In post-independence Greece, *klephtic* heroes figured prominently in nationalist rhetoric.

Although analysis is made problematic by the fact that they often terrorized and robbed peasants and blackmailed the state as well, this fact does not deter contemporary Cretan shepherds from drawing upon such symbols to legitimate their sheep-rustling activities (Herzfeld 1985). In Sicily, Salvatore Giuliano's ambiguous notoriety, created partly through extensive press coverage, derives from his expression of regional aspirations, even though he also massacred peasants.

In Latin America, banditry has had a strong political dimension, especially since the latter nineteenth century. Originally embedded in cattle raising and smuggling in a frontier economy, banditry and violence "linked peon and gaucho, bandit and ranch hand, smuggler and policeman" (Duncan Baretta and Markoff 1978: 616), and was to subsequently imprint a dominant model of the progress of "civilization" over "barbarism." By the late nineteenth century banditry was not pre-political according to Slatta, who finds little evidence of "social" banditry: "unlike social bandits, political bandits show clear partisan (rather than class) leanings. Unlike the pre-political social bandit [whom he dismisses-PSC], political bands were conscious of and loyal to a larger political movement. In Mexico and Cuba, political bandits did not switch sides for financial gain but worked towards a political, partisan and regional agenda" (ibid.: 148). He suggests "groups resorted to banditry if they could not organize or protest through the judicial system" (ibid.: 149). Here it is clear that Slatta and his contributors are talking about banditry in terms of mass and violent sustained resistance and political mobilization, often in the countryside, as a "weaker strategy" available among other strategies, including Scott's "weapons of the weak" (1985).[2] Nevertheless, it is clear that political banditry of this sort conceals (paraphrasing Edmund Burke) "the mean and interested struggle" for wealth and resources. "Political banditry" in the Columbian *Violencia* from the late 1940s to the early 1960s was closely linked with political party struggles, but for various complex reasons it became detached from the evolving political struggle. Bandits delegitimized themselves by their preying on peasants, were abandoned by the parties they had previously supported, and were criminalized by the state (Sanchez and Meertens 1987). Unsurprisingly, in contrast to the powerful myths of the Brazilian Lampiao and others (Chandler 1978), in Columbia "the bandit personifies a cruel and inhuman monster . . . the 'son of the *Violencia*,' frustrated, disoriented, and manipulated by local leaders" (Sanchez and Meertens 1987: 168). One may be tempted to quip that banditry is condemned to be "social" (politically correct but misdirected) in the past, and "political" (i.e., anti-social and politically repressive) in the present.

Ambiguity and the packaging of the myth of banditry in literate state contexts are significant features which cannot be disregarded as mere frills. That bandits often terrorized peasants who appear to have voluntarily supported them is often indubitable yet does not exhaust or even address the significance of why and how banditry emerged, how it was sustained, and the potency of bandit myths at both the local and national levels. Bandits are often romanticized afterwards through nationalist rhetoric and texts which circulate and have a life of their own, giving them a permanence and potency which transcends their localized domain and transitory nature. How bandits are portrayed in the modern nation-state and the way in which such symbols are utilized to legitimate contemporary struggles is as significant as what they actually did and represented.

Banditry in Cyprus

As in many Mediterranean societies, Cyprus had its own share of banditry until the end of the nineteenth and the beginning of the twentieth centuries. This essay examines the most famous band, known as the Hassanpoulia, which operated in the rugged Paphos countryside in the late nineteenth century. In contrast to Sicily, for example, to which nineteenth- century Cypriot banditry initially bears some superficial resemblances (for example, large-scale livestock rustling by ex-pastoralists, and protection rackets), banditry in Cyprus in the twentieth century never reached the spectacular proportions of the Hassanpoulia. Contemporary bandits rarely survived for very long and did not form into large bands until the emergence of EOKA militants in the late 1950s, who largely followed bandit ways.[3] Hence, it is important to ask why banditry on such a large scale disappeared in Cyprus by the end of the nineteenth century for nearly fifty years until the EOKA emerged. Certain anthropologists, as well as military men sent out to hunt bandits, have found answers in the state's increasing control of the monopoly of violence, and the growth of civilization or the civilizing process. I hope to show that these explanations are inadequate.

A distinctive variable of banditry concerns the process of mythification. Bandits in Greece, such as *klephts*, were incorporated into nationalist rhetoric (Koliopoulos 1987). By contrast, banditry in Cyprus never assumed nationalist overtones. Although the Hassanpoulia subsequently enjoyed brief recurrent periods of popular revival, they never became incorporated into nationalist rhetoric. Indeed, when EOKA bands took to the hills in 1955 to fight the British, they traced their spiritual descent not from their early Cypriot forebears, such as the Hassanpoulia, who had been involved in skirmishes with British-led police and the army, but rather from the much earlier and equally dubious mainland Greek *klepht*s who had ostensibly taken up arms against the Turks. This was in fact far from the truth—the *klepht*s had mainly preyed upon Greek villagers.[4]

Between 1887 and 1896, in the early years of British administration, a series of incidents occurred in the Paphos district of Cyprus which were the subject of a lengthy police report by an Inspector Kareklas in 1937 (the reasons why this report was produced so late will be examined later). The report dealt with a band of armed men who committed a series of violent acts, including cattle rustling, livestock theft, abductions, rapes, and at least thirteen murders. These bandits, known as the Hassanpoulia, were mainly Turkish Cypriots, although their ethnicity had little to do directly with the matter, and they included both Greek and Turkish Cypriots among their accomplices and victims.

There were three significant features about the group. First, the police consistently hunted the band, whose members were captured by betrayal, never by being outgunned, as the police themselves often were. Indeed these men often obtained supplies, assistance, and ammunition from the very police sent out to capture them. Second, despite the very large reward offered for their capture,[5] the Paphos villagers did not betray them. Although the Hassanpoulia clearly struck terror in many villages, numerous villagers supported them. They only needed to be known as the *Poulia* (literally, the birds) to get what they wanted, often but not exclusively from local men of authority.

Third, although these bandits were not then voicing a pre-political form of protest, as Hobsbawm claims for bandits generally, popular accounts of them were later used to carry political messages. Although they terrorized many ordinary peasants, as A. Blok claims, their lengthy operations cannot be attributed solely either to protecting the powerful nor terrorizing people at the grassroots level. Additional factors must be invoked to explain the persistence of banditry in Cyprus, and its even stronger presence in other Mediterranean societies such as Greece and Sicily.

The story of how the Hassanpoulia brothers entered their banditry careers is exceedingly complex. It involves two generations, an uncle and his two nephews, all from shepherding backgrounds, who acted as hit men. They had powerful protectors and some support from the local population. Eventually they were betrayed and shot. The incidents set in motion by the Hassanpoulia, not new to Cyprus, indeed date back to the Ottoman administration that ended in 1878. In Cyprus, as in Greece, though with differing emphases, the Ottomans lacked a permanent salaried scribal class of functionaries or a permanent military presence. Instead, they relied upon local potentates to collect taxes and maintain order in return for a guaranteed fixed revenue to the Porte. In Cyprus until 1821 taxes were collected from the Christian Greek population by the Church, whereas in much of Greece local potentates performed this function. In both societies state control over rural areas was rudimentary. Because the groups that were collecting taxes and maintaining order were either identical or closely allied, the system encouraged the dispossession of peasants from their land and its accumulation into large estates or *chiftliks,* which produced primary products for European markets. Dispossessed peasants unable to obtain employment on these large estates fled to the higher mountainous areas that were less subject to oppressive taxation.

The Ottomans also farmed out the organs of the state that maintained order, usually to the same tax-collecting interests. Inevitably, such men were more interested in making their bids pay. In Greece a process of rotation operated. Bands of mainly Christian Greek but also Moslem Albanian irregulars known as *armatoles* were entrusted with keeping away the brigands known as *klepht*s. Through the strategic use of violence, terror, extortion, and theft, *klepht*s often managed to discredit the tax-collecting armatoles to become armatoles themselves. Discharged armatoles in turn reverted back to brigandage in the hope of gaining reinstatement at a later, more opportune, moment. They commonly moved from one band to another, and the leaders of these bands tried to outdo their opponents by attracting followers through bribery, selective magnanimity, and the prospect of looting, usually of sheep. The purpose of the selective use of violence was not banditry per se but rather a routinized form of capital accumulation legalized by the authorities. Official employment as armatoles enabled them to accumulate tax grafts, protection money, land, and so forth. Klephts and armatoles played a dangerous, disingenuous, uncertain, and collusionist shadow-game of musical chairs. In this world, one could never be certain about one's teammates, and crosscutting ties and sudden shifts in alliances militated against the emergence of secure relationships and bases of power. As one *klepht* said, "everyone is in debt to the robber."

In Cyprus, by contrast, a diarchy prevailed. The Church collected taxes from the Christian population, while Turkish beys largely administered separate territories. Revolts by military garrisons over delayed pay were common. As a result, the military class were obliged to support themselves by turning to harsher, more arbitrary pillaging of peasants, dispossessing and usurping titles, and incorporating peasant holdings into *chiftliks*.

The formation of *chiftliks* and absentee landlordism in Cyprus inevitably resulted in the emergence of middlemen as administrators and field watchmen. Such men rented large tracts of land, using some and subletting the rest to the peasants on short-term contracts or for sharecropping. Due to their critical interstitial position, both landlords and peasant-pastoralists depended upon such men; they could, therefore, play one level off against the other. The overseers, usually but not exclusively Turks, were permitted to carry arms, and in the sparsely populated countryside violent acts were easy to execute and conceal. Violence also kept the peasants cowed and docile. The social origin of such overseers and field watchmen was significant, for most came from upwardly-mobile pastoral families. Pastoralism as a way of life encourages aggressiveness and, in the fiercely competitive world of nineteenth-century Cyprus, required the ability to retaliate for any real or imagined wrong. Banditry in Sardinia and Corsica also had a strong pastoral base. Kareklas notes that, "the owners of goats, mares or cows were the richest and, therefore, the leading members in each community. From the life they led on the hills or in the rivers from their childhood one can easily realize what kind of character they had. They were the worst criminals and as such the leaders in the village. The quiet men, who were very few, were considered of no account" (1937: 6).

In 1821, following the mainland Greek rebellion against the Ottomans, the Church in Cyprus lost its monopoly of tax collection. The ensuing power vacuum in the countryside was rapidly filled by these middlemen on large estates. They often worked in conjunction with urban-based merchants, who were immune from prosecution because they were attached to foreign trading consulates. Tax farming, usury, illegal exports along the coastline, the subletting of land, the policing of rural areas, the application of violence to keep the peasants cowed, protection from depredation for a fee, and the disposal of stolen goods reinforced one another and resulted in the establishment of extensive, temporary, informal, and fluctuating coalitions.

Banditry in Comparative Perspective

In Cyprus, like the other Mediterranean examples, especially Sicily and Greece, where banditry flourished for much longer, banditry persisted partly because the state was weak. However, it would be simplistic to attribute the decline of banditry to the state's increasing monopoly of violence, although this is certainly important. Rather, the persistence or decline of banditry depends upon a complex interplay of variables, including the social structure and political ecology of a particular region; the nature and distribution of property and capital accumulation (whether landed, or moveable and precarious such as livestock), and the means available to legitimate it; the presence or absence of trust and its relationship to the development of civil society; underdeveloped electoral processes which may encourage strong-arm tactics; and permanent insecurity rather than permanent misery at the grassroots, the former being more conducive to banditry. The political ideology of local elites and their relationship to the state is also important because bandits may either be co-opted by local elites, as in Sicily, as a means to resist the state, or reluctantly by the state itself, as in Greece, where bandits were used both nationally and locally for irredentist adventures to threaten supporters of rival politicians. The state's policies toward landlordism, peasant cultivators, and pastoralists may also be a significant variable because it may favor one over the other, with radical implications for the practice of illegality—in certain situations the peasants may prefer the traditional depredations of pastoral bandits to the more extensive, sustained ones of the state, such as taxes. In other situations the depredations of the potentates' henchmen may be protected by powerful national interests.

A final important variable is the process of mythification at the local and national levels and its role in the process of nation-state formation. The two levels may be separate and different, but in the Mediterranean literacy and the circulation of popular accounts are particularly significant. In certain cases these accounts interact in complex ways with the creation of the nation-state's history. Bandits may be portrayed in texts as outsiders and hence dangerous, as residues from the past and hence ambiguous, or as insiders and hence admirable. They may move from the outside to the inside and vice-versa. This may affect how bandits are perceived and legitimated, and even how they legitimate themselves. In nineteenth-century Greece, ex-*klephts*, such as Koloktronis, "used their memoirs to glorify their own actions and to denigrate those of their political rivals" (Gallant 1988: 272). Later, parliamentary deputies published books which turned bandits and freebooters of all sorts into national liberators in order to pursue national irredentist claims. Soon, bandit chiefs themselves published pamphlets in their own defense: like good Greeks, they fought the Turks; the Muslim outsiders were the brigands attempting to discredit Greece, and "the vital national interest" often prevented politicians from suppressing banditry (Kolipoulos 1987; Jenkins 1961). Such definitions and redefinitions have created a vocabulary of justification, traces of which remain in contemporary life. In contemporary Crete, extensive livestock theft is legitimized orally by reference to written, highly selective, nationalist accounts of the "freedom-loving" *klephts* of old taught in school books (Herzfeld 1985). In Andalusia, local communists have turned nineteenth-century bandits into proto-regional rebels, symbols in their devolutionist struggles with Madrid (Mario Guarino personal communication; Zugasti 1934). For Corsica, Wilson notes that by the late nineteenth century "bandits of a mercenary type liked to be thought of as 'Robin Hood' figures" (1988: 348). In short, when dealing with banditry, we must be aware that stories have an essentially constitutive role and are often reinterpreted in determinate ways.

The decline of banditry in Cyprus cannot be attributed either to an increase in peasant class consciousness or a growth in the state's monopoly of violence in the countryside. Peasant consciousness only reached collective dimensions by the mid-1940s, and the state's control over the countryside, relatively rudimentary well into the twentieth century, could not prevent the EOKA bands from operating extensively between 1955 and 1959. Instead, banditry's decline is due to major economic, political, and administrative changes brought about at the end of the nineteenth century, which departed significantly from developments either in Sicily or in Greece. At least seven reasons can be advanced for these changes, which together contributed to a change in the old order. The first, the removal of Turkish legal privileges and their replacement by legal equality between Greeks and Turks, implied that the previously dominant ethnic inequality was replaced by economic inequality. Ethnic privileges could no longer be utilized as a stepping-stone to economic and political power. The second, the first full-scale compulsory registration of properties in 1888, made usurpation and dispossession more difficult. The third, the increasing individual or familial appropriation of land, was detrimental of village rights. During this period there was a scramble to transform state land, especially forests, into private property. Large tracts of forest were cleared, and men laid claim to them by possession. This reduced the amount of land available for pasturage. The fourth was the colonial government's support for peasants and the marginalization of shepherds, the mainstay of livestock rustling and shady activities in the countryside. Shepherds and goatherds found that they could not let their animals graze in the forests with impunity. The fifth reason was the establishment of new marketing relations. The religious fairs in which products were bartered in the countryside were replaced by town markets, where cash was the main means of transaction. The British colonial government also introduced a Weberian-type bureaucracy which created new channels of social mobility. Finally, a legislative council was established, and new literate political groups emerged in the towns dominated by bureaucratic, professional, and marketing interests.

As a result, Cyprus was incorporated into a new economic, political, and administrative order which marginalized certain groups. The British tried to encourage the ideal of the small peasant cultivator, not the shepherd or goatherd. Peasant landownership was encouraged; the large estates remained static, although their productivity declined; and a new administration required a vastly larger independent, salaried scribal class which the Ottomans previously lacked.

The evolution of violent rural entrepreneurs in Cyprus thus departed significantly from the example of the western Sicilian Mafia and from the Greek case to which it had hitherto borne many similarities. In all these societies, banditry had a predominantly agro-pastoral base; and in both Sicily and Greece, violent entrepreneurs from pastoral backgrounds managed to create new niches for themselves in the nation-state, especially when the new regime attempted to penetrate the countryside. In Sicily, *mafiosi* were actively involved in the Risorgimento, backing the Garibaldini and managing to wrest effective control of the *latifundia* from the absentee Sicilian aristocracy. They thus shifted their wealth into land, their pastoral backgrounds proving particularly useful both in co-opting bandits and in suppressing peasant unrest. In Greece, banditry was intimately grounded in pastoralism and even had a seasonal cycle based on movements from the plains to the mountains. The age-old conflict between pastoralists and agriculturalists obliged the former to rely on self-help to intimidate peasants, especially in the new Greek state, which radically reduced the amount of land available for pasturage and tried to encourage the expansion of the small peasant cultivator class. In 1871, following the notorious Dilessi Murders, an army officer made the following telling remarks:

> There can be no brigands without a shepherd, and no shepherd without a brigand. I have met and talked to many shepherds, and they usually tell me: "We cannot survive without brigands." Imagine a shepherd group in Karpenisi. The group needs the backing of a band of brigands; or just to be known that they have such backing. Because, when the animals of that group are led down they destroy everything. . . . If the peasants know that the group in question is under the protection of [a bandit] they don't harm the shepherds, but are friendly to them, because they fear them. Otherwise the shepherds are unable to pass: their animals destroy everything, they lay barren whole plains (Quoted in Koliopoulos 1979: 290).

Pressures on pastoralists increased in nineteenth-century Greece, but agriculture remained underdeveloped. As McGrew has demonstrated, the state's policy was ultimately contradictory and "legal insecurity of tenure, labor shortages, absence of capital and the general unprofitability of most of the country's farms . . . made agriculture the preserve of those who had no alternative but to till the soil" (1985: 220). Moreover, no rural landed elite emerged as in Sicily. In such a context pastoralists were uninterested in becoming peasants. Instead, they retained their scorn for cultivators while aspiring, as they had under the Ottomans, to state employment in occupations they understood and at which they were proficient: forming irregular temporary bands to capture the easily transportable booty of animals and cash. Also as under the Ottomans, there were ample opportunities for military opportunists in the new Greek state. Indeed, the new Greek nation-state paradoxically became "Ottomanized" for a considerable part of the nineteenth century. The Greek War of Independence, conducted almost exclusively by irregulars attracted by the prospect of booty, had created an enormous number of refugees, mostly of pastoral origins who were already accustomed to a life of semi-banditry. This left the new state with only the Peloponnese, since Thessaly, Macedonia, Epiros, and Thrace were still to be liberated from Ottoman rule. The new state utilized ex-brigands to foment unrest in the parts of Greece controlled by Turks, because it could not pursue an overt and potentially disastrous war with the vastly superior Turkish forces, because mass desertions from an unpopular regular conscripted army rendered it ineffective in foreign wars and in maintaining internal order, and also because disbanding irregulars could further destabilize Greek society. Hence, rather than allowing bandits to be turned loose on the small peasant class it was trying to create, the state employed them covertly for national causes and politicians utilized them to intimidate supporters of rival candidates. The result was a veritable infestation of the Greek countryside by bandits, especially in the north. Every time conflict with Turkey erupted, the prisons were emptied of brigands, who formed irregular bands. Inevitably such men were much more interested in state employment and in booty than in nationalist causes.

In nineteenth-century Greece, therefore, bandits managed to exploit a new niche for themselves as the vehicle to pursue war and to liberate the portions of Greece controlled by the Ottomans. Some bandits became respected members of society, and others managed to spread their booty through their networks of pastoral kinsmen, but many had relatively short careers. Few invested in agriculture. In any case a regular supply of refugees were desperate for some form of state employment, so banditry remained a significant feature of Greek political life well into the time of Venizelos. By contrast, in Cyprus new sources of wealth were created. The acreage of land increased dramatically to absorb pastoralists, whilst the large estates upon which they had depended declined. The dominance of moveable wealth in herds and flocks, upon which the old elite of violent entrepreneurs had relied, dwindled in relation to other sectors.

When analyzing banditry in a comparative perspective, we must be cautious in treating bandits either exclusively as primitive social rebels (as Hobsbawm [1969] does), or as individual opportunists, or as merely the co-opted henchmen of rural potentates (as Blok [1972] does). Often all these features coexist in particular examples of banditry, although one may dominate in certain contexts but not in others. The particular form and significance of banditry, which is a sui generis phenomenon only to a certain extent, depends largely upon a complex series of factors. Banditry may also hold different and changing significances for different segments or groups across time. We thus have to peel away the different layers in the hope of discovering the original explanation of an incident or series of incidents, although clearly the mythification reinforced through texts is particularly potent and is anthropologically significant.

Banditry traditionally appeared in areas where large-scale landholding coexisted with a relatively permanent intermediate strata of leaseholders or freeholders based upon family-sized plots, such as Sicily, parts of Greece, Cyprus, Peru, and Mexico. In Columbia in the 1950s it was found in areas where different sized properties coexisted, and where there was a cash crop like coffee (Sanchez and Meertens 1987: 161). As in Sicily during roughly the same period, bandit entrepreneurship exploited the gap between the tenant farmer (*agredado*) and the absentee (i.e., fled or murdered) landowner. Bandits were linked to merchants, and like *mafiosi* were protected by powerful urban political party patrons. It appears somewhat puzzling however that bandits could neither legitimate themselves, nor transform their wealth into land holdings, given the large profit inducements offered by coffee.[6] Sustained banditry requires concealable, transportable wealth (e.g., cash, cash crops, animals, alcohol, narcotics, stock-exchange dealings by rogue traders) which leave few traces. In the nineteenth century Mediterranean banditry was particularly strong where pastoralists occupied an intermediate position between small-scale cultivators and large-scale proprietors, as in northern Greece; where overseers and sharecroppers performed that function, as in rural Sicily; or even where pastoralism was prominent in its own right, as in Sardinia and Corsica. Yet there are apparently basic differences between the banditry in predominantly agricultural areas and that in pastoral areas, which are often mountainous. In the latter, banditry appears to have been more resilient, especially where a combination of external factors militated against making pastoralists into peasants. This did not occur in northern Greece but did in Cyprus in the latter part of the nineteenth century. Banditry in more agricultural contexts is usually more controllable and can be tamed more easily, especially when violent men from humble origins acquire secure property and legitimate themselves.

Banditry tended to appear less in areas with large masses of rural proletarians, such as Puglia in Southern Italy (Snowden 1977). Few legal or illegal opportunities were available there for social mobility, and the social relations of production encouraged the emergence of collective solidarity and of anarcho-syndicalism: "The absence of substantial intermediate strata of peasant proprietors, leaseholders and sharecroppers also closed the political safety valve of upward social mobility. There were few examples of men who by toil, initiative and good fortune were able to gain land of their own. Between the mass of the landless there was an unbridgeable void" (ibid.: 73).

Much the same appears to have happened in the Andalusian town of Santaella, where absentee landlords were separated from a mass of largely landless laborers and where rural discontent increasingly took class forms

(Driessen 1983). By contrast, where large-scale estates owned by resident landlords coexisted with small family plots, banditry flourished. Vanderwood quotes a Peruvian judge who found, "little banditry in districts where property was well distributed among the peasants. Unproductive haciendas, however, spawned bandits among their landless peons. On the other hand, commercial farming districts experienced limited brigandage because the capitalistic entrepreneurs had the will, means and police to control it" (1981: 12).

The social structure of a region is, however, only one precondition, though an admittedly important one, for the emergence of banditry. Other conditions include a weak state and an undeveloped electoral process in which politicians are encouraged to utilize strong-arm tactics to widen and patrol their power bases by co-opting ex-bandits as retainers, sometimes for ostensibly national causes, such as in late nineteenth-century Greece (cf., Jenkins 1961). Other conditions include the dominance of moveable and precarious wealth, such as livestock, and, importantly, the absence of trust and permanent insecurity, rather than permanent misery, at the local level (as in nineteenth-century Mexico). This opens a field of anarchic, individualistic opportunism, such as in nineteenth-century Greece and Mexico. Vanderwood observed that, "The business of Mexican bandits was business. They were not the justice seeking precapitalist peasant brigands whom E. Hobsbawm describes. The only thing the Mexican brigands seemed to protest was their exclusion from rewarding sectors of the social system. They wanted profit, position and power, not to overturn society, and many later made good as bandits-turned-*rurales*" (1981: 14). Much the same appears to have occurred in Greece in the turbulent mid-nineteenth century.[7]

The romanticization of banditry, and hence its legitimization, is also a significant feature of the phenomenon. Bandits were often viewed at the grassroots level with some degree of ambiguous and grudging admiration in certain societies, including Cyprus. This issue addresses the crux of the debate between Hobsbawm and Blok. The former takes myth as an amplification of grassroots yearnings for a type of pre-political just, but hierarchical, world. The latter has overemphasized the causative role of terror in suppressing peasant unrest through the cooption of bandits as henchmen by landlords and *mafiosi.* Both Hobsbawm and Blok overemphasize the psychology of terror without analyzing its complex sociology. Furthermore, they do not sufficiently distinguish between violence and terror, and in particular the demiurgic role of violence. In the next section I begin by examining the role of violence as a system of signs, and as a means for the engendering of sacrifice.

Violence, Mutilation, and Sacrifice

Traditional banditry has often been accompanied by extreme violence in both its expression and its repression. Hobsbawm suggests both that "moderation in killing and violence belongs to the image of the social bandits," and also that "they are heroes not in spite of the fear and horror their actions inspire, but in some ways because of them" (1985: 58). There is uncertainty on the significance of violence in Hobsbawm's account: On one hand he asserts that "excessive violence and cruelty are . . . phenomena which only overlap banditry at certain points" (ibid. 63). On the other, he advances various reasons suggesting violence is more central: bandits have a functional need for violence—they need to alternate love and fear; cruelty is inseparable from vengeance (ibid. 63); violence is "associated with particularly humiliated and inferior groups" (ibid. 64). And finally "things just get out of hand" (ibid. 65): when men "cannot be 'heroes,' they then stop acting like heroes" (ibid. 66), but then he says that they need to inspire fear and horror in order to be considered heroes (above).

Hobsbawm's arguments here are thus somewhat circular, and unsatisfactory. They are too psychologistic in a predictable sense; in their circularity, they paradoxically present bandits using anti-social means when Hobsbawm is keen to present them as *social* bandits, even if "primitive" rebels. In our state-dominated, routinized, political worlds it is difficult to conceive of violence except as disruptive. That is the double-Hegelian "cunning of reason" *(list der vernunft)* which de-rationalizes and de-legitimates violence except as the manifestation of the state's right to "protect order/rationality." Rather than a "lack of control," the intensity of violence in banditry suggests a control manifest through the application and signification of violence, however distasteful to our modern sensibilities. In banditry, as in feuding from which it often derives, personalized violence is critical and finely graded. Violence is targeted specifically against persons and things as properties of persons, and is displayed through stories.

Hobsbawm does not distinguish between violence and terror. Terror can be a product of violence, but is not necessarily. It is clearly much more complex because it is a series of representations. Also, Hobsbawm presents violence as theoretically unproblematical. Following Girard (1988),

I suggest violence is more than the producer of terror, and that it is demiurgical. When individuals employ violence in "banditry"-type contexts, and when they are its recipients, they act not just as individuals, but also in almost dramaturgical roles: as the wronged party, the avenger, the fugitive from justice, the victim, etc. Underlying the process whereby "banditry" is generated—a conflict, a killing, flight, becoming an outsider, justice/revenge, retribution, and eventual capture and execution—is a complex structuration of signification through violence that evokes notions such as sacrifice, justice, and retribution. Violence has a structural, almost sacrificial engendering role. The state in its Ancien Regime form is not peripheral but critical to this process. In the public execution of the bandit as dangerous outlaw-outsider, the state transforms him into a sacrificial victim of justice, who whilst being polluted through bloodshed is nevertheless transfigured through his suffering into a popular apotheosis of the populace as victim of the state law. I suggest that Hobsbawm simplifies the figure of the bandit as a modern yet transcendentally valid hero. The bandit is a tragic and deeply ambivalent "hero," a figure of tragedy, which subsequent enlightenment thought simplified and Manicheanized.

Terror and violence had a functional role. Many bandits embarked on their careers through personal vendettas, such as in Corsica, or the Hassanpoulia in Cyprus. Betrayal to agents of the state was always a grave danger, unless the individual were protected by powerful interests. In Corsica, many bandits were obliged to rely on the support of family and kin and thus soon found themselves further enmeshed in family feuds. They used their prepotence and violence to protect their kinsmen's interests, and thus ensure the latter's support against betrayal to the state. Kinsmen and bandits thus depended on each other: the former as protection against enemy depredations, the latter against betrayal. To become a bandit was a "disgrace" and a "misfortune," a point I return to later. Here, violence had a functional purpose as a warning and deterrence. It had to be "overdetermined" to ensure that there was no ambiguity, and that massive retaliation would result. The more protected an individual was, especially by powerful patrons as in Sicily, the less need to use violence to signify itself, and the more opportunities there were to employ ambiguity and courtesy, a point noted by Franchetti and Sonnino (below). Thus the more marginalized a bandit, the more dependent he was on protection, the greater the risk of betrayal, and thus the greater the tendency for violence to appear "gratuitous," that is, to signify itself.

If the genesis of banditry often had a personal element (vendetta, revenge, etc.), its prosecution was also personal. In its ideal form most stories about "bandits" can be reduced to the following pattern: slight to personal/family honor by equal/superior—> response—> violence—> breaking of state law and threat of revenge—> escape to maquis (flight of young man)—> retribution—> death of offender—> further marginalization and involvement of outlaw/bandit in illegal but morally just actions—> betrayal (killing) or capture (execution by state). Violence is polluting. It is significant that the outbreak of violence was usually, in both ancient and other more modern societies, followed by banishment as an alternative to state prosecution (Wilson 1988: 338): "The cause of ritual impurity is violence . . . This impurity is contagious, (thus) . . . the only sure way to avoid contagion is to flee the scene of violence" (Girard 1988: 28). As a nineteenth-century observer for Corsica noted: "The vendetta is a kind of religion . . . The Corsican takes revenge . . . because the affront which he has suffered *separates* him from his peers, and renders him *impure,* like a social *excommunicate.*"[8] In any case, the culprit usually banishes himself both out of fear of retribution by the state, and of the kin if blood has been spilt, or to pursue the retribution if he has been wronged and could not obtain justice, as in the case of Hassanpoulis The Old. A central way to express violence, to damage one's opponent's interests, and to express violence as a series of autonomous signs, was through the mutilation both of individuals and of animals. As an exchange between individuals, banditry thus employed a specific set of finely graded messages involving violence to the body and property of the victim. Violence was targeted specifically against persons and things as properties of persons, and displayed through stories. As the victim's metaphorical representation, his property is subjected to an excess of violence, for example livestock that is disemboweled (*sventrate* in Sicily; cf., Blok 1983) but not killed. This was practiced by one of the Hassanpoulia brothers on the cattle of the man who had reported him. The owner would be forced to complete the bitter destruction of his own herd. In other cases, (such as in Corsica) mules' ears were cut off as a ritual death threat (Wilson 1988: 78). Such actions served as a warning, or an unambiguous omen of further action. Whereas lower animals (e.g., dogs) were destroyed, medium range animals (e.g., sheep) were grievously wounded, and higher animals (bulls, mules, etc.) had marks left on them. The victim was therefore defined taxonomically.

Through the destruction of animals or other property of the offender, or even the killing of some other person, a surrogate victim is created: "By killing, not the murderer himself, but someone close to him, an act of perfect reciprocity is avoided and the necessity for revenge by-passed" (ibid.: 26). The act resembles both a legal punishment and a sacrifice, yet "it cannot be assimilated to either" (ibid.: 26). It resembles sacrifice in that the victim of the second murder is not responsible for the first. But it resembles a legal punishment "because it constitutes an act of reparation, a violent retribution" (ibid.: 26).

However as Girard points out "the difference between sacrificial and nonsacrificial violence is anything but exact; it is even arbitrary" (1988: 40). One might add that it is precisely this overlapping that gives vengeance-banditry its ineluctable momentum. The bandit as killer tends to be drawn into a vortex of violence. This is what Girard has called the "sacrificial crises": "the inability to distinguish between blood spilt for ritual and for criminal purposes." Like figures from Greek tragedy, individuals seem to go insane with the trauma and spilling of blood: "In the early 1920s a party of Orthodox Montenegrans set out to raid the Bosnian villages as men had done from time immemorial. To their own horror they discovered themselves to be doing things which raiders had never done before and which they knew to be wrong: torturing, raping, murdering children. *And they could not help themselves.*"[9] As Girard observes: "Men find it distasteful to admit that the "reasons" on both sides of a dispute are equally valid, which is to say that *violence operates without reason*" (ibid.: 46 original emphasis). The sacrificial crises "coincides with the disappearance of the difference between impure violence and purifying violence. When this difference has been effaced, purification is no longer possible and impure, contagious, reciprocal violence spreads throughout the community" (ibid.: 49).

In killings, there are two main features. First, there is the selection of the victim, and secondly there is (often) the mutilation of the body. Sometimes victims were selected precisely as substitutes. Wilson notes: "There are indications that the killing of children characterized feuds of peculiar bitterness or 'bad feuds' aimed at the total extinction of rival families. *On adults and children, it does not matter. / Even on the women. / Rip out all their guts!,* an aunt enjoined her nephew in a lament" (1988: 209). "All sacrificial rites are based on two substitutions. The first is provided by generative violence, which substitutes a single victim for all the members of the community" (Girard 1988: 269). This is the choice of the surrogate victim, a member of the community, often chosen precisely because he or she is a treasured member of the community (such as women and children), which further compounds the sacrilege, the anathema.

Second, the body has to be "prepared" retroactively, backward as it were, disassembled rather than dressed, in parts rather than whole, blemished rather than pure, to be offered back to the group who "made" it. This is the antithesis of fertility. "Desecration"/mutilation of the corpse performs this function. Significant parts of the body are isolated as targets of extreme violence, often physically detached/removed from the whole body, and reassembled with the corpse as metonyms of disassembled potency and messages of denaturalized personhood. In Corsica in 1846, "Giovan-Natale Fanceschi's head was cut off and his viscera ripped out, while the body of his fourteen-year-old son and another relative similarly treated" (Wilson 1988: 405). Often this follows metonymic associations— the offence itself determined the treatment of the corpse. In other cases sexual organs had been cut off, especially where the victim had been accused of a sexual offence. In Cyprus and Sicily the cut off penis was stuck in the mouth of the victim. In Corsica ears were cut off, especially for those of low status, thus metaphorically treating them as animals/mules of more powerful protectors (Wilson 1988: 407). Sometimes bodies were stripped.

The desecration of the body, its disassembly to be reassembled in a grotesque mimetic parody of the original body, is what Girard has called sacrificial preparation: "Once the victims have been obtained, (ritualistic thought) strives in various ways to make them conform to its original image of the original victim and simultaneously to increase their quotient of cathartic potential. (1988: 272). The defilement of the corpse and the denial of burial in Homeric Greece went "beyond accepted conventions" and was a sentence of exile for the spirit (Campbell 1992), but conventions were often broken, and the initial uncertainty surrounding Patroculus' and Hectors' bodies indicates that anger and violence often tempted men to take this course. Corsicans sometimes "wanted to kill their enemies precisely when they were in a state of mortal sin, so that they would suffer eternally after death," including not being buried on consecrated ground (Wilson 1988: 405).[10] Yet in so doing the bandit embarked on his final transformation. He sets himself up outside the community and thus as the ultimate sacrificial victim. He does not just turn his victims into surrogate sacrifices, but defines himself as the ultimate sacrifice. This is the second component of sacrifice—the true sacrifice: "The only strictly ritualistic substitution, is that of a victim for the surrogate victim. It is essential for the victim to be *drawn from outside the community.* The surrogate victim, by contrast, is a member of the community. Ritual sacrifice is defined as an inexact imitation of the generative act" (ibid.: 269, my emphasis). The bandit must set himself up outside society through his personification of excess unthinking violence in order to be ultimately sacrificed as the *defeat* of violence: "If the sacrificial victim belonged to the community (as does the surrogate victim), then his death would promote further violence instead of dispelling it" (ibid.: 269).

To recapitulate: "the victim should belong both to the inside and the outside of the community. . . . Since there is no category that perfectly meets this requirement. . . the goal is to make the victim wholly sacrificeable. In its broadest sense, then, sacrificial preparation employs two very different approaches. The first seeks to *make more foreign a victim* who is too much part of the community [e.g., through mutilation, my emphasis]. The second approach seeks to reintegrate into the community *a victim who is too foreign to it"* [i.e., the "bandit," my emphasis] (Girard 1988: 272). As Marcaggi noted: "The bandit is a being who has placed himself on the *margin* of society, who is constrained by *no responsibilities,* who has *sacrificed his like in advance,* who will perish sooner or later by *violent means,* and whose only guide is his own whim."[11] We can now more fully appreciate the songs about the hardships of bandit life in Corsica (Wilson 1988: 344), Greece (Politis 1973; Campbell 1992), and elsewhere, and understand why becoming a bandit was far from glorious. Most bandits in Corsica saw themselves as victims; they spoke about their "disgrace," "destiny" and "fate" *(poveru disgraziatu)* (Wilson 1988: 340); in Greece the notions of *atichos* (luckless) and *moira* (fate) were equally prevalent.

The Bandit as State Sacrificial Symbol

Most academic accounts of banditry concentrate on the lives of bandits. In so doing they miss an equally important aspect: their death. That this was the subject of popular accounts should alert us to something distinctive. I suggest that it is not so much through their lives that bandits generated the (sometimes powerful) myth of nobility, but rather in their death. Nor was it because they lived or died "nobly," or some such similar inanity. It was rather by being either betrayed/killed, or (publicly) executed, that they achieved sacrificial status. For the first, they became symbols of betrayal by more powerful vested interests. Second, their public execution as sacrifice became "an instrument of prevention in the struggle against violence" (Girard 1988: 170). The violence of their executions, and the disassembly of their bodies as public spectacle, demonstrated the irrepressible power of the state over the individual. When caught and juridically processed, their bodies became the subject of a publicly demonstrated spectacle of state power. Through their public executions the state generated and imposed order through the slow, measured (rather than through a personal impetuous anger), disassembly of the bodies of its subjects (rather than their mutilation practiced by individuals), whose violence as justice-retribution-emotion threatened the justice-legality-reason of the leviathan. Finally, their lives through their deaths became fated like tragedy, and, as in tragedy, individuals became aware how they themselves assisted in the birth of their own destinies only when they had finally happened. For tragedy is the "balancing of the scale, not of justice but of violence" (ibid.: 45).

As "one of us who always risks becoming one of them," the bandit set himself up outside (not against, but neither for) society. He distinguished himself as a potentially sacrificial being from nonsacrificial beings by one essential characteristic: "Between these (potentially sacrificial) victims and the community a crucial social link is missing, so that they can be exposed to violence without fear of reprisal. Their death does not automatically entail an act of vengeance" (Girard 1988: 13). It follows that the bandit as polluted, as a being set apart from society, must be captured by those outside the community (the agents of the state), even if this still required the concealed complicity and betrayal of members of the community.[12] Offered up by the community to the state, he is returned to the community through and by his death. His suffering is apotheosed as an imaginary suffering collective peasant body. In their public torture and executions, bandits, as examples of criminality (state law both uses justice and travesties it), became spectacles through which the crushing resolute power of the state was manifest and elevated as a theological principle. If, as Foucault has suggested, "the condemned man represents the symmetrical, inverted figure of the king" (1979: 29), then the body and suffering of the "bandit" becomes an icon of the peasant body—mute, inexpressive, almost beast-like, terrible not so much in the revenge he exacts through the bodies of others, but in the silence with which he is made to consecrate his suffering.

The bandit is thus not so much an expression of peasant reaction to its oppression, nor a simple wish fulfillment, but may well be a *transfiguration of peasant suffering*, transformed from (individual) execution to the collective personification of sacrifice. The parallels between bandits and saints, and the linkage in the literature between bandits and monks, is not fortuitous, not just in terms of the social conditions that gave rise to banditry, but also in terms of the iconography and models of suffering.[13] Many bandits whilst in prison become "like saints." Hassanpoulis The Old became a model prisoner, he learned to read and write.[14] By his public execution and suffering the bandit is conjured up as a victim of a terrible state power, and thus as sacrifice. Popular models of suffering were available in the lives and tortures of saints. Foucault notes that the Ancien Regime punishment (and most glorifications of banditry by the peasantry date from the immediate post-nation state establishment period) ran a risk: "The great spectacle of punishment ran the risk of being rejected by the very people to whom it was addressed . . . the people never felt closer to those who paid the penalty than in those rituals intended to show the horror of the crime and the invincibility of power; never did the people feel more threatened, like them, by a legal violence exercised without moderation and restraint" (ibid.: 63).

Accounts of crimes were published, but the effect, like the use of this literature, was equivocal:

> The condemned man found himself transformed into a hero by the sheer extent of his widely advertised crimes, and sometimes the affirmation of his belated repentance. Against the law, against the rich, the powerful . . . he appeared to have waged a struggle with which one all too easily identified . . . If the condemned man was shown to be repentant, accepting the verdict, asking both God and man for forgiveness for his crimes, it was as if he had *come through some process of purification:* he died in his own way, *like a saint.* But indomitability was an alternative claim to greatness: by not giving in under torture, he gave proof of a strength that no power had succeeded in bending. *A convicted criminal could become after his death a sort of saint, his memory honored and his grave respected* (ibid.: 67, my emphasis).

The following account of a Calbarian bandit's execution around 1810 by the French forces brings together a number of the above themes:

> Betrayed and bound by his followers as he slept in the forest of Cassano, Benincasa was brought to Cosenza, and General Manhes ordered that both his hands be lopped off and that he be led, thus mutilated, to his home in San Giovanni, and there hanged; a cruel sentence, which the wretch received with a bitter smile. His right hand was cut off and

the stump bound, not out of compassion or regard for his life, but in order that all his blood might not flow out of the opened veins, seeing that he was reserved for a more miserable death. Not a cry escaped him, and when he saw that the first operation was over, he voluntarily laid his left hand upon the block and coldly watched the second mutilation, and saw his two amputated hands lying on the ground, which were then tied together by the thumbs and hung round his neck; an awful and piteous spectacle. This happened at Cozenza. On the same day he began his march to San Giovanni in Fiore . . . one of the escort offered him food, which he accepted; he ate and drank what was placed in his mouth, and not so much in order to sustain life, as with real pleasure. On the next day, as the hour of his execution approached, he refused the comforts of religion, ascended the gallows neither swiftly nor slowly, and died admired for his brutal intrepidity.[15]

Rather than seeing the violent actions of bandits as a yearning for a pre-political just world, it is in their violent executions that "bandits" witness both the transcendent notions of retribution-justice, and that pre-political just world that can only be realized, like the sufferings of saints, as an imagined utopia outside time.

Terror, Consent, and Complicity

To understand terror, we need to understand the signification of violence, the sociology of terror, and how complicity is spun out of the unintended consequences of one's actions.

One must begin an analysis of terror by examining the physical organization of the countryside. In the cellular structure of such agrarian capitalist or pastoral societies as Sicily and Greece which lack developed means of communication, the effects of violent acts were often necessarily limited. Banditry merely reinforces the fragmentation of peasant collective consciousness but is not its direct cause. This point had been made in an interesting book entitled *Inchiesta in Sicilia,* written by two early Italian politicians, Franchetti and Sonnino. I quote some of their observations because they shed light on the sociology of terror. I am well aware, however, that they problematize the issue from a statist perspective.[16]

"The brigands/bandits are so confident of their prestige, of their authority over all the classes of the population and in considering themselves as forming an integral and recognized part of society, that they often do not demonstrate the need to be brutal, retaining within their most violent acts, the greatest formal courtesy" (1977: 28–29, my translation). The authors were also puzzled by the peasants' compliance with violence: "How can such wrongdoers have acquired such a striking power over people? . . . Indeed, to see people from all classes submitting themselves so easily [to brigands] when all that would be needed to destroy banditry would be to act in unison for a few days is perplexing. The first impression is that this resignation is none other than complicity. . . . This apparent complicity is universal. . . . But in Sicily the appearance of complicity is meaningless. Who can find the means to distinguish the complicity imposed through terror from that which is spontaneous and lucrative?" (ibid.: 31).

Franchetti and Sonnino then tackle the problem of admiration for bandits. They note that this admiration may be found in all classes, especially among those who have not suffered more than is normal from such wrongdoers. One notes peppered in their conversations a certain fondness for the brigand type, a tendency to turn him into a type of legend, a sentiment in short that would be natural in a professor of literature, but which is difficult to explain among landed proprietors who possess *masserie* and combustible granaries (ibid.: 34).

They also observe that although fear and protection are critical components of bandit power, they are not a sufficient cause for their prepotence: "Why do the violent have, in that part of Sicily that they dominate, authority—not only material authority but also moral authority? . . . [Their] authority is not only material [i.e., physical] but also moral. Fear is not a sufficient reason because although it explains why people are silent as regards offences, it does not explain the public reprobation that affects those who resort to constituted authority to be defended from imminent danger" (ibid.: 86–88).

The two authors suggest that bandits do not merely survive because of the fear they inspire, although this is certainly important. A climate of fear would in any case be difficult to maintain if it were to be reduced to the potential actions of a few individuals. Rather, they actually thrive because of the consent they receive at the local level. It is not consent of the positive type, a Hobsbawmian striving for a pre-political just world, nor is it necessarily wrung-out of a hostile peasantry. It is, rather, a type of solidarity against outsiders and outside authority from which they benefit. Codes of behavior, such as *omerta*" (silence) and *dropi* (shame), constitute the very fabric of social relations and define identity and status. Bandits not only draw upon such codes to maintain their hegemony, but even more important, they guide the bandits themselves, for these codes are drawn from the very social strata (peasants or pastoralists) in which such beliefs are strongly expressed. As a result, it is difficult at the grassroots to distinguish between those acts which can be called personal (e.g., a vendetta over a matter of honor) from those that can be labeled political (e.g., reporting crimes to the police). Indeed the latter are often viewed and recounted as illegal or illicit in the sense of utilizing a new and powerful resource to pursue personal strategies, which thus deserve public reprobation.

Clearly such individuals have an *interest* in the interpretation of their actions as being resolutely personal and personalizing, rather than having a social significance. Here the signification of violence is crucial. As noted, banditry often employs a specific set of finely graded messages involving violence to the body and property of the victim in a series of exchanges between individuals. Its violence *has to be given* a specific personalized "logic," "aesthetic," signification, and interpretation. Violence employed in banditry is personalized. It is targeted specifically against persons, and things as properties of persons, and displayed through stories. As his metaphorical representation, the property of the victim suffers an excess of violence as a warning, or an unambiguous omen of further action. In killings, significant parts of the body are isolated as targets of extreme violence, often physically detached/removed from the whole body, and reassembled with the corpse as metonyms of disassembled potency and messages of denaturalized personhood. Gender identities are disassembled and reassembled to reconstitute that person as a simulacrum of a despised profaned alterity. The exposure of such actions as signs, and the excess signification of ferocity as displayed through violated bodies, overloads and predetermines the interpretation of events. "Reason" dictates that such excess "personalized" violence could not but of necessity have had a personal genesis of which it is an expression. Banditry displays itself socially in the form: "retribution as justice," where the ferocity of signification of an imploding vortex of "reciprocity" between two parties, renders it a private affair not to be witnessed to the state.

Thus, activities by bandits which have political implications (e.g., violence which keeps the peasants cowed and docile) are often perceived as personal at the grassroots and hence are of only limited concern, except to the participants. Gallant, who has examined the accounts of Greek bandits written after the war of liberation, notes that far from being lone wolves, most Greek bandit gangs were composed of kinsmen who operated in well-defined social networks; rather than being removed from peasant society, bandit gangs were an integral part of it (1988: 272).[17]

Bandit morals are embedded in, and indistinguishable from, the general morality of society: "Every person interested in maintaining society in its actual form, whatever that society might be, instinctively demonstrates a sentiment of disdain and repulsion for every act that threatens this form of society" (Franchetti and Sonnino 1977: 87). "The wrongdoer who, in the midst of a society, itself founded on private power and force, finds those same norms already in use for all social relations. . . . He has so little need to regulate and accommodate the reciprocal responsibility between himself and other wrongdoers with the preestablished norms of the society, that he even has as his accomplices all the population outside his immediate circle" (ibid.: 92).

Complicity may be either active or passive, yet both are equally significant. The former establishes trust; the latter conceals illegal violent acts. Passive complicity consists of a series of unconnected individual acceptances of the status quo. On the individual experiential level of incidents, banditry employs a set of moral codes drawn and indistinguishable from kinship-based ideas of justice and retribution. Hence a reaction against banditry is often impossible because it conflicts with the moral codes that regulate traditional society. As in many stateless societies, the distinction between the private and the public (that is, civil society) has limited significance. Banditry may certainly possess a cumulative political significance in suppressing peasant unrest, but the actions it employs are embedded in peasant morality.

The absence of peasant agitation, therefore, is not, as Blok (1972) suggests, a by-product of banditry, although banditry certainly contributes to preventing its emergence. Although it is not the direct cause of low levels of peasant consciousness, banditry does emerge in social structures with these low levels of consciousness and collective action. Furthermore, society's reaction to banditry reproduces preexisting low levels of peasant consciousness.

Banditry employs a distinctive and extreme form of personal power and prepotence which has to be reinforced constantly through whole series of actions, such as selective generosity and magnanimity, as well as calculated arbitrariness. These practices emphasize the indivisibility and personality of power from the brigand/bandit or the cognate *mafioso,* contributing to his mythic value, which Gambetta (1988) suggests is an essential precondition for the trust that *mafiosi* and others require to operate. Calculated arbitrariness in imposing one's will and extravagant generosity are two aspects of the same phenomenon. They personalize the *mafioso*'s/bandit's power and prepotence and generate respect and emphasize his inalienable symbolic capital. When Gilsenan refers to the lords of North Lebanon, he suggests that: "The man of power . . . has been a figure bestriding the domains of order and disorder, master of both and creator of both. For his arbitrariness disorders and throws out of kilter the worlds of others. The highest representatives of the collective, who are at the same time its most singular figures, concentrate these two domains in their person or agency. On the one hand the least predictable in their actions against opponents, they are on the other hand the most reliable for those tied to them by services and clientship" (1988: 389).

Stories which circulate about the bandit or the *mafioso* often constitute an essential part of his power; indeed that power is manifested in, and created through, discourse (or often elliptical discourse) or, even in some cases, paradoxically, through silence, which is none other than saying that they cannot be told or, more precisely, by not being told, they say all.[18] Yet those recounted (by others) emphasize both the calculated arbitrariness which generates a climate of fear and unpredictability and the extravagant generosity which personalizes transactions rendering them incommensurable. Blok thus misses part of the significance of the phenomenon when he states, "The more successful a man is as a bandit, the more extensive the protection granted him" (1972: 498). Certainly protection by the powerful is important, but it is not enough, nor does it exhaust the significance of such forms of illegality. Similarly, Blok misses the wider implications of the notion of protection when he narrows it down to harboring or insulating a bandit from prosecution: "Protection of bandits may range from a close though narrow circle of kinsmen and affiliated friends to powerful politicians, including those who hold formal office as well as grass-roots politicians" (1972: 498). The notion of protection, while useful to delimit the degree to which bandits or *malfattori* may operate with impunity, does not take into account the often large sectors of the public involved in maintaining secrecy toward public authorities through codes such as that of *omerta, dropi,* and so forth. Conversely, overt passivity could conceal covert resistance, but even this had personal motivations (Wilson 1988: 362).

If we want to understand passive complicity, we could turn to written fiction, such as Gabriel García Márquez's short story, "Chronicle of a Death Foretold," perhaps because fiction can take liberties in highlighting those incidents which in a real reconstruction or investigation would largely remain embedded and hidden in the folds of everyday memory. Márquez's story deals with the killing of a man by two brothers of a girl who accused him of having seduced her. It is unclear whether the murdered man was actually guilty of the offence; the villagers could not recall any hint of a misdemeanor on his part, although the girl herself stuck to her story. But who was really to know? Furthermore, the villagers themselves were accomplices through inertia or accident to a murder they knew was about to happen; and the condemned man, although warned, shrugs off the threat (through awareness of his innocence, supreme self-confidence, stupidity, or a misplaced faith that his two killers would be apprehended?). But who was responsible here: the two brothers who committed the murder, the sister who named the young man, the murdered man himself for not taking any precautions once warned, the police for making only half-hearted attempts to stop the brothers, or the villagers themselves who allowed the two brothers to commit their deed in view of everybody? Clearly all are involved in various degrees, whether passively or actively.

We must thus exercise extreme caution in our treatment of banditry because it is a phenomenon which is not only often refractory to the investigations of the outside observer but is also concealed from the participants themselves. It is a phenomenon expressed through expressive silences, elliptical statements, grand mythical reconstructions and gestures, as well as ambiguity. Stories about bandits should be treated as texts to be deconstructed. We must be cautious in reducing discernible sociological facts, such as the observation that a bandit successfully managed to evade capture for a long period, to single empiricist causes ("powerful protection"). Likewise, in contrast to Hobsbawm, stories about bandits should not be treated as primary raw data on the bandits themselves nor as simplistically expressive of hidden essentialist peasant aspirations. Rather we must see them as end-results of a process of elaborated discourse (including textual discourse and reinterpretation) about power relations within society. These discourses are often metaphorically constructed, interpreted, and reinterpreted in various ways. In short, discourse on and about bandits in society indicates a great deal about that society and how it conceptualizes power relations including different conflicts of interpretation.

Banditry, Literature, and the Imaginings of the Nation State

"Better occasional murders than frequent adulteries."

> (Boswell, on the advantages of the Corsican justice
> system, quoted in Carrington 1971: 83.)

When Hobsbawm singled out bandits as pre-political rebels against oppression, he was following in the steps of the Enlightenment. The intellectuals of the modern nation state were heavily implicated in the literary and political romanticization of banditry.[19] There were at least two examples in Europe where guerilla-irregular popular uprisings (i.e., "banditry" as an expression for freedom) against outside despotism caught public imagination: Corsica in the mid-eighteenth century and Greece in the early nineteenth century. The uprising of the Corsicans against the Genovese attracted the interest of Rousseau and Boswell (who visited the island). In his *Contract Social* (published 1762) Rousseau singled them out in Europe as the one people fit to produce just laws: "There is still in Europe one country capable of legislation, and that is the island of Corsica."[20] In Rousseau's imagining of the Corsican way of life are contained many of the germinal contradictory notions about bandits that developed in Romanticism, and which have popular currency today. "It will be known" he bragged to Saint Germain "that I was the first to see a free people, capable of discipline, where all Europe still saw only a horde of bandits."[21] Carrington observes "for him their factions and feuds were the direct consequence of their 'servitude' to the Genoese. They had only to revert to their primal condition, barely out of sight, to recover 'concord, peace and liberty'" (1971: 265). Similar views were entertained by Byron for Greek *klephts*. The Rousseauesque utopia inverted traditional wisdoms (certainly the Hobbesian justification of the state, power, and sovereignty), and manufactured the bandit as the first modern primitive on the borders of Europe. The bandit was the distorting looking glass through which European political thought could engage in the process of anticipating the future. Where there was no (state) law, Rousseau apprehended justice; where the people were oppressed, Rousseau anticipated freedom; where the Ancien Regime recognized anarchic bloodthirsty bandits, he discerned exemplary citizens capable of discipline. Bandits were natural men, outside time, but nevertheless potential law makers. To anticipate themselves and the future they had to further recover their bucolic pleasures: the "simplicity, the equality of the rustic life." Previously, bandits were seen as barbarians with whom one could coexist, inhabiting the same time, and whose criminality was predictable, but religiously condemnable. Now, they were seen as living ancestors who inhabited a different time and who had to be tamed in the modern republic. Rousseau had plotted the trajectory of the social bandit even down to scripting a role for the intellectual: "The valor and constancy with which this brave people has known how to recover and defend its liberty well merits that some wise man teaches them to preserve it," he proclaimed with some modesty.

Literary romanticization of bandits was pronounced during the formation of the nation-state and was often coupled with a desire of the urban literati to discover sources of opposition (often to foreign rule) in the countryside.[22] In the middle to late nineteenth century, *klephts* also figured prominently in Greek historiography, representing an often entirely fictional traditional opposition to Ottoman rule. The earliest collection of songs extolling the virtues of the *klephts* was obtained from a Kerkyran nobleman (Gallant 1988: 272). The myth of banditry may well, therefore, have a double function. In the hands of urban intellectuals it points to the bad old days before the establishment of the nation-state, when life and property were not secure. On the other hand banditry suggests that ordinary peasants or pastoralists, the source of national folklore and the social stratum from whom bandits were traditionally recruited, possessed the right ethnic sentiments in rejecting foreign authority, exploitation, and so forth. That such men were often misguided and ultimately shifted their loyalties only serves to demonstrate that peasants are incapable by nature of taking legitimate mass political action unless they are under the leadership of the more enlightened urban elites, as Rousseau intimated. Since national culture of the nation-states is built upon folklore, or even created it where there was none (Gellner 1983), there is no reason to exclude banditry from this type of elaboration, such that "it is difficult . . . to distinguish between myth and fact, especially in a world in which one turns so readily into the other" (Hobsbawm 1969). Such an example emerged in Greece in the nineteenth century (Koliopoulos 1979; 1987).

By the mid-nineteenth century, with the growth of industrialization and mass migration to the cities, most of Europe's periphery was temporalized in a different time zone. The countryside of Europe's periphery became a theatrical topos where the vicarious fantasies, and terrors, of an emergent national, reading bourgeoisie could be collectivized and enacted in literature. In Spain, Sicily, Greece, and Corsica, bandits became important literary, operatic, and iconic subjects. Novelists traveled to remote places to ground their texts in direct experience and observation. Edmond About published *Le Roi des Montagnes* in 1856, with illustrations by Gustave Dore, an ironical story about a Greek bandit leader who kidnaps some Europeans on a tour of classical sites. The themes are resolutely modern: tourism, terrorism, kidnapping, obscure politics, intermeshing hidden political agendas that conceal financial gain, even absurdity and an awareness of "this can't be happening—it's like in a book," are all there. And literature could easily turn into life, even if the ending was not acceptable. In 1865 a kidnapping did take place near Marathon that echoed About's novel, but it went horribly wrong—the tourists were butchered and the brigands cut down. Some Greek politicians tried to exculpate governmental blundering in dealing with the crises by claiming that banditry was an Ottoman heritage and not Greek (Jenkins 1961). In Corsica the mutual interpenetration—life-literature—became anticipatable. Prosper Merimee, then Inspector of Historical Monuments,[23] wrote his novel *Colomba* (published 1840) inspired by a contemporary vendetta.[24] But "fearing the incredulity of his readers, Merimee could not resist adding a footnote to the effect that anyone who doubted the possibility of such a performance could go to the Sartene and learn for himself how 'one of the most distinguished and agreeable citizens' had saved himself in similar circumstances" (Carrington 1971: 107–8). Bandits, however, were no longer the hoary exemplars from the past, and could read. Merimee's naiveté in fabulating and anticipating a Pirandello world, where reality and fiction blended into each other from their respective territories before their time had come in this century, had disastrous consequences. In the eyes of local society, the hero of the novel, after being forgiven by his enemies, had "committed the monstrous injury of boasting of his crime" and was killed (ibid. 1971: 108).[25] Wilson observes "Corsican attitudes towards what was in the main a hostile stereotype were mixed, reflecting an ambivalence towards socially sanctioned violence at least among the elite" (1988: 14).

Banditry did not just become romanticized in the nineteenth century. In Sicily it became regionally folklorized, and eventually nationally problematized; whilst in Greece it became regionally problematized and nationally folklorized (Herzfeld 1985; Politis 1973). In Corsica it appears to have been somewhere in between the two. The noted Sicilian folklorist G. Pitre had presented personal prepotence in existential terms, quoting one of his informants: "Mafia is self-respect/awareness (*coscienza del proprio essere*). The *mafioso* wants to be respected, and to be respected in almost all situations. He knows how to vindicate himself personally." Mafia was then almost a manifestation of local color.[26] In literature, the closer one got to the actual *topoi* of banditry, the greater the tendency to either conceal it (as in Sicily), or to treat it either romantically or negatively, as in Greek *ithographia*.[27] The reports by the northerners Franchetti and Sonnino problematized banditry as a national question of regional public order, a resistance to the state and its undoubted benefits that derived not just from structure, but from culture. Cultural misperceptions and obduracy by all strata prevented the new Italian citizens from realizing their own long-term interests. From the perspective of the state, the two politicians were right. Mafia and brigandage thrived in the early modern Italian state. Mafia and *brigantaggio* became part of the wider *questione meridionale* (the southern question/problem), a "question" that suggested cultural (southern) reasons for its construction and northern (rational) means for its resolution. Brigandage moved away from being a question of individual barbarism which the Ancien Regime had to extirpate by an overdetermining signification (massive repression, or decoration of bandits when they assisted the regime against invasion as in Bonaparte-resisting Bourbon Calabria). Instead it became an issue of collective measurement, documentation, education, and economic development.

Unsurprisingly, this aroused the ire of local intellectuals and politicians. As the contemporary novelist Leonardo Sciascia pointed out, there was "a certain latent racism of the north towards the south" (1983: 140). "As soon as the state conditioned by northern opinion posed the problem of the Mafia (or, in its language, in terms of public security in Sicily) as a problem that is completely Sicilian, typical of Sicily's psychology and history; distancing itself thus from it—then the educated classes in Sicily react by minimalizing the criminal happenings . . ." (ibid.: 140–41). Indeed, the nineteenth-century Sicilian novelist Luigi Capunaa in his *La sicilia e il brigantaggio* accused Franchetti and Sonnino's report of being vitiated with an "original sin." "They went there, like doctors to a sick man's bed, with the preconceived idea that the illness of that poor devil must be something quite out of the ordinary."[28] He then denies the Sicilianity of the Mafia. Mafia may exist in Sicily but is no different than criminality found elsewhere.[29] Sciascia objected that this should not have excused local authors, such as Pirandello, Capuana, and Verga, from recognizing the insidiousness of the Mafia and *brigantaggio*.[30] By the early twentieth century brigandage was a regional stain unless it could be safely nationalized. This is why it was folklorized in Greece but less so in Sicily and Corsica, unless it could be presented as a precursor to modern resistance to the state.[31] "Bandits and brigands are the two subjects on which a Corsican is never expansive," wrote Archer in 1924. "They prefer the foreigner to believe that such things no longer exist." Or, she might have added, "that they never had" (Wilson 1988: 14). Equally, of course, foreigners were keen to have it remembered.

Banditry has thus been surrounded by a mythology and rhetoric which are far from insignificant. Caution must be exercised in treating such myths either as generic expressions of hidden grassroots aspirations (as

Hobsbawm does) or as largely irrelevant to banditry's political functions in the class war (as Blok suggests). The two are not necessarily opposed and indeed may coexist at different levels of analysis. Nor is it possible, or even desirable, to aim for essentialist definitions, and Blok rightly questions the usefulness of the category of social bandits. Yet because what passes as banditry cannot be analytically separated from wide areas of social life, its presentation in discourse is particularly significant. This includes not just the various ways in which strong-arm men are co-opted by the powerful (for it would be surprising if they were not), but also how such men are portrayed by various strata of society, including conflicting interpretations. Banditry is often linked in complex ways to nationalist rhetoric and to writing. Hence, one critical issue is why and how certain bandits from determinate periods are mythicized in certain contexts, while others are not. An answer to this question can help to explain why the Hassanpoulia were never incorporated into nationalist rhetoric in Cyprus, whereas the equally dubious Greek *klephts* were.

Peasant idealization of bandits is also variable and a function of their subsequent political evolution. In contrast to Hobsbawm, I argue that bandits do not necessarily "belong to the peasantry" (1986: 130); they often belong to those groups who sponsor or control the production of these symbols, often in literary form. In certain cases bandits may belong to the peasantry only because those who peddled these images were themselves of recent humble origins and eager to legitimate themselves. This occurred in Greece with ex-*klephts*, such as Kolokotronis and Makriyiannis. In Brazil and elsewhere, through the *literatura de cordel,* bandits belonged to the peasantry because they were incorporated in widely circulated chap books (*folhetos*) which popularized and contemporized bandits, such as Lampiao (Fentress and Wickham 1992). Bandits often belong solely to the peasantry because no other social group has a need for them and because they are often forgotten. In Cyprus and in Greece, and doubtlessly in other parts of the Mediterranean, bandits do not "belong to remembered history, as distinct from the official history of books," as Hobsbawm claims (1985: 133); rather, they belong to remembered history because they were often incorporated in written history, or through other devices such as written ballads and puppet theatre.[32]

Narratives and Politics

Just as we cannot rely on populist accounts of banditry as unproblematical reflections of "reality," we must also exercise particular caution when treating police accounts as disinterested (Joseph 1990: 18). I now examine the particular text upon which this essay is based (Inspector Kareklas' report), and I conclude by positing various reasons why the Hassanpoulia were not mythicized as examples of peasant consciousness in Cyprus, nor provided a model for the EOKA fighters in the 1950s. If, as Barthes (1977) has claimed, writing is never innocent, we need to examine how the Inspector constructed his report for his British superior forty years after the events and the particular context within which the report was produced. Although it is a remarkable ethnographic document, the report is also striking in the way that Kareklas strings details together to produce a type of hidden statement on the values of society as perceived by a policeman. Reduced to its bare essentials, the account reads like a moral lesson. Hayden White has suggested that "the value attached to narrativity in the representation of real events arises out of a desire to have real events display the coherence, integrity, and closure of an image life that is and can only be imaginary" (1981: 23). He suggests that the fiction of having a world already narrativized is "necessary for the establishment of moral authority" (ibid.), that we need such fictions in order to create the idea of a moral authority. Moral authority is concealed under the aesthetic. Moralizing is pursued and concealed through an aesthetic which informs narrativity.

In Kareklas' report two examples of banditry are taken from the same family, which like a tree can yield both good and bad fruit. The bandit from the older generation takes to the hills out of a sense of injustice but eventually gives himself up, keeping his honor intact. Numerous guidelines in the text indicate how the reader is to view Hassanpoulis "The Old." He was "a model prisoner," "learnt to read and write," "protected women," and so forth. The bandits from the younger generation, by contrast, took to the hills for the same sets of reasons but soon became corrupted and utilized by entrenched interests, and lost their honor. Once a man loses his honor, anything is possible, and they were eventually betrayed by people thought to be their friends. This is their fate, or *moira.* Hassanpoulis The Old emerges as a type of hero. His nephews, who fare less favorably, threaten the new social groups then emerging in the early years of the British administration. In the 1930s, when Kareklas wrote his report, the interests of lawyers, merchants, and money lenders dominated Cypriot politics, at a time when it was experiencing a crisis of leadership and a lack of direction (Georghallides 1985). The 1930s were also a time of rapid pauperization and insecurity for many Cypriot peasants, and of incipient class conflict. The popular songs and ditties in circulation at the grassroots level when Kareklas collected his information were composed by popular itinerant story tellers, and poets (*piitharyes*), and have been cleansed and sterilized of the nastier aspects of the Hassanpoulia story. The memory of these bandits survived in a somewhat neutered form at the local level but was never taken up by urban literati. Indeed, no portraits of these bandits exist, in contrast to countless Greek klephtic-heroes. Whilst popular poets, who thrived in the 1930s, did express political and popular sentiments, they became increasingly marginalized by an elite eager to distance themselves from their rural origins. Greek Cypriot political culture increasingly wanted to view itself, and its past, as a variant of mainland Greek culture in such things as language and customs. The Hassanpoulia, as Turkish Cypriots, fitted incongruously in this project, even though during this period ethnic boundaries and identities were probably much more porous—Greek-Cypriots spoke Turkish and vice-versa. Nor were they adopted by the Turkish Cypriots, who increasingly came to rely on the British administration. As prototypical Cypriot primitive rebels, the Hassanpoulia could have achieved some prominence, but the political program of both the Greek and Turkish elites was to progressively ethnicize their histories , not de-ethnicize it (at least until recently). In addition, they were from a wrong period. Had they operated in the Ottoman occupation (1571–1878), this would have been more "ethnic-history friendly," because the Ottoman administration is perceived by Greek-Cypriots as a period of oppression.[33] The Hassanpoulia survived as a trace of a folk memory in the Paphos region in the late 1970s, when I began doing fieldwork there. The Hassanpoulia were never incorporated into the pantheon of national Cypriot heroes, either Greek or Turkish.

On another level, the report, which is implicitly linked to politics in Cyprus in the 1930s, can be read as a moral about trust. The two sets of bandits can be seen as metaphors for Cypriot leadership during this period. By setting themselves up against the law (that is, the written state law imposed by the British) in pursuit of an ideal (justice or *dikaiosini,* different to the laws of the state), the one set of bandits can be seen as analogous to the Cypriot political leadership during the time. The other set of bandits attempted to pursue an ideal based on ethnic sentiment (*enosis* or union with Greece, which came to embody freedom) against the formally imposed written constitutional rules which banished it to the political wilderness. Seen in this light, the political implications of the text become clearer: Individuals of the past, such as Hassanpoulis The Old and the traditional political leadership embodied by the Church, possessed pure ethnic and ethical values even though, like the bandit, they inhabited a world they could sometimes not understand. Yet they were true to their values (kin/women/honor and ethnos) and were not deflected from their aim of justice (*dikaiosini*), despite the conflict with written state law. Indeed, whether rejecting or collaborating with authorities, the bandits maintained their integrity unsullied.

The younger generation of bandits, by contrast, must have appeared to a middle-ranked Greek policeman working for the British authorities as a metaphor for the new generation of Cypriot politicians: well-supplied, more numerous, certainly more dynamic, yet deflected from the aim of justice (enosis) and freedom by entrenched interests and their own bickering. Instead, the bandits unwittingly act as henchmen of protected interests, much as many Greek Cypriot politicians unwittingly served imperial interests by their inability to act in unison and by venal corruption. To a middle-ranked official likely to have been at the mercy of powerful politicians in his more junior days and with direct experience of venal corruption in his professional career, such an analogy would have been obvious. Significantly, food and women are the symbols which bring out this contrast. Whereas Hassanpoulis The Old leads an almost monastic existence, abstaining from sex ("above all he protected women," who are metaphors for the nation in nationalist rhetoric) and taking solitary (but above all "silent," i.e., monastic) meals, by contrast the younger generation of bandits indulge in both sex and lavish noisy feasts.

The linguistic metaphor in Cyprus for patronage which shades into corruption is "to eat"; indeed, when men wish to say that a politician is corrupted they use the word *hortase* (he feasted). Feasting is thus a metaphor for corruption. Although the bandits make desperate attempts to establish trust, they are betrayed. The moral is clear: Trust (i.e., cooperation) can only be established on a permanent basis if men remain true to their ideals. Once abandoned for expediency they embark on a slippery path, lose control over their destinies, and respond piecemeal to events which can only end in disaster. In contrast to Hassanpoulis The Old, who gave himself up, these other bandits were taken over by events in much the same way as the various politicians in Cyprus in the 1930s lost their direction and legitimacy in the events leading to mass riots in the uprising of October 1931, when the constitution and elections were suspended and political life came to an abrupt end.

Significantly, Kareklas wrote this report only a few years after these events. To a Cypriot policeman caught between the Scylla of an undirected ethnic sentiment, apparently abandoned and betrayed by its leaders and the Charybdis of public disorder (which must have offended his sensibilities), the reconstruction of events forty years later must have assumed the nuances of a disenchantment with politics. Pursuing the associations brings this out in greater detail. In rural Cypriot culture the ethic of breaking bread together (*kanoume trapezi,* literally, "to make a table"), is a means to bring nonrelated men together, usually in a feasting and celebratory mode. The clearest example is the *trapezi gnorimias* (the feast of introductions), which occurs after matchmaking has been successfully concluded, when two as yet unrelated potentially hostile kinship groups meet for a feast marked by conspicuous display and consumption. Such an event provides an ideological justification for future cooperation without necessarily committing both parties indefinitely to each other. The idea of holding a feast, usually by and mainly for men, is explicitly oriented toward the outside, toward non-kin, and implies both intentionality and a single specific event. This is in contrast to the mere preparation of food by women for family members, the repetitive cycle of meals in the home, a part of the natural process of marriage. Indeed, the monotonously regular mention of food in Kareklas' report is not fortuitous. Holding a feast was one of the main means of transcending the climate of potential suspicion between unrelated men, of establishing some element of short-term trust in an uncertain world in which men were highly attuned to the real possibility of betrayal. Feasting was in certain ways the opposite of normal eating. At home, there are strong taboos against wasting food, and the quantity and variety of food offered were limited. At a feast, one could throw away food because of the quantity available; vast amounts of alcohol were drunk on these occasions; and the food consisted mainly of meat, usually sheep or goats roasted on a spit. Meat was a rarity in those days, especially for peasants, which partly explains the ambiguous admiration and fear peasants felt for shepherds—ostensibly below them on the social scale, yet above them in terms of the types of food they had greater access to.

Greater access to meat was of course due to the theft of the animals, a standard feature of pastoral societies, and contrasted with the bread consumed by peasants. Meat also has sexual connotations. Eating meat and having sex are metaphorically interchangeable in conversation, and it is often jestingly said: "*to kreas tis gynaikas en glychi*" (the meat/flesh of women is sweet). The metaphor is further reinforced in the report by two facts: First, unrelated men and women feasted together on occasion in the Hassanpoulia band, suggesting the suspension of the normal moral codes of honor and shame. Second, many of the women who consorted with the bandits were wives of other men; like the meat consumed at these feasts, they too had been "stolen" (i.e., abducted).

To complete the metaphorical associations Kareklas tells of a woman of loose character who had voluntarily joined the band. In the villages "she frequented the coffee shops and danced for the public" (Kareklas 1937: 21). These metaphors are mirrors of Cypriot political culture during the 1930s. Just as women become men in this semi-mythicized account of banditry and lack shame, men in the real world of Cypriot politics have become *poushtes* (passive homosexuals), a term of abuse reserved for the most abject of clients and applied also by villagers to politicians by whom they feel abandoned and who thus lack honor. Politicians prey on their co-nationals, instead of representing them, much like the bandits who grew fat on stolen meat and women. It is hardly surprising therefore that the Hassanpoulia were never adopted as national heroes by the urban elite; like the Hassanpoulia, the old guard of Cypriot politicians had been too heavily embroiled in entrenched interests, and the young EOKA men who took to the hills between 1956 and 1960 traced their spiritual descent from the mainland Greek *klepht*s of the nineteenth century, who were even more spatially and temporally distant but were legitimated by national school books and Greek hagiography.

The final puzzle remains as to why an official report detailing such activities was produced so late as 1937. The reasons are contained obliquely in the Governor's preface. From 1931, following nationwide riots in favor of *enosis* (although the reasons had more to do with the depressed state of the economy), the British suspended the constitution and ruled by governorial decree. Governor Palmer, who sponsored this report, was by most accounts far from a liberal. The latter years of elective politics until 1931 had set the British and Greek Cypriots on a collision course, and the latter volubly criticized the lack of infrastructural development, inordinately high taxation, and the prevention of their national aspiration of uniting with Greece. Cypriot delegations had visited the Colonial Office, which also sensitized relations between London and the Governors. British authorities in Cyprus were highly sensitive to these accusations, many of which were certainly well-founded. The report was thus motivated by a desire to demonstrate that British rule had been beneficial to the island, and to discredit Greek Cypriot politicians, who had often been a thorn in the flesh of Governors. Indeed, the Governor's preface makes the connection explicit: "The British administration was at that time dependent on members of a Legislative Council who, to maintain their position had perforce to work through and with those elements . . . [who] maintained their strength by 'gangster' elements" (Kareklas 1937: 3).

He then goes on to state that such incidents "on a smaller and less notorious scale, were far from uncommon up to 1931" (ibid.: 3). The choice of this date is far from arbitrary, for it marked the suspension of limited democracy in a colonial framework. The connection is clear: direct rule has had beneficial effects, in that it has resulted in the decline of banditry and corruption. He ends with the hope that this document would be of value "to a wider circle who are now interested in Cyprus" (ibid.: 3). The political context is thus key. The colonial authorities sponsored the production of a report which insinuated the embarrassing connections between the political elite and banditry in the past. *Ergo,* the suspension of civil and political liberties was not only justified, it was a boon to the population.[34]

Conclusion: Violence, Terror, and Reason

This essay argues that banditry is not a unique phenomenon and that it can take different forms according to specific and particular conditions. Banditry is intrinsically neither a pre-political form of protest nor a means of suppressing peasant unrest, although it may have these functions, among others. Rather, banditry is an aggressive form of illegality and of adventurist capital accumulation found in certain social contexts. In this sense it is a product of political economy. As a category of social behavior banditry employs specific forms of the display of violence for personal ends, and generates terror in specific ways. Banditry is as much a social role as a specific type of rationality and behavior. Terror is the employment of signs according to a certain rationality to affect reason itself. As a legalistic and political-social category, banditry is formed by the impact and interaction of the state on local communities, and its meanings have changed across time to reflect these changing relationships. The myth of banditry, furthermore, is often not a reflection of reality but, rather, may be employed by urban middle classes or peasants as a means of legitimizing political strategies.

On a more substantive level this study attempted to raise questions of a general Mediterranean significance, with particular reference to Cyprus and the Greek world. It appears that, in certain restricted contexts, agropastoralism led to a concentration of power in Cyprus, Sicily, Corsica, Sardinia, and parts of the Greek mainland, in contrast to other areas, such as North Africa, where it led to a more egalitarian society. This may have been partly due to intense competition for scarce resources, the greater capacity of the state to extract taxes (and hence the development of moveable wealth to escape taxation), and greater opportunities for trade in southern Europe, which was more heavily involved in exporting raw products to north-western Europe than was North Africa.

Second, why did banditry as a sustained large-scale phenomenon disappear in Cyprus by the early twentieth century, in contrast to other parts of the Mediterranean such as Greece, Sicily, and Sardinia? Three possible key variables are timing, participation in national struggles in however confused a form, and the ability to enter new occupations and gentrify oneself. In Sicily, *mafiosi* not only participated in national unification struggles but also managed to capture critical resources, such as land, during redistribution, and in Greece they obtained state employment as irregulars. Banditry and strong-arm tactics were also kept alive in Sicily and in certain parts of the Greek Kingdom by pledging votes to urban politicians (cf., R. Jenkins 1961). In short, tough "men of honor" could always move upwards, transforming themselves in the process. Hart has also highlighted the significance of timing for Algerian bandits. Discussing an Algerian bandit in the 1920s, he states, "It is undeniable that bin Zilmad has not acquired the stature of a national hero in the Algerian collective memory. Nonetheless, there seems little doubt that, if he had lived in 1954, bin Zilmad would have been in the forefront of the Algerian struggle for independence" (1987: 44).

In Cyprus, by contrast, bandits and strong-arm men from pastoral backgrounds found it increasingly difficult to transform their social skills into large-scale ownership of land and assume leadership roles. This was partly because the state encouraged the idea of the small peasant cultivator and also because more powerful urban classes of middlemen and merchants controlled the export trade and were fast expanding into land ownership. This does not suggest that Cyprus by the early twentieth century had become a rigid class society. Mobility remained possible for men with certain skills, but pastoralists found themselves increasingly marginalized. This may also help explain why the Hassanpoulia had to a certain extent become idealized in the villages by the 1930s, when usurious rates of interest maintained by town and village merchants created a great deal of social discontent in the villages.

In such contexts, which were far from idyllic, what was often important to villagers and what remained imprinted in their collective consciousness was the extent to which such bandits threatened the dominant ruling groups, rather than the extent to which these bandits preyed upon ordinary villagers, which they undoubtedly did. Due to such sentiments and the uncomfortable relationship of the ruling groups with their own past, the Hassanpoulia were never incorporated in a Cypriot national rhetoric, and subsequent Cypriot *agonistes* modeled themselves on the equally dubious Greek *klephts* rather than their own homegrown variety.

Finally, some concluding thoughts on the nature of violence, rationality and terror may be useful here. To see the issue in terms of the legitimation of violence is to reproduce the authority of the state in a double-Hegelian sense: the state is not just the highest expression *of* reason/violence, but the state is the ultimate *producer of reason/violence.* This "reason" takes two forms: First, it links up the power of the state with violence in almost instrumental, "reasonable" terms (the state as the ultimate guarantor of the rule of law, as having a "monopoly of violence" which can ultimately be deployed if it is threatened by illegitimate means), to therefore ensure the "rule of reason." Second, it is interiorized such that "reason" supports this construction. If we accept, following Evans-Pritchard, that there is reason in magic, and that there is order outside the state, then we should also be attuned to the possibility that the structuration of violence in the modern state is an aspect of a specific form of reason. Taussig has suggested, "there is something frightening, I think, merely in saying this conjunction of reason and violence exists, not only because it makes violence scary, imbued with the greatest legitimating force there can be, reason itself, and not only because it makes reason scary by indicating how it's snuggled deep into the armpit of terror, but also because we so desperately need to cling to reason—as instituted—against the terrifying anomie and chaos pressing in on all sides" (1992: 115). Violence, he suggests, is not a *substance* of power (as Weber seemed to think), but a power that produces the "intrinsically mysterious, mystifying, convoluting"; "violence is very much an end in itself—a sign, as Benjamin put it, of the existence of the gods" (ibid.: 116).

I share this view, but with some qualifications. In contrast to what Taussig is suggesting, violence does not need to have corporality. It does not even need to be applied, it can be extracted from the social world to signify itself. It can derive from, and engender, corporality. Violence is not so much an end in itself, but both a series of signs, and a power of signification, that conjure up and make real from within the social imaginations of men, that which is externally mysterious and internally mystifying.

NOTES

Acknowledgments: This paper derives from an earlier version published in *Comparative Studies in Society and History* (1993), and discussed at the 1994 "States of Violence" conference at the University of Michigan in Ann Arbor. I should like to thank the participants for their valuable comments and observations on the *CSSH* version of the paper, particularly Fernando Coronil, Julie Skurski, Val Daniel, Juan Cole, John Collins, and Setrag Manoukian (who were discussants of my paper and made some very incisive and useful comments), Raymond Grew, and Allen Feldman

1. Military report of 1826 quoted in Wilson (1988: 339).

2. One problem with Scott's view is that it is historically too general.

3. EOKA, The National Organization of Cypriot Fighters, was a guerilla organization commanded by General Grivas that waged a successful struggle against the British from 1955–1959.

4. One main reason was that the anti-colonial struggle was run and legitimated by the Church, rather than being organized by lay political leaders. Other reasons were that Greek bandits later dominated schoolbooks imported from the mainland, and that the Hassanpoulia consisted of both Greeks and Turks and were relatively fresh in popular memory before written populist accounts could swamp public consciousness and induce selective popular amnesia. Hence a number of questions need to be answered: Why did the Hassanpoulia emerge as the last stage of an old social order based mainly upon pastoralism? Why did not subsequent banditry follow until the emergence of EOKA in 1955? And why did the EOKA militants bypass the Cypriot Hassanpoulia to concentrate on Greek *klephts*?

5. £100, a fabulous sum then.

6. Sanchez and Meertens suggest, puzzlingly, that bandits were both class conscious and class active, whilst also being politically partisan and class blind. For the former they note that "bandits began to attack or weaken the economic interests of property owners of *their own party*" (1987: 164, my emphasis), whilst for the latter they observe "acts of violent terrorism were justified as righteous vengeance against representatives of the opposing party, *even through these might be peasants of the same region*" (ibid.: 165, my emphasis). They call this "a fragmented class consciousness" (ibid.: 165). It is hard to fully comprehend such obtuseness if that is the case.

7. Koliopoulos states that "The Kapetanioi were those who often created serious problems for the central power but eventually they became organs of the State" (1979: 19, my translation). Political exigencies certainly encouraged this tendency. In 1843 "one of the first actions of the revolution was to free an unknown number of jailed men, including many bandits among them" (ibid.: 39–40). Uncertain frontiers, especially in the Northern mountainous areas of Epiros, enabled

bandits to shift loyalties easily from Greek to Ottoman paymasters depending upon financial incentives (ibid.: 71).

8. Quoted in Wilson (1988: 405), my emphasis. "To do violence to a violent person is to be contaminated by his violence. It is best, therefore, to arrange matters so that nobody, except perhaps the culprit himself, is directly responsible for his death" (Girard 1988: 27).

9. Hobsbawm, quoting Milovan Djilas (1985: 66, original emphasis). I am not so convinced by the suggestion that individuals do things without being able to help themselves, but it is of interest that they subsequently appeal to the notion.

10. Others were more charitable, and indicate the importance of the concept of grace as an equal component to the study of honor.

11. Marcaggi (1898: 21–22). Quoted in Wilson (1988: 355).

12. Such individuals thus become tainted with the stain of state power and the blood of the victim.

13. In Calabria, banditry was linked to monasteries, and the monk is the spiritual double of the bandit.

14. Even nowadays Cypriots use these metaphors. A highly educated Cypriot leftist told me about a criminal member of a gang (known as the *Ayroporii*) who was recently shot in Limassol: "You would never believe he was such a man. He looked so peaceful, just like a saint."

15. Colletta, quoted in Douglas (1994: 324). Douglas notes that this incident was denied by General Manhes, but this would hardly be surprising, nor necessarily contradict the points made above.

16. I am particularly grateful to John Collins, a discussant on my earlier paper for the Michigan "States of Violence" conference, for his incisive observations on this point. I am aware that the motives of Franchetti/Sonnino were not disinterested. The term *Inchiesta* has legalistic/statist associations, of a (magistrate's) inquest after a crime, etc. Nevertheless, I believe that its insights are worth quoting. All accounts may be suspect, but that does not exclude that they may present an insightful depiction of the world. The internal consistency of a text (or a painting) is an important criterion of its validity.

17. Slatta makes a similar point for Latin America when he observes: "What united people behind outlaw gangs more often were kinship, friendship and egio—not class" (1990: 147).

18. The bandit is sometimes presented as having a "double" who preys on people to extort money. The bandit finally catches up and obliges him to restitute everything he extorted (cf., Wilson 1988: 352). What better way to reinforce the myth than to have a monstrous double?

19. Clearly banditry appears in literature much earlier but bandit literature first becomes a genre from the eighteenth century, such as in the *Rauberromane*. Hobsbawm recognizes this but it is surprising that he does not further explore the relationship between banditry stories and the nation state.

20. Quoted in Carrington (1971: 263). Rousseau was engaged to write a constitution for the Corsicans, a project dashed by the French invasion.

21. Quoted in Carrington (1971: 264).

22. Cervantes' Don Quixote, which features El Guapo, was written soon after the Reconquista.

23. The irony is that a government official in charge of the statist view of time through monuments should have occupied himself with a sympathetic elaboration of local customs and moeurs. He wrote his novel *Colomba* (published 1840) inspired by a contemporary vendetta.

24. The central dilemma in *Colomba* is whether or not to pursue a feud. There is a gender symbolism with the heroine representing the nation remaining faithful to the traditional obligations whilst the brother, who had been educated abroad, is reluctant to do so. The brother represents modernity. A similar opposition is found in the novel *O Archeologos,* by Karkavitsas (cf., Politi 1988).

25. Of course one can never be certain about the veracity of such claims, but what is of interest here is the imagining and envisionability that such possibilities can occur.

26. In *Usi e costumi, credenze e pregiudizi del popolo siciliano* (1889), quoted in Sciasca (1983: 141).

27. Popular literature produced in the later nineteenth century.

28. Quoted in Sciascia (1983: 139). I thank Setrag Manoukian for bringing this text to my attention.

29. Farrell is too harsh in calling it "provincial braggadocio" and "bad faith" (1995: 14). From an anthropological perspective Capuana is absolutely right (1982).

30. He referred to "the paradoxical situation where a literature committed not to betray realism . . . when faced with the mafia, has observed a type of *omerta"* (1983: 143).

31. The myth of banditry continues to be used strategically in contemporary Crete (Herzfeld 1985).

32. The models of the noble bandit in Brazil were in turn based on noble heroes of medieval Europe. (cf., Fentress and Wickham 1992), but even these two authors' excellent work has difficulty in explaining whether this was transmitted, and if so how, or whether these models offer the satisfaction for a "structural need" for justice.

33. Greek Cypriot historians have tended to discover proto-rebels mainly if they were of the "right" ethnicity: "In 1860 both communities objected to the settlement of Arabs, Drusians and other Moslem dregs in the island and thwarted their landing at Larnaca . . ." However, no such reaction is recorded of the Greek "chief-robber" Kattirci-Yiannis, who was in fact a guerilla with a glorious record of fighting against the oppressive authorities around Smyrna, where he surrendered in 1854 and was imprisoned. At Famagusta he became the object of admira-

tion by all" (Kyrris 1976: 149). Most history (including by Greek Cypriots) of the Ottoman administration emphasizes uprisings and violence not so much to suggest inter-ethnic peasant consciousness, but rather as a frustrated reaction to Ottoman oppression.

34. The same sorts of arguments were used in Sicily under fascism during this period.

REFERENCES

About, E. 1861. *Le Roi des Montagnes.* Paris: Librairie Hachette.

Barthes, R. 1977. *Image, Music, Text.* S. Heath, trans. New York: Hill and Wang.

Blok, A. 1972. "The Peasant and the Brigand: Social Banditry Reconsidered." *Comparative Studies in Society and History* 14: 494–503.

———. 1983. "On Negative Reciprocity among Sicilian Pastoralists," in *Production Pastorale et Societe.* N.p.

Braudel, F. 1972. *The Mediterranean and the Mediterranean World in the Age of Philip II, Vols. 1 and 2.* London: Collins.

Campbell, J. 1992. The Greek Hero. In, J. G. Persistainy and J. Pitt-Rivers, eds., *Honour and Grace in Anthropology.* Cambridge: Cambridge University Press, 129–49.

Capuana, L. 1982. *La Sicilia e il brigantaggio.* Rome: N.p.

Carrington, D. 1971. *Granite Island. A Portrait of Corsica.* London: Longman.

Chandler, B. J. 1978. *The Bandit King: Lampião of Brazil.* College Station, Tex.: Texas A & M Press.

Douglas, N. 1994 [1915]. *Old Calabria.* London: Picador.

Driessen, H. 1983. "The "Noble Bandit" and the Bandits of the Nobles: Brigandage and Local Community in Nineteenth-Century Andalusia." *Archives europpeennes de Sociologie* 24.

Duncan Baretta, Silvio R., and J. Markoff. 1978. "Civilization and Barbarism: Cattle Frontiers in Latin America." *Comparative Studies in Society and History* 20: 587–620.

Farrell, J. 1995. *Leonardo Sciascia.* Edinburgh: University Press.

Fentress, J., and C. Wickham. 1992. *Social Memory.* Oxford, and Cambridge, Mass.: Basil Blackwell.

Foucault, M. 1979. *Discipline and Punish. The Birth of the Prison.* New York: Vintage Books.

Franchetti, L., and S. Sonnino. 1977. *Inchiesta in Sicilia, Vol. 1, 11.* Firenze: Vallecchi editore.

Gallant, T. W. 1988. "Greek Bandits: Lone Wolves or a Family Affair?" *Journal of Modern Greek Studies* 6: 269–90.

Gambetta, D. 1988. "Fragments of an Economic Theory of the Mafia." *Archives europpeennes de Sociologie* 24: 127–48.

Gellner, E. 1983. *Nations and Nationalism.* Oxford: Basil Blackwell.

Georghallides, S. 1985. *Cyprus during the Governorship of Sir R. Storrs.* Nicosia: Cyprus Research Centre.

Gilsenan, M. 1988. "The Lords of N. Lebanon," *History and Anthropology* 1.

Girard, R. 1988. *Violence and the Sacred.* P. Gregory, trans. London: Athlone Press.

Hart, D. 1987. *Banditry in Islam. Case Studies from Morocco, Algeria and the Pakistan North West Frontier.* Cambridgeshire: Middle East and North African Studies Press.

Herzfeld, M. 1985. *The Poetics of Manhood.* Princeton: Princeton University Press.

Hobsbawm, E. 1969. *Bandits.* NY: Delacorte Press.

Jenkins, R. 1961. *The Dilessi Murders.* London: Longman.

Joseph, G. 1990. "On the Tail of Latin American Bandits." *Latin American Research Review* 25: 7–53.

Kareklas, M. Ch. 1937. "Report on the Activities of the Hassanpoulia." Nicosia: Government Printing Office.

Koliopoulos, J. 1979. *Bandits. Central Greece in the Mid-19th Century.* Athens: Ermis Editions (in Greek).

———. 1987. *Brigands with a Cause.* Oxford: Oxford University Press.

Kyrris, C. P. 1976. "Symbiotic Elements in the History of the Two Communities in Cyprus." In *International Symposium on Political Geography. Proceedings.* Nicosia: Cyprus Geographic Association, 127–66.

Marcaggi, J.-B. 1898. Fleuve de sang, Histoire d£une vendetta corse. Paris: Privately printed.

McGrew, W. 1985. *Land and Revolution in Modern Greece, 1800–1881.* Kent, Oh.: Kent State University Press.

Moss, D. 1979. "Bandits and Boundaries in Sardinia." *Man, NS* 14: 477–96.

Politi, J. 1988. "The Tongue and the Pen: A Reading of Karkavitsas' *O Archeologos.*" In, R. Beaton, ed., *The Greek Novel A.D. 1–1985.* London: Croom Helm.

Politis, A. 1973. *To Dhimotiko Tragoudi.* Athens: Ermis.

Sanchez, G., and D. Meertens. 1987. "Political Banditry and the Colombian Violencia." In, R. Slatta, ed., [no title or publisher available].

Sant Cassia, P. 1986. "Politics, Ethnicity and Religion in Cyprus during the Turkocratia." *Archives europpeennes de Sociologie* 27: 3–28.

———. 1993. "Banditry, Myth, and Terror in Cyprus and Other Mediterranean Societies." *Comparative Studies in Society and History* 35: 773–95.

Sciascia, L. 1983. "Letteratura e Mafia." In, L. Sciascia, ed., *Cruciverba.* Torino: Einaudi, 139–49.

Scott, J. 1985. *Weapons of the Weak: Everyday Forms of Peasant Resistance.* New Haven, Conn.: Yale University Press.

Slatta. R., ed. 1987. *Bandidos. The Varieties of Latin American Banditry.* Connecticut: Greenwood Press.

———. 1990. "Bandits and Rural Social History: A Comment on Joseph." *Latin American Research Review* 25: 145–75.

Snowden, F. M. 1977. *Violence and Great Estates in the South of Italy. Apulia 1900–1922.* Cambridge: Cambridge University Press.

Taussig, M. 1992. *The Nervous System.* London: Routledge.

Vanderwood, P. J. 1981. *Disorder and Progress. Bandits, Police and Mexican Development.* Lincoln: University of Nebraska Press.

White, H. 1981. "The Value of Narrativity in the Representation of Reality." In, W.J.T. Mitchell, ed., *On Narrative.* Chicago: University of Chicago Press, 1–23.

Wilson, S. 1988. *Feuding, Conflict and Banditry in Nineteenth-Century Corsica.* Cambridge: Cambridge University Press.

Zugasti, de, J. 1934. *El Bandolerismo Andaluz.* Madrid: Espace Calipe.

Of Crowds and Empires: Afro-Asian Riots and European Expansion, 1857–1882

Juan R. I. Cole

Our language about collective violence and the categories into which we fit it have been powerfully shaped by state officials, by elites, and, in the global South, often by colonial authorities. On 11 June 1882, a fight between a Maltese and an Egyptian in the teeming cotton port of Alexandria spiraled into an afternoon of violence between urban Egyptians and those coded as foreign (Maltese, Greeks, Italians, British, and French). At the level of small-group encounters, we have only disconnected accounts of the thousands of individual altercations that went to make up the disturbance. Sayyid the dough kneader said he was stabbed by a European because he took the side of a fish seller in a dispute. Some Europeans reported being fired on by the very gendarmes they expected to succor them. The army finally moved in late in the day and reestablished order, but too late to restore public confidence, for in the next weeks the nearly 100,000 Europeans in Egypt streamed out of the country in panic. How to construe this event that helped determine the political fortunes of the Eastern Mediterranean and of Africa in the subsequent eighty years? Was it a massacre of innocent European expatriates by enraged, fanatical Muslim mobs? Had it been deliberately instigated by the insurgent General Ahmad 'Urabi? European journalists and officials (often one and the same) reported both characterizations in the London press. Their categorizations implied that ancient racial or religious hatreds and Oriental despotism were the natural state of Afro-Asia, from which it could be saved only by enlightened European colonial rule. This chapter attempts to place in question these categories, which have increasingly come under challenge in post-colonial historiography.

I here offer a study, focusing mainly on Egypt, of the nature, political consequences, and rhetorical construction of urban conflicts between local inhabitants and Europeans or their protégés in the age of gradual European imperial expansion in the Middle East stretching from the 1850s to the 1880s. The history of this period has tended to be written as high politics, and its main actors in Africa and Asia have on the whole been appropriated for the purposes of twentieth-century bourgeois nationalist historiography. My aim here, of recovering the subaltern element in this history of resistance, and of questioning the very categories ("massacre of Christians," "military government") by which indigenous movements have been described in most British historiography, has resonances with the "subaltern studies" school of Ranajit Guha, Gyan Pandey and others in India.[1] Collective action by the urban crowd as a social historical phenomenon has a double advantage for the study of the Middle East. First, it has been well delineated by historians, especially the Anglo-Marxist school and American resource-mobilization theorists.[2] Second, it is among the more visible (that is, for the historian, recoverable) activities of ordinary persons in non-European lands.[3]

In the interests of clarity, I should define my own terms before challenging the words chosen by nineteenth-century Europeans. I employ the word "crowd" to indicate any urban collectivity gathered for a collective purpose, whether in regard to ritual, entertainment, or protest, etc. Sometimes crowds turn violent, smashing shops or other buildings and assaulting individuals who symbolize some grievance, all of which governmental authorities tend to call a "riot." The term "riot" is not, as I have been reminded by readers, a neutral word. The American Heritage Dictionary gives its definition in the law as "a violent disturbance of the public peace by three or more persons assembled for a common private purpose." I do not believe that most of the urban crowd disturbances I discuss below had only a "common private purpose," but rather, they often aimed at securing corporate or communal goals. To "disturb the public peace," moreover, makes it sound as though the action were aimless or unjustified, whereas many of the crowd actions discussed below came in response to disruptions of their urban moral economy. Where I occasionally use the word below, therefore, I am not employing it in its official or legal sense, but rather in the sense of "violent collective action by a crowd." Veena Das has suggested that the form of the riot involves three kinds of symbolic structures: "the organization of symbolic space, the temporal structure of riots (different kinds of riots, relating to ritual or political calendars in different ways), and, finally, the repertoire of symbolic actions that is called upon in the case of ethnic or communal conflict."[4] Here, I will attempt to be attentive to all three of these dimensions.

The salience of the suggested periodization derives from the difficulties Europeans, especially the British, faced in extending their domination over the Middle East during these decades. The Great Rebellion in North India (1857–1858) and the 'Urabi revolt in Egypt (1881–1882) demarcated an era of imperial gradualism that ended with the occupation of Egypt and the subsequent scramble for Africa. The histories of colonialism and anti-imperialism are so various that generalization about them is difficult, but both revolutions were children of the mid-nineteenth century. On the one hand, they involved a local response to an increasingly self-assured colonial acquisitiveness, as well as to the impact of nineteenth-century capitalism. Local leadership was more diverse than had been the case in eighteenth-century resistance movements against European encroachments, which had most often involved a diffuse eruption of regional violence led by traditional chieftains such as *nawabs* and *mamluks*. In particular, from the mid-nineteenth century leaders from the intermediate strata became more important, coordinating collective violence on a more nearly "national" scale. In short, a shift occurred in the repertoire of contention. The shift reflects not a teleological unfoldment or a natural history of colonialism, but specific and various responses to macro-historical developments such as industrial capitalism and the increased capacities (owing to technological and organizational advances) of colonial administrations.[5]

Amidst engagements with Europeans and the protégés led by landlords, peasants, and the military during this period of anti-colonial revolts, one cannot help but be struck by the equal importance of urban crowd action. The significant dates and urban battles of these decades conjure up images of enraged mobs trapping the imperial bureaucrat, the freebooting entrepreneur, the indigenous Christian or other minority merchant with ties to foreign consuls: Lucknow and Delhi in 1857, Jiddah in 1858, Damascus in 1860, Alexandria in 1882. (These examples have been chosen for their significance and in the cause of wieldness, not because they exhaust the instances of this phenomenon.)

It is not enough, however, to note the importance of such events to the imperial imagination. The social historian of Africa and Asia will be interested to know what sort of urban structures and political processes formed the matrix of these crowd actions. Albert Hourani, writing of the Ottoman lands in the 1850s, suggested that a number of anti-Christian riots, including Jiddah (1858) and Damascus (1860), manifested the opposition of local notables both to Ottoman centralization and to the increasing political and economic penetration of the European consuls and their clients.[6] This interpretation, a breakthrough at the time it was offered, contains a strong element of truth. But its force is somewhat vitiated by the concentration solely on an elite. Hourani, appealing both to the Weberian notion of patriciate and to the Middle Eastern conception of the *a'yan* or prominent leaders, limited the notables to three groups: the Muslim clergy or *ulama,* the heads of local garrisons, and the landed secular notables. The question we must address is whether the anti-European urban disturbances to which Hourani refers, as well as others occurring in this era, were really led by persons deriving from these three groups, or did the urban crowd act in a more complex and autonomous fashion than such an interpretation would suggest?

Let us turn now to the subject of our case study, Egypt. The age of the Ottoman Viceroy Isma'il (1863–1879) in Egypt, which was followed by the proto-nationalist 'Urabi revolt and the British occupation of 1882, has been an inexhaustible laboratory for historians of the Middle East, much as the second half of the eighteenth century has been for historians of France. The era marks many beginnings: the burgeoning of capitalist agriculture, independent press and publishing houses, modernist thought on social reform, an embryonic form of nationalism within an Ottoman framework, financial indebtedness to Europe, and, finally, colonization.

Historians have virtually ignored the common people in Viceroy Isma'il's Egypt, and one can only speculate that this is so only because these historians believed elites were the primary actors in the important movements of the age.[7] More sophisticated recent work has often simply widened the political sphere to encompass a larger group of notables. The late Gabriel Baer did begin the task of examining Egyptian social history, but as a pioneer he was forced to paint with a broad brush, so that his work only occasionally illumines the specificities of our three decades. The same might be said of Judith Tucker's recent ground-breaking treatment of working women in nineteenth-century Egypt.[8]

At first sight, the thesis of the political uninvolvement or unimportance of the laborers, artisans, and shopkeepers might seem difficult to contest. No guild archives exist; no working-class presses printed Arabic pamphlets for radical Egyptian cobblers. Egyptian government archives are too preliminarily catalogued to be used easily to address such issues.[9] On one area, however, the ordinary folk made a mark of a political nature (or with political implications) too explosive to be overlooked, at least by contemporary observers. They assembled as crowds for violent collective action. Between 1858 and 1882 Egyptian and European laborers in Egypt clashed with some frequency, engaging in vendettas with one another. One may consult the standard political histories without finding most of these disturbances mentioned, despite their size and repercussions. I have discovered detailed accounts of these events reported by the network of British agents in Egypt's cities and towns. Baer first drew attention to, but hardly exhausted, this rich source, which, incidentally, also preserves many Arabic documents.

A thematic argument can be made, moreover, against the inconsequentiality of popular turmoil. Although some of the fracases in the streets of Alexandria, Port Said, or Cairo had few immediate political effects, one urban disturbance helped change the history of the Mediterranean and Africa. The Euro-Egyptian riot in Alexandria in June of 1882, at the height of the 'Urabi revolt, shocked the European public. It helped provoke not only indiscriminate naval bombardment of the city, but also the British military intervention that eventuated in the occupation of Egypt (despite Prime Minister Gladstone's feelings against imperial expansion).[10] The coming of the British into Africa profoundly altered the political and economic complexion of the Mediterranean. If urban laborers facing down acquisitive Europeans helped bring it about, then their action can hardly be ignored as unimportant. But like later historians, the two major imperial powers tended to interpret the riot differently. British officials saw it as a "massacre" instigated by the nationalist figure of Colonel Ahmad 'Urabi and his supporters, thus denying the autonomy of the laborers. The rioters took, in this view, a quite centrally political action, but on direction from notables higher up. The French, on the other hand, tended to interpret the violence as a mere harbor fracas, of a type that often broke out even in European ports.[11] From this perspective the riot was an autonomous action of the laboring and dangerous classes, but without political content or implication. No close observer would now accept either of these views as adequate, though both contain kernels of truth. More important, both fail to locate the context of 1882 in the history of urban structures and struggles during the previous quarter of a century.[12]

The European Impact on Egypt

The Bowring report of 1839 foresaw that Viceregal-Ottoman Egypt would also come into increasing contact with the British as the highroad to India. Although there might be some initial opposition, the report concluded, it would die down when the Egyptians realized that the British were spreading wealth and civilization.[13] The part of the prediction about increasing British influence proved accurate, especially from the late 1850s. The completion of the Cairo-Alexandria railway in 1858 helped open Egypt up to European penetration in a dramatic fashion. The trains shortened the length of a journey from the cosmopolitan port city of Alexandria to the previously more isolated capital of Cairo in the interior from four days to eight hours. From 1862 the blockade of the South in the American Civil War helped provoke a cotton boom in Egypt that further attracted European merchants, investors, and speculators. The treasury receipts from higher tax income allowed the Egyptian government to hire European mechanics, engineers, teachers, and even former Confederate officers. Of course, the opening of the Suez Canal in 1869 created large expatriate communities at Suez and Port Said.[14]

From about 10,000 in 1848, the number of Europeans in Egypt grew nearly ten times by 1882. Although most still lived in Alexandria, large numbers moved to Cairo and even, as landlords and moneylenders, into the provinces. Viceroy 'Abbas had not permitted Europeans to own land, but Sa'id and Isma'il gradually allowed them to acquire land and urban property in fact, though they often had to resort to legal fictions.[15] The sheer numbers of immigrants might have been enough to generate a certain amount of conflict. One thinks of the anti-Irish agitations in eighteenth-century London. But along with large contingents of Southern European workers came a smaller group of northern European merchants and investors. The Europeans were present everywhere the Egyptian worker, artisan, or merchant looked, whether as competitors for work, or as owners acquiring workshops, or as creditors. Europeans demanded cash crops like cotton, transforming the economy. But they also insisted on immunity from Egyptian law and taxation, seeking an advantage over Egyptians in their own country that led to seething frustrations.

The Egyptian archives are beginning to yield new insight into the sources of these frustrations. It is clear, for instance, that Egypt's traditional guilds resented the tendency of European capitalism to privatize formerly public and regulated sectors of the economy. Textile and cotton merchants in Alexandria complained bitterly in 1873 that weighers and measurers, who had once constituted a public guild, had all now gone to work for private European concerns, so that Egyptians could no longer expect fair weighing. European merchants also attempted to interfere in the appointment of guildmasters for guilds such as the brokers of Alexandria, generating potential resentment on the part of rival candidates (including the powerful Sha't family). Even such apparently unpolitical effects of the European influx as the spread of steam boilers for ginning cotton raised alarms among urban Egyptians, who feared that the noisy, polluting machines would spread disease and constituted a fire hazard.[16] A prominent Egyptian merchant and manufacturer complained in the late 1870s that "as for the merchant, he has been impoverished by a stagnant market and forced to cling for shelter to the hem of the foreigner, who can, if he pleases, disgrace him or allow him to remain as he is."[17] The laborer and the artisan, the same writer said, were crushed beneath the weight of taxes (high because of the need to service European debts).

Urban Conflicts between Egyptians and Europeans

The classic accounts of anti-European agitation in the 1860s and 1870s focused on the role of intellectuals, journalists, and the military. But the now-largely-forgotten workings of the crowd formed an important social context for the anti-imperialist and pan-Islamic agitations of intellectuals and holy and learned men. These groups interacted, of course. Muslim sermonizers addressed the public every Friday afternoon at congregational prayers, and some literate artisans read the anti-European press that sprang up in the late 1870s. Indeed, one leading journalist, 'Abdu'llah Nadim, came of an artisan background. Moreover, we must not forget that the urban crowd in this period became increasingly polarized, between Egyptian workers on the one hand, and European immigrants on the other. The Europeans could be as boisterous as the locals, and the rivalries between these groups generated their own history of feuding.

Although the urban clashes discussed below had many proximate causes, some background themes reemerge time and again. Religious and national identities contributed importantly to the crowd's mentality. European workers sought to participate in imperial glory by asserting their superiority over the locals—even their immunity from prosecution for crimes. Not only Egyptian nationalists, but apparently European toughs themselves saw a parallel between the imperialist's usurpation of territory in Africa and Asia with impunity, and the European worker's unpunished acts of burglary and vandalism. The Egyptian crowd, on the other hand, often adopted a rhetoric of defending Muslim honor against Christian encroachments. Events elsewhere in the Muslim world sometimes set off, or influenced the terms of, disturbances in Port Said or Alexandria.

For this reason, not only the Jiddah and Damascus massacres of Christians, but also the Great Rebellion of 1857–1858 in North India formed important background events for the culture of Euro-Muslim conflict in Middle Eastern cities. Here such struggles will be noted for their diachronic context. We will come back to them later for synchronic comparison. Anti-European disturbances sometimes reflected the activities of international networks of Muslim activists who opposed European expansion in India, North Africa, and Eastern Europe. Frequently these activists, drawn from many social strata, had been displaced by the European advance, had gone on pilgrimage to Mecca, and then settled in the Hijaz, Egypt, or Syria.[18]

The British consul in Cairo in 1858 not only reported local Christian and European fears aroused by the Jiddah massacre, but confirmed that the revolt in India, in which Muslims had taken a prominent part, had evoked sympathy among Muslims in Egypt and that local Indian and Iranian residents had fanned that feeling. The vice consul in Suez also reported that some Muslims in that city had shown satisfaction in hearing of the Jiddah massacre, especially the boatmen from Jiddah and other Red Sea coasts and those in direct contact with Hadramautis. He reported that earlier in Suez "native Christians and even [sic] Europeans were openly insulted by a number of natives assembled for the purpose."[19]

Sa'id Pasha's pro-European sentiments gave little heart to Egyptians who wished to protest increasing European influence, though his government's near-bankruptcy did little to foster security in the cities. Bulwer, consul in Cairo, reported late in 1862 that "the equality between Christian & Musulman in all social and civil transactions had been cordially adopted as a principle and maintained as a fact."[20] Sa'id's death and the change of government early in 1863, however, created expectations of change.

For several days after Isma'il Pasha's accession, crowds assembled at the spot where executioners usually dispatched criminals "to see the European who it was currently reported was to be hung by the order of the Government as a mark of the change that had taken place as regards Christians."[21] Of course, this expectation proved a chimera. In February 1863 arsonists set a fire at Khamzawi Khan in al-Mousky, a Christian-owned inn, and attempted to start blazes at several French and Italian establishments. Druze, Afghans, and people from Mecca living in Cairo "it is said are inciting the Musulman mob to commit outrages against Christians."[22]

In the small towns of Upper Egypt, an Indian holy man, fugitive from the Great Rebellion, helped provoke a peasant uprising in 1865.[23] At least a slight fallout from 1839 (the First Anglo-Afghan War) and 1857 in South Asia, from 1858 in the Hijaz, and from 1860 in the Levant therefore continued to rain down upon Cairo in the 1860s through networks of Muslim travelers, merchants, pilgrims, and exiles whose bitterness from experiences in defending themselves from Europeans or fighting local Christians had led them to agitate against them among their contacts in the leadership of urban crowds. The government of Isma'il, however, took firm steps to protect Christians and Europeans in the capital, and the new cotton wealth allowed an expansion of security forces.

Despite the rumors of impending Muslim agitation, and the cases of arson just noted, for most of the 1860s the major incidents originated with the foreigners rather than with the Egyptians. The large number of southern European workers who congregated in Egypt's urban centers from 1862 onward came into ethnic conflict several times with local Egyptians. These Greeks, Italians, and Maltese could ignite fights with slurs on Islam or simply by starting drunken brawls.

Alexandria, with its large European population, witnessed several incidents. In 1865 a fracas between Italian sailors and Egyptian donkey drivers and their Arab supporters threatened the city's tranquility. Working-class Italians formed a crowd and besieged their own consulate, demanding it take stern measures to force an Egyptian apology. In 1870 Greeks went on a rampage in an internal dispute over ecclesiastical leadership. A year later some French subjects who were publishing an unauthorized journal clashed with local police who tried to close it down, causing the French consul to authorize his countrymen to repel force by force.[24]

Other port cities also experienced friction between the Egyptians and European immigrants. The Suez Canal brought extremely rapid growth in the late 1860s to Port Said. In 1870 Nubian guards had an altercation with Greeks, and in 1875 fighting broke out between Maltese Christians and Nubian Muslim guards posted at the customs house. An even more serious incident took place between Maltese and Nubians in 1878, in response to which nearly 2,000 nearby Muslim villagers rushed to help their coreligionists against a European crowd. Khedivial officials narrowly averted a serious confrontation.[25]

The interior of the country seldom experienced Euro-Egyptian conflict before 1876. Cairo, seat of government, saw relatively little violence, though one major brawl occurred between Greek toughs and Egyptians in a coffee house in 1863, sparking a diplomatic incident. In 1872 an altercation with religious overtones involving Greeks erupted at Tantah, the large Delta city with the shrine to the medieval mystic Sayyid Ahmad al-Badawi. The Greeks were said to have cursed the shrine keeper.[26]

The urban disturbances of which I could find records in the 1860s and early 1870s have many elements in common. First, a rivalry or some sort of friction existed between two relatively small groups. Italian sailors and Egyptian donkey drivers, Greek shopkeepers and Nubian guards, Greek Orthodox believers and Muslim shrine officials, Maltese port workers and Egyptian customs-house employees—all came into contact on a small scale fairly frequently. But when the conflict assumed an aspect of public violence, larger networks and loyalties came into play. Maltese and Italians came to the aid of Greeks, Egyptians to the aid of Nubians. Guilds that might otherwise have their own differences with one another would stand together against the foreigner. This unthinking allegiance—and suspension of disbelief about the enormities of which the Other was capable—could cause a minor fracas to escalate into a full-blown riot very quickly. The economic relations of Europeans and Egyptians were frequently unequal and exploitative, and often frustrating for all concerned. These daily frustrations formed a background of continuous prose for the occasional punctuation afforded by the melees. The political content of the Euro-Egyptian conflicts of the late 1860s and early 1870s was largely symbolic: local pride and imperial glory lurked in many a humble bout of fisticuffs. The establishment of European fiscal control over Egypt in 1876, the Russo-Ottoman War of 1877–1878, and the 'Urabi revolt all helped intensify implications of such conflicts for politics and for the shape of state structures in succeeding years.

Debt Crisis, the Russo-Ottoman War, and Student Protests, 1876–1878

In 1876 Egypt officially defaulted on its loans and the Europeans set up a debt commission to exercise control over Egyptian finances, with an eye to ensuring that Egypt made its debt service payments to European creditors on time. This direct foreign role in the administration of Egypt altered the country's relationship with Europe and set the stage for greater anti-European feeling. It coincided with the establishment of Mixed Courts, which gave foreigners the ability to often manipulate the law, even in disputes with local Egyptians, and made them more confident about speculating in Egyptian real estate.[27]

Egypt's debt crisis coincided with the outbreak of hostilities between Egypt and Christian powers, both in the Egyptian-Ethiopian War and, later, in the Russo-Ottoman War (to which Viceroy Isma'il contributed troops as a vassal of the sultan). Rumors of an impending war in Europe between a Muslim and a Christian power raised the communal tension in the Ottoman Empire, including Egypt. Western historiography has emphasized the forceful Ottoman suppression of Balkan Christian secessionists in 1876 and the campaign led by Gladstone on the issue of the "Balkan massacres." But Muslim populations in eastern Europe also suffered greatly during the subsequent war, and this news aroused emotions in Egypt.

As Egyptian troops prepared to embark for Istanbul, anti-European demonstrations took place in Kafr az-Zayyat and Zaqaziq, towns in the Delta. Carr, the vice-consul in Kafr az-Zayyat, reported that Europeans in his vicinity were alarmed by a daily procession formed mostly of students of the local Egyptian schools who paraded the European quarter of town asking for God's help against enemies of the Muslim faith and crying out, "Death to all Christians!" These demonstrations spread in July to Mansurah and in September to Damietta.[28] Despite the complaisance of local officials toward these student protests against Europeans, the central government worked to stop them.

Although previous historians have not seen fit to note these demonstrations by provincial students, they undeniably had political significance. The students' anti-imperialist fervor may be assumed to have reflected the sentiments of at least some of their teachers, and very possibly their parents as well. This literate new middle class often felt most strongly against the hiring of large numbers of foreigners as engineers or bureaucrats, since they felt themselves undervalued in contrast. The venue for these protests suggests that European penetration of the Egyptian interior generated some resentment. The four towns mentioned were all in Lower Egypt, and all were provincial centers where Europeans had become increasingly visible and powerful as investors and landowners after the 1876 opening of the mixed tribunals.[29]

By their very nature, the urban clashes posed a challenge to the state and to the power of informal empire, creating a tradition of urban interaction in which some sorts of conflict between ethnic and religious groups were handled autonomously by them, without reference to the national or even provincial authorities. An imagined slur on the honor of Italy caused working-class Italians to run amuck and even take their own ambassador hostage until they considered that face had been saved. An affray between

French printers and Egyptian police could provoke the French ambassador into acknowledging what the French crowd already took to be the case: Frenchmen could repel force by force without recourse to the authorities. On the other hand, the Muslim crowd at the shrine at Tantah thought they knew how to handle the blaspheming Greeks, and it was not by submitting complaints to the local police. Nubians were involved in major instances of violence with Greeks or Maltese three times in the decade of the 1870s in Port Said, suggesting recurring frustrations and enmities—in short, an incipient urban tradition. Throughout, crowd behavior suggested a lack of respect for the supposed Weberian monopoly a force the Egyptian government should have enjoyed.

What we begin to see happening in 1877–1878, against the backdrop of a major military confrontation between the Ottomans and a European power, is the congruity of altercations such as that in Port Said with urban anti-European demonstration, and the participation, not only of workers and tradesmen, but of students from the middle strata. With the appointment of the Debt Commission and the increasing European penetration of the court system and the bureaucracy, Britain and France had decisively entered the arena of domestic Egyptian politics. Policies that might once have simply elicited popular hatred of the viceroy now conjured up anti-European protesters. As the Egyptian intermediate strata began to seek means of political self-expression, they not only ran up against the Ottoman-Egyptian hammerlock on power, but also found Europeans blocking them at every turn. Especially from their base in the army and police, these strata increasingly allied with the urban crowd in anti-European action during the next three years, in what became known as the 'Urabi revolt. Euro-Egyptian conflict was becoming politicized in new ways.

From Turmoil to the 'Urabi Revolt

The three and a half years beginning with the winter of 1879 saw intensified military discontent and involvement with politics. The most rebellious officers came from rural Egyptian notable families and the troops who supported them came from a peasant background. Discontent with the European-backed status quo engendered antagonism towards Europeans as well among the Egyptians who supported the junior officers' protest.

Military protests in the winter and spring of 1879 centered on the dismissal of large numbers of officers and the placing of thousands more on half pay. The ethnic Egyptian junior officers understood very well that these economy measures derived from the need to devote a substantial portion of the budget to servicing debts to the Europeans. The junior officers demanded the dismissal of the European-dominated cabinet and, with behind-the-scenes support from Khedive Isma'il, actually took the prime minister and the British cabinet officer hostage briefly. Other members of the elite, such as the wealthy clergy and mystics, took these protests as an opportunity to offer their support for the viceroy against the Europeans with the quid pro quo that he move toward constitutionalism and parliamentary rule. Isma'il's attempt to manipulate military and clerical dissatisfaction so as to end direct European representation on the cabinet briefly succeeded.[30] But the European powers, far from being thwarted, intervened to depose Isma'il in June of 1879, installing his son Tawfiq as viceroy with Ottoman acquiescence.

Pandora's box could not, however, be so easily closed. The Egyptian junior officers had discovered that they could cause governments to fall. True, political passions subsided during Tawfiq's first year in office. The authorities deported some activist intellectuals, and the censors closed down the major anti-European newspapers.[31] But in 1880 discontent with the new viceroy began surfacing; the old issues of European penetration and high taxes had not gone away. More important, junior Egyptian officers felt themselves blocked by Tawfiq's policy decisions supporting the Ottoman-Egyptian elite. In September of 1881, Egyptian colonels led by Ahamd 'Urabi and backed by insubordinate rank-and-file Egyptian troops and artillery units confronted the viceroy, demanding better treatment for the army, a constitutional and parliamentary government, and dismissal of the current cabinet, "which had sold the country to the English."[32]

The agitation of the junior officers for reform paralleled a wider movement in civil society toward a proto-nationalism and demand for greater power-sharing within the Ottoman framework. As in any nationalism, no matter how tentative, the contrast provided by the Other proved essential in defining identity. The issue of foreign domination gave Egyptians an image of the Other as the European. Although 'Urabi in his speeches before crowds urged that Europeans be well-treated, as guests in Egypt, the building political tension and Franco-British support for viceregal absolutism created an atmosphere in which anti-European feelings began to surface. Some Egyptian newspapers attacked Europeans for interfering in the 'Urabi movement and attempting to suppress the nationalist press, and tolerance for European criticism of Egypt reached a low point. A report from Tantah in November of 1881 suggested that "business transactions between natives and foreigners are affected and that the confidence necessary in such matters which existed formerly has been greatly impaired."[33]

European consular officials viewed this turmoil with alarm, since it threatened European interests on two fronts. First, the rising Egyptian notables in the Chamber of Deputies began engaging in a tug of war with the British and French for control over the government treasury, threatening the debt servicing and raising the specter of a rollback of European penetration of the Nile Valley. Second, the struggle between 'Urabists and viceregal absolutists affected the authorities' ability to govern, and order began to break down in places like Alexandria. In March of 1881, a mob of Greeks injured several Jews in a blood libel attack.[34] In Suez, later the same year, Egyptian soldiers threatened to massacre the Europeans unless an Italian officer accused of murdering an Egyptian was executed.[35] Such events and such rhetoric frightened the British and French, who began to feel how vulnerable they were.

The double compact the Europeans thought they had with Egypt began to unravel; neither European property (including the milk cow of debt servicing) nor European lives any longer seemed protected. The Europeans' feelings of alarm peaked in late May 1882, when the viceroy dismissed the cabinet, including 'Urabi. But the army and various sectors of the public—including heads of guilds—demanded restoration of 'Urabi as war minister, and the viceroy reinstated him on 28 May. The general fear therefore subsided a bit in the first week of June. Sources of conflict remained, however, since 'Urabi wanted fortifications improved at Alexandria, the likely point of any European attack, and put pressure on the Europeans to remove their fleets from the harbor to avoid "the excitement of the public mind caused by their presence."[36]

By the second week of June passions ran high again. On 7 June a quarrel broke out between some Arabs and Greeks. A European witness said the Arabs greatly outnumbered their Hellenic adversaries and beat them with sticks; then some Egyptian soldiers arrived and joined in the attack on the Greeks, and refused to obey their officers when they ordered them to desist. A hundred Europeans subsequently went to the British consulate and demanded that measures be taken for their protection.[37]

The Europeans had, willy-nilly, been drawn in as players in an Egyptian drama. 'Urabi supporters and dissatisfied Egyptian artisans and laborers viewed themselves as victims of an exclusive political Establishment. The Ottomans and Circassians at the top intended forever to keep the lion's share of wealth and power in their hands. The European powers proved their allies in this endeavor, a cosmopolitan Establishment solidly supporting a provincial one. Many among the Egyptian middle strata and their laboring allies, attempting to break the grip of this twin Establishment, perceived the ordinary Europeans in Egypt as symbols of repression. The 'Urabi movement took on an increasingly nativist coloration, so that some grievances were highlighted more than others, some everyday alliances eschewed for new ones. Coptic Christians and Egyptian Muslims, or Nubians and Delta natives, could make common cause against the dual elite of Ottoman Muslims and European Christians. In a political revolution a Manichean logic comes into play, dividing the world into allies and traitors. Politics, operating like a kaleidoscope, reconstituted the colorful ethnic patterns of cities like Alexandria—with their fractious Maltese, Greeks, Italians, Nubians, and Egyptians—into a black-and-white contrast of "them" and "us."

The Alexandria Riot

On Sunday afternoon, 11 June 1882, Alexandria's seething Euro-Egyptian frictions set off a major conflagration. For many reasons, the social composition, motives, and leadership of this clash became a matter of debate. A mere port riot had little political significance. If, on the other hand, the action could be traced to 'Urabi, then it offered a casus belli to a Great Britain whose men on the spot were eager to intervene. In retrospect, of course, the charges by many Europeans that the disturbance formed part of an orchestrated conspiracy directed from Cairo by 'Urabi (and the 'Urabist riposte that Tawfiq instigated it), remain unsubstantiated by any convincing evidence.[38] Indeed, if one remembers the history of Italian, Greek, and French melees in the preceding two decades in Alexandria, and of clashes between Europeans and their protégés and Egyptians in many other towns during the same period, the riot seems less remarkable. It does seem clear that the forces of order either equivocated about whether to quell the disturbance, or actually joined in the killing and pillaging.

Little benefit would accrue from attempting to establish a fixed chronicle of events on that Sunday in Alexandria between 2:30 P.M. and about 6:00 P.M., when the army moved in to stop the fighting.[39] A typical Christian account, though biased, gives one the flavor:

> On the 11th June last, about 2:30 o'clock P.M., at Alexandria, I left my house and went in the direction of the "Strada delle Monache," when I saw, at a distance of about thirty paces from me, about 200 Arabs. I stopped and inquired what was the matter. I was told that Arabs had attacked Christians, and that a Maltese, having been beaten by an Arab with a stick, retaliated, and wounded him with a knife. A little afterwards, I went to the "Manoli" coffee-house, where there were other Maltese. In the meantime, the Arab crowd increased to about 2,000, all armed with sticks; and they attacked Europeans, breaking open and plundering shops. On seeing this, I ran towards another coffee-house, called "Liculuss," where there were about twenty-five Italians, Greeks, and Maltese. I saw about five or six soldiers with their muskets, followed by about 2,000 Arabs, who broke shop doors and plundered.[40]

Others told similar stories. A fight between a Maltese and an Arab, perhaps begun by a wager, took a serious turn. Greeks came to the Maltese's defense. The Maltese stabbed the Arab to death, and local Egyptians gathered to take revenge on the Europeans. One recalls here the Maltese-Nubian clashes in Port Said. But the crowd did not stop with the Maltese, instead invading the European quarter and engaging Europeans, who wounded as many people with their firearms as did the Egyptians with their sticks. The American consul reported that "it was not until the Greeks and Maltese had commenced firing from their windows and flat housetops upon the unarmed natives, and some of their number had been killed and others wounded, that they were aroused to violent acts of vengeance."[41] Ordinary Egyptians such as the groom Ahmad Abu's-Su'ud, tobacco grinder Ahmad Husayn, cobbler 'Ali Salamah, and pedestrian Sabihah, the daughter of Abu'l-'Aysh, were interviewed in a hospital and reported being suddenly struck down by European sniper fire or unexpectedly beaten up by "Christians."[42] Thousands took part in the disturbances; about fifty Europeans (and European protégés) died that day, and perhaps five times that number of Egyptians (their bodies were removed by family members, making them harder to count, and authorities suppressed the number for fear of further incidents). The wounded included about thirty-six Europeans, thirty-five Egyptians, and two Ottomans.[43]

The Europeans charged the Egyptian crowd with extensive looting, though one suspects that the crowd felt it was reappropriating wealth lost to sharp Mediterranean shopkeepers.

The governor and sub-prefect of police accompanied the British consul to the quarter where the fighting first broke out around 1:30 P.M., and they thought they had quelled it. At 3:30 P.M. the authorities again summoned all the consuls to the police station, since fighting had broken out once more, and this time the mob attacked them. Only the British consul suffered a serious wound. Around 5:00 P.M., the Egyptian crowd had grown so large that the Europeans had to retreat from the street to their houses, where they continued sniping at the Egyptians with revolvers. In this fire two Egyptian guards fell dead, infuriating the other guards who for the first time provided the Egyptian side with firepower. Not until around 6:00 P.M. did army units under the command of the governor of Alexandria move in to halt the hostilities.[44]

Although the Egyptian army thereafter restored tolerable order to Alexandria, tens of thousands of frightened Europeans streamed out of the country. Many expected that the Ottomans would invade and 'Urabi would fight them. In Cairo, on 13 June, a row between a Muslim and a Jew, which led to a stabbing of the latter, caused rumors to fly that a Jew had stabbed a Muslim. Only firm police interference prevented a general Muslim riot against Jews and Christians.[45] The few Europeans who remained in the capital felt acute danger. A Mr. Hamilton of Bulaq works faced increasing insubordination among the Egyptian workers under his supervision, and some finally attempted to kill him. Here, class and national cleavages overlapped so forcefully that workers who rose up against their managers could be seen as 'Urabist heroes.[46] The provinces proved even more difficult to control than the capital. On 26 June rioters killed ten Greeks and three Jews in the Lower Egyptian town of Banha. This event, along with the Alexandria events, helped convince the Earl of Dufferin, then in conference with other European diplomats, that he should support Ottoman military intervention (though the British later changed their minds and invaded Egypt themselves).[47] Viscount Lyons summed up the sentiments of many British officials in late June when he told the French government "that to obtain reparation for the Alexandria massacre appeared to me, personally to be a question of national honour and the safety of European residents in Egypt and other Mussulman countries . . . the necessary preliminary to obtaining either . . . was . . . the overthrow of Arabi Pasha and the Military party in Egypt."[48] The events in

Alexandria were, however, an act of collective protest against European encroachment, and could be better characterized as a massacre of unarmed Egyptians by armed Europeans than as a massacre of Christians. The 'Urabi movement aimed at constitutionalism, cabinet rule, and an effective parliament, and the military formed only one element in this movement, which was fought tooth and nail by most British officials. To characterize it as a "military party" was to caricature it.[49]

The British naval bombardment of Alexandria in July, and the subsequent British invasion and occupation of Egypt radically changed the terms of the Euro-Egyptian relationship. At first, many Egyptians welcomed British troops simply because they rejoiced at seeing the end of the war. But the populace by no means reacted universally in this manner. Even in November of 1882 Britishers in an Egypt colored red on the map encountered great hostility among workers in Cairo, and European residents of the Tantah district could not "attend to their businesses in the villages without being grossly insulted and threatened with violence."[50]

Something of the anarchic events of the 11 June disturbance and its consequences can be pieced together from the Egyptian and European narratives. But eliciting its full social significance requires that we have some idea of who participated in it. Indispensable for this purpose are Egyptian government documents in Arabic relating to the subsequent arrests and trials of participants in the riot. These Arabic lists were shared with the British and have, fortunately, been accessibly preserved among British consular documents. Despite the volumes historians have produced about the high politics of the 'Urabi revolt, these lists of ordinary persons have never been drawn upon in a published work. Their usefulness should have been apparent: they help us define the composition of the crowd and its leadership. This question is of great importance—if the crowd consisted only of laborers engaged in an ethnic rumble, its actions would bear a different significance than those of a crowd mobilized by notables for political purposes.

Despite their value, a few reservations about the roster of the accused must be expressed. One list, of persons tried on charges of complicity in the riot, only identifies the accused by occupation or ethnicity in about one-fourth of the cases. Even then, one must remember the use in Arabic names of family occupations not necessarily followed by later generations. Finally, the selection of persons charged with crimes might reflect score-settling or patronage links after the 'Urabi revolt and so be a poor guide to actual crowd composition.[51] But for all these drawbacks, the information in these lists is substantially better than nothing.

Obviously, given the size of the crowd, large numbers of laborers took part. One eyewitness reported that, "Arab workmen struck the passers-by without any restraint from the soldiers who were near, and immediately after killed or wounded them."[52] Many of the 2,000 Egyptian rioters described by Luca were manual laborers. The crowd also included pastoral nomads from Buhayrah province, in town to support the viceroy.

But can we be more precise? Some sense of the popular participation in the disturbance can be gained from an Arabic-Egyptian government document, "List of sentences passed by the Court-Martial of Alexandria," which gives 211 (in 146 lots) names of persons accused.[53] Some fifty-seven occupations or other identifications are given in the Arabic list. Since police arrested some of the accused for dealing in plundered goods, we cannot always be sure that they actually participated in the looting themselves. I excluded several women from the reckoning below, because police charged them only with buying loot. Other instances are less clear.

The bulk of the occupations mentioned belonged solidly in the core of the urban crowd. In the 1870s the traditional sector of Egyptian industry, producing dyes, food, textiles, leather, metal, and other products, employed about 100,000 men, some 6 percent of the adult labor force (most Egyptians, it should be remembered, were peasants). At least 56,000 of these urban craftsmen were organized in the larger guilds. Many service and transportation workers also had their own guilds.[54] Such men were certainly part of the Alexandrian crowd on 11 June. Killers of Europeans included such unlikely figures as a seller of sweet beverages (*shurbatli*) and someone who wrote about petitions (*'ardhalji*) for others. A dyer, a carpenter, and two oil sellers had loot in their possessions. A street-sweeper rioted; a waiter and a butcher pillaged; another butcher, a barber, and a tailor dealt in loot. In the transportation industry, authorities charged a boatman, a wagon-master, a donkey driver, and three porters.

The government arrested a doorman and three hired private guards, though two of the counts involved were simply neglecting their duty to protect their European employers. The courts tried seven Nubians and a Sudanese, and some of these would probably also have been private guards. The documents identify one man as North African, and in view of the recent French occupation of Tunisia in 1881, anti-European feeling ran high in his expatriate community. Police arrested nine women for looting or possessing loot or for "talking sedition," and nine more for buying loot later (thus, eighteen women were tried, constituting 8.5 percent of those accused). Some of these women came from artisan families—one, for instance, stood trial in the same lot with the carpenter mentioned above.[55] The list showed as suspects some sixteen low-ranking soldiers, seamen, policemen, and employees at military installations. Luca's image of six soldiers followed by a mob of 2,000 Egyptians appears to be a good metaphor for the composition of the crowd. The documents invariably mention military occupations, and altogether they formed 7.6 percent of those tried in Alexandria. Only three European names and that of one Syrian appeared, but it seems unlikely that they are underrepresented, since working-class Europeans had a prime opportunity for pillaging and grudge-settling when order broke down. With the mass exodus of Europeans after the riot, any such European looters could have escaped.

Beyond the ordinary tradespeople and laborers, can persons be described who might have constituted a crowd leadership? Given Hourani's thesis about the notables (which, to be fair, did not apply to Alexandria), one would look for *ulama,* heads of garrisons, and landed, secular notables. We find, however, persons of somewhat lesser stature, not patricians, but leaders of the *menu peuple* often sprung from their ranks. The military court charges two heads of city quarters (*shaykh al-harah*), one accused of inciting rebellion and the other of robbery. Also arrested were three owners of coffeehouses, one accused of robbery, one of possessing loot, and one of attempted burglary. A miller and a broker dealt in stolen merchandise, with the question of where they got it left unanswered. A second trial list identifies other potential crowd leaders: the guildmaster of the tailors and his son (a lawyer), the guildmaster of the porters on viceregal lands, thirteen merchants, a broker, two market inspectors (with connections to the brokers' guild), and a weigher.[56] The appearance of guild officers on the list was to be expected. The guilds, who lobbied strongly for 'Urabi's reinstatement as War Minister in May of 1882, formed a natural constituency for the colonel's movement. Perhaps there was even a traditional basis in their support for constitutionalism. The masters greatly valued their electoral procedures and their ability to influence the choice of guildmaster.[57]

For the most part, the prominent participants in the disturbances so far identified do not fit Hourani's triple definition of notables. List 2 does give names of a few persons who might just fall within the category of secular notables. These were civil servants. The government employees charged with involvement in the riot were distributed as follows: one departmental head, three lower-level bureaucrats, six clerks, an official of the excise department, an interpreter, two physicians, and one other, for a total of fifteen. A few of the higher-ranking persons in this list may have held land or belonged to military families so that they could be called secular notables. But most seem to fit better into a more novel category: the new middle class. The most important pool of secular notables in the 'Urabi revolt was concentrated in the middle and lower ranks of the officer corps. Military men show up in two Egyptian government lists, the first a general one with some forty army officers, who appear to have been arrested all over Egypt and not simply in Alexandria. The other, referred to above in connection with the merchants and guildmasters, bears the title "Officers, noncommissioned Officers, and men connected with the rebellion, the disturbance of the 11th June and the subsequent events." Only four commissioned army officers appear here, with one noncommissioned and four privates, for a total of nine army men. Since the governor had command of the army, which played the main role in reestablishing order, low army participation in the events occasions no surprise. On the other hand, many Europeans remembered the police guards as active participants, and only ten of these appear on List 2, all corporals and privates. Regular police personnel, including couriers and municipal guards totaled eleven. Three private policemen also appear on the list.

If the list has any proportional validity, then we may conclude that the civilian, urban intermediate strata of guildmasters, merchants, and heads of quarters, many of whom perceived themselves to have suffered from the European impact, formed the more important set of likely leaders of the Alexandria riot and rebellion. Another significant group from the intermediate strata, the new petty bourgeoisie—especially civil servants—had likewise often faced rivalry from the 1,325 Europeans employed by the Egyptian government.[58] Both high-ranking policemen and army officers provided relatively fewer rebel leaders in the Alexandria disturbances; in any case few were charged.

In this search for a "leadership" of the crowd, we should not forget that most actions in Alexandria were taken spontaneously and in small groups, so that day laborers, artisans, and other ordinary folk often took the lead.[59] To the extent that any hierarchies survived this liminal setting, those prominent persons who supported the crowd action derived not from the ranks of the clergy, old military families, or rural, landed notables, but from the core of the crowd itself. The head of the porters, the master of the tailors, the Sha't family of brokers whose election bid the Europeans helped defeat in 1878—these were the men Tawfiq's loyalists later fingered as supporters of the rioters. Nor was the crowd itself merely an assemblage of manual laborers and street people. It included literate persons such as the writer of petitions who killed a European, as well as carpenters, dyers, and other skilled craftsmen. The Alexandria upheaval, like most of the urban disturbances in Egypt of 1858–1882, was the work of the urban crowd rather than that of the notables.

Neither the British conspiracy theory nor the French suggestion of riotous port workers, then, stands up to evidence. The whole incident must be seen in a far more complex manner. First, one must note the common occurrence of working-class European riots in Alexandria in the 1860s and early 1870s, which would not have sat well with Egyptian workers and artisans. Although more Euro-Egyptian conflicts had occurred elsewhere in the decade previous to the 1882 disturbances, other conflicts, in Port Said, for example, would not have been unknown among the port's workers. Aside from rivalries among working-class groups of different nationalities, wealthy European merchants often engaged in activities that helped displace or disrupt many Egyptian occupations.

The extensive influence of Christians and Christianity in Alexandria, and Muslim sensitivity to domination by Europeans, also must have played a part. The wave of anti-Europeanism during the Russo-Ottoman War had come only four or five years earlier. The French had established a protectorate over nearby Tunisia just the year before. 'Urabi appealed to the masses partially because he stood up to the Europeans as a Muslim (and though the Ottoman sultan actually opposed him, this did not stop 'Urabi from successfully posing in Egypt as his defender). During the disturbances, both Muslim officials and experienced European observers distinctly remembered religious rhetoric being used to incite the mob. Leaders cried "Kill him, O Muslims!" and "Muslims, help me kill the Christians!"[60] These cries did not echo primordial hatreds. There is no history of significant Muslim-Coptic riots in Khedivial Egypt, for instance, and many Muslims cooperated in various ways even with European Christians, before and after the 'Urabi movement (in the 1870s the Shaykhu'l-Islam, a high Islamic authority, had a business partnership with an Englishman). Rather, the crowd was reworking the symbols of identity to help in the fight at hand, invoking militant Islam versus Christianity for a contingent and bounded purpose. Arabic-speakers such as Maltese and Levantines, who might in other circumstances have been coded as local because they had (or in the case of the Levantines often had) European passports and connections, were lumped together with the British and French. Traditional Islamic law offers Jews and Christians a subordinate protected status as long as they submit to Muslim political superiority, and the Muslim crowd clearly felt that the non-Egyptian Christians were attempting to get the upper hand and so had forfeited protection.

The political atmosphere intertwined with religious frictions. The Anglo-French opposition to a leader of 'Urabi's popularity helped create an adverse image of all Europeans. Provocative acts, such as the dispatch of warships to Alexandria's harbor on 20 May, and the subsequent pressuring of Viceroy Tawfiq to dismiss 'Urabi from his cabinet, increased anti-European feeling. Indeed, many Egyptians took these moves as a signal that the Europeans intended to occupy Egypt. A populist proto-nationalism and a desire to defend Islam thus came together in Alexandria with a set of concrete grievances against working-class and wealthy Europeans to produce the conflagration.

With Europeans and their compradors representing so many evils for the urban populace, from frustrating competitiveness with local concerns to unwarranted interference in the reform of the army and the government, any spark could have ignited such flammable tinder. The crowd and police guards came to the fore in participating in the riot of 11 June 1882. The heads of city quarters, perhaps some guild officers, brokers, and bureaucrats, and even coffeehouse owners gave their moral authority to the attack; some of them even joined in the plunder. The artisans and skilled workers, along with manual laborers, stormed the Christian quarter. This conflict required no military conspiracy directed from Cairo—enough immediate local grievances and enough urban precedent existed to make further explanation inelegant.

Conclusion

What then, was the role of the urban crowd in the anti-colonial disturbances of the mid-to-late nineteenth century? In order to generalize more effectively, let us return to the similar clashes that occurred outside Egypt in this period.

The North Indian city of Lucknow, capital of the kingdom of Awadh (or Oudh), provides a striking parallel to the Egyptian case. In 1856, after a long period of British economic and political penetration of the area, Governor-General Dalhousie annexed Awadh, deposing its king and making the province of "Oudh" a part of British India. In 1857 the entire former area of the kingdom, along with some neighboring territories, formed the site of a bloody uprising against the British, which they misnamed the "Sepoy Mutiny" (mutinous British Indian troops were only one social element in the revolt). Many Europeans in the capital of Lucknow were killed, and the British Residency was besieged. As Gautam Bhadra has argued, the historiography of the rebellion has focused upon the landed elite as the principal actors in it.[61] But Lucknow city saw much urban collective violence undertaken by ordinary folk. A firsthand Persian account says that the capital's mobs included some prominent urban leaders and Muslim sermonizers who led bands of butchers, weavers, carders, and other tradesmen. Crowds as large as 6,000 sometimes attempted to coordinate with rebelling units of the Bengal Army.[62]

In their actions of May and June 1857 the urban rioters were for the most part not led by military men, landed notables resident in the city, or Establishment *ulama.* The crowd leadership was, instead, drawn from the city's intermediate strata of heads of quarters and lower-ranking holy and learned men; local moneylenders and other wealthy men figured among its targets. There is good reason to think that the great secular notables in the city feared for their lives and property during these months, and although many *ulama* supported the rebellion in general, many were wealthy enough to want to avoid urban rioting.[63] Of course, the groups Hourani called "notables" certainly played the leading part in the general revolt. But despite the desire to coordinate with the rebel army in May, the Lucknow crowd appears to have acted to some extent on its own.

Research has shown that the riot against Christians in Jiddah in 1858 conforms much more closely to Hourani's vision of urban action instigated by provincial notables. Artisans and sailors clearly took part in the attack on European consulates and business establishments provoked by a dispute over the nationality of a ship anchored in the harbor (the British and Ottomans both claimed it). A series of Ottoman investigations under British and French pressure finally revealed, however, that the action had been planned by high *ulama* and religious judges, the leader of the Prophet's descendants, an Ottoman official, and the chief of the Hadramauti merchants and boatmen.[64]

On the other hand, Philip Khoury's recent discussion of the anti-Christian disturbances in Damascus in 1860 does not support the thesis of notable responsibility there. He argues that this riot can in part be explained, not only by Muslim resentment toward increasingly favorable economic and legislative conditions for the Christian minority, but also by the decreased authority of Muslim notables over the urban crowd. In this interpretation, the crowds who invaded the Christian quarter, killing inhabitants and smashing looms, acted on their own initiative in opposition to the wishes of most Muslim patricians.[65]

We should see a politics of the crowd, rather than (or in addition to) a politics of the notables, in Lucknow (and other North Indian cities) in 1857, Damascus in 1860, and Alexandria in 1882. Such politics has been confused with that of the notables because of its rarity in an age before mass political mobilization. Hourani rightly guided us to gaze down from the viceroys and sultans to the provincial notables in seeking the background of Near Eastern politics. But in some instances we would be wise to glance even further downward, into winding streets and crowded quarters, in identifying political actors of consequence.

Two sorts of major crisis or radical change formed a prerequisite for these (and other such) disturbances. Each major anti-European or anti-Christian urban melee coincided with a crisis of the state: Britain's annexation of Awadh and abolition of the monarchy there in 1856, the Ottoman empire's adoption of the 1856 reforms granting religious minorities equal rights with Muslims, the junior Egyptian colonels' challenge to viceregal absolutism and Ottoman-Egyptian hegemony in 1881–1882. The paralysis of state structures, including security forces, was a prerequisite for the politics of violent crowd action, since normally the police and army, with their firearms, would prevent such large disturbances.

Each such upheaval also involved a radically changed relationship with Europe. Lucknow had just become a British-administered city, the Ottoman empire had shifted its ideological basis away from traditional Islam toward a Europe-inspired model of the equality of citizens, and Egypt had fallen increasingly under European financial and political control from 1876. Because European economic or political expansionism either directly caused or helped provoke these instances of turbulence, the crisis of the indigenous state also became a crisis of imperialism.

We must separate out the broad revolts from the episodes of urban agitation within them. Without any doubt, the notables—religious scholars, military heads, and landed families—formed the chief leadership for the Great Rebellion in India, the sectarian struggles in the Levant, and the 'Urabi revolt, as broad regional movements. But the specifically urban violence must often be seen as a relatively autonomous attempt to coordinate with the revolt, carried out by the crowd and its subaltern leadership of guild officers, shopkeepers, minor *ulama,* street toughs, and outspoken women ("talking sedition").

By contrast, Jiddah in 1858 represents a different sort of phenomenon, and despite its superficial similarities to other émeutes, involved no spontaneous politics of the crowd. Here we see no crisis of the state (the Hijaz being much more isolated from Ottoman reforms than was Syria), but rather a planned response by the notables resident in a small Red Sea port (population 15,000) to increasing European economic penetration of the area. The politics of the crowd required a larger city, so complex that layers of networks and leadership did not so easily interpenetrate one another. Lucknow's population of half-million people sheltered not only the Awadh royal family and nobility but also notables from the intermediate strata and, finally, prominent persons among the crowd itself. Alexandria with a quarter-million people and the provincial capital of Damascus had a similar layered structure of leadership. The relatively small port of Jiddah, however, possessed no real nobles, and the notables were in enough face-to-face interaction with the populace to possess immediate authority among them. An urban politics of the notables that resulted in a violent engagement with Europeans or their protégés seems to have occurred, as in Jiddah or Tantah (population about 29,000 at the time of the anti-Greek riot of 1872), in medium-sized cities where the Europeans constituted a small but economically increasingly powerful group challenging the town-based notables.

The fights between port and customs-house workers in Port Said, and between sailors and donkey-drivers in Alexandria, on the other hand, constitute yet a third sort of contention—ethnic clashes among laborers. Although typologically distinct, the history of brawls between local workers and the Europeans or their protégés forms an important backdrop to the politics of the crowd, since the repertoire of ethnic violence could be put to new uses during a revolt. Nor may we assume that the crowd had no memory and no window on the wider world. The British consuls, at least, reported quite emphatically that Euro-Muslim conflict elsewhere influenced the terms of local clashes. Modern communications, such as the press and telegraph, were beginning to link the Muslim world even as the European powers sought to divide it up among themselves. Thus, Suez workers approved of the Jiddah affair, many in Cairo sympathized with the Indian revolt, and the Alexandrians were alarmed by the 1881 French occupation of Tunisia.

What drove the politics of the crowd? Some answers have already been suggested, but it may be worthwhile to reprise and expand them by way of conclusion. As with preindustrial crowds in Europe, hatred of the rich and hatred of foreigners appear prominently among crowd motivation in the incidents discussed above.[66] Whether increasingly high food prices played a part is impossible to determine at this point but no indication of such a factor is present in the main sources. Hatred of the rich and hatred of foreigners, moreover, had different implications in Africa and Asia during the age of capital than in eighteenth-century London. The foreigners had the upper hand and were seeking to change the local economy so as to incorporate it into their own industrial capitalism. They brought an increased monetization of the economy, increased wage labor, increased social stratification. They often sought to control the indigenous state. The rich, then, were often also foreign consuls, speculators, and moneylenders, or local men with links to such groups. The foreign coloration or implication also held true at the lower levels of the "rich," whom the crowd saw more often. Even the successful shopkeepers in Alexandria were often Greek, Italian, or Syrian Christian.

The distinction in European historiography between the preindustrial and industrial crowd seems inadequate for African and Asian crowd action in the third quarter of the nineteenth century. The preindustrial crowd is said to have rioted over food prices or changes in the prices of and regulations concerning other essential commodities.[67] With the advent of industrialization one begins to see union organization and strikes instead. The issues addressed by the non-European politics of the crowd were much more complex than food prices, but do not resemble industrial negotiations over salaries and benefits. The Indians, Syrians, and Egyptians, far from being "preindustrial," rioted in a world already transformed by the industrial revolution, but in a context of lopsided Afro-Asian development where urban structures existed not to house factories but to speed the delivery of raw materials to the hungry machines of Europe. For Europeans, reworking or building up cities for this purpose required co-opting, displacing, subduing, or changing local urban groups. The riots here studied simply testify to what dangerous work this could be.

Hatred of the foreigner had many dimensions, one of them the religious, although it is admittedly hard in this instance to separate Christian-Muslim conflict from xenophobia and class conflict. Specifically religious ethnicity and ideology, nevertheless, did form a background to the riots. Here the suggestion by Natalie Zemon Davis that preindustrial religious riots represented a kind of vigilante effort may be applicable.[68] The common folk took it upon themselves to purify their religious environment from outside threats, acting as they thought the civil or ecclesiastical authorities would or should. Lucknow's Muslims and Hindus acted (in the name of the Mughal emperor) to prevent what they saw as an attempt to deprive them of their religious "caste" and impose Christianity on them. The Damascene crowd reacted against growing Christian political and economic power. The Alexandrians, aware of an impasse between 'Urabi and the viceroy, took action themselves on behalf of Islam and of the Ottoman sultan. (As in European "church and king" riots, it did not matter that the sultan actually opposed 'Urabi; from the crowd's point of view he had to lie because he was prisoner to the Europeans). Likewise, the European crowd took on the Alexandrians with firearms, just as they expected the police or offshore Europeans forces should have done.

The politics of the crowd, like the revolts it often accompanied, proved a dismal failure in regard to accomplishing structural change. As with most sorts of collective violence, it tended to be brief and discontinuous. Although 1857 in India probably made the British more cautious about imperial expansion for a while, it obviously did not deter them in the long run. Additional military forces and artillery sent from England reduced Lucknow. The British savagely bombarded Jiddah during the height of the pilgrimage season in Mecca in response to the riot there. European pressure on the Ottomans ensured the execution of many participants in the anti-Christian actions in Damascus and the exile of prominent notables. The troubles in the Levant ended with Ottoman acquiescence to Christian local self-government and changes in law benefiting capitalists over landlords. The naval bombardment, staple of seagoing imperialism, was used again in Alexandria a month after the riot there, a prelude to military conquest. Many notables seem to have understood the danger to their independence posed by the politics of the crowd, but they had lost control during a crisis of the state. Alexandrians, far from cleansing Africa of the acquisitive European Christians, opened the flood gates to an inundation of the continent. If Europeans were not safe under indigenous states, imperial bureaucrats reasoned, then Europe had to rule instead. The rhetorical underpinning of this imperialist sentiment, what Guha calls "the prose of counter-insurgency," was erected by consular officials, journalists, later memoirists and then historians who cast the June 11 events in Alexandria as a "massacre" of Christians and characterized the Egyptian constitutionalists seeking cabinet and parliamentary rule as the "military party."[69]

The significance of crowd politics lies in what it tells us about the agency of the ordinary folk, and about the structuring of urban collective action at any particular time and place. Moreover, the shift in the repertoire of collective action demonstrated by these nineteenth-century revolts boded ill for the long-term ability of Europe to impose itself on Africa and Asia. The politics of the crowd would once more emerge during the nationalist struggles of the interwar period, in conjunction with the bourgeois political parties so central to nationalist historiography. Yet these parties, led by politicians such as Sa'd Zaghlul and Mahatma Gandhi, had significant grassroots support and were taken up by the urban population as powerful additions to their repertoire of collective action, beyond more spontaneous and intermittent crowd violence. The little people of Afro-Asian cities in the twentieth century thereby finally achieved the anti-colonial aims their forebears were denied in the nineteenth. Ironically, the stronger, more efficient colonial state, and the flourishing of peripheral capitalism that it allowed, contributed to the emergence of this new repertoire.

NOTES

Acknowledgments: I wish to thank, for their helpful comments on the earlier version of this chapter, John Markoff, Maureen Feeney, Edmund E. Cole, Fernando Coronil, Val Daniel, and Julie Skurski. It was a treat to have something I had published scrutinized by such an assemblage of interesting minds, and their interventions have been most useful in making revisions.

1. A convenient anthology here is Ranajit Guha and Gayatri C. Spivak, eds., *Selected Subaltern Studies* (Oxford: Oxford University Press, 1988); see also Gyanendra Pandey, *The Construction of Communalism in Colonial North India* (Delhi: Oxford University Press, 1990). Because I wrote my dissertation in the 1980s on Indian history, I encountered the subaltern school, which was one of many unstated influences on the earlier version of this chapter, and I thank Val Daniel for urging me to make this debt explicit.

2. See in general George Rudé, *The Crowd in History: A Study of Popular Disturbances in France and England, 1730–1848* (New York: John Wiley and Sons, Inc., 1964); Charles Tilly, *The Contentious French;* the Tilly family's *The Rebellious Century, 1830–1930* (Cambridge, Mass.: Harvard University Press, 1975); Robert J. Holton, "The Crowd in History: Some Problems of Theory and Method," *Social History* 3 (1978): 219–33; Natalie Zemon Davis, *Society and Culture in Early Modern France* (Stanford: Stanford University Press, 1979), esp. chs. 1, 6.

3. Despite the obvious possibilities, the Middle Eastern crowd in the pre-industrial period has been little studied; but see André Raymond, "Quartiers et mouvements populaires au Caire au XVIIIème siècle," in *Political and Social Change in Modern Egypt*, P. M. Holt, ed. (London: Oxford University Press, 1968), 104–14, and the same author's "Deux leaders populaires au Caire à la fin du XVIIIe et au debut du XIXe siècle," *La nouvelle revue du Caire* 1 (Annual, 1975), 281–398; Gabriel Baer, "Popular Revolt in Ottoman Cairo," in his *Fellah and Townsman in the Middle East* (London: Frank Cass, 1982), 225–52; Ervand Abrhamian, "The Crowd in the Persian Revolution." *Iranian Studies* 2,4 (1969): 128–50; Juan R. I. Cole and Moojan Momen, "Mafia, Mob and Shiism in Iraq: The Rebellion of Ottoman Karbala, 1824–1843," *Past and Present* 112 (Aug., 1986): 112–43; and Bruce Masters, "The 1850 Events in Aleppo: An Aftershock of Syria's Incorporation into the Capitalist World System," *International Journal of Middle East Studies* 22 (Feb. 1990): 3–20.

4. Veena Das, ed., *Communities, Riots and Survivors in South Asia* (New Delhi: Oxford University Press, 1992), 9.

5. In the earlier version of this paper I employed the distinction between primary, secondary, and modern national revolts put forward by T. O. Ranger, "Connexions between 'Primary Resistance' Movements and Modern Mass Nationalism in East and Central Africa," *Journal of African History*, Part I–9, 3 (1968): 437–53, Part II–9, 4 (1968): 631–41; and Eric Stokes, *The Peasant and the Raj* (Cambridge, Cambridge University Press, 1978), 120–39. Comments by Maureen Feeney, John Markoff, and Charles Bright urged me to interrogate this formulation as overly teleological and insufficiently nuanced. I still think useful Ranger's general point, that because of macro-historical processes, an eighteenth-century revolt was not exactly like a nineteenth-century one, but I agree that it is undesirable to use language with teleological overtones, and have tried here to avoid doing so. For the idea of the repertoire shift, see Tilly, *The Contentious French* (Cambridge, Mass.: Harvard University Press, 1986), 390–98.

6. Albert Hourani, "Ottoman Reform and the Politics of the Notables," in *Beginnings of Modernization in the Middle East: The Nineteenth Century*, W. Polk and R. Chambers, eds. (Chicago: University of Chicago Press, 1968), 67–68; see also 44–49 for the definitions involved.

7. See, for example, Georges Douin, *Histoire du règne du Khédive Ismail*, 3 vols. (Rome and Cairo: Société Royale de Géographie d'Égypte, 1933–1941); 'Abdu'r-Rahman ar-Rafi'i, *'Asr Isma'il*, 2 vols., 2d ed. (Cairo: an-Nahdah al-Misriyyah, 1948); Muhammad Sabry, *La genèse de l'esprit national égyptien, 1863–1882* (Paris: Association Linotypist, 1924); idem., *L'empire egyptien sous Ismaïl et l'ingérence anglo-française (1863–1879)* (Paris: Librairie Orientaliste Paul Geunther, 1933); Angelo Sammarco, *Le règne du Khédive Ismaïl de 1863 à 1875* (Cairo: Société Royale de Géographie d'Égypte, 1937). The elite approach to cultural history in this period is as apparent in Rafi'i and Sabry as it is in Albert

Hourani, *Arabic Thought in the Liberal Age* (London: Oxford University Press, 1962).

8. It is instructive to contrast chapter 5 in Roger Owen, *The Middle East in the World Economy 1800–1914* (London: Methuen, 1981), concerning Egypt, 1850–1882, with chapter 6, on the same period in Lebanon, Syria, and Palestine. The former focuses largely on the debt crisis and elite decision making, whereas the latter is mainly concerned with social history. Alexander Schölch studied the elite political history of the 'Urabi period from Egyptian archival documents in his German work, translated as *Egypt for the Egyptians! The Sociopolitical Crisis in Egypt 1878–1882* (London: Ithaca Press, 1981), and F. Robert Hunter looked at bureaucrats in his *Egypt under the Khedives 1805–1879: From Household Government to Modern Bureaucracy* (Pittsburgh: University of Pittsburgh Press, 1984). Both of these studies broke important new ground, but they have not been much supplemented by work that also extends our knowledge of non-elite classes of this period. The partial exceptions are Gabriel Baer, *Studies in the Social History of Modern Egypt* (Chicago: Chicago University Press, 1969), and idem., *Fellah and Townsman in the Middle East* (London: Frank Cass, 1982); and Judith Tucker, *Women in Nineteenth-Century Egypt* (Cambridge: Cambridge University Press, 1985). Likewise, substantial advances in cultural history, such as Nikki R. Keddie, *Sayyid Jamal al-Din "al-Afghani": A Political Biography* (Berkeley and Los Angeles: University of California Press, 1972), and Gilbert Delanoue, *Moralistes et politiques musulmans dans l'Égypte du XIXeme siècle, 1798–1882,* 2 vols. (Cairo: Institut Français d'Archéologie du Caire, 1982), move in the circle of notables if not the old narrow elite, and have not been supplemented for this period by studies of popular culture.

9. Although material relating to guilds and urban disturbances is abundant in Egyptian National Archives, it is only preliminarily catalogued. The European archives remain important, because some events, such as urban riots between Europeans and Egyptians, may have struck the consuls as more worth recording than it did the Egyptian bureaucrats.

10. For this movement see Juan R. I. Cole, *Colonialism and Revolution in the Middle East: Social and Cultural Origins of Egypt's 'Urabi Movement* (Princeton: Princeton University Press, 1994).

11. Great Britain, Public Record Office, Kew, Foreign Office (hereafter, P.R.O., F.O.) 407/20, Extract from the *Journal Officiel* of 14 June 1882, encl. in no. 1018, Lyons/Granville, Paris, 14 June 1882.

12. I should also enter the caveat here, however, that Egyptians in particular reacted rather passively to the influx of often greedy and acquisitive Europeans during the 1860s and 1870s, despite the way in which a few incidents of violence now seem important.

13. P.R.O., F.O., 78/381 Bowring Report, Mar. 1839.

14. Owen, *The Middle East in the World Economy,* ch. 5; Charles Issaw, ed.,

The Economic History of the Middle East (Chicago: University of Chicago Press, 1966), 416–38. Many aspects of this period are treated in Baer, *Studies in the Social History of Modern Egypt,* passim.

15. Nubar Nubarian, *Mémoires de Nubar Pacha,* M. B. Ghali, ed. (Beirut: Librairie du Liban, 1983, 151–52; P.R.O., F.O. 141/125, Vivian/Salisbury no. 53, Cairo, 15 Feb. 1879).

16. Egypt. Dar al-Watha'iq al-Qawmiyyah [DWQ or National Egyptian Archives], Nizarat ad-Dakhiliyyah [Interior Ministry], Arabic Correspondence, Mahfazah 11, Muhafiz al-Iskandariyyah/Nazir ad-Dakhiliyyah, 21 Jumada 11 1290/16 Aug. 1873 (for the privatization of weighing); for the European interference in guild elections see DWQ, N.D., Ar. Corr. 26, Muhafiz Iskandariyyah/Nazir ad-Dakhiliyyah, 18 Sha'ban 1295/18 Aug. 1878; for protests about the steam boilers, DWQ, N.D., Ar. Cor. 14, Muhammad 'Asim Wakil al-Muhafazah/Nizarat ad-Dakhiliyyah, 13 Sha'ban 1291/25 Sept. 1874 and Ar. Corr. 13, Mansurah Petition of Safar 1291/Mar.–Apr. 1874, and enclosures.

17. Ibrahim al-Muwaylihi, in *al-Watan,* Vol. 2 (1 Feb. 1879/10 Safar 1296).

18. Throughout the nineteenth century, Arabs who had emigrated to India in search of patronage were forced to return to their homelands when local courts were conquered. 'Ali al-Muzayyin, ancestor of many of the prominent Shi'i az-Zayn clan in Southern Lebanon, returned home from India in 1810 after participating in battles against the British: see 'Ali az-Zayn, *Fusul min ta'rikh ash-shi'ah fi lubnan* (Beirut: Dar al-Kalimah li'n-Nashr, 1979), 132. A decade after the 1857–1858 Indian revolt, the British consul in Jiddah estimated the number of Indians in the Arabian peninsula at 10,000, so they were hardly insignificant. And although less than a thousand British subjects registered in Egypt in the 1860s, one consul suggested that they actually numbered about 10,000. Many of these would have been Indian Muslims. See P.R.O., F.O., 141/62, Sandison/Reade no. 33, Jiddah, 10 June 1867; F.O. 141/68, Francis/Stanton, Alexandria, 17 Feb. 1869. Indians in Cairo and even in the provinces were numerous enough to have chosen their own local leaders or *"shaykhs"*: F.O. 141/111, Carr/Wallis, no. 19, Kafr Zayat, 22 Dec. 1876. Even the secondary effects of the indigenous struggle against European expansionism could be significant. The Iranian Sayyid Jamalu'd-Din Asadabadi "al-Afghani," as a young man in Bombay, began to cultivate his anti-imperialist fervor in 1857, later bringing it with him to Egypt in 1871 on his arrival in Alexandria; see Keddie, *Sayyid Jamal al-Din "al-Afghani."*

19. P.R.O., F.O. 141/36 Pt. 1, Walue/Green, Cairo, 5 July 1858; F.O. 141/36, Pt. 1, West/Green, Suez, 5 July 1858.

20. P.R.O., F.O. 141/49, Bulwer/Russell, Cairo, 15 Dec. 1862. Sa'id drastically reduced his police force, leading some unemployed former policemen to turn to looting and vandalism: Dar al-Watha'iq, Dabtiyyah [Police], Mahfazah 1, Sa'id/Ma'mur Dabtiyyat Misr, no. 115, 25 Rajab 1276/17 Feb. 1860; Sa'id/Ma'mur, no. 116, 3 Ramadan 1276/26 Mar. 1860.

21. P.R.O., F.O. 141/48, Drummond Hay/Colquhoun, Cairo, 18 Feb. 1863.

22. Ibid.

23. P.R.O., F.O. 78/1871, Colquhoun/Russell, no. 41, Cairo, 24 Mar. 1865; see also earlier dispatches in this series, no. 27, Mar. 1865, and no. 32, 11 Mar. 1865; I am the first to note the Indian connection reported by Colquhoun here. See also Isma'il Sarhank, *Haqa'iq al-akhbar 'an duwal al-bihar,* 2 vols. (Bulaq: al-Matba'ah al-Amiriyyah, 1895–1898), 2: 281; Baer, *Studies in the Social History of Modern Egypt,* 99.

24. P.R.O., F.O. 78/1871, Colquhoun/Bulwer, no. 2, Alexandria, 22 May 1865; Colquhoun/Russell, no. 56, Alexandria, 25 May 1865; Colquhoun/Russell, no. 58, Alexandria, 27 May 1865; 78/2139, Stanton/Clarendon, no. 3, Cairo, 7 Jan. 1870; F.O. 141/71 Lane Clarendon, Alexandria, 15 Jan. 1870; F.O. 78/2186, Stanton/Granville, no. 5, Alexandria, 29 June 1871; Stanton/Granville, no. 60, Cairo, 14 Dec. 1871; Numbar, Mémoires, 394–97.

25. P.R.O., F.O. 141/72, Zarb/Stanley, Port Said, 21 Feb. 1870, encl. w/Stanley/Stanton, Alexandria, 24 Feb. 1870, arch. no. 92; 141/72, Zarb/Stanley, Port Said, n.d., encl. w/Stanley/Stanton, 5 Mar. 1870, arch. no. 104; 141/72, Stanley/Zarb, 28 Feb. 1870, encl. w/Stanley/Stanton, 5 Mar. 1870; 141/92, Baker/Cookson, Port Said, 15 Sept. 1875, arch. no. 406; 141/20, Captain Beamish/Vice-Admiral Hornby, no. 32, Alexandria, 17 June 1878; F.O. 141/115, Vivian/Salisbury, no. 21, Alexandria, 22 June 1878. For context, see Zayn al'Abidin Najm, Ta'rikh Bur Sa'id (Cairo: al-Hay'ah al-'Ammah li'l-Kitab, 1988).

26. Viceroy/Muhafazat Misr, 25 Ramadan 1279/19 Mar. 1863, tr. in Amin Sami, *Taqwim an-nil,* 3 vols. (Cairo: al-Matba'ah al-Amiriyyah and Dar al-Kutub al Misriyyah, 1916–1936), 2: 466; P.R.O., F.O. 141/68, Joyce/Stanton, Cairo, 6 Mar. 1872, no. 118 arch.

27. DWQ, Mahfuzat Majlis al-Wuzara' [Cabinet Papers], Haqq, 2/1 Qawanin Mutanawwa'ah, Ministry of Justice dossier dated 1882, "Commisions de conciliation dans l'Égypte," undated memorandum [late 1870s]. The author discusses the disadvantages to peasants of the newly introduced court system vis-à-vis Europeans and invokes Algerian revolts and 1857 in India as arguments against such a rapid change in local law and custom.

28. P.R.O., F.O. 141/111, Carr/Borg, no. 32, Kafr Zayat, 31 May 1877; 141/111, Borg/Atkin, no. 15, Cairo, 30 July 1877; 141/107, Vivian/Derby, no. 298, Alexandria, 29 Sept. 1877.

29. P.R.O., F.O. 141/120, Carr/Borg, no. 14, Tantah, 11 June 1878.

30. P.R.O., F.O. 141/128, Borg/Vivian, no. 1, Cairo, 18 Feb. 1879; F.O. 141/125, Vivian/Salisbury, no. 57, Cairo, 15 Feb. 1879; F.O. 141/125, Vivian/Salisbury, no. 59, Cairo, 19 Feb. 1879; F.O. 141/25, Vivian/Salisbury, no. 71, Cairo, 22 Feb. 1879; see Schölch, *Egypt for the Egyptians!,* 66–73; and Hunter, *Egypt under the Khedives,* 215–16.

31. DWQ, Afghani Dossier [uncatalogued].

32. A hitherto unexploited autobiographical account of military and bureau-cratic dissatisfaction in this period is Muhammad Effendi Fanni, "Baqiyyat al-mutamanni fi tarjamat Fanni," MS 1126, pp. 65–91, Tarikh Taymur, Egyptian National Library, Cairo. See also Ahmad 'Urabi, *Taqriri 'an al-hawadith,* Trevor LeGassick, ed. and tr. (Cairo: American University in Cairo Press, 1982), pp. 5–19 of the Arabic text. For a British view see P.R.O., F.O. 141/144, Report of A. Colvin, encl. w/ Cookson/Malet, no. 233, Political, 10 Sept. 1881; the Khedive's reaction is in DWQ, Mahafiz ath-thawrah al-'Urabiyyah, Box 41, Khedive/Sultan, 9 Sept. 1881 (telegraphic).

33. Quoted from P.R.O., F.O. 141/144, Malet/Granville, no. 335, Cairo, 17 Nov. 1881; see for 'Urabi's urging graciousness towards Europeans in speeches in Sharqiyyah province, F.O. 144/149, Felice/Malet, no. 22, Zaqaziq, 21 Oct. 1881; for other points, see F.O. 141/144, al-Hijaz, no. 8, 17 Shawwal 1298/12 Sept. 1881, encl. w/ Malet/Granville, no. 251, Cairo, 23 Sept. 1881; F.O. 141/144, Malet/Granville, no. 313, Cairo, 31 Oct. 1881. See also Schölch, *Egypt for the Egyptians!,* 160–72.

34. P.R.O., F.O. 141/148, Cookson/Malet, no. 6, Alexandria, 23 Mar. 1881. For incidents of blood-libel persecution of Jews by European Christians and their protégés in the nineteenth-century Middle East, see Bernard Lewis, *The Jews of Islam* (Princeton: Princeton University Press, 1984), 157–59; this libel was not gen-erally a feature of Muslim-Jewish conflicts.

35. P.R.O., F.O. 141/149, Mieville/Malet, no. 44, Suez, 18 Dec. 1881.

36. P.R.O., F.O. 407/20, Mallet/Granville, no. 933, Cairo, 6 June 1882; P.R.O., House of Commons Accounts and papers, ZHC1/4460, Adm. Seymour/Sec. Admiralty, Invincible at Alexandria, 16 June 1882; Schölch, *Egypt for the Egyp-tians!,* 231–43. For the role of merchants and artisans, see Latifah Muhammad Salim, *al-Quwa al-ijtima'iyyah fi'th-thawrah al-'urabiyyah* (Cairo: al-Hay'ah al-Misriyyah al'Ammah li'l-Kitab, 1981), 337–58.

37. P.R.O., ZHC1/4503, *Correspondence Respecting the Riots at Alexandria on the 11th June, 1882,* Granville/Malet, 17 Aug. 1882, enclosure, Statement of Carmelo Polidani.

38. Schölch, *Egypt for the Egyptians!,* 250; 'Urabi's foes among the pro-vice-regal forces also attempted to blame the riot on him: see "Safinah biha mukatabat li ru'asa' ath-thawrah al-'Urabiyyah," MS 500, pp. 110–13, Shi'r Taymur, Egyptian National Library, Cairo. For an examination of the high politics of the riot, and a verdict that it was either spontaneous or at least partially encouraged by the Khe-dive Tawfiq, see M. E. Chamberlain, "The Alexandria Massacre of 11 June 1882 and the British Occupation of Egypt," *Middle Eastern Studies* 13, 1 (1977): 14–39.

39. Accounts by Egyptians wounded in the conflict are in DWQ, Mahafiz ath-Thawrah al-'Urabiyyah, Box 18, Dossier 1, and stress the Europeans' indiscri-nate use of firearms. Other important early Egyptian attempts at such narratives are translated in Wilfrid Scawen Blunt, *Secret History of the English Occupation of*

Egypt (London: T. Fisher Unwin, 1907; repr. Cairo: Arab Centre for Research and Publishing, 1980), app. III.

40. *Correspondence Respecting the Riots,* Granville/Malet, 17 Aug. 1882, Statement of Giacomo Luca; Granville's report quotes many similar accounts taken from Maltese, Greeks, and Italians.

41. Elbert Eli Farman, *Egypt and Its Betrayal, An Account of the Country during the Periods of Ismaœil and Tewfik Pashas, and of How England Acquired a New Empire* (New York: Grafton Press, 1908), p. 304.

42. DWQ, Mahafiz ath-Thawrah al-'Urabiyyah, Mahfazah 18, dossier 1, testimony of the wounded at the government hospital, report dated 4 Oct. 1882.

43. P.R.O., F.O. 407/20, Calvert/Granville, no. 903, Alexandria, 12 June 1882, 1:58 P.M. (telegraphic); Medical report of European Consular Corps in Alexandria, encl. no. 7 in No. 1447, Alexandria, 12 June 1882.

44. P.R.O., F.O. 407/20, Cookson/Malet, Alexandria, 16 June 1882, encl. no. 1 in Cookson/Granville, no. 1447, Alexandria, 20 June 1882; Mr. A. A. Ralli/Mrs. Ralli, Athens, 17 June 1882, encl. in no. 1553.

45. *Correspondence Respecting the Riots,* Granville/Malet, 17 Aug. 1882.

46. P.R.O., F.O. 141/161, Beaman/Malet, no. 46, Cairo, 4 July 1882.

47. P.R.O., F.O. 407/21, Dufferin/Granville, no. 332, Therapia, 28 June 1882.

48. P.R.O., F.O., Confidential Print 4716/1, Viscount Lyons/Earl Granville, 30 June 1882, in Kenneth Bourne and D. Cameron Watt, eds., *British Documents on Foreign Affairs,* Part 1, Series B, 15 vols. (Washington, D.C.: University Publications of America, 1984), vol. 9: 44.

49. I make this argument in a more elaborated way in *Colonialism and Revolution in the Middle East,* chapter 9 and the conclusion.

50. P.R.O., F.O. 141/161, Carr/Borg, no. 15, Tanta, 2 Nov. 1882; Borg/Malet, no. 60, Cairo, 3 Nov. 1882; Felice/Borg, Zaqaziq, 29 Oct. 1882; for the events of summer and autumn, 1882, see Schölch, *Egypt for the Egyptians!,* 258–305.

51. Muhammad 'Abduh maintained that 'Abdu'r-Razzaq Alwan, court-martialed for complicity in riots at Damanhur, had actually attempted to protect Christian lives, but was victimized by the triumphant viceregal officials: Blunt, *Secret History,* 507. Although some prominent individuals may have been wrongly charged, it seems unlikely that hundreds of ordinary people were.

52. "Correspondence Regarding the Riots," Herbert/Tenterden, Downing Street, 14 Aug. 1882, enclosure, Statement of E. Violaras, Larnaka, 27 July 1882.

53. "Kashf 'an bayan al-ahkam al-mutawaqqa'ah min majlis 'askariyyat Iskandariyyah 'ala madhkurin nazaran li ta'alluqihim bi'l-'isyan wa ishtirakihim fi'l-waqa'i allati hadathat," enclosure in F.O. 141/161, Jafo/Malet, 28 Oct. 1882. An English précis of this document, also enclosed, for the most part only gives names, omitting much crucial detail concerning occupation and ethnicity. (I was unable to locate the original of this document in the Egyptian archives.)

54. See Owen, *The Middle East in the World Economy,* 148–49, for estimates of

numbers. The Egyptian Interior Department's own list of specifically craft guild membership in 1870, with 55,808 members, preserved in P.R.O., F.O. 141/75, archives no. 147; cf. P.R.O., ZHC1/3496, Stanton/Granville, 17 Nov. 1870. 'Ali Mubarak, writing in the early 1880s, gives guild membership in Cairo alone at 63,487, but includes groups beyond the craft guilds; *al-Khitat at-tawfiqiyyah al-jadidah,* 20 vols. (Bulaq: al-Matba'ah al-Kubra al-Amiriyyah, 1304–1306/ 1886–1888), I, 99–100. A general work is Gabriel Baer, *Egyptian Guilds in Modern Times* (Jerusalem: Israel Oriental Society, 1964).

55. For working women in urban centers, see Tucker, *Women in Nineteenth-Century Egypt,* esp. ch. 2.

56. These Egyptian documents are enclosed in P.R.O., F.O. 141/161, Jafo/Malet, no. 4, Alexandria, 28 Oct. 1882.

57. Guild members' respect for elective procedure and anger when officials attempted to subvert it are apparent throughout the guild petitions in the Ministry of Interior correspondence files for the 1860s and 1870s; see among others, DWQ, Nizarat ad-Dakhiliyyah, Arabic Correspondence 20, "'Ardhal kayyalin" [Petition of the weighers], with Nazir ad-Dakhiliyyah/Muhafiz Misr, 14 Dhu'l-Qa'dah 1293/2 Dec. 1876, and Ar. Corr. 24, "'Ardhal ta'ifat as-samasirah" [Petition of the brokers], rec'd. 29 Shawwal 1294/6 Nov. 1877. One is aware, of course, of the British conviction that guild leaders had been coerced into supporting 'Urabi, but the trial of some of them indicates genuine support.

58. P.R.O., F.O. 407/21, Roswell/Tenterden, 14 July 1882, no. 522, enclosure. Apart from the 203 Europeans employed in the judicial and administrative staff of the tribunals of the reform, 1,112 persons drew a total of LE 315,600 or L 232,490 sterling from the Egyptian government in salaries.

59. I am grateful to Maureen Finney for urging me to strengthen this point.

60. "Correspondence Respecting the Riots at Alexandria," Herbert/Tenterden, 14 Aug. 1882, Statement of Christo Argiri, Limassol, July 1882; Statement of Franz Lanzon, Limassol, July 1882. (Corroborated in DWQ, Mahafiz ath-Thawrah al-Urabiyyah, Box 18, Dossier 26, Statement of Ahmad Qabudan.)

61. Gautam Bhadra, "Four Rebels of Eighteen-Fifty-Seven," in, Guha and Spivak, eds., *Selected Subaltern Studies,* 129–75.

62. "Zafarnamih-'i vaqa'i'-i ghadr." Persian MS 431, India Office Library, foll. 17a–b, 21a, 31–32. For the role of urban forces in 1857, see C. A. Bayly, *Rulers, Townsmen and Bazaars: North India Society in the Age of British Expansion, 1770–1870* (Cambridge: Cambridge University Press, 1983), 359–66. For recent general work on the rebellion see Rudrangshu Mukherjee, *Awadh in Revolt* (Oxford: Oxford University Press, 1984); and Juan R. I. Cole, *Roots of North Indian Shi'ism in Iran and Iraq: Religion and State in Awadh, 1722–1859* (Berkeley and Los Angeles: University of California Press, 1988), ch. 10.

63. Martin Richard Gubbins, *An Account of the Mutinies of Oudh and the Siege*

of the Lucknow Residency (London: Richard Bentley, 1858), 39–40; Cole, *North Indian Shi'ism,* op. cit.

64. The 1858 Jiddah riot is analyzed in detail in William Ochsenwald, *Religion, Society and the State in Arabia: The Hijaz under Ottoman Control, 1840–1908* (Columbus: Ohio State University Press, 1984), 140–52.

65. Philip S. Khoury, *Urban Notables and Arab Nationalism: The Politics of Damascus 1860–1920* (Cambridge: Cambridge University Press, 1983), ch. 1; see also for corroboration Kamal S. Salibi, "The 1860 Upheaval in Damascus as Seen by al-Sayyid Muhammad Abu'l-Su'ud al-Hasibi, Notable and Later Naqib al-Ashraf of the City," in *Beginnings of Modernization,* Polk and Chambers, eds., 185–202.

66. Rudé, *The Crowd in History,* 61–64.

67. See E. P. Thompson, "The Moral Economy of the English Crowd in the Eighteenth Century," *Past and Present* 50 (1971): 76–136; Elizabeth Fox Genovese, "The Many Faces of Moral Economy: A Contribution to a Debate," *Past and Present* 58 (1973): 159–68; William M. Reddy, "The Textile Trade and the Language of the Crowd at Rouen 1752–1871," *Past and Present* 74 (1977): 62–89; Alan Booth, "Food Riots in the North-West of England 1790–1801," *Past and Present* 77 (1977): 84–107; Dale Edward Williams, "Morals, Markets and the English Crowd in 1766," *Past and Present* 104 (1984): 56–73.

68. Davis, *Society and Culture,* ch. 6: "The Rites of Violence."

69. Ranajit Guha, "The Prose of Counter-Insurgency," in Guha and Spivak, eds., *Selected Subaltern Studies,* 45–86.

Ethnic Violence on the
South African Gold Mines

T. Dunbar Moodie

Elsewhere, I have identified a moral economy that operates on the South African gold mines as an implicit contract (Moore 1978), setting broad limits on arbitrary management power through collective action by black workers, often organized along "tribal" lines (Moodie 1986). Occasionally such protest action might turn violent, especially against mine property. Deaths and injuries usually occurred as a result of management or state police efforts to suppress such moral economy protests. I shall not discuss such collective violence in this paper however, concentrating on the much more difficult question of "black-on-black violence" that has always been referred to on the mines as "faction fighting." Faction fights are only partially products of management structures or the outcomes of general conditions of exploitation. Exploitative management structures are endemic on the mines and yet faction fights are fairly rare. Furthermore, their incidence fluctuates over time and between mines. What I hope to do in this paper is to provide an explanatory context for factional violence on the mines, both for its incidence and for recent changes in its form.

For the purposes of this paper, I define "violence" as action which causes or threatens to cause physical hurt to the person or property of another. This is not to deny structural violence built into the disciplinary organization of social formations.[1] However, this paper deals with violent *action,* and its focus is *collective.* Although acts of individual violence may precipitate collective violence, they do so only under certain conditions. There is an organizational component to group identities which is short-circuited by psychological explanations. While collective violence may reinforce social networks, it seldom, if ever, forms them on the spot. Potentially violent group identities already exist in the taken-for-granted beliefs, interactions, and practices of everyday life. Within the exploitation of the mine migrant system, ethnic violence implies specific choices by more or less formal groups of particular actors rather than free-floating aggression. Collective violence, I suggest, is the practice of politics by violent means.

Probably the most widely read account of violence in South Africa is Rian Malan's book, *My Traitor's Heart* (1990), which takes a position directly at odds with the argument of this paper. Malan sums up his own understanding of the meaning of his South African upbringing in the following words (p. 93): "That is how it has been all my life, from the moment my eyes first opened. It was quite clear, even to a little boy, that blacks were violent, and inscrutable, and yet I loved them. It was also clear that they were capable, kind, and generous, and yet I was afraid of them. The paradox was a given in my mind, part of the natural order of things. It was only later, when I was old enough to be aware of what was happening around me that the paradox starting eating me."

He wrote his book, he says (p. 103) "to seek resolution of the paradox of my South African life in tales of the way we killed one another." Violence, then, lies at the core of Malan's account of South African reality. As he describes it, violence is the heart of the South African situation, and it is irredeemable, irrevocable, "tribal" violence, provoked by "ancient and primordial" rage (p. 328), that is shared by white and black alike. Thus, for Malan, violence in South Africa is inevitable, rooted in deep-seated ethnic identities and entrenched in the violent common sense practices of everyday life in modern South Africa. A gifted crime reporter, he piles story upon story of murder, torture, massacre and execution, graphic in horrific and bloody detail, claiming that such accounts of free-floating "tribal" aggression get to the heart of South Africa social reality.

I make no effort to deny the fundamental role of violence in male socialization in South Africa (Beinart 1992). As a rather puny youngster growing up in a South African elementary boys' school, I was subject to some of it myself. Historically, violence has been an aspect of becoming a man, black or white, in South Africa as in many parts of the world. Corporal punishment is still held to be character-forming for boys and young men alike. Recourse to violence in disputes is common enough for South African males of all groups for it to be taken for granted as a strategic option. It is Malan's neo-Freudian notion of free-floating aggression and his reified "primordialist" conception of ethnic identity that is at odds with my understanding of faction fights on the mines.[2]

I want to argue that ethnic violence in South Africa is not an arbitrary expression of uncontrollable anger, but rather strategically motivated in terms of special interests fueled by group solidarities. Such solidarities may be more or less fixed depending on the historical situation, but they are always socially constructed and seldom monolithic in the modern world. Recourse to violence focuses actors on particular memberships and clearly labels them and the others. While ethnic identities certainly need to be reckoned with in South Africa, data from the gold mines demonstrate both that their boundaries are not fixed and also that they may be fomented and manipulated for political ends. Since strategy can be met by strategy, and successful strategies take into account various and cross-cutting interests and solidarities, ethnic violence is not inevitable. Given the increase in so-called "black-on-black" violence in South Africa since 1985, there are political as well as theoretical reasons for questioning primordialist arguments there.

Rian Malan's language would not be unfamiliar to those who have interviewed South African state officials or mining managers about ethnic violence on the gold mines. Their assumptions also tend to be stereotyped and couched in reified terms like "tribalism" (except that, unlike Malan, they exclude themselves from such interpretations). The comment of a Welkom CID officer is typical. He said, "I don't know why they're beating each other to death, management doesn't know and I'm damn sure they don't know themselves" (Argyle n.d.). I shall unpack that statement historically by asking who "they" are, how they "beat each other," and how they themselves have explained their actions in different periods.

Solidarities, Motivations, and Styles of Violence
before the 1970s

There can be no reliable historical count of factional violence on the South African gold mines. Since faction fights were regarded as a "normal" aspect of mine life, not all such skirmishes made their way into the newspapers or even the archives. For example, a police report (NA 81, F164) about a 1910 Christmas fight between "Mxosas" and "East Coast boys" concluded by saying that "this is the fourth disturbance the Mxosas at this compound have caused during the year." There is no record of the other three. Indeed only seven disturbances are recorded for all the mines for 1910 (BBNA 1910: 391–92). Four years later, James Millar, compound manager at Langlaagte B, told Native Grievances Commissioner

H. O. Buckle that fights between "Xhosa" and "Basutos" were lessening (NGI, 27/1O/14: 35). "On Block B four or five years ago we had faction fights once a week regularly," he said. In March 1914, James Douglas, Deputy Commissioner of Police in Johannesburg, reported to Buckle (NGI, 6/3/14: 2) that frequent but manageable trouble on the mines was "due to faction fights and [they] often start by a paltry incident between two boys of different tribes." In his report (par. 509), Buckle referred to African workers' "ancient habit of faction fights."

In the past (as with Rian Malan now), with rare exceptions incidents of "intertribal" violence were taken by whites to be primordial and inevitable, precipitated by individual squabbles, no doubt, but unavoidable in dealing with primitive, "uneducated natives" (NGI, Douglas, 6/3/14), who came to the mines with fixed tribal identities. Policy was one of containment and deaths were taken for granted, almost as with rockbursts underground. What is rather extraordinary is that there were so few deaths. Faction fights on the mines before the 1970s seem often to have been ritual events which operated according to their own rules of combat and were often remembered with excitement by those who had fought (Gordon 1978). There is one wonderful account of a rollicking and obviously celebratory fight on Christmas and Boxing Days in 1917 at City Deep and in Prospect Township, with wild drunkenness and typically rough stick play (NLB 197, 1440/14/48). An account of a fight at Langlaagte B in July 1914 also suggests the joy of fighting—this time of BaSotho (NLB 185, 1169/14/48, NA JHB West, 9/7/14). One might add testimony from Johannes Rantoa of whom Guy and Thabane (1987: 447) write:

> There is an atmosphere of intense enjoyment in Rantoa's description of the fights in which he participated: the fight is something of a game, just as football, in his accounts, has something of the fight. There can be no doubt that the exhilaration of physical combat gave relief in general conditions of severe social deprivation:
>
> We were stronger than those people, there was not another reason (for fighting). It was just the enjoyment of fighting and it was as if people were not satisfied during their time of herding. It was nice that thing of fighting each other like that, even though it was dangerous as it caused so many deaths.

Although all groups (however defined on the mines) engaged in factional violence if they felt driven to it, until the middle 1970s the rules for faction fighting seem to have been derived from the mores of cattle-herding boys in Transkei and Lesotho. Ms. Ndatshe and I found in Pondoland, as did Guy and Thabane in Lesotho, that, "All our informants have stressed the importance of their boyhood herding to the development of their characters. It was then, in the struggle for dominance within herding groups, in the physical privation, in the rivalry amongst different groups, that the fighting skills, the physical toughness and the aggression which one needs to deal successfully with the world were developed" (Guy and Thabane 1987: 44).

Young boys, while herding cattle, learned to fight with sticks (and to fight fair) from somewhat older boys. In their later teen years they formalized such practices in battles between regional youth groups. Individuals might get carried away in the heat of battle, but hitting an opponent when he was down was deeply deplored. Thus, while stick-fighting was rough play, it was play nonetheless, with its own rules and sport-like rituals.[3] When they become men, traditional Xhosa were supposed to put away such childish things and learn the *imiteto* (sing. *umteto*), the laws and discipline of manhood. Young men settled squabbles with sticks, but responsible adult men talked things through to a conclusion founded in the rules of a consensual order they call law (*umteto*). Throughout all stages of life, Xhosa and Sotho rural practices were subject to careful regulation by peer groups. On the mines, however, such controls might be lifted in the hurly-burly of mine life, especially when confronted with its real inequities. Sotho informants insisted to me that "we don't fight after we have been circumcised." However, one Sotho man on President Steyn mine told the mid-1980s joint NUM/Anglo-American inquiry into mine violence: "Treat us like boys and we'll behave like boys" (Leatt et al. 1986).

The solidarities and activities of compound life made mine labor bearable for mine workers as long as they had access to land in the countryside and were earning capital to fund rural homestead production (Moodie 1994). The social basis for maintenance of rural self-conceptions was the home-friend network, and miners would go to much trouble and take much pleasure in maintaining these rural links. Mine-workers preferred, indeed insisted, on being housed near or with home-friends, and management not only permitted but also encouraged such solidarities by housing persons from similar linguistic regions together, although work teams were always mixed and management definitions of "tribal" groups differed according to recruitment patterns. Thus "Bomvana," "Mpondo," "Baca," or "Xesibe," all of whom speak Xhosa, might be housed separately or with other Xhosa-speakers depending on management inclinations or compound management conceptions of "tribal" identities. Ethnic identifications, hypostatized by management housing and job assignment policies, were adopted by disparate groups of workers themselves both for wider mutual solidarity and to protect their occupational and recreational "territory." The rhetoric of violence was important in this regard, since acts or threats of collective violence help to define the group committing the violence and also to define their opponents. Violence, in its immediacy and perturbation, heightens group solidarities. Indeed, violence is almost always perceived as legitimate by the group committing it, as an expression of moral outrage and often as a response for symbolic or physical violations of members of one's own group or groups by the "others."

The policy of ethnically segregated housing along with home-friend networks thus provided informal networks which formed the terrain for faction fights, but fluidities of definition complicated these events. Xhosa-speakers might stand together, for instance, but sometimes "Mpondo" and "Bomvana" (both groups renowned for their belligerence and both of them Xhosa-speaking) would fight one another. As an example of fierce Mpondo and Bomvana independence from any simple "Xhosa" identity, consider the following summary of a 1942 police report (NTS 7675, SAP Krugersdorp, 12/9/42) about a fight at Venterspost Number One:

> Bomvanas returned to #1 compound from a beer drink and attacked Xhosas sleeping on the lawn in the compound (5/9/42). On Sunday (6/9/42) the Xhosas attacked the Bomvanas in retribution. Police from Randfontein restored order. However the Mpondo heard a rumor that three Mpondo had been stabbed by Bomvanas on a nearby farm so they attacked the Bomvanas in the compound, killing one and smashing everything in their rooms. Mine police were driven out of the compound and the compound manager who tried to pacify them had to retire under a rain of missiles. Police came and chased them to their rooms where they put up a violent fight. Eventually the Mpondo and Bomvana's were disarmed and the police collected a cartload of sticks, pieces of iron, hammers, etc.

Even when "tribal" identities (cutting across a common language) were reinforced by such violent affairs on particular mines, however, their boundaries were not fixed for all situations. In socializing in the compounds after work and engaging in the various "sidelines" (hair-cutting, knitting, clothing and shoe repair, illicit brewing, drug dealing, bicycle repair, and so on), everyday practices might reinforce local networks, but they often cut across them. Many mine workers whom Vivienne Ndatshe and I interviewed in Pondoland, for instance, mentioned mine gatherings which included persons from several Pondoland villages and even Xesibe and Bhaca Xhosa-speakers. Since work-teams were always ethnically integrated, camaraderie underground often led to inter-ethnic individual friendships in the compounds. Home-friend networks did not preclude wider friendships.

Ethnic identities themselves shifted, with ethnic boundaries defined as much by the numbers of home-friends or common language-speakers who happened to end up on any particular mine as on fixed or universal ethnic boundaries.[4] If one had many home-friends on the mine one would, of course, identify with them. In the absence of home-friends one might find others who spoke the same language—or related languages (so Sotho and Tswana would hang out together, or Xhosa and Zulu). Mpondo, for instance, who speak Xhosa, but do not circumcise like the Xhosa, would be ranked as Xhosa unless their numbers warranted their being defined as a "tribe" on their own. Although faction fights were important as assertions and confirmations of "ethnic" solidarities among mine workers, and rural masculine socialization played a role in the inclination of Sotho-, Xhosa-, and Zulu-speakers to use violent methods, the composition of the mine labor force or the compound and underground seniority structures were quite as important in fixing the boundaries of such "tribal" identities as was any sort of "primordial" ethnic heritage.

Unfortunately, most accounts of faction fights before McNamara's (1985) pioneering work on the 1970s rested upon common sense generalizations about "tribalism." Police reports in particular explain collective violence on the mines in terms of "jealousy between groups," "race prejudice," "tribal difficulties of old standing," and so on. Many reports cite the importance of drunken attacks upon individuals in igniting ethnic rivalries. Such accounts obviated the need for further investigation by the authorities. Often tribal fights were said to start in nearby towns or at *shebeens* (speakeasies) on farms in the vicinity and then were imported into the compound. While such evidence may indeed have been the sole available explanation (see also McNamara 1985: 222–43), occasional closer investigations, usually by members of the Native Affairs Department, revealed deeper structural reasons.

On Modder B on 4 January 1926, for instance, following a massive

Christmas faction fight, "East Coast natives" killed six "Cape Colony natives" and one British Basotho (NLB 365, 28/26/48). At that time recruitment from the Cape was picking up, and on Modder B Mozambican numbers had been limited. This shift in numerical balance, which represented a long-term threat to the more numerous Mozambicans, was almost certainly part of the problem (statement of mine detective Day, 5/1/26). H. S. Cooke, the Director of Native Labour, himself undertook an immediate review, found that the compound manager had disarmed the Cape workers but not the East Coasters, and with the support of mine management and the NRC, suspended the compound manager on the spot. Such careful investigations were few and far between, however. Matters most frequently were left to the South African Police and the compound authorities to sort out.

Take a case on Crown Mines in 1938, as an example of management mediation of a "Xhosa/Pondo" fight which on the face of it seemed to be about the cultural practice of circumcision. Xhosa feel superior to uncircumcised and irascible Mpondo "boy-men" who fail to carry on their bodies the marks of manhood. That the Mpondo do not circumcise is clearly an issue that cuts across their shared linguistic heritage. The issue of circumcision was explicit in the 1938 police account of the fight on Crown Mines X compound (NTS 7674, 99/332, 10/6/38), on which Ms. Ndatshe and I obtained further testimony from an old man in Pondoland in 1984. It was not the predominant factor, however. On 9 June 1938, a force of police were called out to X compound. According to Jackson Yaca, a Mpondo participant who vividly remembered the event forty-six years later, the battle was caused by underground *boss boys* (work-team supervisors), most of whom were Xhosa and Sotho, "bothering the Mpondo, who did very hard work as lashers and timber-boys." He also mentioned widespread tension between Mpondo and Sotho/Xhosa on the "uncircumcised boys" issue. No doubt assaults underground by white miners and their *boss boys,* that were endemic anyway, were exacerbated by such attitudes.

On that particular day in 1938, the Mpondo held a meeting after work to discuss their treatment by the *boss boys.* Their leader was a machine driller from Lusikisiki, who was respected for his knowledge of mine ways. They went to the *induna* (black supervisory official) who, being Xhosa, according to Yaca, took no notice of them, so they went straight to the chief compound manager. According to the police report, the *induna* had approached the compound manager but the matter had not been "adjusted to the satisfaction of the Pondos." Yaca remembered that all the Mpondo "gathered at the office of the chief compound manager to complain of their treatment at the hands of the *boss boys.*" When the manager asked them their problem, they all shouted their support for their spokesman. "The compound manager promised to investigate their complaints, but by this time they were so angry that they went to fight . . . Then "khakis" [white policemen] came with batons to disperse them," said Yaca. The chief compound manager investigated the matter immediately and, according to the police report, dismissed two Xhosa *boss boys* to appease the Mpondo.

While collective violence both asserts instrumental goals, making a claim to the opponent about one's own rights and privileges, and reinforces group solidarities, it also sends a message to the dominant class (on the mines, management) about group identities and grievances. Not only did the Mpondo beat up the Xhosa in the case above, but management was persuaded by the riot to dismiss some of the hated *boss boys.* The message could hardly have been lost on other Xhosa *boss boys* on this mine. The efficacy of violence was explicitly affirmed by a Mpondo, Mtilisho Mdibaniso when he told us in 1984:

> The compound manager would sack a man if he thought his case wasn't good, or he was a trouble-maker in the compound. I do know of cases, where the compound manager would favor the Sotho because the Mpondo had a reputation for making trouble. The Mpondo accepted this because the manager's word was final. The Mpondo were very strong on the mines, however, so the manager was careful not to offend them too much. Their strength made him wary of injustice against them. The Mpondo were the miscreants on the mines—they were always fighting with the Sotho.[5]

Thus did a reputation for belligerence help protect group interests. In a similar case at East Rand Proprietary Mines on 27 December 1941 (NTS 7675, 1O2/332, SAP Boksburg, 16/1/42), Barotse, relative newcomers to mine work, attacked Sotho because they claimed that continuous underground assaults were ignored by the compound manager. "The Compound Manager did not make it his business to see that their complaints received the attention of the Law as it should," so they told the police. The compound manager stated that it was seldom possible to get sufficient evidence for the courts to prosecute in such cases. The Barotse alleged, in their turn, that in that case the law was no good and did not give them a fair deal. They wished to deal with such assaults their own way. To the policeman who wrote the report, their demands simply confirmed his assumptions about primitive tribalism: "It was evident that the Barotsis, being a tropical tribe and owing to their undeveloped minds, did not or could not understand the procedure of the Law as far as prosecutions are concerned." The actions of the Barotse were hardly "lawless," however. Rather, they had a different understanding of legal procedures and justice than their white rulers.[6] In this case, the Barotse were given a warning and no further action was taken.

From such examples we may conclude that faction fighting has historically been rooted in more than merely symbolic solidarities. Often collective violence would break out along already established ethnic lines, but it was much more likely to be supported by group members when perceived real interests were at stake. Collective violence is seldom merely moral or symbolic. It is generally instrumental as well.

Moral outrage that risks violent action seems to require a practical basis. Some of the most serious fights occurred on mines where there had been a large influx of new workers from one particular region who would tend to be supervised (and assaulted) by established workers from another group. More generally, ethnic violence involved retribution by members of one group over real or alleged assaults upon one perceived as a fellow. Over the entire period from 1910 to 1950, I was unable to discover any consistent or recurrent "ethnic" patterns in group rivalries on the mines. Full explanation of faction fights thus cannot rest upon assumptions about presumed group solidarities alone, but must take account of the capillaries of power and configurations of interest on and around the mine. The category of "tribe" tends to obscure such factors. To understand "factional" mine violence, one needs to know when the different groups arrived on each mine, the specific work they were assigned, with whom they were housed, how large a complement they formed on the mine, whether or not they were assigned their own compound policemen and/or an *induna,* their prior experience of mine or other wage labor, and who controlled the various rackets in the compound—meat, alcohol, "boys"—and the *shebeens* (speak-easys) and eating houses round about. Thorough investigation must be undertaken on a mine-by-mine basis. At issue is not a reductionist denial of the importance of "ethnic" solidarities, but rather an insistence on their historical character, their shifting context and relativity to local conditions. More generally, I would argue that no social scientific explanation, whether for Yugoslavia, Russia, Somalia, India, or even Canada (Johnstone 1990), can be satisfactory unless it historicizes and contextualizes the notion of ethnicity as I have sought to do in this paper.

Sotho-Xhosa "Faction Fights" in the 1970s

We have seen that "ethnic" violence on the South African gold mines before the 1970s was handled by a combination of authorities. Where local mine management paternalism was insufficient, the formal authority of the South African Police was invoked. The informal authority of management-appointed and worker-accepted "tribal" black officials, and the operation amongst some worker groups of migrant organizations and cultures with their own rules for fights both encouraged and contained violence. In the context of such rules before 1973, contestation tended to arise over local and particular rather than industry-wide issues. The 1970s brought a series of fundamental changes on the mines.

With the dramatic rise in the price of gold in the early 1970s, the gold industry, for both strategic and moral reasons, decided to raise wages substantially. In 1973 there were more workers on the gold mines who were from Malawi (109,731), Mozambique (83,390), and the combined ex-High Commission territories of Lesotho, Botswana, and Swaziland (101,671), respectively, than workers from within the borders of South Africa itself (81,375). The perilousness of such dependence on foreign labor was dramatically demonstrated in 1974, when President Hastings Banda decided to withdraw all Malawians from the mines as their contracts expired. Malawaians in the mine labor force dropped from over 100,000 in 1973 to fewer than 500 by 1976. At about the same time, the changeover of governments in Mozambique cut the Mozambican labor supply almost in half.[7]

Armed with the new wage scales, and aided by the collapse of homeland subsistence production and mechanization of white farming, the Chamber of Mines mounted a massive and successful recruiting campaign within South Africa and Lesotho. By 1983, the Sotho labor complement on the South African gold mines had increased by one-half to 95,731, and South African labor had gone up three-fold to 239,065 (most came from the Transkei and Ciskei, but also from urban areas, white farms, and rural resettlement areas, which were growing rapidly as commercial farming mechanized in the early 1970s). The ethnic complexion of the mine labor force thus changed radically and very rapidly with the recruitment of a more wage-dependent labor force. Thus the changes during the 1970s took place on two fronts, as the class composition of the labor-force changed along with its "ethnic" make-up.

Almost at once, in 1974, ethnic strife between Xhosa- and Sotho-speaking workers broke out on Welkom Mine in the Orange Free State. Unlike similar disputes in the past, however, the dispute on this mine spread rapidly to others. The incidence of disputes with management also increased. Thus, rapid systemic changes between 1973 and 1982 brought with them changes in the nature and incidence of collective violence both among workers and against management. One might have expected greater conflict with management as a more proletarianized work-force was recruited from within South Africa, but why also an increase in so-called "tribal violence?"

What is most striking about intergroup clashes during this period is that over 40 percent of them (37 of the 88 cases—including almost all the fights in the Orange Free State) involved conflicts between Sotho (sometimes allied with Tswana) and Nguni (Xhosa- or Zulu-speaking) workers. Such ethnic consistency on the part of mine "faction fighters" was unique in the history of the mining industry and lent credence to primordial interpretations (notice however that almost 60 percent of faction fights were not between Sotho and Nguni-speakers). Even Kent McNamara (1985: 217), upon whose excellent analysis of this period I rely heavily, writes of a "feud." However, he also provides several other interpretations. Two explanatory factors seem particularly convincing.

The first important issue is not directly mentioned by McNamara although it is implicit in much of his analysis. This is the question of proletarianization. As we have seen, by raising wages and actively recruiting "South African" labor from townships and rural slums in the mid-1970s, the South African mining industry did not merely increase the "South African" proportion of its labor force. For the first time in its history, it hired large numbers of fully proletarianized, if still migrant, workers, although this extremely rapid process of proletarianization was uneven and is still proceeding, with pockets of "traditional" workers continuing to live by the old migrant values. The impact of the new workers on the industry was volcanic, however. They were better educated, with urban tastes in dress, music, and entertainment (and styles of violence, for that matter), and far more intolerant of crowded living conditions and mistreatment at work and in the compounds. They tended to regard their blanket-garbed fellow-workers as country bumpkins and to reject the authority of illiterate *indunas* and mine police, as well as Sotho and Shangaan *boss boys,* now rebaptized "team leaders."

Persons entirely dependent on wage-labor for their livelihood, working to support dependent families in far flung rural slums—if they had not already abandoned them for town women (Moodie and Ndatshe 1992)— were not inclined to sit around the compound and share stories of rural life with home fellows. Instead they looked for excitement away from the mines in local *shebeens,* or they drank to get drunk every evening and on weekends in the mine liquor outlet. These new mine workers were no longer insulated from the liberation struggle going on in South Africa; more and more, many of them were part of it. Paternalist mine authorities impressed them not at all. They expected due process and proper worker representation.

Proletarianization did not mean that conflict around wages and labor conditions would not be interpreted in ethnic terms. The new workers, the large majority of them Xhosa-speakers, did not find the well-paid jobs with ample authority to which they perhaps expected their education entitled them when they first began to come to the mines in the early 1970s. Instead they were allotted the lowest-paid jobs in the most marginal mines, and subject to all the constraints and assaults on their dignity that mine work in South Africa has implied over the years.

The second major factor in understanding Sotho-Xhosa faction fights follows from the first. Migrants from Lesotho tended to dominate the better-paying jobs on the Orange Free State mines (McNamara 1985: 211). With the departure of Malawians in the late 1960s, Sotho-speakers had become team leaders or *boss boys,* machine operators, winch and locomotive drivers. Even the easier unskilled jobs in timber support and maintenance were dominated by Sotho on the Free State mines, whereas Xhosa-speakers were relegated to the most menial underground laboring jobs. Sotho dominance of better-paid and less arduous work was the outcome of 1963 South African legislation which forbade citizens of Lesotho from working in South Africa except on the mines. Migrants from Lesotho on the Free State mines (like Mozambicans in the Transvaal before them) worked longer contracts on the mines and returned more regularly, building up seniority. Many of them were also better educated and more wage-dependent than other workers during the 1960s. Thus in the early 1970s thoroughly proletarianized (i.e. wage-dependent) and better-educated Xhosa-speaking workers were recruited for the most strenuous and least well-remunerated jobs on the Free State mines, and were subject to intense production pressure from largely Sotho-speaking supervisors. Little was needed in the way of precipitating factors to pitch Xhosa-speakers into faction fights with Sotho.

Moreover, the very nature of violence on the mines had begun to change. Before the 1980s (and even to some extent during the period of transition in the 1970s), despite the frequency of collective violence, its ritualized forms and traditional methods meant that deaths were relatively infrequent. Nowadays, new methods of fighting more typical of slum streets than country cattle-herding have led to wide-scale slaughter. The *Weekly Mail* for 23–29 January 1987, declared that during the preceding year, 113 black mineworkers had been killed by other black miners on South African gold mines. The mines included Kloof, Vaal Reefs, Western Deep Levels, Kinross, President Steyn, and Beatrix. The list did not include a death at East Rand Proprietary Mines (ERPM) in April (*Star* 21/4/86), or one at Grootvlei in December (*Sunday Times* 21/12/86) which bring the total to 115. While these figures pale in comparison to the preliberation carnage in contemporary Natal and the Transvaal townships, they are large compared to earlier experience on the mines and are very disruptive of production.

In response to the unrest, some mining houses have begun to rationalize white and black managements at the local level, gradually replacing paternalistic authority with bureaucratized supervision and armed security forces along police lines. As a result, on Anglo-American mines *indunas* have become "unit supervisors" without ethnic responsibilities, and local compound managers have been disempowered. In addition, Anglo-American, the wealthiest of the mining houses, permitted, even encouraged, the founding of the black National Union of Mineworkers (NUM) in the early 1980s. The corporation's intent was to create a labor conciliation system which would oblige the NUM to control and discipline its own members. However, disputes on the mines have deep structural and historical causes which could not be controlled or removed by the creation of a trade union. If anything, the NUM, by empowering its members in local contestations, made matters worse for old-style local management's patriarchal control. Let us turn to the links between faction fighting and the eroding authority of local managements by considering events at Vaal Reefs Number One Shaft in November and December of 1986. The five thousand pages of evidence to the Bregman Commission provide a uniquely detailed account of this faction fight and the events leading up to it.[8]

Collective Violence on a Contemporary Gold Mine

The NUM, when it established itself on the mines after 1982, was obliged to organize a changing and differentiated work force in which class and ethnic divisions sometimes coincided, but often cut across one another. Workers were divided along class lines, between the older traditional miners with their roots in the countryside and more fully proletarianized recent recruits. The allocation of jobs, which followed such class lines, also potentially coincided with ethnic divisions. These might be manipulated by management or security forces to build up resentment against the union. Organizing on such contested and shifting terrain, in the face of different management strategies of control (both among the various giant mining houses and between senior and lower-level local and head-office management), posed problems of great complexity for the union. Furthermore, closer identification of a "South Africanized" labor force with the liberation struggle in the country eventually obliged the NUM, along with other Congress of South African Trade Unions (COSATU) unions, to take a stand on political issues, despite the risk of dividing the mine labor force (Seidman 1994; James 1991).

For several years after the founding of the NUM in 1982, its immediate successes in curbing unfair dismissals and in confronting safety issues led to widespread support. Initially it targeted team leaders, but it soon learned that this was a shaky strategy since team leaders are in intercalary positions which force them to choose between their responsibility to management and their identification as workers. Team leader's identification as workers were further threatened when management on many mines gave them higher wage raises, provided separate and superior housing for them, and built special messes where clerks, team leaders, and other black supervisors could dine in finer style. The union thus shifted its attention to machine drillers. This inadvertently meant a shift from organizing mostly Sotho to concentrating on Mpondo. In both cases, however, the union was organizing older, more established workers. Since the formation of COSATU in 1985, with NUM's explicit support of its strategy of "political" or "social movement unionism," the union has moved onto more controversial terrain in which support from the new breed of mine workers has come to the fore. At the same time, support from more traditional miners, although they remain members, has become less overt. While many of the old divisions in the work force still exert their influence, they have now been overlain on the local level by new struggles between unionists and management.

A convenient beginning for the events on Vaal Reefs Number One compound is the killing in mid-February 1986 of four Sotho-speaking team leaders on Vaal Reefs Number Five compound which, like Number One, is located in the East Division on Vaal Reefs. According to union members on Number Five, the team leaders had tried to break up a union march in the compound and been pursued to their rooms and killed by angry rank-and-file members. On 24 February, an NUM shaft steward on Number Five, one Mgedezi, was arrested along with four others by the South African Police in connection with the team leader killings. Early on the morning of 25 February, NUM shaft stewards went from room to room in No.1 Compound urging workers to stay away in sympathy with Mgedezi. There was a total strike on all three shafts in East Division.

A group of NUM pickets gathered at Number One shaft gate. However, "Seven" Mojakisane, a gang supervisor from Lesotho who was renowned amongst the workers as a traditionalist of great integrity, decided to go to work, as he said (AAC/VR: 5120, 5103), "because some of my Sotho people were already killed and I was not afraid to be killed. I said to myself I would be the same as the other Sothos who were already killed and the strike was also not legal . . . I was also told that [one of the team leaders who had been killed was from my home district] and had fought viciously in defense of himself."

Having deposited his belongings with a friend in the white quarters, Seven returned to the compound and walked to the shaft area to report for work, ignoring a request to attend an NUM meeting from Thabang, a dynamic Sotho shaft steward, who seems to have been one of the union's most charismatic leaders on Number One shaft. At the Training Centre he picked up a couple of dozen newcomers to the mine, who had allegedly been threatened by management with dismissal if they did not accompany him (AAC/VR: 4286). They went from room to room together, dressed in their work clothes, donned blankets and armed themselves (AAC/VR: 5116). They then marched through the picket lines and went underground. No others went to work that day. However, the consensus had been broken and when they went to work the next day, again armed and blanketed, everyone followed their example. The influence of Thabang seems to have been crucial in the decision to avoid confrontation, else "there would be violence and the name of the trade union would be smeared" (AAC/VR: 1508).

Shortly thereafter local management gave Seven thirty days leave. Of course no action was taken against him or the others for going underground armed, although that was strictly against the regulations. Mlamli Botha, an outspoken Mpondo shaft steward, expressed his disgust in no uncertain terms, saying that it was "the first time in the history of this mine to see people with all sorts of dangerous weapons, passing next to Management, going straight to work with all those weapons" (AAC/VR: 1504). The point to note is not just the integrity and consistency of both Seven's position and that of the shaft steward, but also their incommensurability. Seven's outrage at a strike in support of the killings of Sotho home-fellows who were also fellow underground supervisors was as deeply felt as Mlamli Botha's disgust at Seven's management-supported and armed strike-breaking. Notice that in the contemporary situation, ethnic collectivities and cleavages have been complicated by the coming of the union, whose membership cuts across ethnic divisions. Despite widespread support for Thabang, who was from Lesotho, Seven expressed himself in explicitly ethnic terms, whereas Mlamli Botha's deepest resentment was aimed at local management.

Perceived senior mine management inaction continued to rankle NUM shaft stewards in Vaal Reefs East Division. On the weekend of March 1 and 2, they met and decided to propose to the workers that they engage in a short-day strike, working only four hours a day (roughly half-time). Black miners on Number One shaft began such a strike on Wednesday, 5 March. During the afternoon, union activists paraded around the compound carrying the NUM flag, dancing and singing songs of defiance. On the night of 5 March, the *indunas'* cars were damaged by commercial explosives hurled into the locked building where they were garaged. The following day, four elderly mine clerks who elected to work a full day were dragged from their offices by the militants, assaulted, and roughly forced to parade about with them, carrying the flag. They had to be hospitalized with quite serious injuries.

Management, furious at the short-day strike and the accompanying violence, obtained a court order against the strike, closed the shaft on Friday, 7 March, and obliged workers, in the presence of armed security personnel, to sign a document reaffirming their conditions of employment and their willingness to continue working on the mine. On Saturday night,

8 March, presumably in retaliation, a bomb was exploded outside the bedroom of the Sotho chief *induna*. Compound rumor attributed the bombs to two sources: Thabang, the militant Mosotho shaft-steward, and the Xhosa *induna*, Machain. Indeed, Thabang was believed to be in cahoots with Machain (AAC/VR: 2737). There were those who said that Thabang, who was a dynamic leader in the union and among Sotho-speakers, coveted the Sotho *induna*'s position (AAC/VR: 4550). This was nonsense in any formal sense, not least because the position of *induna* itself was being phased out by head office management, but it does demonstrate the popular respect accorded to Tabang by a substantial number of Sotho-speakers. Indeed, shaft-stewards were taking over many of the *indunas'* traditional functions on the mine—representing workers in individual grievance cases, for instance, and caring for their general welfare (AAC/VR: 3939–43).

Be that as it may, a group of traditionalists from Lesotho at once set up an armed guard over the Sotho *induna* and declared themselves ready to settle with Tabang and Machain and the "Xhosa" (AAC/VR: 2736). It is not clear exactly how they conceived of the "Xhosa," but opposition to the union came to be identified in popular worker belief—or at least in the eyes of local management—with migrants from Lesotho. By implication, Xhosa-speakers were perceived by local whites to be NUM supporters. On Monday, 10 March, everyone went to work. However, that night—or Tuesday morning at 2 A.M. to be precise—a group of about twenty "Sotho," armed and wearing blankets, stomped around the compound, blowing whistles and calling their fellow-countrymen to arms. Workers emerged sleepily from their rooms, puzzled by the commotion. Since in this hostel workers were housed ethnically by room but blocks were arranged by work group, the rooms of the various ethnic groups were scattered about in the compound. The armed "Sotho" announced that they wanted the head of Thabang, the charismatic Sotho-speaking shaft-steward perceived as a threat to the Sotho *induna*, and they named other Sotho- and Xhosa-speaking shaft stewards as well. According to another account, as a result of the whistles, many men from Lesotho milled about shouting, "Let us go and attack Xhosas." At least in the minds of these Sotho-speakers, the union was identified with an enemy ethnic group, even though officials of the union included some of their own people—no doubt perceived as ethnic sell-outs. Eventually close to one hundred had gathered with their blankets and their weapons outside the Sotho *induna*'s room (AAC/VR: 995). Ethnic identities were becoming paramount on the mine.

Someone, probably the Sotho *induna* himself, called mine security, who entered the compound in two armored vehicles (Hippos), told the now wide-awake workers to go back to their rooms and to bed, shot off one or two tear gas canisters for effect, and put a guard on the compound gate. The *induna* called off his warriors from their declaration of war. For such it was. No-one slept that night. Sotho- and Xhosa-speakers alike spent the remainder of the night feverishly making weapons that they might defend themselves in the battle they knew lay ahead (AAC/VR: 1000, 1693–98). Underground that day, also, time was devoted to weapon construction. Welding torches were used to produce weapons from metal found underground and no mine policeman dared to disarm workers emerging from the crush at the shaft head.

Mlamli Botha, the Mpondo shaft-steward, accompanied senior Xhosa-speaking black compound officials, including the *induna* and the sub-*induna,* early in the morning to report to the Hostel Manager, "Tsotsi" Wilden, about the ruckus of the night before. They wanted the *indunas* with two representatives from each group to meet to iron out the matter. Wilden sent them to a clerk to make formal statements, but did no more. Mlamli Botha, realizing that nothing would be done, went off to town to Orkney and bought himself a serrated sword. In the afternoon, Wilden ignored a union delegation and went home.

By eight that evening the two groups had lined up facing each other, the Sotho in their blankets, many of the Xhosa-speakers in white sheets. Asked who made up the "Xhosa," Mlamli Botha replied (AAC/VR: 1003): "When I say Xhosa, I mean the Xhosa-speaking people. It might be Pondos, Bhacas, Bomvanas, Xhosas, but they are Xhosas. Also from Ciskei." The standard-bearers from Lesotho blasted their whistles and their group attacked. They were a distinct minority, since many of their fellow-citizens had chosen not to join the fight, and the "Xhosa" pushed them out of the compound. At that point, security arrived in four Hippos and, openly promising aid to the militant Sotho, advanced into the compound firing rubber bullets at white-sheeted workers. The Sotho war group returned to the compound behind the Hippos, hurling stones to accompany the security bullets. The fighting Xhosa-speakers were hemmed up into one corner of the compound.

Sotho-speaking rioters looted and rampaged through "Xhosa" rooms, smashing lockers and stealing and destroying belongings. A Sotho and a Swazi mine policeman led the security guards from one Xhosa-speaking room to the next, so that security could roust them out for target practice with rubber bullets. In the rush to escape the bullets, people "were just getting into rooms that they could come across near them, so that it was just a mixture in the rooms. Sothos and Xhosas mixed . . ." (AAC/VR: 4561). One man was reportedly hacked to death in his room in the presence of the mine police (AAC/VR: 1837–41). Apparently one Sotho-speaker was killed in the original rout from the compound, although the number of fatalities is vague. Many from both groups were seriously wounded. Ethnic divisions were by no means set in stone, however. The Sotho-speaking shaft-steward Thabang was rescued by a group of Xhosa-speakers and smuggled out of the compound. He later left the mine for good. A certain Sigayi, a young Xhosa-speaking activist "comrade," was chased by security rubber bullets into a "Sotho" room where he was promptly loaned a Sotho blanket and where he spent the night (AAC/VR: 4344–46).

It is particularly striking how little eagerness there was for the fight on both sides. Mlamli Botha said of the Xhosa-speakers that "we were ready for anything" and admitted that he had personally participated in the fight "to defend myself because I was attacked" (AAC/VR: 1696–99). When asked why he returned with his weapon rather than staying in town or elsewhere off the mine, he replied: "I knew that that thing was not only directed to me alone . . . it was directed to all the Xhosa-speaking" (AAC/VR: 1761–62). There was no joy in this expression of solidarity, however. When Commissioner Bregman asked him directly whether he would have been disappointed had there been no fight, he answered simply: "I would have been exceedingly happy" (AAC/VR: 1710).

Matsepe Mokheti, a Sotho worker on the night shift, went down that evening unsure whether there would be a fight until a white shift overseer came eager with the news. Mokheti at once told his work mates, Sotho- and Xhosa-speaking alike. One of the consultants to the Bregman Commission asked him later whether there was "a change of atmosphere underground? Whether you continued working just normally, or whether now there was tension or something like that?" Mokheti replied that "we continued working normally until the end of the shift. [Then, because the cage came up late] we started preparing ourselves underground and we took roof bolts to make weapons. . . . we did this jointly. We were even helping each other as to how to make weapons." His interlocutor was astounded: "But Xhosas helping Basuto? And Basuto helping Xhosa? How does it come about that you did not desert or fight there and then?" "There was a suggestion from one of the Sotho chaps that these Xhosa should be fought here underground," said Mokheti, "[but] one of the guys opposed this and said it would be illegal and [you] could be sent to jail if you fight underground." "So instead you decided to help each other to make arms?" "Yes, until the cage came" (AAC/VR: 2749–51).

On coming to the surface, they found the rest of the night-shift, ethnically mixed and by now fully armed, locked together in the clocking-in room on the surface. Shortly they were released, but the compound gate was manned by security who would not let them in. There was no sign of fighting. They stood there a long time, that mixed group of night-shift workers with their weapons at rest. Finally, at about five in the morning they were disarmed and allowed into the hostel.

Mokheti was asked why they were so eager to get into the hostel. Did they want to fight? He responded simply: "We were hungry because we were from work and we wanted to go to the kitchen . . . we had already heard that there was no fighting going on." When asked if they would have joined in if fighting had been going on, he said: "I believe that if we found that there was fighting going on we were also going to fight" (AAC/VR: 2755). However, Mokheti's entire testimony hardly depicts primordial thirst for blood. Instead, like that of Mlamli Botha, it implies unenthusiastic acceptance of the taken-for-granted and mutually assumed responsibility to follow through on the obligations of ethnic group membership once that had become salient through violence.

Once inside, the night shift finally separated, Lesotho citizens going to their folk and Xhosa-speakers to their own. The hostel manager, "Tsotsi" Wilden met them at the gate and guided the "Sotho" to the kitchen, saying as he went that they should fight "the Xhosa" if they came. "He was really encouraging the fight," said Mokheti, "he assured us that security was going to help us [with tear gas] if the Xhosas were defeating us . . . He said Xhosas were troublesome people. They are the cause of strikes" (AAC/VR: 2758, 2761). The Sotho night shift got special food that day, but Xhosa-speakers went hungry.

On this mine at least, there is ample evidence that local management and mine security exploited traditional ethnic solidarities to its own advantage against the union. I do not wish to be misunderstood here. Actions of local NUM activists were certainly provocative on this compound, but local compound management did not seriously try to negotiate with the local union structure. Instead, with the cooperation of lower-level security personnel it used ethnic solidarities to try to arouse hostility against union activists.

After the Sotho night shift had eaten, all the workers were shunted out to the sports stadium and the general manager of East Division announced that the fight had really been between tribal supporters of the two *indunas*. The *indunas* solemnly shook hands. No-one queried "Tsotsi" Wilden's behavior. Nor was any action taken against security, although at a meeting on 14 March between senior East Division management and ministerial delegations from Lesotho and Transkei, four security officers were named as having taken sides (AAC/VR: KVD45). The two whistle-blowing Sotho-speaking battle leaders were acquitted in the local magistrates court of any wrong-doing. Although many workers from Lesotho had refused to participate in the fight, management was clearly unable to think in other than ethnic terms. Moreover, the looting of Xhosa-speakers' lockers by victorious warriors from Lesotho reinforced ethnic identities on the mine, especially among traditionalist Mpondo with their long history of belligerence.

Local compound management and mine security had tried an experiment in union-bashing that had failed, but they would try again. It is surely no coincidence that the state police began to foment "black-on-black" violence at about the same time as this Vaal Reefs affair (Haysom 1987). Traditionalist black miners learned that violence against perceived union supporters had the support of management and the security forces. Local management's tendency to blame the union for all political intimidation by mine workers was deeply resented by union officials. Two incidents on Vaal Reefs Number One brought their anger to the boil. The first had to do with a conservative white mine official named Porky Rheeders. The story is a simple one, and harks back to similar stories told over the past century on the South African gold mines about intense black worker outrage around delays in hoisting. Complaints about delays in hoisting blacks from underground are as old as deep-level mines themselves. Since workers are paid for hours spent at the workplace rather than bank-to-bank, it is understandably a sore issue.

In this case, on 4 July 1986, mine overseer "Porky" Rheeders "stopped [black] people [on 59 level] from getting to the lift while they were knocking off. He said to the workers that 'this is not a lift for the kaffirs [niggers], this is a lift for the whites'" (AAC/VR: 1041), and proceeded to the surface with the cage almost empty. When the cage returned, the black workers refused to be hoisted, saying that they wanted the "kaffir lift." White officials who went down were totally unable to break the sit-down strike and had to call in representatives of the union to negotiate with the workers. Three shaft stewards went down and eventually, after gaining some concessions from management, were able to get the workers at 59 level to leave the mine. Two days later, Meshack Lange, the shaft steward who had made most of the running in the negotiations and essentially talked the striking workers to the surface, was detained under state-of-emergency laws and held by the South African Police. Outraged workers demonstrated in front of the hostel manager's office. In Mlamli Botha's words (AAC/VR: 2189), "People were really angry about this because Porky who started the whole thing was not arrested under the state of emergency whereas the shaft steward who came to assist . . . was consequently arrested. . . . I believe he was arrested since he made the workers listen to him [so that] management was of the view that he was also responsible for inciting the workers to refuse to go from underground." In addition, said Botha in disgust, although he had heard that management had censured Porky Rheeders, they did so in private, out of the presence of the shaft stewards at the inquiry.

The second case led to what local union officials believed were several totally unjust dismissals. At eight o'clock on the morning of 8 October 1986, the section manager on Number One "received information that employees were going to refuse to come out of the mine" (AAC/VR: KVD59). Accordingly, he dispatched mine overseers to various levels to clear the mine of workers and to take note of any who refused to come up. That the section manager was willing to disrupt production on the basis of rumor demonstrates how rattled management must have been by the Porky Rheeders sit-down strike. At 66 level, several workers boarded the cage reluctantly and twenty-seven remained behind. When they refused the command of the mine overseer to enter a cage he had ordered especially for them, he summoned mine security officers who batoned the workers into the cage. Only sixteen of them turned out to be NUM members. Seven were found guilty and dismissed from the mine on the spot. They appealed to the production manager who reprieved two of them but sustained the discharges of the other five.

Mlamli Botha represented some of the accused at the disciplinary hearing presided over by Fulscher, the section manager. He pressed their case strongly, with typically astute arguments and his characteristic sense of justice and outrage at arbitrary power (AAC/VR: 1058–59):

I asked Mr. Fulscher whether a worker could be taken out of his job even before his time has some for him to get off. To which he said on this particular day he had arranged that people should knock off early.

I asked Mr. Fulscher whether prior he had told the people about this to which he said "No," he said that it was only his own right. I asked Mr. Fulscher as people were striking underground according to him with which shaft steward did he go down in this incident. He said he did not call any shaft steward. I reminded him about the July incident when he had called a shaft steward to underground when people were refusing to go out. I asked him why then not this time. . . . He did not give an answer. I asked him [whether he considered it just] to do this type of thing. He just said that I am dismissing these people because they refused to get to the lift. I wanted to know what type of evidence did he have because it was work time when he forced these people to the lift. People at Station 65, their lift begins at quarter-to-three to take them up. You, at half-past-eleven at work time you are taking them up, you are telling them to go to the lift. He did not even answer, he just said "I am dismissing these people." Then I told him that you are exercising your own right and that is illegal.

To Mlamli Botha, management was behaving most arbitrarily. The "law" that Fulscher was contravening was the new *umteto* of a mine with an active union presence. Whatever rumors he might have heard about a threatened underground sit-down, Fulscher should have checked with the shaft stewards before taking action, Botha believed, as had been done in resolving the Porky Rheeders affair.

The handful of men who were actually dismissed were all "comrades" (AAC/VR: 2428), militants who were openly associated with the union and thus liable to victimization by management because of their singing and dancing in the compound. In Botha's opinion, it was their close identification with the union, rather than their refusal to ride the cage as such, which distinguished them from those non-unionists who had behaved similarly underground but who were acquitted. Thus the dismissals could be construed as a direct assault on union structures and activities on the compound.

There can be little question that production management at Number One had been severely shaken by the Porky Rheeders sit-down strike underground. Like the four-hour go-slow which preceded the March faction fight, the "Porky" affair had affected mine production. No doubt management thought it had the potential to be far more disruptive of production in the future since it had demonstrated management's impotence without union cooperation. This time they were no doubt determined to act forcefully without union participation, for in the sphere of production, mine management is openly and avowedly despotic.

When the production manager dismissed their appeal, on 31 October, the shaft stewards asked the hostel manager for permission to hold a meeting on 4 November for "feedback" (AAC/VR: 179–81 and 1065–66). Mlamli Botha told the Bregman Commission (AAC/VR:1066–69) what occurred there:

> We talked to the people as they were upset. We told them that some of them, the workers, had been dismissed as a result of this [Fulscher] incident. We told them further that we tried to represent them to the management to our best, but our appeals were fruitless. We told them now we have come back with this report and we are now waiting for your mandate as you are the people who elected us. . . . We then waited for their mandate. . . . The hall was full, in fact there was even some overspilling. . . . The people said in that case then we will boycott the liquor outlet, because they did not come to the mine to drink. And that is our own way of punishing the management until it succumbed . . . so that they can . . . cancel the dismissals.

The first point to make about liquor outlet boycotts is that they were a last-ditch strategy devised by workers out of weakness rather than strength. The most effective way for workers to impress management is to withhold their labor—to strike. "Illegal" wildcat strikes, or even protest assemblies, were no longer an option, however, since workers were under a court injunction and there was a government state of emergency in effect. With "legal" strikes under South African law, one has to show one's hand so far in advance that they are not very effective in redressing local injustices, especially unjust dismissals.

Thus, for both tactical and moral reasons, the local union chose alcohol as a rallying point. Because boycotting the liquor outlet did not directly affect production, management could not declare it illegal and seek a court injunction. The workers believed that the boycott would nevertheless deal a blow to management profits. Furthermore, the new breed of workers tended to see black drunkenness as a strategy deliberately used by whites to keep blacks in submission. Supporters of the boycott insisted that "we are not here to drink, but to earn money for our families!" Such arguments won unanimous approval at the union meeting.

The first day of the boycott, 5 November 1985, the bar was empty. The next day a group of traditionalist "Mpondo" workers marched into the liquor outlet clad in sheets and heavily armed and sat down to drink.[9] Nothing happened. Next day the bar was as busy as ever, with all the regulars back at their customary stations. The boycott was over. When Mlamli Botha (himself from Pondoland, but also a union leader) spoke to the "Mpondo" boycott-breakers, they admitted their fault in going against the decision of the union meeting, but insisted that if there was to be another boycott, the union should allow a day for the heavy drinkers to lay in a stock of liquor to tide them over.

Two weeks later, on 19 November, a second liquor boycott aborted when, in its enthusiasm, the union meeting ignored the informal terms negotiated with the strike-breakers and called for immediate action. By its precipitous action in ignoring the Mpondo drinkers request and simply belaboring them at the meeting, the local union succeeded in alienating not only the toughs of the Mpondo dance-team, but virtually the entire Mpondo (and much of the Bomvana and Baca) community on the mine. The more traditionalist Xhosa-speakers were outraged. In retrospect, the local union had made a most serious strategic error.

This time, "Mpondo" drinkers felt no moral obligation to respect the boycott call, meeting or no meeting. The only sanction now was a threat of coercion from union militants. That threat they were happy to meet in their own belligerent style. On Friday, 21 November, armed and clad in the white sheets that constituted Xhosa battle-dress, the Mpondo dance-team once again marched into the liquor outlet (unhindered by the mine police) and broke the boycott a second time. Within an hour a motley group of regular drinkers from various groups on the mine were back at their favorite tables in the outdoor enclosure near the bar.

The local branch of the union, whom management regarded as unruly "agitators," were by far the most representative group on the mine, earning respect and representing just and proper order for the large majority of workers—including even the least proletarianized amongst them. Furthermore, for most workers, local management had lost any shred of legitimacy and maintained its hegemony by racheting up the level of coercion in order to maintain the barest consent from most of their black employees. Mpondo grievances against the union represented another opportunity for a local management intent on union-breaking to make use of "ethnic" divisions. This time it was more successful. From senior management's point of view, however, things got out of hand. Management forgot that traditionalist Xhosa-speakers also carried deep grievances against the workers from Lesotho (and by implication all Sotho-speakers) who had raided their lockers with management protection in the March ruckus.

Between six and seven in the evening of 21 November, the day the "Mpondo" from the rooms of the dance team "opened" the bar at Number One Vaal Reefs, a shaft steward lobbed a petrol bomb over the roof of the bar and into the drinking enclosure (AAC/VR: 2353–58). The armed "Mpondo" at once burst out of the liquor outlet and began a systematic room-by-room search for shaft stewards and other union activists. That night Ernest Kang, the Sotho chief shaft steward, was beaten up by the armed group. The other shaft stewards and union militants changed quickly out of their union T-shirts and most of them chose not to sleep in their beds that night. Several witnesses reported that the "Mpondo" claimed that they had been given immunity by management in their harassing of shaft stewards. Certainly, all witnesses agreed that the entire compound staff chose to ignore the shaft-steward hunt going on in full view for a couple of days. Nine months after the events here described, on 17 August 1987, in the midst of the three-week-long 1987 miners' strike, a shaft steward at Vaal Reefs Number One mentioned in a handwritten message to the NUM head office that: "Mr. de Graeve [the white shaft personnel officer] stated that the blacks won't go on strike because he organized the faction fight instead." De Graeve figures nowhere in the Bregman records, but very few of the white local management testified before the commission, and there is no reason to doubt that his shadowy figure initiated the events at Number One.

On the night of Saturday, 22 November, two men were killed: Patrick Masela, a Xhosa-speaker from the Western Transkei, who was not a shaft steward but "was always among us" and led the songs at union meetings, and Alton Mhlamvu, a Zulu-speaking shaft steward who also sang with the "comrades." Mhlamvu was killed in the street in the mine village for married couples, and there is little evidence about how he died. Patrick Masela was battered to death in a most gruesome fashion on the stairs of a compound room.

After Masela's death security men moved about from room to room, ostensibly investigating, but instead, according to Matshepe Mokheti, "asking us why we were not chasing the shaft stewards" (AAC/VR: 3693–94), Some answered, because "they are our representatives," but most made no reply. That night Mokheti did not sleep. Instead, he said, he was "sitting, watching what is going to happen." No doubt few of the compound residents slept very well. Next morning, on Sunday, 23 November, the groups of Xhosa-speakers who had been hunting for shaft stewards left through the back gate of the compound, near the liquor outlet, for one last house-to-house search of the married quarters where Mlamvu had been killed. They were armed and clad in white sheets and said as they left that "all people who 'tete' [speak with clicks], that means all Xhosa speaking people," should join them (AAC/VR: 3706). Those who stayed in the compound, they said, would be dealt with on their return.

Apparently this was the point at which the hunt for shaft stewards took on a consciously ethnic dimension. Only those who spoke Xhosa were included in the last stages of the attack on shaft stewards. The reasons for the shift are somewhat obscure. Perhaps the "Xhosa" resented that they had been left to do the dirty work for the entire multi-ethnic band of drinkers whose peace had been disturbed by the petrol bomb, or perhaps they were unhappy that they had been left to break the liquor boycott alone. Their ethnic solidarity may have been deliberately primed by local management. Most important, I think, the looting of Xhosa-speakers' lockers during the March faction fight still rankled with the Mpondo, who now had management support and were no doubt determined to right that perceived wrong.

Some other Xhosa-speakers followed the leaders to the married quarters, numbering in the end about four hundred persons. Sotho-speakers armed hastily (AAC/VR: 3747–828, 2889–973). At this point they were joined by the many "Xhosa" who had chosen not to go to the married quarters and who therefore also felt threatened by the return of the vengeful Mpondo-led mob. Having set a guard at the liquor outlet gate, this armed group ("most of the Sothos . . . a big group") waited silently just inside the main gate of the compound for the return of the "Mpondo." "There was no whistle blown, we were standing there . . . only standing there, guarding," said Mokheti (AAC/VR: 3742, 3749): "When they entered the hostel they found us standing next to room 16. . . . We wanted only to see whether it is true that we were going to be attacked together with the Xhosas that remained with us."

As they came through the gate, the vanguard of the Xhosa-speaking group saw the armed and largely Sotho-speaking crowd standing and waiting. At once, one of the Mpondo sounded on his horn, the others responded with a Sotho whistle, and the two groups ran toward one another and met in a flurry of action. Two Xhosa-speakers died on the spot and the "Mpondo" withdrew, encircled the compound, and entered again at the back gate. At this point, for reasons that are obscure, Xhosa-speakers who had been left in the compound switched sides and drove

Sotho-Tswana speakers out of the hostel. The hunt for shaft stewards had become a full-scale faction fight. Mine security officers arrived and placed their armored vehicles at the hostel gate, effectively keeping the "Sotho" from retaliating. Fouche, the chief security officer, entered the compound and found armed and white-sheeted Mpondo immediately inside the gate and a motley group of Xhosa-speakers farther back. For the rest of the night, members of the mine security patrolled the compound and escorted out two non-Xhosa-speaking workers who had barricaded themselves in their rooms when the fight started. Meanwhile, the Mpondo systematically raided the lockers of their Sotho-speaking enemies.

In the morning, when everyone was marched to the adjacent soccer stadium, the latter were understandably upset about having been locked out of the compound and having heard their lockers being smashed for much of the night. They also feared that their antagonists, disarmed in the soccer stadium, would have hidden weapons in the hostel to use at a later date. Eventually, however, they reluctantly agreed to make peace. Everyone was searched on the way back into the compound, and the next day, while workers were underground, security and the mine police broke open lockers and searched thoroughly for weapons. Security filled more than one tip-truck load with weapons found in and around Number One that day. For twelve days, an uneasy calm descended on the compound.

On 5 December, a different faction fight, this time between "Mpondo" and a combination of "Xhosa" and "Sotho" (notice again how on different mines ethnicity continues to be perceived differently), started on the neighboring compound at Number Two Shaft. It seems that the Mpondo dance team initiated the conflict on that compound, but there are few details. Refugees poured into Number One compound. On the night of 6 December, a fight started in the liquor outlet at Number One, apparently because a worker from Lesotho accosted a Mpondo wearing a shirt he claimed had been taken from his locker on 23 November. At once, Xhosa-speakers attacked the Sotho in Number One compound and drove them out through the main gate. The "Xhosa" conducted mopping-up operations throughout the compound. Nine persons were killed, seven of them from Lesotho, one Tswana and one Baca. Sotho-speakers had been taken by surprise. They were afraid to return to the compound and when management gave all who refused to work the ultimatum of going home, it was citizens of Lesotho who availed themselves of the opportunity. Two-thirds of the 700-odd workers who resigned were Sotho, whereas only about seven percent of the Xhosa-speakers left the mine.

The Bregman commission heard insufficient testimony on the 6 December affair at Number One to enable careful analysis. We have only two full accounts—those of Fouche (AAC/VR: 525–50) and Matsepe Mokheti (AAC/VR: 3845–922). While neither could explain how the fighting began, episodes from the stories of each of them once again cast doubt on primordial explanations of such "tribal" strife. They point up how everyday attachments and obligations cut across "ethnic" allegiances in myriad ways. Even in the midst of collective violence, cross-cutting everyday commitments cast doubt on totalistic primordialist assumptions.

Mokheti reported that although workers from Lesotho were not happy about the way security had handled the 23 November affair, they certainly did not expect trouble on 6 December. When Xhosa-speakers attacked, some of them were asleep, others were in the change houses—"we were divided, we were scattered." People ran away, jumping walls and diving through windows. Mokheti, who was cornered in the quadrangle at Section 13, watched a compatriot being butchered. Another was already lying dead beside him. Mokheti himself escaped by slipping down a side passage—and then he got away only because of the kindness of one of the Mpondo. As he said (AAC/VR: 3851–53): "I managed to go through that passage because one Pondo called Goduka stopped these 'people from attacking me and then I was able to manage to go through that passage. . . . I believe they would have killed me. . . . [Goduka was not a personal friend of mine, but I did help him] by sewing his pair of trousers and [he] did not have any money so [I] told him to forget the debt. . . . [He] went through that passage with me and . . . he instructed me to run. . . . I ran.' Thus did Mokheti's 'sideline' and the generosity with which he practiced it, save his life."

This account of Mokheti's rescue by a Xhosa-speaking acquaintance should come as no surprise to readers of this essay, where the contextual nature of collective violence has been so carefully argued. However, Fouche, the security officer, who fully accepted primordial accounts of "tribal" violence, was astonished when those "Sotho" who had opted to resign from the mine were escorted into the compound to collect their belongings. He told the story as follows (AAC/VR: 547–48):

When we entered the hostel I did not see one weapon, I did not see people moving around. As a matter of fact they were all sitting. . . . And I really could not understand it, up to today I cannot understand it. When those Sothos went out of that hostel they greeted some of the Pondos and Xhosas with their hand when they walked out with their belongings. Do not ask me why, I just cannot clarify it. They were friends, they were really friends in the hostel when we took them in. . . . [A] man coming out of the room with his . . . goods in a bundle in a blanket over his shoulder, he will go to a man who is sitting in the hostel who must be a Pondo or a Xhosa, talking to him, shaking hands and leaving. I saw a lot of them doing it.

Conclusion

What is most interesting about the Bregman testimony is the extent to which, in the midst of the apparent chaos of "tribal" or "racial" strife, a wider sense of social order prevailed. Ethnic violence, in this case, and I would submit in almost all cases, is not free-floating, uncontrollable, or indiscriminate. Instead, as I have argued, it is focused, strategic and deliberate, for all the powerful sense of solidarity that fuels it. Indeed, in the contemporary situation at Vaal Reefs, management's union-bashing strategies set ethnic solidarities over against the authority of the new union local organization. When ethnic conflict erupted on the mine, however, senior local management washed their hands of responsibility, either claiming the inevitability of primordial "tribal" sentiment or, more frequently, blaming the union.

What is most surprising about the evidence, however, is the cogency of the sense of order which continues to structure even situations of apparently primordial ethnic violence. Compounds have been presumed to be tinderboxes for "tribal" conflict rooted in the alienation of the "inmates'" existence. Why then does "law" keep coming up in the testimony of the mine workers themselves? Although the authorship of the "law" (*umteto*) differs in the different periods, "laws" as "proper ways of acting" both constrain and encourage black worker action at every point. Indeed, perhaps the most important everyday function of the NUM is to generate such "laws" (*imiteto*), which hold workers accountable and bind them to a common purpose, at the same time that it represents their interests to management. Management reactions are increasingly seen as despotic, arbitrary, "lawless" in both policy and practice. The law of the union, on the other hand, is representative because it is generated from the "meeting," and respect for the decisions of the "meeting" extends even to those who dislike their effects. Of course, ethnic solidarities and the "laws" which establish social order have both been important taken-for-granted terrains for strategy in the struggle for power on the mines. Ethnic conflicts and solidarities on the mines have always presupposed a wider social order, management-imposed in the past, but now increasingly in the hands of the union.

Divide-and-rule can be an important strategy in the maintenance of control. However, management is discovering that the exacerbation of ethnic divisions on the mines can have seriously deleterious effects on production. It is clear from minutes of meetings held with branch and national representatives of the NUM after the 6 December fight, that top management panicked at the massive loss of experienced Sotho workers who chose to leave the mine (AAC/VR: 11/12/86, 14/12/86). Indeed, with the decay of the old compound manager/*induna* system, as a matter of policy and of fact, the union is management's only recourse when its downward communication system disintegrates.

Anglo-American top management would like a working relationship with the union. However, such a relationship implies a different and much more democratic philosophy of management on the ground at the local level than has ever existed on the mines before. Power-sharing, which is time-consuming and may interfere temporarily with production, does not come easily to mine managers accustomed to absolute rule, and even less easily to local white and black officials and security officers—not to mention their buddies in the South African Police. But the old days when management could impose *imiteto* and force workers to strategize within the parameters of management authority have gone for good—if they ever existed in pure form. Unionized African mine workers have created new *imiteto* amongst themselves. These new "laws" are entrenched in the (more or less) open debate of union meetings which empower shaft stewards to talk back to managers and demand compromises from them. Such a democratic style is anathema to old-style local managers (many perceive it as revolutionary agitation), and they do their best to manipulate latent divisions to disrupt the union. The problem for local managers is that if they are successful in using conservative workers to challenge union organization, the resulting chaos makes rational management impossible.

The cases in this paper have ranged from early examples of ethnic violence on the mines, which are little more than mentioned in archival records, to a detailed account of a full-scale event whose ramifications persist to the present day. In all this material—and the argument becomes more convincing as more detailed testimony becomes available—there has been no need to fall back on primordial, "Africanist" explanations rooted in aggressive instinct or violent emotion. Individual violence may sometimes have libidinal roots, and people certainly identify powerfully with perceived group interests and solidarities, but ethnic violence has a logic which implies strategic choices, brutalized and brutalizing, perhaps, but directed to sensible purposes. Indeed, opting for violence is often an act of moral outrage at entrenched injustice that is itself violently imposed. Ethnicity, however, can also be manipulated strategically by the powerful for their own unscrupulous ends. The old-style ethnic violence on the mines, constrained as it was by the sport-like *umteto* of stick-fighting societies and the heavy hand of management control, now threatens to get out of hand as management's strategic use of ethnic violence confronts the union's new order on the mines.

Of course, participatory democracy, so typical in African village societies, can suppress dissent and lead to intimidation in larger groups. On the one hand, those of us whose own practices presuppose an intense degree of individualism must be careful not to overlook the communitarian sense in which African mine workers may have willingly (if not always eagerly) accepted decisions which they personally disliked for the sake of what was perceived to be the common good, often despite the particular interests of certain (even "ethnic") groups. On the other hand, a stress on decisions of "meetings" as "lawful" has the potential to paper over real divisions and differences of interest which may emerge later as dangerously disruptive—especially in situations where outside powers consciously exploit such divisions to further their own interests.

Senior management and union leadership alike tend to hold each other responsible for actions of the other's subordinates when they clearly have no intention of disciplining their own. Given the rapid growth of the union, its popular democratic principles, and the constraints under which it is obliged to operate, and given management's aspiration to firm control, it seems to me that management must bear the primary responsibility in such cases. This is a responsibility which it tends to eschew in the interest of an imposed order which simply sets the scene for renewed conflict. I suspect that similar conclusions could be drawn from the role of the de Klerk government and the South African Police in "black-on-black" violence between 1985 and 1994.[10] Matters have quieted down on Anglo-American mines since management and the union signed a code of conduct. Time will tell whether the recent elections will have a similarly chastening effect on "ethnic" violence on the national scene.

NOTES

Acknowledgments: An earlier version of this paper was published in the *Journal of Southern African Studies* 18, 3, September 1992. In its present form, much of it has been culled from my 1994 book with Vivienne Ndatshe, *Going for Gold.* That work provides a wider context for understanding black miners' lives, although the focus of the argument regarding ethnic violence in this paper is more pointed than in the book and owes much to the discussion at the States of Violence conference.

1. Structural violence and hegemonic control in South African mine work and mine compounds are discussed in *Going for Gold* (Moodie and Ndatshe 1994: 44–118).

2. For useful discussions and critiques of primordialist notions of ethnicity, see Eriksen (1993) and Thompson (1989). Hank Johnston (1985) insists on the importance of what he calls "primordial ethnic identity" in the pre-mobilization phase of Catalonian nationalism, stressing the importance of pre-existing solidarities in response to ethnic competition theory (Olzak and Nagel 1986), but in redressing a balance he is nonetheless far from Malan's reified primordialism. Royce's (1982) notion of "ethnic identity" is closer to that of Malan, and reifications of "culture" abound in contemporary American popular culture. In fact, Malan's book strikes me as peculiarly "American" in its ambience.

3. On a more individual level, corporal punishment ("beatings" of youth by elders and women by men) was a standard aspect of all African societies. Such punishments were seen as character-forming and important for the maintenance of social order.

4. For a nuanced account of the situational nature of ethnic identities and their implication in power relationships between men and women in the countryside in Northern Natal, see David Webster's superb essay (1991).

5. The recollection of a feud between Mpondo and Sotho is not supported by surviving archival documents. Almost certainly it stems from a pattern that began in 1974.

6. For a classic account of African understandings of legal processes (based on fieldwork in Botswana) see Comaroff and Roberts (1981).

7. Crush, Jeeves, and Yudelman (1991), provide a full discussion of changes in the mine labor force.

8. For alternative accounts of the events on Vaal Reefs Number One, see the Report of the Bregman Commission of Enquiry (1987: 44–126), and Shanafelt (1989). The transcript of evidence to the Bregman Commission (cited as AAC/VR) is available on microfilm from the Center for Research Libraries.

9. On Vaal Reefs Number One at this time there were relatively few Mpondo— no more than 200—but they had not been simply absorbed into the Xhosa-speaking community. Rather, in typical Mpondo style, they maintained an organized identity as Mpondo. Mlamli Botha, for instance, was no traditionalist, but he

seems to have known his Mpondo home-fellows quite well. However, although the boycott-breaking and shaft-steward-hunting group of workers are called "Mpondo" in the records, it is clear from the evidence that, while the majority of them were from Pondoland, they had been joined by rural toughs from other parts of the Transkei, perhaps because they were all members of the dance team. Once again, the apparent impermeability of ethnic boundaries is revealed as mythical (a charter myth for the majority of those from Pondoland, no doubt, but a myth nonetheless).

10. For useful discussions of contemporary township violence which follow the lines of my argument in this paper, see Segal (1991) and Sitas (1992).

REFERENCES

Archival Sources

AAC/VR. Transcript of Evidence to the Bregman Commission, 1986–1987, microfilm at Yale University Library.
BBNA. Blue Book on Native Affairs.
NA. Files of the Department of Native Affairs (early years), National Archives, PTA.
NGI. Evidence to the Native Grievances Inquiry (also called the Buckle Commission), National Archives, PTA (fragmentary).
NLB. Government Native Labour Bureau, Transvaal Archive.
NTS. Files of the Department of Native Affairs, National Archives, PTA.

Books and Articles

Argyle, J. n.d. "Explaining Faction Fights." Unpublished paper, about 1987.
Beinart, W. 1992. "Political and Collective Violence in Southern African Historiography." *Journal of Southern African Studies* 18, 3.
Comaroff, J. L. and S. Roberts, 1981. *Rules and Process: The Cultural Logic of Dispute in an African Context.* Chicago: University of Chicago Press.
Crush, J., A. Jeeves, and D. Yudelman. 1991. *South Africa's Labor Empire.* Boulder: Westview Press.
Eriksen, T. H. 1993. *Ethnicity and Nationalism.* London and Boulder: Pluto Press.
Gordon, R. 1978. "The Celebration of Ethnicity: A Tribal Fight in a Namibian Mine Compound." In, B. M. du Toit, ed., *Ethnicity in Modern Africa.* Boulder: Westview Press.
Guy, J. and M. Thabane. 1987. "The Ma-Rashea: A Participant's Perspective." In, B. Bozzoli, ed., *Class, Community and Conflict.* Johannesburg: Ravan.

Haysom, Nicholas. 1987. *The Rise of the Right-Wing Vigilantes in South Africa.* Johanesburg: Johanesburg Centre for Applied Legal Studies. University of Witwatersand (Occasional Paper No. 10).

James, Wilmot. 1991. *Our Precious Metals: African Mine Labor in Modern South Africa.* Capetown: David Philip.

Johnston, H. E. 1985. "Catalan Ethnic Mobilization: Some 'Primordial' Revisions of the Ethnic Competition Model." *Current Perspectives in Social Theory* 6.

Johnstone, F. A. 1990. "Quebec, Apartheid, Lithuania and Tibet: The Politics of Group Rights." *Telos* 85.

Leatt, J., P. Zulu, M. Nchewe, M. Ntshangase, and R. Laughlin. 1986. *Reaping the Whirlwind? Report on a Joint Study by the National Union of Mineworkers and the Anglo American Gold Division on the Causes of Mine Violence.* Johannesburg: NUM and Anglo American Corporation (version including interview protocols).

McNamara, J. K. 1985. *Black Worker Conflicts on South African Gold Mines, 1973-1982.* Ph.D. dissertation, University of the Witwatersrand.

Malan, R. 1990. *My Traitor's Heart.* New York: Vintage.

Moodie, T. D. 1986. "The Moral Economy of the Black Miners' Strike of 1946." *Journal of Southern African Studies* 13, 1.

Moodie, T. D. and Vivienne Ndatshe. 1992. "Town Women and Country Wives: Migrant Labour, Family Politics and Housing Preferences at Vaal Reefs Mine." *Labour, Capital and Society* 25, 1.

———. 1994. *Going for Gold.* Berkeley: University of California Press.

Moore, Barrington. 1978. *Inequality: The Social Bases of Obedience and Revolt.* White Plains, NY: M. E. Sharp.

Olzak, S. and J. Nagel. 1986. *Competitive Ethnic Relations.* Orlando: Academic Press.

Royce, A. P. 1982. *Ethnic Identity: Strategies of Diversity.* Bloomington: Indiana University Press.

Segal, L. 1991. "The Human Face of Violence: Hostel Dwellers Speak." *Journal of Southern African Studies* 18, 1.

Seidman, G. 1994. *Manufacturing Militance.* Berkeley: University of California Press.

Shanafelt, R. 1989. "Worker Solidarity, Differentiation, and the Manipulation of Ethnicity: Conflict at Vaal Reefs, 1984–1986." Typescript. University of Florida, Gainesville.

Sitas, A. 1992. "The Making of the 'Comrades' Movement in Natal, 1985–1991." *Journal of Southern African Studies* 18, 3.

Thompson, R. H. 1989. *Theories of Ethnicity.* New York, Westport, Conn., and London: Greenwood Press.

Webster, D. 1991. "*Afafazi Bathonga Bafihlakala:* Ethnicity and Gender in a KwaZulu Border Community." *African Studies* 50, 1&2.

Violence in the Big House:
The Limits of Discipline
and the Spaces of Resistance

Charles Bright

Because prisons are both producers and containers of violence, the problem of violence in prison poses difficult analytic, as well as custodial, conundrums. If I choose to emphasize the "pains of imprisonment," the deprivations, brutalities, and unrelieved grimness of life inside, and make this the framework for considering prison violence, I identify myself as liberal and humane, and presage an argument about the structural evils of the institution. If, on the other hand, I stress instead the viciousness of modern-day criminals, their wicked, mean spirited, and incorrigible natures, or the violent, dysfunctional worlds from which they spring, I establish myself as tough-minded and stern, and begin an argument for the effective institutional management of bad people. The latter position, which sees violence as imported to the prison by its inhabitants, focuses attention on the individual rather than structural causes of violence.[1] This puts the spotlight on violence among prisoners—the stabbings, assaults, rapes, and bullying that give vent to violent dispositions crammed together unwillingly behind the walls. The former position, by contrast, looks past incidental and isolated acts of violence to the structural determinants of violence *in* prison. This draws attention to the more collective manifestations of inmate frustration and communal grievance, especially violence directed at prison keepers, and ends up focusing on the problem of prison riots.[2] Both points of departure are loaded with remnants of old arguments and gauged to political preferences; neither provides much insight into the effects of custodial, or official violence in the production of inmate violence, and either can be made to fit the available evidence, which is sparse, incomplete, and difficult to compare.[3]

Behind the walls, violence materializes in two basic ways, along the fault line between keeper and kept and in intramural conflicts among prisoners. A "successful adjustment" to the institution, which custody demands of all inmates, is full of unwanted rubs and unfamiliar gratings that hone resentment and foster violent encounters. The techniques of control—of regimentation, surveillance, and punishment—bear down upon inmates as verbal harassment, shake-downs, strip-searches, "tickets," disciplinary hearings, losses of privilege, beatings, chainings, and the hole. These are all designed to establish dominion over prisoners, to force them to accept their fate and what the institution has in store for them. But while this official violence may impose compliance, it breeds, at the same time, deep hostility among the incarcerated who, perhaps inevitably, "reject their rejecters."[4] Prisoners fight back, but they also duck, dissimulate, drag out, and sham compliance, swallowing a lot of rage in the process. These accumulations of bile are then spit out, in moments of desperation or bravado, as acts of violence directed at authorities, at each other, and at themselves. Because power relations in prison are so asymmetrical, inmate resentment towards their keepers generally gets displaced laterally along interior channels of expression where it becomes ever more compressed in the narrow and unyielding spaces behind the walls. Prisons ooze a kind of anchorless anger. A pervasive undercurrent of violence physically charges all encounters among prisoners, conditioning the organization of space, property, sex, and status inside. Many felons with no history of violence outside commit violent offenses inside. Sometimes authorities see violence among prisoners as an acceptable alternative to violence directed at themselves, but at all times prisons must deploy a panoply of deeper sanctions—the "hole," the adjustment center, the "maxi-maxi" units—to manage the violence generated by incarceration itself.

One could leave it at that. Prisons are nasty places; a lot of hard and wicked people are sent there, and the institution must deploy force to manage such a menacing assemblage. This would direct our attention to the managerial discussions that have long been a part, and now seem to dominate, the penological literature.[5] But if we want to problematize prison violence, we must grapple with a formidable tradition in American sociology that has made the prison a kind of microcosm of society, and prison violence a force of functional coherence inside. Indeed, whether prison violence is generated inside, by the peculiar pressures of the institution, or imported from the streets by convicted felons carrying their violent ways with them, has long been, at least implicitly, at the center of scholarly debate about the prison.[6] An earlier and extremely influential tradition treated the prison as a separate society, cut off and bounded by walls, behind which flourished a distinct culture, with its own rituals and argot, that socialized convicts to deviant stances and blocked all attempts to change or rehabilitate them. A later generation of revisionists, responding to changes in the legal status of prisoners and to the growth of gangs inside, preferred to emphasize the continuous traffic of people and cultural influences moving between the cellblocks and the streets. They treated the prison as part of society, not a separate world, its interior culture suffused with the mores and practices of the world outside which, imported into the prison, remained so strong and were so continuously replenished that the prison had little if any effect on its charges, one way or the other.

These sociologies of prison have always been chiefly preoccupied with what works, or with finding explanations for the apparent, and seemingly persistent failure of the prison to reform its charges. They thus adopt, implicitly, a custodial frame of reference, noting official violence, but treating it not as a systemic feature of prisons, but as only a woeful lapse or lack of professionalism that will be eliminated with the progress of penology (itself implicitly assumed). Ultimately the answer to the question "Does violence in prison arise from the structure of the institution or from the behavioral dispositions of its inhabitants?" is bound to be "a bit of both," and thus the discussion tends to go in circles. The prison deploys violence to suppress violence by violent felons which is, at least in part, a response to their being in prison. This underwrites the prevailing functionalism of the earlier sociologies, in which violence was read instrumentally—as marking boundaries, shaping expectations, enforcing accommodations, conditioning social roles, and in all, forging a separate society behind the walls. In recent years, as sociologies have come to stress the porous and interactive nature of prison society, they have treated prison violence as an import from outside, and have become increasingly oriented to the custodial preoccupations of control: violence (among inmates, that is) must be assumed, given their wicked natures; its control reflects the capacity of prison managers to govern their institutions effectively, its spread marks the interruptions in the patina of custodial control that must be closed. Thus the rationally deployed violence of the keepers becomes the only appropriate antidote to the irrational impulses of the kept.

Alternatively, we could develop a more anthropological approach and turn the discussion of violence into a reflection on resistance. Prisons are especially dramatic sites of domination, and their inmates (who also happen to be criminals) can be seen as locked in the position of the powerless and downtrodden everywhere, deploying the weapons of the weak against their all-powerful masters. Resistance—less perhaps a social movement among prisoners than the collective effect of the seething hostility and defiance produced by incarceration itself—takes shape, following Scott,[7] in "sequestered settings where, in principle, a shared critique of domination may develop." The act of scratching out "hidden transcripts" beyond the gaze of authority can be seen as, first and foremost, an act of negation, but from the marginal autonomies of "safe speech," subordinates can mobilize counter-understandings that transform the rhetoric and promises of authority into claims and entitlements that can sometimes inflect the regimes of domination into spheres of potential empowerment. This helps move discussion, at least partially, from the sources of violence to a consideration of its effects. But prisoners are obviously not peasants, and the cellblock cannot be made over into a communal village. Because authority is "right in your face," the space for action—even for a limited personal privacy—is extremely limited in prison, and the "sequestered sites" beyond surveillance where collective acts of negation can take place or transcripts hidden are extremely hard to find and easily disrupted. Perhaps for this reason, prisoners rarely feel the need to mask their resentment at being in prison, and their defiance is often a full-throated expression of verbal aggression and violent sentiments.

Moreover, the equation that makes resistance a necessary obverse of domination establishes a pathway of reduction which we ought to avoid: if resistance is regarded as an essential category in prison, it is tempting to interpret all forms of violence—even verbal aggression, pointless acts of intimidation, and idle cruelty—in terms of the eternal cold war stand-off between keeper and kept. A circle then closes around a circle: violence that is inevitable, given the combination of official domination *and* inmate resistance, must arise from either (or both) the structural contradictions of the prison or (and) the violent nature of its inhabitants.

In what follows, I want to resist a functional sociology and a structural anthropology, while appropriating the insights of both. The whole essay is in many ways a meditation on resistance, and I have drawn heavily on the early sociologies of prison to frame my more historicized discussion. Since general models of the prison apply generally to all cases, but to none when encountered in "real time," I want to draw on work I have done in the history of a single penitentiary, the state prison at Jackson, Michigan, in order to develop a historical context for the recurrent violence of prison. In doing so, I have tried to see in the rich sociological tradition less a movement toward some clarified ideal-type—"the" prison—than a commentary on, or series of historically conditioned snapshots of, a continuously changing institution. At the same time, I have been concerned with recapturing the agency of prisoners, not as something derived from structures or inherent in criminal essences, but as the work of incarcerated people, compelled very much against their wills to carve out a life for themselves in the perpetual din, crowding, scarcity, indignities, and danger of prison, and to defend these "life spaces" against the continual pressure that custodial containment brings down upon inmate inventiveness. This enterprise has collective or communal implications but it is also, first and foremost, a desperately lonely and isolated struggle. To establish the precarious interplay between individual defiance and collective resistance, I will turn, first, to the autobiography of one prisoner.

Finally, in trying to keep the many-sidedness of prison violence open and to set my analysis of it among the prisoners, I have been led to consider, less the communal formation of "hidden transcripts" than the more complex Brechtian maneuvers of space-taking and self-activity which Alf Ludtke, in another context, has called *Eigensinn*.[8] Indeed, the practice of cooperating while holding out, getting along without going over, playing the game without buying into it—seeking a space to be that is, also, neither in resistance nor in complicity—captures, in prison, precisely that ambivalence of compliance that Ludtke saw as fundamental to the patchwork of appropriation and response, acceptance and distance, that defines "workers' spaces" as their own; being by oneself or with one's mates, but in all events, "'winning distance' from the commands or norms from above and from the 'outside.'" *Eigensinn* ("self-reliance" in Ludtke's translation) suggests the tenuous balancing act, *within* oppositional stances, between individual toughness and collective grievance. This is not only an implicit space in prison life, a zone of non-acquiescent resignation or non-compliant consent (which prison authorities actually promote in their oft-repeated, twin injunctions to "get with the program" and "do your own time"), but it exists precisely at the intersection of compliance and defiance where the tatty embattled worlds of inmates, wrested in the teeth of surveillance, confront the all-powerful resources of authority, and where intramural, often individual, violence among prisoners finds its commonality in more polymorphous forms of grumbling, back-talking, conniving, pilfering, evasion, and sabotage—*the effects* of which amount to a collective refusal of the prison and its minions. This opens a way of seeing violence in prison, not in terms of causes or sources, but rather of spaces and the possibilities these spaces create for the practice, individually and collectively, of self-reliance.

Violence in the Panopticon: The Case of Jack Abbott

"[V]ery few people know much about violence in prisons," Jack Abbott told Norman Mailer in the first of a remarkable series of letters from *In the Belly of the Beast*.[9] At the time, Abbott was well past thirty, and except for a six-month hiatus between sentences when he was eighteen, and a six-week spree when he escaped from the Utah State Penitentiary, he had been incarcerated since he was twelve. He got his education in prison, learned to read and write in prison, ploughed his way through the classics of Western culture and philosophy in prison, and became a disciple of Marx. He was, as he said, "state-raised," with a vocabulary he had mostly never heard spoken and an ability to write with powerful clarity about his predicament. And as his letters make plain, he was a permanent rebel, always defiant, repeatedly trying to escape, frequently in solitary confinement (fourteen of his twenty-five years in prison), and continuously on what he called "the captain-doctor-broken-rule merry-go-round."[10] He writes of all this as a kind of ritual ordeal in which physical toughness and willpower became exercises in self-invention and mental cleansing. He tells of ten-mile walks in a ten-foot cell, of pitch black isolation units and months in the hole on starvation diet, of listening to his mind in a sensory-deprivation cell, of strip-cells, chained naked to floorboards in permanent light, hand-fed by guards and defecating on himself, of savage beatings and tear-gassing, and terrifying, mood-modifying drugs; and through it all he remained utterly and absolutely defiant, with a kind of macho-bravery and steely resolve that Norman Mailer, researching *The Executioner's Song*,[11] found utterly captivating.

Abbott was no innocent. Originally sent to prison for passing bad checks ("insufficient funds"), he committed a robbery while in flight during his escape and later killed another prisoner in a fight. But serving time on an indeterminate sentence, he was again and again passed up for parole because of his unbroken refusal to adjust and his defiance of prison authorities who tried to make him do so. And he knew this: "I have never accepted that I did this to myself . . . That is the only reason I have been in prison so long." And again: "I am not responsible for what the government—its system of justice, its prisons—has done to me. I did not do this to myself."[12] This implacable refusal to accept responsibility for his own incarceration—to "become indoctrinated" as he saw it—defied one of the key precepts of the rehabilitative or therapeutic prison of the 1960s, namely that you take responsibility for your crimes, admit you have a problem, and then work though it with the help of counseling towards parole and eventual freedom. This places Abbott's defiance in a specific historical context to which I must return. But because his defiance repeatedly postponed his parole, Abbott's continued incarceration became, in fact, something he did do to himself. Resisting "the game" in the name of dignity, personal responsibility, self-respect, or autonomy—all terms he used—only pushed him deeper into the disciplinary channels of the prison that had made him and now defined him as incorrigible. The promise of release, which would only become real if he capitulated, evaporated because he could not give way and yet remain, in his own eyes, free. Defiance of authority was the way he constituted himself as an autonomous, self-reliant individual. The contradiction was complete: Abbott was only free in the deepest recesses of disciplinary segregation.

There is in his grim story, of course, some of the implacable logic of Foucault's carceral discipline. Abbott was fully a product of the disciplinary order   a state made individual who was, also, the target of its disciplinary technique. His resistance meant nothing in this context: whatever Abbott did in defiance was duly noted, labeled, classified, converted into the typologies of criminality, sickness, or insanity, and filed. His resistance was thus securely attached to, and thereby transformed into, the codified knowledge that arose from surveillance and became an aspect of the "constituted" and thereby "known" target of further disciplinary action. Thus the delinquent Abbott was created: ". . . the little soul of the criminal, which the very apparatus of punishment has fabricated as a point of application of the power to punish and as the object of what is still called today penitentiary science."[13]

In Foucault's terms, Abbott's individuality descended upon him in the ceremonies of objectification that were at the core of disciplinary surveillance; he could not live outside the prison frame. Indeed, when Abbott finally won parole (with Mailer's vigorous intervention) and became a celebrated author, he was unable to break free of the carceral order that had made him; within six months of parole, he stabbed a waiter in a stupid argument at an all-night restaurant and went back to prison, probably forever.[14]

In these courageous, self-defeating, and in the end, almost tragic, acts of defiance, Abbott created a series of binary oppositions that enabled him to constitute himself over against his keepers who, in labeling him a troublemaker and misfit, returned the compliment in full measure. Defiance thus confronted discipline directly, not as a series of gaps or interruptions (as in Foucault's story of the judge and the vagabond[15]), but as moments of stark and intensely physical contestations, in which Jack Abbott's body—the object of power and disciplinary inscription—became also the site of deepest resistance. From this isolated space, Abbott threw a revealing light back at the panopticon which stands as the central metaphor of Foucault's disciplinary archipelago. The constant, noiseless operation of surveillance in the panopticon appealed to Foucault because, in his reading, it created permanent effects even though the act of surveillance itself was not continuous; precisely because the system operated upon the mind, grounded in an expectation of being watched and seen, it so internalized normative codes that surveillance (imagined more than real) intervened before the offense. The prisoner-criminal learned to check himself. In this way, Foucault argued, power could be intensified while coercion was lightened, its actual exercise even rendered unnecessary. Yet Abbott's defiance revealed that the smooth operation and silent effect of the panopticon only works if the person under surveillance cares (or can be made to care) very much if he is seen. The prison makes its famous claim to a surplus on the penalty (turning punishment into correction) on the assumption that the offender being punished will want to be reconciled and reunited with the society that punishes—or more precisely, that the process of surveillance, of expert knowledge and its applications in corrective discipline, will *create* a delinquent soul eager to be free and anxious to do whatever is required to secure release. The panoptic science—and Foucault's use of the panoptic metaphor—rests on the twin pillars of exclusion (punishment) and the promise of re-inclusion (correction). Abbott's refusal of the proffered terms crippled the incentives for compliance and exposed the extent to which the smooth operation of the panopticon, the very embodiment of carceral discipline, depends upon a tier of implied sanctions, the existence of which are only revealed when someone says, "I don't care what you see." By stubbornly enduring punishment, Abbott showed that, while the carceral order could not perhaps be overturned, its panoptic effects could be resisted.

He also gained from this a singular insight into the workings of violence in prison. Explaining to Mailer "the way violence is inculcated in prisoners," he spoke first of the guards, whom he always called "pigs" and about whom he could not "imagine a time I could ever have anything but the deepest, aching, searing hatred."[16] The daily humiliations—the bossing, pushing, herding, beating—were, in his view, designed to destroy him, reduce him, dominate him: "always, *always*, every guard in prison is a tyrant and prisoners are his subjects." At a personal level, this had to be resisted in the name of "dignity and sanity," without which "we would truly be broken completely." The only alternatives to defiance were insanity, suicide, or "co-existence [by which] I mean becoming a *tool* of those who govern us in prison."[17] By enduring the ferocious pressures of authority, he sheared away all traces of implication "with the man," eliminated any reservation about his refusals, and found a kind of autonomous space, by himself, where resistance was pure—not outside, but at the heart of discipline. He also enured himself in a highly gendered discourse, in which manliness, measured as toughness, found expression in flat refusals and the endurance of punishment. Abbott believed that the legendary figures in prison (and he considered himself one) were those who stood up to authority and did not buckle. Somewhat implausibly in his isolation, he made himself over into the voice of a revolutionary vanguard: "The 'working code' of a convict is at bottom to best the man, the pig. To do what he can to get his time done and get out of prison. There are some things he can't do and still be a man . . . At that point, he rebels. He has no 'revolutionary ideology,' true. But eventually he'll run into me in the hole and I'll tell him things that will clear this confusion and give his rebellion a cause. Its happening all over the country now . . . And when he rebels alone, if I see him fighting a squad of pigs on the yard or in the hole, I will never hesitate to dive in. We are brothers under the skin. His fight is my fight."[18] Even in these reveries (wherein we hear echoes from the outside), Abbott never lost sight of the deep difference between keeper and kept: "they obey violence . . . [while] a prisoner does not."[19] From inside, the cycle started with "their" violence and ended with "our" struggle for liberation.

Lest we think this is some aberrant move that leads only to the iron cage conundrums that trapped Jack Abbott, we might consider this from his contemporary, George Jackson: "What if there was nothing on earth that could be taken away from me which could result in my discomfort. What if a person was so oriented that the loss of no material thing could cause him mental disorganization? This is the free agent. He is nameless . . . without habit, without the weaknesses of the flesh . . . Only the free agent can win for us the necessary control over the direction of our unrewarding lives." And later: "Where face and freedom are concerned I do not use or prescribe half measures. To me life without control over the determining factors is not worth the effort of drawing breath. Without determination, I am extremely displeased."[20]

And a few pages on, "This is one nigger who is positively displeased." Another "state-raised" convict who embraced Marxism, Jackson, like Abbott, found in isolation the purified ground of revolution; the more custody sought to cut him off and silence him, the more he came to see himself (and to be constructed by others) as the embodiment of revolutionary struggle. As his racial self-identification and powerful evocation of the collective "us" indicate, he moved rather more quickly than Abbott from personal acts of defiance to a collective stance that spoke for others and found wide echo in the Muslim protests and insurgent movements among African American prisoners at the end of the 1960s. Yet in many ways, Jackson's politics, which for all their eloquence became pretty delusional, are less instructive than his stance: inside Soledad and San Quentin prisons, his charismatic presence and undoubted eagerness to spread the revolution carried conviction among other prisoners, less for the power of the word than because of his reputation as a brawling, strong-arm yard hustler, not afraid of a fight and willing to take on the guards. It is perhaps no surprise that his second book, *Blood in the Eye,* where Jackson began to make himself over into the revolutionary persona that had been constructed for him by outside admirers, he came to rely upon a notion of vanguard violence, the so-called "foco" theories that he borrowed from Debray and that later informed the "tactics" of the Symbionese Liberation Army, which saw the revolution arising, not from the mobilization of the people, but from the demonstration effects of insurrectionary activity carried on by a few who made revolution by practicing it before masses of witnesses.[21]

There are, of course, many avid readers of Marxism-Leninism in prison, and during the early 1970s, it was one of the tropes of the radical cult of the prisoner/outlaw to assume that collective solidarity would triumph over self-interest. But with prisoners, it rarely does. The techniques of discipline work to divide, isolate, and individualize prisoners who are no more likely to escape these entangling effects than to find positions of resistance that are outside discipline. Under the relentless pressure of custody, wrote Abbott, prisoners "are inculcated by acts of violence so constant and detailed, so thorough and relentless, as to develop a kind of defensive automatic suspicion of everyone." In the interest of control, the keepers actively foster distrust and animosity among the kept. Not surprisingly, prisoners learn to hate each other, fear each other, and above all, watch each other. Suspicious and observant, they mark every move and see each act of violence, intimidation, or humiliation; because custody is always on top of them, crowding them, peering into their spaces, they become adept at reading signs, detecting veiled signals, and sensing things in the air. Fights are rarely "out in the open" for authorities to see; violence is usually more covert, in the look, the posture, the dare, more stealthy, in passageways, the showers, and the corners of the yard, and up close, with the "shiv" or knife—that most intimate of weapons. The knowledgeable see and read the signs, right under the noses of authority, and communicate with one another through the very tension their covert violence generates. Violence, then, is a coded dialect of prison: "You try only to keep yourself together because others—other prisoners—are with you. . . . The manifestation of the slightest flaw is world-shattering in its enormity. It is as if you very discreetly passed wind in a huge stadium and suddenly the thousands of people grow silent and look at you in condemnation. This is what prisoners do to each other."[22]

In Abbott's understanding, this is how prisoners police each other, school themselves in the "hard code" of toughness, and teach newcomers how to hold out against the destructive forces of the prison, withstand the pressures of "the man," and preserve their precious, desperately narrow spaces of autonomy—or conversely, how to avoid becoming one of "the many broken men" in prison. If prisoners hold violence in high esteem, it is because violence is the means of their self-reliance, both individual and collective. "It is what makes us *effective.*" For it is through hostile encounters with each other and with their keepers that prisoners define, clarify, and make their worlds visible to themselves, in the alert gaze of witnesses, under the watchful eye of authority, and in the teeth of official hostility. Violence is a tool for measuring the spaces and testing the boundaries of self-activity and autonomy. In this context, the bold defiance of Abbott or Jackson—and their dramatic (self-)destruction—becomes a marker of the outer bounds of possibility, a tracer probing gray areas. Violence is thus a practice of self-reliance in prison, and *Eigensinn* arises from this quotidian violence to become, in turn, a condition of possibility for more dramatic acts of resistance.

Reflections on the insights of an individual can only take us so far, but a few points may be drawn here. First, and most obviously, the panoptic discipline that Foucault elaborated at the heart of his carceral archipelago draws its power from its capacity to constitute the individuals who are also the objects of discipline, and more broadly, to constitute the social domains that become also the targets of rationalized intervention. There is no site of resistance outside this disciplinary process. But we should bear in mind that what in Foucault's compelling imagery swarms out across other social institutions and diffuses into the microcircuits of social relations, becoming ever more omnipresent and silent, is also, simultaneously, concentrated behind prison walls. The small irritations and anxieties that you and I may feel about omnipresent surveillance and implied or panoptic disciplines become congealed into powerful hostilities and paranoiacs inside the prison. It is from this violence that self-reliance arises and its spaces are defended, not vice-versa. For even as the panoptic effects are intensified behind the walls, the gaps and limits of discipline are also made more plain to see by the very activity of taking space and watching how far it may stretch. Where little is held in reserve and the realm of possibility most constrained, human ingenuity becomes, as it were, concentrated as well and more sharply focused on the forces bearing down. Prisons are thus not only the anchors of a disciplinary archipelago extending out across society; they are also the containers of deep struggles (chaotic, perhaps aimless, usually disorganized and inchoate, often mute and muddled) between discipline and its objects.

Thus, secondly, while defiance and oppositional posturing in prison rarely deflect the dominant order—certainly cannot overthrow it and may only serve to reinforce it—it is impossible to understand how a prison works without taking seriously Lila Abu-Lughod's suggestions about the "diagnostic" possibilities of resistance.[23] We may study systems of domination themselves (their logic and operations) or how domination bears down on people (documenting oppression), but it is only when we pay close attention to how domination is contested that we actually "see" it working. And here I would press Abu-Lughod's point: for it is not just that "we" (as scholars or outside observers) can see, through resistance, how domination works; seeing, like surveillance, produces useable knowledge, and what Jack Abbott, George Jackson, and indeed all prisoners, watching each other, come to "know" about how domination works becomes, for them, in practice, a kind of oppositional surveillance that constitutes counter-identities and amplifies their abilities to contest the official regime, carve out spaces of self-activity, and survive with what Abbott called "dignity and sanity." In this context, to say that resistance does not work or only reinforces domination misses the point, by placing the limited and often contradictory effects of resistance ahead of its practice.

Yet this practice is, finally, anything but straightforward. There is no unilinear progression, no directional spiral of clarification, leading from individual defiance, to the self-policing of separate spaces, to a collective resistance of authority. The prison deploys enormous counter pressures at every point, and though, as Abbott recognized, the very ferocity of the disciplinary riposte clarifies the ground of resistance, it also disrupts inmate spaces and defeats their self-activity. Not only are oppositional practices covert and highly coded, but prison authorities, seeking a comprehensive supervision, often see resistance where there is none, readily assuming that malingering, wandering, gossiping, space-taking, and other signs of inmate self-activity betoken insubordination. Moreover, prisoners who defy a rule or challenge a guard can just as easily find their resistant stance duly noted and filed, transformed into the typologies of "childishness," "criminal disposition," "perversion," or "madness" and incorporated into the knowledge that arises from surveillance. There are no secure positions in the ever-hostile, mutual entanglement of keeper and kept. The official regime—the way it distributes prisoners, segments the day, orders carceral spaces, and calibrates routine—registers a quest for knowledge, for information about, and comprehension of, inmates that necessarily incorporates the calculations and inventiveness of the incarcerated in its program. In this sense, discipline not only constitutes its subjects, but is constituted by them. And within the official regime thus devised, prisoners inhabit the spaces, invest the order with human smells and passions, live across its categories, challenging and reshuffling its distributions, and appropriate its classifications as claims, statuses, and openings that can transform disciplinary domains into terrains of limited, but real possibility. Patterns of resistance, of space-taking and self-activity, and of individual defiance all reflect, but also inflect, the regimes of domination they face.

Sociological Interventions: A Case for History

Cast in these somewhat timeless terms, our analysis begins to echo the great sociologies of the American "big house" that flourished in the 1940s and 1950s.[24] We have situated violence in the structure of the prison, flowing from three distinct sources: the authorities use it to enforce their will upon inmates; prisoners use it to challenge and defy authority; and they deploy it against each other, both to define autonomous spaces and to align these spaces in an oppositional stance toward authority. From here we could retreat to the functionalism of the standard sociologies and seek to understand the role that violence plays in the reproduction of prison society.

Indeed, the description Abbott gives of his own dogged defiance of authority and of the hostile, tension-filled solidarity among prisoners against their keepers is a general reprise of Donald Clemmer's seminal study of "inmate culture" two score years before. For Clemmer and many of his disciples, the prison was a separate society with its own roles, argot, rituals, and solidarities. This distinct social world was made up partly from elements of the "criminal underworld" which were imported into the prison as a "thieves code" of silence and stand-offishness, but it was primarily a creation of the grating, hostile encounters between keepers and kept on the inside. The disciplinary pressure that custodians brought down upon their charges in an effort to break and control them was answered with sullen refusals, choked submissions, and suppressed rage. But the front of solidarity which the convict code put up in the face of custodial hectoring was, for Clemmer, only barely able to mask the deep hatreds and tensions that roiled among prisoners. Intra-prisoner violence became, along with gossip, taboos, and stir-wise dogmas, part of a panoply of social controls which prisoners used in organizing themselves over against authority. To some extent, in Clemmer's treatment violence among prisoners isolated them and broke up tentative expressions of solidarity, while in other respects it also simultaneously disciplined inmates to a code of defiance that presented authorities with a rejectionist front of non-compliance. Thus emerged Clemmer's matchless descriptions of the "thwarted, unhappy, yearning, resigned, bitter, hating, [and] revengeful" people behind bars,[25] and his central thesis that the key to understanding why prisons did not reform criminals lay in recognizing that any adjustment to prison life—"prisonization" in his terminology—only deepened deviant defenses, inured prisoners in anti-social behaviors, and annealed them to a life of crime.

A postwar generation of sociologists added important interactive dimensions to this grim stand-off behind the walls. To Clemmer's analysis of the resilient and impervious "inmate culture," Gresham Sykes and others added the official regime and its needs in order to complete the picture of a separate social world in the prison. With this move they exposed for analysis the tacit accommodations and trade-offs that were forged between prison subcultures and the prison administration in the interests of a peaceful and smooth-running institution. Indeed, Sykes reached the "glaring conclusion" that "despite the guns and the surveillance, the searches and the precautions of the custodians, the actual behavior of the inmate population differs markedly from that which is called for by official commands and decrees."[26] Unable to win voluntary compliance and unwilling to rely on force in all encounters, custodians fell back on an elaborate system of incentives and rewards, buying inmate cooperation and compliance in exchange for a series of marginal concessions of power. Tacitly and by degrees, custodians let prisoners "run the joint," holding sway less through the power of guns than through dense layers of personal relations, connections, and even friendships with selected inmates, often extending over many years and involving long, invisible records of reciprocity. For Sykes, this produced the central paradox of prison: "they can insure their dominance only by allowing it to be corrupted."[27]

Sykes argued for an instrumental understanding of prison violence. Custodians, with a monopoly of legitimate force, deliberately withheld it in exchange for inmate cooperation in keeping the peace; prisoners, especially those able to establish themselves as leaders in a position to broker deals, used violence internally to police the prison and enforce the contract with authorities. Just as custodians always retained an implicit threat of force if prisoners crossed the negotiated thresholds, prisoners could always resort to violence if authorities made untoward changes in the rules of the game. Actual violence was not necessary as long as the threat of violence was credible. Like nuclear deterrence, the possibility of violence made accommodation by both sides a desirable alternative to open warfare, yet the credibility of the threat depended upon a violence-laden culture, full of dare, intimidation, and show-down. The main beneficiaries of such a system, in Sykes's view, were the guards, who had ample force to call upon, and strong-armed inmates who were able to make themselves "useful" to custodians by subordinating other prisoners. It was their collusion that insured peace and organized the social world of the prison, and it was their interest in a stable accommodation that made them the most resistant to change.

These pictures of prison society, while powerful in their functional coherence and in their sharp observation of detail, remain nevertheless strangely static. Seeking to model a social whole, they tend to collapse historical time into the ceaseless, rhythmic oscillations of prison life. Abstracting back from particular cases (Clemmer studied Menard Prison, and Sykes the New Jersey Penitentiary) in search of universally applicable general statements, these studies essentialize the oppositional culture of inmate society into the abiding and recurrent "given" of prison life. The people producing this culture remain faceless and nameless, their presence acknowledged only generally, in behaviors, patterns, and dispositions. Neither of them is quite prepared to see inmate society as volitional, the product of creative actions or self-activity among prisoners, produced in specific and changing conjunctures that are neither given nor timeless.

In what follows I want to push against these sociologies in two specific ways. First, I would like to shift the focus from the sources or causes of prison violence to its effects, to see in inmate defiance and intramural violence the agency that constructs, in the face of custody, limited spaces of self-activity and autonomy within the prison. Prisoners were never in control of the terms of their lives but they were always engaged in the terms as they found them, and the spaces they created with the means at hand oscillated and shifted continuously. Thus I would like also to see these zones of self-reliance (*Eigensinn*) as historically conditioned and contingent, forming and reforming along the intersection of what custody demands in the light of its changing and not always coherent control strategies and what prisoners are able to make of the opportunities left open or made available to them by the gaps in discipline. To do this, we must move in time.

Zones of Autonomy and Regimes of Control: The Case at Jackson Prison

Late in 1944, the year Jack Abbott was born, Joseph Medley, a shambling, long-time prisoner serving thirty to sixty years for armed robbery, left the State Prison of Southern Michigan on what was called an "outside detail" and went into the town of Jackson, escorted by an Officer Freeland.[28] He was taking $800 collected in a war bonds drive in Prison Industries to the bank. He and the officer first went for breakfast and then drove over to the bank, where Medley left Freeland waiting in the car and went in to make the deposit. He never returned. Captured three months later in Washington D.C., he was charged with several robberies and a murder, for which he was eventually executed.

How could such a dangerous criminal have been let loose on the town and allowed to walk away with so much cash? Medley said, according to the press, that Jackson prison was a "damn sandbox"—"easiest thing in the world to walk away from"—and the public demanded explanations. An Attorney General's investigation quickly opened a large can of worms.

It turned out that Medley was one of about fifteen or twenty so-called "big shots" at Jackson, inmate satraps who had divided the prison into a series of overlapping rings that organized illicit activities, employed hundreds of other prisoners as gophers, go-betweens, bag-men, lookouts, and dealers, and defended their turfs and monopolies through strategic alliances, elaborate treaty systems, and gangs of enforcers. The state's investigation turned up a remarkable diversity of "scams" and "hustles" by which inmates tried to make life more tolerable or accumulate a little working capital in a society of scarcity. Some were quite legal: concession stands (for candy, tobacco, pencils, handkerchiefs) which required a pass and a "streetcorner" that could be had for a fee, split between the hall captain and the inmate clerk in charge of placements; or hobbycrafts, including canary raising, cage making, and handicrafts, which involved elaborate subcontracting and a covert traffic with outside suppliers, arranged through a "big shot" and his custodial allies. Some were illegal: loan sharking operations that handled hundreds of dollars at amazing rates of interest; pawnshops that held collateral against loans; and widespread, well-organized pilfering:

> Morris Glover [manager of the chicken farm] admits that he gave a chicken away "here and there," but he cannot account for the loss of 4000 chickens in the last three years. . . . He claims that many died, many were stolen by inmates working on the farm. He says some were taken by people who would drive by the chicken farm at night and be handed out some chickens by inmates, who took cash. On one occasion, a truckload of inmates were being taken from the farm to 16-Block to attend a movie and somebody pulled an unexpected shakedown on this truck and much contraband was found including cooked chickens, raw chickens, [live chicks], and eggs.

One officer and his wife ran the kitchen at the Jackson County Country Club, using chickens supplied covertly and at cut-rate prices by inmates.[29] Some scams were harmless but proved shocking to investigators and made lurid headlines: it was apparently possible for a prisoner to "run up" his temperature and be sent to the infirmary where an inmate nurse, for a fee, would provide a private setting and an officer, for a fee, and would leave the prisoner alone with a female visitor—there were even photographs of the curtains enclosing this "Cupid's nest for lovelorn inmates." Some were clearly big business operations: investigators figured that there were at least a dozen stills operating in the prison, mostly in industrial facilities and out-buildings, which depended on pilfered sugar from the kitchen and jars from the canning plant. Their products sold inside for $20 per gallon. Gambling and bookmaking, centered on the gym (where the athletic director took a cut) but organized throughout the institution by networks of "big shots," were even more profitable, turning over hundreds of dollars, especially on holidays and Sundays when prisoners would set up gambling shop on the yard, sometimes paying guards for an early unlock so that they could place their blankets in the best spots.

But what most alarmed the public was news that prisoners were regularly being taken into Jackson on "outside details" to visit a whorehouse, or on trips to Detroit for a baseball game and a visit to O'Larry's bar on the Westside, hangout of Detroit's notorious Purple Gang. The Deputy Warden, D. C. Pettit, and his Captain of the Guard ran a tab at O'Larry's (which was owned by the brother of the warden's inmate chauffeur) and regularly carted cases of whiskey back to the prison which were shared with inmate "big shots" in after-hours parties "with women present." State officials were most appalled by evidence of widespread collusion between keepers and kept; by the extent to which guards seemed implicated in illicit activities, directly involved in liquor production, bookmaking, gambling, and the smuggling of contraband, or aware of it and prepared, for a fee, to turn a blind eye, or parasitical upon it, using a selective enforcement of the rules to leverage a cut for themselves; by the obvious complicity of the deputy warden, whose office controlled job and cell placements, reviewed disciplinary actions, and monitored the movements in and out of the prison and who was able, through his clerks to place allies and retainers throughout the prison, protecting their monopolies in return for a cut of their take; and by the fact that the warden, Harry Jackson, a tough old-pro who had run the prison since 1925 and been largely responsible for building the new facility that had opened in 1934, apparently knew exactly what was going on and condoned it.

All these goings-on were scandalous, of course, or could be made into a scandal as they were detached from their context in the prison and re-presented in the public arena where media outrage and political posturing destroyed all attempts by the warden and his cronies to explain themselves or reclaim the narrative. "The cons ran the joint": this was the conclusion of most observers at the time and, indeed, a recurrent refrain about the "big house" penitentiary in the 1930s and 1940s. It was a damning charge when leveled at prison managers, because it turned the world of righteous distinctions upside down and disturbed the boundaries between the criminal and the law abiding that a prison was supposed to make and keep plain. But it is intriguing, too, in its suggestion that Clemmer's "oppositional culture" may have taken over, or deeply conditioned, the official regime. Indeed, a few years later Gresham Sykes seemed to explain, even normalize, these apparently deviant practices with a sturdy sociological account of the collusion between keeper and kept in the everyday operations of the "big house." Yet between the scandalously deviant and the sociologically normal lay other possible accounts. The evidence generated by the scandals at Jackson prison, mid-way between Clemmer's and Sykes' studies, suggest not timeless, but dated developments—specific, not generic, and best explained historically, not sociologically. Indeed it would seem best to read the great prison sociologies of this period not as the general laws of penal motion but as time-lapsed exposures of changes going on inside the "big house"—historically specific descriptions of the industrial penitentiary and its embattled evolution, and in particular of the openings, opportunities, and oppositional possibilities that this kind of prison offered to its inmates.

As far as I can tell, there were no inmate "big shots" at Jackson prison during the 1920s, nor anything like the highly organized internal satrapies that came to dominate the terrain inside during the 1940s. But it was during this decade that the penitentiary in Michigan became fully industrialized. By the mid-1920s, the state had commenced construction of a huge new facility at Jackson, a kind of "River Rouge" of industrial prisons, that when finished a decade later was commonly reckoned to be the largest walled institution in the world.[30] Although something of a unique departure in American corrections, this behemoth "big house" captured many general movements in the relationship of work and corrections during the early decades of this century.[31] Throughout most of the nineteenth century, moments of hard labor (often meaningless, make-work in quarries, rock piles, and coal heaps) had been carefully blended by prison managers with the rigors of reflection (silence), repentance (Bible reading) and pain (corporal punishment) in the pursuit of correction. Jackson prison, which first opened in the 1840s, never employed the segregate system of isolation and silence that was pioneered by the Quakers in Pennsylvania and later exported to France, where it shaped the reforms Foucault studied. Like penitentiaries elsewhere in the United States, Jackson prison turned early to the congregate system of gang labor employed by outside contractors on lease from the state doing mostly sweat and piece work, ostensibly under rules of silence. The driving force in these developments was not a theory of punishment or reform agenda, but profits: in the 1870s and 1880s, Jackson prison was able to pay its way using the proceeds of prison labor. But a rising population and mounting costs during the 1890s produced growing deficits, and wardens came under increasing pressure to devise new and more productive ways to use prison labor power and raise revenues. Thus in the first decades of the twentieth century, just as European (and especially British) penology was moving back toward a strict reaffirmation of segregation, silence, and make-work routines,[32] and many American prison systems were finding the productive use of inmate labor constricted by hostile trade unions,[33] Michigan prisons plunged headlong into full-fledged industrialization.

Why and how this happened is less important for our purposes than the effects of the transformation; several features bear notice. There was, first of all, a continuous and dramatic expansion of productive facilities at Jackson prison, which was owned and operated by the state, under quasi-professional management, and produced an impressive array of goods—binder twine, cloth, shirts, blankets, mattresses, cots, chairs, utensils and tools, brushes and brooms, tombstones and markers, brick and tiles, license plates and road signs, cement and canned goods—all sold competitively on the open market as well as to state agencies (the sales catalogue of Prison Industries was thick, slick, and professionally done by the institutional printing press). The rapid expansion of industrial production brought about, secondly, a notable shift in disciplinary techniques at the prison. The introduction of machine technologies and mass production techniques went hand-in-hand with the abolition of striped uniforms, whips, and the strange accouterments of the nineteenth-century custodial repertoire: the water treatment, wooden horse, wire cap, iron collar, foot clogs, treadmill, and rock pile. The last vestiges of the old silent system faded. As the prison came to replicate a factory, the key sites of discipline shifted; though corporal punishments were by no means abolished, direct physical violence, control of the body through pain, drill, and silence, became less crucial as a tool of institutional control or reformation. The regimented forms of domination associated with the lock-step shuffles and enforced silence gave way, gradually and partially, to the comparatively less rigid routines of the factory floor and machine-paced order. Global coercions, working on expectations rather than bodies, came more fully into play; a precise articulation and expanded use of parole, coupled with the inauguration of indeterminate sentencing (which gave the Parole

Board its broad discretionary powers) were used in the prison to secure inmate compliance with work routines. Until the late 1930s, the warden at Jackson retained a powerful voice in parole decisions, and by linking a good work record to the promise of release he was able to squeeze work out of inmate labor power (which was, after all, not easily cowed by the threat of the sack). Finally, this industrialization of the prison, coupled with a system of parole, was wrapped in the rhetoric of modernity and deployed as a coherent, internally consistent account of what the prison was doing, to whom, and with what effect. The prison took shiftless, thriftless criminals who had never been taught the virtues of work and never held down a steady job; it disciplined them to the rigors and rhythms of real industrial labor (work that also helped pay their room and board and thus built in them pride and self-respect); and it released them when they were deemed ready to move, smartly and under continuing supervision, into the ranks of the industrial work force and decently-paying jobs. This narrative was at the center of carceral ideologies by the 1920s.

In re-centering the carceral regime around industrial labor, the "big house" penitentiary abandoned some of the key elements of Foucault's panoptic regime: isolation, silence, the precise monitoring of movement, the compartmentalization of the body in daily routine—all gave way at least partially to a mass industrial society, in which days were divided between work/no-work, months into workdays and weekends or holidays, and inmate life was organized around the relative sociability of the shop floor. The work place in prison was actually less closely monitored—movement less regulated, spaces less closely ordered—than the home or cellblock. And it is striking how quickly the work place became the site of other activities, unassociated with the labor process or production. It was in prison industries that illicit activities were most often concentrated—the stills, the stashes of contraband, the drug dealing, the business conferences and peace negotiations, as well as the fights. It was in the movement to and from the work place, in the unmonitored halls, passageways, and paths across the yard or out onto the farms, that plans were laid, information exchanged, goods and weapons passed. The rapid expansion of prison industries, especially in the 1920s, also offered amplified opportunities for pilfering; tools, utensils, clothes, canned goods, and in the highway road camps, gasoline, tires, and spare parts, moved into and through the circuits of an inmate commodity exchange. In the 1920s, the large number of prisoners coming and going between work sites scattered over the new production facilities inside (some working night shifts), the farms outside the prison walls, the road camps and construction sites further afield, were difficult to monitor and, together with the petty venality of guards, made possible an enormous traffic in contraband goods, exchanged among prisoners and between inmates and local citizens. By all accounts, Jackson was "wide open" in the 1920s.

These might be called the "tolerated illegalities" of the industrial prison.[34] While the space for such illicit doings was probably greater at Jackson than in many other prisons for reasons specific to place and time (the peculiar role of state politics, the personality of the warden, the aggressive expansion of prison industries in Michigan, and the unusually heavy use of inmates on construction sites outside the prison), the fact of this widespread and full-blown inmate self-activity suggests how far the industrial prison expanded opportunities for prisoners to take and organize parallel spaces and to construct networks of exchange and remuneration beyond effective surveillance or direct custodial control. In the sprawling, bustling industrial plants, prisoners were able to scratch out domains of their own; as long as they worked hard and kept up production, custodians did not press too hard or look too closely at their covert activities, and inmates tried to make them as inconspicuous as possible. Though widespread and relatively flush, these enterprises remained quite decentralized and fluid; the violence associated with them tended to be sporadic and not murderous, largely it seems because there was plenty to go around and showdowns over access or turf could often be settled by expansion and redistribution. Nor were these oppositional activities marked by great defiance of authority; prison managers were clear about their carceral project, grounded in industrial discipline, and they were prepared to leave room for inmate self-activity so long as it did not compromise productive or correctional goals. This tended to channel inmate entrepreneurial (and criminal) energies into the production of parallel worlds which mimicked, tested, evaded, and resisted the formal structures of custody, without challenging custodial control. It was this pattern that Clemmer then studied and theorized.

The fact that illicit activities were so broadly tolerated suggests, in turn, that prison authorities, whatever their rhetoric, were less concerned with the consistent and unbroken applications of discipline than with appearances. It was less important that prisoners actually step up to the mark, learn regular work habits, and reform themselves than that they *seem* to do so, and in exchange for the appearance of compliance in a smooth-running institution, prison officials were willing to give something back, or at least to let the prisoners have space to pursue parallel agendas. This was, of course, a gritty, uneven, continuously tested and contested standoff, but that prisoners were not so much reformed as invited to appear so, points to a certain "lie" at the heart of discipline. Prisons were not only expressions of the disciplinary intent and character of a well-ordered, industrial society; they also embodied the lie of non-completion, of partial compliance, of cynical, self-interested and resigned consent that also continued, in the same moment, to express resistance, non-compliance, and a refusal to cave in. Inside everyone knew this, but prisoners cooperated with their keepers in the production of public testimonials of reformational success so that, outside, appearances could be maintained. The prison and its lie of compliance thus sustained an illusion that discipline was intact, when in fact most all the objects of discipline were both compliant and complaining, outwardly conformist and inwardly subversive. And it was precisely this illusion that enabled the prison to produce the characteristic delinquent of that age—the shiftless, undisciplined, thriftless (and in the time of prohibition, probably inebriated or bootlegging) layabout (probably foreign) who needed a strong dose of discipline and regular work habits to make good. This figure too was a fabrication, a composite that also contained a lie about the world, but it permitted a plausible link to be established between public images of criminals and the techniques of the corrective process, and this enabled prison managers to deploy a coherent, legitimating narrative of what they were about.

The crisis of the industrial prison in Michigan began with the depression and lasted until the early 1950s. At its most manifest level, the economic crash idled plants and laid off workers in the prison, destroying forever the dreams of self-sufficiency that had guided the industrial expansion of the 1920s and radically contracting the supply of partible resources available for illicit business. This produced two kinds of problems for prison managers and they came up with competing solutions, framing rival currents that did battle for control of Michigan corrections for over a decade. In practical terms, idleness produced control problems at the prison. The new Jackson facility, completed in 1934, was geared entirely to industrial purposes, and in the absence of work, it had to contain nearly 6,000 prisoners without the architectural means to properly segregate them or the staff resources to fully supervise them. On the other hand, the collapse of the industrial model of corrections snapped the narrative link between hard labor in prison and successful re-entry, under parole supervision and the disciplines of the labor market, to the world outside. Constructing a plausible ideological line for the correctional project required reformulating the synaptic connections between punishment and crime and rethinking what was being done to prisoners, in prison, with what putative effects.

At the prison itself, the warden and his deputies had no solution to the second problem, but they faced the custody crisis every day, at every turn. Without industrial work or the steady stream of illicit resources to stoke an informal economy and fire inmate compliance, authorities fell back on the informal circuits of power among inmates which the industrial model had fostered, seeking supplements for the vanishing industrial discipline. The sphere of inmate self-activity expanded and deepened, but within a sparser, less affluent environment and in the face of authorities who had lost a coherent account of the carceral project. This produced a more thoroughly organized, hierarchical social order inside, as rival rings scrambled to control scarcer resources and corner available markets. It was in this recomposition of power inside that the "big shots" seem to have emerged in the late 1930s; intramural struggles, apparently accompanied by considerable violence among inmates, produced tighter networks of internal subordination that the prison administration, actively seeking allies among the "strongmen," came to rely on to "keep the lid on." It was this reconfiguration of the industrial prison that Sykes then studied and theorized.

During the early 1940s, prisoners effectively colonized the day-to-day administration of the prison. In large measure, this reflected the growing role and significance of inmate clerks and office workers, whose numbers grew with depression cutbacks and wartime shortages of custodial and clerical staff and the general shrinkage of civilian employees that accompanied the collapse of industrial operations. These inmate clerks, who were usually "big shots" themselves or their loyal lieutenants, handled and mishandled much of the quotidian routine and paper traffic in the institution and were able, through these nodal points, to facilitate a much tighter, more centralized organization of inmate activities. Those who emerged on top of these reorganized power relations and could, by virtue of their clout inside, make themselves useful to hard-pressed authorities. They could now afford to "come out," as it were, and enjoy the special privileges that went with their status: the "big shots" were all locked together in 15 Block (called "Aristocrat's Row") and received regular care packages of candy, fresh fruit, and sardines ("the boys like sardines in oil, not sauce") from O'Larry's Bar in Detroit. They enjoyed immunities from custodial hassles and disciplinary actions, and they had access to forbidden pleasures—invitations to Pettit's house or lake cottage, parties with girl friends, rides in the deputy's convertible. An infamous photograph produced by the Attorney General's investigation showed nine of these "big shots," dressed neatly in white shirts and ties, lounging in the deputy's red roadster; ostensibly they were waiting tables for the wedding of Pettit's son Pinky, but the picture captured precisely the ambiguity of their relationship with the deputy warden—were they servants or friends?

One might say that Pettit and other prison officials "went over" to the cons. The deputy warden was by far the most popular official at the prison, where he had worked since 1919; he was reputed to know every inmate by name, and he took great pains to make personal contacts and follow up on individual needs. He also had his hand in everything, drawing a large, informal (in other words, criminal) income from his allies among the prisoners. He caroused with his "big shot" pals and knew their families, and if we follow circumstantial evidence he probably gave two Purple Gangsters at Jackson a pass for an outside detail and the use of his car, in order that they could run up the M-99 and do a gangland hit on a state senator who was involved in a grand jury investigation of gambling.[35] It is apparent that at some point Pettit lost precise control over the trade-offs. Prisoners were naturally inclined to push as far as they could go, opening any door the keepers left unattended, and concessions of control, once made, proved difficult to reclaim or even to restrain. The ever deepening need for discretion—to "keep the lid on" in the double sense of control and secrecy—afforded ample room for blackmail, and the "big shots" were able to continually ratchet up the terms of their cooperation, forcing authorities to add sweeteners to keep everyone in play. The boundaries between keeper and kept became increasingly fuzzy, as the fiction of compliance was purchased through an ever more explicit criminalization of authority, and the "hidden transcripts" of the prison became, in effect, the operating manual of the institution.

Yet it would be a mistake, despite appearances, to conclude that the "cons" really ran the joint. If we listen to the stories of the hundreds of small-time operators whose affidavits piled up in the Attorney General's files, we encounter a more complicated, multivalent struggle, one that was stamped by deep inequalities and highly stratified relations of power. It is, to be sure, difficult to reclaim prisoners for history; they are forever cocooned in the records of the institution that kept them, their words coming to us as they were recorded and represented by others, in a bureaucratic paper trail that was almost entirely independent of, and in most respects antagonistic to the worlds and world views of the prisoners it encoded. But what appeared to outsiders as collusion between custody and criminals seems to have been, for most prisoners, an ever-shifting, capricious zone of contestation in which the everyday struggles to get by and make life agreeable grated against the formal rules and the venal demands of corrupt authorities, on the one hand, and against the accumulated privileges and the tripwires of informal power laid down by powerful inmate rings, on the other. They were caught in a double grip. We have no idea how voluntary their participation was, or how much violence and intimidation was deployed to insure compliance, for as custody retreated and inmate spaces expanded the need for discretion and silence grew as well. If prisoners had never had it so good, they could not let on, and if anyone objected, they were subjected to heavy pressure from prisoners and guards alike to keep quiet. Defiance was necessarily muted by the collusion between Pettit and the "big shots," and it was in no one's interest to reveal how far the social order of the prison had come to rest upon the self-activity of prisoners and a systematic corruption of custodial discipline.

The growing gap between the ideological claims and the operational realities of the prison could not be concealed forever—especially since by the mid-1940s an alternative current in penology had begun to take shape around new power centers in the state capital. A reorganization of the Department of Corrections, and in particular the creation of an independent Parole Board in Michigan, produced a cadre of administrators who were determined to rein in the autonomous wardens, and who turned a critical eye not only on management practices at Jackson prison, but on the industrial-model penitentiary whose crisis had produced D. C. Pettit's collusive solutions. In their view, following Clemmer's analysis, the industrial prison had produced unintended lapses and spaces behind the walls which facilitated the kind of counter-activity among inmates that enabled them to resist its disciplinary effects and under certain circumstances to gain control of the prison itself. This had to be stopped; the prison had to be disciplined—the more so because the central narrative of industrial discipline was now permanently disrupted. In a world where the links between inmate labor and the industrial labor market were attenuated if not wholly severed, and the possibilities of reviving industrial labor inside as a means of discipline, correction, or control were pretty much gone. Thanks to the depression and the growing power of trade unions in its wake, the notion that there was much connection between what prisoners learned inside and employment opportunities outside became increasingly unconvincing. The newly reconstituted Parole Board, insisting on its independence and professionally suspicious of the warden's recommendations for release, tightened the screws on parole, claiming that no useful correction was going on at Jackson and no prospect of gainful employment existed on the outside.[36]

From this current of criticism within the department there emerged a new narrative of corrections, one that sought to plausibly reconnect the disciplinary regime inside with a program for release and reintegration into a changing society outside. The solution that took shape gradually over the decade was first to supplement, then replace industrial labor with other improving activities. Imprisonment in this conception was still supposed to correct the wayward impulses of criminals and restore them whole and rehabilitated to the community. But hard labor in factories was no longer the exclusive, nor even the primary means of achieving this result. Work was displaced as the central pivot of prison life. Industrial as well as institutional and maintenance jobs were to be repositioned on the sidelines as ancillary and contributory activities, and classification was given pride of place as the new coordinating science, around which the satellite arts of education, vocational training, group counseling, and individual therapy were assembled in a "total program" geared though diagnostic tests and classification procedures to individual inmates.

At the center of this new therapeutic penology was the professional or trained expert, equipped with diagnostic findings, case histories, test scores, normative standards, and measured results. The intended effect of the new order was to invert basic social relations in the prison, for the process of elevating the expert and legitimizing the ascendancy of professionals required that the objects of corrections be transformed into the opposite of the expert—into dysfunctional, incompetent, disturbed, even psychotic misfits. Prisoners had to be altered into something clinically distinct in order to affirm the expert's claim to control and correct. This necessitated a new distance—a rupture—between keeper and kept which would cut against the continuum of collusion between guards and inmates that had, in the industrial order, made informal collaboration, face-to-face accommodation and secret recognitions possible. Indeed, for all the attitudes of helpfulness and support embodied in the treatment stance, its dominant message to prisoners was one of separation, segregation, classification, differentiation, and individualization. It promised an atomized world in which each prisoner, his particular problem and needs distinguished from all others, was attached as an individual case to a counselor who combined, ambiguously, the roles of helper and authority, friend and disciplinarian. And this atomization was powerfully reinforced by efforts to expand the discretionary power of the Parole Board through ever-broader indeterminacy in sentencing. Indeed, the head psychiatrist at Jackson thought everyone should be given a sentence of one to one hundred years: "Then it would be up to a group of trained experts to decide when release would be granted."[37] The superior knowledge of the expert would then confront the lowly, witless prisoner and keep him guessing. Worn down by diagnostic pressures to "admit you have a problem," subject to a withering barrage of strange labels and diagnostic prescriptions, he would move through an unfamiliar maze of programming, groping for the magic formula of release, and arrive before the Parole Board where the results of his therapeutic program would be already known and his chances of release would be determined at a professional distance: "There is little, if anything, that the individual could advance in his own behalf that is not already known to the board."[38]

On paper, the new therapeutic model provided a reasonably coherent narration that resonated well with post-war cultural notions about deviance and public trust in medical expertise.[39] It also offered a clear ideological position from which to batter the management at Jackson, and it was from this high ground that the warden's enemies struck when Joseph Medley walked away from his outside detail in November 1944 and made a public scandal possible. Harry Jackson and all his subordinates at the prison were immediately fired, and a new regime was installed with instructions to crack down. Strict controls imposed on inmate movement and a uniform enforcement of custodial rules broke down differentials of status and privilege, as a far-reaching custodial assault—including shakedowns, searches, and harsh discipline in the hole[40]—tore into the delicate webs of reciprocity and favor that had built up in the industrial prison. The effects can be seen, not only in a growing number of hostile encounters between guards and prisoners, but in an upsurge of petty squabbling and fighting among inmates. This apparently registers both the proliferation of smaller factions and cliques—the remnants of shattered networks—and the deep uncertainties that the new wave of official violence imposed upon the interactions and spaces of prisoners. But the upsurge in violence inside, and the signs of resentment and anger that were uncovered in further official investigations of the prison during the late 1940s,[41] captured not only the radical narrowing of inmate spaces but also the implicit infantilization of prisoners that the new therapeutic rhetoric implied. Not only were inmates forbidden to organize their own order inside, they were now categorized as social incompetents who could not be relied on to act in socially constructive ways. They were encouraged, instead, to depend on the experts, in particular, on a new program of individual counseling and group therapy that was installed at Jackson prison in 1949 under the direction of a new Deputy Warden for Individual Treatment. A complex new filing system that combined disciplinary and work records with diagnostic tests and professional assessments was developed to facilitate classification and treatment programs and to guide the Parole Board in its deliberations over conditional release.

But in a prison the size of Jackson, little was changed by this. The ten counselors were forced to carry an impossible case load and felt that "if we could get a 'good morning Joe' on an individual basis to every man in the prison three times a year, it would . . . be an advance for treatment."[42] The new programs for education and vocational training proved inadequate, and the Parole Board seemed to show little interest in inmate participation in these or any other therapeutic programs. Indeed the Delphic and imprecise procedures of the board were a source of immense frustration among prisoners. This was compounded in 1950–1951 by deep tensions between guards and counselors. While the older structures of custodial control were by no means effaced by the intrusion of college-trained counselors behind the walls, the power of the latter as agents of the new ideological order set off endless squabbles among the keepers that further disturbed the alignments of keeper and kept, and produced a thicket of stories and cautionary lore among inmates about "how to work the system." In practice, inmate spaces were squeezed and attenuated in the disciplinary crackdown, leaving prisoners less able to organize order themselves. This made them more dependent upon authorities, but the new managers failed to consolidate the elements of a new order, or to provide an alternative narrative that could establish coherent links between the disciplinary regime inside and the proffered paths to release. As the gap between rhetorical promise and operational reality widened, the lines of antagonism between keepers and kept deepened.

The first fruit of reform was a major riot at Jackson in 1952.[43] Completely spontaneous in its origins and quickly contained to the disciplinary block of the prison, the insurrection soon turned into a siege in which several hundred inmates, holding hostages, negotiated with authorities for several days to find a peaceful resolution. In the initial stages, however, several buildings were burned, the kitchen was plundered and sides of beef roasted in impromptu barbecues on the yard, prison offices were looted and records destroyed, and there were several beatings and assaults—all of which allowed state politicians and prison officials to write off the upheaval as a senseless orgy of violence led by a psychopath, or what the press persistently called "an inadequate personality." The official investigation afterwards could find little point or meaning in the riot either. But Gresham Sykes, studying a similar upheaval in New Jersey that same year, offered some sociological insight. He applied his collusive model of prison management, in which authorities insured their dominance by allowing it to be corrupted, to the problem of riots, and argued that custodial power, once conceded, became extremely difficult to reclaim. Any attempt by prison authorities to reverse the flow of concessions, limit the corruption of their power, and reassert their dominion would inevitably, Sykes argued, tear into the web of reciprocities and tacit understandings, undercutting the cohesive forces within inmate society, displacing settled hierarchies, and up-ending established inmate leaders whose positions hinged on corrupt collusions and who had a positive interest in institutional peace. Discontent and instability would produce a riotous brew as the prison in transition moved toward another expression of Sykes' central paradox: "The system breeds rebellion by attempting to enforce the system's rules."[44]

It certainly appears to have been the case at Jackson prison that the disciplinary crackdown that dismantled Harry Jackson's regime had also undercut the settled hierarchies of informal order among prisoners who had once had a stake in preserving peace. The bitter rivalries and turf fights among prisoners in the late 1940s surfaced as intramural violence in the riot of 1952; and the very disorganization of prisoners in revolt may be read as the effect of the new regime's efforts to destroy those networks of allies and retainers among inmates. These same networks, in an earlier period, might have allowed prison authorities to reach down into the yard or cellblocks and assert control. In the standoff that followed insurrection, negotiations eventually fell, by default, to a single inmate thrown up by events and the Deputy Warden for Individual Treatment. Over several days these two carried on a dialogue that came to resemble a therapy session, deeply personal, replete with threats, dares, and tantrums, and punctuated by emotional reconciliations. The strange nature of these negotiations, which faithfully mimicked the new therapeutic regime, ultimately discredited the substance of the settlement they produced. But if we take seriously the demands formulated by the besieged prisoners (which no one did at the time), we gain insight into the silent struggle going on over the terms of change inside. Prisoners denounced the brutality of hard-line guards, producing strap chains, "wrist-breakers," and rubber hoses as evidence of the violence used in the disciplinary block; they called for an inmate review committee to discuss disciplinary rules and, at first, they demanded the abolition of the Parole Board and the restoration of fixed sentences, later modifying this to the removal of the hated Chairman Pascoe. But they did not demand the restoration of the old regime; there was little sign of nostalgia for Harry Jackson's prison nor any indication that the "big shots" of yore were fomenting rebellion in an effort to retrieve lost privileges. Instead, inmate demands pressed for better educational and vocational programs, more therapy, and greater influence for counselors in disciplinary hearings and punishment procedures, and they spoke of the need for clearer parole guidelines and greater weight for rehabilitative efforts in parole decisions. Clearly, prisoners were trying to use the space created by the riot to affect the terms by which the prison was being overhauled. Their voices, which had been silenced by the disciplinary crackdown and filled with anger and frustration by the official failure to organize coherent pathways to release, were now heard again. In the context of a violent challenge, they sought to articulate the terms of a coherent order in the absence of an official one by hastening promised changes, but also by bending these in ways that weakened capricious authority and increased predictability.

And, we might add, with some success. In the wake of the riot, the therapeutic model was consolidated as the anchor of a reasonably coherent account of carceral practice in Michigan. The population at Jackson was dramatically reduced by the late 1950s, the number of rehabilitation programs grew steadily, and the grand independence of the Parole Board was swiftly curtailed, its decisions harnessed to more systematic procedures for hearings and release. All of this tended to bring the practices and techniques of punishment into line with the claims of rehabilitation, offering a narrative of corrections that spoke, simultaneously, to multiple audiences: to the public, about how prisons made them safe; to politicians, about how punishment was being put to constructive social purposes; to prison officials, about the aspirations and quotidian routines of the system; and to prisoners, about what they had to do to win release. If this narrative of carceral practice did not always work, it was, to all appearances, what ought to have worked, and to this extent it proved plausible. And for all its drawbacks, the new therapeutic prison, like the industrial penitentiary before it, provided the terrain and openings for prisoners to take and shape their own spaces of self-activity. Indeed prisoners picked up on the promises of therapy far faster than their keepers, and they anticipated opportunities in the new model that were wholly unintended and quickly stretched beyond official control.

The governing discourse of the therapeutic prison sought to transform the convicted felon into the maladjusted, emotionally disturbed, and inadequate personality who did not fit for reasons of mental or emotional impairment and whose crimes were born of individual deficiencies which could be overcome with expert intervention and remedial help. In producing this new and (for the 1950s) characteristic delinquent, the therapeutic prison placed enormous emphasis upon getting prisoners to admit that they had a problem that could then be made the object of corrective intervention. "We quickly learned," wrote Malcolm Braly, a prison writer who captured the empty cynicism of therapy better than anyone,[45] that "we were expected to view this journey through prison as a quest, and the object of our quest was to discover our problem." From an insider's point of view there was deep irony, not to say deception, in the public rhetoric of rehabilitation, but if cures were wanted, cures could be presented. In the interest of getting out, inmates did their group counseling, played cat-and-mouse with the therapists, occupied spaces in rehabilitative programs, pursued education, and cultivated the ruse of the remade man for the benefit of the Parole Board. But in producing behavior that mimicked the public rhetoric of rehabilitation, prisoners were also engaged in more artful inflections of treatment: they used participation in treatment programs to evade custodial routines; they turned art and writing classes into vehicles of self-expression to speak bitterness about the prison and society more generally; they invoked the counselor's commitment to treat the "whole man" in order to legitimate complaints about the continuing brutality and arbitrariness of prison discipline; they discovered in the relaxation of communications control and the official encouragement of productive encounters with the outside world openings through which to acquire books, publicize conditions, launch lawsuits, and cultivate support groups of sympathizers; they became writers (getting past the constraints and formulas of sanctioned writing to produce some powerful, revelatory prose[46]) and earned money from their publications (whether to purchase contraband, sex, and other forbidden pleasures inside or to hire lawyers to further court appeals outside); and they captured control of many educational programs in the institution, turning the approved curriculum for uplift into Marxist study groups or seminars on religious, political, or legal questions, often taught by sympathetic outsiders. A budding inmate intelligentsia—jailhouse lawyers, preachers, teachers, and political activists—operating within the treatment modalities, sustained by the late 1960s and early 1970s a growing prisoners' movement which, linking up with activists on the outside, became more self-confident and politicized in its confrontations with authorities. As rehabilitation opened untoward avenues of inmate self-activity, prison officials became increasingly alarmed about the security of their institutions and guards. Facing the brunt of inmate insubordination, they became increasingly inclined to crack down hard.

Clearly an old pattern was here reproducing itself in the therapeutic context. The new model prison had been spawned in the 1940s, not only by a crisis of industrial production in the big house and the loss of carceral coherence that went with the collapse of industry, but also by a crisis of control that arose when the specific counter-spaces which inmate self-activity had been able or permitted to produce in the industrial prison threatened to take over effective control of the lower rungs of the institution. In breaking up the privileged hierarchies of the "big shots" and radically constricting the scope of inmate self-activity, prison administrators sought to deploy a more centrally managed alternative regime of dependency, grounded in individualized treatment. Although academic classes and group counseling sessions presented inmates with an entirely different terrain for self-activity than the bustling shop floors and informal economy of the 1920s, prisoners found new opportunities for self-reliant activity. In the production of these spaces of quotidian *Eigensinn,* violence was always present, moving with and through them along continually changing vectors. Official violence, which was capricious, very physical, and aimed at policing the tolerated illegalities of the informal economy in the 1920s and 1930s, became increasingly selective, individualized, and mental by the 1950s and 1960s. Intramural violence among inmates, which was channeled into struggles for control of the spoils during the 1920s and 1930s, and then deployed by "big shot" enforcers to impose subordination during the 1940s, was broken up into running feuds and turf fights by the disciplinary crackdown, before turning into a more individualized form of stand-off and personal testing under the treatment regime of the 1950s and 1960s. By then, finally, the ritual exercises in therapy and the feigned reformations that prisoners concocted in the pursuit of release were reproducing again, in a therapeutic context, the lies of compliance and the illusions of disciplinary wholeness that made the public narrative of corrections plausible.

Reading this rather breathless historical sketch of the highly unstable, shifting ground of inmate self-activity in the era of the "big house," sociologists might choose to emphasize the continuities in the story and turn these to a reinforcement of prevailing models. Yet the history traced here is not an example of some timeless law of penal motion working itself out. It was not some essential, structural characteristic of the prison that produced the texts of complicity which made cooperation necessary and self-activity possible. The need for a "corrupt bargain" arose from the ideology of rehabilitation which was, despite many contradictions and interruptions, at the core of penitentiary science in both its industrial and therapeutic moments. This is not to claim that rehabilitation ever "worked," in the sense of solving the crime problem or redeeming lost souls, but rather to suggest that all efforts to make a carceral narrative cohere around rehabilitation made necessary the participation of prisoners and thus framed the possibilities of self-activity inside. Foucault's conception of the modern penalty depended, as we saw, upon a reading of the panopticon as a vehicle of exclusion (punishment) and re-inclusion (correction): "The carceral network . . . takes back with one hand what it seems to exclude with the other."[47] Predicated upon notions of (re)inclusion, rehabilitational penology expressed a fundamentally Gramscian kind of hegemony, in which consent was won (whether by conviction, purchase, or sham) through promises, proffered "to subordinate groups by way of explaining why a particular social order is also in their best interest."[48] It partook of a prevailing liberal discourse in the public sphere that held out the promise of inclusion to those on the margins as an invitation and rationale for their compliance, and which understood power struggles in terms of contests for control of the pathways and mechanisms of inclusion, on the assumption that command of the gateways and rules of access also entailed control of those trying to gain access. In its relatively rare moments of operational coherence, the carceral regime of rehabilitation combined a strategy of corrections, which provided prison authorities with a continuous narrative of what imprisonment was about—what was done, to whom, with what effects, measured by what yardsticks, and to what end—with a strategy of compliance, which provided inmates with a clear idea of what they had to do to get out with the least cost in terms of personal dignity. This combination formed a logic of incarceration on which keeper and kept alike relied to produce order and render it meaningful. The goal of re-inclusion anchored the pathways of release in a rhetoric of reformation which, enshrined as a public rhetoric of corrections, made necessary those exercises in deception inside that left room for the cultivation of the spaces of *Eigensinn*. Ultimately, then, in a carceral regime of (re)inclusion, the dream of a well-ordered prison, like that of a well-ordered society, depended on some form of consent from the governed, whether sincerely given, feigned for convenience, or constituted in the disciplinary process itself. It was this necessarily collusive relationship that sustained the patterns of mutual surveillance to which I have alluded. It was within a regime requiring obedience but needing consent that both sides came to study each other, to judge intentions and read actions in a context of mutual, if antagonistic understanding. It was in this framework that violence was contained, or at least channeled into circuits and spaces that custody could tolerate and inmates could use. It was in this context that Abbott's refusal to play the game acquired its power, and the harsh responses of authority took on a wider meaning. And it was from within this framework that both prisoners and guards, watching each other, could interpret violence. For in a carceral regime that sought to present a coherent narrative of rehabilitation, violence could be "read" as a response to the failure of promises, or as an attempt by inmates to gain better terms or more consideration within an established set of proffered pathways, or as a move by authorities to narrow options and restrict inmate self-activity. Even riots invited remedial responses as well as repression. The sociologies of prison in the 1940s and 1950s, at the height of the rehabilitational era, could thus infer function to inmate violence and treat it as a crude but instrumental form of address. And the institution itself could deploy receptors to register and record inmate activities in the process of producing a surer knowledge of the delinquent, and shaping the regimes of control that the inmates contested.

Conclusion: The Narrative of Exclusion in Postmodern Penology

It is from this perspective that we may mark, in a broadly more speculative way, the very different character of contemporary corrections. For it is precisely the absence of any rehabilitational intent that characterizes the current situation in American penology. Since the mid-1970s, prison professionals and politicians have abandoned the notion that prisons can reform criminals and jettisoned the rhetoric of individualized treatment, together with the ideology of rehabilitation that underwrote it. In state after state, indeterminate sentences have been replaced by fixed terms, flat time, and a no-nonsense, back-to-basics incarceration predicated upon the centrality of custodial management and control. What Jack Abbott and George Jackson once refused has now been simply withdrawn; the promise of eventual re-inclusion and the program of rehabilitation that sustained that promise and anchored it in the free world have been shut down across the board, and exclusion—the language of dumping, warehousing, and three-strikes-you're-out—now runs its course unchecked and unleavened. Explanations for this turn have varied.[49] But any historical treatment must account for both the crisis of the treatment model in corrections and the simultaneous collapse of the rehabilitational ideal. For while the former disrupted the coherence of the carceral narrative and opened the ground for another reformulation in correctional policy, such as occurred in the 1910s and 1940s, the latter was a historic watershed in the history of punishment which repositioned the prison in the carceral terrain and reconfigured the relationship of penalty and society in late twentieth-century America.

Treatment penology grew out of the collapse of industrial jobs inside the prison, a crisis of labor that proved permanent and made prison the first community in the United States to experience systematic deindustrialization and universal unemployment. Yet the treatment model continued to rely heavily upon the availability of jobs outside. Indeed during the 1950s and 1960s, the coherence of the treatment ideology depended upon the capacity of parole procedures, now coming into their own, to provide a plausible assurance of continuing control through its supervision of former prisoners at work and in the community.[50] As the bridge of re-inclusion, parole was anchored in the treatment programs in prison that led to conditional release, on the one hand, and in the labor market and social supports of free communities, on the other. Its effectiveness as ideology and as practice was thus doubly conditioned. During the 1950s and 1960s, two related and parallel developments combined to throw the treatment model into crisis.

On the one hand, a reconfiguration of the industrial labor market, especially a rapid deterioration at its urban and low-skills end, spread systemic unemployment through the communities from which many criminals came and to which, on parole, they returned. As larger swatches of the population, primarily though not exclusively in the old industrial centers, were permanently disconnected from the labor market, and their communities decayed, the structures of discipline that had once anchored a plausible narrative of rehabilitational treatment and parole disintegrated. At the same time, inside the prison the growing number of incarcerated African-Americans—approaching and in the case of Jackson prison exceeding 50 percent of the population during the 1960s—as well as the solidarity and growing politicization of these prisoners, combined to stand American society on its head behind the walls. The Black Muslims made their first appearance at Jackson in the late 1950s, and they were joined by the Black Panthers and other militant groups during the 1960s.[51] Their challenge was initially to the prison order, displacing the presumptive claims of white inmates to spaces and preeminence and contesting through direct action official policies that kept blacks in an inferior position. All prisons experienced deepening racial tensions on the yard and in the cellblocks during the 1960s, as white, black, and Hispanic inmates taunted, jostled, and fought one another along racial or ethnic lines and as authorities, especially guards on the line, sought to use these tensions in the interest of control. Most prisons also saw a sharpening of antagonism between black (and in California or the southwest, Hispanic) inmates and "the man" which generated ugly frictions and provoking deep unease among custodians.[52] More than anything, the racial solidarity among African American prisoners cut to the quick of the therapeutic model, confronting its individualizing ethos, which was supposed to dissolve the negative solidarities of inmate culture in the name of rehabilitation. It did so with a phalanx of opposition that was not easily or peacefully broken up by custodial pressure. Most blacks came to see rehabilitation as a white man's game, cast in a white image of redemption. The counselors' helping hand could not reach across the racial divide because with black prisoners, despite good intentions and appeasing rhetoric, difference was already a given, and therapeutic efforts to make them *be* different—that is, to admit they had a problem and to take responsibility for their incarceration, in order to begin redemptive correction—only exposed the fact that "their" difference was not redeemable in the eyes of white society. Many militant blacks took this as a mark of distinction that reversed the injunctions of treatment and resisted its condescensions: as prisoners, black males were representatives of an incarcerated people—prisoners in their own country—and their presence in prison was not aberrant, but expressive of a communal fate in the face of a common oppression.[53] These stark lines of hostility frightened prison officials, and by the early 1970s the therapeutic obsession with turning (white) prisoners into useable objects of corrective intervention had been replaced, among custodians, with an obsession with the control of dangerous and incorrigible (black) criminals.

The crisis of the therapeutic model behind the walls and the erosion of the anchors of parole in the labor market and community outside briefly open up space for experiments and new possibilities in the early 1970s. It was during this period that the most trenchant critiques of carceral claims, the broadest reevaluation of treatment methods, as well the most bizarre experiments in behavior modification, were made,[54] and it was in this moment that practical essays in community corrections, deinstitutionalization, inmate democracy, and, at Jackson prison, "the responsibility model" were attempted.[55] But these efforts to meet the crisis of treatment modalities with experimental departures were quickly swamped by the conservative political mobilizations which, by the mid-1970s, had effected a massive reformulation of prevailing discourse about crime and its control. Indeed, the economic restructuring that drained jobs and residents from urban centers helped feed the right-wing current in a number of complex ways. As the middle class fled the city for the suburbs and inner-city populations lost regular contact with the labor market, a new or starker concentration of poverty produced a "spatially specific" crime problem. This enabled the symbolic politics of law and order, which drew heavily on fear, to criminalize the crisis of employment and social cohesion in the inner city. And, in a dual and simultaneous motion, it racialized the crime problem, turning it into a moral, behavioral, and genetic commentary on black people and generating the images of black predators menacing "society" that amplified fear and concentrated its focus on specific groups. As the people of the inner city were redefined as a "dangerous class," "their perceived dangerousness reinforce[d] their isolation," forging an underclass which, in Simon's words, "no longer provide[d] a coherent target for the strategies of integration and normalization" that had been the hallmark of rehabilitational corrections.[56] The deployment of the markers of danger—young, black, male, inner city, unemployed—and of the images of dangerous places, gutted streets, disorganized neighborhoods, and pathological family structures, framed instead an excluded population that needed to be contained and managed by the criminal justice system.[57] And with prisoners being released into marginal communities that were marked as both irredeemable and dangerous, prison became merely an extension of now permanent circuits of exclusion, engaged in what Simon calls "waste management" rather than redemption.

As the operations of criminal justice turned increasingly toward exercises in exclusion, the ever-mounting investment in private security, police, and prisons during the 1980s—what Diana Gordon named the "justice juggernaut"[58]—succeeded, not so much in reducing crime or the public's fear of criminals, as in clarifying, with the help of comprehensive electronic records, the dimensions of danger and the zones of the excluded. This may be taken as the coercive moment in the shift to a post-modern, post-Fordist, and post-liberal society, in which uneven growth and minimal upward mobility foreshorten opportunity and limit access. A record, or lack of it, becomes a kind of permanent computerized quarantine that channels large segments of the population and categories of people without good credentials away from jobs, and whole sectors of employment into perpetually marginal, excluded statuses. But we should also mark a deep alteration that has taken place in the disciplinary project that Foucault imagined. For at the margins, the workings of the panopticon are now reversed, and surveillance has become preoccupied, not with forming the thresholds of conformity and the ritual subordinations entailed in the taxonomic project of orderly compliance and inclusion, but with marking those who do not belong and are to be permanently excluded.[59] Here the illusions of compliance that the prison once sustained are no longer necessary, because in a regime of post-liberalism, inclusion is no longer a goal and willing compliance no longer expected of those with no prospect of access. Public assurances that discipline is intact now depend upon the technical competence of security forces in keeping "them" away.

This realignment has produced what many regard as a systemic incoherence in modern corrections. As community constraints and the social disciplines of the labor market erode—and with these, the very norms to which corrections aspires—the narrative certainties that linked carceral disciplines with free society and made a regime of punishment cohere have collapsed. Without a program of inclusion, there is no strategy of corrections to combine with inmate strategies of compliance to produce a logic of incarceration, nor any parole strategy that can convincingly link this logic to assurances of control after release. There is, as a result, little connection these days between the corrections profession and academic disciplines—little research, few interesting ideas, and no philosophical debate going on anywhere in the field. The profession, says one long-time observer, "seems to have lost its moral defense—its sense of purpose. Corrections appears to have become an institution without an ideal—a set of practices without purpose or direction."[60] To be sure, the spreading conviction that prisons cannot change criminals, only hold them, coupled with the massive growth in prison populations during the 1980s, has produced a more practical, policy-relevant prison sociology which professes its impatience with "overly complex" academic sociologies. It finds it "difficult to swallow the notion that the 'society of captives' was somehow beyond better government," or that it is necessary to acquiesce in collusive strategies with inmates to insure peace. It calls for a "policy oriented knowledge" that will enable prison managers to govern their institutions, dominate their violent and resentful charges, and present society with assurances that the criminal element has been safely put away.[61] This is part of a broad movement in contemporary penology and parole toward managerial strategies of control, procedures that rely heavily on the latest technologies of risk management and generate internally-driven standards of performance with fewer ties to the outside world and little need to measure "effectiveness" in social terms.

The ultimate expression of this logic in penology can be found in the Pelican Bay (California) and Florence (Colorado) facilities, or the dozens of other "maxi-maxi" units that are being modeled on them.[62] Here, in so-called "special housing units," prisoners designated as unruly, troublesome, or violent are kept on twenty-four-hour lockdown in their cells; they see no one and have no contact with other inmates; guards deal with them from control booths, through television monitors and intercoms, and doors open and shut by remote control; food is passed through an opening in the cell door; all movement outside the cell is in manacles and leg-irons; prisoners may not decorate their cells, hold personal belongings, work, or pursue hobbies; reading material is strictly limited and counseling or educational programs do not exist; recreation consists of a brief pass in a concrete yard, alone. And because these are (routine) administrative procedures, not measures of punishment, prisoners remain in deep uncertainty about their duration or the terms of "release" to ordinary confinement. "[T]he isolation of the convicts guarantees that it is possible to exercise over them, with maximum intensity, a power that will not be overthrown by any other influence; solitude is the primary condition of total submission."[63] Here, key features of the most modern of prisons hark back to the incarceration of perfect isolation and silence that the Quakers sought to attain in the first penitentiary at Eastern State in Pennsylvania, but without any of the redemptive intent of the earlier essays in punishment. Professional management nowadays seeks absolute control which can exist only in isolation—static spaces frozen in time.

The "maxi-maxi" units are primarily used to house those who have committed violent offenses while in prison. I do not wish in any way to minimize the growing violence and insecurity that plagues poor communities or to enter a debate with prison professionals over whether today's prisoner represents a new breed of vicious predator beyond approach. But it is worth considering, briefly, the extent to which the new carceral strategies of risk management condition both the patterns and interpretations of violence in contemporary prisons. The proliferation of gangs behind the walls has been the most striking phenomenon of prison life in the last twenty years. A problem in only a few jurisdictions at the beginning of the 1970s, gangs spread to more than half the prison systems in the country during the 1980s and became the major management preoccupation of prison officials.[64] The strategies adopted to control prison gangs—segregating the leaders (a practice that made systems with the most serious gang problem pioneers in the construction of "maxi-maxi" units) and, in some states, separating gangs among different institutions—may have been, as John Irwin argued at the time, a "self-fulfilling prophecy": "the more attention you pay to the gang, the more gang-like it becomes."[65] Certainly the classificatory responses developed by prison officials, none of whom shared Irwin's view, tended to over-determine the saliency of gangs and to push some prisoners to opt for gang association. By closely monitoring gang activity, trying to foster divisions within gangs or to flush defectors from them, prison officials actually promoted tension and violence among gang members. Cummins reported that since the only way to get out of the Special Housing Unit at Pelican Bay was to "debrief" or name gang members, anyone coming back to general population was assumed to have "snitched" and thus became vulnerable to retaliatory attack.[66] Over time, the proliferation of gangs inside, and the extensive ties between gangs in prison and on the streets, forced prison officials to adopt more flexible forms of response, based on computerized tracking systems and "early-warning" assessments of what, in the Federal system, were called "security threat groups."[67] Authorities were convinced that ignoring gangs until they show up on disciplinary sheets was too risky, and they determined to leave "no room for negotiating with gangs . . . no message . . . that implies sanctioning their organizations or activities." They thus came to regard themselves as being at war with gangs, declaring no terms and no quarter.[68] Draconian use of "maxi-maxi" confinement was a logical corollary of this policy, as prison officials sought to master the gang problem while continuing to deny the relational processes that were producing this impasse.

A power that seeks to erase all autonomy in the subordinate rules out all relational connection with its objects. The preoccupation with custodial ascendancy effectively denies space for inmate *Eigensinn* and refuses to invite inmate consent. The internal regime is no longer anchored in strategies, however tatty and contradictory, for re-inclusion, and there are, consequently no linkages, however tacit or implied, between keeper and kept upon which to establish common ground or negotiate the terms of a social contract. Prisoners, denied the spaces of self-reliance from which to surveil authority and act on that knowledge, are in no position to contest—or to give consent to—the carceral order. Without the context of mutual collusion to frame events and give meaning to what is observed, there are no signs or messages being exchanged; the prison has fewer receptors calibrated to read what inmates say or do as purposive or meaningful. Violence thus cannot be interpreted: there are no promises to betray, no terms to negotiate, no need for authorities to channel a self-activity that is denied. Riots can have no point, and prisoners finding no one to address can make no point through insurrection, except to declare despair.[69] Violence that has no meaning invites, not proactive response, but vigorous repression and deeper tiers of penalty. Thus while official violence is securely anchored in the legitimating imperatives of control, "their" violence becomes an anchorless eruption that marks "them" as different from "us"—an expression of what we expect of them—and calls attention to the lapses in the patina of carceral domination that need to be closed. Prisoners are thus triply effaced: they are no longer objects of rehabilitation, or subjects of collusion, or authors of purposive action.

A sociology of coping designed for a carceral project without purpose save containment may be fully in accord with prevailing discourse about crime and its control. But its general aimlessness may also mark the outer limits of carceral discipline itself. For the failure to renew the promise of re-inclusion and the creation of permanent, non-negotiable categories of exclusion suggests that the production of useable delinquencies (the representative criminal figures that "sum up symbolically all others"), which Foucault regarded as central to the carceral project as a whole, has now moved outside the prison. More precisely, the prison can no longer be found where Foucault tried to locate it, "at the point where the codified power to punish turns into the disciplinary power to observe . . . at the point where the redefinition of the juridical subject [the offender] by the penalty becomes a useful training of the criminal [the inmate]."[70] Perhaps this is because surveillance is now more complete, more generalized, diffuse, and total, and thus no longer needs an anchor in the prison. The panoptic project moves onto the streets and into the squad cars, the rap sheet replacing the prison record in the production of useable delinquents. But this is possible precisely because the "representative" delinquent in our time is the black male, who is constituted as criminally dangerous prior to imprisonment and is put in prison as a confirmatory act, part of a continuing and generalized process of exclusion. The carceral archipelago in this interpretation has slipped its anchor and now floats free of core practices in the prison. For its part, the prison, now relocated to one side, cauterizes itself in the interest of more perfect control, its custodial instincts droning on without coherent narration of purpose or substantive links to the outside world, mindlessly producing carceral cocoons for the excluded, simply because no alternative procedure has been dreamed up (except in the movies).

NOTES

1. "What all importation explanations of prison violence have in common is the location of the source of prison violence in the offender." James Jacobs, "Prison Violence and Formal Organization," in Albert K. Cohen et al., eds., *Prison Violence* (Lexington: D. C. Heath, 1976), p. 80.

2. Discussions of prison violence often veer off into a meditation on prison revolts. See for example, the essays collected in, Michael Braswell, et al., eds., *Prison Violence in America* (Cincinnati: Anderson Publishing Co., 1985).

3. Information on violence in prison is hard to come by: data compiled by state departments and the Federal Bureau of Prisons tend to focus on violence directed at prison staff and on homicides that can yield successful prosecution. The press picks up on the spectacular moments of violence, such as the shocking riot in New Mexico in 1982 (where inmate-on-inmate violence was especially brutal) or the surge of inmate killings in Texas in 1984–1985 (fifty-two killings in one year, more than in the previous fifteen years combined). But most quotidian violence among prisoners goes unreported. From the episodic and scattered evidence available, it is almost impossible to get a comparative picture of prison violence, over time or across the country. See, the impressions of James Jacobs about Illinois prisons, in "Prison Violence and Formal Organizations" p. 80; the somewhat dated analysis by Lawrence Bennett, "The Study of Violence in California Prisons: A Review with Policy Implications," in Albert K. Cohen et al., eds., *Prison Violence* (Lexington: D. C. Heath, 1976), pp 149–68; reports on Texas in Sheldon Ekland-Olson, "Crowding, Social Controls, and Prison Violence: Evidence from

the Post-Ruiz Years in Texas," *Law and Society Review,* 20 (1986): 389–421; and Salvador Buentello, "Combating Gangs in Texas," *Corrections Today,* July 1992.

There is indirect evidence that more violent offenders are being incarcerated: between 1980 and 1992, the fastest growing categories of arrest and conviction were for drug offenses and crimes against persons; the arrest rate for "serious" crime rose 38 percent in this period, and incarceration rates raised the ratio of commitments from 120 per 1000 to 148. Most of this increase was for "aggravated assault." Generally, then, it is possible to argue that, as the overall population of American prisons grew from one-third of a million to one million inmates in twelve years (an increase of 187 percent), the proportion of violent offenders in this mix increased as well. See Bureau of Justice Statistics, *Bulletin: Prisoners in 1993* (U.S. Department of Justice, 1994).

4. The phrase belongs to McCorkle and Korn, from "Resocialization within Walls," *Annals of the American Academy of Social and Political Science,* 293 (1954): 88–98.

5. A good recent example of this approach is John Dilulio, *Governing Prisons: A Comparative Study of Correctional Management* (New York: Free Press, 1987). See also Mark Fleisher, *Warehousing Violence* (Newbury Park, Calif.: Sage, 1989).

6. Compare, for example, the work of Donald Clemmer in *The Prison Community* (Boston: Christopher Publishing House, 1940) with James Jacobs' *Stateville: The Penitentiary in Mass Society* (Chicago: University of Chicago Press, 1977). Or compare John Irwin (with Donald Cressey), "Thieves, Convicts and the Inmate Culture," *Social Problems* 10 (1962): 142–55; with Jacobs, "Street Gangs behind Bars," *Social Problems* 21 (1974): 395–409.

7. James Scott, *Domination and the Arts of Resistance: Hidden Transcripts* (New Haven: Yale University Press, 1990), p. 45.

8. Alf Ludtke, ed., *The History of Everyday Life: Reconstructing Historical Experience and Ways of Life* (Princeton: Princeton University Press, 1993); also "Cash, Coffee-breaks, Horseplay: Eigensinn among Factory Workers in Germany, circa 1900," in Michael Hanagan and Charles Stephenson, eds., *Confrontation, Class Consciousness, and Labor Process* (Contributions to Labor Studies #18); "Organizational Order or Eigensinn: Workers' Privacy and Worker's Politics in Germany," in Sean Wilentz, *Rites of Power: Symbolism, Ritual, and Politics since the Middle Ages* (Philadelphia: University of Pennsylvania Press, 1985).

9. Jack Henry Abbott, *In the Belly of the Beast: Letters from Prison* (New York: Random House, 1981).

10. Ibid., p. 37: The round would begin in altercations with guards, go to disciplinary hearing where defiance would get him referred to "the shrink" ("when the captain . . . cannot control you, you are handed over to a 'psychiatrist,' who doesn't even look at you and who orders you placed on one of these drugs") and "after stammering like an idiot" for a few months, it leads back to general population, where another incident with a guard would start it again.

11. Norman Mailer, The Executioner's Song (Boston: Little, Brown, 1979).

12. Abbott, *Belly of the Beast,* p. 15–17.

13. Michel Foucault, *Discipline and Punish: The Birth of the Prison* (New York: Vintage, 1979), p. 255.

14. The story is told by Michael Israel, "Jack Henry Abbott, American Prison Writing, and the Experience of Punishment," *Criminal Justice and Behavior* 10, 2 (Dec. 1983). See also, Jack Katz, *Seductions of Crime: Moral and Sensual Attractions of Doing Evil* (New York: Basic Books, 1988), pp. 294–96.

15. Foucault, *Discipline and Punish,* pp. 290–92.

16. In what follows, I am drawing on Abbott's chapters "The Prison Staff" and "The Inmates," from *Belly of the Beast,* pp. 54–86.

17. Ibid., p. 91.

18. Ibid., p. 68–69.

19. Ibid., p. 62.

20. George Jackson, *Soledad Brother* (New York: Bantam, 1970), pp. 119, 204.

21. On the construction of George Jackson as a revolutionary, see Bruce Cummins, *The Rise and Fall of California's Radical Prison Movement* (Stanford: Stanford University Press, 1994), ch. 7.

22. Ibid., p. 86.

23. Lila Abu-Lughod, "The Romance of Resistance: Tracing Transformations of Power through Bedouin Women" *American Ethnologist* 17 (1990): 41–55; "A Community of Secrets: The Separate World of Bedouin Women" *Signs* 10 (1985): 637–57. Note also James Scott's working assumption that even "the most severe conditions of powerlessness" are diagnostic, in *Domination,* p. x.

24. Donald Clemmer, *The Prison Community;* Gresham Sykes. *Society of Captives* (Princeton: Princeton University Press, 1958); Donald Cressey, *The Prison: Studies in Institutional Organization and Change* (New York: Holt, Rinehart and Winston, 1961); and the work of the "Group on Correctional Organization" (including Donald Cressey, George Grosser, Richard McCleery, Lloyd Ohlin, Gresham Sykes, and Sheldon Messinger) sponsored in the late 1950s by the Social Science Research Council, collected in Richard A. Cloward et al., *Theoretical Studies in Social Organization of the Prison* (New York: Social Science Research Council, 1960).

25. Clemmer, *Prison Community,* p. 297.

26. Sykes, *Society of Captives,* p. 42.

27. Ibid., p. 58.

28. What follows is drawn from my study of Jackson prison, *The Powers That Punish: Prison and Politics in the Era of the "Big House," 1920–1955* (Ann Arbor: University of Michigan Press, 1996).

29. Interviews with Morris Glover, 22 May 1945. Attorney General, Investigations, SPSM, Box 1, File 11. State Archives, Lansing, Michigan.

30. I have discussed the building of this new facility in "Political Patronage and

the Construction of the Jackson State Prison in Michigan" *Michigan Academician* 16 (1983): 5–22.

31. See Glenn Gildemeister, *Prison Labor and Convict Competition with Free Workers in Industrializing America, 1840–1890* (New York: Garland Publications, 1987); and Howard Gill, "The Prison Labor Problem," *Annals of the American Academy of Political Science* 157 (1931): 83–101. Useful background on the changing nature of prison labor is provided by Blake McKelvey, *American Prisons: A History of Good Intentions* (Montclair, N.J.: P. Smith, 1936; reissued, 1977); and Jonathan Simon, *Poor Discipline: Parole and the Social Control of the Underclass, 1890–1990* (Chicago: University of Chicago Press, 1993).

32. David Garland, *Punishment and Welfare* (Brookfield, Vt.: Gower Press, 1985).

33. David Rothman, *Conscience and Convenience: The Asylum and its Alternatives in Progressive America* (New York: Little Brown, 1980), pp. 137–48.

34. I adopt this term from Foucault, who used it in describing the quotidian deviance of the *ancien regime* that came under disciplinary gaze and became criminalized.

35. The murder of Senator Warren Hooper is a wonderful and complex story, zestily retold by Bruce Rubenstein and Lawrence Ziewacz, *Three Bullets Sealed His Lips* (East Lansing, Mich.: Michigan State University Press, 1987).

36. This only deepened the collusive conundrum inside the prison, for the warden, unable to promise inmates release, had to rely instead on a steady expansion of favors and status inside to insure inmate cooperation—all the while railing at the board as a "dirty bunch of sons-of-bitches."

37. Statement by David Philips, who was first hired at Jackson under the reform administration of Governor Frank Murphy in 1937, in the *Jackson Citizen Patriot,* 27 May 1937.

38. Statement by board chairman, A. Ross Pascoe, know as "Mr. Parole" in Michigan corrections, and as "the blowtorch" by prisoners, 30 Jan. 1945. "Parole Inquiry," Attorney General Files, Criminal Investigations, Box 1. State Archives, Lansing, Michigan.

39. On the links between therapy, parole, and public attitudes in California, see Simon, *Poor Discipline,* ch. 3.

40. Donald Clemmer, on a survey of Michigan prisons in 1951, concluded that the conditions in "solitary" were "more severe than in many other northern prisons." Staff Report to the Michigan Joint Legislative Committee on Reorganization of State Government, No. 15, March 1951, pp 17–18.

41. There was a state senate investigation in 1946, further probes by the Attorney General in 1947, a survey by Noel Fox for the new Democratic administration in 1949, and visits by Austin MacCormick of the Osborne Association (1947 and 1949), and Donald Clemmer (1951) leaving reports and recommendations.

42. Quoted in Noel Fox, *Survey of Michigan Corrections,* 20 June 1949, p. 68.

Papers of G. Mennan Williams, Box 14. Michigan Historical Collections, Bentley Library, University of Michigan, Ann Arbor.

43. Contemporary accounts of the riot are found in John Barlow Martin, *Break Down the Walls* (New York: Ballantine Books, 1953), ch. 8; and Vernon Fox, *Violence Behind Bars: An Explosive Report on Prison Violence in the United States* (New York: Vantage Press, 1956), pp. 86–144. The Governor's Special Commission's investigative report is in the Williams papers, Box 83, Michigan Historical Collections.

44. Sykes, *Society of Captives,* pp. 123–24.

45. Malcolm Braly, *False Starts: A Memoir of San Quentin and Other Prisons,* 1976), from which this quotation is taken (p. 156); and *On the Yard: A Novel* (Boston: Little, Brown, 1967). Braly was a product of San Quentin's "bibliotherapy" program and a thorough non-believer in it.

46. Braly describes getting around the restrictions on prisoner writing at San Quentin. Eldridge Cleaver produced some transparent "uplift" writing on his way to *Soul on Ice* (New York: McGraw Hill). See Cummins, *Rise and Fall,* ch. 5.

47. Foucault, *Discipline and Punish,* p. 301.

48. Scott, *Domination,* p. 72.

49. Francis A. Allen. *The Decline of the Rehabilitational Ideal* (New Haven: Yale University Press, 1981) stressed the exhaustion of liberal penology and the mounting empirical evidence of the failure of treatment (the classic statement of which was offered by Robert Martinson, in "What Works?—Questions and Answers about Prison Reform," *The Public Interest* 35 (Spring 1974). Stanley Cohen, *Visions of Social Control: Crime, Punishment, and Classification* (Cambridge: Polity Press, 1985) traced the combined impact of left and right challenges in the early 1970s, which crushed liberal penology in an ungainly pincher movement. The most eloquent critique of treatment penology from the left came from the American Friends Service Committee's *Struggle for Justice: A Report on Crime and Punishment in America* (New York: Hill and Wang, 1971). See also Jessica Mitford, *Kind and Usual Punishment: The Prison Business* (New York: Knopf, 1973). For the attack from the right, see Ernest van den Haag, *Punishing Criminals: Concerning a Very Old and Painful Question* (New York: Basic Books, 1975).

50. By far the best study of parole in the modern era is Jonathan Simon's *Poor Discipline.*

51. "What do we do about the Muslims?" came the question from the cellblocks. "Muslim! What the hell is Muslim?" was the initial response of the Deputy Warden, quickly contextualized by the warden in a report to his superiors: "We are getting quite a few complaints from a group of colored inmates who call themselves Muslims. They will not eat pork or anything that is derived from pork, and they are demanding that we set up a special menu for them. They have also demonstrated on numerous occasions and you know that I have segregated these people because I don't feel they should run the institution" (Letter, Warden William Ban-

nan to Gus Harrison, 8 July 1958, including Incident Reports. Directors File, SPSM, Michigan State Archives, Lansing, Michigan). On the radicalization of prisoners in California, see Cummins, *Rise and Fall.*

52. See Min S. Yee, *The Melancholy History of Soledad Prison, in which a Utopian Scheme turns Bedlam* (New York: Harper's Magazine Press, 1970); Erik Olin Wright, *The Politics of Punishment: A Critical Analysis of Prisons in America* (New York: Harper and Row, 1973); and Theodore Davidson, *Chicano Prisoners: The Key to San Quentin* (New York: Holt, Rinehart, and Winston, 1974).

53. See H. Bruce Franklin. *The Victim as Criminal and Artist: Literature from the American Prison* (New York: Oxford University Press, 1978).

54. See note 48 above. See also, Robert Sommer, *The End of Imprisonment* (Oxford: Oxford University Press, 1976). On behavior modification, the seminal statement is J. V. McConnell. "Criminals Can be Brainwashed—Now," *Psychology Today,* Apr. 1970. See also, P. Sanford, "A Model, Clockwork-Orange Prison," *New York Times Magazine,* 17 Sept. 1972; and Philip Hilts, *Behavior Mod* (New York: Harper's Magazine Press, 1974), ch. 6.

55. For the experiments in inmate councils (the "citizenship model") at Washington State Penitentiary at Walla Walla, see Charles Stastny and Gabrielle Tyrnauer, *Who Rules the Joint? The Changing Political Culture of Maximum-Security Prisons in America* (Lexington: D. C. Heath, 1982). For a study of the problems of representation and "pluralism" in prisons in California and New Jersey, see Robert Berkman, *Opening the Gates: the Rise of the Prisoners' Movement* (Lexington: D. C. Heath, 1979). And see John Dilulio, *Governing Prisons* for a critical study of Michigan's "responsibility model." Andrew Scull, *Decarceration: Community Treatment and the Deviant: A Radical View* (Englewood Cliffs, N.J.: Prentice-Hall, 1977) is a programmatic statement. See also the essays in Y. Bakal, ed., *Closing Correctional Institutions* (Lexington: D. C. Heath, 1973).

56. Simon, *Poor Discipline,* pp. 253, 255.

57. On the markers of exclusion, see Thomas Dumm, "The New Enclosures: Racism in the Normalized Community," in Robert Gooding-Williams, ed., *Reading Rodney King/Reading Urban Uprising* (London: Routledge, 1993), pp. 178–95.

58. Diana Gordon, *The Justice Juggernaut: Fighting Street Crime, Controlling Citizens* (New Brunswick, N.J.: Rutgers University Press, 1991).

59. I have in mind here Mike Davis' panoptic shopping centers, in *City of Quartz: Excavating the Future in Los Angeles* (London: Verso, 1990), ch. 4.

60. Peter Scharf, "Empty Bars: Violence and the Crisis of Meaning in the Prison," in Michael Brasell, Steven Dillingham, and Ried Montgomery, eds., *Prison Violence in America* (Cincinnati, Oh.: Anderson Publishing Company, 1985).

61. Here the writing of John Dilulio is representative: see his *Governing Prisons,* from which the quotations are taken, pp. 3, 12, and 172; and more recently, *No Escape: The Future of American Corrections* (New York: Basic Books, 1991).

62. "A Futuristic Prison Awaits the Hard-Core 400" *The New York Times* 17 Oct. 1994. The sophisticated control techniques deployed in these units have a genealogy that runs back to the START program and special disciplinary units at Marion Federal Penitentiary in the 1970s. Marion went on permanent lock-down in 1982, and the "lessons" learned were then incorporated into the Pelican Bay Special Housing Unit (SHU), and from there found their way into the new federal maximum security unit at Florence, Colorado. What little is known about the SHU unit comes from the Pelican Bay Information Project in San Francisco, which has been seeking to document practices and consequences through interviews. See the discussion in Cummins, *Rise and Fall,* pp. 270–74, and by Bill Dunne, in "The U.S. Prison at Marion, Illinois: an Instrument of Oppression," in Ward Churchill and J. J. Vanderwall, eds., *Cages of Steel: The Politics of Imprisonment in the United States* (Washington, D.C.: Maisonneuve Press, 1992). None of this colors John Dilulio's applause for "better management"; see *No Escape,* pp. 25–26 for his discussion of Marion.

63. Foucault, *Discipline and Punish,* p. 237.

64. California and Illinois were the first states to experience gangs in their prisons, and they remain, today, the state systems most dominated by the gang presence. The head of the Illinois Department of Corrections has claimed that 70–80 percent of inmates have some gang affiliation. See Michael Lane, "Inmate Gangs," *Corrections Today,* July 1992; and George M. Camp and Camille G. Camp, *Prison Gangs: Their Extent and Impact on Prisons* (New York: Criminal Justice Institute, 1985).

65. See Irwin's comment on a report by George W. Sumner of the California prison system, "Dealing with Prison Violence," in Cohen, et al. *Prison Violence,* p. 177.

66. Cummins, *Rise and Fall,* p. 272.

67. See Craig Trout, "Gangs: Taking a New Look at an Old Problem"; and Salvador Buentello, "Combating Gangs in Texas," *Corrections Today,* July 1992.

68. Cummins, *Rise and Fall,* p. 272. The quotes are from Lane, "Inmate Gangs."

69. See, as a case in point, the interpretations of the New México prison riot of 1980 in Bert Useem, "Disorganization and the New Mexico Prison Riot of 1980," *American Sociological Review* 50 (1985): 677–88; and in his book with Peter A. Kimball, *States of Siege* (Oxford: Oxford University Press, 1989). A helpful corrective is Mark Colvin, *The Penitentiary in Crisis: From Accommodation to Riot in New Mexico* (Albany: SUNY Press, 1992).

70. Foucault, *Discipline and Punish,* p. 224.

Sexual Violence, Discursive Formations, and the State

Veena Das

Sexual violence against women is constitutive of social and political disorder in India. Widespread violence against women occurred at the time of the Partition of India, when more than one hundred thousand women were abducted from each of the two parts of the Punjab alone (Butalia 1993; Menon and Bhasin 1993). Not only were women abducted and raped, but slogans like "Victory to India" and "Long Live Pakistan" are said to have been painfully inscribed on women's private parts. Although a Fact Finding Organization was set up to enquire into these atrocities, its findings were never made public. I have argued elsewhere that the bodies of women became political signs, territories on which the political programs of the rioting communities of men were inscribed (see Das 1995). Although the judicial silence regarding this occasion is a stunning fact of history, I suggest that in order to read this silence it is necessary to juxtapose it with other occasions when judicial discourse has engaged in separating "normal" sexuality from "pathological" sexuality. We must ask whether the very logic by which courts of law in India bring out this separation does not "normalize" violence against women during periods of disorder. In the face of the disorder of collective violence the state seems to absent itself, so that we cannot guess how the judicial discourse would have constructed pathological sexuality. But I submit that we do have evidence of how, "individual pathology" is constructed in rape trials during normal periods; and further, that in the dense discursivity of the state as it engages in separating the normal from the pathological, we find a production of bodies (both male and female) that normalizes sexual violence, at least for purposes of the law.

393

Rape in the Judicial Discourse

The pervasiveness of sexual violence at every level of social organization has been decisively demonstrated by feminist scholars. Many have claimed that everyday heterosexual practices and the practice of rape participate in the same structure of relations defined by patriarchal ideologies. For example MacKinnon has argued that "sexuality is a set of practices that inscribes gender as unequal in social life. On this level sexual abuse and its frequency reveal and participate in a common structural reality with everyday sexual practice" (1992: 126; see also 1989). But there is a peculiar puzzle here. If sexuality in everyday life, sexual ecstasy, and sexual abuse all have complex, albeit discontinuous linkages, then how is it that the state steps in through its judicial institutions to "problematize" the assumptions of everyday life regarding men's uncontested rights over women's bodies? If the law were only interested in treating sexual offences on analogy with offences against male property, as many have alleged, it would be difficult to explain the importance of the notion of consent in case law as it has developed in India and elsewhere. Indeed, "consent" of the woman turns out to be the most significant category for distinguishing between non-punishable sexual commerce with a woman and the offence of rape against her. In this context, Smart (1989) considers the significance of the category of consent to be that it helps to systematically transform rape into consensual sex within the legal system. More recently Matoesian (1993) has identified courtroom talk as the site for examining how the victim's experience of sexual violence is delegitimized, and the acts in question are decriminalized by their conversion into consensual sex. "Courtroom talk captures the moment to moment enactment and reproduction of rape as criminal social fact" (Matoesian 1993: 27).

There is a genealogical link between the argument made here and Foucault's understanding of the relationship between power and sex. In his *History of Sexuality,* Foucault (1980) essentially understood power as that which seeks to dictate its law to sex. This means first of all that sex is placed by power in a binary system of licit *versus* illicit; permitted *versus* forbidden. In this reading, the effects of power take the general form of limit and lack. Yet Foucault above any other thinker has emphasized that sexuality in modern societies is not so much a product of judicio-political prohibitions as of the will to knowledge/power that lies behind discourses defined by techniques of confession and scientific discursivity. Hence, "We must not think that by saying yes to sex, one says no to power" (Foucault

1980: 157). This seems to imply that the search for freedom in the pleasures of sex is ironically what places a person under the domain of power. Here the distinction between sexual pleasure and sexual subjugation becomes blurred. It is this very play between pleasure and subjugation, I shall argue, that defines techniques of confession in judicio-political discourse, so that the woman's body is made to confess *against her explicit speech;* subjugation is read as pleasure. The court room trial and the structure of sentencing demonstrate how a woman's "no" to sex can be converted into a "yes" through the operation of judicial grammar and sentencing. It is in these practices that we shall see what consent means in the dense discursivity of a field defined by the juridical domain.

The Judicial Discourse

One way of conceptualizing judicial discourse is to see it as a crossroads for multiple transactions by which a particular way of talking about rape sorts women into categories that bring law and social practices into congruence. In their path-breaking work on a semiotic understanding of judicial discourse, Greimas and Landowski (1976) describe how the legislative function of this discourse first separates the licit and illicit comportment of human desires though normative enunciations. These desires, they argue, are then classified and hierarchized through processes of judicial verification by an application of such distinctions as nature and culture, and individual and social.

The legislative function in the discourse is a function of enunciation: it belongs to the order of being by which legal objects are brought into existence in the process of being named. The adjudicatory level, on the other hand, belongs to the order of doing. The linguistic practices encountered in judicial prose orient one toward thinking that the processes of adjudication belong to a reality that exists prior to being named. But in fact it is the legislative function that gives direction to those elements of the world that will be selected for reference. Thus the order of doing is the operational sphere of semiotic objects that have already been brought into existence by legislative enunciations or the legislative definitions of reality.

The juridical domain is defined by the combinations of prescriptions and interdictions, "that create a solid and immobile architecture." However, since the production of rules is constantly subject to verification, the undifferentiated domains of non-prescriptions and non-interdictions that initially define the non-juridical domain can move into the juridical domain through the application of juridical phrases. In the final analysis, then, the juridical discourse splits into the two poles of grammar and semanticity. The legislative level is the level of grammar without content, while the adjudicatory processes relate to the level of judicial verification through which content is given to the judicial grammar. The level of non-judicial discourse—devoid of both judicial grammar and judicial semanticity—constitutes a virtual world, elements of which may enter the judicial world through judicial production and verification. It is this double process of judicial production and verification that negotiates the "reality" of societal categories and fits it into frames of law. In the process, the judicial discourse comes to mediate the everyday categories of sexuality and sexual violence, sorting and classifying the normal and the pathological in terms of marriage and alliance. It is because of the manner in which categories of alliance are brought into the process of judicial verification—separating women into "consenting" and "non-consenting"; regulating male desire by channeling it toward women of appropriate categories—that we can see why judicial discourse becomes silent when rules of alliance stand suspended during periods of collective violence. Let me try to flesh out this argument through a consideration of rape law in India.

Rape in Indian Case Law

Within the codification of law, rape constitutes an offence against the body. At one level, it may be seen along with other crimes in which force is used against a person, resulting in grievous harm or death of the victim. Yet by separating and codifying a separate category under the heading of sexual offences, the Indian Penal Code directly recognizes the right of the state to regulate sexuality. It is important, therefore, to note that although in the sentencing structures judges are compelled to distinguish constantly between rape proper and grievous bodily harm caused by attempted rape, in the penal code itself sexual offences are classified through a binary distinction between "rape" and "unnatural offences." The deployment of the concept of nature, as we shall see later, allows rape to be viewed as an offence which is "natural" and men as falling into a natural state when the ordering mechanisms of culture are absent.

The law relating to crimes in India was codified in 1860 by the colonial British Government by the introduction of the Indian Penal Code (see Dhagamwar 1992). The Code identified rape as an offence and made it punishable under Section 376, which defines rape as follows:

A man is said to commit "rape" who, except in the cases hereafter excepted, has sexual intercourse with a woman under circumstances falling under any of the five following descriptions:

First—against her will.

Secondly—Without her consent.

Thirdly—with her consent, when her consent has been obtained by putting her in fear of death or of hurt.

Fourthly—With her consent when the man knows that he is not her husband, and that her consent is given because she believes that he is another man to whom she is or believes herself to be lawfully married.

Fifthly—with or without her consent, when she is under ten years of age.

Explanation—Penetration is sufficient to constitute the sexual intercourse necessary to the offence of rape.

Sexual intercourse by a man with his own wife, the wife not being under ten years of age is not rape.

The original age of ten years in the fifth clause has since been amended through a series of legislative amendments so that it now stands at sixteen years.

Even from a cursory reading of the text it is clear that in defining the offence of rape the concern is with regulation of sexuality, rather than protection of bodily integrity of the woman. One of the commentators on the present paper, Stacy Cherry (1994), noted that the description specifying a woman giving consent because she believes herself to be lawfully married to an "alleged rapist" seems particularly problematic. What kind of circumstances must exist, asked Cherry, for a woman to believe that she is married and yet not be married? To my mind, this clause clearly brings out the manner in which social reality is mediated through the judicial discourse. Thus, for instance, a man may commit bigamy without the knowledge of the second woman he marries. The woman may believe herself to be married to him, but the marriage is null and void in law. Hence, although he may not have used any force in having sexual relations with her, and indeed, the woman may have consented to the sexual relationship, legally he would be defined as a rapist. When we read this along with the clause which does not consider it judicially possible for a husband to "rape" his wife if she is above the age of sixteen, we can see that the offence of rape is about the regulation of sexuality and not about the protection of the bodily integrity of women. An examination of the case law shows that the consent of a woman can be read as non-consent, and the absence of consent can be read as consent, depending upon where she stands in the system of alliance. What rape as illegal sexual commerce offends, it seems, is not the body of the woman but the correct ordering of sexual relations as defined by societal norms.

It is not that the law is not concerned with the question of consent—at the level of judicial verification, the question of injury to the body becomes crucial in finding evidence of consent. Yet at the level of judicial enunciation of norms the question of consent in the definition of rape is a very complicated issue indeed. This becomes even clearer when we see the subsequent Section 377, which defines "unnatural offences" and prescribes punishments for these.

Section 377 reads as follows: "Whoever voluntarily has carnal intercourse against the order of nature with any man, woman or animal, shall be punished with imprisonment of life, or with imprisonment of either description for a term which may extend to ten years and shall also be liable to fine." The explanation states that: "Penetration is sufficient to constitute the carnal intercourse necessary to the offence described in this section," while a Comment to the Section clarifies that this particular offence consists of carnal knowledge against the order of nature.

I regret that I do not have information about the case law that developed around the category of unnatural offences, but it seems important for us to examine this law to better understand the notions of "nature" deployed in the judicial discourse. For the present I simply note that in contrast to the law on rape, in which the notion of consent plays a very important part, reference to this is absent in defining offences "against the order of nature." Thus, in law, a man cannot be raped, by definition, and a woman submitted to sado-masochist practices by a man through the use of force could not be said to be raped. One is compelled to conclude that *rape is not an unnatural act*. Indeed, as Charles Bright (1994) stated succinctly in his comments on this paper, "the whole question of female consent becomes a process of positioning the male to do what comes naturally—that is to act from and in nature, in full accord with both body (desire) and speech (will)." I think the point is sufficiently clear that the rape law is not oriented toward protecting the bodily integrity of a woman, but towards the regulation of sexuality, and that the category of nature is deployed as an important category for effecting this regulation.

In recent years there have been important amendments to the rape law (see Agnes 1992). A crucial year was 1979, when serious gaps were identified in the law and a push toward reform was initiated. The precipitating event was, as is well known, the Supreme Court judgment in the case of Tukaram versus State of Maharashtra, A.I.R. 1979, S.C.185. The facts of the case were that a young girl, Mathura, was summoned to the police station on a complaint of abduction lodged by her brother against her lover. She came to the police station along with her relatives, including the brother. She alleged that while the relatives were asked to wait, she was taken to the rear of the main building where the Head Constable raped her while a second Constable attempted to rape her, but was unable to because of his inebriated condition. The accused were acquitted by the Sessions Court, which found no evidence of force having been used. The High Court, on appeal, reversed the finding of the Sessions Court on the grounds that it had failed to distinguish between "consent" and "passive submission." Subsequently, the Supreme Court in appeal held that because the victim had not raised any alarm, her allegations were untrue. In the course of pronouncing the judgments, several statements were made in the respective courts regarding the girl that included description of her as a "shocking liar" and frequent references to her having been habituated to sex. These were given considerable weight by the Supreme Court toward discrediting her account of the event. Four law teachers strongly protested the judgment (Baxi, Dhagamwar, Kelkar, and Sarkar—see Baxi et al. 1979). Their agonized formulations led to a country-wide mobilization of women's groups to press for changes in rape laws. After discussions in Parliament and submissions of the Law Commission, the rape law was amended in 1983 to address both procedural and substantive issues. In the amended law, efforts were made to tighten the law in favor of victims. More specifically, the category of custodial rape was defined. The burden of proof was shifted to the accused in cases of custodial rape, and a minimum punishment of ten years rigorous imprisonment was prescribed. Under this provision, gang rape, and rape with a woman known to be pregnant, would also bring a minimum of ten years imprisonment (Dhagamwar 1992).

The 1983 amendment cited more than 100 cases in order to clarify the different clauses. A compilation of these cases, undertaken by Pratiksha Baxi,[1] shows that there are two major concerns in the case law: one pertains to the definition of consent, and the second to the judicial definition of what constitutes "penetration."

Regarding consent, the case law evolves in the direction that consent cannot be obtained after the act; that a woman who is sleeping or is intoxicated cannot give consent; that a woman who is not of sound mind cannot give consent; and that if she misunderstood the act then she cannot be said to have given consent. It seems from these cases that consent is defined in the process of judicial verification as an act of reason and will. This is clearly spelt out in Idan Singh 1977 Cri LJ 556 (Raj), in which it is stated that consent is an act of reason in which there is a conscious and voluntary acceptance of the act of sexual intercourse. Yet there is a counter text which assumes consent to be not only a matter of cognitive and moral recognition, but also a choice that a woman makes between resistance and assent (Rao Harnarain Singh 1958 Cri LJ 563). Here we see two things set in opposition to each other: the will of the woman as expressed in her speech, and the body of the woman as providing evidence of acceptance or rejection. As we shall see, the body is often made to speak, as under torture, against the idea of consent as constituting a cognitive category ALONE. Finally, since the underlying idea is that sexual intercourse with a woman, defined as vaginal penetration, is an act of *nature,* it is rarely asked what constitutes the act of sexual intercourse that a woman consents to. For example, in Jarnail Singh 1972 Cri LJ 824 (Raj), it is stated that if consent is given prior to sexual intercourse, no matter how tardily or reluctantly, and no matter how much force has been used in the act of intercourse, the act does not amount to rape. In each of these areas, a way of reading the relation between signs inscribed on the surface of the body and the "depth" of female subjectivity is established.

Regarding the second point pertaining to penetration, a number of cases state that partial penetration amounts to penetration for purposes of the law; that it is not necessary that the hymen be ruptured, and that medical evidence may be added to other evidence but cannot be treated as sole evidence of rape having occurred, since rape is a legal category and not a medical category. As was stated in Joseph Lines 1844 I C & K 393, "to constitute penetration, it must be proved that some part of the virile member of the accused must have entered within the labia of the pudendum of the girl, no matter how little."

The 1983 amendments were expected to make it easier for victims to seek redress, and case law since then has introduced the idea that mere absence of injury on the body of the prosecutrix does not constitute evidence of consent; neither is corroborative evidence always necessary. Surprisingly, however, the rates of conviction are steadily declining. According to the statistics provided in *Crime in India,* the percentage of convictions in rape cases was in the range of 35 to 38 percent between 1980 and 1986, but it declined to 8 percent in 1988, and then to 9.1 percent in 1990. Although many of these cases did not involve custodial rape, and several of them were already in courts of law before the amendment was passed, one would have expected that the new directions given for interpreting consent would have made conviction easier rather than more difficult. The question of why rates of conviction have declined is one to which I have no ready answer. However, it is worth considering the possibility that the underlying assumptions of judicial production and verification—especially the normalization of rape through its naturalization—have made the process of judicial reform much more difficult than was anticipated.

Judicial Grammar and Judicial Semanticity

In terms of the two poles of judicial grammar and judicial semantics proposed by Greimas and Landowski (1976), we can piece together the following taxonomy: At the pole of judicial grammar the law defines two circumstances: the first in which rape cannot occur by definition, and the second where no judicial verification of consent is necessary. The former covers cases of sexual intercourse between a man and his wife, regardless of whether the wife consents or not . The possibility that a man could force his wife into having sexual intercourse is in the realm of judicial nullity. The second circumstance is the case of a girl below the age of sixteen, in which case only the fact of intercourse has to be established in order for the offence of rape to have occurred. A wife who has been forced into submission by her husband, and a man who has obtained the consent of a girl under sixteen, are both subjects in the "real" world, a reality that judges encounter in the courts again and again. But because from inside the law the real world is seen as a virtual world, it needs the mediation of judicial phrases to negotiate the "messy" reality. As we shall see, there is a tension between judicial grammar and judicial verification, so that a judgment may take into account that a man does not have a right to inflict grievous bodily harm on his wife in the process of having sexual intercourse with her, although within the limits of the judicial grammar this cannot be classified as rape. In the converse case, when judges have encountered evidence of a girl's consent to sexual intercourse, even if she is proved to be under sixteen (but not much below this age), this has been taken to constitute mitigating circumstances, and reason for reducing prison sentences.

The judicial grammar then leaves a whole domain of sexual commerce to which the distinction between force and consent comes to be applied in order that the difference between "sexual intercourse" and "rape" be judicially demonstrated. It is in the play of power to define sex that we find here that distinctions between nature and culture come to be articulated, in order to dramatize masculinity and femininity as capability. The following sections depend heavily upon evidence taken from modes of reasoning applied in judgments in rape cases. The judicial prose, with its own stylistic peculiarities, is embroidered with my own prose, but I hope that it retains its mark of "otherness."

Force and Consent

In the process of judicial verification, the concepts of force and consent are deployed along two different axes constituted by reading the signs on the body, and relating them to the speech of the woman. In every case, the speech of the woman is pitted against her body for the production of truth. In the process of judicial verification, the judges find that either the body bears witness to the truth of the statements of the prosecutrix that she had been forced into submission, or contrarily, it provides evidence to negate her statements.

While in all cases pertaining to the violation of bodily integrity it is inevitable that the body will be objectified in the process of judicial verification, here the body is objectified as a *sexual body*. The female body is defined in this discourse primarily as one which is marked by the impress of male bodies on it, leading to a gendered reading of this process of the body's objectification.

The first question that the judges in a rape trial investigate is whether sexual intercourse has occurred. A whole way of talking about the sexualized body comes into play here: Is the hymen intact? How much of a finger could be inserted into the vagina under medical examination? Is penetration to be understood as vulval or vaginal? and so forth.[2] In this way the court creates a topology of signs that move on the surface of the body, territorialize it, and constitute it as a sexual body, fit or unfit for exchange. The body is objectified in ways that become a kind of judicial pornography. Allow me to give an example of this particular mode of verifying whether an offence is to be classified as a sexual one, or is better treated as non-sexual.

In this case[3] (S.C. 58/1986 decided on 20 Jan. 1987, per P. N. Santhakumari, Sessions Judge, Ernakulam, Kerala), the prosecution accused a boy, age seventeen, of committing assault and rape on a two-year-old girl. The child's mother had left her briefly in the care of her seven-year-old brother) while she went to post a letter. The mother returned to find her son standing in the corridor and crying. The accused was in a room with the baby, and the door was locked and did not yield to her repeated attempts to push it open. Looking through the window, she saw the accused, half-naked, lying on the baby. He was sexually assaulting her, having laid her on the floor while he held her mouth shut with his hands. When she finally was able to get into the room, the mother found that the girl was bleeding profusely from injuries on her private parts, and she was rushed to the hospital. In the medical evidence it was stated that there was a perineal tear on the girl's private parts, and profuse bleeding. The doctor had deposed that he could not examine the girl completely because she needed urgent medical care to save her life.

In arriving at the sentence in this case the judge had to decide whether the offence committed by the accused constituted rape. She summarily dismissed as absurd the plea of the defense that it was a case of false accusation. Nevertheless, her judgment was that the offence was one of attempted rape and not rape proper. The judge's reasoning was as follows:

> Now the question arising for consideration is whether there was penetration to the vaginal canal so as to justify the term rape. In cases of rape the prosecution, in order to prove sexual intercourse, needs to prove penetration in the vaginal canal. Penetration is enough so as to constitute rape, whereas without penetration the offence or the act cannot be termed "rape." . . . The girl being two-years old, penetration would appear to be difficult. Still, there is a perineal tear . . . There is no concrete evidence of penetration into the vaginal canal of the girl, despite the perineal tears on the private parts of the girl, which could probably have been caused by criminal force. The presence of the seminal stains and human sperm heads on the girl's frock, and the evidence of the mother that the accused laid upon the girl does not prove penetration, although it does prove sexual assault. Thus the act does not come within the purview of "rape" as defined in S.375 I.P.C. . . .
>
> The accused having laid the girl on the floor, shutting her mouth by his hands, and being half-naked lying against her as seen by the mother, and having completed the sexual act by the discharge of semen which the mother saw him wiping off from his own private parts and also from

the body of the girl, the accused having taken the girl to the room and having committed the act with the determination and the intention to commit the offence of rape, though he had completed his sexual acts there being no evidence as to the penetration which is the most essential ingredient for rape, it is only sexual assault and attempted rape.

This lengthy quotation has been given here, not because it represents the typical way in which judges define penetration—there are many other cases in which the judges have held that partial penetration is sufficient to constitute penetration under the law—but rather to show that while the same act is constituted as a sexual act for the man, there is an ambiguity as to whether a little girl's body can be treated as a sexual body in the commission of this very act.

I will give one more example in which the judges came to an opposite conclusion, viz., that though the girl had not sustained any injuries the offence *was* that of rape. The case seems to suggest that the question of whether the girl had been sexualized by the experience is an important one in determining whether the offence is sexual in nature. It shows that the movement between surface and depth, between reading the body and reading the woman as subject, provides the underlying grammar of judicial verification.

In this case the respondent/accused was a medical officer staying in a joint family. One day he tricked a young friend of his niece, who was then eight years old, to come to the house when he was alone with his niece. He then compelled the young girl to commit fellatio on him and also slightly inserted his penis into her vulva and had an ejaculation. Although the girl did not relate this to her parents immediately, because he had threatened her with dire consequences if she did, the story came out in the next few days. On being confronted by the girl's enraged father, the accused confessed that he had frequently abused other girls in a similar manner, including his own niece. In court the statements made by the accused were treated as having been an extra-judicial confession made in the presence of the girl's father and his own relatives. In this confession he clearly stated that he had "raped Tulna and had also committed the same kind of sexual assault on earlier occasions with Richa, Priti, and other girls of that locality, but being a doctor he had been careful enough not to rupture their hymen."

The case had come up before the High Court of Madhya Pradesh, which had accepted the entire evidence of the prosecution but had nevertheless entertained a doubt as to whether the offence could be classified as rape. The High Court held that since there were no signs of injuries on either the girl or the accused, the offence was not one punishable under either the provisions of rape or of causing grievous bodily harm, but only under Section 354 IPC, on the ground that the respondent had outraged the modesty of a young girl.

The decision of the High Court created a scandal in the international press. Although the State did not prefer an appeal, the father of the girl appealed in the Supreme Court against the judgment. In its review of the case, the Supreme Court held that there was enough evidence that the respondent "without completely and forcibly penetrating the penis into the vagina of the girl had slightly penetrated within the labia majora or vulva or pudenda without rupturing the hymen and thereby satisfied his lust after ejection of semens." The Supreme Court held that this was sufficient to constitute the statutory definition of penetration which was necessary to prove rape, and handed out punishment accordingly.

In contrast to the first case, in which the girl had suffered grievous bodily harm, in this one the girl was forced to cooperate with the accused and had hence escaped injuries on the body. The accused, being a doctor, had the technical skills not to rupture the hymen. In the case of the two-year-old child the offence was declared to be a non-sexual one. In the second case, the Supreme Court concluded that it was a sexual offence that had been committed.

I suggest that underlying the discussion of what constitutes penetration, and hence rape, is another discourse, one that crisscrosses the discourse on sexuality: the discourse on alliance. In Hindu society the young girl, with her body unmarked by the sexual desires (lusts) of men, is considered the appropriate gift in marriage that establishes alliances between men. A girl's awakening into sexuality is considered not as the work of her own desire, but rather the working of male desire, which in the code of alliance is, most appropriately, the desire of her husband. The sexual offence of rape against a young girl thus becomes an offence against the code of alliance, although this is only obliquely alluded to in the judicial discourse. Hence in the case of Tulna, the Supreme Court having defined the offence as that of rape, went on to state the following: "We are told at the bar that the victim who is now nineteen years old, after having lost her virginity still remains unmarried undergoing the untold agony of the traumatic experience and the deathless shame suffered by her. Evidently the victim is under the impression that there is no monsoon season in her life and that her future chances for getting married and settling down in a respectable family are completely marred."

Without making every qualification, I would like to suggest that judgments on rape in cases involving young girls (especially if a girl is a virgin), lie at the intersection of the discourse of sexuality and the discourse of alliance. Therefore, the question of whether a sexual offence has been committed is decided, not by recourse to the opposition between force and consent, but rather according to whether the body has been so sexualized by the experience as to make it unexchangeable in marriage. Thus it is not only a matter of regarding the signs on the surface of the body, but also of constructing an "inside," much as Foucault talks of the inside as being in the nature of a fold. Hence, in the first case, involving the two-year-old child, the offence came to be constituted as one of having caused bodily injury, but not rape, even though the injuries were on the private parts of the girl. In the second case, although the girl did not sustain any injuries and her hymen was not broken, the act was clearly defined as sexual in nature. I suggest that this may be attributed to the fact that the two-year-old child, although badly injured, was not seen as having been "sexualized" by the act, whereas the eight-year-old girl, by having been compelled to *experience* male sexuality, had been so sexualized as to be unremittingly shamed by her experience.[4] Indeed, the judges in their verdict quoted from her account to show that what she experienced could be appropriately termed a sexual violation. For example, she had stated that "Nawal Chacha (uncle) put his male organ inside my vagina and since it was fat it kept slipping out. After that my vagina was paining." The judge's reference to her feelings of shame in recalling these events shows that it is not only changes in the body but also in the construction of the self as a sexual being that determines "marriageability" of a girl. This is why the judicial discourse dwells on her memory of the event as much as on bodily harm as constitutive of rape.

Whereas in cases of a child or a virgin the question is whether a body previously unmarked by the impress of male desire on it has been "sexualized" through the offence under trial, in cases of women who may be defined as "sexually experienced," the discourses on sexuality and alliance intersect at a different point. This is the point at which a slippage occurs in which the offence against the body and the will of the woman is transformed into an offence against the rules of alliance. These rules implicitly state that men may only treat as sexually available those women who are not integrated into the structure of alliance. Thus those men who *recognize* each other in the "matrimonial dialogue of men," to use the evocative phrase of Lévi-Strauss (1969), are normatively required to constitute the women as signs, as women carrying *significance* in this dialogue. If, on the other hand, a woman is not chaste and is therefore without *significance* in exchange between men, then she may be seen as available for sexual experimentation. In all such cases, the rape trial becomes a dramatic enactment, showing how force may be used against the will of the woman but is likely to be converted into consent by the application of judicial reasoning. An example of the first kind of reasoning—the offering of judicial protection to a woman who is integrated into the structure of alliance—is found in a judgment delivered by the Karnataka High Court in Criminal Appeal No. 79 of 1983, D. II–II–1986, in the case of the State of Karnataka (Appellant) and Mehaboob and Others (Respondents). In this case the prosecutrix was a married woman, normally resident in Bangalore, who had gone to another town by bus to visit her ailing father. From the bus stand she took an autorickshaw driven by one of the accused. On the way the driver stopped and at his whistle another accused entered the autorickshaw. Instead of going to the residential colony where the woman's father lived, the driver took her to a lonely place. The prosecutrix was threatened and bodily carried to a ditch where she was raped. The defense plea was that the absence of injuries on her body or on the accused showed that the prosecutrix did not resist and therefore her accusation was a tissue of lies. The Sessions Court had acquitted the accused on the grounds that injuries were not found on the woman or on the accused, and that there was a lack of other collaborative evidence to prove rape. In an appeal against the order of acquittal, the Appellate Court held that it was possible that the woman did not physically resist for fear of being assaulted, and that absence of injuries did not constitute lack of proof of a sexual offence having been committed on her. The Court also held that it was now settled law that corroboration was not essential for conviction and that the necessity of corroboration was a matter of prudence. In this case, since the prosecutrix was a respectably married woman, her testimony did not need collaboration. The order of acquittal was thereby reversed. This case is a good example of the manner in which femininity as capability is constructed, and illustrates how a rape trial may become a dramatic enactment of the division between good women and bad women, placing the norms of femininity on display.

The defense of the accused in this case had been that the prosecutrix had been abandoned by her husband and had taken to prostitution. They alleged that the police had foisted a false case against them, and that because the woman was of an immoral character her evidence was not credible. The defense had also relied on an earlier case (Pratap Misra vs. State of Orissa, AIR 1977, SC 1307: [1977 Cri LJ 817]) when it had been held that absence of injury either on the accused or the prosecutrix showed that the prosecutrix had not resisted.

In its judgment, the Appellate Court admitted that, according to the medical officer, the woman had not complained of any pain in her private parts. However, "as stated by the medical officer herself further, there would be such pain or injury only if the victim is virgin and admittedly PW-1 was a married woman and used to sexual intercourse. Therefore, the fact there were no injuries on the person did not necessarily mean either the story of PW-1 regarding the incidence was unreliable or that she was a consenting party."

The judges went on to state further that "We have gone through the evidence of PW-1 with utmost care, particularly the version of the case the defense has tried to present regarding the character of PW-1, but regarding the suggestions in the cross examination, which she has strongly denied, there is nothing to even remotely suggest that she is a woman of such easy virtues."

We shall see a little later that how judges interpret the absence of injuries depends upon their understanding of the character of a woman, and more precisely whether a woman "habituated to sexual intercourse" is firmly bound within the structure of alliance, or whether she can be treated as someone outside it. In this particular case, the dividing practices by which good women and bad women are separated is even clearer, since the judges gave an elaborate discourse on the meaning of consent. It is worthwhile to quote this at some length.

And whilst the sands were running out in the time glass, the crime graph of offences against women in India has been scaling new peaks. This is why an elaborate rescanning of the jurisprudential sky through the lenses of "logos" and "ethos" has been necessitated. In the Indian case refusal to act on the testimony of a victim of sexual assault is adding insult to injury. Why should the evidence of a girl or a woman who complains of rape or sexual molestation be viewed with the aid of spectacles fitted with lenses tinged with doubt, disbelief or suspicion? . . . We must not be swept off our feet by the approach found in the Western world, which has its own social milieu, its own social mores, its own permissive values, and its own code of life. Corroboration may be considered essential to establishing a sexual offence in the backdrop of the social ecology of the Western world. It is wholly unnecessary to import the said concept on a turn-key basis and to transplant it to Indian soil, regardless of the altogether different atmosphere, attitudes, mores, and responses of the Indian society and its profile . . .

Having established through spatial differentiation the difference between a social milieu which is permissive (i.e., the West) and one in which girls live in a "tradition bound non-permissive society" (i.e., India), the judges map this spatial difference onto a difference between women of two kinds. They give no less then twelve reasons why one may presume that women in India would not make false allegations of sexual assault, "with the rare exception of one or two cases coming from possibly amongst the urban elite." These twelve reasons define the limits within which sexual desire may move. Thus a woman admitting to sexual assault against her would be conscious of social ostracism; if she is unmarried she would apprehend the difficulty of securing an alliance with a suitable match "from a respectable or an acceptable family"; she would risk losing the love and respect of her husband; she would feel extremely embarrassed in relating the incident to others on account of her upbringing in a tradition-bound society where, by and large, sex is taboo.

I need not labor the point further that a woman whose testimony is likely to be believed is normatively defined as one who is "tradition bound," who displays the appropriate modesty with regard to male desire, and who is in danger of losing the love and respect of her husband if it turns out that she has consented to sexual intercourse with another man. This brings me to the issue of how judicial logic is applied to issues of consent when the woman does not come within these defined limits, and hence violates the definition of a good woman.

I should like to take my examples of this sort of judicial reasoning from two cases: one (State of Orissa vs. Pratap Misra) was quoted in the previous judgment, and the second, Tukaram vs. State of Maharashtra, more popularly known as the Mathura case, was alluded to earlier. It may be recalled that Mathura, a young girl had been raped at the police station. The Sessions Court had acquitted the accused,, while the High Court, on appeal, reversed the decision on the grounds that passive submission by the girl could not be read as consent. The judgment that we shall be considering is that of the Supreme Court which reversed the decision of the High Court and set aside the conviction.

Let us see how Mathura is portrayed as a social persona in the judgment. "Mathura (PW-1) is the girl who is said to have been raped. Her parents died when she was a child and she is living with her brother, Gama (PW-3). Both of them work as laborers to earn a living. Mathura (PW-1) used to go to the house of Nushi (PW-2) for work and during the course of her visits to that house, came into contact with Ashok, who was the sister's son of Nushi (PW-2) and was residing with the latter. The contact developed into an intimacy so that Ashok and Mathura (PW-1) decided to become husband and wife."

Following this, Mathura's brother Gama had lodged a report at the police station alleging that his sister had been kidnapped by Nushi. At the police station the Head Constable asked Mathura to wait while he asked the others to leave. It was while her companions were waiting outside that the Head Constable took her to a toilet situated at the rear of the police station, loosened her underwear, lit a torch, and stared at her private parts. He then dragged her to a charpoy, felled her to the ground, and raped her, despite her protests and stiff resistance. After this a second constable fondled her private parts but was unable to rape her because he was intoxicated.

The main contention of the appellants before the Supreme Court was that there was no direct evidence of rape, no marks of injury were found on the person of the girl and "their absence goes a long way to indicate that the alleged intercourse was a peaceful affair and that the story of stiff resistance put out by the girl is all false." The High Court had found evidence of passive submission, and believed the victim when she stated that "immediately after her hand was caught by Ganpat, she cried out. However, she was not allowed to raise a cry when she was being taken to the latrine because she was prevented from doing so. Even so, she had cried out loudly. She stated that she had raised an alarm even when her underwear was loosened at the latrine, and also when Ganpat was looking at her private parts with the aid of a torch." The Supreme Court, however, held that the cries and alarm were a concoction on her part. It said that it was preposterous to suggest that she was so over-awed by the persons in authority and the circumstances that she could not resist. The judges supported the judgment of the Sessions Court, including the version that, "Finding Nushi angry and knowing that Nushi would suspect something fishy, she (Mathura) could not have admitted that, of her own free will, she had surrendered her body to a Police constable. The crowd included her lover Ashok and she had to sound virtuous before him."

How is it that in the State of Karnataka vs. Mehboob and Others the judge made such a strong case for giving full credence to the woman's claim that force had been used against her, despite the absence of injuries, while in the present case the Supreme Court assumed that the girl had actively participated in the act of intercourse, even though her brother and lover were waiting outside. One must to in the structure of alliance relations within which the girl/woman was placed to see why her body was perceived to contradict her speech. Mathura had already been cast in the social persona of a woman who had taken a lover, and so her claim that she had protested could be dismissed as a lie. In support of the judge's contention, medical evidence was read to show how habituated to sexual intercourse she was. "Her hymen revealed old ruptures. The vagina admitted two fingers easily." Thus the reading of the surface of the body is made to conform to the judge's reading of the "inside" of her being; to his conviction that she was a particular kind of girl who would be so overcome by her sexual desire for the constable, whom she had encountered for the first time, that she would surrender her body to him while her lover waited outside, and then make false accusations of rape so as to appear virtuous. Taken together, these two judgments show that judicial belief or disbelief in a woman's version of the events is a matter of the classificatory practices through which good women are separated from bad women. It has less to do with protecting the bodily integrity of women and more to do with the regulation of sexuality in accordance with rules of alliance. Far from problematizing practices of sexuality in this regard, judicial discourse normalizes the dividing practices. Sexual violation cases provide the opportunity for courts of law to become sites of dramatic enactment of the judicial norms through which the relationship between the surface of the body and the depth of the feminine being can be read. The court can thereby create the female as the subject, though by necessity a fragmented subject since her body and speech are put at war with each other.

If further proof were needed of the classification of women suggested by the case law, one could refer to State of Orissa vs. Pratap Misra. In this case a pregnant woman who was staying in a holiday resort with a man was raped by some N.C.C. students. Despite the presence of corroborative evidence, what weighed most heavily with judges in pronouncing the sentence of acquittal was the finding that the man accompanying her was not her husband but her lover. The absence of injuries on her body was then seen as a sign of her consent and it was assumed that the man had contracted with the students to make her available for sexual intercourse. Even the miscarriage she had following this sexual assault was seen as unconnected to the event of rape.

We are now in a position to give a concise description of the classification of women that emerges in these rape trials. There is first a binary distinction between a girl who is a virgin and a woman who is sexually experienced. Desirable women are those who can be integrated into the system of alliance as virgin girls given as a gift in marriage to "respectable and acceptable" families, or women who have already been so integrated. Sexual desire in these women is regulated by the structure of alliance, and therefore an offence against them constitutes a sexual offence because it violates the codes through which the matrimonial dialogue of men is conducted. By the same logic, however, women who are described as of easy virtue, "habituated to sexual intercourse" with men who are not their husbands, do not have rights to the protection of the state. In their cases, the body always speaks to negate their speech. By declaring them to be shocking liars, the courts construct a category of women in whose cases a "no" to sex can be converted to a "yes" by the application of judicial reasoning. I shall now argue further that judicial discourse does not simply blot out such women from sight, but actively constitutes them as available for the satisfaction of male lust by the judicial phrasing of the relationship between surface and depth. This is the logic within which we can understand the concern of case law to define, first, what is penetration and, second, what is consent. The first re-orders the body as surface on which the judicial gaze can read different kinds of signs, establishing either complicity with or resistance to sexual intercourse. Her body provides evidence of her place in the division between virtuous and wanton women. The second concern, to establish consent, requires inference about the will of the woman. It thus turns on how depth, or the woman's interior motive, may be made to appear by reading the surfaces of the body through the judicial gaze. Female subjectivity is made transparent as the judicial gaze moves from the surface to the depth of the body. Thus the integrity of her being is shattered in the rape trial and the whole question of female consent becomes a "process of positioning the male to do what comes naturally—that is to act from and in nature, in full accord with both body (desire) and speech (will)" (Bright 1994: 3).

The Construction of Male Desire

The discourse on male desire is a veiled one. Nevertheless, the judicial phrases uttered in judgments show clearly that the concept of nature is deployed to define men's desire for female bodies as "natural." Then the classification of women between good and bad—is used to direct such "natural" desires toward the appropriate categories of women.

Desire for female bodies is seen as "natural," a counterpart to rape being seen as an offence that does not violate the order of nature, and so the judicial discourse on male sexuality is engaged in the creation of a "social savage" (Greimas and Landowsky 1976). This social savage is tamed by the application of rules of alliance on the basis of which men may be constructed in relation to each other. Thus desire in the male is schooled by placing men in particular positions relative to each other, and the desire for female bodies is regulated through social recognition that men grant each other in the system of alliance. Male desires are then judicially classified in accordance with the points of intersection between the discourse of sexuality and the discourse of alliance.

Desire for the female in a young male is classified as *instinct,* provided it is directed toward a woman who is not integrated into the system of alliance and can therefore be categorized as a woman of easy virtue. The judicial construct of "young male acting out his natural sexual instincts" is deployed in the sentencing structure in the course of hearings on mitigating circumstances granted to the accused. It may be evoked in the context of acquittal, or in cases when judges are laying out their reasoning as to why the offence should be treated as a grave one. Independent of the context, the judicial phrasing (emphasized in the following texts) makes this construct of a "natural sexuality" residing in the male available for thought. This is particularly striking because women who the courts classify as of "easy virtue" are not seen as acting out natural instincts which would be common to all women.

In the case discussed earlier (S.C. 58/1986, Ernakulam) of the two-year-old child who was sexually assaulted by a young man, the Assistant Sessions Judge gave her reasoning for reduction of his prison sentence: "It is indeed a cruel and wretched act to commit sexual assault or attempt to rape an infant girl of 2 years, especially in the circumstance that the accused was sharing his stay in the residential apartment of the family of that girl along with them. At any rate *the accused could have refrained from whatever his sexual instincts may be while around the child. Still, in due consideration of the prime of youth of the accused and his tender age of 17 at the time of the act . . ."* (my emphasis).

The second case is that of an unmarried woman who was raped by a hospital attendant after he had taken her to an empty room on the pretext that he was taking her to the ward where her niece was admitted. After rejecting the defense plea that the prosecutrix could not be believed because she was not a virgin and that there were discrepancies in her account, the Court observed: "The beastliness and atrocity of the crime are evident from the injury that resulted from the thrust. According to PW-2, the doctor, about thirty stitches were needed for the ragged tear inside the vagina and a blood transfusion also had to be given. There is no evidence of any provocation or enticement from the side of the victim. *There is no evidence that the prosecutrix is of easy virtues. The accused is thirty-two years old and the crime evidently is not the result of any impulsive act due to the irrepressible sexual urge of an adolescent or youngster"* (my emphasis).

Many other examples could be given of this form of reasoning. I hope the point is sufficiently clear that in the process of judicial verification courts construct a category of young males who are acting out their impulses and "irrepressible sexual urges" when they rape women. The judicial intervention is not directed towards the protection of all women from such males on the prowl. What the courts do is define the category of women upon whom these urges may be acted out, and separate them from the women upon whom these acts may *not* be committed. The former are defined as women of "easy virtue," while the latter are women who in future may be integrated into the system of alliance or are already within it.

I believe it is this definition of a certain kind of sexual violence as stemming from the order of nature which allows agents of the state such as policemen to commit rape and sexual assault on women who have come within their jurisdiction due to disturbances in the code of alliance. In the case of Mathura, it was the complaint lodged by the brother against her lover that allowed the police constables access to her. The judicial phrasing of the Supreme Court judgment was also based upon the fact that, "she had a lover, she was habituated to sexual intercourse, and the hymen had shown 'old' tears." It was as if it were "natural" for such a woman to agree to sexual intercourse with the constable whom she had not even known before, right in the police station while her relatives, including her lover, waited outside. In other cases of custodial rape also, a common feature has been that the woman has violated the code of alliance and thereby become a field on which men may gratify their sexual instincts.

In the eyes of the courts, when does sexual instinct become unholy lust? I have suggested that this occurs when the sexual act has made unmarriageable a girl who was previously suitable for being given in marriage. We saw this reasoning applied in the case of Tulna, the eight-year-old girl. In that case the appellants and the defendants belonged to "respectable families," a point emphasized quite strongly in the judgment, which noted that the girl's father was a journalist who had traveled abroad, and the people involved were men of "status." The same reasoning, viz., that the offence of rape consisted in having made the girl unmarriageable, may be found when the accused has a higher status than the girl, except that in such cases the judges may seek to correct the injustice by insisting on a marriage between the victim and the offender, or the punishment may be that financial compensation has to be paid to the girl to secure a bridegroom who would be willing to marry her.

Rose Varghese (1992) cites a case (Braja Kumar Chauhan vs. the State of Orissa) in which the judge first tried to arrange a marriage between the prosecutrix and the accused. After the attempt failed, the judge then reduced the sentence of imprisonment of the accused and fined him Rs. 3000, to be paid to the prosecutrix. He stated that the prosecutrix "now a young girl, will be left at lurch on account of the stigma" due to the publicity that the case must have locally received, and prospects for her marriage appeared bleak. However, she could be rehabilitated if she received some financial assistance. Clearly the court was instrumental in engineering a "trade off" in this case so that a man of a lower social status might be provided with financial incentive to marry the woman who has otherwise become unmarriageable. The concern is again not with protection of the bodily integrity of the woman but with correcting a disturbance in the system of alliance[5] which has been violated by "untamed" male desire.

The judges are also likely to treat sexual desire as "unholy lust" in cases of gang rape if the husband is present at the time of the sexual assault, that is, provided the man is *recognized* as an appropriate partner in the matrimonial dialogue. In one case, three men broke into a house, committed robbery, and gang raped the wife while the husband was held at knifepoint. In the First Information Report, the husband did not report the rape "due to fear of loss of reputation."[6] However, after the accused were identified and arrested he reported the rape, saying that "this should not happen to any *husband* in future" (cited. in Varghese 1992: 159; my emphasis). In awarding the sentence of ten years imprisonment, the court noted the heinous nature of the crime. Although the woman had not physically resisted the rapists, the judges noted that this was "due to fear of death of her husband, herself, and her child." As Purvi Shah (1994: 4) astutely noted, "This court's decision is not based on any injury to the woman's body or lack of consent. Rather, it is framed within the context of the harm her husband, family and she—within the context of her family—may face. Indeed, this woman has been made into a wife or mother rather than a woman. The cases whereby the court renders decisions of rape involve subjects seen as wives, not as women." Not only is the husband's respectability seen as the central factor in this case. This privileging of the husband echoes the power granted to a father. For instance, in the rape case involving the eight year old, part of the case's validity stemmed from 'the girl's enraged father' who was responsible for appealing the case." Thus "natural instinct" is transformed into "unholy lust," in judicial phrasing, if acting out this instinct leads to stigmatizing men as husbands or fathers. In arranging and aligning women and positioning them *in relation to men* as either available for sex or protected within systems of alliance, the courts construct male desire in a manner that leads to either the naturalization of rape as legally consensual, or to its criminalization it as a challenge to patriarchal alliance systems.

Similar facts, however, of a woman raped in the presence of her husband have a different appearance in judicial reasoning if it turns out that the woman was not legally wedded to the man. In the case of Pratap Mishra vs. State of Orissa, referred to earlier, the woman was sexually assaulted by three N.C.C. cadets while on holiday with a man. In this case the judges of the Supreme Court disbelieved the woman's version—even though she suffered a miscarriage after the rape—and assumed consent on her part. An important factor for the judges was that the woman was only a "concubine" of the man. Vasudha Dhagamwar (1992: 246), in an excellent critique, quotes from the judgment: "We do not mean to suggest even for a moment that PW-2 was a pimp, but the fact remains that the appellants undoubtedly wanted to have negotiations with him before insisting that he open the door. This is also a circumstance that militates against the case of rape and shows that PW-2 himself connived in the sexual intercourse committed by the appellants with his concubine."

One is stunned to observe in this case that what counts for the judges is the assumed relation among the men; the circumstance that militates against the case of rape is that "*PW-2 himself connived in the sexual inter-*

course committed by the appellants with his concubine." Neither the injuries on the body of the woman, nor her own will, count; the female body and will are placed in the "custody" of the male to be disposed of as he wishes.

The third construction of the rapist is of a man securing vengeance against another man by violating the latter's wife, daughter, or sister. Here again the woman's body is merely the sign through which men enter into relationships with each other. In the Indian courts this comes up frequently in the context of policemen going on a rampage of looting, destruction, and mass rape in order to punish the population of a village or a locality. Varghese (1992) quotes from the case of fourteen policemen who went on a rampage against the women in a small village in order to avenge an insult to one of their colleagues (quoted in Varghese 1992, and Dhagamwar 1992). The Court acquitted the policemen on the grounds that the women in the village, who were from the lower castes, could not be equated with "such ladies who hail from decent and respectable societies," since they were engaged in menial work and were of questionable character.[7] The judge further added that, "It cannot be ruled out that these ladies might speak falsehoods to get a sum of Rs. 1000, which was a huge sum for them."

Because the naturalization of male desire is connected to systems of alliance, the whole question of marital rape is removed from the arena of judicial discourse. The satisfaction of male desire within the confines of matrimony is considered legitimate, no matter how it is fulfilled. The legal code does not recognize marital rape—hence at the level of judicial grammar the category does not exist. In the process of judicial verification, however, the judges can find instances when grievous bodily harm has been done to the wife in the process of the husband's exercise of his conjugal rights. In such cases the courts have held that while a husband can cause grievous bodily harm to his wife, this cannot be classified as a sexual offence. The first and best-known case of this kind was reported in 1890 when Phulmoni Dasee—who was a little over ten years old—died when her husband tried forcibly to have sexual intercourse with her. The husband was convicted under section 338 of the Indian Penal Code which deals with causing grievous hurt by committing an act so rashly as to endanger human life or the personal safety of another. Subsequently the age of consent was raised to twelve, and it has continued to rise to where it now sits at sixteen (see Dhagamwar 1992). The law clearly takes recourse in the idea that marriage is the prescribed institution for the satisfaction of "natural" sexual instincts, and therefore sexual intercourse within marriage cannot be considered a sexual offence. If a woman incurs injury during sexual intercourse with her husband, this is to be treated as are other non-sexual offences of a similar kind. Thus in the case of a conjugal couple, the surface of the female body has no information to convey for determining the nature of the "inside," for she does not exist as a subject for purposes of rape law.

Pratiksha Baxi (1995) argues that the discourse on marital rape, not only in the courts but also in parliamentary debates, has normalized the use of force in sexual intercourse within marriage. She points out that in the report of the Joint Parliamentary Committee on the proposed amendments to the rape law, a separate category of "illicit sexual intercourse not amounting to rape" was created to cover cases in which a man who is separated from his wife forces her to have sex with him (J.P.C. Report 1982: 8). In defense of this amendment it was stated that "The Committee feel that in a case where the husband and wife are living separately under the decree of judicial separation, there is a possibility of reconciliation between them until a decree of divorce is granted. Hence, the intercourse by the husband with his wife without her consent during such period should not be treated as, or equated with, rape. The Committee are of the opinion that intercourse by the husband with his wife under such circumstances should be treated as illicit sexual intercourse" (J.P.C. Report 1982: 8; cited in Baxi 1995: 73). As Baxi insightfully observes: "The distinction between rape and sexuality from the woman's point of view gets blurred, for the state permits force in sexual intercourse, not only for describing it as normal but by normalizing it for the sake of "reconciliation." Here power is deployed to constitute a married woman's sexuality as "passive," for the capacity to say "no" to sex within marriage is not recognized by the law as a legal right."

In Foucault's *History of Sexuality* (1980), power was understood as essentially that which dictates its law to sex by dividing sexuality between licit and illicit and between permitted and forbidden compartments. In looking at the relationship between power and sexuality as it is revealed in the judicial discourse in India, I suggest that it is encountered not in the form of limit and lack, but in its dynamic, active form of production of bodies and speech, both male and female. The sites of judicial discourse are the female body and male desire, while there is a corresponding silencing of the discussion on female desire and male bodies. As we have seen, it is male desire which is considered "natural," hence "normal," and the female body is seen as the natural site on which this desire is to be enacted.

Women are not seen as desiring subjects in the rape law—as wives they do not have the right to withhold consent from their husbands—although the state invests its resources in protecting them from the desires of other men. Paradoxically, women defined in opposition to the wife or the chaste daughter, that is, women of easy virtue, as the courts put it, also turn out to have no right to withhold consent. Unlike the case of the wife, however, it is not through the application of judicial grammar but through judicial semantics that this right, though legally granted, is taken away in the course of court hearings. As Purvi Shah puts it, "A reading of female desire as interpreted by the courts demonstrates that while men are seen to be acting out their 'natural' urges when engaging in 'illicit' sex, women who show any sort of desire outside the confines of marriage are immediately considered 'loose.' By escaping the confines of male-centered discourses of sexuality and alliance, these women are then castigated by becoming the objects of any sort of male desire. Rape is not a crime but is reduced to an act that she herself deserves or seeks. . . . Under the court's adjudication of these rape cases, every man thus becomes not an object of female desire, but rather these women who show 'illicit' desire become consensual objects of male desire even against their will" (1994: 6).

Thus it is clear that a woman's "yes" to sex outside of marriage puts her in a position in which she is rendered judicially incapable of constructing desire in the singular. Her illicit desire places her within the power of *any* man and especially within the power of the agents of the state such as policemen. It would, however, be a mistake to think that this is only a disciplining of female desire. It is equally a disciplining of male desire. By constructing male desire as "natural," it is also generalized, so that once the system of alliance is suspended in thought, one woman is considered as good as any other for the satisfaction of this desire. Thus the judicial discourse cannot admit desire for a particular woman even in the male subject. One may recall the evidence in the case of the *chowkidar* (watchman) of the guest house in the Pratap Misra, who had found the man crying helplessly outside the room in which the N.C.C. cadets raped the woman, presumably his lover. Similarly Mathura's brother and husband were made to wait outside the police station while she was raped by the constable.

Just as there seems to be no place for the woman as a desiring subject in the judicial discourse, while there is an elaborate vocabulary for describing the female anatomy and the impact of sexual intercourse on it, correspondingly there is no reading of signs of sexuality on the surfaces of the male body for establishing sexual offences, nor any understanding that desire in the male may be for a particular woman rather than for a generalized, standardized female body.[8] About the only question that seems medically relevant to the courts is whether the accused is capable of sexual intercourse or not, and whether there are signs of injury, especially on the sexual organs of the male. In both of the two cases of the violated two-year-old and eight-year-old children, the judges found evidence of sexual acts on the part of the males. In both cases the judges only considered the question of penetration, although in one case partial penetration was considered sufficient to constitute rape while in the second case it was not. An alternative way of constructing rape would be to consider the evidence on the male body—reading its surface as conveying information about the nature of the offence—as sufficient for establishing that a sexual offence has occurred. In that case, the whole question of what constitutes penetration would become irrelevant because both male and female subjects would be constructed in their wholeness.

Concluding Observations

In this paper's introduction I raised the question of whether an understanding of how judicial discourse constructs normal and pathological sexuality at the level of the individual could help us to understand the widespread violation of women during episodes of collective violence, and the judicial silence that we encounter in the face of such grave disorders. I do not think that I have provided any final answers, but I do think I have charted a useful direction for future enquiry. The combination of judicial production and verification (judicial grammar and judicial semantics) that we have considered produces a discourse on rape which places itself essentially at the intersection of the discourses of sexuality and alliance, and fulfills the essential function of protecting the alliance system rather than the bodily integrity of women. Therefore, the law can only function so long as certain normal classifications remain in place: those of marriageable and non-marriageable women, and those of men who *recognize* themselves as being partners in alliance as opposed to men for whom such recognition is withheld since they are not likely partners in alliance. Since the function of law is to sort out women, and to position them in terms of availability and non-availability with reference to different categories of males, the entire judicial discourse falls silent when these categories collapse. This does not explain why the desire to assert collective identity—whether of nation or of community—should become metamorphosed into the desire to humiliate men of other nations or communities through violent appropriation of "their" women, but I believe that my analysis lays the foundation for understanding why the judicial institutions of the state become silent in the face of such disorder. I cannot find even the rudiments of a jurisprudence in the Indian legal system (perhaps this can be generalized for other legal systems) that could address the problem of rape in contexts in which the problem is not that of ordering and sorting women, but of protecting their bodily integrity against brutal rape and abduction.

NOTES

Acknowledgments: I am grateful to the participants in the "States of Violence" conference who commented on this paper. I would like especially to thank the student commentators, Carole McGrahanan, Purvi Shah, and Stacy Cherry, as well as Charles Bright for his comments that proved extremely challenging to me while I was revising the paper. Thanks are due also to the editors for their close reading of the paper and for their suggestions. Discussions with Upendra Baxi, Pratiksha Baxi, and Kalpana Viswanath were very fruitful in helping me to formulate the issues.

1. I am grateful to Pratiksha Baxi for compiling the list of these cases for me.

2. The female body is objectified as a general body—all women are assumed to have "normal" bodies that undergo the same kinds of changes as a result of sexual activities.

3. Many of the cases analyzed here are cited in Varghese (1992) painstaking report on sentencing structures in rape cases.

4. Pratiksha Baxi has argued that the link between shame and sexual violence often results in rape being seen as "worse than death," an interpretation that she says the Indian Women's Movement has consistently tried to reject (Baxi 1995). See also Kalpana Viswanath (1994), who shows how the idea of shame and sexuality as a linked pair are internalized by women.

5. We may compare this with mediation in feuds—another system in which men recognize each other through the exchange of violence—in which the party that is on the verge of losing may be persuaded to accept blood money to terminate the feud.

6. The question of how temporality enters the judicial discourse is a very important one, not only at the level of judicial grammar, but also at the level of judicial verification. Delay in reporting rape seriously prejudices the prosecution's case, outcome of prosecutions for them, not only because of the difficulty of obtaining medical evidence, but also because judges are less likely to believe the woman. In the Indian judicial system, the delays in arriving at a judgment can make time itself a resource in the hands of litigants.

7. When the exchange of violence is within the framework of the institution of feud, strict rules control the styles of violence used. The sexual violation of women by the feuding parties is strictly outside of the normative frame (see Das and Bajwa 1994). What we witness in the case of policemen going on a rampage against lower-caste women cannot be derived from rules of feud, within which only men of equal status are said to "recognize" each other. Instead, it emerges from a perverted theory of punishment in which the illegitimacy of state practices combine with a working of caste hierarchy to produce such outcomes.

8. Desire for a male sexual partner is similarly generalized as a enactment of unnatural desire—an offence against nature.

REFERENCES

Agnes, Flavia. 1992. Review of a Decade of Legislation, 1980–1989: Protecting Women against Violence? *Economic and Political Weekly* 7: WS19–WS33.

Baxi, Pratiksha. 1995. The Normal and the Pathological in the Construction of Rape: A Sociological Analysis. Unpublished M. Phil. Dissertation, University of Delhi.

Baxi, U., et al. 1979. An Open Letter to the Chief Justice of India. *Supreme Court Cases* 4: 17–22.

Bright, Charles. 1994. "Comment on 'Sexual Violence, Discursive Formations and the State,'" by Veena Das, at the *CSSH* conference "States of Violence," University of Michigan, Ann Arbor, 16–18 April.

Butalia, Urvashi. 1993. "Community, State, and Gender. On Women's Agency During Partition." *Economic and Political Weekly* 17: WS12–WS24.

Cherry, Stacy. 1994. "Some Comments on Veena Das' 'Sexual Violence, Discursive Formations and the State.'" Presented at the *CSSH* conference "States of Violence," University of Michigan, Ann Arbor, 16–18 April.

Das, Veena. 1995. *Critical Events: An Anthropological Perspective on Contemporary India.* Delhi: Oxford University Press.

Das, Veena, and R. S. Bajwa. 1994. "Community and Violence in Contemporary Punjab." In, D. Vidal, G. Tarabout, and E. Meyer, eds., *Violences and Non-violences in India.* Special issue of *Purusartha* 16: 245–61.

Dhagamwar, Vasudha. 1992. *Law, Power, and Justice: The Protection of Personal Rights in the Indian Penal Code.* Delhi: Sage.

Foucault, Michel. 1980. *The History of Sexuality, Vol. 1: An Introduction.* Robert Hurley, trans. New York: Vintage Books.

Greimas, A. J., and E. Landowski. 1976. "Analyse semiotique d'un discourse juridique." In *Semiotique et science socials,* by A. J. Greimas. Paris: Seule.

Lévi-Strauss, Claude. 1969. *The Elementary Structures of Kinship,* rev. ed. J. H. Bill and J. R. von Sturmore, trans., Rodney Needham, ed. London: George Allen and Unwin.

MacKinnon, Catherine A. 1989. *Toward a Feminist Theory of the State.* Cambridge, Mass.: Harvard University Press.

———. 1992. "Does Sexuality Have a History?" In *Discourses of Sexuality: From Aristotle to AIDS.* Ann Arbor, University of Michigan Press.

Matoesian, G. 1993. *Reproducing Rape: Domination through Talk in the Courtroom.* London: Polity Press.

Menon, Ritu, and Kamla Bhasin. 1993. "Recovery, Rupture, Resistance. Indian State and Abduction of Women during Partition." *Economic and Political Weekly* 17: WS2–W12.

Shah, Purvi. 1994. "How to Get on Top of the Social Savage." Comment, at the *CSSH* conference "States of Violence," University of Michigan, Ann Arbor, 16–18 April.

Smart, Carol. 1989. *Feminism and the Power of Law.* London: Routledge.

Varghese, Rose. 1992. *Sentencing in Rape Cases: Legislative Cases and Judicial Practice in the Context of Gender Justice and Atrocities against Women.* Bangalore: National Law School of India University.

Viswanath, Kalpana. 1994. "Shame and Control: Feminism, Sexuality and the Body." Paper presented at the conference "Femininity, the Female Body and Sexuality in Contemporary Society." Delhi: Nehru Memorial Museum and Library, 21–25 November.

Violence and Vision: The Prosthetics and Aesthetics of Terror

Allen Feldman

> Such the confusion now between the real—how say the contrary? No matter. That old tandem. Such now the confusion between them once so twain.
>
> —Samuel Beckett

One of the few photographs I associate with my fieldwork in Northern Ireland shows a burly mustached man in a tank top, wearing aviation sun glasses.[1] He proudly displays a second photograph of a woman seated at a desk cluttered with papers, an ashtray, and telephone. Her eyes smile at the camera lens; her friendliness is contrasted to the almost ominous dark background. He is the author of this second image. The picture within the picture is notable for its high definition; in its expert use of lit foreground and darkened background creating perspectival depth it is a competent example of visual realism. I use the latter term, following John Tagg, as pertaining to the evidentiary, typified, and mimetic dimension of photography: a core attribute which establishes its privileged claim on truth, facticity, and intelligibility.[2] This picture is a souvenir that I needed to bring home for it communicates a visual ideology that permeates the structure and experience of political violence in Northern Ireland. It is a photograph that addresses some of the urgent issues raised by the conference "States of Violence," in which considerable debate was devoted to the "aestheticization of violence" as evidenced by recent ethnographic writings. Ethnographic depiction was accused of nurturing a literary voyeurism and distantiation from the reality of violence. A social-scientific realism was invoked by this critique as a corrective, although some speakers seemed to find any "graphic" representation of violence distasteful and sensational-

425

istic. This essay will explore this photograph as an aesthetic artifact that effectively challenges the assumptions of the realist, aestheticization, and sensationalistic critiques of ethnographic representations of violence.

Visionscapes

Among my raw data from fieldwork in Belfast, such first-hand photographic artifacts are rare.[3] Photography in the policed zones of working class Belfast has been a dangerous avocation during the course of the conflict. The photo lens is considered equivalent to the gun sight and the pointed rifle. The British army, the Royal Ulster constabulary, even the Belfast fire department react angrily and precipitously if they find a camera pointed at their bodies and activities. The police and army have been known to rip film out of the cameras of accredited foreign photo-journalists, who are then arrested. The security apparatus claims that photographs of state personnel doing their duty can find their way to the IRA and other Republican paramilitary groups and serve to identify off-duty soldiers, policemen, and firemen for assassination.

Visual depiction is feared to the extent that it interdicts role distancing, collapses the space between public and private lives, and spreads terror and violence into the everyday recesses of government functionaries. The police and the provincial army reserve particularly fear assassination when they are away from the front-line, in mufti, in their homes, and pubs, among family and/or friends, relaxing and recreating.[4] Republican paramilitaries relish such attacks as eloquent inversions of the mutation of their own homes into war zones by these same representatives of the state.[5] Repeated pre-dawn raids of the domestic space by the police and army has been a commonplace event in working class Catholic neighborhoods for the last two decades. Bereft of any domestic insularity themselves, paramilitaries assume that the war's front-line can and should be everywhere as an objective condition of social life.

Republican and Loyalist paramilitaries also fear iconic capture, seeing it as a sure harbinger of sudden death. Both paramilitaries and non-combatants have been subjected to a totalizing optical surveillance by the state where they live and operate, particularly in Catholic communities. This includes video cameras mounted on street corners, and covert photography conducted from behind special slits cut into delivery vans or mounted from the roofs of high-rise buildings, or from helicopter over-flights covering political demonstrations and funerals. The appearance and dress of many residents in Catholic working class communities are registered and cross-referenced in extensive computer files that are accessed by police, army patrols, and their respective road blocks. An informant (male, thirty-two, Catholic), living in the Divis Flats housing project that lies under the gaze of British Army video cameras mounted on an adjacent high rise building, declared: "They know the patterns of your wall paper and the color of your underwear!" Here the linkage between the penetration of the domestic space and the penetration of the body directly captures the psychic effect of the surveillance grid—private life is lived on the outside and by inference political activism, which must be kept hidden from the state's gaze, is correlated with privacy. And indeed a good deal of political violence in Northern Ireland is aimed at domestic spaces and is disruptive of the private sphere. Visual surveillance authorizes other forms of bodily invasion. Young males fourteen years old and upward, the group most frequently subjected to stop-and-searches on the street, have been known to return home and take a shower after being body-frisked in public by the "security forces." Such tactile invasion extends visual surveillance, and is experienced as dirtying the self in much the same manner that scopic penetration contaminates private space and lives.[6]

I attended a meeting between activists at Divis Flats and representatives of the British National Mine-workers Union in 1984; the latter were recounting the surveillance/harassment techniques they had been subjected to by police on the British mainland.[7] The housing project activists nodded with quiet recognition until a woman from Divis Flats silenced the miners by pointing to the window behind the union representatives remarking "Their cameras are on you even now" as we all followed her gaze out the window and upward to the high rise with its crown of electronic sensing antennas and video cameras.

In 1986, over a drink in a suburban home located in a residential enclave for policemen, a Loyalist paramilitary, discussing his frequent arrests by the security forces, related the following rumor to me. The persons named below are either well-known IRA or Loyalist paramilitaries and politicians, many of whom had been killed by assassination, firefights, and ambushes.

There was a member of the security branches and they've seen a board with various photos on it in one of their briefing rooms.[8] The last person who had a face on it was a fellow called Bryson.[9] On one side of the board there were photos of all Republicans and on the other side there was the Paisleys, the Bill Craigs, the Tommy Herrons, and mine.[10] Joe McCann of the Official IRA was up there, he was dead, Bryson was dead, a few others were still alive. But it appeared that most of them on the other side of the board were Republicans and they were dead. Red X's through them like it was something out of the comics or 007.

The dead men's photo display story was repeated to me by Republican paramilitaries. The tale evokes rituals of the state: arcane rooms, conspiratorial conferences, unforgiving archives where individual deaths are subject to rational planning, and the sympathetic magic of manipulating personhood through visual replicas.[11] Such rumors, true or not, are a necessary complement to the secret knowledge systems that accompany the counterinsurgency campaign; they ascribe to the half-hidden state apparatus an authorial center, a visible place from which its aggressive activity emanates. As such, this ascription is a reaction to the actual diffuse capillary threading of state surveillance and power through the warp of everyday life. Resisting this cohabitation of the state and private life takes the form of rumoring. There is a frisson here between the precision optics of the state—the rationalization of political subjects by visual grids and archives—and the imprecise, out-of-focus and floating quality of rumor. Rumor becomes a vehicle for evading the rationalization of existence under state surveillance. It is the very imprecision of rumor that drives it as a counter-narrative against the seemingly electronic wall of the state's gaze.

Not only do such fears, insecurities, and rumors about photographic depiction inhibit documentary picture taking, they reveal to what extent visual perception after more than two decades of clandestine and not so clandestine war is informed by, if not actually modeled on, acts of violence; seeing and killing, being seen and being killed are entangled and exchangeable in the ecology of fear and anxiety. Further, visual appropriation, because it is always pregnant with the potential for violence, has become a metonym for dominance over others: power lies in the totalizing engorged gaze over the politically prone body, and subjugation is encoded as exposure to this penetration. In the war zones of Northern Ireland, vision can be aggressive and weapons, in turn, become instruments of political image making—weaponry makes ideological objects objectives and scenography appear; this is the politically visible, that horizon of actors, objects and events that constitute the world view and circumscribed reality of the political emergency-zone—the gathered and linked components of crises.[12] This symbiosis means that political subjects are formed, in part, within a circuit of visual prosthetics: the surveillance camera, the helicopter over-flight, the panoptic architecture of the interrogation room and prison,[13] and the aimed gun. These instruments of fatal vision can be divided into hardware and software technologies, and among the latter must be included in the human gaze, subject to a high degree of spatial and temporal extension and electronic supplementation. In turn, the fabrication of the politically visible implies the concomitant creation of that which is politically invisible. The circuit formed by vision and violence is itself circumscribed by zones of blindness and inattention.[14]

Foucault conceived of Bentham's panopticon apparatus within an evolutionary trajectory that progressively distanced punition from the practice of visible hands-on violence. I find little historical evidence for this sanitized application of ocular aggression in Northern Ireland nor in other neo-colonial situations. Foucauldian optical rationality is not "contaminated" by "exceptional" violence in Northern Ireland; compulsory visibility is the rationality of state counterinsurgency, and of neo-statist paramilitary violence. This is evident in the visual staging and technological penetration of the body by cameras, high velocity bullets, or digitized bombs, which unite both seeing and killing, surveillance and violence in a unified scopic regime.[15]

By a scopic regime I mean the agendas and techniques of political visualization: the regimens that prescribe modes of seeing and visual objects and which proscribe or render untenable other modes and objects of perception. A scopic regime is an ensemble of practices and discourses that establish the truth-claims, typicality, and credibility of visual acts and objects and politically-correct modes of seeing. In Northern Ireland, each sectarian assassination victim, each detainee interrogated and tortured, each prisoner incarcerated, each army or police patrol ambushed, have been subjected to a ritualized gaze, an ex-posture that is an endowment of power to the aggressor. The violent imagination in Northern Ireland is a visual imagination that extends from the surveillance and imaging of bodies living and dead to the public imaging of projected yet non-existent national entities such as a United Ireland or a British Ulster.

Scotology

The particular photograph under discussion, taken in-doors and with a subject posing for the camera, seems free of the complicity imposed upon vision by violence.[16] The ex-Loyalist paramilitary shows the ethnographic camera a picture of a smiling middle-aged woman sitting at a desk busy with papers. In contrast, the desk he sits at is vacant. The woman in the photograph has accumulated her clutter because she reads, she looks and smiles with her eyes at the lens, her sight is captured by the camera lens. The ex-paramilitary is framed by an empty desk devoid of papers and files, not because he is idle, but because he is blind. The photograph he holds up to the camera is one he has recently taken. Since he lost his eyesight to sectarian gunfire, photography has become an avid hobby. When he was sighted and militarily active he would, with equal enthusiasm, "do snipes," looking through the scope of a 303 Enfield rifle picking off Catholics across Belfast's Crumlin Road, the sectarian divide that separates his neighborhood, Woodvale, from the predominately Catholic Ardoyne. Even fourteen years after his wounding he would rhapsodize over the scopic powers of particular rifles. However he was not blinded while sniping, but during the sectarian rioting of 15 August 1969.[17] His paramilitary career was cut short when an Ardoyne resident fired a shotgun loaded with pellets into his face as the photographer was standing guard by a recently erected neighborhood barricade. The erection of these barricades in working class neighborhoods transformed these areas into "no-go areas," cutting them off from the outside world and placing them under virtual paramilitary rule until the British army tore the barriers down in 1972. When I met him in the mid-1980s the blind photographer was working at a community center, a respected figure who has exhibited his work.

Made by a blind former gunman, this photograph is emblematic of crucial dimensions of my ethnographic experience in Belfast; it evokes the perceptual possibilities that emerge during and in the aftermath of violence. This image of vision captured by sightlessness, evokes the words of another paramilitary, in this case a Republican, who summed up his experience of violence in the city: "An eye for an eye will make the whole world blind." The saying distills the exchangist structure of political aggression identified in my ethnography of violence and the body in Northern Ireland, *Formations of Violence*.[18] When I first heard this Gandhian maxim, I envisioned a cosmic darkness, but considering this photograph's juxtaposition of images, of vision and non-vision, its realism both fabricated and objective, I now imagine the sensory alterity of aggressors, the wounded, the maimed, and the terrified. How does one perceive during and after chronic political violence? What knowledge emerges from the terror zones and at what cultural sites does it appear? Where does violence emerge into visibility and what visibility does violence create? What are the *perceptual and somatic* coordinates of political depiction and imagining in Northern Ireland? Within the visual regimes under which the blind former gunman was formed, where does the rifle scope leave off and the camera lens begin? Can we presume that he pursues photography partly in order to remain within an empowering scopic regime, and not simply because it is a media for rehabilitating the disabled—providing them with a hobby or therapy?

The photo taken by the blind man is fictive, he has seen nothing shown by that photograph and he has not seen the photograph that repeats these things which he holds up for others to see. It is artifice posing as documentary, the most fabricated aspect being the photo's realist aura that most of us, educated since childhood in photo-realism, would initially accept as an adequate and intelligible representation of a woman seated behind a desk. Yet, the image is autonomized, it is solely a product of a prosthetic—the automatic focus camera. Though the photographer may have used sensory capacities like sound and touch to make it, the picture captures no human vision on the other side of the camera lens. The visual artifact itself gives birth to the optical circuit that makes it intelligible.

The validation of this particular photograph's intelligibility is beyond the blind photographer's optical capacities and dependent on an external witness—a sighted viewer, or in this case a second camera. The photographer poses himself behind the picture and holds his photograph as an emblem of the mimetic adequacy of his non-existent vision. Positioned behind his creation, he borrows from the metaphor of receding perspective to claim authorship. Since the photographer is sightless, his picture poses the realist gaze, just as much as it poses a woman behind a desk. Thus his blindness foregrounds another ironic and allegorical schema: the elimination of an actual human eye here reinforces the unmediated naturalness of the photograph. Visual realism is created through the defacement of the human eye and through the cultivation of a certain type of non-seeing; for one of the artifacts created by realist representation is the very normative eye that apprehends the image—seeing supposedly does not exist outside the realist frame, or so we are conditioned to assume.

As an artifact of realist conventions the photograph aesthetically replicates many of the optical values that are deployed in the sensory configuration and aesthetics of that political violence, which blinded the photographer in the first place. It is my contention that the photo partakes of past socio-perceptual coordinates of its author when he saw and placed others between the cross hairs of his rifle scope. The absence of sight is at the origin of this photograph and yet it preserves a gaze (here momentarily pacified) that also channels and materializes violence as a sensory ecology. The reified character of that gaze is all the more stark here because it is detached from the eye.

The gaze is ex-orbited and in this detached state can be more readily appreciated or ex-posed as a potential instrument of technical aggression. For *who* really looks in a panoptic or scopic regime, whether state sponsored or otherwise? The question is better put as "what sees in the scopic regime?" We know who and what can be watched, but what sees? It is simply not enough to say the state, or the assassin or sniper—the former is too general and the latter too particularistic. Neither response accounts for the political agency of seeing. There is no original and literal eye of the scopic regime. Behind the hegemonic facade of multiple insect-like envisioning orifices there is a core of blindness: a dis-association between making the visible and receptive cognitive seeing in which the latter is simply an imprecise anthropomorphic figure—a fictive terminus for the images created and consumed by the scopic machine. For the ultimate claustrophobic attribute of the scopic regime is that dominant vision is autonomized and requires no singular authorial eye, only the circuit of visibility and the power relation ignited within this circuit between autonomized technical instruments of visualization and those surveilled and objectified by vision and/or violence. Thus in the interrogation rooms of Castle Reagh, the prominently displayed video cameras that are meant to monitor interrogation, and forestall human-rights abuses, are either unattended, turned off, or manned by police who turn a *blind eye* to any violence taking place. The detainees are frequently blindfolded, for being seen and surveilled requires the removal of their vision and the monopolization of that sense by the state. A scopic regime, like Foucault's panopticon or Lacan's mirror stage, is an apparatus behind which lies no one who sees, for *seeing,* no matter how privileged, is but one position in, internal to, and a function and product of the total scopic apparatus and is not the mechanism's point of origin. Hence the distinction between the eye and the gaze. The latter is a mechanics of power,[19] the former a sensory organ that can be socially appropriated to channel and materialize normative power in everyday life. Here human vision becomes an adjunct, an instrument and an automaton of the scopic regime.

In the discussions that emerged from the conference upon which this volume is based, aestheticization of violence was proposed as the representational failing of the theorist of violence, a by-product of the imputed voyeurism of those who watch but do not partake in violence as actor or recipient, who do not share in its material consequences, and who therefore write.[20] However what I propose here is that watching and acting may not be polarized positions in the field of violence, that visual regimes can have a deadly materiality. This means that acts of violence and relations of the body which precipitate and emerge from aggression move perceptual aestheticization into the core of a political culture grounded on violence and the objectified body. Unconscious aestheticization of political violence does not have to be an unavoidable effect of a naive writing violence, but should certainly be a primary object of ethnographic inquiry as it may be the pre-condition for writing in and from the emergency zone. Politicized aestheticization in the emergency zone may draw upon residual cultural influences like photographic realism, the synoptic visual styles of the electronic media and cinema, but it takes on new valences and offers new things to see once these artifacts of visual culture are drawn into the reconfiguring maelstrom of chronic political aggression.

Ethnic Landscapes as Visual Culture

Belfast, from the early nineteenth century onwards, was characterized by the rapid expansion of industrial capitalism, an ethnic/religious division of labor, and residential segregation enforced by populist sectarian violence. In Belfast the reproduction of an ethnic division of labor among the working class rested on (1) kin-based and therefore sectarian labor recruitment, (2) the creation of a predominately Catholic labor reserve through rural to urban migration, (3) a segregated or ghettoized settlement pattern, and (4) endogamous marriage practices based on religiously bifurcated descent systems. The urban settlement pattern was also determined by the punctuation of overt crowd violence by the Protestant majority (frequently abetted by the sectarian state), alternating with more silent forms of covert intimidation which enabled the social engineering of ethnic populations and classes into urban reserves that were associated with economic cores and peripheries, that is, to major and minor industries, each with their own confessional, ethnic, and topographic associations. The sectarianization of labor and settlement promoted an ethnicized visual landscape of confessional neighborhoods, Catholic and Protestant commercial and manufacturing zones, and in-place and out-of-place bodies.

Violence and urbanism underwrote the colonial experience in Northeast Ireland. Urban development in Belfast not only advanced through

massive industrialization and rural in-migration but through ghettoization. Said has termed geography the imperial methodology, and ghettoization in Northern Ireland implemented imperial and colonial agendas
by using geographical control to constrain and rationalize social and
therefore bodily and perceptual contact between sundered populations.[21]
In Belfast, visual experience in everyday life was intimately linked to ethnic contact avoidance as a typified somatic posture in the urban setting.
The perceptual organization of working class Protestants and Catholics
was and is organized around the metaphysics of "telling"—discerning who
was Protestant or who was Catholic. "Telling" mobilized imaginary and
projected images of embodied ethnicity and body politics.[22] Visual imaginaries, once transcribed onto the physiognomy, dress, and body comportment of the encountered ethnic Other, played a crucial role in the construction of identity in urban everyday life. In Belfast, the social logic of
telling is so encompassing that even the foreign visitor may become
engulfed in the inferential visual classification of ethnicity. Neighborhood
segregation of Protestants and Catholics provides an environmental frame
for such visual quick-studies of ethnic identity, though telling is more frequently and forcefully applied to potentially out-of-place bodies and to
ethnically plural spaces, such as the mass transport system or the downtown commercial center.

Current sectarian political violence in Belfast continues many of the
ocular strategies of ghettoization. Victim selection in sectarian violence
frequently fuses social space, the body, and ethnicity in a visual diagnostic
for homicide, and this can directly result in the killing of someone from
one's own group in space classified as Other; a consequence that reveals
the discrepancy between the visual-spatial imaginary and the real. The
ocular character of ethnic classification indicates that contact avoidance is
not only the immediate precipitant of sectarian violence, but inhabits the
very infrastructure of its enactment. Contact avoidance can be indexed in
the way in which visual distancing organizes victims and aggressor into
stylized postures and poses, as has been shown in the assassination narrative above.

"Telling" practices are the oldest organizer of the politically visible, but
other ideological imaginaries deploy rigid discriminatory and context-
bound classification grids in language and discourse to create the politically visible and the politically unseen. Moral discrimination and ethno-
historical context are the basic mechanisms for differentiating one act of
violence from another. Moral discrimination takes on a particular charac-

ter in Northern Ireland because the dominant morality is not a matter of choosing non-violence over violence but rather of morally legitimizing one act of violence in another. Political discourse harbors a visual logic that enhances its credibility. Ideological objects in Northern Irish political culture are subjected to a high-contrast binary optic based on exclusive and opposing ethnic, confessional, and political categories—Protestant/Catholic, Loyalist/Republican, state/anti-state—in which nothing is blurred, thus enabling their polarity to antagonistic ideological objects. This high-contrast visual figure is also formed of foregrounds and backgrounds or perspectival regression that set the truth-claims of any political act or statement. The Northern Irish ideological object is forged through strategies of receding or regressive historical perspective and typification; contemporary political acts of insult and injury are proposed and popularly received as reenactments, replications, analogies and echoes of earlier acts in a linear trajectory that eventually recedes towards an elusive historical horizon-line of first injury, first assault, and first death dating back to the Cromwellian Plantation, if not earlier. Thus ideological objects possess distinct foregrounds—literal commonsensical presence—and supportive backgrounds—spatial origin, historical genealogy, and social causation. Any act of personal destruction and social disfigurement is typified by being immediately absorbed back into this regressive and mimetic temporal schema where each act of violence repeats another, and where each act of violence both epitomizes and renews the dualism of the political culture in time and space. Typification is not guaranteed in advance and may always be contested, but without it no act of paramilitary violence is legitimized in support communities.[23]

I term this schema the historiography of excuse, where prior acts of violence extenuate the committal of present and future acts.[24] The rationality of excuse depends on recursive time and mimetic resemblance as narrativized by political discourse and popular memory. Through temporal mimesis and regression each act of violence becomes typified insofar as it participates in, and takes its validity from, a prior aggression. Typification, considered by John Tagg[25] to be an important attribute of the realist percept, entails the instantaneous transference and extraction of usually stereotypical and fetishized cultural codes to and from the act of violence. In Northern Ireland these codes are organized around sectarian ethnic classifications, law and order imperatives, or antiquated pro- and anti-British Empire discourse. Ernst Bloch anticipated Tagg's linkage of typification to realism in describing the latter as the *cult of the immediately*

REALISM *ascertainable fact.*[26] Rapid fact setting is dependent on the recognition codes built into any violent enactment, which are the foundation of its typicality. In terms of the sheer materiality of acts of violence, these acts are basically undifferentiated in terms of their concrete human consequences. They are polarized and differentiated through the instantaneous infusion of idealizing nationalist, ethnic, and other cultural codes into the material performance and its debris, rendering the latter excusable. The fusing of realist frame and material act is so overdetermined that the act of violence can be a visualizing apparatus, a lens, and a narrativizing frame all at once. The wrack and ruin of dead, wounded, maimed bodies and buildings is already a representational configuration; a created or artificed scene that is prepared in advance for an ex-post-facto second representation by the media, and various apologetics or condemnations.

Typification and mimesis allow violence to function as collective memory because violence is grounded on the moral aesthetics of reenactment in Northern Ireland. The meaning and memory of any political act is prepared in advance by an accumulation of mimetic moments and reenactments that weave together fate and fatality. As one Republican paramilitary answered in response to my question about the ultimate effectiveness of repeated acts of violence: "Because people forget." Violence, repetition, and memory create the circumscribed and enframed space of the politically real, that is, of political totality in Northern Ireland. While much attention has been paid in the literature on the conflict to official ideological discourse, which can certainly be dissected for its realist narrative, little has been said about the performative infrastructure of acts of violence and of the political iconography they project. This even though it is this actual enactment of violence upon the bodies and spaces of others that constitutes the material substrata, and the material culture of the conflict. To move to the performative is to ask, what does violence visualize in Northern Ireland and in what forms of seeing are these visions possible?

Targets

The weapon in Belfast is a perceptual instrument, one that organizes urban prospects, frames a historical landscape before itself; a political spectacle of targets as moral objects. The built environment records the effects of this scene making, and not only with literal ruins. The walls of the red brick houses where snipings have occurred are subsequently painted black up to a height of six feet by the British army to block optical acquisition by IRA snipers, so that "no profile would come in" as one IRA member put it. Places where previous snipes or bomb attacks have occurred are marked with white paint by the army and police: "Look Here, Look Up," so that violent vision has a history and a geography. Other graphics include numerous wall murals and graffiti dedicated to the neighborhood dead. The gun when it is pointed—not even fired, but pointed—possesses a manifest power to alter the material surroundings and to temporarily freeze life. The ideological rationality that informs the aiming of a weapon and the final act of assault against the body establishes the weapon as a field of vision, a relationship that can frequently invert rendering specific acts of perception akin to the infliction or reception of violence. In Belfast I have felt perceptual assault, like an itch at the back of my head, as I sensed the scopes of patrolling British soldiers framing my body as they traced my crossing a street with a movement of their gun barrel.

A blind man makes a picture that gives us the real; previously he shot at Catholics through a gun-scope to create the political. In its fixation of poses, in framing political targets and objectives, the weapon intersects with the perceptual infrastructure of the camera; they are both prosthetic instruments. The gun translates visual acquisition into tactile destruction. The weapon in Northern Ireland's military-political culture is comprehended by the actors and audience of violence as an icon making device; it is a prosthetic instrument that extends ideology and visions of history into the depth of the human body, leaving the dead and the depicted in its wake.

The scopic dimension of targeting and weaponry plays at several levels in the following narrative about an attempted *coup de etat* within the Ulster Defense Organization, with 10,000 members the largest Loyalist paramilitary organization. The attempted assassination described below halted a split in the organization. The West Belfast component of the Ulster Defense Organization initiated an armed take-over of the organization's headquarters on the Shankill Road, located in the heart of the Loyalist community. The ejected leadership countered this move with a plan to assassinate the coup leader, one Harding Smith.

There's a fish store in the Shankill Road, Frizell's . . . Above this fish shop is the UDA headquarters, and on the opposite side of the street there was an optician's and the Brits go into it because they couldn't go anywhere else in Belfast for their glasses without getting sniped—this man must have had a contract to supply glasses to the army. The opti-

cians across from the headquarters was a vantage point, a spying point.
There was this sort of scenario. They placed a kid to sit there in a long
black coat and mustache reading the *Daily Mirror,* under the coat is a
machine gun, next to him there are these two young birds—receptionists—he's the lookout. The lads [two gunmen] move in and take the
optician up the stairs. They stuck the machine gun out, "any nonsense
you're fucked, you're getting the message. We know the Brits come in
here, if youse want to live with these Brits go up and tell them their gear
is not ready—get them out. "Now they were sitting there upstairs and
downstairs for hours. The receptionists were asking the young buck
"Do you do all this all the time? Are you a professional?" The strategy
in the game was you put a kid who doesn't do any thinking. If the kid is
young enough he smells no or knows no danger. And he's sitting with
these wee girls. And the Brits come in between, "I'm sorry you will have
to come back in the afternoon your order is not ready" [imitating a
woman's voice]. "You see, the girls were that fascinated. While the boy
downstairs is sitting with a machine gun, the boys are up the stairs, one
with some sort of handgun stuck to the optician's ear or up his nose or
ass. Wherever it was stuck it was very impressionable because the optician seemed to respond.

Because the way the windows on the block opposite were set a wee
bit lower, they opened the sash at the top, commonly known in Belfast
as the fanning light, making a foot-square gap. They were leaning on
the table and your man puts a chair on the top table, takes the gun and
sits and watches like Roy Rogers. So he sees the two top men [of the
other faction] through the two windows of the office [across the street],
Tucker Little and Bucky McCullough. There were these two windows
and they were standing there, one moved over to the other and the two
were standing by the one window waiting on Harding Smith coming
[the leader of the coup]. All I'm telling you this was in the police reports
so I am not telling you any tales out of school—because I wasn't there
nor was I involved in the conspiracy [laughter], I was in East Belfast [the
other side of town] waiting on the other end of the phone line [more
laughter].[27]

The next thing it was they titting away at this wee man [the optician]
"See you walking down the road every day." "Well I just get the bus at
Oxford Street." "Oh I know where you get the bus all right, don't you
dare tell me, I know where you get the bus all right! [said with exagger-

ated menace]. They had looked at his wallet, found his photo ID and knew that he lived in Donaghadee and given it back but the wee man was so terrified he didn't even realize all that. "We know you get the number 56 to Donaghadee. "Oh Jesus Christ! You know where I live an all—what sort of people are you?" "We have to do [kill] someone but we'll not hurt you now, we know all about your family. "Don't hurt my daughter because her man's not well." So they find out all about the wee man's personal business. He starts panicking and they were winding him up—so the wee man is so wound up like a big spring so he goes blank off their identification. It's a whole ploy. While the wee girls down the stairs are fascinated by this professional killer. He was like Lee Marvin—he killed dead ones.

The next thing it was they lift the phone and ring and this is what the wee man heard: "We got two men here, McCullough and Little. Will we shoot them ones and come back for your man? [Harding Smith]. The optician said, "He put the phone down and replied to his partner, "Don't shoot them ones, the man says we can shoot them ones any time, we're not worried about them ones, we want to shoot Smith and get rid of him now. We can touch them ones any old time and the rest of their family" [other members of their faction, West Belfast UDA].

The first thing Smith does when he arrives he stands and looks out the window. "Lovely day boys." That was his common thing to do, he done it regular as clockwork and watching the cars go up and down as if he was someone important. They were forty yards across the street— they seen the wee window opened. They hit him with an M-1 carbine and he spun around like a pirrie about a half dozen times and the only thing that saved him was that he didn't drink nor smoke and was as fit as a fiddle. He spun around like a pirrie and every time he spun around they kept banging him and every time they spun him they hit him on the rebound and actually skimming him. There was just flesh wounds in him, they put a couple through him anyway but they went right through the stairs . . .

While he was lying in the fucking hospital after the shooting his men, McCullough and Little, were at a peace conference selling him out. It was psychological: the two men picks up the phone, one says, "Will we do these two wee bastards?" and the other one says "We can get them ones any time." Well that scared the shit right out of them ones; that the boys were standing there for two hours waiting on Harding Smith and they could've been dead, how easy it was for them to die and how determined the other ones who were watching them for two hours. They couldn't believe it; it just blew their minds.

The cinematic aesthetic of the narrative is both sophisticated and self-conscious. The narrator locates the assassination in the midst of the banal particularities of a shopping district. It builds tension with jump-cuts between the upstairs, the professional assassins, and the downstairs—the "kid" and the receptionists—a repetitive turn between foreground and background. The optician is repeatedly characterized as "wee," a diminutive indicating smallness and vulnerability; in the narrative he occupies the same visual position as the targets forty yards across the street. It is as if he is being viewed down the barrel of a miniaturizing lens. The convergence of scopic signifiers is almost pun-like and most are borrowed from the aesthetics of visual realism—framing of visual objects, foreground and background action, synoptic action sequences, and the formatting of the killing ground as a proscenium stage. Narrative structure and value can be found as much in the visual values as in the described action or ideological rationale of the attack. Consider the choice of the optician's as the staging ground of the killing, the window frames of the target that set up a Hitchcockian mise-en-scene for murder, and the repeated thematic of surveillance as a form of image-making that implies impending death. This motif runs from the manipulation of the optician's photo I.D. to the deferral of material violence against the targets for the pleasures of watching—"them ones"—who could be made targets at any time in the future. The pleasures of seeing without being seen empowers the act of violence, the invisibility of the killer is crucial to the optical reduction of the victim. Both the optician and the paramilitaries not shot at are devastated by the fact that they have been invisibly surveilled. Scopic power over the target is the source of fear and compliance, the gun as prosthetic vehicle both augments the human eye and materializes vision in physical assault and trauma; in terms of the creation of fear and dominance there is very little differentiation here between physical assault and scopic power, each reinforces and, more importantly, simulates the other. Finally, with its cinematic references to Roy Rogers and Lee Marvin films, the tale winds around itself disclosing the optical metaphors and convergences of the narrative as not only functioning as literal descriptions of the event but as pleasure-endowing keys or punctuations where the alchemical substances of dominance are stored, tapped, and remembered.

The Genealogy and Gender of the Real

I mean to show that realist strategies of depiction can be found, not only in discourse and conventional practices of visualization like photography, but in the perceptual infrastructure of acts of domination and violence. To link visual realism to post-colonial violence in Northern Ireland is to remove the former from a purely expressive domain and to uncover the uses of visual realism: what it does to situations and persons, what it makes, alters, and transforms. These issues explicitly challenge visual realism as passive reflection, or naturalized mimesis. The ethic of the correctness of the gaze, the concept of *homoiosis*—the resembling gaze that matches perception to what *should be sighted*—is the ground of realist aesthetics and should be placed under question in any inquiry into politicized vision. I seek to reverse the conventions of photo-journalism, the cinematized eye and legal representation.[28] Rather than solely treating realism as the privileged depictive vehicle for the expression of violence as advanced by the afore-mentioned cultural institutions, I am interested in approaching violence as the depictive blade that inscribes realist aesthetics onto a social landscape and uses these aesthetics to uphold truth-claims about the power and efficacy of political violence.

Emily Apter has identified a plurality of realisms in colonial and post-colonial societies.[29] Alongside the synoptic realism associated with nineteenth-century literature and twentieth-century cinema, she locates a related but distinct colonial visual realism akin to tourist and ethnological depiction that is exemplified by the tourist postcard. To this can be added the mathematical imagery of colonial census taking—the multiplication and division tables of ethnic, caste, and tribal counts—that Arjun Appadurai identifies as essential to the surveillance technology and governmental imagination of imperial administration. John Tagg, in his archeology of nineteenth-century criminal and phrenological photography, identifies visual realism with various legal, penological/disciplinary regimes,[30] while Anson Rabinbach links the realism of nineteenth-century scientific kinesthetic photography to Fordist labor discipline applied to the body of the worker on the factory floor.[31]

To recognize a multiplicity of realisms, visual or literary, and to map a genealogy of visual realism historically rooted in diverse socio-cultural locales and media implies that the political agenda of realist modes of depiction and perception must be established in specific historical circumstances and institutional contexts on a case-by-case basis. Different utilities have been found for visual realism in various socio-historical circumstances. I could not describe seventeenth-century Dutch still life and interior painting, or the photography of Eugene Atget, as politically invested in domination as is the surveillance system or ocular aggression in Northern Ireland. The molding of realist modes of depiction into a hierarchy of credibility and fact-setting and as a public form of truth-claiming and depictive legitimation was a long and fragmented historical labor that emerged in a variety of discontinuous but overlapping social sites, and not all at one time if we consider the respective development of state archiving, juridical rules of evidence, popular media, optical experimentation, art movements, and the commodification of visual experience.

Terry Eagleton has characterized "literary" realism as the dominant narrative genre of external and internal colonialism in nineteenth-century Ireland and the United Kingdom, respectively. Realism for Eagleton is suited for nation-building projects and expansionist and centralizing bureaucracies is "the form par excellence of settlement and stability gathering individual lives into a whole . . . realism depends on the assumption that the world is story-shaped—that there is a well formed narrative implicit in reality itself."[32] For Eagleton, narratological realism harbors a decidedly visual project of totalization: "[realism] . . . springs from a characteristic way of seeing.[33] In the complex industrial milieu of nineteenth-century England social relations are diffuse and opaque . . . the dense intricate texture of social life is notably hard to totalize, and secreted behind each social persona is some hinterland of inscrutable private experience, which only the *omniscient authorial eye can decipher*" (my emphasis).[34]

Here realism is identified as a scopic project committed to the domination of space, to the appropriation of bodies that move through space, and to the recuperation of the "hidden" private lives borne by these bodies. The creation of a unified spatial/perceptual field and mastery over that terrain, which animates the realist scopic regime, readily lends itself to nation-building projects which are grounded on the presumption or desire for spatial/cultural/racial/ethnic homogeneity.

The tableau of a blind male photographer displaying and portraying a woman introduces a pervasive gender dimension that I would contend is also integral to the realist construct, particularly as it pertains to violence and vision in Northern Ireland. I suggest that the militarized gaze and the realist gaze have been historically crossed with the male gaze, if not identical with it. The Western male gaze—played out in painting, cinema, pornography, social science, and the network of glances that form daily visual culture—situates femininity in a state of passivity and receptivity, the feminine is something fixed, pictorial, framed, and sculptured. It is masculinity, and the male gaze that is activity in itself, that both rigidifies and informs the feminized body as the bearer of socio-political values and imaginary and symbolic networks. In nationalist and ethnic politics the feminine is permitted to be an image but women are not readily positioned as authors of national imagery, as Partha Chaterjee has pointed out in demonstrating the gendering of development/nation-building ideology.[35]

The moment of iconic capture is the pre-eminent realist event, whether it is effected by cameras, rifle scopes, or discourse, and it is frequently a gendered and politicized event. As Mary Ann Doane[36] proposes, the camera/subject nexus mobilizes relations of power, the authority of the distanced observer or the off-screen or out-of-frame voice who commands and frames the scene, staging and molding the depicted: "smile, don't smile; move here, move there." Contained within this disciplining of the body there is a politics of the pose. In the performance culture of the pose, visual subjects, male or female, receive a veneer of iconic femininity in order to become depictable as though the condition of the feminine were synonymous with the pose. Posing and being posed can be a mortification of the flesh, a freezing and rigidification by way of being submitted to the Medusan gaze of the Other.[37] This politics speaks to the "pose" as both a bearer of ideological codes and as a state of embodiment in which social fictions are rendered tangible and literal.

To talk of a "politics" of the pose is to take an aesthetic act and show how it can be politically magnified, fetishized, and institutionalized. This is not to mechanically assert that all painting or photography or depiction are automatically political or gendered violence. One must examine what is done to bodies to create these images, to enforce their legitimacy, and to substantiate their typicality. It is not only a question of how an iconography of poses is made to bear normative social codes, but also of how heterogeneous bodies are made to bear desired poses. I suggest that political violence is a crucial medial in transcribing prescriptive poses onto bodies that never volunteered for such portraiture in the first place.

Within this framework, acts of political violence and the human debris they leave in their wake engage and enlarge the politics of the pose and its material consequences. For instance, in Belfast acts of political violence can be linked to the gendering of aggressors and victims as well as to imagery of rigidification, petrifaction, and mortification—the politically encoded corpse can be re-read in light of the politics of the pose. In Belfast the noun and image "stiff" describes the victim of political violence, and the verb to "stiff" or "stiffing" refers to the actual act of homicide and gives the latter a dynamic visual contour. The stiff is vernacular for a corpse, but in the last two decades the term has narrowed and the noun and verb forms largely refer to those corpses created by political and sectarian violence. In Belfast the stiff and the act of stiffing are related to other body imagery that metaphorize bodily harm and political punishment. In paramilitary vernacular a targeted male victim prior to being stiffed is "a cunt," a targeting phrase. To "knock his cunt in" refers to killing or beating. To stiff someone is also to "give him the message."

Violence is a transfer of political signs from self to Other. In the working class vernacular "giving the message" pre-dates the civil violence and was slang for the male role in heterosexual intercourse. Bearing in mind its pre-political nuances, "giving the message" now implies the feminization of the object of political violence as a "cunt." In turn the "cunt" is understood as a passive recipient prior and during the infliction of violence. The stiff is not only given the message, but is meant to display these messages of visceral intimidation and manifest power to prescribed audiences.[38] The petrified dead are first posed by acts of violence, and then by justifying narratives that excuse or condemn these acts. The "stiff" created by political violence is statuary—a frozen bearer of unyielding ideological agendas and an unavoidable spectacle for a community of witness. And the montaging of a female sex organ onto male victims is a prescription for how one should see and consider the enemy dead. Gendered inflections of aggression and victimage distribute masculine and feminine essences between agents and recipients of political violence—the posers and the posed. And it is no coincidence that the domestic space, which has explicit gendered connotations in Northern Ireland, has been the social unit most frequently violated by the surveillance apparatus and by sectarian assassination.

The male gaze, like the realist percept, is blind to itself, the eye and the gaze are split. To the extent that it obliterates its gendered, embodied, and positioned origins, the male gaze establishes its realist, transparent, and naturalist truth-claims. "Realism, so the Formalists instruct us, works by concealing its mechanisms."[39] Both visual realism and the male gaze have in common the tendency to obscure the constructed origins of their perceptual apparatus and advance themselves as natural, unchanging, and ahistorical.[40] Visual realism and the male gaze are in symbiosis in this strategy of naturalization because they both stand for the correctness of vision, for a pre-determined adequation between the viewer and the viewed, which actually entails the reduction of the viewed to the coordinates of gaze—a process which I would call posing.

The political nexus between the male gaze, the mortification of the viewed body, and the rigidity of the pose is expounded upon in Lacanian theory.[41] For Lacan, executive organs of the body are detachable objects; through sensory specialization and hierarchy, vision is retooled as an instrument of technical aggression.[42] The visually constructed world must also be intimately connected to the engineering and aggressive encoding of social space. For Lacan, the enclosure of experience within a "self preserving" fetishized vision in "full forward flight" characterizes the drive for scopic domination as a kind of vertigo displaced onto unmastered, unending space as the pre-eminent visual object.[43] Social space and somatic spaces are both terrains of disorder and desired objects of visual control requiring vectoring, and bounds the rationality of societal margins and edges that cannot be crossed without being surveilled, borders that can be planted on the body or on a social-scape. In a scopic regime subject formation and spatial command intersect—visual command of the body of the Other is both the command of a unit of space and a reduction of the visual object to a spatial determination. Projects of surveillance regulate movement between spaces and create a spatialized social life mediated by rigid and normative geographies. Lacan's correlation of visual objectification, vertigo, and the drive to spatial domination implicitly connects scopic regimes with the spatialized politics of nationalism and related projects of topographic control.

Lacanian space is not empty, and he returns us to the politics of the pose, for Lacanian social space is punctuated by vertical beings, by ideological statuary—exemplary figurines and emblems of mastery or subjugation, upon which humanity projects itself, generating a world of fetishized identity-objects. The Lacanian social-scape is an assemblage of authoritative and authorizing postures rigidified and supported by vision, mimesis, and desire. This mirror-stage of the political is a museum peopled with immobile images, petrified hieratic monuments of domination/subjugation: stiffs or heroes.[44] The gaze of political mastery stands "ex-posed" and mirrored before itself in the form of the postured Other. The world is composed of statues "in which man projects himself" and "produces himself in front of himself" creating automata—ideological sculpture, a garden of sexual and political figureheads.[45] Ideological projects throw up statuary which form a continuum of stasis, of things, identities and substances stabilized by vision and mimesis. Mastery is constructed through forceful bodily projection onto a subordinated posed Other who then is consumed or read for the domination codes that can be extracted from the mirror effects of its objectified and petrified embodiment. In Northern Ireland the victim posed in violence and death is the mimetic artifact, the detachable part of the master gaze and a metonym of spatial domination.

Being Seen: Rumor and Realism

Oral testimony about war experience in Belfast usually approaches the scopic regime from the position of being seen, of being registered in the politically visible. Some of these narratives trace the symbolic ecology of the scopic regime as it is inserted into the crevices of everyday life and into the body itself. In arrest and interrogation situations, the scopic regime is felt at the level of the socially constructed nervous system and in the form of rumor-consciousness. As I have written elsewhere:

> In zones of violence, *the terror of everyday life is risk and rumor felt on the body.* Rumor is somaticized as the dream of the executioner borne within the imputed victim's body. Through rumor and risk-perception embodiment is doubled: expected victimizer and potential victim are intermingled in the same form. The body becomes transitive and historicized by the conjuncture of chance and finality. Torture and assassination become rumor materially enacted upon other people's bodies[46] which then, in turn, can be transmuted into rumor as they are first subtracted by violence as living entities and then frequently made to vanish altogether as both persons and corpses by state silence and/or popular incomprehension.[47]

To the extent that it visually fixes and reduces its victims to manipulable surfaces, the scopic regime of the state can effectively de-realize the body and the self. The state uses visual disinformation to create rumor, disorientation, and fear. When the interrogated are to be released, the police stage photographs showing the interrogated and tortured shaking the hands of their aggressors in order to create the impressions of collaboration, and as if to create an institutional memory of the physical intimacy they have shared. These photographs can be used to blackmail the interrogated, or they can be disseminated in the community of the prisoner, thereby discrediting the suspect and possibly setting him up for assassination as an informer by paramilitary organizations. Another staged photograph appears to show the suspect receiving a check from the police. After release, these checks can be publicly delivered by the police to the suspect's home. It goes without saying here that, as in other instances, the photograph and the politics of the pose can kill.

Rumor consciousness fed by the scopic-regime and its fictions seems to cultivate its own special perceptual array that weaves new sensibilities between personhood and the state—vectoring the body in unexpected fashion. The following stories are taken from both Republican and Protestant paramilitaries and concern their experience of "the warning." In these stories the force of being seen and thus targeted by the state is not experienced as a human act of perception, but rather is apprehended as affect within the body that is scripted by the state.

First Arrest Narrative: The police had an occasion to look for me. Their normal thing is to come out at a quarter to six in the morning. That's to disorient ye, so ye don't know what's happening. I'm lying there awake in bed, can't sleep at a quarter past five. You get a gut feeling about this. Sure as God above you know when there's a raid on. And you know there's somebody coming for ye. I'm lying in bed and I have this terrible gut feeling that they're coming for me. I says to the wife, "I've got to get dressed. I'm just about to put my trousers on" . . . Bang! Bang! Bang! Knock comes to the door. I had a blanket up the previous night behind the front door so the peelers couldn't see me if I came down the front stair past the door. I grabbed my trousers in my hand and my shoes, no socks on, scarpers down the stairs out the back, leaps over the top of the back fence, didn't get my trousers on till I was half way down the street. There was me running down the street bollick naked (male, loyalist paramilitary).

Second Arrest Narrative: You ask my ma. I would wake up in the middle of the night and tell her, "The house will be hit today, so be expecting." You have that feeling inside you. Things weren't just right. You'd have been picking up bits and pieces of info from other guys that were getting picked up and interviewed. Sometimes it added up, other times it mightn't. But then always at night the feeling would come onto you and you knew you were for it. A load of times out of nowhere I would wake the mother and tell her the house would be hit. I told her a load of times (male, Republican paramilitary).

Third Arrest Narrative: When they came for me . . . I was up at half five in the morning. I had been up the same time the Monday and Tuesday before. Though I hadn't been involved for some time I knew they were coming for me. I'm thinking, "Will I keep the door open?" Here's me, Sure, when they come I'll rap the window for to let them know I'm expecting them. I went back to sleep for an hour, woke up and told the wife to get up because the house is getting done today. At a quarter past six I hear the Land Rover coming up the street. Before the peelers could get to the door I jump up and rap the window.

The peeler says to me, How did you know that we were coming? Here's me: "I'm psycho." He says, "If you're psycho, you could have saved me from getting out of my bed and coming down to lift you. You could have come down to Castlereagh [interrogation center] yourself." He got me on that one. I says, "You think I'm going to fucking do your job for you?" I was asked again and again in the interrogation. "How did you know we were coming for ye?" (male, loyalist paramilitary).

 In these accounts, rumor consciousness functions as a somaticized symptom or specialized organ of sensory perception. The bodily registration of rumor as warning is indexed in such phrases as "terrible gut feeling," or as a nocturnal sensation, "at night the feeling would come onto you." The liminality of the night is crucial to the somatic shift for it magnifies the encompassing capacities of state vision. This dis-ease of the body records the other and affective side of scopic claustrophobia and penetration: these sensations and apprehensions are seismic traces of visual power and violence at the level of the socially mediated nervous system. The stories encode the subjective experience of the hyper-visibility of the targeted body and the tangible invisibility of scopic aggressors.

The warning tales above come close to describing somaticized rumor/danger as "nerves," a term which is not used by these male narrators because it is associated with female disorders in working class Belfast. The gendered concept of "nerves" is used by working class women to explain their overuse of barbiturate and other sedatives because of the personal losses and terror many have experienced. Nerves is a condition that continues the mourning process stemming from the trauma accruing from arrest, torture, imprisonment, and death of immediate family, kin, and neighbors (mainly males). Self-medication with barbiturates prolongs the numbing effects of trauma stemming from these events and thus perversely extends the mourning process through the alternation between attacks of nerves and chemical sedation. For these women, nerves is a political disease come by through the structures of everyday life in Belfast; "nerves," like rumor, becomes a micro-language of terror that is conveyed by gesture and expression from body to body in everyday muted contact. In working class Catholic neighborhoods "nerves" is state terror sunk into the lived body. However, nerves are also recognized as a condition of war that can cut across adversary lines linking others in a unified field of fear. The following stories emerged from a conversation with two "Catholic" mothers at a daycare center in West Belfast. The second story was presented as a commentary on the first.

First narrator: The Brits here are constantly taking nerves and cracking up—being taken away screaming hobnob to the hospital. There was a fairy ring in McCort's fort where the British soldiers are situated. And when they moved into the fort they ploughed the land up and dug the ring up. Everybody was shouting at them: "You'll regret it. You'll regret it." So some of these Brits who had dug the ring up were lying in bed and red light hovered over them every night. And another cracked up because he kept seeing these wee men around the fort. So they took him away.

Second narrator: When the Brits used to come into this area raiding we would tell the yarns about Riddle's Field [where the ghost of a Protestant factory owner haunts his own property]. An army barrack had been built on the site. We would say, "Old Riddle will come and get you!" This old Brit would be standing at the door of your house while they were tearing it apart and say tell, "Tell us that again!" Then they would tell us of incidents that happened to them that they couldn't explain. One of them saw a horseless carriage with an old man sitting on it. A couple of them (British soldiers) were supposed to be taken away from that.

The first story connects the contemporary dynamics of military occupation to the violation of pre-Christian sacred space, the faeryring. Such stories have a long history in rural Irish oral culture as commentaries on British colonial occupation in the west of Ireland in the eighteenth and nineteenth centuries. In the Belfast story sequence an equation is tacitly made between the transgression of historicized and/or sacred space and the violation of contemporary domestic space: occupiers are people out-

of-place who do you out of your place. This is indexed in the ironic juxtaposition of the second narrative where, as they tear apart the narrator's
house, the British soldiers ask her about the legends and rumors attached
to the site of *their* domicile. McCort's Fort and its faeryring is a remnant
of pre-historic Ireland, while Riddle, a classic Dickensian figure, exemplifies an earlier form of colonization from Belfast's age of industrial capitalism. The non-synchronicity of these places with the present calls into
question the unlimited capacity of the counterinsurgency apparatus to
domesticate the urban landscape, to control its time and space. These
judgments are concentrated in the disordering or de-rationalization of the
soldiers' vision, their major vehicle of spatial control and command. I am
drawn to the fact that it is the vision of these agents of the state, with all of
its potencies and instrumental rationality, that is subjected to a supernatural, that is, anti-realist, interruption. These supernatural visitations constitute a blind spot in the military visual apparatus. The soldiers may share
these phantasmic apparitions with the locals, but they are ultimately culturally alien and antagonistic to the military gaze generating nerves and
various mental disorders.

These rumors and legends of the colonized speak about unfinished historical experiences and unreconciled pasts which, through the uncanny,
remain contemporaneous with the current experience of foreign domination and social dislocation. The infiltration of the uncanny in the warning
and visitation stories, the somaticization of the state's gaze and the disordering of that gaze, imply that scopic rationalization can be reframed by a
counter-narrative that taps into the popular memory of the supernatural,
and rumor.

The locus for the reversibility of violence and vision and the axis around
which any space of death and terror is congealed is the body. Any consideration of the unreal as historiography, any assertion that the phantasmic,
the oneiric, and the fictive have a purchase on historical experience must
turn to the body as the phenomenological site of the nexus of the real and
the unreal, of perceptual certitude and perceptual fabrication. Foucault
has described the working of the phantasmal on the body as a kind of sen-
sory-ideational violence, as a reterritorializing, or a re-sectioning of the
body into new perceptual sectors and vectors. For Foucault, the phantasmal condition undermines the clear distinction between the real and its
"contrary"; it is a delimitation of the real at the level of bodily experience,
one that abandons any distinction between appearance and essence:

It is useless to seek a more substantial truth behind the phantasm, a truth to which it posits a rather confused sign (thus the futility of "symptomatologizing"); it is also useless to contain it within stable figures and to construct solid cores of convergence where we might include on the basis of their identical properties, all its angles, flashes, membranes and vapors (no possibility of "phenomenalization"). Phantasms must be allowed to function at the limit of bodies; against bodies, because they stick to bodies and protrude from them, but also because they touch them cut them break them into sections, regionalize them, and multiply their surfaces; and equally outside of bodies, because they function between bodies according to laws of proximity, torsion and variable distance—laws of which they remain ignorant. Phantasms do not extend organisms into an imaginary domain; they topologize the materiality of the body. They should consequently be freed from the restrictions we impose upon them, from the dilemmas of the truth and falsehood and of being and non-being (the essential difference between simulacrum and copy carried to its logical conclusion); they must be allowed to conduct their dance, to act out their mime, as "extra beings."[48]

Rumor consciousness, as both the effect of hyper-objectification by the scopic and its violence, and resistance to the latter, is rooted in the body rendered phantasmic. We also glimpse this counter-real in the premonition tales of arrest and the stories of "extra beings" visited upon the occupying British Army. In her archaeology of African-American rumor-lore as cultural resistance, Patricia Turner[49] identifies the origin and thematic content of African-American rumor with the institutionalization "of the bodies of blacks as disputed terrain."[50] Black rumor registers the cultural prognosis that, "the dominant culture remains intent on destroying blacks—one body at a time."[51] This is a conclusion with which many Catholics and most paramilitaries in Belfast would identify. Turner identifies a preoccupation with the protection of bodily boundaries and integrity in African-American rumor traditions. She relates the emergence of African-American rumor to a highly stratified informational and communication economy that is instrumental in the reproduction of dominant world-views from which African-Americans have been historically estranged.

Ann Stoler,[52] in her dissection of the polyphonic and conflictual reports of local violence in colonial Sumatra, also identifies rumor as either reacting against or responsive to a "hierarchy of credibility," depending on the social strata in which rumor originates. Rumor emerges when different social groupings have unequal access to a the "colonial lexicon." For Stoler, the emergence of rumor mills in relations of colonial domination confounds the cultural construction of truth based on a hierarchy between "hearsay as *opposed to visually confirmed facts.*"[53] Vincente Rafael, in his reconstruction of the rumor-lore that emerged in the Philippines as a form of resistance to the Japanese occupation, associates rumor with the divorce of "believing from seeing."[54]

These case studies of coercive colonial labor conditions and military occupation confirm Turner's thesis that subaltern rumor encodes the experience of devastated bodily boundaries, transgressed bodily orifices, and bodily subjection. In both Stoler's and Rafael's essays, the epistemologies mobilized by rumor and the fantastic are polarized to canons of facticity grounded by vision as a privileged truth-claim of colonizer and occupier. Both Gayatri Chakravorty Spivak and Homi Bhabba have, within the context of subaltern consciousness, explored the anti-canonical character of rumor, its relation to the production of phantasmagoria and its subversion of colonial modalities of objectification and realist depiction. Spivak writes of the epistemological role of rumor in the work of the Subaltern Studies group: "I would submit that it is more appropriate to think of the power of rumor in the subaltern context as deriving from its participation in the structure of illegitimate writing . . . rumor is not error but primordially (originally) errant, always in circulation with no assignable source. This illegitimacy makes it accessible to insurgency."[55]

While Bhabba links rumor to phantasmagoria through "the performative rhetoric of circulation/panic" which mobilizes a host of "slender narratives," rumor and panic refract and give birth to "the unheimlich space for the negotiation of identity and history." The "unheimlich" is the phantasmal, and the uncanny which for Bhabba originates in the eminently anti-realist historical terrain of "the not there," the "excluded, excised evicted."[56] Rumor is expressive of "a traumatic moment of the 'not there' or the indeterminate or the unknowable . . . around which the symbolic discourse of human history comes to be constituted."[57]

In overturning factual hierarchies, communicative stratification, and authorized sites of discourse production, rumor practices of the subaltern dismember the corporate communicative or informational body of domination in a fashion that resembles the exaggerations, inversions, and distortions of the grotesque as described by Bakhtin.[58] Rumor's fixation on part-objects and fragments captures at the level of narrative form the socially evocative distortion and dismemberment of body parts that frequently serve as metaphors and as real artifacts of social violence. Bakhtin's maxim that in carnival "the kitchen and the battle meet and cross each other in the image of the rent body"[59] may well be applied to the inversion/subversion of dominant truth-claiming systems, such as scopic regimes, by vernacular rumor and the phantasmic. The exaggerated narrative of rumor directly communicates with exaggerated and grotesque bodily protuberances and distorted orifices which originate in material experiences of terror and violence.

To move from ideologies of the real to the experiences of the phantasmal is to enter the zone where one phantasm shifts into another, where the realism of political instrumental rationality and the literalism of political ideology become estranged and transformed. In this slippage, a *metaphysics* of power can be discerned within the *microphysics* of practices such as violence and vision. It is from this point that instrumental political violence can be connected to the war sensorium in Belfast.

A Bestiary

During a night of late drinking, a Loyalist paramilitary described to me a rumor and a legend of his organization, about a faceless assassin known as "The Jackal." Jackal stories circulated throughout the Loyalist paramilitary community. The Jackal killed Catholic males by moving in and out of Catholic areas, silently slipping into their bedrooms at night and slitting their throats while they slept—the body to be discovered by the unsuspecting family members or the wife who had been asleep beside the victim the next morning. His silent intrusions and subsequent surveying of Catholic domestic scenes magnified the Jackal's aura for the narrator. As he described the silent invisibility of the Jackal's movements in and out of people's homes, he invoked an almost dream-like creature who he apparently found to be exotic, frightening, and admirable for his technique. As he talked I could not shake the realization that the elegiac tone of his discourse, the far-away look in his eyes, his intimacy with details of specific acts of murder indicated that he was relating stories about a double, a secret sharer, who may have been himself—a self that was and was not in the room, that was also far way, haunting other rooms and other nights.

The presence of animal imagery in the name "The Jackal" can be considered integral to the phantasmagoria of violence. In Belfast there was the figure of the Blackman associated with the sacrificial death of animals, whose rumored appearances and murders congealed accumulated perceptions of the uncanny urban space brought about by kaleidoscopic terror.[60] There is also the association of the name "The Jackal" with a popular film concerning a professional killer, whose elaborately crafted rifle fitted with a custom-made magnifying scope was as much a personality in the film as the assassin. Like the Loyalist killer, the film's character was also a master of incognito.

There is a scopic subtext encased in the name of the killer. In Belfast, the zoological jackal is not popularly known as a predator or hunter, but as an eater of carrion, consuming bodies already dead, already rendered inert. Does this say anything about the practices of the Loyalist killer of the same name? I would suggest that embedded in the animal image and the killing methods of the Jackal is the recognition that the actual physical death of his victims was a secondary act of violence. The Jackal invades and visually commands the nocturnal domestic space, an eminently feminized terrain in Belfast and a fitting stage for the politics of the pose. His victims are first assaulted by ocular aggression when the killer infiltrates their privacy and surveys these sleeping, unknowing bodies. The Jackal is a morbid echo of Terry Eagleton's characterization of the realist observer as an "omniscient authorial eye" penetrating a "hinterland of inscrutable private experience" secreted behind each "social persona."[61] Surveilling the private sphere behind the public persona of Catholics has a particular frisson because of the polarized ethnicities of victim and killer—their mutual estrangement and their physical intimacy in death. The Jackal indulges in the pleasures of seeing before killing. Sleep observed anticipates petrifaction and mortification; the gaze of the killer imprints these qualities on the body and the act of violence leaves a forensic record of these operations. Here vision robs the victim of material subjecthood in transforming the target into an iconic object. The second theft of the Jackal takes life itself. Physical death is a redundant action after piercing by the gaze of the killer, which has already frozen the victim. The Jackal leaves for others the concretion of his invasive vision: the petrified body of his victim. The Jackal's vision is only visible in the displayed corpse, for as the name implies, there is no human source for this sight and its inhumanity is tied to its invisibility.

The body left by the Jackal is both a *materialization and a memory of the killer's vision.* These associations continue and transpose many of the motifs of the attempted assassination through the window discussed above, and add another element to that zone of mediation where ocular aggression and visual hierarchy transmute into the phantasmic. An important element in both accounts is the invisibility of the observing aggressor. The externality of the spectator/killer to the scene of violence establishes the potency of the latter by removing this figure from perceptual fixation and framing—the gaze in the scopic regime is off-frame, it cannot be posed for it is that which poses, it has no site because it is the author of sites.[62] And yet this potency requires materialization in the act of physical assault that leaves marks not solely of tactile but of ocular contact on the body. The site-less gaze is located and seen only in the bodies of the viewed, posed, and harmed. The victim becomes the reminder, the remainder, and the visual record of the invisible killer.

The rumors of the Jackal exceed any individual act of violence or any individual killer they describe, and circumscribe an objective condition, a political and sensory situation by which the killers themselves, among others, narrate the historical fulcrum from which they carve out their political identities with acts of visual and violent acquisition. Such stories evade the neat argumentation and historical logic of formal ideological rationale. They seem to have nothing to do with elevated projects of nation building and ethnic assertion, yet they capture a spatial substrate: the locus where aggression, vision, and the body covertly come together in the production of power and historical agency which, in turn, colors the experience of violence as an intermediate yet efficacious plateau of dominance. It is in this material geography, hidden in ideological cellars, upon which more grandiose and dematerialized nationalist edifices rest and stake their territory as viable political forces in contemporary, postwar Northern Ireland.

Aestheticization and Iconoclasm in Writing Violence

At this juncture the reader might ask what type of knowledge does contemporary political terror engender? We can envision discontinuous circulatory corridors of discourse and practices which emanate from the ethnographic and historiographic field site, and which move between various public cultures and academic disciplines. These transmutations eventually find their way back to the field site as transmitted text or in the very person of the ethnographer that arrive at the field site like a canceled piece of returned mail. In this context the ethnography of violence and the reactions it ignites can be approached as a field site unto itself. The reader's response to the ethnography of violence can be distributed along the entire temporal and spatial trajectory of the ethnographic project, whether it is embodied in the person of the ethnographer or in the peculiar persona of the text. I am suggesting that when it comes to an ethnographic reading of violence and other subjects there are three types of sites: a pre-ethnographic or culturally residual site, an ethnographic site of dialogical mutation, and a post-ethnographic site of discursive regulation and normativity.

By this division I do not mean to indicate discrete spaces, but rather different epistemic conditions that may or may not conform to a temporal structure of before, during, and after; the epistemologies of the pre- and post-ethnographic site are often the unspoken premises of the initial ethnographic project leak into in its very unfolding in the field. Consequently, there can be a valid ethnography of the pre-and post-ethnographic which can illuminate the epistemological conditions of the anthropological inquiry. It is my contention that the pre- and post-ethnographic are sites for surplus, repressed content that exceeds the discursive closures of what is conventionally considered to be "ethnographic," and that these whitened spaces are an ethnography's condition of possibility.

When I returned to the United States after fieldwork on political violence in Northern Ireland, I encountered a concern for violence and memory in the discipline. However, this concern was not with the existential costs of memory acquisition in Belfast, which was the focus of my research there, but rather with the preservation of canonical and institutional memory over and against disturbing ethnographic content. I turn to this experience because I suggest that the essays in this volume are fated to be read in terms of the iconic normativity that I encountered post-Northern Ireland, which goes to the core of my discussion of realism and violence. For when it comes to modern political violence there is a canon of quasi-silence in anthropology and related human sciences. For by and large, the discipline seems to have little to say about the intersubjective structuration of contemporary violence, and many people have decided opinions on *how not to say it.* Much of this is confined to what George Marcus calls "corridor talk," but such talk exerts canonical authority to at least the same degree as a published literature review.[63] A scholar reproached me in a conference corridor with the declaration: "How could you write such a sad book?"; the author absorbs the pathogenesis of violence he/she has known and written about.

In anthropology, writing violence has long been acceptable only if it is archaicized and abstracted and subjected to protective thematic insulating cushions such as cannibalism, sacrifice, ecological carrying capacity, modes and relations of production, discourse and ideology. An expert on aborigines once cautioned me that researchers of Australian aboriginals had "over-ritualized" local contemporary violence to protect "their" informants from further stigmatization by Australian whites. Without the provenance of the pre-modern, the ritualistic and the ceremonial, he claimed, any depiction of Aboriginal violence would be a betrayal of local informants. This was what I was in fact doing, he felt, by making violence the main subject of my research in Northern Ireland, a place where one does not have the cultural insurance of pre-modernity on which to fall back.[64]

Through a series of such incidents I was given instruction on disciplinary etiquette, in other words, on how discourses of violence become permissible. I experienced these lessons as a form of cultural regulation, Cartesian rules for the production of text and silence and the rules of iconic interdiction on which anthropological discourse is based. Violence and culture were conceived as external to each other, and not as historically complicit. In order to write about violence and culture one had to create an insulated space protecting the latter from the former. The polarity between structural violence and transacted violence was a crucial element of this depictive interdiction. It was always preferable to write about structural inequity which coincidentally held both *moral* and methodological priority over violence as transacted, performed, and instantiated. Writing on violence had to double-back on itself through strategies of sequestration. As in the daily ideological contents of political emergency zones one had to find rationalizing excuses for violence or be conflated with its pathogenesis. Those speaking as disciplinary representatives advised me that I could speak correctly on violence only if my speech were adequately moral or prescriptive; condemnation and cure were presented as two sides of the same ethical currency. One could not write violence if one was devoid of textual emotion nor if one displayed too much emotion. I was instructed that the ethnographer of violence must not give in to voyeurism and other practices of distantiation, but if he/she became too involved the analyst would be stigmatized as morbid and violent.

To write about violence meant that the author should be subjected to normalization in direct relation to the perceived 'abnormality' of the subject. After the publication of my monograph on Northern Irish violence I was met with a series of false rumors: (1) I had fought alongside the IRA; (2) I practiced "parachute ethnography"—a peculiar military-invasive image; (3) I was Irish; (4) I was pro-Republican; (5) I was anti-Republican; (6) I had been killed in action in Belfast. The iconic fuzziness of violence had been readily transferred to the ethnographer as the author of a violent text. The way to confirm me as the author of a violent/violating text was to transmute me into a rumor, a Foucauldian phantasm.

The iconoclastic stricture against aestheticizing violence foregrounds the deep-seated internal contradictions within the human sciences on the subject of violence. If the aestheticization of violence is where the discipline of anthropology stands or falls, then we are going to need some new foundations. For I cannot reconcile the stricture against making pleasure-giving images of violence and the oft-repeated requirement that one subordinate ethnographic depiction of violence to rules of taste. Did not the discrete image or narrative become discrete because it gave pleasure, in not giving pain? If so, wouldn't the ethnographer be aestheticizing violence in the very act of depicting it in conformity with rules of taste and distaste, within certain regularities of discourse and scholarly consumption?

I propose that any system of discourse regulation that prescribes and proscribes images, practices of representation, depictive codes—alphabetic, numerical, visual, aural, realist, or surrealist—is implicitly an aestheticizing practice. If a discourse subordinates image making and depiction to rules of exclusion and inclusion, legislates the production of forms and codifies protocols of consumption, and memory, thereby insuring the pleasures or at least the decencies of reading, it practices aesthetics. In turn, such practices of discourse are invariably practices of power, a willing of truth and canonical memory. As Nietzsche and Foucault have taught us, such truth-claiming procedures are reflexive of, and embedded in, wider institutional configurations. In this context the aestheticization of violence is not merely a writing effect, a symptomatic reaction to chronic violence, but a crucial practice within the political emergency zone, one that begs inquiry and analysis of the type presented in this essay.

There are two further disturbing aspects of the aestheticization critique. It tends to polarize writing and violence, to render them external to each other in a Cartesian fashion; writing is equated with a dematerializing mind, and violence is equated with the negativity of matter. However I have shown that in Northern Ireland, the practices of violence were part and parcel of institutional cultures of writing, such as in high-technology surveillance, computer registration of everyday population movements, media-censorship, interrogation-torture and penal incarceration. Secondly, this criticism seems to bar ethnographic practices of writing from an intertextual relationship with literary writings on violence, such as the work of Kafka, Malaparte, Kosinski, Levi, Wiesel, and Morrison, among others, who have deeply explored the patterns of twentieth-century political violence and terror.

In discussions of violence, visuality is problematized precisely because of the powerful and seemingly holistic truth-claims it throws up. However at the level of theorization and non-theorization, the presupposition that the visual is the primary vehicle for the theoretical capture of violence and that it remains voyeuristically external to the act of violence must be structurally complicit with its other side: the assertion of iconoclastic rules of representation—rules for promoting the *in-visibility* of violence by controlling its imagery and imagining. The accusation of sexual voyeurism that is frequently applied to the ethnographic study of violence itself expresses an escape from history in its assumption of estrangement, personalized voluntarism, and privatized consumption of violence and collective trauma. The question remains: are we condemned to either iconoclastic censure or voyeuristic distance and seduction? Are there other strategies for writing violence that take into account the complicity of violent acts in their cultural depiction, particularly by supposedly non-aestheticized modes such as narrative and visual realism?

Conclusion: Piercings

The blind man's photo possesses a disturbing clarity. It appears to be the ultimate triumph of realist aesthetics, establishing its existence independent of human subjectivity. Yet once contextualized in blindness and war, the photo imposes an estrangement effect on visual realism. The "ethnographic photo" stands at the fulcrum of this bivalent visual nexus. It seemingly shows someone's sight yet shows nothing of the sort; rather it *elicits* the viewer's consent to realist conventions such as typification, intelligibility, and perspective. However the photograph's "realist description" is disfigured by contextual and wider cultural implications to such an extent that the sensory medium of vision falls into ethnographic crisis and serves more as a sign-post of the perceptual crisis of both ethnographer and informants than as an authoritative description of the ethnographic object. In this sense it is a figure of double aspect, what Salvador Dali called the "paranoiac image": "The way in which it has been possible to obtain a double image is clearly paranoiac. By a double image is meant such a representation of an object that it is also without the slightest physical or anatomical change, the representation of another entirely different object."[65]

Such figures are anamorphic, an image or form arising from or out of another form without the cancellation or disappearance of the first image. If realist fixation fabricates an eternal present of social permanence, the anamorphic percept is the equivalent of historicity in motion and of its indeterminate signification. Merleau Ponty describes the anamorphic figure in terms of temporality that fractures realist domestication: "The assumed plenitude of the object and of the moment only appears in the presence of the imperfect nature of the intentional being. A present without future or an eternal present is precisely the definition of death, the living present is torn between a past and a projected future. It is therefore essential for the thing and the world to present themselves as open to project us beyond their predetermined manifestations and constantly to promise us other things to see."[66]

If critiquing the truth-claims of visual realism proceeds by establishing its genealogical linkage to domination and to colonial and post-colonial hegemony, then it is also important to connect this critique to movements of perceptual and depictive decolonization within the imperial metropole as the center of realist cathexis and capital. The exponents of Dada and Surrealism, such as Dali, may have presented themselves as afflicted by realist closure, but they elaborated a sophisticated iconographic critique of visual realism that connected it to forms of military, technological, and economic violence that bear relevance to the perceptual culture of the political terror zone.

At the end of World War I, the Dada and Surrealist movements characterized the depth penetration of modernity as bodily trauma and perceptual shock, thus putting the realist percept into crisis and fragmentation. This judgment largely originated in the complementary experiences of the World War I battlefield with its unprecedented mechanized assault on the human body, and in the accelerated commodification and refunctioning of culture of which war technology was a part.[67] The war created 11,000,000 disabled veterans, bodies patched up with artificial limbs and prosthetics, images of post-war everyday life that informed Dada and Surrealist aesthetics of the human figure; alterations to human proportions implicated corresponding mutations in human identity and its perceptual coordinates. The confrontation of organic life with mechanized violence was experienced by the exponents of Dada and Surrealism as a denaturing and de-realization of the body. Disfigurement could be as abruptly violent and dramatic as on the battlefield, or it could be a silent accretion within the structures of everyday post-war urban life. In this manner the mundane oneiric practices associated with Surrealism transmogrified the everyday into a sensory war zone. The infamous opening scene of the film *Un Chien Andalou* (1929) by Luis Buñuel and Salvador Dalí directly evoked this theme of perception as gendered somatic trauma and shock: a razor cuts across a woman's eye which fills the screen with its open wound. This image was both description and manifesto. Under the perceptual razor of modernity, the transformation of executive organs meant their wounding and bifurcation through their encounter with aggressive objects. There was an inherent inversion linked to the mutilation of an eye: inasmuch as the eye could be victimized and be pierced, it could also assault what it viewed—the camera is the razor in this scene.

The "picture shock" (*Bildshock*) aimed at by the film's imagery was the aesthetic equivalent of the shell shock of war experience. Max Ernst's collages of the 1920s frequently show body parts, particularly hands pierced by sharp objects and/or amputated implying the technological detachment, specialization, and autonomization of the perceptual organs in which they achieve new capabilities and produce new perceptual objects. This violent decontextualization of the sensory organism was an attempt to apprehend perception within new socio-historical coordinates.

The Surrealist inheritance offers a critique of the fetishized integration of realist aesthetics into warfare and everyday life, but also the possibility of rehabilitating anti-realist perceptual postures within the sensorium of war. The record of these postures points to the historical possibility of a post-war counter-memory to the canonical ideological narratives and positivist event histories that prescribe the manner in which violence is to be remembered, depicted, and recorded and reproduced as consciousness and agency. Can we preclude the possibly of counter-memory arising not only from artistic and theoretical critique, but also from the marginalized practices of popular culture and memory grounded in vernacular idioms. The ethnographic encounter with such anti-memories may well recuperate the slender narrative of the dehistoricized. Dehistoricization is a perceptual, experiential, and depictive after-effect of certain practices and representations of violence, of cultural anesthesia that represses or makes inadmissible multi-form sensory-experience.[68] Counter-memory is thus contingent on the recovery of multi-form sensory alterity and its re-historicization.

In Belfast the dehistoricized can be partially located in the shifting spaces of the uncanny, the phantasmal, and the rumored which are not merely external to political-military realism, but can be found within anxieties about the nature of the politically real. Thus the stories I have related are double-edged. They attest to the dominance of visual paradigms in the prosecution of political warfare and in its culture of representation, and yet at the same time they register the limits of vision and violence as vehicles for claiming truth.

This essay has been an analysis of the decay of realism towards its margins—towards anamorphic fracture that promises us other things to see. I began with the emblematic—a visual souvenir, a post card from my fieldwork—and proceeded to fashion an ethnography of emblems: of realism as an emblem, and of visual linguistic and corporeal emblems of realism which seem fixed but are constantly shifting and unstable. Ethnographic inquiry is constantly confronted with and itself generates paranoiac and anamorphic figures that bar ethnography from a naive acceptance of visual and other forms of realism and their perceptual coordinates. My aim is not to exorcise visual or synoptic realism from ethnographic depiction, but to clarify their constructed, perceptually relative, and historically determined character as an inherited complicity of both ethnographers and informants.

To assume an iconoclastic posture on realist depiction would be to repeat the very stratifying gesture that allows realist representation to monopolize the construction of facticity in modernity: this is the customary strategy of a crude post-modernism. Realism, in its ejection and repression of alternate perceptual postures, has been the most successful iconoclasm to date. Indeed I have marshaled realist depictive procedures, from photography to history, to situate realism in its historical contingency.[69] The critique of realist aesthetics can only take place from within the cultural inheritance of realist depiction itself; the latter is but one vector of a multi-plex dialogical terrain whose complexity has been made invisible by the realist gaze in the process of describing the visible.

In Belfast the political efficacy of violence itself is contingent on norms of visual realism and perceptual circuits of visibility and invisibility, that is, on an aesthetic efficacy that provides pleasures of consumption and reception, of iconicity and stylization. These aestheticized relationships, moreover, are not confined to writing or academic analysis but inhabit the core of political praxis. At the same time, the rigid geometry of scopic realism and power may be relativized at the margins of experience by the phantasmic, the rumored, and the uncanny.

As opposed to continuing the "post-modernist" tendency of aestheticizing domination, this analysis identifies acts of aestheticization as intrinsic to political power, thereby moving the aesthetics of political violence into the center of a political anthropology concerned with war. Aestheticization is the civilizational heritage of all depictions of violence and all empowered discourses. There are counter-aesthetic positions that one can take: rehabilitation of historicity against dominant history, and of sensory alterities that problematize the aesthetic continuum of domination. But I doubt one can find a purely pre-aesthetic ground from which to write against domination. The circuitry of scopic domination and violation in Northern Ireland, the visual realism it deploys and elevates and the sensory alterities it suppresses and yet instigates remains the epistemic terrain where the metaphysics of political violence in Belfast and elsewhere will have to be de-mystified. Like rumor, the warning sensation of impending arrest, or tales of ghosts, faeries and banshees, the latent politics of realism is a hieroglyph that requires its own decipherment and archaeology. This project would aggravate the iconoclastic strictures of realism at work in the public culture of both the ethnographer and the victim of violence. But this endeavor might also return us to the agendas and emblems of the Surrealists who countered the *realist eye* that cuts and pierces with another orb, neither totally blind nor all-seeing, the eye that weeps with memory in the face of violence.

NOTES

Acknowledgments: This essay in part originated in the rich dialogues on violence and aesthetics that took place at the conference "States of Violence" in March 1994, organized and sponsored by *Comparative Studies in Society and History* and the Department of Anthropology at the University of Michigan. I would like to thank the conference organizers and volume editors E. Valentine Daniel, Julie Skurski, Fernando Coronil, and Raymond Grew for facilitating my thinking on these matters. In addition, I am grateful to various colloquia in 1994 and 1995 at the Department of Anthropology, Princeton University, and the Anthropology Board, The University of California Santa Cruz, and the conference, "Violence and Political Agency," sponsored by the Social Science Research Council and the Rajiv Gandhi Foundation, which facilitated the development of the theoretical frameworks presented here. I would also like to acknowledge the insightful readings of this paper by the editorial collective of *Public Culture,* and Pamela Reynolds, Nadia Seremetakis, and Paul Stoller, all of whom were instrumental in turning my attention to the anthropology of the senses.

1. Samuel Beckett, *Id., Ill Seen, Ill Said* (New York: Grove Press, 1980), p. 40.

2. John Tagg, *The Burden of Representation: Essays on Photographies and Histories* (Boston: University of Massachusetts Press, 1988).

3. Fieldwork was conducted in County Tyrone during the years 1978–1980, and in Belfast in 1984–1987, 1990, and 1992.

4. Under the current tenuous truce conditions, which at the time of writing the IRA no longer observes, it is difficult to ascertain whether these descriptions of assassination logic should be in the past or present tense.

5. See Allen Feldman, *Formations of Violence: The Narrative of the Body and Political Terror in Northern Ireland* (Chicago: University of Chicago Press, 1991, pp. 85–105) on house raiding by governmental "security forces" in Northern Ireland.

6. The state's counterinsurgency program drastically altered civil life, including the civil character of law enforcement, through the suspension of common rules of law, enhanced powers of arrest, detention and interrogation (the latter frequently culminating in torture), altered rules of evidence, and trials without jury. This panoptic apparatus is applied with greater force and violence to the Catholic working class community than to the Protestant working class community. Such ethnic imbalance is always considered to be politically motivated in Northern Ireland. The Catholic populations subjected to this surveillance perceive it to be explicitly political and an invasive erosion of their personal lives, effectively criminalizing the latter. The majority of people subjected to this surveillance are not engaged in either political or "criminal" activity; this is an intervention system designed by the state to intimidate mass populations.

7. This was during the massive coal mine strike of 1984.

8. There are many covert informational and military linkages between Loyalist paramilitaries and certain sections of the police and army reserves which are largely composed of Protestants.

9. Bryson was a legendary IRA gunman of the first years of the conflict who was shot to death by the British army.

10. Ian Paisely and William Craig are leading Loyalist politicians and Tommy Herron was a legendary leader of the Ulster Defense Association who was assassinated. This is a Loyalist pantheon with which the narrator is associating himself, deservedly or not.

11. See Michael Taussig, "Malefacium: State Fetishism." In, Emily Apter and William Pietz, eds., *Fetishism as Cultural Discourse* (Ithaca, N.Y.: Cornell University Press, 1993).

12. I do not distinguish here between the actual use and the theatrical display of weaponry, for both acts create political iconography.

13. See my discussion of the panopticon technology in Northern Ireland (*Formations of Violence,* pp. 115–38).

14. The thematic of vision circumscribed by, or organized around a core of

blindness can be found in the works of Merleau-Ponty, Lyotard, and Derrida, and is conspicuously absent in Foucault.

15. Here only the aggressor strives to remain invisible, or cultivates a mediated visibility in the material record of bodies wounded, killed, captured, and tortured.

16. From the term scotomization—a psycho-somatic blind spot that appears in vision where something is too threatening to be seen. *Skotos* in Greek means darkness.

17. See *Sunday Times* Insight Team, *Ulster* (Penguin, 1972) for a comprehensive account of these events. The aftermath of this crowd violence precipitated the rapid growth and institutionalization of paramilitary organizations in both Protestant and Catholic working class communities.

18. For discussion of the exchange structure of violence see Feldman, *Formations of Violence,* pp. 72–74, 100–102, 234–35.

19. Obviously the gaze as a technique of power has its own cultural history that is both continuous and discontinuous with the development of human vision, for we must also allow for resistance to the politicized gaze by vision and other senses. See Susan Buck-Morss, *The Dialectics of Seeing: Walter Benjamin and the Arcades Project* (Cambridge, Mass.: MIT Press, 1989); Christoph Asendorf, *Batteries of Life: On the History of Things and Their Perception in Modernity* (Berkeley: University of California Press, 1993); Jonathan Crary, *Techniques of the Observer* (Cambridge, Mass.: MIT Press, 1991).

20. Nor are writing practices external to the scopic regime or the practice of violence. See my discussion of writing and violence in "Ethnographic States of Emergency," in, Carolyn Nordstrom and Antonius Robben, eds., *Fieldwork under Fire: Contemporary Studies of Violence and Survival* (Berkeley: University of California Press, 1995).

21. On the sectarianization, racialization, and ghettoization of social space see David Smith, *Apartheid City and beyond Urbanizations* (London: Routledge, 1992); Margeret C. Rodman, "Empowering Place: Multilocality and Multivocality," *American Anthropologist* 94, 3 (1992): 640–56; David T. Goldbery, "Polluting the Body Politic: Racist Discourse and Urban Location," in, Malcom Cross and Michael Keith, eds., *Racism, the City and the State* (London: Routledge, 1993); Doreen Massey, *Spatial Division of Labour: Social Structures and the Geography of Production* (London: Macmillan, 1984); Rob Shields, *Places on the Margin: Alternative Geographies of Modernity* (London: Routledge, 1991).

22. See my discussion of ethnicity and embodiment and the practice of "telling" in Feldman, *Formations of Violence,* pp. 56–59.

23. State violence is usually legitimized by the Loyalist political culture, though not always. This community embeds state violence in its own local genealogies whether they approve of it or not. See the recent disputes of ceremonial marching in which the police along with Catholics became objects of Loyalist antagonism.

24. For fuller discussion of excuse rationality, see below.

25. Tagg, *Burden of Representation.*

26. Ernst Bloch, *Heritage of Our Times,* N. Plaice and S. Plaice, trans. (Cambridge, Mass.: MIT Press, 1990).

27. In fact the narrator planned the assassination.

28. See my discussion on violence, racism, and visual and legal realism in "On Cultural Anesthesia: From Desert Storm to Rodney King," *American Ethnologist* 21 (1994): p. 2.

29. Emily Apter, "Ethnographic Travesties: Colonial Realism, French Feminism and the Case of Eliss Rhais." In, Gyan Prakash, ed., *After Colonialism: Imperial Histories and Postcolonial Displacements* (Princeton, N.J.: Princeton University Press, 1995).

30. Tagg, *Burden of Representation.*

31. See Anson Rabinbach, *The Human Motor: Energy, Fatigue and the Origins of Modernity* (New York: Basic Books, 1990).

32. Terry Eagleton, *Heathcliff and the Great Hunger: Studies in Irish Culture* (London: Verso, 1995), p. 147.

33. In the nineteenth century, "realism" was associated with modes of narration and visualization that presumed an omniscient observer detached from and external to the scenography being presented. It was linked to formal pictorial perspectivism and narrative linearity with all its assumptions about causality, space, and time (Crary, *Techniques of the Observer*).

34. Eagleton, *Heathcliff,* pp. 174–75.

35. Partha Chaterjee, *The Nation and Its Fragments: Colonial and Post-Colonial Histories* (Princeton, N.J.: Princeton University Press, 1993).

36. Mary Ann Doane, "Women's Stake: Filming the Female Body" *17 October* (Summer 1981): p. 24.

37. In modernity, the gender reversal in the transfer of Medusan powers to the male gaze is traced back to the demonization of the female in the Medusa myth. Medusa is the radical and monstrous image of the Other who threatens the male self and is defeated when Perseus uses a mirror effect to turn that gaze back upon her—indicating a male channeling and mediation of the powers of vision. A full mythography of this myth and its cultural replication in modernity is beyond the scope of this paper.

38. I have subjected these terms to a more expanded discussion elsewhere (*Formations of Violence,* pp. 68–74). However, the issue of posing compels a different reading of these terms than I originally generated.

39. See Eagleton, *Heathcliff,* p. 148.

40. The gendering of vision here in the phrase "the male gaze" is based on several historical processes: the Western civilizational pattern that associates visual empowerment with dominant elites, monopolized technologies, hierarchies of credibility, and truth-claiming (Crary, *Techniques of the Observer*); the history of Western painting and sculpture and the historical formation of vision as a commodity form closely associated with pleasure and mobile consumption, as in

Baudelaire's and Benjamin's notion of the flaneur—again a male figure whose female counterpart for Benjamin was the prostitute (Buck-Morss, *The Dialectics of Seeing*). The adjective "male" does not mean that only men "see" in a scopic regime. I am not arguing for an essentialized male gaze but for the male gaze as a mobile cultural form—so both men and women and trans-gendered persons can engage in the male gaze as a mode of objectification. It is to avoid essentialization that I argue that in a scopic regime there are only positions of vision *internal* to the apparatus, and no anthropomorphic vision at the source or as the author of the apparatus. A woman behind the scope of a rifle in Northern Ireland, or behind the video-camera in the torture chamber, is engaging the politics of the pose and positioned within the male gaze as a practice of domination as much as any man.

41. Jacques Lacan, *Ecrits: A Selection,* Alan Sheridan, trans. (New York: Norton, 1977), pp. 2–3, 16–17, 28.

42. The intersection between the historical formation of the senses and the division of labor is first discussed by Marx in *The Economic and Philosophical Manuscripts,* which indicates that there is a dense stratigraphy of modern perceptual techniques that links the economic, aesthetic, and political spheres—a history that has been only partially explored. Karl Marx, "The Economic and Philosophical Manuscripts." In, Rodney Livingstone and Gregor Benton, trans., *Early Writings.* (Hammondsworth, New York: Penguin in association with New Left Review, 1992).

43. Lacan, *Ecrits,* p. 28.

44. The theory of the pose is based on Lacan's discussion of the Mirror Stage, in which the child displaces its identity and origin to the posed image of its body in the mirror—the first statue relation, so to speak. This pose image is introjected by the child through mimetic play (Lacan, *Ecrits*).

45. See Lacan, *Ecrits,* 2–3; and Mikkel Borch-Jacobsen, *Lacan: The Absolute Master,* Douglas Brick, trans. (Stanford: Stanford University Press, 1991, p. 60).

46. See Feldman, *Formations of Violence.*

47. Feldman, "Ethnographic States of Emergency," p. 234. The cultural elaboration of terror can simply involve the emergence of traumatized persons and bodies from the bowels of the interrogation space or in the production of indifference by the state engaged in disappearances and their subsequent denial.

48. Michel Foucault, *Memory, Counter Memory and Practice: Selected Essays and Interviews,* Donald F. Bouchard, ed. (Ithaca, N.Y.: Cornell University Press, 1988), pp. 169–70.

49. Patricia Turner, *I Heard It through the Grapevine: Rumor in African-American Culture.* (Berkeley: University of California Press, 1993).

50. Ibid., p. 200.

51. Ibid., p. 201.

52. Ann Laura Stoler, "In Cold Blood: Hierarchies of Credibility and the Politics of Colonial Narrative," *Representations* 37 (Winter 1992).

53. Ibid., pp. 179, 183.

54. Vincente Rafael, "Anticipating Nationhood: Collaboration and Rumor in the Japanese Occupation of Manila," *Diaspora* 1, 1 (Spring 1991): 67–82.

55. Gayatri Chakravorty Spivak, "Subaltern Studies: Deconstructing Historiography," in *Other Worlds: Essays in Cultural Politics* (Routledge, New York, 1988), p. 215.

56. Homi Bhabha, "In a Spirit of Calm Violence." In, Gyan Prakash, ed., *After Colonialism,* pp. 331–32.

57. Ibid., p. 338.

58. Mikhail Bakhtin, *Rabelais and His World* (Cambridge, Mass.: MIT Press, 1968). Though political terror and carnival emerge in distinctly different socio-economic contexts, they share a structure of inversion. But what I refer to is the carnivalesque inversion of dominant truth-claiming. Needless to say, carnival has not been devoid of its own practices of violence.

59. Ibid., p. 197.

60. Feldman, *Formations of Violence,* pp. 81–84.

61. Eagleton, *Heathcliff,* pp. 174–75.

62. Those who have experienced the "warning" sensation prior to their arrest can attest to this.

63. Personal communication.

64. His warning explains why many theorists working on Northern Ireland frame Republican violence in pre-modern emplotments of Catholicism, Protestantism, and tribalized ethnicity that emphasize an ahistorical ritual-ceremonial logic and de-politicize Republican violence.

65. Salvador Dalí, "L'ane pourri," in *Le Surrealisme au service de la Revolution* 1 (Paris, 1930), pp. 9–12.

66. Maurice Merleau-Ponty, *Phenomenologie de la Perception* (Paris: Gallimard, 1978), p. 38.

67. See Jan Martin, *Downcast Eyes: The Denigration of Vision in Twentieth-Century French Thought* (Berkeley: University of California Press, 1993); Kenneth Silver, *Espirit de Corps: The Art of the Parisian Avant-Garde and the First World War, 1914–1925* (Princeton: Princeton University Press, 1989); Sidra Sitch, *Anxious Visions: Surrealist Art.* (New York: Abbeville Press, 1990).

68. See Feldman, "On Cultural Anesthesia"; and Reinhart Koselleck, "Terror and Dream: Methodological Remarks on the Experience of Time during the Third Reich," in *Futures Past: On the Semantics of Historical Time* (Cambridge, Mass.: MIT Press, 1985).

69. I owe this insight to James Boon's insightful critique of an earlier version of this paper, which influenced a more Derridean take on the realist archive.

Contributors

SILVIO R. BARETTA is a native of Brazil, where he grew up and attended Brazilian schools, obtaining his B.A. at the Universidade de Passo Fundo, RS, Brazil in 1969. He earned his doctorate from the Department of Sociology, University of Pittsburgh, in 1986. He has published a variety of articles with John Markoff on economic and political development in Latin America in Journals such as *Comparative Politics* and *Comparative Studies in Society and History.* He is currently a senior partner of a consulting firm focused on economic development and strategic planning for the nonprofit and public sectors.

CHARLES BRIGHT is Professor of History in the Residential College, University of Michigan, teaching in the areas of world history, Detroit urban history, and the history of prisons and punishment. His most recent book is *The Powers That Punish: Prisons and Politics in the Era of the 'Big House,' 1920–1955* (1996). His current work on the history of globalization, with Michael Geyer, includes "World History in a Global Age" in *American Historical Review* (1995); and "Where in the World Is America? The History of the United States in a Global Age" in, Thomas Bender, ed., *Rethinking American History in a Global Age* (University of California Press, 2002).

PAUL SANT CASSIA is Reader in Anthropology at the University of Durham, U.K., and Editor of *History and Anthropology.* He previously lectured at the University of Cambridge, U.K., where he was Curator for the Anthropology Collections at the Cambridge University Museum of Archaeology and Anthropology. He has been visiting Professor at the Universities of Paris (Nanterre), Aix en Provence, and Malta. He has conducted anthropological research in the Mediterranean (Cyprus, Greece, Tunisia, and Malta), and has published on politics, oratory, property transmission, and family and kinship. He is an author, with Constantina Bada, of *The Making of the Modern Greek Family* (Cambridge University

Press, 1992). His latest book, *Bodies of Evidence: Burial, Memory and the Recovery of Missing Persons in Cyprus,* is soon to be published by Berghahn (Oxford, U.K.).

JUAN R. I. COLE is Professor of Modern Middle East and South Asian History at the History Department of the University of Michigan. He has written extensively about modern Islamic movements in Egypt, the Persian Gulf, and South Asia. His most recent book is *Sacred Space and Holy War* (I.B. Tauris, 2002). Among his other books are *Colonialism and Revolution in the Middle East: Social and Cultural Origins of Egypt's 'Urabi Movement* (Princeton, 1993), and the edited volume *Comparing Muslim Societies* (Michigan, 1992).

FERNANDO CORONIL, a Venezuelan citizen, teaches in the Departments of Anthropology and History at the University of Michigan and is the Director of the Doctoral Program in Anthropology and History. His research focuses on contemporary historical transformations in Latin America and on theoretical issues concerning the state, modernity, and postcoloniality. His publications include, *The Magical State: Nature, Money, and Modernity in Venezuela;* the introduction to *Cuban Counterpoint: Tobacco and Sugar,* by Fernando Ortiz, and "Beyond Occidentalism: Towards Non-Imperial Geohistorical Categories." He is completing a book on the coup against President Chávez of Venezuela as a Fellow at Harvard University's David Rockefeller Center.

E. VALENTINE DANIEL is Professor of Anthropology at Columbia University. He has carried out extensive research in Sri Lanka, his country of origin, and with Tamil refugees. His writings include many articles on violence, culture, and meaning, as well as the books *Fluid Signs: Being a Person in the Tamil Way, Charred Lullabies: Chapters in an Anthropography of Violence,* and the co-edited volume, *Mistrusting Refugees.* He is the Director of Columbia University's Southern Asia Institute.

VEENA DAS is Professor of Anthropology at Johns Hopkins University. Her extensive research in India concerns the workings of cultural logics in contemporary events, and moments of rupture and recovery. Her recent work has focused on questions of violence, social suffering, and subjectivity, and addresses the processes through which violence is produced and testimonials are created. Her current collective research project concerns disease and health-seeking among the urban poor in Delhi. Her publications include, *Critical Events: An Anthropological Perspective on Contem-*

porary India, the edited volume, *Mirrors of Violence: Communities, Riots and Survivors in South Asia,* and the co-edited books on issues of violence, *Social Suffering, Violence and Subjectivity,* and *Remaking a World.*

DAVID B. EDWARDS is a graduate of Princeton University and the University of Michigan, where he received his Ph.D. in anthropology in 1986. He is currently Professor of Anthropology at Williams College in Williamstown, Massachusetts. He first lived in Afghanistan from 1975 to 1977, when he was an English teacher in Kabul. He subsequently returned to Peshawar, Pakistan in 1982 as a Fulbright Fellow conducting his doctoral research on Afghan refugees and Afghan political parties in Pakistan. He lived in Peshawar for two years between 1982 and 1986, and had the opportunity to visit refugee camps throughout the North-west Frontier Province and Baluchistan, and also to travel with a mujahidin group inside Afghanistan. He made return trips to Afghanistan and Pakistan in 1995 and 2001. He is the author of many articles on Afghanistan and two books: *Heroes of the Age: Moral Fault Lines on the Afghan Frontier* (Univ. of California Press, 1996) and *Before Taliban: Genealogies of the Afghan Jihad* (Univ. of California Press, 2002). He is the director of the Williams Afghan Media Project.

ALLEN FELDMAN is an anthropologist who works at New York University's Steinhardt School of Education. He has conducted ethnographic field research in Northern Ireland, South Africa, and with the homeless in New York City. He has taught at Central European University— Budapest, Institute of Humanities Studies—Ljubljana, and the Department of Performance Studies, NYU. His interests include visual culture and violence, the political anthropology of the body and the senses, and the archeology of media and technology. Feldman is the author *Formations of Violence: The Narrative of the Body and Political Terror in Northern Ireland.*

JOHN MARKOFF is Professor of Sociology, History, and Political Science at the University of Pittsburgh. His publications include *Waves of Democracy* (1996), and *The Abolition of Feudalism* (1997), winner of the Distinguished Scholarly Publication Award of the American Sociological Association, the Pinkney Prize of the Society for French Historical Studies, and the Sharlin Prize of the Social Science History Association. His most recent book, *Revolutionary Demands* (1998), co-authored with Gilbert Shapiro, was also awarded the Pinkney Prize.

T. DUNBAR MOODIE is professor of sociology in the Department of Anthropology and Sociology at Hobart and William Smith Colleges. He is the author of *The Rise of Afrikanerdom,* and *Going for Gold,* as well as many articles. His most recent work deals with changes in the everyday lives of black South African miners in the course of the twentieth century, with special attention to the impact of wider South African economic, political, and social changes. His most recent work is an analysis of the rise of the National Union of Mineworkers on the South African gold mines.

JULIE SKURSKI teaches in the Departments of Anthropology and History at the University of Michigan and is the Associate Director of the Joint Doctoral Program in Anthropology and History. Her research concerns the intersections of national, racial, and gender relations in Latin America, and developments in global feminism. Her publications include "The Ambiguities of Authenticity in Latin America: Doña Bárbara and the Construction of National Identity," in *Becoming National.* She is currently completing *Civilizing Barbarism,* a book on gender, *mestizaje,* and the state in Venezuela.